D0205696

Essentials of Christian Theology

ESSENTIALS OF CHRISTIAN THEOLOGY

Stanley J. Grenz
John B. Cobb, Jr.
Sallie McFague
Serene Jones
Robert W. Jenson
Hughes Oliphant Old
Ellen T. Charry
Paul F. Knitter
Richard J. Mouw
Noel Leo Erskine
David S. Cunningham
Kathryn Tanner
Clark M. Williamson
Leanne Van Dyk
Letty M. Russell
Michael Battle
J. A. DiNoia, O.P.
Ted Peters

edited by William C. Placher

WJK WESTMINSTER JOHN KNOX PRESS
LOUISVILLE • KENTUCKY

© 2003 Westminster John Knox Press

All rights reserved. No part of this book may be reproduced or transmitted in any form or by any means, electronic or mechanical, including photocopying, recording, or by any information storage or retrieval system, without permission in writing from the publisher. For information, address Westminster John Knox Press, 100 Witherspoon Street, Louisville, Kentucky 40202-1396.

Scripture quotations from the New Revised Standard Version of the Bible are copyright © 1989 by the Division of Christian Education of the National Council of the Churches of Christ in the U.S.A. and are used by permission.

The chapter by Clark M. Williamson was originally published as "Neighbors along the Way: Humanity" in *Way of Blessing, Way of Life* and is used by permission of Chalice Press, 1221 Locust St., Suite 1200, St. Louis, MO 63103.

The chapter by J. A. DiNoia is a slightly edited version of an essay originally titled "Christian Universalism," which was published in *Either/Or: The Gospel of Neopaganism,* ed. Carl E. Braaten and Robert W. Jenson. It is reprinted here by kind permission of Wm. B. Eerdmans Publishing Co.

Book design by Sharon Adams
Cover design by Jennifer K. Cox

First edition
Published by Westminster John Knox Press
Louisville, Kentucky

This book is printed on acid-free paper that meets the American National Standards Institute Z39.48 standard. ♾

PRINTED IN THE UNITED STATES OF AMERICA

05 06 07 08 09 10 11 12 — 10 9 8 7 6 5 4

Library of Congress Cataloging-in-Publication Data

Essentials of Christian theology / Stanley J. Grenz . . . [et al.] ; edited by William C. Placher.
p. cm.
Includes bibliographical references.
ISBN 0-664-22395-8 (alk. paper)
1. Theology, Doctrinal—Popular works. I. Grenz, Stanley, 1950– II. Placher, William C. (William Carl), 1948–

BT77.E69 2003
230—dc21

2003047906

Contents

Contributors

Michael Battle is Assistant Professor of Spirituality and Black Church Studies at Duke Divinity School. His books include *Reconciliation: The Ubuntu Theology of Desmond Tutu* and *The Wisdom of Desmond Tutu*. He is an Episcopal priest.

Ellen T. Charry is Margaret W. Harmon Associate Professor of Systematic Theology at Princeton Theological Seminary and editor of *Theology Today*. Her books include *Franz Rosenzweig on the Freedom of God*, *By the Renewing of Your Minds: The Pastoral Function of Christian Doctrine*, and *Inquiring after God: Classic and Contemporary Readings*. She is an Episcopalian.

John B. Cobb, Jr. is Professor Emeritus of the Claremont School of Theology and is codirector of the Center for Process Studies. His books include *God and the World*, *Christ in a Pluralistic Age*, and *Transforming Christianity and the World*. He is an ordained minister of the United Methodist Church.

David S. Cunningham is Professor of Theology and Ethics at Seabury-Western Theological Seminary. He is the author of *Faithful Persuasion: In Aid of a Rhetoric of Christian Theology*, *These Three Are One: The Practice of Trinitarian Theology*, and *Reading Is Believing: The Apostles' Creed through Literature and Film*. He is a member of St. Luke's Episcopal Church, Evanston, Illinois.

Joseph Augustine DiNoia, O.P., recently became Undersecretary of the Congregation for the Doctrine of the Faith in Rome. This essay was written while he was Professor of Theology at the Dominican House of Studies in Washington. His books include *The Diversity of Religions: A Christian Perspective*, *The Love That Never Ends: A Key to the Catechism of the Catholic Church*, and *Veritatis Splendor and the Renewal of Moral Theology*. He is a priest of the Dominican Order.

Noel Leo Erskine is Associate Professor of Theology and Ethics, Candler School of Theology, Emory University. He is the author of *Decolonizing Theology* and *King among the Theologians*. He is an ordained minister of the Jamaica Baptist Union.

Stanley J. Grenz is Pioneer McDonald Professor of Theology, Carey Theological College, Vancouver, B.C. His books include *The Social God and the Relational Self: A Trinitarian Theology of the Imago Dei*, *Renewing the Center: Evangelical Theology in a Post-Theological Era*, *Theology for the Community of God*, *A Primer on Postmodernism*, and, with John R. Franke, *Beyond Foundationalism: Shaping Theology in a Postmodern Context*. He is an ordained minister in the Baptist Union of Western Canada.

Robert W. Jenson is Senior Scholar for Research at the Center of Theological Inquiry in Princeton, New Jersey. His books include *Systematic Theology* (in two volumes), *Essays in the Theology of Culture*, *Unbaptized God: The Basic Flaw in Ecumenical Theology*, *America's Theologian: A Recommendation of Jonathan Edwards*, *Visible Words: The Interpretation of Practice of Christian Sacraments*, and *The Knowledge of Things Hoped For: The Sense of Theological Discourse*. He is an ordained Lutheran minister.

Serene Jones is Associate Professor of Systematic Theology at Yale University Divinity School. Her books include *Feminist Theory and Christian Theology: Cartographies of Grace* and *Calvin and the Rhetoric of Piety*. She is jointly ordained in the Christian Church (Disciples of Christ) and the United Church of Christ.

Paul F. Knitter is Emeritus Professor of Theology at Xavier University in Cincinnati. His books include *No Other Name? A Critical Survey of Christian Attitudes toward World Religions*, *One Earth, Many Religions: Multifaith Dialogue and Global Responsibility*, *Jesus and Other Names: Christian Mission and Global Responsibility*, and *Introducing Theologies of Religions*. He is a member of the Roman Catholic parish of Bellarmine Chapel in Cincinnati.

Sallie McFague is Distinguished Theologian in Residence at the Vancouver School of Theology and Carpenter Professor of Theology, Emerita, Vanderbilt University. Her books include *Models of God*, *The Body of God*, and *Life Abundant: Rethinking Theology and Ecology for a Planet in Peril*. She is a member of the Anglican Church of Canada.

Richard J. Mouw is President and Professor of Christian Philosophy at Fuller Theological Seminary. His books include *The Smell of Sawdust: What Evangelicals Can Learn from Their Fundamentalist Heritage* and *He Shines in All That's Fair: Culture and Common Grace*. He is a member of the Presbyterian Church (U.S.A.).

Hughes Oliphant Old is a member of the Center of Theological Inquiry and a visiting lecturer at Princeton Theological Seminary. His books include *The Reform of the Baptismal Rite in the Sixteenth Century, The Reading and Preaching of the Scriptures in the Worship of the Christian Church* (four volumes so far), and *Leading in Prayer*. Formerly he was pastor of Faith Presbyterian Church in West Lafayette, Indiana.

Ted Peters is Professor of Systematic Theology at Pacific Lutheran Theological Seminary and the Graduate Theological Union in Berkeley, California. He is editor of *Dialog: A Journal of Theology* and most recently author of *GOD—The World's Future* and *Science, Theology, and Ethics.* He is an ordained pastor in the Evangelical Lutheran Church in America.

William C. Placher is the Charles D. and Elizabeth S. LaFollette Distinguished Professor in the Humanities at Wabash College and winner of the American Academy of Religion's 2002 Award for Outstanding Teaching. His books include *A History of Christian Theology, Unapologetic Theology, Narratives of a Vulnerable God, The Domestication of Transcendence*, and *Jesus the Savior*. He is an elder in the Presbyterian Church (U.S.A.).

Letty M. Russell is Professor Emerita of Theology at Yale University Divinity School. Her books include *Church in the Round: Feminist Interpretation of the Church, Household of Freedom: Authority in Feminist Theology, Feminist Interpretation of the Bible*, and *Dictionary of Feminist Theologies*. She is an ordained minister in the Presbyterian Church (U.S.A.).

Kathryn Tanner is Professor of Theology at the University of Chicago Divinity School. Her books include *God and Creation in Christian Theology, The Politics of God, Theories of Culture*, and *Jesus, Humanity, and the Trinity*. She is an Episcopalian and presently a member of the Theology Committee, which advises the Episcopal House of Bishops.

Leanne Van Dyk is Professor of Reformed Theology at Western Theological Seminary in Holland, Michigan. She is the author of *Believing in Jesus Christ* and editor of the forthcoming *Theology and Worship*. She is a member of the Presbyterian Church (U.S.A.).

Clark M. Williamson is Indiana Professor of Christian Thought, Emeritus, at Christian Theological Seminary in Indianapolis. His books include *A Credible and Timely Word: Process Theology and Preaching, A Guest in the House of Israel*, and *Way of Blessing, Way of Life*. He is ordained in the Christian Church (Disciples of Christ).

Acknowledgments

Both the basic idea and the title for this book came from Donald McKim, and I am more grateful than I can say to him both for his encouragement and for entrusting his own "baby" to me as its editor. Some of my editorial work was done with the support of a grant from the Louisville Institute, and I am thankful to Jim Lewis both for the grant and for permission to turn to this task from what I was really supposed to be doing. I did my work in the pleasant surroundings of the Martin Marty Center of the University of Chicago Divinity School, and I owe thanks to Richard Rosengarten, dean of the Divinity School, and Clark Gilpin, director of the Center, for their hospitality. Matt Miller fixed nearly endless last-minute computer problems. Above all, I am grateful to the authors of the essays included in this book, who took time from very busy schedules to undertake this work because of their belief in the importance of introducing students to theology. Some of them even finished on schedule.

W.C.P.

Why Bother with Theology?

An Introduction

WILLIAM C. PLACHER

Several times, introducing me to a church group, a well-meaning person has said, "Bill Placher is a theologian, but I think you'll find what he has to say very interesting." That *but* always worries me, yet it captures something honest about contemporary attitudes to Christian theology. It is not surprising that many religious skeptics dismiss theology as meaningless superstition, but many Christians also think of theology as technical, complicated, irrelevant.

What is puzzling about this attitude is that all Christians do theology all the time, for *theology* just means thinking about our faith.[1] When a child dies and we say, "God didn't want that to happen," or, "Now she's in heaven," or even, "I don't know how to make sense of this"—whatever we say, we are doing theology. In less dramatic moments, if we pray, "If it be your will, help my mother to get well," or explain, "No, your friend can't take Communion; she hasn't been baptized," or sing, "Jesus loves me, this I know, for the Bible tells me so," all of that too is, or at least presupposes, theology.

> All Christians do theology all the time, for *theology* just means thinking about our faith.

The responsibility to think about our faith and how its elements fit together falls particularly on those who preach and teach. The twentieth-century Swiss theologian Karl Barth used to call theology "the conscience of preaching." A preacher can carefully research the biblical texts, reflect on the situation of the congregation, and preach on one scriptural passage this week, and then another one next week, and give thoughtful sermons. But if someone in the congregation says, "Those two sermons seemed contradictory," or, "I don't see any connection between those ideas," then, in order to explain, one has to start doing theology—and maybe should have done it before preaching!

Similarly, a pastor can help plan the church budget, provide helpful pastoral counseling, and get involved with organizing the community against a local polluter. But how do the way we allocate church funds, the advice we give, or the stands we take connect to our Christian faith? When we think about such questions, we are doing theology. Theology thus orders and connects our faith and our practice. If Christians pretend not to think about theology, we end up with unexamined theology, sometimes in forms that are silly or even dangerous.

It is possible, of course, to build a church around friendly community, helpful counseling, social outreach, and good music on Sunday morning without worrying much about how we articulate our faith. But social clubs, psychiatrists, political action groups, and choral societies can do all that as well or better. What sets churches apart is that we claim to have challenging but joyous news (after all, *gospel* just means "good news") about God, ourselves, and the world in which we live. In order to do well what only the church can do, we need to get clear on that news in our own minds and figure out how to teach it to our children and explain it to our neighbors. There again, we are doing theology.

Theology, then, serves a variety of purposes, but it is also just fun. Many "professional" theologians, truth to tell, may have started out with varied interests in philosophy, history, anthropology, cosmology, and any number of other fields. Then we found this subject called theology for which *all* our interests were relevant. Once you start thinking about God, after all, it can lead anywhere. Some of the greatest minds of history have devoted their lives to Christian theology, and it is rewarding to think in their company, even as we try to connect what we are thinking with concrete problems down the street or around the world. As the contemporary theologian Thomas Oden puts it, watching good theologians "play theology is like watching Willie Mays play center field or Duke Ellington play 'Sophisticated Lady.'"[2] Theology can bring people hope and help transform the world, but the seriousness of the task should not detract from the joy of observing the grace of the performers.

CONTEXTS FOR THEOLOGY TODAY

The authors of the book share a passion for theology. They are good writers who can effectively communicate their excitement. All are Christians, but they are other things as well—women and men, white and black, of different sexual orientations, Lutherans, Presbyterians, Methodists, Roman Catholics, Disciples of Christ, Episcopalians, Baptists. Those characteristics, and many others, shape the way they think about their faith. All come from North America, and all of them live at the beginning of the twenty-first century. Those contexts too, of course, contribute to the theological issues that seem important to them, and the ways they approach those issues.

At the risk of drastic oversimplification, let me just mention five factors that shape the doing of Christian theology in North America at the beginning of the twenty-first century:

> At least five factors shape the doing of Christian theology in North America today: modernity, the Barthian challenge, ecumenism, pluralisms, and postmodernity.

1. Modernity. What historians mean by *modern* is a complex and contentious matter. For our purposes, suffice it to say that, beginning sometime in the seventeenth century, most Christians acknowledged: (a) that the discoveries of modern science shape at least some important aspects of the way we understand the world (at minimum—this was the first big controversy—that the earth revolves around the sun, not the opposite), and (b) that people of different religious beliefs can find ways of living more or less peacefully together under the same government. As many of us have recently learned, in some (not all) Islamic societies *all* education is based on the Koran and none but Muslims are allowed to teach their religious beliefs in public. Most predominantly Christian societies are very different from that, and that difference illustrates the fact that Christians have pretty much accepted modernity, while Islam is still debating whether or not to do so.

2. The Barthian challenge. Karl Barth (1886–1968) is the one twentieth-century theologian who simply cannot be ignored. His liberal German teachers had taught him that theology has to adapt to its culture. Barth (who was Swiss) grew alarmed when those teachers supported the German war effort in World War I. Under the Nazis, he denounced church officials and theologians who compromised Christian faith in order to get along with the government. Barth drew a much different conclusion: Christianity, he said, should *never* compromise its principles to fit the culture around it. Even theologians who disagree with him have to face his challenge. If we are willing to adjust to a relatively nice society in order to fit in, do we have strong enough principles to resist and preserve our own values and beliefs if Nazis take over some day?

3. Ecumenism. Fifty years ago, denominational loyalties meant a lot to most Christians and to most Christian theologians. Preachers and theologians regularly denounced other denominations passionately. Things have changed. The Second Vatican Council (1962–1965) opened Roman Catholicism to all sorts of new influences—to freer conversations with non-Catholics and even non-Christians, to critical biblical scholarship, to trends in modern science and philosophy.

Catholics continue to debate whether Vatican II went too far, just the right distance, or not far enough, but all would agree that it changed their church in fundamental ways. The second half of the twentieth century saw all sorts of ecumenical conversations between Catholics and Protestants and among different Protestant denominations (and to a lesser extent Eastern Orthodox groups). Certainly among Protestants, and even among Catholics, labels such as *liberal, conservative,* or *evangelical* have now come to be more important than *Lutheran* or *Baptist.* Conservative or liberal Presbyterians, for instance, will often feel they have more in common with conservative or liberal Methodists or even Catholics than with the opposing party in their own denomination.[3]

4. Pluralisms. Fifty years ago nearly all those with academic training in theology were white and male. Women, African Americans, and Hispanics are now beginning to be well represented among theologians in North America. Moreover, in 1900, two-thirds of all Christians lived in North America and Europe; in 2000, the figure was only one-third. Europeans and North Americans can no longer take ourselves for granted as the mainstream of Christian theology when we represent only a minority of Christians. Even in Europe and North America, furthermore, Christians live with far more non-Christian neighbors. Muslims or Hindus are not just distant objects of curiosity or missionary activity; they live down the street. All these forms of pluralism make a difference in how we think about theology.

5. Postmodernity. If it is hard to define what *modern* means, it should be no surprise that what supposedly comes after it—the *postmodern*—is even trickier. *Postmodern* has become a faddish word among many writers, but they often mean very different things by it. For example, modern architecture aimed for simplicity and functionalism. The boxlike skyscraper seeks to be "rational" by providing office space and elevators as efficiently as possible. Postmodern architecture, by contrast, calls attention to itself as architecture: the top cut off at an odd angle, the arch perched on the top of the building. Similarly, postmodern novelists do not consistently help readers lose ourselves in the story; they keep interrupting to call attention to the fact that we are reading a piece of fiction. Even TV shows where characters turn to address the audience directly, as if to remind us that we are watching a program, can claim to be postmodern.

In philosophy and other fields, *postmodern* often refers to the idea that, after the carnage of World Wars I and II and the horrors of the Holocaust, it is hard to be as optimistic about human progress and the power of reason. The stories we tell about humanity must therefore be more ironic and fragmentary (and more conscious of their own character as stories) than the big stories (*metanarratives*) that intellectuals used to tell concerning how history as a whole is really about intellectual progress, or the growth of Western culture, or the eventual triumph of the working class. The "modern" idea that science and civilization have or soon will overcome barbarism looks doubtful. Some even wonder if "modernity" was such a good idea. At any rate, looking at a simple, Stone Age tribe in the Amazon jungle, postmoderns hesitate to say with confidence that we are better than they are.

If one had to summarize a very complicated idea in one word, one might say that postmodernism teaches theology to be *suspicious*—suspicious of optimism about human nature, suspicious of easy answers (whether from the left or the right), more comfortable with ambiguity, irony, and fragments. (It follows of course that postmodernism teaches us to be suspicious of short definitions!)

ORGANIZATION, LANGUAGE, AND SOME FINAL WORDS

Nine chapters follow this introduction. They represent a fairly standard list of some of the big topics of Christian theology (though others certainly might have been included; I am particularly conscious of the lack of a separate chapter on the Holy Spirit). The structure represents a combination of three of the most common ways of organizing Christian theology:

1. Following the outline of history as the Bible presents it: First there is God, then God creates the world, then human beings fall into sin, then God works to save them in the history of Israel, the coming of Christ, and the activity of the Holy Spirit, shaping the life of the church and the lives of individual Christians as well as other elements of the world until all history comes to an end.

2. Organizing according to the Trinitarian pattern of the creeds: first the "Father" and the work of creation, then Christ and salvation, then the Spirit, the church, and the last things.

3. The *exitus-reditus* ("going out and returning") pattern particularly common in medieval theology: Creation flows out from God and in sin people turn away from God, but then Christ begins the process of returning us to God, which will be completed only at the end of history.

These three organizing schemes overlap enough to make compromises among them fairly easy. Thus, the following chapters discuss: (1) revelation and authority, by way of introduction; (2) God; (3) creation and providence; (4) human nature and human sin; (5) the person and work of Jesus Christ; (6) the church and its worship; (7) Christian life; (8) Christian understanding of non-Christians; and (9) eschatology—(the study of the last things).

Two theologians will address each topic from different points of view. Sometimes they will disagree strongly; in other cases, they will illuminate different aspects of their topic from similar perspectives. In inviting these particular writers, I sought to avoid lining them up in two clear "teams." Theological debate is more complicated than that, and the points of view here represented reflect that situation. You may well love some and hate others; perhaps it is worth remembering that some other readers will probably like best the essays you most dislike. Strong disagreement may well generate your own best theological thinking. The philosopher Alasdair MacIntyre has defined a *tradition* as an ongoing argument. The authors of this book share in the Christian tradition; that will not stop them from arguing. You are invited to join the tradition by joining the argument.

Doing theology does involve operating in a tradition. It is significant that a textbook in chemistry, for instance, might have a few pages at the start about the history of the field but would move quickly to the current state of the discipline. Introductions to theology, by contrast, always contain great chunks of history all the way through, and every chapter in this book will begin with some form of historical survey. In his essay for chapter 1 of this book, Stanley Grenz offers two reasons for studying history as part of studying theology. First, it offers us both good models and warnings of pitfalls. Second, Christians are necessarily part of a community (more on that in chapters 6 and 7), and attending to theology's history affirms our membership in a community of thinkers that extends through the centuries. If we ignored that history completely, we would be placing ourselves outside the body of Christian believers.

Paying attention to a tradition, however, does not always mean agreeing with it. Nor does "the Christian tradition" always speak with one voice. A tradition, remember, is an ongoing *argument.* Even the language we use in writing theology is a matter of ongoing debate. Like all of those writing theology these days, the authors of this book have to think about the proper language to use, particularly as regards gender. Like other writers in English, theologians used to say "men" in a way that, more or less, meant "men and women" but also in a way left women out. It is usually easy enough, and certainly better, to say "people" or "men and women" or "women and men."

Like all of those writing theology these days, the authors of this book have to think about the proper language to use, particularly as regards gender.

Other changes raise harder questions. Jesus spoke to and of one he called his "Father." Was he just reflecting the patriarchal patterns of his society? Or was he using God's true name, which we should not change? Theologians disagree. Christians generally agree that God is beyond gender—neither male nor female. Some conclude that we should not use male pronouns of God. Others find the use of female pronouns an unacceptable break with the tradition, and argue that avoiding personal pronouns at all makes God an impersonal "it" who could not love us and to whom we could not pray.

Passions run high on these topics. Some women who have suffered discrimination or, even worse, abuse, find that using male language to refer to God reinforces the cultural patterns of which they are victims. Some men agree. Other women and men are convinced that changing language changes content and breaks with the faith that the Christian tradition has taught. Different authors in this book follow different practices in these matters. It seemed inappropriate to edit them into a common usage (even if they would have let me!), since the appropriate usage is itself an important issue in theological debates.

I have written a brief introduction to each chapter, laying out some of the history and some of the key terms that concern that issue, so that the other authors can plunge immediately into stating their own theological ideas. I have also added some summary statements at key points in the text and provided questions for reflection and lists of books for further reading at the end of each chapter. These aids may be particularly helpful to those reading this book on their own, rather than as a member of a class.

Throughout, I have tried to function as much as I could simply as a historian and summarizer, but smart readers will recognize that I too have my perspective and my prejudices. I am nevertheless pleased that my role as "introducer" has generally freed the other authors from needing to summarize and review so that they can get on with the excitement of doing theology. Samuel Johnson, the eighteenth-century English writer, was once asked if he believed in infant baptism. "Believe in it?" he replied. "Why I've seen it done!" An introduction to theology, it seems to me, should not just describe for readers what it would be like to do theology; it ought to give them a chance to see it done.

I earlier mentioned a number of reasons for doing theology; I have saved one for last. The Westminster Shorter Catechism, a famous seventeenth-century summary of Reformed faith, opens by declaring that the chief end of human beings is to glorify God and to enjoy God forever. Theology can sometimes be a rather ponderous way of glorifying God. Still, just as God gave the cheetah its speed, the elephant its strength, and the otter its playfulness, so God has given us humans intellect and imagination. When we use those gifts to think about God, we give God glory. So—to the glory of God.

FOR FURTHER READING

The works cited here (and at the end of subsequent chapters) are all from the last hundred years and mostly from the last twenty-five. The footnotes and bibliographies of these recent books should lead you to older ones. Books listed here generally survey the whole range of theological topics. Many theologians who are just as important but whose most significant books address only one or two topics in theology will appear in the lists following later chapters.

Introductions to Theology

The Common Catechism. New York: Seabury Press, 1975.

Evans, James H., Jr. *We Have Been Believers: An African American Systematic Theology.* Minneapolis: Fortress Press, 1992.

Fackre, Gabriel. *The Christian Story.* Grand Rapids: Wm. B. Eerdmans Publishing Co., 1978.

Gilkey, Langdon. *Message and Existence.* New York: Seabury Press, 1981.

Grenz, Stanley J. *What Christians Really Believe—and Why.* Louisville, Ky.: Westminster John Knox Press, 1998.

Guthrie, Shirley. *Christian Doctrine.* Rev. ed. Louisville, Ky.: Westminster John Knox Press, 1994.

Migliore, Daniel L. *Faith Seeking Understanding.* Grand Rapids: Wm. B. Eerdmans Publishing Co., 1991.

Edited Introductions

Braaten, Carl E., and Robert W. Jenson, eds. *Christian Dogmatics.* 2 vols. Philadelphia: Fortress Press, 1984.

Fiorenza, Francis Schüssler, and John P. Galvin, eds. *Systematic Theology: Roman Catholic Perspectives.* 2 vols. Minneapolis: Fortress Press, 1991.

Hodgson, Peter C., and Robert H. King, eds. *Christian Theology: An Introduction to Its Traditions and Tasks.* Philadelphia: Fortress Press, 1982.

LaCugna, Catherine Mowry, ed. *Freeing Theology: The Essentials of Theology in Feminist Perspective.* San Francisco: HarperSanFrancisco, 1993.

Introductions to the History of Theology

Bromiley, Geoffrey W. *Historical Theology* Grand Rapids: Wm. B. Eerdmans Publishing Co., 1978.

González, Justo L. *A History of Christian Thought.* 2 vols. Nashville: Abingdon Press, 1970–1971.

Kelly, J. N. D. *Early Christian Doctrines.* 5th ed. New York: Continuum, 2000.

Pelikan, Jaroslav. *The Christian Tradition.* 5 vols. Chicago: University of Chicago Press, 1971–1989.

Placher, William C. *A History of Christian Theology.* Philadelphia: Westminster Press, 1983.

Classic Works of the Twentieth Century

Barth, Karl. *Church Dogmatics.* 13 part vols. Various translators. Edinburgh: T. & T. Clark, 1936–1969.

Moltmann, Jürgen, *Theology of Hope* (1967), *The Crucified God* (1974), *The Church in the Power of the Spirit* (1975), *The Trinity and the Kingdom of God* (1981), *God in Creation* (1985), *The Way of Jesus Christ* (1989), *The Spirit of Life* (1991), *The Coming of God* (1996). Trans. Margaret Kohl and others. Minneapolis: Fortress Press.

Pannenberg, Wolfhart. *Systematic Theology.* 3 vols. Trans. Geoffrey W. Bromiley. Grand Rapids: Wm. B. Eerdmans Publishing Co., 1991–1998.

Rahner, Karl. *Foundations of Christian Faith.* Trans. William V. Dych (New York: Crossroad, 1982.

Tillich, Paul. *Systematic Theology.* 3 vols. Chicago: University of Chicago Press, 1967.

Feminist, Womanist, and Mujerista Theology

Carr, Anne E. *Transforming Grace.* New York: Harper & Row, 1988.

Isasi-Díaz, Ada Maria. *Mujerista Theology.* Maryknoll, N.Y.: Orbis Press, 1996.

Jones, Serene. *Feminist Theory and Christian Theology.* Minneapolis: Fortress Press, 2000.

McFague, Sallie. *The Body of God.* Minneapolis: Fortress Press, 1993.

Ruether, Rosemary Radford. *Sexism and God Talk.* Boston: Beacon Press, 1984.

Russell, Letty M. *Human Liberation in a Feminist Perspective.* Philadelphia: Westminster Press, 1974.

Williams, Delores. *Sisters in the Wilderness.* Maryknoll, N.Y.: Orbis Press, 1993.

Evangelical Theology

Bloesch, Donald G. *Essentials of Evangelical Theology.* 2 vols. San Francisco: Harper & Row, 1978–1979.
Grenz, Stanley. *Theology for the Community of God.* Grand Rapids: Wm. B. Eerdmans Publishing Co., 2000.
Henry, Carl F. H. *God, Revelation, and Authority.* 6 vols. Waco, Tex.: Baker Book House, 1976–1983.
Jewett, Paul K. *God, Creation, and Revelation.* Grand Rapids: Wm. B. Eerdmans Publishing Co., 1991.
Packer, J. I. *Knowing God.* 2nd ed. Downers Grove, Ill.: InterVarsity Press, 1993.
Thielicke, Helmut. *The Evangelical Faith.* 3 vols. Trans. Geoffrey W. Bromiley. Grand Rapids: Wm. B. Eerdmans Publishing Co., 1974–82.

African American Theology

Cone, James H. *A Black Theology of Liberation.* 2nd ed. Maryknoll, N.Y.: Orbis Books, 1986.
Evans, James H., Jr. *We Have Been Believers.* Minneapolis: Fortress Press, 1993.
Roberts, J. Deotis. *A Black Political Theology.* Philadelphia: Westminster Press, 1974.
Williams, Delores. *Sisters in the Wilderness.* Maryknoll, N.Y.: Orbis Books, 1993.

Third World Theology

Battle, Michael. *Reconciliation: The Ubuntu Theology of Desmond Tutu.* Cleveland: Pilgrim Press, 1993.
Gutiérrez, Gustavo. *A Theology of Liberation.* Trans. Caridad Inda and John Eagleson. Maryknoll, N.Y.: Orbis Books, 1973.
Koyama, Kosuke. *Waterbuffalo Theology.* Maryknoll, N.Y.: Orbis Books, 1974.
Oduyoye, Mercy Amba. *Hearing and Knowing.* Maryknoll, N.Y.: Orbis Books, 1986.
Segundo, Juan Luis. *The Liberation of Theology.* Maryknoll, N.Y.: Orbis Books, 1976.
Sobrino, Jon, and Ignacio Ellacuría, eds. *Systematic Theology.* Maryknoll, N.Y.: Orbis Books, 1993.
Song, Choan-Seng. *Third-Eye Theology.* Rev. ed. Maryknoll, N.Y.: Orbis Books, 1990.

Other Contemporary Theologians (Protestant)

Cobb, John B., Jr., and David Ray Griffin. *Process Theology.* Philadelphia: Westminster Press, 1976.
Hall, Douglas John. *Thinking the Faith* (1989), *Professing the Faith* (1993), *Confessing the Faith* (1996). Minneapolis: Fortress Press.
Hodgson, Peter W. *Winds of the Spirit.* Louisville, Ky.: Westminster John Knox Press, 1994.
Jenson, Robert W. *Systematic Theology.* 2 vols. New York: Oxford University Press, 1997, 1999.
Kaufman, Gordon D. *In Face of Mystery.* Cambridge, Mass.: Harvard University Press, 1993.
Macquarrie, John. *Principles of Christian Theology.* New York: Charles Scribner's Sons, 1966.
McClendon, James William, Jr. *Systematic Theology.* 3 vols. Nashville: Abingdon Press, 1986–2000.

Peters, Ted. *GOD: The World's Future.* Minneapolis: Fortress Press, 1992.
Torrance, T. F. *The Trinitarian Faith.* Edinburgh: T. & T. Clark, 1988.

Other Contemporary Theologians (Roman Catholic)

Balthasar, Hans Urs von. *The Von Balthasar Reader.* Ed. Medard Kehl and Werner Löser. Trans. Robert J. Daly and Fred Lawrence. New York: Crossroad, 1985.
Küng, Hans. *On Being a Christian.* Trans. Edward Quinn. Garden City, N.Y.: Doubleday, 1976.
Ratzinger, Joseph. *Introduction to Christianity.* Trans. J. R. Foster. New York: Crossroad, 1988.
Tracy, David. *The Analogical Imagination.* New York: Crossroad, 1986.

Web sites

Christian Classics Ethereal Library: *http://www.ccel.org/*
The Ecole Initiative: *http://cedar.evansville.edu/~ecoleweb/*
The New Advent Catholic Web site: *http://www.newadvent.org/*
Religion Online: *http://www.religion-online.org/*
Wabash Center Guide to Internet Resources:
http://www.wabashcenter.wabash.edu/

Chapter 1

How Do We Know What to Believe?

Revelation and Authority

"Our church teaches you have to be baptized as an adult."

"I just can't believe in the Virgin Birth."

"Homosexuality is a sin—it says so in the Bible."

"You can't take the Bible literally."

We hear such comments all the time, and they remind us that Christians disagree with each other about what to believe. Sometimes individual Christians even disagree within ourselves—new ideas come into conflict with the faith we were taught as children, and we struggle to make up our minds.

If two people disagree about the answer to a math problem, we go back to check our figures. If two scientists reach different conclusions, they go back to review their data. How do Christians argue? How do we decide what to believe?

REASON AND REVELATION, SCRIPTURE AND TRADITION

We might try to decide theological questions the same way a mathematician or scientist would—through the use of our *reason*. Two hundred years ago, the great

German philosopher Immanuel Kant tried such an approach in a book entitled *Religion within the Limits of Reason Alone*. Brilliant as the book is, most philosophers think it reaches beyond the limits of reason, and most theologians argue it falls far short of Christianity. A long tradition in theology has held that, even if people could reason their way to belief in God and some sort of moral code, Christian doctrines like the Trinity and salvation through Christ are inaccessible to reason.

The role of reason in theology, however, cannot be explained by drawing a sharp line between what reason can know and what it cannot. Whatever other topics it addresses, theology inevitably talks about God, and Christians generally agree that human reason by itself is inadequate for understanding God. To start with, God is infinite, and we are finite. We are too limited to be able to make sense of God. Moreover, sin has corrupted what capacities we have, and any idea we developed of God on our own would be distorted on that account.

Theologians have disagreed about the extent of that distortion. Historically, Roman Catholics have held that, even though we are finite and sinners, our reason can provide some truths about God. Aquinas, for instance, began his discussion of God with five philosophical arguments for God's existence (more of that in the next chapter). The Protestant Reformers Luther and Calvin both believed that whatever truth reason might provide about God was, thanks to sin, so mixed with error that it was best not to depend on it. Both Protestants and Catholics, however, have agreed that we cannot figure out for ourselves anything like an adequate knowledge of God. For that, we have to depend on something God gives us—*revelation*.

To emphasize that *all* our knowledge of God comes from God, theologians sometimes call what we can figure out by our reason *general revelation*, in contrast to what God gives us in Scripture or other particular sources, which they call *special revelation*. *Natural theology* is another name for general revelation—the part of theology we learn through the study of nature rather than Scripture. As noted in the introduction, the great early-twentieth-century theologian Karl Barth warned against natural theology. He argued that human reason is shaped by our culture, and therefore natural theology, based on reason, can lead us away from Christian faith into beliefs about God shaped by the values and assumptions of our particular culture.[1] Theologians thus fall along a spectrum, from those at one end who trust almost entirely in reason, to those like Barth at the other, who put all or almost all their trust in revelation.

Theologians thus fall along a spectrum, from those at one end who trust almost entirely in reason, to those like Barth at the other, who put all or almost all their trust in revelation.

Catholics and Protestants have also traditionally seemed to disagree on where to find that revelation. *Sola scriptura* ("Scripture alone") was one of the slogans of the Reformation. When his opponents sought to prove him wrong by appealing to decisions of popes and councils of the church, Martin Luther, in a famous and dramatic moment in 1521, stood before the emperor and assembled nobles of Germany and declared,

> Unless I am convinced by the testimony of Scripture or by clear reason, for I do not trust either in the pope or in councils alone, since it is well known that they have often erred and contradicted themselves, my conscience is captive to the Word of God. I cannot and will not retract anything.[2]

In response, at the Council of Trent a generation later, the assembled Catholic leaders made explicit what Catholics had widely assumed for a long time—that there were unwritten traditions passed down through the church which had authority alongside that of Scripture.[3]

Recent discussions between Protestants and Catholics have found more agreement than the slogans of the Reformation era would imply. There were Christians, after all, before there was a Bible. Protestants have to admit that those first Christians must have been dependent on traditions passed down among them and that traditions still shape the way we read the Bible. Catholics acknowledge that traditions function primarily to point us back to the truth of Scripture.

However much theology depends on revelation, and wherever theologians look for that revelation, revelation requires *interpretation*, and that generates further questions. From the early centuries of Christianity some theologians argued that some passages in the Bible could not be literally true and therefore must be understood in some other sense.[4] If the Bible talks about the "hand of God," for instance, it does not mean that God literally has hands. Likewise, it seemed to most medieval interpreters that the rather erotic poetry of the Song of Solomon could not be literally about a love affair between a man and a woman. It must refer to the relation between Christ and the church, or God and the soul. Eventually, medieval theologians discerned four senses in Scripture: the literal sense, the allegorical sense (which applied to Christ and the church, and could also be used as a general term for any nonliteral sense), the tropological sense (which applied to our lives), and the anagogical sense (which applied to the last days or heaven). So, for example, when the Bible talks about Jerusalem, it can refer to the city in the Middle East (literal), the church (allegorical), the soul of the believer (tropological), the heavenly Jerusalem (anagogical), or all four—or some combination of them.[5]

> Medieval theologians discerned four senses in Scripture: the literal, the allegorical, the tropological, and the anagogical.

Even in the Middle Ages, theologians debated how much emphasis to put on the nonliteral senses. While the Reformers did not abandon allegorical interpretation altogether, they did emphasize the literal sense. Still, they exercised considerable freedom in interpretation. Luther thought that justification by grace through faith was the core of biblical teaching. He treated texts that did not speak to that theme with indifference or hostility. He admitted that he did not know quite what to make of the book of Revelation and dismissed the Letter of James as a "letter of straw," claiming that "it does not amount to much."[6] Calvin was more cautious, but he too acknowledged that the Gospel writers "were not very exact as to the order of dates, or even in detailing minutely every thing that Christ said and did."[7] The truth of the Bible did not depend on the literal truth of its every proposition.

In the seventeenth century, however, debates among the different branches of Christianity intensified, and pressure grew to "prove" that one was right and one's opponents were wrong. In an age when science was growing in importance, many people adopted one version or another of the scientific method as the definition of a good argument. The Westminster Confession of Faith, written by Reformed Christians in England in 1647, already says that everything that we need to know for our salvation "is either expressly set down in Scripture, or by good and necessary consequence may be deduced from Scripture."[8] Like scientists, the Westminster Fathers claimed they could deduce their conclusions from indubitable assumptions. In the centuries since, many theologians have continued to follow that model of looking for clear *starting points* for theology in revelation, but in thinking about revelation, they have chosen either a *propositional model*, a *historical model*, or an *experiential model*.

> In the seventeenth century, pressure grew to "prove" that one was right, and many theologians adopted one version or another of the scientific method as the definition of a good argument.

THREE MODELS OF REVELATION

1. A *propositional model* of revelation, already implied by Westminster's language of "expressly set down in Scripture," has taken clearest form among conservative American Christians beginning in the nineteenth century. As the evangelical theologian Carl F. H. Henry puts it, "The whole canon of Scripture . . . objectively communicates in propositional-verbal form the content and meaning of all God's revelation."[9] Quoting Gordon Clark, Henry states succinctly, "Aside from imperative sentences and a few exclamations in the Psalms, the Bible is composed of propositions. These give information about God and his dealings with men."[10]

For the most uncompromising propositionalists, biblical truth is an all-or-nothing deal. The Bible is a set of propositions. If we start questioning any of them, then there will be no place to stop, and soon we will not be able to trust the truth of anything in the Bible. Therefore, the Bible must be *inerrant*—all of its propositions must be true. But even within a propositionalist model there is room for alternatives. Some who insist on the inerrancy of the Bible as originally written (the *autograph*) acknowledge that the biblical manuscripts available to us differ, and therefore admit that existing biblical texts can contain minor errors. Others go further and say that God's purpose in giving us the Bible is to lead us to salvation, so only what concerns salvation in it need be true.

To take some contemporary North American evangelicals as examples: Harold Lindsell holds that the original biblical writings were inerrant and that God has protected key manuscripts so that we still have inerrant texts. Carl Henry says that the original texts were inerrant but minimal errors may have slipped into the manuscript tradition since then. Clark Pinnock defends the inerrancy of the intention and meaning of the texts as we have them, but not of their specifics. Bernard Ramm believes the Bible is inerrant with respect to knowledge needed for salvation, but not concerning historical and scientific matters. Donald Bloesch affirms the inerrancy of major theological assertions, but holds that some religious and moral assertions in the Bible, as well as historical and scientific claims, may be in error.[11] The unqualified inerrantists face the challenge of explaining what seem inconsistencies in the Bible or defending claims it makes about science or attitudes it takes toward slavery or the position of women or other issues where what the Bible says makes many readers today uncomfortable. They in turn challenge those who introduce qualifications as to how they can know where to stop once they have admitted the possibility of some biblical errors.

> For the most uncompromising propositionalists, biblical truth is an all-or-nothing deal. The Bible is a set of propositions. If we start questioning any of them, then there will be no place to stop.

2. The German Lutheran theologian Wolfhart Pannenberg is the most distinguished representative today of a different approach, a *historical model* of revelation. For Pannenberg, God is revealed not in the propositions in the Bible but in the events that they report. God is revealed, for example, not in the fact that the Bible says Jesus was raised from the dead, but in the fact that Jesus was raised from the dead. Believers in the propositionalist view have to explain how we *know* that the Bible is inerrant by some appeal to faith. In contrast, Pannenberg insists that on his view: "The historical revelation is open to anyone who has eyes to see. . . . God has proved his deity in this language of facts."[12]

> For Pannenberg, God is revealed not in the propositions in the Bible but in the events that they report.

Pannenberg argues that history tests the truth claims of various religions. For instance, worshipers of Marduk in ancient Babylon believed that Marduk was the most powerful of gods and would always bring them victory. But the Babylonian empire was ultimately destroyed. History proved them wrong. Religious folk dream dreams and make prophecies, but "signs are either borne out or not. Dreams come true" or not,[13] and such results determine the truth of the religious claims.

Since religious claims concern the whole of reality and we are only in the midst of history, Pannenberg admits, we can only say that the evidence so far *tentatively* supports Christian faith. But Jesus' resurrection anticipated the end of history; what happened to him offers the central clue about how all of history will turn out. Since Pannenberg thinks there is good evidence that Jesus was raised from the dead, he concludes that Christians are justified (if still tentatively) in their convictions concerning the shape of history as a whole and therefore in their beliefs concerning what God reveals in history.

Back in the 1950s, many adherents of the "biblical theology" movement made a similar appeal to history as the locus of revelation. The Old Testament scholar G. Ernest Wright published a widely used textbook on the Bible called *The God Who Acts*, emphasizing that the Bible is "a history book" which points to God's acts in history. Most followers of the biblical theology movement, however, did not believe in literal miracles. They thought, for instance, that only a few Israelites had ever been enslaved in Egypt and that the story of the parting of the Red Sea had grown up as a legend from some rather limited, nonmiraculous starting point. Thus, as Langdon Gilkey pointed out in a particularly devastating article, it was hard to know exactly what they meant by talking about God's actions in history.[14]

Pannenberg's position is less easily refuted. For one thing, he really does believe that Jesus was objectively raised from the dead, that his disciples saw him, that his tomb was empty. On the other hand, he would admit that much of the Bible, from the creation stories to the book of Job, is not "history" in that same sense. Are such stories then not revelation, or is "history" an inadequate category for the Bible as a whole? Pannenberg also struggles between saying that Jesus was raised from the dead (the evidence is in, and the facts are clear) and saying that history is incomplete (we still need faith, and Christian claims remain tentative). It is not clear how strong a claim he intends to make concerning the current evidence of God's revelation in history.

3. The propositional model and the historical model both claim to focus on objective realities. Out there, outside of me, there are scriptural propositions or historical events, true or false, real or imagined. An *experiential model*, by contrast, looks inward for certainty. The religious individual comes to know truth about God through direct personal experience, and nothing can challenge, it would seem, the immediate certainty that that experience provides. How do I know that the book in front of me is red? I just look at it and see—what could be more certain? How do I know that God is loving? If I have experienced God's love for me, then I will have no doubt. As the American philosopher William James once observed, such experience may not persuade anyone else, but it is decisive for the person who has experienced it.[15]

The propositional model and the historical model both claim to focus on objective realities. An experiential model, by contrast, looks inward for certainty.

Such an appeal to experience has often attracted those who would like to challenge traditional doctrines. If I dislike something in the Bible or the teachings of the church, I can say, "That is not how I experience God." The road to God through experience can also seem more democratic. It takes some education and expertise to make judgments about the meaning of the biblical text or the events of history, but each of us is the ultimate authority on our own experience. The appeal to experience can generate more tolerance, for many of those who adopt the experiential model say that at the deepest level the experience of the divine is much the same in the world's different cultures and religious traditions. It is only the inadequate language in which it is reported that creates apparent differences.[16]

Christian communities have generally been nervous, however, about putting too much weight on appeals to religious experience. Cynics will observe that those with institutional power feel threatened by the claims of religious experience, and no doubt there is truth in that observation. At the same time, fanatic cults and individuals remind us that religious visions can lead people to odd and dangerous beliefs and actions.

Questions about how far we can trust experience arose early in Christian history. In the middle of the second century, a Christian from Asia Minor (modern Turkey) named Montanus claimed that, when he fell into a trance, the Holy Spirit spoke directly through him. The church historian Eusebius quotes one of Montanus's critics:

> A recent convert named Montanus . . . was filled with spiritual excitement and suddenly fell into a kind of trance and unnatural ecstasy. He raved, and began to chatter and talk nonsense. . . . Then he secretly stirred up and inflamed minds closed to the true Faith, raising up in this way two others—women whom he filled with the sham spirit, so that they chattered crazily, inopportunely, and wildly, like Montanus himself.[17]

In response to these "Montanists" and others like them, the early church came to put more emphasis on a canon of Scripture (a list of the books that counted as authoritative and would be included in the Bible), on creeds, and on hierarchical officials as the sources of authority. If a Christian claimed that God had spoken to him or her in a vision, one could evaluate the vision by seeing if it accorded with the Bible or the community's confession—or one could ask the local bishop. The church grew more structured, with all the advantages and disadvantages that implies. (One effect, in a society where official positions were almost always held by men, was to decrease Christian women's opportunities to speak with authority).

Debates about the authority of religious experience have continued down the centuries. Medieval mystics wrote of their profound religious experiences, but some of them were suspected as heretics. Luther denounced the experiential claims of his opponent Thomas Müntzer, remarking that he seemed to have "swallowed the Holy Ghost, feathers and all."[18] In seventeenth-century England, the Quakers began to speak out their own beliefs, often at risk of imprisonment or persecution, under the guidance, they said, of an Inner Light.[19] In one debate in a seventeenth-century English parish, when one speaker, challenged about his theological opinion, said he had "found it by experience," a majority of the parishioners declared, "We desired him to prove it by the scriptures, for we would not be ruled by his fancy."[20]

At the beginning of the nineteenth century, the great German theologian Friedrich Schleiermacher developed a classic statement of the experiential model of revelation. He insisted that revelation cannot be a matter of a "system of propositions." Rather, it comes in a "moment of inspiration" where God makes a direct impression on our self-consciousness.[21] From that experience, we derive a "sense of absolute dependence," whose object "is to be designated by the word 'God,' and . . . this is for us the really original signification of that word."[22] Originally, for Schleiermacher, *God* thus means, first of all, not the one witnessed to in the Bible, or the one who raised Jesus from the dead, but the one with respect to whom I have a feeling of absolute dependence.

Our experience never comes pure but is always shaped by the culture and language we bring to it.

Schleiermacher already recognized what others have since pointed out: Our experience never comes pure but is always shaped by the culture and language we bring to it. Schleiermacher experienced a "sense of absolute dependence" in part because he was a nineteenth-century German with a particular intellectual and religious background. In its less sophisticated forms, the experiential model assumes that we can have some pure experience and that religious language can then be judged by its adequacy or inadequacy to that experience. But people from different cultural backgrounds experience the world differently. The South Sea Islanders who saw Captain Cook's three-masted ship sailing into their harbor saw it differently than the sailors on board. So too with religious experiences. The pious Jew trusting in the Lord and the Buddhist hoping for nirvana are not using different words to say the same thing. We cannot appeal to the raw experience behind all culture as the criterion by which we measure the ways various cultures describe their experience.[23]

IS THERE A FOUNDATION?

So how do we decide what to believe as Christians? Reason does not in itself suffice to teach us about God. Some appeal to Scripture, or Scripture and tradition; others to history; still others to experience. Some in the Methodist tradition speak of a "quadrilateral" of Scripture, reason, tradition, and experience.

Two generations ago, debates on such topics went on, at least in seminaries and graduate schools, primarily among relatively privileged white males. The conversation now often takes place in much more diverse communities, and that changes what gets said. Feminists sometimes experience the Bible as written by men, about men, and for men. They want to critique it in terms of their own experience.[24] African Americans and other traditionally oppressed groups, in contrast, argue that the Bible was written by oppressed people and that it speaks with particular power to them.[25] They find their own experience giving the Bible authority, even as it shapes how they understand it, and, doing this, they remind us that *everyone* interprets the Bible in terms of their own experience.

Other contemporary scholars, influenced by some strains in contemporary philosophy, wonder if it is right to talk about a "starting point" at all. At the beginning of this introduction, I mentioned that efforts to "prove" that one's own religious answers were right took fully developed form only at the beginning of the modern age, in the seventeenth century. The French philosopher René Descartes, writing at that time, used the metaphor of *foundations*. We had to erect the edifice of knowledge on absolutely secure foundations or else it would collapse.[26] Scientists looked for indubitable first principles or unambiguous sense-data as starting points free of doubt. By analogy, Christians turned to Scripture, or church tradition, or experience as their starting points.

Much of twentieth-century philosophy, though, challenged Descartes's metaphor. "I have arrived at the rock bottom of my convictions," the philosopher Ludwig Wittgenstein declared, "and one might almost say that these foundation-walls are carried by the whole house."[27] Neither in science nor in religion nor anywhere else do we really start with a blank slate, "nonfoundationalists" argue. We always find ourselves beginning with a set of beliefs, assumptions, ways of looking at the world. None of them is unchallengeable. If relativistic physics explains more and more things but conflicts with the basic rules of Euclidean geometry, maybe those rules need reexamination. If overwhelming evidence indicates that the friend I thought I saw yesterday was in fact in China, then maybe I was mistaken. I hold on to the beliefs that best help me make sense of the world around me and live my life. Some are more fundamental than others, but I cannot predict in advance which ones I might end up having to change. Scientists have learned to live this way; perhaps theologians can too. Recognizing the interconnectedness of the webs of our beliefs might provide a richer understanding of how we judge what we believe and of the meaning of revelation.

> Stanley J. Grenz, writing from an evangelical perspective, maintains that the propositionalist models of revelation traditionally favored by evangelicals are too simple. Noel Erskine shows how cultural context shapes our understanding of revelation with examples from his own background and in dialogue with Emil Brunner and Elizabeth Johnson.

In the first of this chapter's essays, Stanley J. Grenz, writing from an evangelical perspective, maintains that the propositionalist models of revelation traditionally favored by evangelicals are too simple. His analysis draws insights from a recent school of philosophy called *speech-act theory* and from recent work in the social sciences. While he insists that Scripture is indeed the "norming norm," the ultimate criterion for evaluation in Christian faith, he emphasizes how the Holy Spirit speaks *through* the biblical text and how both the Christian tradition and our contemporary cultural context inevitably influence how we understand the Bible.

In the second essay, Noel Erskine shows how cultural context does indeed shape the understanding of revelation with examples from his own background of growing up in Jamaica, where thinking about revelation could not be separated from thinking about salvation. Then, in dialogue with the mid-twentieth-century Swiss theologian Emil Brunner and the contemporary American theologian Elizabeth Johnson, he reflects on the problems of how we can talk about God. He worries that Brunner does not situate theology concretely enough in the context of oppression, while Johnson does not sufficiently emphasize that salvation depends on divine initiative, and he looks for an approach that would combine the best of both these accounts.

Both these authors, then, warn us against simplistic answers to the question of how Christians can know what we should believe. When it comes to beliefs about God, even the greatest theologians are like little children listening to lectures on quantum physics, mostly only catching a familiar word here and there. We trust that God's self-revelation will not lead us astray, but we are most faithful to it when we admit how often we are unsure of how much we understand.

Stanley J. Grenz

At one time or another most people raise questions about the meaning of life: Who am I, and why am I here?[1] What is God like, if there is indeed a God? What happens when I die? When people reflect on such questions, their responses generally take the form, "I believe that. . . ." This suggests that attempts to engage credibly the most perplexing yet crucial questions of human existence and the nature of the universe lead inevitably to the realm of belief. Although Christianity is not simply about beliefs, they remain an important aspect of it, for the Christian faith involves a mosaic of beliefs, and this mosaic offers a stance regarding the big questions we all raise.

Viewed from this perspective, Christian theology may be described as the discipline that seeks to discover, articulate, explore, and clarify the Christian belief-mosaic. This aspect of the theological task raises a question that Christian theologians have explored throughout the history of the church: How can we know what to believe? That is, what is the ultimate basis for determining which beliefs ought to be deemed genuinely Christian? Interpreting this question in its prescriptive rather than simply its descriptive sense leads to the crucial matter of authority in theology: On what basis can a theologian conclude that a particular set of beliefs comprises *the* teaching of the church? Or what makes accepting a specific doctrine incumbent on Christians? Grappling with this question of authority has traditionally led theologians to the parallel theme of revelation: What is the source of the beliefs of the Christian faith?

The word *source*, as it appears in this query, may be understood in several ways. One manner of viewing the term, of course, is to see it as a reference to revelation in the strict sense. In this understanding, Christian theology is the intellectual enterprise in which correct religious statements (or doctrines) are deduced from some type of divine disclosure. Rather than engaging with the topic of revelation directly, in the following pages I will offer an understanding of revelation and its place in theology that moves in a somewhat indirect manner, namely, by means of an exploration of another way of understanding *source*.

> Theology emerges from a particular source, namely, Scripture—viewed as its "norming norm"—read within the trajectory of the church's theological heritage and in the context of the culture in which the theologizing community is situated.

In addition to connecting *source* directly to *revelation*, the term can also be seen as raising the question of theological method: To what ought the theologian turn, or what ought the theologian consider when engaging in theological exploration? Even when described in this manner, the word *source* remains open to multiple interpretations. One possibility is to understand the term in the more general sense of *resource*. Seen from this perspective, theological construction is dependent on certain considerations that the theologian must keep in view in the task of theological construction.

Source may also be understood in a stronger manner. Theology's source is whatever ought to determine its design and content. *Source* in this sense is interchangeable with *norm*, insofar as theology's source carries normative weight. The two understandings are not as separable as they may appear to be. Nevertheless, in the first section of this essay, I will use *source* primarily in the stronger sense, whereas in the second section it will largely carry its more general meaning. My goal in what follows is to explicate the thesis that theology emerges from a particular source, namely, Scripture—viewed as its "norming norm"—read within the trajectory of the church's theological heritage and in the context of the culture in which the theologizing community is situated—and all these together comprise theology's resources.

SCRIPTURE: THEOLOGY'S NORMING NORM

Most people would not find the inclusion of Scripture in a discussion of the source of theology at all surprising, for Christians have always been a "people of the book." In a sense, we might suggest that the church is by its very nature called to be a biblical community, a people who base their lives and their life together on Scripture. This might well be a sufficient reason to surmise that the Bible's central role in theology is a given. Because the Bible is the universally acknowledged book of the Christian church—because it is the foundational document of the faith community—it simply is the accepted norm for our theological reflections. Yet the crucial question still remains: In what sense ought Scripture to be afforded this status? To this query may be added another: How does the Bible function in the community? Actually, the two questions are interrelated, for the answer to the second provides a basis for responding to the first.

In the opinion of many theologians, considering the role of Scripture in theology leads immediately to the concept of revelation, for the Bible is often defined as inscripturated revelation. Furthermore, such descriptions of the Bible have repeatedly been found within elaborate theological introductions that follow the sequence: revelation, inspiration, biblical authority, illumination.[2] Hence, the typical introduction to what has become the "classical" theological system routinely begins with the affirmation of God's self-disclosure in general and special revelation before turning to the Spirit's past work of inspiring biblical writers to inscripturate (form into a sacred text) special revelation and then concluding with the Spirit's present work in illumining the reader to understand its content. Despite its long pedigree, modern theologians have found this approach deficient, largely because of its focus on the divine character of Scripture at the expense of a sufficient sense of its human aspect.

The desire to recast the doctrine of Scripture in a manner that avoids the difficulties posed by the classic approach has led a variety of modern theologians to separate divine revelation from Scripture. Despite their different opinions over what the Bible is, they are in agreement that, rather than being revelation, the Bible is a *witness to* revelation. Although this change of perspective has opened new vistas from which to understand both revelation and the role of Scripture, in the end the various alternative proposals have tended to drive too great a wedge between revelation and Scripture. Moreover, they do not arise out of an awareness of the chief difficulty in the classical approach, namely, its elevation of the Spirit's completed work in inspiration to the detriment of an adequate emphasis on the continuing activity of the Spirit speaking in Scripture.

> In contrast to what has been the reigning paradigm in modern theology, I would assert that the Bible is indeed revelation, but the connection between Scripture and revelation emerges only indirectly. Scripture is authoritative in that the sovereign Spirit has bound authoritative divine speaking to this text. As a consequence, the church of all ages looks to the biblical texts to hear the Spirit's voice.

In contrast to what has been the reigning paradigm in modern theology, I would assert that the Bible is indeed revelation. I must quickly add, however, that the connection between Scripture and revelation emerges only indirectly.

Developing this connection requires the introduction of the concept of authority, together with an understanding of the Bible as the Spirit's book.

The Westminster Confession of Faith, written in England in the 1640s, offers what many Reformed theologians see as the classic statement of what might be called the Protestant principle of authority:[3] "The Supreme Judge, by which all controversies of religion are to be determined, and all decrees of councils, opinions of ancient writers, doctrines of men, and private spirits, are to be examined, and in whose sentence we are to rest, can be no other than the Holy Spirit speaking in the Scripture."[4] In keeping with the Reformation concern to bind Word and Spirit together, this statement suggests that the authority of the Bible lies in its role as that in which the Spirit has chosen to speak. Scripture is authoritative in that the sovereign Spirit has bound authoritative divine speaking to this text. As a consequence, the church of all ages looks to the biblical texts to hear the Spirit's voice.

The classic Christian declaration that the Spirit speaks in Scripture raises the question of the manner in which the claim is to be understood: How does the Spirit speak in the text? The answer to this query is crucial because it not only indicates the sense in which Scripture may be deemed revelation, but it also offers a basis for acknowledging the Bible as the norm for theology.

We can be assisted in our attempt to understand what it might mean to say that the Spirit speaks in Scripture by taking a cursory look at the speech-act theory of a linguistic philosopher such as J. L. Austin.[5] Austin views speech as an act entailing three components: the locution, the illocution, and the perlocution. These may be seen as corresponding roughly with enunciating a sentence, what the speaker is doing by this enunciation, and what the speaker achieves (or seeks to achieve) by the act of enunciating.[6] For example, suppose I say, "John, close the door!" The *locution* consists of my actual uttering of the words "John," "close," "the," "door." The *illocution* is the act of addressing the particular command, "Close the door!" to a specific person in the room, named John. The *perlocution* is John actually getting up from his seat, walking to the door, and closing it.

Obviously, when I say that the Spirit speaks in Scripture I am not thinking of a locution. The Spirit does not actually speak the words of the Bible. Nevertheless, I am claiming that through the words of the text, the Spirit does in fact address us, just as I addressed John in my hypothetical example. Hence, to say that the Spirit speaks in Scripture is to claim that the Spirit performs an illocutionary act. The ongoing task of the community of Christ, in turn, is to ask continually, What is the Spirit saying to the church (Rev. 2:11)? Or, stated in terms of speech-act theory, What illocutionary act is the Spirit performing in our midst on the basis of the reading of Scripture?

Allow me to preclude a potential misunderstanding here. The Spirit's illocutionary act ought not to be viewed as somehow occurring independently of what is commonly called "the original meaning of the text." Exegesis remains crucial in theology. Nevertheless, the Spirit's address is not bound up simply and completely with the text's supposed internal or original meaning. Indeed, as certain contemporary proponents of "textual intentionality" (such as Paul Ricoeur) remind us, although an author creates a literary text, once it has been written it takes on a life of its own, insofar as it speaks in various ways to the various people who read it. Applied to the Bible, this observation reminds us that the Bible is the living book of the living Spirit. Consequently, we must never conclude that our attempts to come to know the mind of the author of a biblical text can exhaust the Spirit's speaking to us in the text. Although the Spirit appropriates the text in its internal meaning and hence "what the author said" places limits on what the Spirit can possibly be saying in the text, the Spirit's ultimate goal is always to communicate to *us* in *our* situation.

What perlocutionary act does the Spirit seek to accomplish in his act of speaking in Scripture? The answer may be stated quite simply: The Spirit creates "world."

In describing the speaking of the Spirit in Scripture as an illocutionary act, we are not yet at our goal in describing the role of the Bible in theology. Rather, we must take Austin's speech-act idea a step further and ask, What is the *goal* or *product* of the Spirit's speaking? What perlocutionary act does the Spirit seek to accomplish in his act of speaking in Scripture? The answer may be stated quite simply: The Spirit creates "world."

To understand how this is true requires a short detour into the discipline of sociology. Sociologists such as Peter Berger have pointed out that the world we inhabit as humans is not merely given to us. Instead, we live in a world of our own creation; we inhabit a social or cultural world. World construction entails above all the imposition of a meaningful order (what Berger calls a *nomos*) upon our variegated experiences. This ordering of experience involves "knowledge," which Berger understands not as a body of objective statements about the universe as it actually is but the "common order of interpretation" that a society imposes upon experience.[7] Throughout history, religion has played a decisive part in this world-construction process.[8] By locating a society and its institutions within a sacred frame of reference, by bestowing on participants in a society a sense of being connected to ultimate reality, and by giving cosmic status to the *nomoi* (or common orders of interpretation) of that society,[9] religion legitimates the socially constructed world that participants in any society inhabit. Sociologists point out that religion fulfills its role in part by devising a set of beliefs that together comprise the specifically religious view of the world that participants in a society share. Moreover, these beliefs are articulated in texts, that is, "scriptures."[10] For this reason, as Paul Ricoeur has noted, the meaning of a text always points beyond itself—it is "not behind the text, but in front of it"—for it projects a way of being in the world, a mode of existence, a pattern of life, and it "points towards a possible world."[11]

The Bible is the literary vehicle through which the Spirit constructs the new world that we are to inhabit. Rather than being simply the world surrounding the ancient text, the world the Spirit creates is the *eschatological* world that God ultimately intends for creation, as disclosed in the Bible. This future world is a world centered in Jesus Christ, who is the one through whom all things find their connectedness (Col. 1:17). In appropriating the Word written, therefore, the Spirit creates a world centered on the Word incarnate[12] and invites us to live now in that world. Furthermore, the Spirit-authored world is communal; it is a community of the Word, a fellowship of persons who gather in the name of Jesus the Christ, who is the Word. The way in which Scripture functions in the Spirit's work of creating a new communal world indicates how the Bible is theology's norm. To take this final step requires that I introduce two additional concepts: paradigmatic narrative and interpretive framework.

A *paradigmatic event* is a historical occurrence that captures the imagination of a community in such a manner that it shapes the community's way of conceiving the totality of reality as well as the community's understanding of its ongoing experience of reality. Because of the event's wide-ranging influence, the community preserves its memory, while both reinterpreting the event in the light of the subsequent situations in which the community finds itself and discovering in it the source of a renewed hope for the future. A paradigmatic narrative is a set of events that connects the community and its participants with the past and the future. Through their appropriation of these events, succeeding generations understand themselves in relationship to past experiences of the community and in anticipation of a future that will mark the actualization of the community's ideals. By functioning in this manner, a paradigmatic narrative is not merely a collection of occurrences in history, for this narrative has the potential to create a meaningful present. A paradigmatic narrative fuses past and future with the present in a manner that calls forth a new world in the here and now, so that the community that inhabits this world takes its identity from, and becomes the contemporary embodiment of, the paradigmatic narrative itself.

> A paradigmatic event captures the imagination of a community in such a manner that it shapes the community's way of conceiving the totality of reality.

The Bible narrates the primary paradigmatic events that shape the identity of the Christian community. A central aspect of the Spirit's appropriating of the biblical narrative is to connect us with the primal events that originally constituted the Christian community, especially the life, passion, and resurrection of Jesus, together with the sending of the Holy Spirit, as understood in the context of the Old Testament story. As the narrative is retold (or reread), the Spirit transports its contemporary hearers (or readers) into the text. Or, stated in the opposite manner, the Spirit re-creates the past as narrated by the text within the present life of the community. Rather than ending with the paradigmatic events of "long ago," the Bible also anticipates a future, new creation in which humans live in harmony with each other, with God, and with all creation (see Rev. 21:1–22:5).

In addition to connecting us with our narrative past, therefore, in speaking in Scripture the Spirit links us to God's glorious future. The Spirit appropriates the biblical vision of the divinely intended new creation, so that we might view our situation in the light of God's future and as a result open ourselves and our present to the power of that future, which is already at work in and among us (see Rom. 8:9–30).

By narrating our foundational past and disclosing our glorious future, the Bible provides a paradigm of life for the believing community and as participants in that fellowship. Furthermore, through the appropriated biblical text, the Spirit forms in us a communal way of looking at life that is in keeping with the new world we are called to inhabit. The Spirit leads us to view ourselves and all reality through lenses that are unabashedly Christian and specifically biblical, so that we might understand our world and respond to the challenges of life in the present, conscious that we are a contemporary embodiment of a faith community that spans the ages.[13] We might say that scripture mediates to the reader a specifically Christian *interpretative framework.* By leading us to view life in accordance with this particular interpretive framework, the Spirit creates in the present a foretaste of the eschatological world and constitutes us as an eschatological people who serve as a sign pointing to the new creation that God is already fashioning.[14]

> By leading us to view life in accordance with a particular interpretive framework, the Spirit creates in the present a foretaste of the eschatological world.

The world the Spirit creates is simultaneously communal and personal. That is, the Spirit creates a new community composed of persons who enjoy a new identity. Contemporary social psychologists point out that we do not create our own identity; our sense of self is socially produced.[15] More specifically, identity develops through the telling of a personal narrative in connection with which one's life makes sense,[16] a narrative that is always embedded in a transcendent story, that is, in the stories of the communities in which we participate.[17] This narrative forms the foundation for participation in the community and, in turn, for the sense of personal identity as a member of the social group. Applying these insights to participants in the Christian community yields the assertion that the Spirit is the agent of the Christian identity-creating process. The Spirit authors a new personal identity, as the Spirit brings a person to reinterpret his or her own life narrative in accordance with the paradigmatic narrative disclosed in the Bible. Hence, the Spirit appropriates the "old, old story of Jesus and his love" to lead people to view all of life from the perspective of that story, that is, from an unabashedly Christian interpretive framework.

These observations lead us, finally, back to theology. Christian theology is closely connected to the biblical, paradigmatic narrative that constitutes the Christian community and to the interpretive framework by means of which this community understands the world. More specifically, the theologian looks to

Scripture with the goal of discovering, articulating, exploring, and clarifying the interpretive framework of the Christian community, that is, the Christian belief-mosaic. Hence, the process of theologizing draws primarily from the biblical narrative of what God has said and done, and what God intends yet to do, as well as the scriptural record of what the early faith communities thought and did on the basis of their consciousness as a people belonging to the God of the Bible. In this manner, the Bible serves as the informing and forming source for theology throughout the ages. Or as the older theologians put it, Scripture emerges as the "norming norm" for theology.

HERITAGE AND CULTURAL CONTEXT

At first glance, we might anticipate that the chapter ought to end here. From what I have said thus far, we could conclude that theology simply systematizes what the Bible actually says. Indeed, on the basis of this assumption about the nature of theology, some theologians suppose that once we have outlined an understanding of the Bible as norming norm for theology, we have stated all that needs to be affirmed about theology's source and in the process have brought to completion the discussion of such programmatic themes as revelation and authority. To draw such a conclusion, however, is to assume (erroneously) that we can read the Bible from a disengaged, neutral, objective, and culture-free standpoint. Alas, there is no neutral reading of Scripture. Exegetical aids can help us get closer to the original recipients of the texts, but we will never be totally successful in our attempts to understand a text through the eyes of its original readers. In the end, all our readings of the text remain *our* readings. Moreover, theology is not exhausted by the attempt to discover "what the Bible says," were it even possible to do so, for theology moves as well to the task of articulating and exploring the Christian interpretive framework. Consequently, theologians must take seriously two additional dimensions of the one source of theology. These two dimensions form a resource for the theological task.

> Alas, there is no neutral reading of Scripture. All our readings remain *our* readings.

Heritage: Theology's Hermeneutical Trajectory

We are not the first generation since the early church to seek to understand what it means to be the community of Christ in the world. On the contrary, we are part of a historical trajectory that spans church history. From the patristic era to the present, the church has sought within ever changing situations to listen to the voice of the Spirit speaking in Scripture and to discover, articulate, explore, and clarify the Christian belief-mosaic for the sake of its ongoing life in, and its mission to, the world. This centuries-long dynamic comprises a theological heritage, a *tradition* (if I might use the older, albeit often misunderstood, term). The historical deposit—the church's theological heritage—in turn, provides a rich resource for theology in the present, for it puts us in contact with the wisdom and insights that emerged from the Spirit-guided reflection on Scripture that engaged our forebears in the faith.

How is this heritage a resource to theology? Stated simply, it provides the hermeneutical trajectory in which our own theological discourse can properly transpire. (*Hermeneutics* is the theory of interpretation.) This role arises in two basic ways.

First, the theological heritage comprises a hermeneutical trajectory for our theologizing in that it consists of a set of reference points—a signpost—that offers guidance in the construction of a theology that is truly Christian. It comprises a signpost in a negative manner insofar as the history of theology is littered with far-reaching miscues and theological failures, many of which bear the traditional label *heresy*. Looking to the theological history of the church, therefore, alerts us to some of the pitfalls we should avoid, some of the land mines that could trip us up, and some of the cul-de-sacs or blind alleys that are not worth our exploration. Awareness of the formulations of the faith that the Christian community has rejected also leads us to appreciate more fully the crucial theological work of our forebears who guided the church along the orthodox pathway. As Roger Olson rightly concludes, it is "almost impossible to appreciate the meaning of orthodoxy without understanding the heresies that forced its development."[18]

The theological heritage functions as a signpost in a positive manner as well. The work of our forebears points us in directions that hold promise as we engage in the theological calling today. Especially important in this respect are those theological works that have come to be regarded as "classics." The writings of the theological "masters" that have survived the test of time and thereby have remained an integral part of the community's life not only provide a rich resource of insight into perennial religious questions but also offer models for how we can best engage in the task of theology.

The idea of a deposit of classic theological statements leads to a second way in which the heritage of the church functions as a resource for theology. Because we engage in the theological task conscious that we are members of a community of faith that spans the centuries and hence that we participate in the one church of Jesus Christ, we naturally desire to retain continuity of basic doctrine with the church throughout the ages. In this task, we can gain great assistance by paying attention to the doctrinal formulations—the confessions of faith—that have gained broad acknowledgment among Christians and have thereby bound the people of God together confessionally throughout the centuries. For example, the nearly universal acceptance by the worldwide Christian community of ecumenical statements such as the Apostles' Creed and the Nicene Creed suggests that these "classic" symbols of the faith ought to be afforded a special ongoing significance for the work of theology.[19] Such statements have not only acted as markers indicating the boundaries of what the church has considered to be orthodox; they have also given insight to generations of theologians who have sought to articulate the faith in quite different contexts.

Moreover, in confessing the one faith of the church, we become a contemporary embodiment of the legacy of faith that spans the ages and encompasses the entire chain of faithful confessors, including both our forebears who have made this confession in ages past and our successors who will do so in the future. Because we are members of this one community of faith, the theological tradition of the church must be a crucial component in the construction of our contemporary theological statements, so that we might maintain our confessional unity with the one church of Jesus Christ.

Let me add, however, two cautionary notes. First, in using the term *heritage* I am not intending the medieval Roman Catholic idea that tradition is a source of truth standing alongside the Bible. Rather, I intend that the term serve as a reminder that the biblical text is always read through the lens of a hermeneutical trajectory. Some theory of interpretation, explicit or implicit, always shapes our reading. We should therefore engage in the theological task conscious that we are participants in one particular hermeneutical community, namely, the trajectory constituted by the ongoing theological history of the church of all ages. Furthermore, because we come to the text as those who seek to understand the whole of Scripture as the instrumentality of the Spirit's speaking to us, we do well to keep in view what the church through the ages has considered this biblical "whole" to be. Stating the point in another manner, as Christians we desire to read the Bible "christianly" and construct thereby a truly Christian theology. This process is advanced as we take seriously the attempts of our forebears to engage in the hermeneutical task that now occupies us. Furthermore, the attempt to remain in hermeneutical fellowship with all the people of God enjoins on us the goal of constructing a truly catholic theology, even though we might come to conclusions on some theological issues that differ with past luminaries.

> We should engage in the theological task conscious that we are participants in one particular hemeneutical community, namely, the trajectory constituted by the ongoing theological history of the church in all ages.

A second cautionary note is equally important. Despite the important role they play as a theological resource, past creeds, confessions, and theological formulations in and of themselves are not binding on theology. Nor dare they usurp the normative place of the Bible, for they must continually be tested by the norming norm, the Spirit speaking in Scripture. In addition, in our reading of the great theological literature we must keep in mind the culturally situated nature of all such statements. Hence, it may well be the *intent* of the creeds, confessions, and formulations, and not necessarily the specific construction and wording, that becomes significant for contemporary theology.

Perhaps a metaphor from the performance of a symphony might illumine the function of heritage as a hermeneutical trajectory in the task of theology. The goal of the orchestra in a concert is to offer an authentic rendition of the symphony chosen for the event. In this process, the score of the symphony is, of course, authoritative. Yet every performance constitutes a particular interpretation of the score, and not all interpretations are equally legitimate. Determinations about the legitimacy of specific interpretations emerge within the ongoing history of the performance of the symphony.

Purpose of Goal of theology

The ultimate purpose of theology is not simply to establish "right belief" but to assist the Christian community in its vocation to *live* as the people of God in the particular historical-cultural context in which it is situated. Hence, the goal of theology is to facilitate what we might call authentic "performance" of the Christian faith as it is "scored" in Scripture. Like the performance of a symphony that has only one score but many possible interpretations, the scriptural score has been subject to numerous interpretations over the centuries. The history of theology provides a crucial resource for contemporary attempts to facilitate authentic performance of the biblical score or vision of the Christian faith. By functioning as the hermeneutical trajectory for our theologizing, the church's theological heritage allows for creativity in addressing new situations, while offering a basis for identifying interpretations that are not consonant with the one church of all ages.

Culture: Theology's Contemporary Context

The suggestion that the church is called to "perform" the Christian faith in new situations leads to a final consideration regarding theology's source. The task of the church is to listen to the Spirit's speaking in Scripture. In keeping with this, the theologian engages in the process of discovering, articulating, exploring, and clarifying the Christian belief-mosaic. Yet this composite enterprise always occurs in a particular historical-cultural context. Consequently, the manner in which the one faith of the church is understood and conceptualized will always be related in some way to the context in which the performing, theologizing community is situated. For this reason, culture must be viewed as a resource for theology.

In pointing out the importance of culture to theology I am not saying anything new, of course. Christians have always sought to understand and articulate their faith within the context in which God calls them to live and minister. Although theologians from the time of the early church to the present have disagreed about the role culture ought to play in theology, there is broad agreement that the quest for a culture-free theology is both ill-founded and unwarranted.

How then does culture function as a resource to theology? The answer to the question is dependent in part on what we mean by *culture*. Many of us today understand the term in accordance with the modern conception that emerged in the 1920s. This perspective views culture as consisting of the language, customs, and rituals of a particular social group, including the specific pattern of behaviors that distinguishes any given society from all others.[20] More helpful in describing the connection between theology and culture, however, is a more recent understanding, which highlights the connection between culture and meaning. Culture, as one contemporary cultural anthropologist declares, denotes "the framework of meaning, of concepts and ideas, within which different aspects of a person's life can be related to each other."[21] Culture, therefore, is related to the forms and symbols that a particular group finds meaningful. Moreover, rather than a fixed entity, culture is the product of social interaction, and hence humans are active creators, rather than passive receivers, of culture.[22] This process of culture construction occurs as participants in a particular society struggle over the meaning of the symbols they hold in common and through which they express and communicate to each other their understandings of the central aspects of life.

> Insofar as theology entails the process of meaning-making, it is a cultural practice.

The contemporary perspective suggests that insofar as theology entails the process of meaning-making, it is a cultural practice. Obviously, because the Christian meaning-making process occurs within the circle of those who acknowledge the God of the Bible, theology may be described as the meaning-making activity of the people who comprise the community of Christ. Viewed in this light, theology is the "in-house" conversation regarding the meaning of the various symbols that Christians share, with the goal of setting forth a cogent delineation of the belief-mosaic of the Christian social group. Furthermore, Christians who are embedded in a wide variety of historical and cultural contexts will naturally bring aspects of these various perspectives to the theological conversation, producing thereby a culturally connected theology.

Equally significant is the idea that theology involves the process of meaning-making within the larger society in which the church is called to live and minister. Our initial response to this suggestion might well be to understand the role of culture as giving the theological task a character that would focus on mission, that is, as highlighting the importance of what we might term a *relevant* theology. A theology that is culturally relevant seeks to articulate Christian beliefs in a manner that is understandable to people within the wider society in which the church ministers. Consequently, the theologian draws from the cognitive tools—including language, symbols, and thought-forms—by means of which people in the host society view and speak about their world, so as to engage in a kind of "translation" task in which the categories of a society, including its philosophical conceptions, become the vehicles for the expression of the Christian belief-mosaic. A relevant theology likewise seeks to address the problems, longings, and ethos of a particular culture. The theologian, therefore, explores the specific issues raised by the wider social context, in order to develop a delineation of the faith that responds to the perceived needs and questions posed by people in society. Furthermore, a relevant theology takes seriously the discoveries and insights of the various disciplines of human learning, drawing from the so-called secular body of knowledge to assist in the process of understanding Christian doctrine, while also critiquing contemporary perspectives when they are deemed to stand at odds with Christian convictions.

The idea of theological relevance does not express completely, however, the relationship between theology and culture. There remains yet the deeper aspect of theology as meaning-making within the wider society, that is, what we might call the *public* character of theology. Although the church constitutes in some sense a distinctive social group, our calling is not to be a society completely separated from humankind. On the contrary, we are not called to be anything but truly human. This being the case, we ought to view ourselves as coparticipants with people around us in an ongoing conversation about what it means to be human, a conversation that always occurs within a specific cultural context. What makes Christians unique in this conversation is our desire to engage in the broader process of meaning-making from a particular vantage point, namely, as those who view all reality in connection to the God of the Bible who we believe is revealed supremely in Jesus Christ.

In the conversation about the big questions that humans face, we can expect not only to offer our perspective as Christians but also to gain insights from other participants that will trigger deeper understandings of the Christian belief-mosaic itself. The theological basis for such an expectation takes us back to the Spirit who speaks. In contrast to those Christians who assume that the church is the *only* location in which the Holy Spirit is operative, the biblical writers display a broad understanding of the Spirit's presence, a presence connected to the Spirit's role as the life giver (Gen. 1:2; 2:7) and life sustainer (Ps. 104:29–30; Isa. 32:15). Because the life-giving Spirit is present wherever life flourishes, and Spirit-induced human flourishing evokes cultural expression, Christians can anticipate hearing overtones of the Spirit's voice in many media, including human culture. I must quickly add, however, that the Spirit speaking in the Bible offers the only sure canon for hearing the Spirit in culture, because the Spirit's speaking everywhere and anywhere is always in concert with this primary speaking in Scripture.

To conclude: The Christian faith entails living out, under the guidance and empowerment of the Spirit—i.e., it entails the performance of a particular vision of—the nature of reality and our place within it. The goal of theology, in turn, is to foster genuine listening to the Spirit and consequently legitimate performances of the faith by seeking to discover, articulate, explore, and clarify the Christian vision, that is, the Christian belief-mosaic. To this end, theologians look to theology's source, which is the Spirit speaking in Scripture as heard in accordance with the hermeneutical trajectory of the church's theological heritage and within the specific historical-cultural context in which the gathered people live as the community of Christ.

> Although they differ significantly from each other in the roles they play, Scripture, heritage, and culture nevertheless compose a single, interrelated, threefold source for theology.

Although they differ significantly from each other in the roles they play, Scripture, heritage, and culture nevertheless compose a single, interrelated, threefold source for theology. And even though they may be treated conceptually in isolation from each other, in practice they are nearly inseparable. We do not first get our understanding of the Bible straight and then look to our common heritage to make sure we are orthodox before finally seeking to understand these matters within our social context. Rather, regardless of the particular "text" being "read" in the moment—whether it be the "text" of Scripture, of heritage, or of culture—we always read it together with the other two partners within the one interconnected dance that comprises the theological art. Or, stating the point in another manner, Scripture, heritage, and culture do not comprise three different moments of the Spirit's speaking and hence of our listening. Rather, just as the Spirit who speaks is one Spirit, so also the Spirit's speaking is one speaking. Theology assists in the hearing task by seeking to explicate a truly scriptural, unabashedly Christian, and completely contextual conceptualization of the Christian belief-mosaic for the sake of the church's calling to be, on the basis of its primal past, the sign in the present of the glorious eschatological future of all creation.

NOEL LEO ERSKINE

We often regard any new insight as *revelation,* but such a broad use expands the original meaning of the term. Fundamentally, *revelation* means "removing the veil"—there is a disclosure, something previously hidden is revealed, that which is mysterious becomes less mysterious.

In the Bible, revelation often is expressed through different mediums: trees, stones, a burning bush, visions, a nation, or a book. However, what is of decisive importance is that these mediums do not reveal themselves and should not be confused with the revealing subject. The transcendent chooses to use finite means through which to express revelation, but the means should not be confused with revelation itself. William Hordern puts the issue succinctly:

> When the Israelite people were prone to suppose that they could be identified with God, they were rudely reminded that judgment begins with the household of God (1 Pet. 4:17). Although Israel was the chosen people, Israel's acts were never simply the acts of God. God stood in judgment over them. Although Jesus made claims for himself that made his revealing function clear (e.g., Matt. 10:32, 16:13–28), he could nonetheless ask why men inquired of him what was good when there is only one that is good, God (Matt. 19:16, 17). Although Paul called the church the Body of Christ (1 Cor. 12:27), in the same letter he could force the Church to face its sinfulness in a radical manner (1 Cor. 1:11–14, 5:1–6:11). Although Christians hold to the Bible as the supreme book of God's revelation, they have had to learn painfully that it is not itself divine.[1]

The transcendent chooses finite means to communicate with human beings, since such means are translatable and understandable to us. Paul underscores this when he reminds us that, "we have this treasure in earthen vessels" (2 Cor. 4:7). In Christian faith it is above all the person of Jesus Christ who reveals the transcendent.

It is of first importance to grasp that even though a revelatory experience may occur at any place or through any means, for the Christian faith revelation in Jesus Christ is normative. Part of what is special concerning Jesus Christ as the bearer of revelation is that the church traces its foundation back to this original revelation. As the contemporary British theologian John Macquarrie puts it, "A community of faith, within which a theology arises, usually traces its history back to what may be called a 'classic' or 'primordial' revelation. This classic revelation, a definitive disclosive experience of the holy granted to the founder or founders of the community, becomes as it were the paradigm for experiences of the holy in that community."[2]

For the Christian, Jesus Christ is this classic revelation, which is constantly renewed in the life of the community of faith. It is precisely at this point that Macquarrie is insistent on the close relationship between experience and revelation. Experience points to participation in the community of faith and to the appropriation of revelation, which is given in the birth of the community. Revelation cannot be manufactured or forced; it has a gift-like character and has to be received: "If, in general terms, we say that what is disclosed in revelation is the dimension of the holy, then, in the revelatory experience, it is as if the holy 'breaks in' and the movement is from beyond man to man."[3] In the phrase "from beyond man to man," Macquarrie points to the structure of revelation—the revealing object and the receiving subject. As Paul Tillich noted, there can be no revelation without someone to receive it: "Revelation, as revelation of the mystery which is our ultimate concern, is invariably revelation for someone in a concrete situation of concern. . . . There is no revelation 'in general.'"[4]

Perhaps a better way to articulate this encounter between the transcendent object and the receiving subject is to talk not about object-subject relationship but subject-to-subject relationship. Here we posit revelation as a disclosive event between the divine and human subject. Revelation is not the imparting of truths from or about God but rather an I-Thou encounter with the transcendent. This recalls the classic text of the twentieth-century Jewish philosopher Martin Buber, *I and Thou,* in which, after discussing the "I-Thou relationship" that can exist between two people, he speaks of the transcendent as the *eternal* Thou. Over against the I -Thou relationship, he posits an I-It relationship in which the other is encountered as object rather than subject. The I-Thou relationship is a reciprocal one in which the revelatory occurrence happens between the revealing and receiving subject.[5]

Revelation then is not the sharing of information but the communication of one mind to another. As human beings, we do not know God as we know objects in the physical world. We know God only as God reveals God's self to us in the context of the freedom of God. Revelation in a biblical sense is never the revelation of an object to a subject. This would be to make the transcendent an object.

The revelation that is unveiled is that of the transcendent subject sharing itself with the human subject. The movement within which revelation occurs is from subject to subject. However, we cannot allow this identification of revelation as movement from divine subject to human subject to mislead us into positing mutuality between the transcendent mystery and humanity. We must be mindful that this revelation "from beyond humanity to humanity" is the will and purpose of God. What is being revealed is the mystery of God disclosed in the life, death, and resurrection of Jesus Christ. Revelation is about God's saving action in the world on our behalf.

> Revelation then is not the sharing of information but the communication of one mind to another.

Another dimension of this knowledge of God has to do with the problem of human alienation and sin. A state of alienation and sin has disrupted the relationship between the human and the divine, and this fundamental malaise affects our reception and perception of revelation. Because the basic human condition is sin and not ignorance, in the Bible people do not inquire, "What may we know?" but rather, "What must we do to be saved?" (John 3:3).

I take the theologian Paul Tillich seriously in his claim that "revelation, as revelation of the mystery which is our ultimate concern, is invariably revelation for someone in a concrete situation."[6] Therefore, in this essay, I would like to look at the church's understanding of revelation in my social context—Jamaica, West Indies—and explore in a situation of oppression and suffering what issues emerge as the people there seek to make theological sense of revelation. Further, I would like to place the insights that emerge in conversation with two theologians who have also taken the church seriously as a critical context for talk about revelation. We will look at revelation as encounter in the understanding of Emil Brunner, and revelation as the experience of women from the perspective of Elizabeth Johnson.

REVELATION AND SOCIAL LOCATION

Nurtured in the Christian church in Jamaica, I realized at an early age that there is an indissoluble connection between salvation and revelation. The church teaches that through divine revelation manifested in Jesus Christ it is the will and plan of God for all people to be saved through Jesus Christ. This offer of salvation through revelation is seen as not only a promise and possibility but an actuality afforded by the revelation made plain in the life, death, and resurrection of Jesus Christ. As I reflect on those formative years in the Jamaican church, I realize the central question was the same, whether one entered the Roman Catholic, Episcopal, or Pentecostal Church. The question is not "What may we know?" but "What must we do to be saved?"

Freedom from ignorance is not seen as the central issue, but rather freedom from harsh suffering, grinding poverty, and sin, which is understood as the root cause of the problem of suffering and poverty. In a social and political situation in which economic insecurity, injustice, deprivation, scarcity of essential resources, and terminal poverty are omnipresent, it should not come as a surprise that the church links salvation and revelation. For some time, the people of Jamaica have sought to make a connection between revelation and history as we look back to the event of our liberation from slavery. We have invested August 1, 1838, with revelatory significance, as that is the day that slavery was abolished. For the Jamaican people, it represents one of the mighty acts of God that led us out of slavery. Although this is an event outside the church, it is interpreted within the church. Jamaica is reminded that the God who is revealed in Jesus Christ is also the Lord of history.

On August 1 every year, there are commemorations of deliverance from slavery during which the populace crowd into local churches to participate in Emancipation Day, as the remembrance of the victory over slavery is called. In this remembrance, which provides hope for a new future, the church finds evidence of the saving activity of God in our history.[7] The Jamaican church is clear that this activity in history makes theological sense within the church because people are set free, and the event is interpreted in the light of the full revelation manifested in Jesus Christ.

It is in the light of this revelation in Christ that we understand other revelations. Moreover, the bottom line is that people need to be free from sin. The church maintains that sin is the root cause of poverty, crime, and social and economic injustice. Sin is not merely seen as a state into which everyone is born, but it is understood as a destructive power that human beings cannot handle on their own. Seen as endemic and systemic, sin holds humanity in slavery. The wage sin pays is death, and the instrument of sin is the flesh, which points to our relationship to the world, our weakness and mortality. The challenge is that Christians will not live *kata sarka* ("according to the flesh"). To live *kata sarka* is to rely on one's own strength and ingenuity to gain freedom from slavery to sin. The answer to this slavery to sin is manifest in the revelation of Jesus Christ expressed in emancipation, justification, and reconciliation.

Perhaps it is because the symbols of slavery and emancipation are part of our culture that we construe salvation as revelation and see emancipation as a response to the bondage of sin.

Perhaps it is because the symbols of slavery and emancipation are part of our culture that we construe salvation as revelation and see emancipation as a response to the bondage of sin. Emancipation as it relates to revelation means the breaking of the yoke of slavery to sin and the curse of the law. It recalls the deliverance of the children of Israel from Egypt with whom Caribbean people always compare themselves. "You were bought with a price" (1 Cor. 6:20) is a popular text that speaks to this price as the purchase paid for the emancipation of the Jamaican people. God pays the ransom for our emancipation, a ransom we cannot pay for ourselves. Emancipation conjoined with revelation is seen as the breakthrough of grace—expressed in the life, death, and resurrection of Jesus Christ—that saves us from servitude to powers other than God.

Another consequence of our long sojourn in slavery and our lost battle with poverty is that the Jamaican people feel cursed and condemned. Jamaicans often characterize themselves as living with a sense of worthlessness and refer to our marginal existence as the consequence of God's punishment. The response of the church to this existential plight is that God offers us justification in the revelation manifested in God's Son, Jesus Christ. The way the church understands justification is not primarily in terms of being made righteous but in receiving the gifts of pardon and forgiveness. The church feels that these gifts, manifest in the death of Jesus Christ on the cross, should be the basis of the Jamaican forgiveness of self.

The cross of Christ lifts the curse and condemnation, and reveals a glad acceptance of us as we are and not as we ought to be. This existential situation points to a gulf between where we are and where we want to be or what we want to become. The good news as the church understands it in the disclosive love of God demonstrated on the cross is that God accepts us as we are because God sees us not in our sinful condition as defined by poverty and different kinds of slavery but in the light of the justifying work of Christ on the cross. The good news is that God accepts us as we were and as we are. For this revelatory moment to be complete, we must then accept ourselves.

We need a new relationship, which will be a consequence of the new life made possible by justifying grace. What we need is a new relationship with ourselves, others, and God. The acceptance of divine forgiveness and pardon means a new standing in these relationships. The church insists that what needs to change is not merely our legal status, and this insistence is of critical importance since we are no longer slaves and can witness that emancipation has come. What will change is our lives—lives in which emancipation and justification are powerful witnesses to the revelatory activity of God in Jesus Christ, which we describe as the third expression of divine activity. A central biblical key for us was, "In Christ God was reconciling the world to God-self" (2 Cor. 5:19). The good news is that God is active in saving revelation, in reconciling the world to God-self. It is divine love that is the source and the cause of reconciliation, and it is God who is at work reconciling the world to God-self.

The revelation manifest in Jesus Christ is the place in which God expresses divine love. This is the basis for our reconciliation, and it reconnects in an environment in which we experience oppressive encounters with the master class and those who seek to perpetuate the aristocracy of slavery. The oppressive encounters are the basis for the class stratification within Jamaican society. The lower class is actually the largest sector of the society, followed by a relatively small middle class, and a minuscule upper class. The frequent conflicts among these classes still evoke patterns from the time of slavery.

Another way in which oppressive encounters manifest themselves is in the role of color in the society. The upper class is composed primarily of those with lighter pigmentation who see themselves as white, while those in the lower class are all of African ancestry. The following gradations illustrate the problem of color in the society:

Mulatto: the child of a black woman and a white man
Sambo: the child of a mulatto and a black man
Quadroon: the child of a sambo and a white man
Mustee: the child of a quadroon and a white man
Mustiphini: the child of a mustee and a white man
Quintroon: the child of a mustiphini and a white man
Octoroon: the child of a quintroon and a white man[8]

The goal of this gradation is the obliteration of the "black stain." In nineteenth-century Jamaica, an Octoroon was legally white and therefore free. This is the existential context in which the church teaches and proclaims Jesus Christ as reconciler. The walls that separate and alienate are broken down as eyes are opened and the people become cognizant that relationships are to be empowering and liberating instead of oppressive. We understand revelation as a new way of being in the world. It now represents a method of identifying self, coming to understand that we are no longer slaves but sons and daughters of God (2 Cor. 6:18). Reconciliation has become a pathway for structuring the just community in which persons are not valued because of skin color or gender or sexual orientation, but because God gives God-self to us in communion: "For if while we were enemies, we were reconciled to God through the death of his son, much more surely, having been reconciled, will we be saved by his life" (Rom. 5:10).

The walls that separate and alienate are broken down as eyes are opened and the people become cognizant that relationships are to be empowering and liberating instead of oppressive. We understand revelation as a new way of being in the world.

As the Jamaican church deals with the existential situation of alienation and poverty through emancipation, justification, and reconciliation, it is clear that revelation is not only something that *has happened* but also something that *is happening* and that *may happen* in the future. The activity of God in saving revelation is not only a past experience but also a present one. God through Jesus Christ is active in the present moment through saving revelation. Revelation is a progressive event, and the word that captures this for us is "sanctification."

Retrospectively, we do not only see the accomplishments of God through Jesus Christ, but the church also emphasizes the enabling power of God through continuing revelation. From this perspective, saving revelation is both a gift and a task. The church teaches that we are to work out our own salvation in fear and trembling all the time, being aware that God is at work in us (Phil. 2:13). There is no mistaking that Jesus Christ is our authority, and that our faith in Christ leads us to act in certain ways and provides a basis for our attitude toward self, neighbor, and God. Because Jesus Christ is normative concerning our understanding of revelation, he becomes the focal point of centeredness and integrity. Revelation as encounter with Jesus Christ affects our speech, our values, and our actions. This revelation manifest in Jesus Christ becomes the basis for a change in perspective and orientation. The oppressive encounters with those who rob us of our identity give way to encounter with revelation through Jesus Christ as a way of planning a new future. Ours is now the confidence that belongs to the children of God. Our style of life is to reflect this new confidence manifest in Jesus Christ as the revelation of God. A biblical text from John provides a basis for this new confidence:

> In the beginning was the Word, and the Word was with God, and the Word was God. He was in the beginning with God. All things came into being through him, and without him not one thing came into being. What has come into being in him was life, and the life was the light of all people. The light shines in the darkness, and the darkness did not overcome it. (John 1:1–5)

In Colossians there is an equally important foundational text:

> He is the image of the invisible God, the firstborn of all creation; for in him all things in heaven and on earth were created, things visible and invisible, whether thrones or dominions or rulers or powers—all things have been created through him and for him. He himself is before all things, and in him all things hold together. (Col. 1:15–17)

As we look at the existential situation in Jamaica, marked by alienation and poverty, we acknowledge that the underlying problem is sin, characterized as oppressive encounters. We note that as Jamaican Christians seek to make theological sense of their social location, they join salvation and revelation. They contend that the central question in the Bible as in their existential situation is not "What may we know?" but "What must we do to be saved?" They posit an indissoluble relationship between salvation and revelation.

REVELATION AS ENCOUNTER

I now turn to the work of the mid-twentieth-century Swiss theologian Emil Brunner, whose vision of revelation as encounter, I believe, speaks with specificity to all situations where human encounters are oppressive. While it is not possible to give an exhaustive study of Brunner's work on revelation at this time, I would like to highlight six emphases he makes that are instructive as the church seeks to address situations of oppressive encounters.[9]

1. Brunner points out that revelation always means the unveiling of mystery. When we turn to biblical revelation there is an added dimension, as revelation has to do with *absolute* mystery. Not only is the mystery awesome, but the revelation that takes place is the revelation of the absolute. This means among other

things that revelation may not be acquired as one would acquire ordinary knowledge through research, observation, and different forms of study: "In the Bible, God and revelation are so intimately connected that there is no other than that which comes to us from God, and there is no other knowledge of God than that which is given through revelation."[10] Revelation is divine self-communication, and what is especially hopeful for human beings is the personal communication of God with humans in a personal way. To know God is not the same as to know about God, but to be personally encountered by God.

2. A presupposition of revelation is bondage or darkness. Revelation is given in situations of oppression. In the Bible, bondage or darkness always has a personal character and an absolute dimension: "Being estranged from the living God by the fall, man goes about constructing by his reason an *idea* of the transcendental, the Absolute, which moves ever in the dimension of the abstract, the impersonal."[11] This means that without revelation, persons not only lack knowledge that it would be nice for them to have, but they are lost in darkness. This state of lostness not only affects persons in their outer being, but at the very core of their being. This state of lostness points to a negative relationship with God. This negative relationship is sin. The good news is that sin is never the first word. It is never the beginning, but always comes second. Sin is the turning away, the break in a positive relationship with the God who is never God-in-God-self but always God-for-humanity. The essence of revelation points to the God who wills to be in a positive relationship with humanity, and turns to humanity. In this turning to humanity, the divine offers not *truths about* the divine self, but the divine self. The receiving of this gift transforms humanity. In this sense, revelation is not about increase of knowledge but about self-transformation.

Without revelation, persons not only lack knowledge that it would be nice for them to have, but they are lost in darkness.

> Sin therefore presupposes an original revelation. As the darkness or bondage of man, the negative presupposition, is raised to its highest power by the concept of sin, so the revelation to the sinner is raised to its highest power because it points back to an original revelation. The "second" revelation is revelation in a quite different sense from the first; in an intensified sense it is personal and unconditioned.[12]

3. Brunner insists that in revelation unusual knowledge occurs, which we must differentiate from secular knowledge. In our knowledge of objects, we primarily engage our cognitive processes. On the other hand, our knowledge of subjects or persons is entirely dependent on an act of self-disclosure. What I am able to discover by my own thought processes points to mastery over objects. In revelation, the revealing subject shares the mystery of the *Thou* which encounters my *I* and makes community possible. This disclosure is not ordinary knowledge

but an encounter. In revelation we encounter persons, not things. Brunner proceeds to identify three characteristics of revelation:

a. In acquiring secular knowledge, we seek to become experts in some field of study. The knowing subject is always superior to the object because the subject is more than the object. In any discipline we study, the goal is mastery. The relationship of the self to the object of study is always one of superiority. "But in revelation the opposite is the case," affirms Brunner. "God, through His revelation, becomes Lord over me; . . . by this very fact I become free, and indeed only then do I develop my true 'I.'"[13]

b. While acquiring ordinary knowledge has the effect of enlarging my sphere of knowledge, it will not necessarily transform me. This knowledge may enrich me, but it may not change me. In contrast, "The knowledge of revelation . . . transforms *me myself*; it changes the one who receives it. For this process of transformation, the Bible uses the strongest expression possible: rebirth, the death of the old, and the resurrection of the new man."[14]

c. Another characteristic of ordinary knowledge is that I, as an individual, must appropriate this knowledge. This would be the case even if I were a student in a large class. The bottom line is that I process this knowledge for myself and usually by myself. One of the problems with natural knowledge is that its goal is not the formation of community. In the case of revelation, the opposite is the case. When God makes God-self known to me, I am no longer solitary. I become a member of a community because revelation knowledge is saving knowledge and thus creates community with other human beings based on communion with God. "In the Bible, when the knowledge given through revelation is mentioned, the one who knows and that which is known change places; the one who receives the revelation is one 'who is known by God,' and to be 'known by God' means to have communion with Him."[15] The key here for Brunner is that the love of God revealed in Jesus Christ is at the very heart of the revelatory disclosure. The revealing, generous, and self-giving love of God meets the receptive love of human beings who then reflect back God's love. There is unique occurrence in a revelatory encounter: "This transformation from the objective kind of knowledge of the other to the Thou-relationship is simply the 'love of my neighbor,' which becomes possible and actual in the fact that I receive the love of God. This love of my neighbor therefore is the natural effect of the reception of revelation."[16]

4. Revelation is concerned not merely with aspects of life but with life itself. The darkness and bondage that revelation takes on concern death, disaster, ruin, and destruction. The light and freedom that revelation offers is salvation and life. Revelation, the gift of life, is not merely an enrichment of knowledge but a transformation of that which is evil and destructive. Revelation saves. Revelation gives life. Brunner maintains

When God makes God-self known to me, I am no longer solitary. I become a member of a community because revelation knowledge is saving knowledge and thus creates community.

that revelation and salvation are inextricably linked and their histories are interchangeable. God gives God-self in revelation, and, in receiving this gift, we share in the divine life.

5. The amazing grace of God is the foundation for understanding revelation. The miracle that surrounds revelation is that God elects to reveal God-self to a people who break faith with God and are openly rebellious. In revelation, we meet the God who shares forgiving grace: "God does not owe love to his creatures. His love is always and everywhere a free gift. He loves one from whom he gains nothing; His love is *agape,* not *eros,*[17] a 'giving' and not a grasping love, a love which does not seek a reason for loving the other, but which loves him simply because he wills to do so. He does not only love the lovable, but makes the unlovable lovable."[18] In revelation, humanity discovers that God reaches out to human beings, creates a new righteousness that puts aside all moral and legal requirements, and offers restoration and forgiveness. The human being-who-is-from-God meets the God-who-is-for-humanity.

6. Finally, Brunner turns to the unique and unrepeatable revelation, Jesus Christ. The personal self-communication of God is manifested in him: "If Jesus Christ is really the Redeemer, then it is evident that 'in no other is there salvation,' that in his name every knee shall bow."[19] It is in this sense that revelation, which is ultimately disclosed in Jesus Christ, is unrepeatable. All other happenings are by their very nature repeatable and subject to variation, but not this event. Brunner views the cross of Christ as the decisive event that discloses the love of God. In the cross, we experience a manifestation of God who loves us *in spite of* and not *because of* who we are. Christ is the meaning of love. Speaking of the love of God revealed in the cross of Christ, Brunner states:

> Here, in *the* history which is in the strictest sense of the word on the very borderline of historical happenings, there takes place that which all other history seeks in vain: salvation, the rescue from the powers of destruction. Here therefore the real revelation takes place, the revelation of the holiness and the mercy of God, of His nature and His will, of his plan for humanity and the world.[20]

REVELATION AND WOMEN'S EXPERIENCE

The contemporary Roman Catholic feminist theologian Elizabeth Johnson considers three loci particularly important for discussing revelation. Placing revelation in conversation with the Roman Catholic tradition, she highlights (1) the hiddenness or incomprehensibility of God, (2) the role of analogy in speech about the divine, and (3) the many names of God. Johnson contends that focusing on these perspectives may help shape a hermeneutic of experience that can delimit patriarchal dominance in naming God, guiding speech in new directions, and providing support for a theology that is inclusive and intellectually responsible.

Divine Incomprehensibility

The Judeo-Christian tradition has always highlighted the transcendence and holiness of God. God is the *mysterium tremendum* ("terrifying mystery") who is transcendent and yet immanent and cannot be controlled or manipulated. There is an infinite qualitative difference between the creator and the creature. God, who is totally unlike the created order, may not be circumscribed or captured in words, concepts, or deeds. Because of this distance between the creator and creatures, human beings cannot on their own understand God. Even if one posits the claim that God communicates the will and purpose of God, this does not minimize the incomprehensibility and inscrutable nature of God. That which is mysterious does not lose its essence when revealed. Of this, Johnson writes:

> Johnson highlights (1) the hiddenness or incomprehensibility of God, (2) the role of analogy in speech about the divine, and (3) the many names of God.

> At times theologians have forgotten the mystery they were dealing with and have created the impression that because of revelation the unknown God is now available for inspection, caught within narratives or metaphysical concepts. Revelation, however, no matter by what model it is interpreted, does not and cannot dissolve the mystery of God. In its light we see ever more clearly the incomprehensibility of God as mystery of free and liberating love, love that draws near, chooses us without our deserving it, accompanies and bears us, walks the path of struggle, promises victory, dwells among us to gather us in.[21]

In a revelatory disclosure, the mystery does not lessen but deepens. God remains the wholly other. Johnson reminds us that, although there is not a doctrine of revelation as such in the Hebrew Scriptures, themes of divine hiddenness, holiness, and transcendence are expressed through God's action in history:

> I am the LORD your God, who brought you out of the land of Egypt, out of the house of slavery; you shall have no other gods before me.
>
> You shall not make for yourself an idol, whether in the form of anything that is in heaven above, or that is on the earth beneath, or that is in the water under the earth. You shall not bow down to them or worship them; for I the LORD your God am a jealous God. (Exod. 20:2–5)

The revelation manifested in Jesus Christ does not lessen the incomprehensibility of God. The history of the God of the covenant remains and provides a horizon within which to interpret the life, death, and resurrection of Jesus Christ. The God who raised Jesus from the dead remains in light unapproachable. "Indeed," says Johnson, "there is a sense in which the mysteriousness of God is brought to a more intense pitch in the experience of divine saving love poured out in Jesus Christ."[22] According to Johnson, the witness of

Scripture is that the one true God cannot be exhaustively known and that even in the revelation manifested in Jesus Christ the mystery remains. The most complete knowledge of God is knowing that we do not know God. Johnson adds:

> Suffering adds a sharper edge to this doctrine of divine hiddenness. Jewish reflection on the European holocaust and liberation theology's search for God in situations of extreme poverty and violence, point up the incomprehensibility of God not as a philosophical doctrine but as datum of faith shaped by the anguish of history. Only lament and the courage of hope enable the community to continue walking by divine light, inextricably darkened by the power of evil.[23]

The problem of human suffering makes the issue of the incomprehensibility of God on the one hand and Christian revelation on the other even more complex. It does not help that we bump up against the limits of language and culture in our attempt to theologize about the mystery of suffering and God. A suggestion of the way forward is through analogy.

Analogy

If God is incomprehensible beyond human words or thoughts, how may we talk about this God? If language cannot capture the meaning of God, what then is the significance of words, images, and concepts? Can it be that it does not all depend on us as revelation speaks? Johnson agrees that as inadequate as language is to capture the meaning of suffering and God, we have to use language, as that is part of what it means to be human. Nevertheless, she suggests that one way in which we may go forward that includes, but is not limited to, language is through the "ontology of participation." [24]

> All creatures participate to some degree in "being," the very dynamism of existing which God in essence is. Thanks to this ontology of participation, every creature in some way shares in divine perfection, although in no way does God resemble creatures. Looking at creatures we can glean clues about the characteristics of that primordial fire which is their origin and sustenance.[25]

The process of revelation involves persons. There are clues given to human experience that provide a basis for our understanding of the divine mystery. Because of these clues given to experience, we may speak of God as rock, fire, or a pillar of cloud.

The Many Names of God

For Johnson, God dwells in light unapproachable, and no name, image, or concept can capture the meaning of God. God is essentially inscrutable. The way forward is to acknowledge that language about God is analogical. The advantage of this point of departure is that it values human experience. Because of the ontology of participation, each community has something to contribute to naming God, as each community may appeal to the authority of its own experience. Johnson cites the African theologian John Mbiti, who called attention to the many names for God in Africa. The names of God reflect the indigenous situation of the people pointing to their clan or tribal affiliation.[26]

The many names of God point to the diversity of experience. While names cannot fully capture the meaning of God, they point to the one ineffable source of mystery. The names of God even if taken all together cannot exhaust the reality of the divine mystery. Johnson teaches us to respect the authority and meaningfulness of each community's symbol or name for God as each name points to the uniqueness of human experience and one aspect of divine mystery. The naming of God by each community serves as corrective to any that pretend completeness.

The many names of God point to the diversity of experience. While names cannot fully capture the meaning of God, they point to the one ineffable source of mystery.

A Hermeneutic of Experience

In a rather creative section in *She Who Is,* Elizabeth Johnson points to emancipatory speech that values the experience of women as a central and compelling motif of revelation. Although there are egalitarian impulses in the Bible, Johnson states that the texts are written primarily by men for men in a patriarchal context. For example, "the story of salvation is told from a male point of view, while the creative reflection and participation of women is neglected or marginalized, most often restricted to the one important function of bringing forth sons for the men who are the bearers of promise."[27] Johnson indicates that we are not to be surprised that in keeping with the social location of biblical authors, the images and language used to refer to God are primarily from the world of patriarchy. Images of God as king, lord, and father proliferate. When we note that biblical writers were men bound by their social locations and that the writings of the Bible are regarded as the literal inspired word of God, we should not be astonished that these writings equate the revelation of God with maleness. Revelation becomes a way of denying the dignity of women and placing brakes on the articulation of the mystery of God. Johnson states:

> Undergirding this kind of appeal to Scripture is a certain idea of revelation, namely, that it is conceptual truth given by God to human beings in verbal form, either directly through the mind of the Evangelist or indirectly through founding historical events. This doctrinal model locates revelation in rational, linguistic statements communicated by God without error that give information about divine mystery and dealings with the world. In this view, revelation is equated with the very words of the Bible.[28]

The problem with regarding revelation as propositional truth is that it excludes women because the words and traditions are unchangeable. On the other hand, when a liberating impulse guides interpretation, it links revelation with emancipatory discourse. It is precisely at this point that Johnson begins to talk about salvation as the lens through which to interpret the revelation of God. She affirms the principle that all Scripture is given for our salvation:

> Augustine had written that although the sacred writers may have known astronomy, nevertheless the Holy Spirit did not intend to utter through them any truth apart from that which is profitable for salvation. Aquinas, too, had argued that things which do not pertain to salvation do not belong to inspiration. In sum, the veracity of God and the inerrancy of the biblical authors are engaged precisely where it is a matter of salvation.[29]

The inerrancy of scripture pretain to salvation

We must judge the intent of Scripture in terms of its commitment and service to the word of salvation. Scripture becomes inspired as the community wrestles with the biblical text in the light of the existential problems in the community.

THE HERMENEUTICAL CHALLENGE

Both Johnson and Brunner relate salvation to revelation. Brunner makes it clear that revelation is not primarily about increasing knowledge but about the transformation of persons and the destruction of the forces of evil. The core of the revelatory event has to do with personal communication of God to us through Jesus Christ. It is in this person Jesus Christ that the name and the mystery of God are fully and decisively revealed. In Jesus Christ, humanity learns about the God-who-is-for-humanity and at the same time the humanity-who-is-from-God. To be human is to exist in relationship to self, others, and God; therefore, the dignity of humanity is in relationship. In Jesus Christ, we also learn that the identity of God is in relationship in the Trinity. God, however, elects also to be in relationship to humanity. This is precisely where the liberating possibilities lie in Brunner's understanding of revelation.

In revelation, God encounters humanity as *Thou* through the Word addressed to humanity in the existential situation. The revelatory word of God elicits a response from humanity, and in that response we find the dignity and responsibility of humanity. It is as the human *I* is related to the divine *Thou* that human beings experience the divine who stands over against them in ultimate authority. As Paul Jewett summarizes Brunner:

> Responsibility is not an attribute of humanity, but its substance. Our understanding of responsibility is incomplete, however, until we realize that its proper content is love, *agape*. God is love, and the revelation of this love to man is God's own work. . . . God says to man, "I love thee," and the echo of that word in the heart of man, the reply, "I love thee," is what makes a man true man. . . . [L]ove is the meaning of all responsibility.[30]

The love of God that is always "love in spite of and not love because of" is the revelation of God. The supreme expression of this revelation is in the cross of Christ, where we encounter the self-surrender, the self-sacrifice, and the self-communication of God. To be human is to respond to this revelation of the love of God, and our only choice is to respond.

The hermeneutical key for Brunner is the self-communication of God manifest in Jesus Christ. For Elizabeth Johnson, it is the experience of the struggle of women against injustice as this experience is enabled and enriched by Scripture. The Bible is not itself the word of justice and emancipatory praxis. The source of authority concerning revelation is not Scripture or Jesus Christ but the experience of struggle of women for justice. The problem with Scripture is that alone it often reinforces the oppression of women. Johnson reminds us that we may not use the words of men to describe the being of women. Jesus cannot be the source of authority either, because for women to focus on the Son of God as source of authority increases the oppression of women.

The hermeneutical key for Brunner is the self-communication of God manifest in Jesus Christ. For Elizabeth Johnson, it is the experience of the struggle of women against injustice as this experience is enabled and enriched by Scripture.

The advantage of valuing the experience of women as point of departure for Johnson is that she takes the social situation seriously and focuses on political and human liberation in a way that is not accessible to Brunner. For example, when she talks about the diversity of the divine names, it is not only because she values diversity of social locations but also because revelation is given in the social situation. Johnson addresses this in her formulation of ontological participation in which she reminds us that we participate in God; therefore, there are clues of the divine in our situation. Revelation is given to the experience of women, and they do not have to go outside their own experience to encounter truth.

Women, like other oppressed groups, are able to name God out of their own experience, constantly remembering that there is not one name, concept, or image that can capture the meaning of God. What happens if we name God after ourselves? If we identify God as "woman," "black," or "Father"? Brunner poses for us the possibility that God shares the name of God with us. God speaks for God-self. However, in what way does God in the self-revelation of who God is relate with specificity to our social, political, and economic situation? Is the name of God a saving name? This I believe is the critical question that joins the theological and sociological perspectives. "She will bear a son, and you are to name him Jesus, for he will save his people from their sins" (Matt. 1:21).

While Johnson speaks of the names of God, as this enables her to focus on the sociological context of revelation, Brunner in contrast points to the name of God as expressed in Jesus Christ. Johnson's emphasis allows her to join the political context with the human quest for emancipation. What is neglected is the work of God in salvation in the forgiveness of sin and the call to communion and fellowship. The advantage that her emphasis affords, as she calls attention to the centrality of the experience of women, is an analysis of structures of oppression and a commitment for transformation. For Johnson, revelation occurs in the struggle of women to change the world rather than in divine disclosure. What is needed here is a spirituality that informs the practice of liberation.

The converse is the case for Brunner. While God shares the name of God with humanity through Jesus Christ, and through this name there is an invitation to personal transformation, Brunner does not identify the revelation of God with any human struggle. For Brunner, revelation means Jesus Christ. His work lacks sociological concreteness and an analysis of oppressive structures. Because of this deficiency, Brunner does not name oppression.

It seems to me then that the next step is clear. As revelation expands to include salvation, we must speak of revelation as salvation from sin and admission to the reign of God. The root cause of our oppression is sin. Revelation is for our salvation. Further, revelation must include the diversity of human experience and see salvation from oppression as a critical meaning of revelation. Avery Dulles captures the significance of social analysis for liberation theologies: "They [liberation theologies] seem to assume that God preeminently reveals himself when believers enter into solidarity with the victims of racism, sexism, classism, militarism, and ecological pollution and engage in the struggle to transform the social structures responsible for these evils."[31]

Finally, revelation as salvation must have an eschatological horizon as we look toward a new future, toward the age that is to come. Revelation signifies a midpoint in history from which we may look back from the cross and the resurrection but also look forward to the new heaven and new earth: "For now we see in a mirror, dimly, but then we will see face to face. Now I know only in part; then I will know fully, even as I have been fully known" (1 Cor. 13:12). Revelation as salvation signifies the openness to a new future.

QUESTIONS FOR REFLECTION AND DISCUSSION

1. What is "natural theology"? What did Barth identify as its dangers? What advantages might it have?

2. What are the propositional, historical, and experiential models of revelation? What do you see as the strengths and weaknesses of each?

3. How does Grenz define the Bible's authority in terms of speech-act theory? In this view, what does the Bible *do?* How is this view different from the models mentioned above?

4. How does Grenz think tradition and culture play roles in how we interpret the Bible? Does this view oppose the Reformation ideal of "Scripture alone"?

5. How did his youth in Jamaica shape Erskine's understanding of revelation?

6. How does Emil Brunner understand revelation? How does Elizabeth Johnson

understand it? What strengths and weaknesses does Erskine see in each understanding?

FOR FURTHER READING

Barr, James. *The Scope and Authority of the Bible.* Philadelphia: Westminster Press, 1980.

Brunner, Emil. *Revelation and Reason.* Trans. Olive Wyon. Philadelphia: Westminster Press, 1946.

Dulles, Avery. *Models of Revelation.* Maryknoll, N.Y.: Orbis Books, 1983.

Fackre, Gabriel. *The Doctrine of Revelation.* Grand Rapids: Wm. B. Eerdmans Publishing Co., 1997.

Fiorenza, Elisabeth Schüssler. *In Memory of Her.* New York: Crossroad, 1983.

Henry, Carl F. H. *God, Revelation, and Authority.* 6 vols. Waco, Tex.: Word Books, 1976–1983.

Kelsey, David H. *The Uses of Scripture in Recent Theology.* Philadelphia: Fortress Press, 1975. Republished as *Proving Doctrine.* Harrisburg, Pa.: Trinity Press International, 1999.

McKim, Donald K. *The Bible in Theology and Preaching.* Reprint, Eugene, Ore.: Wipf & Stock Publisher, 1999.

Niebuhr, H. Richard. *The Meaning of Revelation.* New York: Macmillan, 1941.

Pinnock, Clark. *Biblical Revelation—Foundation of Christian Theology.* Chicago: Moody Press, 1971.

Russell, Letty M. *Household of Freedom.* Philadelphia: Westminster Press, 1987.

Thiemann, Ronald F. *Revelation and Theology.* Notre Dame, Ind.: University of Notre Dame Press, 1985.

Tillich, Paul. *Dynamics of Faith.* New York: Harper & Brothers, 1957.

Trible, Phyllis. *Texts of Terror.* Philadelphia: Fortress Press, 1984.

Chapter 2

What Do We Mean by "God"?

The Doctrine of God

Looking down this book's table of contents, even an atheist could accept the legitimacy of most of the topics: How do we know what to believe? What is the nature of human beings? How is the universe going to end? Atheists would give different answers than Christians would, but they would accept the questions. They would also mostly acknowledge that there was a person named Jesus and that we can talk about who he was and why he is (or is not) important, and that there is an institution called the church, whose influence (for good or ill) is worth studying.

But what about God?

For many people in our society, talk about God just doesn't make any sense. God is an obsolete idea, a figment in the imagination of religious people. Such widespread skepticism tempts Christians to seize anyone who believes in God at all as an ally who basically agrees with us, but that strategy has its own dangers. Christians cannot be satisfied with belief in any old God. Some beliefs about God are very different from what Christians believe; some may, in the way they picture God, even justifiably contribute to atheists' rejection of God.

The two essays which follow illustrate two basic alternatives for addressing these problems. John Cobb debates skeptical scientists and philosophers on their own turf. He thinks that many of the common modern beliefs that result in leaving no place for God are wrongheaded. For instance, he denies that

—the world is made up only of matter;

—the world is created by human minds;

—we can only know things of which we have sense experience; and that

—we can explain the development of living things without reference to purpose.

If we reject such assumptions (as Cobb thinks there are good reasons to do), then the idea of God starts to seem a plausible hypothesis—but not the God of much traditional theology and philosophy, who is all-powerful and unaffected by anything in the world. That picture of God, Cobb agrees, is not worth our belief, and he sets out to offer an alternative, drawn out of the school of process theology in which he is one of the most distinguished figures.

David Cunningham takes a different approach. He is much more skeptical of philosophical arguments for the existence of God. He would, I think, be dubious about trying to make the existence of God seem plausible. Rather, he believes that we know about God only because of God's self-revelation. Starting with human efforts, we would never even approach God. If we start with God's self-revelation in Christ as known through the Holy Spirit, however, then we can hardly talk about God except as Trinity.

> John Cobb debates skeptical scientists and philosophers on their own turf. David Cunningham believes that we know about God only because of God's self-revelation.

These alternatives on how to approach talk about God are an old story in Christian theology. In the most widely used theological textbook of the early Middle Ages, Peter Lombard began with a chapter called "On God," whose first section he entitled, "On the Mystery of the Trinity." When Thomas Aquinas was studying theology, Lombard's *Sentences* was his textbook, but, when he wrote his own book for theology students, the *Summa Theologiae*, he changed the order of things.[1] His chapter on God begins with a section, "On the One God," which discusses the existence and attributes of God.

He famously begins with five arguments for God's existence: God is the first mover, the first cause, the necessary being, the highest good, and the one who shapes the universe. Take the argument about God as first mover for an example: Everything that moves is moved by something else, but the series of movers has to have a first mover to start it off. So there must be some being that causes motion but is not itself moved, "and this everyone understands to be God." Similarly, the "fifth way" argues that the natural world seems to involve order or design. The planets and the seasons follow a pattern; living things are wonderfully adapted to their environment. But neither plants nor planets have the intelligence necessary to plan such an order. Therefore, "some intelligent being exists by whom all natural things are directed to their end, and this being we call God."[2]

Take the "five ways" as philosophical arguments and they can be judged like any other such argument: Do we know the truth of their premises? Do their conclusions follow from those premises? Many of his recent interpreters, however, have shown just how complicated the relation of reason and faith is in Aquinas. It is not even clear whether he presents the "five ways" as his own arguments or simply as summaries of other people's philosophical positions. Nevertheless, these arguments, and a good bit more about "the one God," all come up before he gets to the Trinity.

In Aquinas's theology, even if it was not the first topic, the Trinity turned out to be very important, but as time went on, it became steadily more peripheral to many philosophical and theological discussions of God, until, in much eighteenth-century theology, it virtually disappeared. The greatest Christian theologian of the nineteenth century, Friedrich Schleiermacher, introduced the Trinity only in the last thirteen pages of his seven-hundred-page masterpiece, *The Christian Faith*.[3] In the early twentieth century, Karl Barth again reversed the pattern and began his theological masterpiece, *Church Dogmatics*, with a lengthy discussion of the Trinity.[4]

Such debates about where to start the doctrine of God may seem trivial, but they relate in an important way to matters discussed in the last chapter. Theologians like Schleiermacher and Cobb, who think we can start by talking about the one God, are often more optimistic about what human *reason* can figure out about God—this is what has usually been called *natural theology*. Theologians such as Barth and Cunningham, who start with the Trinity, are skeptical about natural theology and assume that we can learn about God only through *revelation*.

TALKING ABOUT GOD

However we come to know about God, what do we mean by the word *God?* Christian theologians have united in affirming how hard it is to answer that question. God is a mystery. All our thought and language break down when we try to apply them to God. The closer we get to seeing God, Gregory of Nyssa wrote in the fourth century, the more we realize that God is invisible.[5]

In his discussion of the one God, Aquinas followed his reflections on whether God exists with what seems a list of properties or attributes that God has. God, he said, is simple, perfect, good, infinite, immutable, eternal, and one. Such lists are common in discussions of God. The Westminster Confession of 1647, for instance, begins its account of God by saying that God is "infinite in being and perfection, a most pure spirit, invisible, without body, parts, or passions, immutable, immense, eternal, incomprehensible, almighty, most wise, most holy, most free, most absolute."[6]

It is at first puzzling that Aquinas introduced his list of God's properties by saying that "because we cannot know what God is, but rather what He is not, we have no means for considering how God is, but rather how He is not."[7] This seems to advocate negative theology, the long tradition, especially influential among mystics, that says we cannot make positive statements about God. We can only say negative things—what God is not. But how then do we explain the list of attributes? As Aquinas developed them, they turned out to be careful specifications of things we cannot say about God: We cannot identify any parts of God, or set any limits on God, and so forth.

The problem with a purely negative theology is that it does not point us in any direction for thinking about God. If God is not X, does that mean God is better than X, or worse, or altogether different, or what? Aquinas therefore added the idea of speaking of God *analogically*. We use a word *univocally* in two cases, he said, when we mean the same thing by it both times: The building is tall; the tree is tall. We use a word *equivocally* when it has completely unrelated meanings in the two cases: In English we use the same word for the "bark" of a dog and the "bark" of a tree, but the meanings are completely different. *Analogy* is somewhere between univocity and equivocity. For instance, a *healthy person* is healthy in a quite different sense from a *healthy diet*. It makes no sense to ask which is more healthy—they are healthy in quite different ways. Yet the use of the same word in these two cases is not just accidental. A healthy diet helps *cause* health in a person; there is that clear relation between the two. So, Aquinas says, if we speak about God as *wise,* we do not mean that God is just like Einstein only even more so. God is wise in a radically different sense from our wisdom, and yet, since God is the cause of our wisdom, there is an analogy between the two uses.[8] Thus, Aquinas gets beyond purely negative theology while preserving God's mystery. We can use words about God, but their meanings are indescribably different from their meanings when applied to other things.

> Aquinas gets beyond purely negative theology while preserving God's mystery. In his account of analogy, we can use words about God, but their meanings are indescribably different from their meanings when applied to other things.

Those who came after Aquinas often neglected his careful distinctions. The issue of how God is related to other things provides a good example of this. Aquinas was deeply influenced by the fourth-century B.C. Greek philosopher Aristotle, whose philosophy was being rediscovered in Western Europe in the thirteenth century and represented the cutting edge of scientific thought in Aquinas's time. Aristotle had said that God's perfection meant that God was unchanging. If God changed, he reasoned, then either God got better or worse—and either way God would then not always be perfect. He further concluded that God was *impassible,* that is, God could not be affected by anything else. After all, if God paid attention to events in the world and grew sad at tragedies and joyful at good moments, then God would be changeable.[9]

Aquinas argued that, when a creature is in relation with God, that relation really affects the creature, but "being related to creatures is not a reality in God."[10] Imagine a dog sitting next to a pillar. If we remove the pillar, the dog will notice, and therefore a change will take place in the dog. If the dog wanders off, however, nothing changes for the pillar; it remains exactly as it was. God, Aquinas says, is more like the pillar than the dog. Whatever changes take place in us have no effect on God's nature, which, as Aristotle said, remains eternally unchanging.

> There was always something odd about identifying Aristotle's "unmoved mover" with the passionate, engaged God of the Bible.

For Aquinas, at least in some interpretations, this analysis was mostly a way of reminding us of how careful we should be in talking about God—of things we should be careful *not* to say. Later theologians and philosophers, however, came to insist that impassibility was a clear and important property of God. There was always something odd about identifying Aristotle's "unmoved mover," the God who causes motion in other things but is unaffected by anything, with the passionate, engaged God of the Bible, a God who takes sides with Hebrew slaves against their oppressors and dies on a cross. Yet many theologians came to insist on a God of impassible power. In the twentieth century, however, theologians from a variety of perspectives began to criticize that point of view.

One form of criticism (more about this later) involved new attention to the doctrine of the Trinity. Another came in the work of process theologians such as Charles Hartshorne[11] and John Cobb, who were deeply influenced by the English philosopher Alfred North Whitehead. In philosophical ideas he laid out in the 1920s, Whitehead argued that the world was not, as so many previous philosophers had claimed, made up of substances, each existing separately and independently. Rather, Whitehead maintained, the universe is composed of interrelated processes. Things are what they are because of the way they are related to the things around them, and things are better the more richly they are related to other things. Even in Aquinas's example, the dog is superior to the pillar because the dog is aware of what is going on around it; it has a richer set of relations. God is perfect, therefore, *not* in being most distant from and unaffected by the world, but in being maximally related to and thus maximally affected by everything that goes on in the universe. "Are not five sparrows sold for two pennies? Yet not one of them is forgotten in God's sight" (Luke 12:6).

Process theologians argue that too much traditional theology lost sight of the God of compassion we encounter in the Bible and put too much emphasis on a God of power and control. They define God, in Whitehead's phrases, as "the poet of the world, with tender patience leading it by his vision of truth, beauty, and goodness,"[12] and "the great companion, the fellow-sufferer who understands."[13] For process theology, God changes, God evolves, God is involved in human suffering—and, in contrast to Aristotle's view, these characteristics contribute to God's perfection rather than threatening it. This is a picture of God very attractive to feminist theologians, not only because it undercuts the image of the all-powerful "Father" God but because it sees God at work by persuasion rather than force, and thus in ways many cultures have (however stereotypically) traditionally identified as feminine.[14]

In the next chapter, Kathryn Tanner's essay will argue that we should not think of God and creatures as in competition over power at all, since they operate at completely different levels. Like other critics, she believes that the process thinkers have misunderstood what many theologians before them were really saying. But, process theologians would reply, much tradition theology *has* seemed to treat the relation between God's power and ours as a zero-sum game. And, if we think in those terms, insisting that God has all the power makes us puppets and God a tyrant.

THE TRINITY

The doctrine of the Trinity addresses some of the same issues about God and relationship. Indeed, it sees relatedness as at the heart of who God is, but it begins with very different concerns. Not until the fourth century did Christians fully develop a doctrine of the Trinity, but from the very start their encounter with God led them to struggle with the issues which led to that doctrine.

Most of the first Christians, like Jesus, were Jews, and they took for granted the one thing that most distinguished Judaism from the religions around it: a belief in only one God. They also believed in Christ's divinity. The first surviving Christian sermon outside the New Testament declares, "We must think of Jesus Christ as we do of God."[15] The first Roman report about Christians describes them as gathering to pray "to Christ as a God."[16] As they remembered the story of Jesus, they described him as praying to, and acting in obedience to, one he called his "Father."[17]

> There is one God, Christ is God, but Christ is not the Father.

Thus, there is one God, Christ is God, but Christ is not the Father. To complicate matters further, Christians began to say about the Holy Spirit some of the same things they said about Christ. They encountered God in the Holy Spirit working in their lives. They read (Luke 1:35) how Jesus was conceived when the Holy Spirit came upon Mary. They baptized "in the name of the Father and of the Son and of the Holy Spirit," so that it seemed that whatever Christian faith said about "Father" and "Son" ought to include "Holy Spirit" as well.

These issues came into sharper focus in Egypt around the beginning of the fourth century. On one side were the "Arians" (named after one of their leaders, Arius). They said that Christ was a divine being but not really equal to God. Athanasius, eventually named patriarch of Alexandria, was their great opponent. If the Arians were right, he said, then Christians were no longer monotheists, since they believed in more than one divine being. Moreover, while Arians worshiped a sort-of-divine Christ, behind Christ was a greater God unknown to them. That would make nonsense out of Christian faith.

In 325, over 300 bishops gathered at the Council of Nicaea and adopted the Nicene Creed. It said that the Son was "of the same substance" (*homoousios*) with the Father, not just "of similar substance" (*homoiousios*). Christ was really God, not merely another being like God. The Arians had lost the day. Like many negotiated agreements, however, the Nicene Creed turned out to be open to different interpretations and left many questions unanswered. It took more than a hundred years to develop terminology to clarify ideas stated at Nicaea.

Educated Christians at this time generally spoke either Greek or Latin, and by the fourth century Greek-speaking and Latin-speaking Christians (the dividing line was down the Adriatic Sea between Greece and Italy) were beginning to drift apart. The Roman Empire divided politically into two halves, and cultural interaction between the two parts steadily declined.

Three great fourth-century theologians from Cappadocia in northern Turkey—Basil, his brother Gregory of Nyssa, and his good friend Gregory of Nazianzus—led a successful campaign to persuade Greek-speaking Christians to say that God was three particular beings (*hypostases*) in one essence (*ousia*). Juan, Susan, and Kevin, for instance, are three particular human beings who share the essence of humanity. In this human example, however, each individual has a different body, and they can disagree with each other and go their separate ways. The three *hypostases* of God, in contrast, are not physically embodied and are always perfectly in accord. So in this case they are inseparably one even while they are three.[18]

Latin-speaking Christians came to adopt terms introduced by the North African theologian Tertullian (the first major Christian theologian to write in Latin) around 200. Two hundred years later, Augustine was still using Tertullian's terminology: "For the sake, then, of speaking of things that cannot be uttered . . . our Greek friends have spoken of one *ousia,* three *hypostases,* but the Latins of one *substantia* . . . three *personae.*"[19] In English, we can fairly straightforwardly translate *substantia* as "substance" or "essence"; *persona* is more complicated. One of its meanings referred to the masks actors wore in Greek and Roman plays. A mask represented a particular character; one actor could play several roles by wearing different masks. The Latin terms thus suggested one God who plays three different roles, but that made God's "threeness" seem only a matter of appearances. Christians meant that God was "three" in a stronger sense than that, but, particularly in the Latin-speaking West, they struggled to find ways to make that clear.

The differences were not just linguistic. Though with any number of exceptions on both sides (and recent scholarship has emphasized just how oversimplified this picture is), Greek-speaking "Orthodox" Christians tended to emphasize God's threeness; Latin speaking "Catholic" Christians emphasized God's oneness.

> Greek-speaking Christians emphasized God's threeness; Latin-speaking Christians emphasized God's oneness.

As Augustine acknowledged, either way theologians were attempting to speak "of things that cannot be uttered." God remains a mystery in the face of which *all* our terminology is inadequate. We have to find ways of talking about God, if only to avoid formulas that would lead us astray, but all formulas generate problems.

One of those problems goes way back in history. The early forms of the Nicene Creed all said that the Holy Spirit "proceeded from the Father." By 800 at the latest, Latin-speaking Christians had come, when they said the creed, to add that the Spirit proceeded from the Father "and the Son" (*filioque*), and many Greek-speaking Christians were horrified. The difference reflected different ways of thinking about the Trinity. For Greek-speaking Christians, the unity of the Trinity resided in the Father, from whom the Son was "begotten" and the Spirit "proceeded." (Since Scripture describes the Son as "only-begotten," theology had to find another word for the Spirit's means of production and settled on "proceed," sometimes used just of the Holy Spirit, sometimes of both Son and Spirit.) Adding another "procession" of the Holy Spirit, this time from the Son, complicated things in a way that made no sense to them. They said it made the Spirit seem to be the Father's grandchild.

Christians who spoke Latin, by contrast, had come to think of the Spirit as the bond of love that united Father and Son. They thought that that love needed to be mutual, and that the Spirit therefore had to proceed from both the Father and the Son. The Greek world was further annoyed that the West had changed the Nicene Creed without consultation, and all sorts of cultural bitterness on both sides added to the tension. In 1054 the pope and the patriarch of Constantinople (principal leader of the "Orthodox" churches) excommunicated each other, and, in spite of many efforts, the breach (which involves other issues too) has not yet been healed.

Other problems in talking about the Trinity have come to the fore more recently. In most modern European languages, *person* or the equivalent term has come to mean an *I*, a center of consciousness. But the idea of three different consciousnesses makes for stronger distinctions than the classical doctrine of the Trinity wanted to affirm. Oddly enough, while the Latin word *persona,* with its connotations of three different masks, originally did not emphasize God's threeness enough, the English word *person* (and its equivalents in other modern European languages) risks overstating the threeness. Two of the greatest theologians of the twentieth century therefore proposed alternatives to *person,* the Protestant Karl Barth suggesting "modes of being,"[20] the Catholic Karl Rahner, "distinct modes of subsisting."[21] Any change in terminology, however, fights against long tradition.

That is equally true concerning objections to the language of *Father* and *Son* as introducing inappropriate male emphasis into our talk about God. For a while, it was popular to refer to the three persons as *the Creator, the Redeemer,* and *the Sustainer,* but many have pointed out that this language makes it sound as if the divine tasks were sharply divided among the three persons. All three persons, however, have traditionally been thought to be involved in all divine activities. David Cunningham, in his essay here as well as earlier work, explores the use of *Source, Wellspring,* and *Living Water* as alternative images for the three persons. It is powerful imagery, though some of his critics have pointed out that it replaces personal language with impersonal, and that something thus gets lost when we move from *Father* to *Source.* In this book's chapter on Christology, moreover, Robert Jenson argues that only *Father, Son, and Holy Spirit* is an appropriate term. This is not just one set of images, but the *name* of God and, like the rest of us, God dislikes being called by someone else's name. Such debates continue among those who discuss the Trinity.

Even as old and new debates go on, the development of the doctrine of the Trinity has accomplished some important goals in Christian thinking about God. The Arians (like many non-Christians in the ancient world) imagined a God very distant from our world and thought that only a series of mediating beings could connect God and world. They could not imagine that God could get involved in the dust and pain of this world; if Christ did that, Christ must be a lesser being than God. Athanasius and those who followed him affirmed that God's love can reach from the highest reality of all straight down to us. Indeed, Gregory of Nyssa, one of the fourth-century Cappadocian theologians involved in developing the Greek terminology for the Trinity, insisted that this reaching down in love is not at all a sign of divine weakness. In fact, he said, we learn how *great* God is precisely in God's ability and willingness to come to "our weak nature."[22] A God who could not reach out in love would be a lesser God.

Athanasius and those who followed him affirmed that God's love can reach from the highest reality of all straight down to us and that relationship is fundamental to God.

Without the Trinity, belief in one God also would invite thinking of God as the single top of the cosmic hierarchy. The doctrine of the Trinity affirms that relationship is fundamental to God, that within God's oneness there is also community of perfect love.[23] Love and community are therefore built into the structure of the universe and the way we ought to live our lives. In that, like process theology, the doctrine of the Trinity emphasizes God's compassion and relatedness, in contrast to monarchical power.

JOHN B. COBB, JR.

DOES IT MAKE SENSE TO TALK ABOUT GOD?

At the outset of this new millennium, can we, even in the church, continue to speak about God? By placing God at the center of our faith, do we show that Christian belief now has no real place? Does our language about a divine Creator and Redeemer correspond with that about the flat earth so far as intelligent and well-educated people are concerned? Is belief in God a sign of mental illness? Does it even cause such illness?

These are serious questions for the church. What many Christians have meant by *God* fits as poorly with the rest of our most reliable belief system as the idea that the earth is flat. Some of what has been called religious experience is clearly pathological. And some Christian beliefs about God that have played a large role in the church have led to the slaughter of "heretics," Jews, and "witches," to patriarchy, to sexual repression, to ruthless exploitation of nature, and to condemnation of other great religious traditions.

But perhaps the incredibility and harmfulness of many beliefs about God only add to the importance of thinking about God in credible and beneficial ways. The unending task of theology is to do that. The question is whether theology can succeed. Is there a credible and beneficial way of thinking about God today?

In the contemporary intellectual world, the burden of proof is placed on the one who claims that the answer is yes. The pervasive assumption is that our culture has outgrown theistic belief, that the world is better understood without God, and that we are mentally and spiritually better off when we are freed from that belief. Indeed, this set of assumptions is now so commonplace that those who hold them feel no need to defend or even explain them. Since, in fact, textbooks in history and the sciences explain everything without reference to God, most intellectuals find it evident that introducing God into our accounts of the world is superfluous, arbitrary, and incredible.

Those who believe in God must either show that scientists and historians have been wrong in leaving God out of their accounts, or else explain that God is related to the world in a way that does not preclude explaining the world without reference to God. The latter has been the more common strategy. The theistic interpretation of the world can then lie alongside the natural/historical one, never impinging upon it—two different accounts, each valid in its own way. This allows a place for the church to do its thing, but over the years it has made that "thing" seem quite irrelevant and a bit silly. It may be time for believers in God to counterattack. Perhaps the nontheistic interpretation of natural and human events finally has failed, and, if that is the case, it may be time to say so. Perhaps the various nontheistic systems that have driven theistic ones out of the marketplace of serious ideas are themselves incredible and pathogenic. On a level playing field, Christian theism might have a chance.

This is my belief. In my opinion, all the major intellectual moves that have brought us to the present state of the discussion are a bit crazy. No one can really live and think as if the ideas that have been so widely professed were true. These ideas have led us to the brink of ecological self-destruction, and yet the intellectual life of the secular world is hardly open to their being challenged. Certainly their proponents expect no effective challenge from theists!

> Perhaps the nontheistic interpretation of natural and human events finally has failed, and, if that is the case, it may be time to say so.

Consider a few determinative modern moves. First, there was *the transformation of nature into a machine.* The seventeenth-century philosopher René Descartes played a large role in this. He taught that only human beings have minds, so that, while animals look as if they are suffering pain or experiencing pleasure, they really do not—only beings with minds can really have experience. According to Descartes, animals are like robots designed to look as if they feel emotions.

It is true that we treat our livestock much as we would treat machines, as if they did not suffer from our abuse, but does anyone really believe that that is true? Does anyone really believe that our pet dogs and cats have no subjectivity, no feelings at all? If we do not believe that, is it sensible or salutary to build our scientific and intellectual system on such false assumptions?

What follows from this starting point is even crazier. Modernity had two choices. It could locate humanity, including its own beliefs about the world, as part of the machine of nature. Some did this and became thoroughgoing materialists. Or it could follow Descartes in holding that there are two radically different orders of being—*mind* and *matter*—that operate on different principles and cannot influence one another. He then had to try to explain, not very successfully, how mind and body seem so closely connected in the case of human beings.

It is hard to say which of these choices is crazier. If we are part of the machine, our continuing to discuss such matters makes no sense. Reasoning of this kind is not a reasonable activity for machines, even if people can make them replicate many of the patterns of human reasoning. On the other hand, our continual experience of the intimate interconnection of our feeling and thinking and deciding with our bodily experience makes it impossible really to believe that mind is totally separate from matter.

Another widely held assumption is that *all our knowledge of the world originates in sense experience.* This does not seem so absurd on the surface. Its error becomes manifest only as its implications are drawn out. For example, if our knowledge all arises in sense perception, then there is no knowledge of the past. Memory cannot be what it seems to be at all. Indeed, there is no reason to suppose that there has been a past. Yet if we did not think and act as if there had been a past about which our memory somewhat accurately informs us, we would certainly be viewed as insane.

There is much in ordinary experience that makes no sense if all knowledge arises in sense experience alone, but causality is the example that has played the most important role in the actual course of Western thought. If the world is a machine, then one movement causes another and so forth. Causality is the essential relationship determining everything that happens. But in the eighteenth century, the philosopher David Hume pointed out that if all knowledge arises from sense experience, then our usual idea of causality, as one thing making another happen, cannot be justified. The contents of sense experience simply succeed one another, and even that succession is not given in sense experience! In any case, one set of data does not necessitate the next. The idea of causality implies some *necessary* connection between cause and effect, and we can never have a sense experience of necessity.

There is much in ordinary experience that makes no sense if all knowledge arises in sense experience alone, but causality is the example that has played the most important role in the actual course of Western thought.

Since it was assumed that science provides causal explanations, the discovery that sense experience could not explain how we know causal relations was deeply troubling. But this did not lead nineteenth-century thinkers to examine other dimensions of experience in quest for the empirical source of the idea of causality. Instead, Western thought moved massively to idealism. *The mind, according to idealism, creates the world.* For some idealists, such as Immanuel Kant, all minds create the world in much the same way. For others, beginning with G. W. F. Hegel, each culture creates its distinct world. For still others, one's social location has a lot to do with the way one constructs the world. But all believed that a world cannot exist unless there is a mind to think it.

Much has been learned by emphasizing the creativity of the human mind. Many ideas that were once viewed as accurate and inescapable descriptions of an objectively given world are now seen as expressions of particular points of view. Many features of society that were once thought to be expressions of necessary social order are now seen as the constructs of those who benefit from them. But it is quite insane to suppose that the human body and nature in general place no limits on these constructions. It is insane not only in that no one can live on such a basis but also in that it distracts attention from the actual degradation of nature by human actions. We all know that there is a real natural world that is independent of our minds and to which we need to pay attention. Yet this belief is rejected by most of our sophisticated theories. The result is far less attention to the natural world on the part of humanists and social theorists than is needed if we are to stop our destructive practices and begin to restore a livable environment.

The attribution to the human mind of the creative powers once ascribed to God is crazy. The belief that mind is radically separate from body is crazy. The belief that there is no mind in distinction from matter is crazy. The belief that the natural world is nothing but matter is crazy. In one sense, everyone knows this and continues to live on another basis, so one could say it does not matter. Unfortunately, it does. The disconnection between avowed beliefs and actual life makes for craziness. And avowed beliefs, when institutionalized in the educational system, have enormous effects on how we really think about important matters. One of these important matters is God. The disappearance of God from sophisticated conversation is partly caused by these beliefs.

Another contribution to the eclipse of God has been the craziness of inherited ideas about God. One of the craziest was the idea that, *for any reality to be considered* God *it must have* all *the power*. This is the doctrine of omnipotence that has been so closely associated with theism in its Western forms. The implications are appalling.

> One of the craziest of inherited ideas about God is that, for any reality to be considered *God* it must have *all* the power.

If there is one being that has all the power, then no other being has any power at all. Everything that happens must be directly caused by the one power. Our normal experience of making choices that make a difference is an illusion. Only God makes decisions.

To call the One who is supposed to decide everything unilaterally "good" only adds to the craziness. Since so much that happens appears not to be good, enormous energy has been expended by theists to prove that what is apparent to all is not really the case. Actually, assigning all power to God has much the same effect as assigning all power to the world machine. It implies that all that we know most intimately and certainly about ourselves and our world is illusory! It declares false the beliefs that are needed to operate sensibly in the world. To reaffirm this traditional idea of God against the craziness of atheistic modernity is of no help whatever.

Our question is whether there is any way of thinking available to us today that is not crazy. In particular, our question is whether such a way of thinking has a place for God. Clearly, it has no place for the omnipotent God to whom so many still cling. Western thought has replaced an incredible and pathological belief in God with an incredible and pathological atheism. Returning to the craziness of traditional theism from the craziness of modern atheism will not help. But these are not the only choices.

If the issue of God's reality is not identical with the question of whether classical theism is correct, then we need some minimal definition of *God* that can guide us in deciding whether a credible and salutary belief in God is possible today. This is not primarily a philosophical question. What is important is the question whether religious believers are justified in their basic beliefs. But even here, difficulties arise. What is basic to the beliefs of religious believers?

For some, no doubt, basic among their beliefs are some that are incredible and pathological. But for many, even among those who affirm such beliefs, these are not fundamental. The actual practice of believers who affirm divine omnipotence is rarely consistent with their professed beliefs.

Another complication in deciding what must be in order that we may affirm the reality of God is the diversity of theistic traditions. In this essay, our focus is on Christian belief in God. Hence, we can posit that for us to say that God is, there must be that which Jesus called *Abba*. Since Jesus was a Jew, the affirmation of the Christian God in all probability will entail the affirmation of the God of Israel and Islam as well. But it is best for Christians to leave that question to Jews and Muslims.

WHAT CHRISTIANS BELIEVE ABOUT GOD

In deciding what must be the case in order that Christian belief that God is vindicated, a good place to begin is with the act that is the primary corporate Christian response to belief in the reality of God: worship. To believe in God is to believe that there is something that pervades the whole of things that is worthy of worship. What Christians worship is a reality that has to do with all things and excludes the reality of other parallel beings. Christianity is, in this sense, monotheistic. The issue for Christians is not the reality of gods but of God. This is most clearly expressed in the Bible by depicting God as Creator of heaven and earth, that is, of all things other than God.

That has often been interpreted to mean that only if there is "creation out of nothing" is there God. That is an overstatement that has led to many problems. The actual biblical account is better understood as ordering the chaos. In the void or chaos there are no "things," but chaos is not nothing in the sense usually meant by creation out of nothing. The point for the Christian is that *no thing* came into existence or comes into existence apart from God. We owe our existence and the existence of all things to God. The one we worship is our Creator. If there are "gods," God is their creator as well. God alone is truly worthy of worship.

The doctrine of divine omnipotence, already critiqued, has been closely connected with the doctrine of creation. Some Christians have drawn from the teaching about creation the conclusion that God is in total control of everything, that God, indeed, determines everything that happens just as it happens. The belief in divine omnipotence has even affected the translations of the Bible. In English translations, especially in Genesis and Job, we often find the expression "God Almighty" or simply "the Almighty," so we suppose that this is the way the biblical writers thought. However, this is actually a quite arbitrary substitution for one of the proper names for God—El Shaddai. A more literal translation would be "the breasted One"!

If one presupposes that God is "almighty," then it may be justified to introduce the term into the text of the Bible. But we must be clear that the Bible itself does not use this language. Christian language of omnipotence has crept into our worship, but from a biblical point of view, what we worship does not determine everything, including human actions, to be just what they are. The Bible depicts

God as having great power, but it does not deny some power to creatures as well. The drama of history is not that of God manipulating puppets. The implications of the doctrine of divine omnipotence have been one main cause for the loss of credibility of Christian theism and the charge that it is spiritually harmful. A credible and salutary Christian belief in God will return to biblical sources.

We may recognize as worship the sacrifices that in some religious traditions are designed to appease an angry God, but whatever reality may attach to what is there worshiped, it is not the one Jesus addressed as *Abba.* That God does not require appeasement by us. Some formulations of Christian teaching imply that once God did require such appeasement but that this was accomplished once and for all in Jesus, whose sacrifice makes all further sacrifice unnecessary. Others, more plausibly, believe that the change is on the side of human understanding of God. Either way, what is worshiped by Christians is characterized more fundamentally by love and grace than by wrath. For Christians to affirm the reality of God is to affirm that there is in reality a creative power that is characterized by love and is gracious toward human beings.

The Bible depicts God as having great power, but it does not deny some power to creatures as well. The drama of history is not that of God manipulating puppets.

The biblical depictions of this reality are generally anthropomorphic—human shaped. In the ancient Near East, using the human form distinguished biblical depictions from those that used animal figures, especially the bull. In any case, the Hebrews rejected depictions of God as *physically* anthropomorphic, and to overcome that kind of anthropomorphism they forbade any images at all. God differs from human beings not only in power and immortality, like the Greek gods, but also in being inherently invisible. What is left of anthropomorphism is personal language. God thinks, feels, and wills. God interacts with human beings in a personal way.

On the other hand, the Hebrews were vividly aware that God's ways are not our ways. As creatures relating to our Creator, ours is a highly dependent condition. God is often spoken of as King, an image that suggests both a great distance and onesidedness in the relation. Unfortunately, the Hebrews' distinction of God from human beings never went so far as to de-gender God. God was almost always depicted as male, and this bias was continuous with the patriarchal structure of society. One of the ways belief in God has been damaging has been in undergirding male domination.

In Jesus' language, the personal character of God is retained, even heightened. Jesus' distinctive address to God as *Abba* establishes or expresses a remarkable intimacy. Paul thought that the ability of a believer to address God in this intimate way was a consequence of the indwelling Spirit (Rom. 8:15–16).

In any case, Christian worship relates to God across this whole spectrum. It has the note of praise and awe toward one who is transcendent creator, ruler, and judge. It also expresses the most intimate personal relations. It seems that, in traditional language, the Christian God is both transcendent and immanent.

Does this mean that God as believed in by Christians is a person? One difficulty with answering this question is that the notion of *person* is not found in the Bible. What *person* meant in the Hellenistic world at the time is not what we mean by the word today. In classical terms, God was said to be three persons, not one, a complication to which we will return. In terms of our normal meaning of person, this Trinitarian expression is polytheistic. It is *our* meaning, of course, that governs our questioning as to whether God is a person, but that too is vague. Let us sort it out a little.

A *person* thinks and purposes, feels and responds. Does God do so? The assumption of the biblical writers is surely that God does something like that. Yet they also know that God does not think as we think, or feel as we feel. They are not philosophers, so they do not try to describe the similarities and differences. There is a wide range of acceptable interpretation among Christians. But if there is no cosmic, or transcosmic, creative reality beyond and above human beings that resembles human beings in thinking, purposing, feeling, and responding, then the great majority of Christians have been mistaken in their belief in the reality of God. What Christians mean by *God* is not merely an object or an abstract principle. It must have reality for itself as well as for others, in short, be a subject.

What Christians mean by *God* is not merely an object or an abstract principle.

On the other hand, to be a person normally means to be one person alongside others. For God to be a person would then seem to locate God at one place rather than others. God would be finite in ways that Christians have never supposed, or divine transcendence would be translated into spatial distance. In all such senses, God is not a person. But even if we decide that we cannot call God a person in our modern sense without depicting him in creaturely terms, we can, and indeed must, say that God relates to us in personal ways. A reality that does not do so is not the God Christians worship.

OVERCOMING ALIEN ASSUMPTIONS

A description of the God Christians worship is not evidence for the credibility or beneficial character of Christian theism. It does make possible a serious discussion of these questions. Is belief in a cosmic creative subject who is graciously disposed toward us credible? Is it salutary?

Consider briefly the reasons for a negative answer lying in the basic assumptions of the modern tradition. If the whole of reality, or everything other than the human mind, is a machine, then the only creative act can have been the one that started the machine running. But if that initiatory act only precipitated the big bang fifteen billion years ago and all else has occurred by the necessity of mechanistic laws, any talk of gracious relations with human creatures appears ridiculous. One may, and some do, argue that the initial creative act established, against all odds, the conditions that led to the evolution of human beings. One can understand that as expressive of a gracious disposition. But as long as the mechanistic doctrine is intact, the biblical vision is kept at a great distance.

If mechanism is rejected and all creatures are understood to have a life and power of their own, the distance to the biblical vision is greatly reduced. A God whose initial act of creation envisions the possibility of sensitive and responsible creatures can then be understood to work through billions of years to bring such creatures into being. God can be imagined as eliciting from the more elementary creatures that were brought into being by the initial creative act the decisions needed for the emergence of more complex beings, and eventually human beings. When that goal is reached, God continues to interact with these human creatures for their good.

Is this credible? It does not contradict any actual scientific knowledge, even if it does not fit into the scientific worldview. But it runs up against another major assumption of the modern mind, namely, that a causal relation cannot be affirmed between God and the world. We saw that this follows from belief in the primacy of sense experience. If we limit ourselves to this, then, as Hume insisted, causality can only be a regular succession of sensory data. "The flame causes the water to boil" simply means that I have experienced flame followed by boiling water over and over again. Since we have no sense perception of God, God cannot be a part of such a relation in any way.

If, on the other hand, as Kant proposed, we posit the creative activity of the mind as imposing a causal interpretation on successive sense data, that helps us not at all with respect to God: We still have no sense perceptions of God. And if, as idealists suppose, the human mind is the true creator of the world, then God is, at most, a creature of the human mind and cannot be a prior or independent agent.

Whether we follow Hume (saying that we derive our idea of causality simply from the repetition of the same pair of sense experiences) or Kant (saying that the human mind imposes a causal interpretation on our sense data), the result with respect to God as agent is much the same. Since sense experience is affirmed to be primary, there can be no experience of that which is not sensuously given. Since God is not sensuously given, God cannot be experienced. God can then only be an inference from what is given in the senses. But our beliefs about causality only apply to objects of sensation, and therefore a causal relation cannot be affirmed between God and the world. The affirmation of God's creative activity is excluded in advance.

For the theistic interpretation to be credible, we must reject the premise that all knowledge of what is not ourselves comes through sense experience. *Radical* empiricism has arisen to challenge sense empiricism on this point. Just as nature contains much more than the mechanistic elements absolutized by modern thinkers, so also human experience contains much more than sense data and the mental operations worked upon them. Radical empiricism tries to attend to *all* the elements of human experience. Our experience of our bodies and of our past, for instance, is not sensory. Our hopes and fears and values are just as fundamental as sense data.

Relationships to other entities existed throughout nature long before there were sense organs. These physical relations do not cease to exist in human beings because of the sense organs. In other words, there is a physical experience of the world that is deeper than the conscious mental one in which sensory experience plays so large a role. These feelings are of the causal influence of the world upon us. All of us in fact know that what happens in the body causally affects our subjective experience. There is no longer any good reason to deny that knowledge. Indeed, there is also good evidence of what is called extrasensory perception and of other parapsychological phenomena that have played a large role in religious literature all over the world. In the context of this much richer understanding of real relationships, it is no longer necessary to assume that experience that is felt to be of God is always delusion. Those who experience God as a causal factor in their lives may be interpreting their experience accurately.

> For the theistic interpretation to be credible, we must reject the premise that all knowledge of what is not ourselves comes through sense experience.

The point thus far is simply that much of the reason for dismissing theism arises from assumptions that, on closer examination, lack plausibility. There may be other reasons for dismissing theism. Indeed, there are excellent reasons for rejecting some ideas about God that have played a large role in the discussion, but this does not exclude the reasonableness of affirming the reality of the one Jesus addressed as *Abba.*

EVIDENCE FOR CHRISTIAN THEISM

Even if a form of Christian theism can be formulated that is compatible with what we know from science and history, is there any reason for adopting it? Are there any known features of the world that are better interpreted in this way than by atheism? If atheism can handle the interpretation just as well, should we not avoid unnecessary and useless hypotheses?

I have hinted at answers above, but they should be systematically stated. They can begin with the currently dominant cosmogony (theory of the origin of the universe), namely, the big bang theory. Other theories challenge it, and theology must always avoid too close a relation to particular scientific theories. Its task is to show that efforts to explain everything without God tend to leave some things out, or to be less convincing. This does not prove the existence of God, but it indicates that such belief fits well with the current state of knowledge. At the moment, the task is to show that a theistic account helps in explaining the big bang.

This is not difficult. Actually, many scientists have recognized this fact. If the big bang is truly the beginning of the cosmos, then it is astonishing that it had just that character that made possible the emergence of life in general and of sophisticated forms of life as well. So many things that appear arbitrary in themselves had to have just the character they had and have in order for this to be. The role of a cosmic intelligence concerned for the emergence of complex forms of life would be a natural explanation.

Why is it so widely rejected? The answer is not that it is implausible but that, for most scientists, it is not "scientific." To be scientific a theory must either establish necessity or explain what happened as a matter of reasonable chance. Furthermore, in the tradition that goes back to Descartes in the seventeenth century, science is not allowed to include mind as a causal factor in physical events. That prohibition definitely includes the divine mind; indeed, it was enacted primarily to keep God out of science. Accordingly scientists have trouble coming up with an explanation.

Since scientists cannot show any necessity in what happened, and since the chance of matters being as they are appears infinitesimal if this is the only cosmos, some have preferred to speculate that this universe is but one of many. If there are innumerable universes, and if these arbitrary elements differ in each, then the fact that one of them happens to have the characteristics of this one is not so remarkable. The character of our universe can then be attributed to chance. Hence, without any evidence whatsoever for the existence of other such universes, this speculation has been rather widely adopted. Its only apparent merit is that it avoids theism. It seems that if the prejudice against theism were not present, the theistic hypothesis would seem quite plausible.

At the opposite end of the spectrum, theistic religious experience seems on the surface to have some evidentiary value. If we are convinced a priori that experience of God is not possible, then of course our task is to provide other explanations of experiences felt by their possessors to be of God. Since we all assume that delusion occurs, we cannot rule out the possibility that all such experience is delusion. Many apply this same principle to extrasensory perception, assuming that it is all delusional regardless of its empirical support.

But if we show that much about human experience and the world can be explained when we acknowledge that sense experience is only part of the way that experience relates us to what is not ourselves, then we can discriminate between delusional and nondelusional experience. Some theistic experience seems on the surface to be nondelusional. The burden would then be placed on those who insist on its delusional character to provide better explanations. So far they have not done very well.

What about the vast period between the big bang and the emergence of human religious experience? Are there any events there for which the working of God would be a helpful explanation?

Yes, there are. The evolutionary process on this planet, which fits so poorly with the idea of an omnipotent God, can be better understood if God is seen as playing a creative role than if God is excluded altogether. Actually, the situation is quite similar to that with the big bang. Scientists adjust their theories to avoid allowing an opening to theism rather than considering the theistic hypothesis on its merits.

In this case, evolutionists from an early point systematically excluded purpose from biology as a possible explanatory factor. They were especially concerned to avoid any explanation of the process as a whole as an expression of divine purpose. They wanted to find explanations through detailed study of the mechanisms involved. They were correct in wanting to find the detailed explanations of how evolution worked, but their decision to do so by treating biological organisms like machines reduced their ability to deal with the facts. The evidence is that purposive behavior on the part of individual animals plays a significant role throughout the process of evolution. Sometimes the intelligent decisions of animals have dramatic importance. An evolutionary theory that ignores and denies this characteristic of the actual process is inadequate and rightly evokes the many criticisms it has received.

> The evolutionary process on this planet, which fits so poorly with the idea of an omnipotent God, can be better understood if God is seen as playing a creative role than if God is excluded altogether.

Why then do evolutionary theorists not include animal purposes among their explanatory principles? It seems to be because they see that once they open the door to purposes, the question of the source of purpose in the world may arise. This opens the door to consideration of the divine purpose. They are right in their fear, but wrong in fearing it. If God's activity plays a role in the evolutionary process, then a real and honest science would acknowledge it. To shape theory in order to prevent a hypothesis from being introduced is indirect evidence that the hypothesis, once allowed, might have some plausibility.

Thus far, mainline theologians have been so influenced by basic features of late modern (or deconstructive postmodern) thought that they have avoided these kinds of challenges. They want to formulate theology in a way that leaves science in charge of shaping our understanding of the natural world. They have left the challenging of dominant formulations of scientific theories to conservatives who have sometimes presented ideas in conflict with well established scientific conclusions. Mainline theologians have then rushed to the defense of the sciences, even when the conservative criticisms revealed real weaknesses.

When mainline theologians have given reasons for belief in God at all, they have done so on metaphysical grounds. (Metaphysics is the part of philosophy that has to do with the most basic questions about reality in general.) These too have some convincing power. For example, we may ask: Why is there anything at all? or Why is there any order at all? as well as, Why does this world have the remarkable characteristics it has? Or we may wonder why, as each present perishes, another is born. Or we may ask why there is freedom in the world, why it is not, as so many assume, simply a deterministic process. Of those who take these questions seriously, many find theistic answers persuasive.

Partly for this reason, the dominant modern mind has been at pains to undermine this kind of questioning. Metaphysics has been caricatured and given a bad reputation indeed. It is often implied that metaphysicians assume that they can escape all conditionedness and relativity and arrive at final certainty. This would, indeed, be arrogant and self-deceptive. The human mind, we are told, is not adapted to questions of this sort and should stick to the issues immediately at hand. Of course, there are metaphysicians, as there are critics of metaphysics, who make exaggerated claims for their judgments. But the enterprise of metaphysics can be pursued with humility as easily as can the work of those who oppose it. The issue is whether the questions are meaningless or of no importance, and the evidence that this is so rests chiefly on the doubtful assumptions of modernity. Metaphysics can add its bit to the plausibility of theism.

CHRISTIAN EXPERIENCE OF GOD

God's role in the totality of things is important for the Christian believer. Understanding the world as God's creation provides direction to action in the world and to understanding oneself as creature. However, for many believers concern centers on how God makes a difference for the believer now. How is that best understood?

Much of what the church has taught and now teaches centers on the effect of our believing that God has a certain character and has shown this in certain acts. We appropriate the fruits of this revelation by faith. Since the revelation occurred in Jesus Christ, we sometimes speak of faith in him. Paul explains that whereas we earlier experienced God as wrath apart from this revelation, God has now displayed in Christ that the justice we so feared is actually merciful love. Believing that God is love frees us from the need to prove ourselves to be good people. We can acknowledge our sin and foolishness without losing our self-esteem. That self-esteem is now grounded in our knowledge that God loves us and has acted in our behalf. Being free from our defensiveness, we become open to others, able to love them for their own sake. The Christian life is, then, the life of love.

Is this account of who God is and what God has done convincing? Against the background of the basic assumptions of modernity, of course, it is not. But if we reject those assumptions, as I have above, it has a better chance. It requires acceptance of the central Christian claim that God has acted for our salvation in Jesus Christ. We can most easily understand this as saying that we have come to know God as love through the events centering in the historical Jesus. For those who believe that God is real and that God relates to the world in love, this is not hard to affirm. If we believe that God is active in the world, it is not hard to believe also that God was significantly active in the life, death, and resurrection appearances of Jesus. We will return to the question of God's mode of acting in the world shortly.

Meanwhile, the question is whether believing that God relates to us lovingly has the consequences attributed to it. Are Christians really freed to love others just by the knowledge that God loves? Surely the claim is exaggerated. Relations to other human beings play an enormous part in determining our ability to love. The ecstatic language of the New Testament about the profundity of the effects of faith in this revelation does not come naturally to us. But surely the belief that God loves us cuts in a beneficial direction. The claims for it are not false.

Some Christians have so focused on God's presence in Christ that they depict it as wholly discontinuous with the way God relates to all others, including believers. These Christians believe that God actually entered the world in Jesus, and nothing even somewhat analogous happens with anyone else. On the other hand, in the New Testament accounts, this distinction is not so sharp. The entry into the Christian life comes when we appropriate by faith the truth that God loves us as revealed in Jesus. But when this has happened, then God begins to work within us through the Holy Spirit. The way God is in us in Christ or in the Holy Spirit (Paul does not make much of a distinction) may not be drastically different from the way God was in Jesus (Rom. 8:16–17).

The way God is in us in Christ or in the Holy Spirit may not be drastically different from the way God was in Jesus.

Many Christians have found all language about the divine presence within the human difficult to understand. They have minimized it or interpreted it in terms of the consequences of the belief in God's loving acceptance instead of seeing it as a distinct, additional way that God relates to us. This has led to interpreting Christian experience in terms of what we believe about God and the effects of that belief rather than in terms of God actually working directly in us. On the other hand, for many other Christians, the immediacy of the relation to God is of primary importance. If it can be understood in a plausible way, then the church will be less suspicious of it. This process of explanation can also throw light on how God is effective in the world everywhere.

The main place where the church did wrestle with the question of how God could actually indwell a human being was in relation to Jesus. There were two extreme possibilities that were conceptually understandable. Those who thought in psychological terms could understand that Jesus' will was attuned to God's so perfectly that they became one. Jesus willed God's will. If one thought in ontological terms (ontology is the part of philosophy that studies the nature of being), on the other hand, one could suppose that some aspect of God displaced some aspect of the human Jesus. For example, one could suppose that although Jesus' body was human, Jesus' mind was really divine, or one could suppose that whereas Jesus had a human mind, his human will was displaced by God's.

Despite their conceptual acceptability, the church was not satisfied with either of these explanations. It rejected the psychological account because it believed that the incarnation did have an ontological character. God was really in Jesus. It rejected the ontological option because that theory denied that Jesus was fully human. The belief that Jesus was genuinely human was based partly on the obvious meaning of the New Testament and partly on an understanding of Jesus' saving work as requiring him to share the human condition. The problem was, then, how to show that God was genuinely in Jesus without setting aside some aspect of Jesus' true humanity.

We may be in a better position to answer that question than were the theologians of the early church. The categories with which they worked were substantialist. That is, they took the model of reality from physical objects like stones or human bodies that endure relatively unchanged through time. They knew that two such objects cannot occupy the same space at the same time. Yet they were committed to God being genuinely in Jesus without taking away anything from his humanity. The results were powerful affirmations with no intelligible explanation. Ever since then, the church has had the problem of arousing an incredulous response to its teachings. It has responded too often with appeals to mystery and authority. In any case, there was little incentive to try for an intelligible explanation of how the Spirit indwells believers.

Today, centuries of problems with the consequences of substance thinking have weakened its hold. Whereas substances have often been understood to be the kinds of things that remain what they are, while their relations to other substances change, many now believe that this is not a good way to understand human experience. For experience, relations are fundamental. Its relations constitute what an experience is. There is not first an experience that is complete in itself and then its entry into relations with others. There are relations with others—the body, past experiences, external objects, and other people—that together constitute the experience. Our bodies and our past as well as other people dwell in our experiences. The presence of others in the experience does not replace anything. It enriches the whole.

This is an ontological statement, and it is crucial to an intelligible account of causality as well as relationality. A cause participates in constituting its effect. The effect actually includes the cause. That is how the cause functions as a cause.

Now let us suppose that the relation to God is also a factor in a human experience. Then God, too, indwells that experience. That indwelling does not replace or displace something of the self that would otherwise be there. It enriches the whole.

The indwelling of the Spirit in the believer is said to strengthen, empower, liberate, and transform. Paul lists its fruit. He also knows that it can lead to ecstatic experiences (1 Cor. 12:8–11; 14:1–5). But the main point here is that the human being in whom the Spirit works most powerfully is not rendered thereby less human. On the contrary, the more effective is God's influence in one's experience, the more fully and joyfully is that experience truly human. That Jesus could be said to be fully God and fully human is not quite so strange when viewed in this light.

Does the Spirit indwell only in Jesus and in believers, or is God present in all creation? Both ideas are present in the Bible. They need to be combined in some way. The prologue to the Gospel of John is suggestive. There the language is about the Word, but at this early point in the development of the Christian tradition, terms of this sort had not been sorted out in a consistent way. It can be interpreted equally well in terms of God's Spirit or Wisdom. The passage (John 1:1–5, 14, 16) provides a sense of escalating intensity of involvement. Everything was made through the Word. What came into being through the Word was life. This life was the light of all people. This Word takes on flesh in Jesus. Perhaps we too can understand that God's creative presence in physical things before the advent of life was not very effective. Physical things are largely determined in their behavior by other physical things. Nevertheless, the working of God in them eventually led to living things in which it was more effective. Its presence in people gave them intelligence. Finally, the Word was uniquely embodied in Jesus. From this incarnation we have received grace, which elsewhere can mean the work of the Spirit within us. Paul focuses on the final two stages, but this need not exclude the presence of the Spirit as the breath of life in all animals, which is attested in other parts of Scripture.

> The more effective is God's influence in one's experience, the more fully and joyfully is that experience truly human. That Jesus could be said to be fully God and fully human is not quite so strange when viewed in this light.

THE TRINITY

An account of Christian experience leads quickly, inevitably, into Trinitarian language. But it does not determine the outcome of debates about how the key terms are to be understood, or even which terms should be taken as key. There is no way of arriving at a system of usage that fits all biblical passages. But we can say something about the issues, why they are important, and how they were resolved.

When Jews and early Christians spoke of God, they had in mind the one whom Jesus addressed as *Abba*. However intimate the relation, there is no identity. Jesus was not praying to himself. Also, typically, when the thought was of God's presence in the world, it was expressed in terms of God's Wisdom, or Word, or Spirit, or Son. God as God was thought of as transcendent and as one who was encountered externally, not found within. In the passage in John just noted, God's presence in Jesus is described in terms of God's Word being enfleshed. This passage played a key role in Trinitarian thought, although the creeds substituted *Son* for *Word*. The divine that was in Jesus was understood to be not the Father to whom Jesus prayed but God's Son. The key question then was how the Son was related to God. However closely they might be related, they could not be simply identical. The final outcome of the debate was the judgment that the Son and the Father were both, equally, God, even though the Son was begotten of the Father. The remaining question was about the Spirit that indwelt believers. Was that also God? The church said yes.

> The church affirmed that the transcendent divine, the divine in Jesus, and the divine in us are all equally divine.

We can be grateful that the church affirmed that the transcendent divine, the divine in Jesus, and the divine in us are all equally divine. As a result, we are not confronted with a mythology of multiple divine beings. But beyond that point, we can only remain puzzled. What does it mean to call all three *persons?* The East and the West answered this quite differently, and neither meant by *persons* what the word means to us today. Also, is it really the case that the three act separately from one another? Surely not! The church decided that all act in the acts of all—with the ad hoc exception of the incarnation. But if so, was there really any point in the complex distinctions?

Today, many theologians find a value in the Trinity that has little to do with the formulation of the original doctrine. They point out that, apart from this doctrine, the monotheistic idea of God could lead to a self-contained and self-sufficient individuality. In our day we stress that people are people in the context of community. This is much better supported, we are told, when we image God also as a community of persons rather than a sheer individual.

Much of this argumentation assumes that we are talking about images and their importance for us. That is a very important topic. The problem is that the move from images to ontological assertions is a common one. Can we really make sense of God as a community of divine persons? While we may draw some benefits from that view, would it not renew the incredulity that so many experience with respect to Christian teaching? It seems to be an idea quite disassociated from any evidence, even the evidence of Christian experience reported in the New Testament.

Let this problem illustrate the fact that, however far we go toward making sense of our received tradition, we will always remain beginners. Fortunately, we do not have to solve the problem of the Trinity in order to believe in God as we have come to know God through Jesus Christ, and as the Word, the Wisdom, or the Holy Spirit, dwelling within us, testifies to us.

But it is also the case that experiencing God through Jesus Christ and the Holy Spirit can be inhibited when our thought patterns cut markedly against the relevant beliefs. Intelligible beliefs are spiritually important. Nothing is more needed in the church today than to restore deep confidence in the truth of its teachings. That requires that we find credible and salutary ways to think about the God in whom we believe.

My own judgment is that we make the point about community better in our time by emphasizing the community between God and the world. We have seen that God is immanent in all creatures. God dwells in us as Holy Spirit.

The same understanding of the nature of reality as relational leads us to add that we also dwell in God. In God we live and move and have our being (Acts 17:28). Paul describes the Christian life as "in Christ." God's empathy with us is such that our experience participates in constituting the divine experience. What we do and feel contributes to the content of God's life. God weeps with those who weep and rejoices with those who rejoice. Whereas in the world the past fades quickly into oblivion, in God it lives vividly on. This conviction rounds out our central belief: that God loves all creatures, including us, and that we are called, in return, to love God and all those whom God loves.

DAVID S. CUNNINGHAM

It would be difficult to imagine anything more fundamental to the Christian faith than its belief in God. Without this belief, none of the other claims that Christians make—about themselves, the church, or the world—would make much sense. Yet throughout Christian history, theologians have emphasized how little we can expect to know about God. In fact, many believe that the only appropriate way to think about God is through negative theology: expressions of what God is *not*. Even through our most refined intellectual efforts, we can gain no adequate perspective on who God *is*.

And yet, "in spite of everything, we go on saying 'God.'"[1] All other Christian claims—about revelation, creation, the church, the world, and the end of it all—depend upon our ability to say something, however inadequate, about God. We speak provisionally and with humility, always knowing that our best insights may be nothing but straw. But we do speak—as witnessed by the statements of faith that have circulated among Christians for almost two thousand years: the "I believe in God" of the Apostles' Creed, and the Nicene Creed's "We believe in one God."

To do Christian theology in any form requires that we speak of God, even as we realize that we will need God's help to do so. "Nowhere," wrote Augustine, "is erring more perilous, nor seeking more laborious, nor gleaning more bounteous."[2] Yet the peril and the labor are justified by the bounty of the harvest, for the Christian belief in God is that element in which all other beliefs find their center.

THE ORIGIN OF CHRISTIAN BELIEFS ABOUT GOD

Jesus of Nazareth was a Jew, and the movement that sprang up around him two thousand years ago was initially a Jewish phenomenon. Consequently, the assumptions about God that were most basic to the followers of Jesus were the same as those that had been established among the Israelites for a thousand years and more. Eventually, Christianity came to adopt many of the fundamental features of the Jewish understanding of God, particularly its claim that there was only one God. "Hear, O Israel: The LORD is our God, the LORD alone," proclaims one of the best-known Hebrew prayers (Deut. 6:4). A second such belief was that God had created the world and all its inhabitants, and had created humankind in God's own image (Gen. 1:26–27). Moreover, God had called Abraham and Sarah into a covenant and had thereby elected Israel as a chosen people in order to bring the whole creation back into a right relationship with God. "In you," God tells Abraham, "all the families of the earth shall be blessed" (Gen. 12:3). Finally, God had shown extraordinary faithfulness to this people, even when they sought to abandon this relationship and go their own way. Like a jilted lover (Hos. 2), God relentlessly pursued the people, reminding them of this covenant and calling them back into a relationship of friendship and mutual desire.

Jesus underscored these aspects of God's love for the people. He emphasized God's desire to save them from their misdeeds and to establish a peaceful divine reign that would put all other rulers and temporal powers to shame. He emphasized God's willingness to forgive, but also reminded his hearers of their need to confess their faults and to turn toward the good. He quoted injunctions from the Hebrew Bible, urging people to love God with their whole being and their neighbors as themselves (Matt. 22:34–40 and parallels, quoting Deut. 6:5 and Lev. 19:18). In all these ways, the God of whom Jesus preached, and to whom he prayed, was very much the God of Israel.

But in their encounter with Jesus, many of his followers believed that they had witnessed not just another prophet or teacher whom God had sent to keep them on the right path. They believed that, somehow, in Jesus, they had experienced God's actual presence on earth. Those who chronicled Jesus' story describe him as "the Son," hinting at a very special relationship between Jesus and God. Mark first identifies it at Jesus' baptism (Mark 1:9–11); Matthew pushes it back to his birth (Matt. 1:18–25), and notes Jesus' ancestry back to Abraham (1:1–17). Luke also emphasizes the birth stories and pushes the ancestry all the way back to Adam and thus to God (Luke 3:23–38). John says that in Jesus, the Word of God—who was in the beginning with God and indeed *was* God (John 1:1)—took flesh and dwelt among us (1:14). While they differ in their ways of doing so, all four evangelists express the early Christian conviction that, in the person of Jesus, his followers had not just heard about God; they had, in some sense, encountered God firsthand.

> Many of his followers believed that, somehow, in Jesus, they had experienced God's actual presence on earth.

Obviously, this belief had profound implications for their understanding of God. For one thing, the words and deeds of Jesus became to them (and by extension, to us), the outward and visible expression of the will of God. God is no longer understood as dwelling *only* in light inaccessible (where we, like Moses, are unable to look upon the divine face: Exod. 33:20). God has taken on human flesh and has been revealed to us in human form. Our encounter with Jesus thus provides us with some of our most basic beliefs about God: care for the marginalized and the outcast, deep compassion and a willingness to forgive, the refusal to adopt strategies of violence and revenge, and a desire that all people should live in community and be at peace with one another. Christians believe these claims to be true of God because they have seen them at work in the life of Jesus.

We also believe that, in Jesus, God was on a mission: God was redeeming the world from its fallenness into sin, reconciling the world, and strengthening its relationship with God. This work on God's part is not categorically different from what had previously been the case. God was always in relentless pursuit of the people, regardless of their waywardness. God calls us into covenant, again and again. God sends us judges, kings, and prophets to correct our steps. God even makes use of our enemies to remind us of our proper allegiances. Nevertheless, in the person of Jesus, something radically different occurs: God actually enters the created order—taking on fragile flesh, suffering the world's slings and arrows, and even being willing to die at our hands—all in order to reconcile us to God. By his wounds, we are healed.

But the life of Jesus, like all human lives, has a finite span on earth. Even though the narratives of our faith tell us that God raised Jesus up from the grave, and even though we continue to speak of his presence and his care for us, we also believe that we are not to "hold on" to him (John 20:17). Jesus has, in some sense, taken our humanity up into full participation in God. Luke paints the picture most dramatically; both in his Gospel (24:51) and in his chronicle of the Acts of the Apostles (1:9), Jesus is described as ascending directly into heaven—taken out of our sight.[3]

On the Jewish feast of Pentecost, God once again comes into the realm of human life. The Spirit of God, prophesied of old, comes into the minds and hearts of the followers of Jesus.

Yet this divine "absence" does not last long. On the Jewish feast of Pentecost, God once again comes into the realm of human life in a direct and dramatic way—but not, this time, as a single human being; rather, as the rush of a violent wind and as tongues of fire (Acts 2). The Spirit of God, prophesied of old (Joel 2:28–32), comes into the minds and hearts of the followers of Jesus, inspiring them to proclaim the good news of God's great work to a much wider range of people than had encountered Jesus in the flesh. The inspiring work of the Holy Spirit brought people together in assemblies, living a common life and sharing their resources, and thereby providing an avenue for more people to enter into a closer relationship with God (Acts 2:43–47).

Their experiences of Jesus and the Spirit convinced the earliest Christians that, even though God continues to dwell beyond our time and space and to transcend all our categories, God has nevertheless entered into our world in a direct and definitive way—twice. First, the Word of God became a human being; God thus walked and lived upon the earth, experiencing the same joys and sorrows that we experience, including suffering and death. Second, the Spirit of God became active in the earliest Christian communities, giving them wisdom and strength to carry out God's mission in the world. These two manifestations of God within the created order, in addition to the longstanding belief in a transcendent God beyond all our categories, meant that people had known and believed in God in three different ways. As the Source of all things, God was transcendent and without a physical body. As the Word incarnate, God was immanent in creation and very much a fleshly body. And as the Spirit inspiring the earliest church communities, God took on a new kind of body—not that of a single human being, but that of a corporate body, the church, knit together by its members' common allegiance to the good news of Jesus Christ. Three experiences of God—three ways of believing in God.[4]

And yet, only one God. The lasting influence of Judaism remained very strong; the narratives of that faith are filled with refusals to bow down to idols and false gods. This commitment to the oneness of God was reemphasized by Christianity's early encounter with the thought-world of ancient Greece and Rome. Admittedly, these cultures told of gods and goddesses who warred and toyed with one another and whose exploits sometimes spilled over into the human world. But these popular stories, however much they may have shaped certain aspects of day-to-day life, were not taken very seriously by the intellectual world of the first century. That world was dominated by Plato, Aristotle, and their many successors, almost all of whom believed in a single God who brought all things into being. This philosophical worldview thus provided fertile ground for the Jewish and Christian claim that there was only one God. It also provided some excellent resources for struggling with the problem of how to make sense of the Christian community's three very different experiences of the one God.

Eventually, Christians came to understand God as having the dimensions of both unity and multiplicity; more specifically, God was thought to be *both* one *and* three. Such a claim requires a good deal of careful explanation and the postulating of precise philosophical distinctions. Indeed, it took Christians the better part of four centuries to work it out in sufficient detail that it might become the standard Christian teaching about God. But work it out they did, and so it comes down to us in the form of the doctrine of the Trinity. Christians believe in the triune God, the One who is also Three.

THE DOCTRINE OF THE TRINITY: A THUMBNAIL SKETCH

From very early on in Christian history, theologians began to speculate on how to uphold the claim that "these three are one" (1 John 5:7, Vulgate). However abstract their speculations may sometimes seem, they represent authentic attempts to make sense of the early Christian experiences of God, Jesus, and the Spirit. It might seem easier to concentrate only on what God does *for us,* and leave aside any inquiry into who God *is.* But if we fail to think about God's inner life, we tend to fall into a fairly passive role in the relationship; we accept God's gifts, but never inquire into the character of the giver. If our relationship with God is to be an intimate one, we will want to know as much as we can—not just about God's actions but also about God's character and inner life.

The doctrine of the Trinity postulates an integral connection between God's character and God's actions with respect to the world. These two aspects of our understanding of God are sometimes referred to as the *immanent* and *economic* approaches to Trinitarian thought: The immanent Trinity is a description of God's nature and character, whereas the economic Trinity refers to God's relationship with the created order—to God's "management of the household" (the Greek word is *oikonomia,* from *oikos,* "household"). But while this distinction can be useful as a means of organizing our reflections about God, the two must ultimately hang together: God's character is integrally related to God's actions. In addition, our knowledge of God's character and actions is itself given to us by God in revelation. The doctrine of the Trinity thus seeks to hold together three strands that are always threatening to unravel: the character of God's inner life, the nature of God's relationship with the world, and God's role as the ultimate source of all our knowledge about God. I want to braid these strands together, using the metaphor of *producing.*

The immanent Trinity is a description of God's nature and character, whereas the economic Trinity refers to God's relationship with the created order.

The Producing God

The verb *produce* shares with all transitive verbs a threefold aspect, implying a subject and object as well as an action. There can be no producing without a producer and a product; the product owes its existence to the producer, and the producer is responsible for the product. In this sense, producing can be understood as an *engaged* activity, in which agent and object are bound together in a close mutual relationship.

Moreover, the word *producing* (as I am using it here) implies more than simply creating an object and leaving it to its own devices. *Producing* describes the activity of, for example, a gardener, who must not only sow good seed but must take care that the plants are not choked by weeds or allowed to go too long without water. Or consider our use of the word *produce* to describe the process of putting on a play or making a film. The creation and assembly of the raw materials—script, space, equipment, money—is a necessary, but not sufficient, condition for the production of the play. Scripts need abridgement and emendation, actors' disputes need to be settled, equipment needs to be repaired and maintained. Producing, in this sense, cannot be a matter of simply beginning something and then abandoning it to take care of itself.

These analogies, of the garden and the play, may shed some light on our interrelated descriptions of God, of God's acts, and of God's role as the source of our knowledge of God. In all three cases, we can employ the language of producing—a complex, fully engaged process of superabundant love and willing donation. First, *God produces God;* more specifically, God's Word and God's Spirit are divine *processions,* manifesting internal difference in God. In addition, *God produces the world*—not merely creating it, but caring for it, redeeming and sustaining it. Finally, *God produces our knowledge of God* through the definitive revelation in Christ, but also in empowering us to receive this revelation through the work of the Spirit in the practices of the church.

> First, God produces God. In addition, God produces the world. Finally, God produces our knowledge of God.

One of the clearest systematic statements of the way in which "God produces God" may be found in the *Summa Theologiae* of Thomas Aquinas. He begins by considering what we may know of God on the basis of what has been revealed to us, and answers that we may know that there are two processions in God. There is the procession of the Word, which he calls *generation* or *begetting.* Jesus is the Word of God whose origins are in God; as he says of himself, "I proceeded and came forth from God" (John 8:42 RSV).[5] And there is also the procession of the Spirit, which is regularly described in the biblical text as issuing from God (sometimes in the form of breath or wind, or as divine love, or as divine wisdom).

Through revelation, then, we learn that God is an internally self-differentiated being. God is one, but within this one God there is multiplicity and difference. This is not merely a self-duplication on God's part; it is an act of self-abandonment, a giving up of oneself in order that there might be an Other to oneself. This self-abandonment does not take place at a particular moment in time; rather, from all eternity, God generates the Word and issues the Spirit. God is thus always about the business of giving place to a divine Other, giving God's own self over to the difference within God, in an act of passion and compassion.

This idea of an internally self-differentiated being is a difficult one; in the created order, there are no perfect analogies to describe it. Nevertheless, some concrete example will be useful to us here. The best one, in my view, is the example of pregnancy. The mother gives her own self to the "other" within her, becomes "other" to herself; yet she does not thereby become two distinct beings as long as the child is in the womb, nor does she diminish herself through this internal procession. The analogy has its imperfections; nevertheless, it may help us think about the concept of internal, self-differentiating processions.

According to Thomas, the two divine processions within God imply multiple *relations* within God. If the procession of the Word is a going forth of God from God, one can consider it in the active voice or in the passive voice—just as we can think of the act of speech as active (speaking) or passive (being spoken). And if the issuance of the Spirit is also a procession, one can similarly consider it as active (breathing out) or passive (being breathed out). According to Thomas, these internal relations within God constitute the divine persons: God speaks, and God is spoken; God breathes out, and God is breathed out.[6]

This way of thinking about relations may seem counterintuitive to us, because we assume that there must first be individual entities with an independent existence who *then* enter into relations with one another. A relation, to the modern mind, seems dependent upon the presupposed beings or persons that are "in relation." But granting such priority to persons over their relations obscures just how much we depend on our relations for our identity. Consider, for example, how we come to know our friends and acquaintances, or how we learn about the characters in a novel. Rarely does this take place through statistical information of the sort found on a driver's license. Rather, we observe how people interact with others; we discover how they relate to one another. Through our experience of another person's relations, we come to know who she or he "really is."

The process is similar for God: We come to know the three persons of the Trinity only as God's complex internal relations. They cannot be understood in the absence of one another: The Word must be *spoken by* someone; the Spirit must be the *spirit of* someone. Although theologians speak of "three persons" in God, these three should not be understood as individuals who begin life alone and then come into relationship. They are not endpoints, between whom there are relations; they are, simply, relations. Human beings may *have* relations, but God *is* the relations that God has.[7]

> We come to know the three persons of the Trinity only as God's complex internal relations.

To explicate the idea of internal relations, the example of pregnancy will again be useful, but in order to provide an analogy to the *two* divine processions, we will need to make it a bit more complicated. In a pregnancy, a woman must go forth from herself and become other to herself *twice:* first in conception, and again in the production of an organ of mediation between mother and child (the placenta). If we were to name the relations that thereby develop within pregnancy, we might call them "motherhood" and "childhood"; and the production of the placenta creates an additional relation of (let us say) "mediating." Note that these relations are not simply "among" three separate entities; the mother, child, and placenta are all interconnected and, at times, not even clearly distinguishable from one another.[8]

The advantage of this analogy is that it underscores the dynamic nature of God's internal relations. This is not static language of isolated individuals, who first existed independently of each other and then decided to enter into a mutual relationship. Rather, both in pregnancy and in the inner life of God, the internal processions and relations tend to *imply* one another, and thus to evoke movement and flux.

Trouble in the Land of Names

Unfortunately, the most common English terms for referring to the threeness of God—the nouns *Father*, *Son*, and *Spirit*—do not automatically remind us of the internal divine processions and relations to which these nouns refer. Instead, we are encouraged to think of the three as separate entities, as distinct individuals. As a result, one of the most important claims of Trinitarian theology—that the three are most fundamentally *relations*—is lost from our view. (We could note a similar problem with the use of nouns to designate the relations in pregnancy: Once we begin to speak of "mother" and "child," we begin to define them in isolation from each other—a tendency that is evident on all sides in the current politics of pregnancy.) Indeed, I suspect that *any* naming of the divine persons by nouns will make it difficult to remember that they are relations.

The persons of the Trinity cannot become separate

Another difficulty inherent in the common English formula "Father, Son, and Holy Spirit" is its heavy reliance on masculine language. It is true that Jesus was male; it is also true that the narratives describe him as using, to address God, a word that Greek-speaking readers of the Gospels would have used to identify a male parent. But in its more philosophically reflective moments, the Christian tradition has expressly denied any attribution of gender to God.[9] Unfortunately, our cultural assumptions about biology, gender, and sexuality often get absorbed into theological claims, and so Christianity's production of language and symbols for God have been dominated by masculinity.[10] Many theologians now believe that, because the traditional formula of "Father, Son, and Holy Spirit" can mislead us toward highly gender-specific and excessively individualistic interpretations, our naming of God needs to be rethought.

Of course, the biblical names for God form something of an architectural patchwork; they are greatly varied and highly unsystematic. Christians believe in one God, but the stories they tell about this God are diverse. Thus, a variety of names have been employed to describe God and God's work—not only in the biblical accounts but throughout the history of the church as well. This variety of names for God underscores the claim mentioned at the beginning of this chapter: that God transcends all our categories and our assumptions, dwelling "where our understanding and our concepts can gain no admittance."[11] It is therefore quite appropriate that we attempt to develop alternative Trinitarian formulas—not to replace but to use alongside the currently accepted names for God. Of course, not just any name will do; new formulations should call to mind God's internal difference and yet also make it possible to hold fast to the oneness of God.[12]

As an example of how we might develop one possible new formula, let us imagine a spring of water coming up out of the ground and then flowing out to nourish the surrounding landscape. Here we have movement, procession, a going-out-from-itself-to-itself. Such a procession implies internal relations—relations of initiation and fruition and emergence. Among the many advantages of this analogy are, first, that it is possible to understand the spring as a unified whole but also to recognize its internal difference. Its source is not immediately accessible to us, but we know it must come from somewhere. The wellspring that comes forth from the ground is different from the water that flows out away from the spring, yet we would be hard pressed to say where one stopped and the other started. This analogy has strong biblical roots (see, for example, the description of God and of the Holy Spirit as "living water" in Jer. 2:13; 17:13; John 4:10–14; 7:38–39), and it was employed in many variations among the writers of the early Christian era.

> This variety of names for God underscores the claim mentioned at the beginning of this chapter: that God transcends all our categories and our assumptions.

In my own theological writing and teaching, I continue to use the traditional language in some instances, often pausing to emphasize its relational character. I also employ the analogy of pregnancy with some frequency. Typically, however, I use language that draws on the analogy of the spring, and refer to the Trinity as "the Source, the Wellspring, and the Living Water."[13] As with any analogy, this alternative has its limits; nevertheless, it does begin to address some of the problems that we have identified in our more common naming of the Trinity. I believe it is an improvement over the traditional translation for the present context of English-language theology.

The Character of God

The foregoing reflections on Christian beliefs about the inner life of the triune God suggest, in turn, certain claims about God's character. I have already made reference to some of these: God is characterized by compassionate love, by superabundant donation, and by passionate involvement with that which is other than God. A large number of additional characteristics could be cited. To conclude this section, I offer three examples of characteristics that seem to be implied by the unity and self-differentiation of God. I will note what these characteristics suggest about our own lives as we seek to live into, and to participate in, the triune life of God.

Mutuality, interdependence, and equality. God's relational nature is necessarily nonhierarchical; the divine Three depend absolutely on each other for their existence and meaning. There can be no child without a parent, but neither can there be a parent without a child. As descriptions of human beings who fulfill particular roles, the one called "parent" must precede the one called "child"; but here again, we are misled by thinking of them as *individuals*—that is, the people who take on the role of parent or child. If instead we think of them as pure *relations,* the terms *parent* and *child* become fully mutual and reciprocal. Neither one comes first: The parent does not become a parent until the child is born. As relations, the parents are as much caused by the children as the children by the parents. Similarly with the analogy of the spring: The Source is not prior to or more important than the Wellspring or the Living Water; all three depend completely on one another for their internal relationality.

This suggests a nonhierarchical understanding of the Trinity. It underlies the Nicene Creed's claim that the Son is "*eternally* begotten of the Father," ruling out any notion that one of the Three existed prior to or independently of the others. The result is a theology of coequality and mutual reciprocity, entailing important claims about equality and mutual reciprocity in the everyday practice of Christian life. We too are called to this life of mutuality, equality, and "giving place to the other" that marks the life of the triune God.

We too are called to this life of mutuality, equality, and "giving place to the other" that marks the life of the triune God.

Diversity and difference. The Three are sufficiently different from one another that they cannot be considered mere modes or manifestations of God; indeed, they mark a real multiplicity in God (yet without denying God's unity). We most fully live into God's triune life when we are able to see such multiplicity and difference as something for which we can rejoice and be thankful, rather than something that needs to be suppressed by our desire for homogeneity and uniformity.

One analogy that can help us think through God's internal difference is that of polyphonic music. In music, more than one thing happens at a time; multiple notes can be played or sung, even at the same time, whether by one person or by a group. In fact, entire melodies can be played in differing and overlapping sequences. When we hear more than one note or line being played at once, we do not usually consider this to be contradictory or confused. Harmonious difference is not only accepted; it is encouraged and rewarded. By analogy, Christianity proclaims a polyphonic understanding of God, in whom there is *difference* rather than a monotonous homogeneity. Yet this difference is not a source of exclusion; attention to any one of the divine Three does not imply a diminished role for the others. All have their distinctive melodies, and all are "played" and "heard" simultaneously, without damage to God's unity. We too are called to polyphonic lives, committed to diversity and difference, not because of a vague faith in pluralism or democracy but from our participation in God, who *is* difference-in-unity.

Peaceableness. God is eternally in the process of giving. The Trinitarian dynamic describes a God who is always going forth, proceeding, and is therefore constantly involved in relations of gift and reception. God is always in the process of "giving place," of moving out of the way so that a new divine manifestation can be recognized as fully God.[14] The Wellspring is always coming forth from the Source (again: "eternally begotten of the Father," in the most common English translation of the creed), and the Living Water is always flowing out to nurture the believing community.

These acts of God are acts of pure gift, rather than occurring as a process of economic exchange (in which one party withholds something until the other has paid the necessary price). Consequently, God's internal relations, as well as God's relations with the world, are essentially peaceful and peacemaking relations. They do not posit a scarcity of resources which would lead to conflict; neither do they suggest that anything is being withheld such that it would have to be taken by force.[15] In contrast to the violence and competition that lies hidden in the heart of our current worldview, the Christian doctrine of God sets forth a narrative of peaceful, superabundant donation.

THE DOCTRINE OF THE TRINITY AND OTHER CHRISTIAN BELIEFS

Having examined the Christian understanding of God's internal relations—how "God produces God"—we now turn to God's external relations with the created order. To do so, we need to take up a number of themes that are explored more fully elsewhere in this volume. This is as it should be, for our beliefs about God are integrally related to every other aspect of Christian belief. Here I simply want to provide an account of how these beliefs might be woven into our belief in the triune God, by extending the metaphor of *producing*.

Creation: God Produces the World, Act I

God's processions are wholly contained within God; they do not flow forth and transform themselves into the created order. From the Christian perspective, the world is not created out of God; it is created out of nothing (*ex nihilo*). God and creation are thus separated by what the nineteenth-century Danish writer Søren Kierkegaard called an "infinite qualitative difference." Yet this difference does not necessarily imply distance, and even less does it imply a lack of concern, care, or involvement. God creates the world as something wholly other than God, and gives to it the gift of life, in order that the world might return the gift to God.

Human beings, in particular, are given a rather extravagant degree of freedom. Created in the image of God, they possess even the power to turn away from God. They alone are capable of choosing not to return the gift. And because such creatures are part of the divine plan from the outset, God's relationship to the world is not exhausted by the divine activity of setting things in motion. God awaits our response, our Yes, our return of the gift. Of course, even those who do eventually say Yes are still free, and they may turn away again. But God seeks to sustain them in their

> God's "producing" of the world may be compared to the work of a gardener who will stay with the project through thick and thin.

willingness to return the gift, taking them up into the divine life and giving them a foretaste of its glory.

God's "producing" of the world may be compared to the work of a gardener who will stay with the project through thick and thin—"through hell and high water" as my grandfather used to say (a Kansas wheat farmer is, after all, a gardener of sorts). Before the seeds are planted, before the garden is even laid out, a decision is made to do whatever it takes to bring these frequently obstinate creatures into full flower. Some may eventually refuse to bloom, but the good gardener does everything possible to get them to do so. The biblical parable of the vineyard plays on this image explicitly: God is the owner of the vineyard, who continues to care for it despite being out of sight; in the end he even sends his beloved son, handing him over to the wicked tenants, and all for the sake of the vineyard (Matt. 21:33–46 // Mark 12:1–12 // Luke 20:9–19).

Here again, an analogy of parents and children may help. Good parents recognize that bringing a child into the world involves more than a mere act of "making a baby"—a pleasurable sexual event that initiates the child's life. Children are not fully under the control of their "creators"; they have the freedom to turn away. Parents who wish to remain in communion with their children know that they must also provide a means whereby children can turn a defiant No into a willing Yes—and they must find ways of sustaining that decision by means of a long, fully engaged process of reconciliation. At its best, parenthood is not simply a series of emergency measures, each undertaken as a way of coping with the willful otherness of the child. Good parents know from the outset that children cannot simply be "made" and left to their own devices.

God is the best of all possible parents. Having created human beings, God redeems them from their isolation and alienation, providing a means by which they can be taken up, once again, into the divine life. Through the Spirit, the Living Water, God also endows them with the power to sustain this return of the gift: God sanctifies them, setting them apart from those elements of the world that set up obstacles to this process of reconciliation, giving them strength and courage to do God's work in the world.

Redemption and Sanctification: God Produces the World, Act II

Christian theology has traditionally spoken of two divine "missions": We can describe them as missions of incarnation and inspiration, or as the "sending" of the Son and the Spirit, or perhaps as the raising up of the Wellspring and the pouring out of the Living Water. The two missions (like all of God's external actions) are singular actions of God and are in no way divided among the Three; the agent of each of them is the triune God. The two missions, though differentiated, are not merely reactions to the course of the world's history, as though, having noticed that things have gone awry, God needed to make an emergency intervention and then to spend the rest of history trying to maintain the world's rather precarious state by means of sanctification. Redemption and sanctification are part of the divine plan from the outset, even though, from our temporal perspective, they only come to pass in the fulness of time. Their "right time" is the moment of the annunciation to Mary, or more precisely, the moment when she actively accepts God's initiative: "Let it be with me according to your word" (Luke 1:38). The Word of God becomes incarnate in the flesh of Mary through the power of the Holy Spirit. Thus, the mission of the Word and the mission of the Spirit begin, from our perspective, at the same time, even though the Spirit's mission is at first focused only on the person of Christ. After the resurrection, and most clearly on the day of Pentecost, the mission of the Spirit reaches its full breadth, as the Living Water is poured out upon the whole world.

God thus carries out the redemption of the world not by an external imposition but through free human acts—the willingness on the part of Mary and Jesus to return to God the gift that we have all been given. Mary accepts her role as God-bearer, gives of herself in pregnancy and breastfeeding, and provides the love and care required to raise a child. Jesus accepts his baptism and his mission; he teaches, heals, and performs signs and wonders; and is willing to suffer and die. But although these are free human acts, they must also be shared by God: a divine willingness to be born into the world, to speak to it and to suffer it, and indeed, to be killed by the world. Again, this is not a temporal decision on God's part, made at some point after things had gone awry; rather, "God chose us, in Christ, before the foundation of the world" (Eph. 1:4).

The mission of inspiration—the pouring out of the Living Water—is the means by which God brings about the sanctification of the world. Until the resurrection, its focus is on the person of Jesus. The Greek word *pneuma* (usually translated with reference to spirit or breath) describes that which animates and empowers Jesus to carry out the will of God. It rests on Jesus at his baptism (most clearly in Matthew's account, where it is described as "descending like a dove and alighting on him," Matt. 3:16), it drives him into the wilderness at the outset of his ministry (Mark 1:12 and parallels), it empowers his teaching in Galilee (Luke 4:14), and he commends it back to his Father as he dies (Luke 23:46). But after his resurrection, Jesus breathes it out on the disciples (John 20:22), and in Acts it is described as being poured out on all flesh on the day of Pentecost (Acts 2:17). It empowers those who have been incorporated into Christ to keep their hearts and minds focused on God, to whom they have been reunited through God's act of redemption.

The mission of inspiration—the pouring out of the Living Water—is the means by which God brings about the sanctification of the world.

The divine missions link the internal divine processions (which constitute God's triunity) to our experience of God in history. In other words, our salvation can be carried out as it is (in the Wellspring and through the Living Water) only because God is already self-differentiated. Imagine, for a moment, that there were no internal processions in God: This would make it very difficult to speak of God "becoming" flesh, and dying, and being raised up by God. Similarly, we could make little sense of the claim that God is both the one who "pours" the Living Water (or "breathes" the Spirit) upon the world, and yet God is also that which is being poured (or breathed). In producing the world, God is simultaneously agent, activity, and completed act.

Traditionally, God's long-term involvement with and care for the world has been emphasized through the theological category of grace. In creating the world, God wills into existence something radically other than God, but the world's otherness is not something that cuts it off from God. There is thus no "pure nature"; nature is always graced. And it is graced not just because it was created by God long ago, but because God is always actively redeeming and sustaining it. God becomes flesh, suffers the world for our sake, and becomes active within the world, moving us to a more profound faith and a more faithful life.

Revelation: God Produces the Knowledge of God, Act III

The analogy of producing can be extended further. God also produces the knowledge of God; that is, what we know about God is revealed to us *by God.* This aspect of Christian belief has already been examined in the previous chapter. Here it is worth observing that this revelatory process—this divine *production* of the knowledge of God—bears a similar structure to the other acts of producing that we have discussed. God's production of the knowledge of God is a Trinitarian event, just as are God's production of God and of the world.

The definitive focal point for God's revelation is the person of Christ. God's willingness to enter the world provides us with the most complete and definitive knowledge of God that we can hope to have. At the same time, however, it should be noted that this "complete and definitive" form of revelation comes not as a statement, nor as a set of propositions, but as a human life. Hence, this knowledge is marked by all the beauty and the ambiguity inherent in any knowledge that we gain from another human life. In order to "come to know" something through the life of another, we have to interpret that person's words and actions, to ask for clarification (when it is possible to do so), and to rely on the testimony of others. In Christ, God is revealed to us—but this is obviously not the end of the story. We must still interpret, for ourselves and for the world, what the apostles saw with their eyes, what they looked at and touched with their hands (1 John 1:1).

Fortunately, we are not left to our own devices in order to do so. As in the case of God's producing of the world, God recognizes that an act of initiation is not sufficient. We are free and fallible beings, and adequate knowledge of God cannot be assured by one definitive act of unveiling, just as an adequate attitude toward God cannot be assured by one definitive act of creation. Instead, God provides us with ongoing interpretive guidance; this is part of the mission of inspiration, in which the church is enlivened by the Living Water to proclaim the Word and administer the sacraments. These ongoing practices help to give shape to our encounter with Christ, such that we learn to read the biblical narratives as God would have us read them—testifying to Christ as the one point of contact, the definitive revelation of God. The production of the knowledge of God begins with the mission of incarnation, but it does not end there, for many have read those narratives in wholly privatized ways and have then barricaded themselves away in the company of their own "personal Jesus." True knowledge of God is only possible through a communally normed reading of the biblical narratives that is made possible by the Spirit-filled church.

True knowledge of God is only possible through a communally normed reading of the biblical narratives that is made possible by the Spirit-filled church.

But this is not all. The knowledge of God, given to us in the incarnation of the Word and interpreted to us through the pouring out of the Living Water, must still be rendered intelligible, concrete, and persuasive. This task requires us to draw on the widest possible range of resources and tools, to "take every thought captive to obey Christ" (2 Cor. 10:5). We believe that God produces the world, and does so for the sake of the incarnate Word ("all things have been created for him," Col. 1:16); thus, there is a certain sense in which the world expresses, and thereby resembles, God.[16] This does not mean, however, that we can know what God is like simply by looking at the world; in fact, we cannot understand the world at all unless we know that it is created, redeemed, and sustained by God—in short, that it is *produced* by God. Any knowledge of God that we can glean from the world must be produced, ultimately, by God.[17]

THE PLAY'S THE THING

In this chapter, I have occasionally referred to the analogy between God's action in the world and the production of a play. This analogy has been used by a number of theologians throughout Christian history, but it is particularly well developed in the work of the twentieth-century Swiss Catholic theologian Hans Urs von Balthasar.[18] Balthasar describes our salvation as the production of a play that takes place upon the world stage, in which God is simultaneously the author, the primary actor, and the director. God has written the script, and so is the ultimate source of the action; God performs the play, entering the world to enact the script that has been written; and God directs the play, bringing the other actors into a proper relationship with the central actor, and providing the necessary promptings to ensure the successful enactment of the drama.

The analogy is a rich one, and Balthasar uses it to make a number of important points about the Trinity. It reminds us that God's external actions are undivided; the missions are not a division of labor among the Three, but a single endeavor to which each of the Three contributes. The author always writes with some ideas about how the actor and director might work with the script; indeed, many authors may imagine how they themselves would undertake these tasks, and write accordingly. Authors thus have something of a continuing effect upon their works, an effect which "extends to the sphere of the actor and director—not tyrannizing them but providing them with an area for creativity."[19] Similarly, the director has to take account of both the author and the actor(s), but has a particular responsibility for the drama's enactment, such that it will eventually have an appropriate effect upon the audience. And yet, in the actual performance of the play, the director will not be seen (nor will the author); only the actor(s) can "incarnate" the action to which all three have contributed.

As Balthasar is well aware, the analogy is not a perfect one; we will misunderstand its point if we try to make God into three separate people (who quarrel and rebel and try to assert their individual egos). Nor will it do to think of those playwrights who have also starred in and directed their own plays; for here, the three activities become merely separate tasks or modes, taken up at different times for different purposes. The point of the analogy is not to provide one-to-one resemblance with the triune God, but to give us a sense of why the divine missions are integrally related to the internal self-differentiation in God. It reminds us that the missions and the processions are bound to one another and that we can never really separate the *immanent* from the *economic* Trinity, let alone privilege one over the other.

Thus, it should not surprise us that, in the major confessions of faith that have dominated Christian worship throughout the ages—the Apostles' and Nicene Creeds—God's internal and external relations are woven together into a single tapestry of faith. What we discover throughout the creeds is a producing God—a God of superabundance and willing donation—with respect both to God's own self and to the world. God's producing involves not only creation (God as the source of God and of the world) but also redemption and sanctification, signifying God's eternal love and care. And so we are called to return the gift of producing—a gift bestowed on us by the triune God, who created the heavens and the earth, whose Spirit moved over the waters of the deep, and without whose Word was not anything made that was made.[20]

QUESTIONS FOR REFLECTION AND DISCUSSION

1. How much can we know about God apart from revelation?
2. Can things in the world produce changes in God? Does God have all the power?
3. John Cobb rejects a number of common modern assumptions that would leave the world with no place in it for God. Do his arguments persuade you?
4. How does radical empiricism involve factors other than sense experience?
5. What does it mean to think of God as personal? Is that important for Christians?

6. How does Cobb compare the way God is in Christ with the way God is in us? Do you agree?

7. What were the key factors that led Christians to think of God as a Trinity?

8. Is the masculine language usually used about the Trinity (*Father* and *Son*) a problem? What do you think of Cunningham's alternative?

9. What implications does thinking about God as a Trinity have for ethics?

10. How is the way "God produces God" like and unlike the ways God produces the world and our knowledge of God?

FOR FURTHER READING

Bobrinskoy, Boris. *The Mystery of the Trinity*. Trans. Anthony P. Gythiel. Crestwood, N.Y.: St. Vladimir's Seminary Press, 1999.

Boff, Leonardo. *Trinity and Society*. Trans. Paul Burns. Maryknoll, N.Y.: Orbis Books, 1988.

Cobb, John B., Jr. *God and the World.* Philadelphia: Westminster Press, 1969.

Cunningham, David S. *These Three Are One.* Oxford: Basil Blackwell, 1998.

Farley, Edward. *Divine Empathy.* Minneapolis: Fortress Press, 1996.

Gilkey, Langdon. *Naming the Whirlwind.* Indianapolis: Bobbs-Merrill, 1969.

Hartshorne, Charles. *The Divine Relativity.* New Haven, Conn.: Yale University Press, 1948.

Johnson, Elizabeth A. *She Who Is: The Mystery of God in Feminist Theological Discourse.* New York: Crossroad, 1992.

Jones, Major J. *The Color of God.* Macon, Ga: Mercer University Press, 1987.

Kasper, Walter. *The God of Jesus Christ*. Trans. Matthew J. O'Connell. New York: Crossroad, 1986.

Kaufman, Gordon D. *God the Problem.* Cambridge, Mass.: Harvard University Press, 1972.

LaCugna, Catherine Mowry. *God for Us.* San Francisco: Harper, 1991.

McFague, Sallie. *Models of God.* Philadelphia: Fortress Press, 1987.

Moltmann, Jürgen. *The Trinity and the Kingdom*. Trans. Margaret Kohl. San Francisco: Harper, 1991.

Peters, Ted. *God as Trinity.* Louisville, Ky.: Westminster/John Knox Press, 1993.

Rahner, Karl. *The Trinity*. Trans. Joseph Donceel. New York: Crossroad, 1997.

Torrance, Thomas F. *The Christian Doctrine of God.* Edinburgh: T. & T. Clark, 1996.

Welker, Michael. *God the Spirit*. Trans. John F. Hoffmeyer. Minneapolis: Fortress Press, 1994.

Wijk-Bos, Juliana W. H. van. *Reimagining God.* Louisville, Ky.: Westminster John Knox Press, 1995.

Chapter 3

Is God in Charge?

Creation and Providence

As the previous chapter discussed, Christians believe in a powerful and loving God, however they sort out the relations between God's power and love. But sometimes the world around us does not look like the creation of such a God. Someone we love dies of a horrible disease. Terrorists murder thousands of people. Would God make a world like this?

Moreover, if God is really *all*-powerful, then what happens to our freedom? Are we just puppets jerked around by a divine puppeteer? If so, does it make any sense to blame us or punish us for anything we do?

Theologians have been worrying about such questions for a long time. In the Greco-Roman world, early Christians faced opponents with challengingly different answers. Traditionally, Greeks and Romans believed in many gods, who often quarreled with one another and did not necessarily care for the welfare of human beings. One deity could upset the plans of another, for good or evil. Many philosophers in the ancient world believed in Fate, an impersonal power that determined the activities of gods and human beings alike.

Alternatively, Manicheanism, a religion founded by a man named Mani who lived in the third century in what is today Iraq, taught that there were two gods, a good one and an evil one. Manicheanism was for a while a serious competitor to Christianity (the great theologian Augustine was a Manichean for a while before he converted to Christianity, and Manicheanism spread from Rome to China). Its adherents saw the world as a battleground between their two gods and believed that it is our job to help the good God whenever we can. But since the evil God is also powerful, there is nothing puzzling about the fact that evil exists in the world. What is hard is to explain why evil exists if Christians are right and there is only one all-powerful and loving God and that God made the world.

CREATION IN GENESIS

To address such challenges, Christians often went back to the beginning of Genesis. The opening chapters of Genesis seem to include two originally separate stories. A very ancient one starting at Genesis 2:4 explains, through the story of Adam and Eve in the garden, some basic features of human nature and our relation to God and the world. (The tradition behind this story is called *J,* since it uses *YHWH* or *Jahweh* as the name for God.) A later "priestly account" (scholars call it *P*) begins at Genesis 1:1 and is very much concerned with the order of the universe and the importance of the Sabbath.

The P account emphasizes that there is one God who made all things and made them good. The J account moves from creation to the story of the fall and emphasizes that human beings have a responsibility to care for the earth and that at least some of the evil in the world is the fault of human choice. Some of these issues belong to the topic of the next chapter—human nature and human sin—but some of them are central to this chapter's concerns.

First, in Genesis God makes everything. Indeed, much Christian theology has taught that God created *ex nihilo*—out of nothing. Some contemporary biblical interpreters, however, call our attention to the "formless void and darkness" of Genesis 1:2. Some sort of chaotic something-or-other out of which God brought order was arguably already present. Still, Genesis pictures God acting effortlessly and without challenge. God speaks, and it comes to be.

> Whatever explanation will be offered about the existence of evil, it cannot be blamed on some preexisting matter independent of God—or on the evil deity of the Manicheans.

In contrast, in many creation myths from other cultures, creation occurs only as the result of struggles between good and evil forces. In the Babylonian creation story *Enuma Elish* (which people in Israel might well have known), for instance, the god Marduk has to subdue the chaos monster Tiamat before making the world out of Tiamat's dead body. The world's elements of evil grow inevitably out of the evil from which it was made.

Many Greek philosophers too imagined a recalcitrant preexisting matter out of which God made a world whose imperfections followed necessarily from the character of its raw material. In Genesis, by contrast, as the Old Testament scholar Walter Brueggemann puts it, "God is serenely and supremely in charge. There is no struggle here, no anxiety, no risk."[1] Whatever explanation will be offered about the existence of evil, it cannot be blamed on some preexisting matter independent of God—or on the evil deity of the Manicheans.

Further, God repeatedly declares the world thus created to be good. Earth, sea monsters, wild animals, and every creeping thing—all are God's creation, and all are good. A long list of Christian heresies have argued that matter or human bodies are evil things to be overcome, but this is a point of view which Genesis, and indeed the Bible generally, does not support.

Why did God make this world? A lovely poem by the great poet James Weldon Johnson imagines God saying, "I'm lonely—/I'll make me a world."[2] It makes for good poetry, but most of the Christian tradition would have said that it was bad theology. God does not make the world out of some need or lack or incompleteness. (One of the implications of the mutual love within the Trinity is that God is *not* lonely.) God is, in Karl Barth's phrase, "the one who loves in freedom,"[3] acting out of no external necessity but freely creating simply because love seeks to share its goodness.

Like most Christian theologians, Barth was assuming that God is radically separate from the world God created. In her essay for this chapter, Sallie McFague would identify this picture as the model of God as monarch or agent. The opposite of that view is pantheism, the belief that God is the sum total of everything that exists. The seventeenth-century philosopher Baruch Spinoza, for instance, held that *God* is simply another name for the totality of nature.[4] Panentheism represents a view partway between the model of God as monarch or agent and pantheism. Panentheists hold that God is neither radically separate from the world nor identical to it. In the work of the early twentieth-century philosopher Alfred North Whitehead and that of the process theologians influenced by him, for instance, God both defines the possibilities for what can exist, and then realizes and responds to everything that is actual. God is thus not simply equal to the world but also not distant and unchanging. Rather, God is most fully engaged with everything that occurs in the world, rejoicing in all joys and sorrowing with all pains.[5] (John Cobb's essay in the previous chapter offered a good example of one form of process theology.)

McFague, with her model of the world as God's body, and some other feminist theologians have found various forms of panentheism particularly compatible with maternal images of God.

McFague, with her model of the world as God's body, and some other feminist theologians have found various forms of panentheism particularly compatible with maternal images of God.[6] In the physiological process of giving birth, after all, a man simply ejects his sperm. A woman encloses and nurtures the fertilized egg. Passages such as this one from Isaiah present a more maternal (and more panentheistic) picture of the creator God than the opening of Genesis:

> Listen to me, O house of Jacob,
>   all the remnant of the house of Israel,
> who have been borne by me from your birth,
>   carried from the womb;
>   . . . .
>   even when you turn gray I will carry you.
> I have made, and I will bear;
>   I will carry and will save. (46:3–4)

Much contemporary debate about Genesis, of course, concerns its relation to the conclusions of modern science. I am persuaded that the opening chapters of Genesis are what Karl Barth, following the Jewish philosopher Martin Buber, called *saga*—"an intuitive and poetic picture of a pre-historical reality of history."[7] The authors of Genesis did not own watches or clocks and were not concerned to make claims about just how long it took God to create or what exact order God followed. Using powerful poetic language, they sought to make points already noted here: that God made all things, that what God created is good, and so on. They had no particular interest in *how* God went about creating things, and indeed do not offer explanations of the sort that would compete with those of science.

If scientists say, "The world is self-generated and has no creator," or, "The world is random and has no purpose," Christians will disagree. They will find, I suspect, that the scientists are in such cases not acting as scientists, that is, by basing their conclusions on empirical evidence, but offering their own philosophies as an alternative to traditional religious views. Once Christians have affirmed the reality and purposes of God the creator, on the other hand, I think we can give science great latitude in explaining how (and how long) the processes of creation developed.

Contemporary science has also made us aware of the fragility of the environment and the importance of ecology, and the Bible has come under some criticism on this score. Here again, much of the debate goes back to some brief passages in Genesis. In the creation story beginning at Genesis 1:1, God gives humankind "dominion over the fish of the sea, and over the birds of the air, and over the cattle, and over all the wild animals of the earth, and over every creeping thing that creeps upon the earth" (Gen. 1:26). God tells the human male and female, "Be fruitful and multiply, and fill the earth and subdue it" (Gen. 1:28). In the J story, God puts the man in the midst of the garden of Eden "to till it and keep it" (Gen. 2:15—the Hebrew word translated "keep" has the connotation of "care for").

Many recent critics of Christianity have argued that Christian interpretations of human *dominion* over nature and God's command to *subdue* it have done a great deal of harm. On this model, they say, creation is ours to plunder as we will; it has no value except as it benefits us.[8]

Historians continue to debate the degree to which Christian theology did produce these harmful results. Did traditional Christian (or Jewish) societies really harm nature more than Chinese or Native American cultures? Did the real harm begin under Jewish or Christian auspices, or only in the more secular industrial age? Serious scholars argue a variety of positions. Whatever the historical conclusions, many theologians today agree that Christians should think more of our responsibilities to nature. The world is not "unclaimed property," the contemporary theologian Jürgen Moltmann remarks, but *God's* creation, of which we are at most the stewards.[9] We should think of ourselves more as keepers of a garden than as subduers of a wilderness. McFague's essay, indeed, proposes that, when we think about the doctrine of creation, we should think more about the Where, the neighborhood in which we find ourselves and our responsibilities for it, than the Why, the ultimate causes behind the universe.

> The world is not "unclaimed property," but God's creation, of which we are at most the stewards.

PROVIDENCE AND EVIL

To say that we have responsibilities over creation is not to say that God has stopped paying it any attention. Christian theology has traditionally followed discussions of creation with accounts of God's providence, which means, John Calvin said, "not that by which God idly observes from heaven what takes place on earth, but that by which, as keeper of the keys, he governs all events."[10] In the seventeenth and eighteenth centuries, this became a matter of particular debate. Some who believed in God—namely, the Deists—thought that God had simply made the world and then set it off to operate on its own. Such thinkers were not necessarily less religious. For the seventeenth-century German philosopher and mathematician Gottfried Leibniz, for instance, who believed that God had initially designed the world so perfectly as to require no further interference, it was blasphemous to think that God needed to intervene in or supervise creation. Such need would imply that God had done a bad job of making it in the first place.[11]

Most theologians, however, argued that a God who was not somehow actively engaged with the world was just not much of a God. They affirmed a doctrine of divine providence which (to quote the Belgic Confession of Reformed Protestants written in 1561) "affords us unspeakable consolation, since we are taught thereby that nothing can befall us by chance, but by the direction of our most gracious and heavenly Father, who watches over us with a paternal care, keeping all creatures so under his power that not a hair of our head (for they are all numbered), nor a sparrow, can fall to the ground, without the will of our Father, in whom we do entirely trust."[12]

Reformed theologians in the seventeenth and eighteenth centuries (partly to clarify their own views in reaction to the Deists) distinguished, within providence, between God's preservation, concurrence, and governance. *Preservation* refers to the idea that creation does not have its own independence even after it is created. If it were not at every moment preserved by God, it would cease to exist. *Concurrence* means that God sustains not merely the existence of created beings but their every action. *Governance* indicates that God is guiding all this activity to some goal or purpose.[13]

> Reformed theologians in the seventeenth and eighteenth centuries distinguished, within providence, between God's preservation, concurrence, and governance.

Put all three together, and they yield a radical affirmation of the Gospel's insistence that God watches over every sparrow. Kathryn Tanner's essay later in this chapter develops a contemporary version of such a position. It is a viewpoint that raises important questions about the character of evil and of human freedom. Tanner thinks of *creation* as defining an ongoing relationship between God and the world rather than something that happened back at the beginning of time; other theologians would feel this view collapses important distinctions between creation and providence.

The question of why a good and all-powerful God would allow evil to occur is one of the deepest puzzles of Christian faith. All sensible theologians acknowledge that mysteries lie here which we cannot understand. Yet simply acknowledging the mystery does not seem enough. At least four sorts of answers to the question of theodicy ("God's justice," from *theos,* "God," and *dike,* "justice") have regularly appeared:

> Why does God allow evil? Here are four possible answers: (1) some goods are possible only if certain evils exist; (2) human freedom is a particularly great good, but free humans may do evil; (3) we become fully human only by being tested against evil; (4) perhaps there are limits on God's power.

1. Most generally, some goods would be impossible without certain kinds of evil. The thrill and grace of balancing on a balance beam would be severely diminished if no one ever fell off. The pleasure of a good meal would be less without the pangs of hunger. Thomas Aquinas offered even tougher examples: "A lion would cease to live, if there were no slaying of animals; and there would be no patience of martyrs if there were no tyrannical persecution."[14] God, who knows all things, allows evils whose absence would diminish even greater goods.

2. More particularly, human freedom is a very great good. But if God makes human beings truly free, it follows that they will sometimes misuse that freedom and do evil. Still, it is better to have free beings that sometimes do evil than a world full of robots. The philosopher Alvin Plantinga, author of the best-known contemporary version of this "free will defense," admits that it explains social

evils like wars and murders better than natural evils like earthquakes and disease. It is harder to explain how human freedom could produce most natural evils. But sometimes, he notes, apparently natural evils in fact have a human cause—deaths result not just from the fact of the disease but from our failure to inoculate its victims. Failing all else, Plantinga says, there may be nonhuman agents (angels/demons) who cause natural evils but whose freedom is also a great good.[15]

3. Alternatively, following the ideas of the second-century theologian Irenaeus, the contemporary philosopher John Hick has proposed that human beings become fully human only by being tested and confronted by challenges and difficulties. Evils thus contribute to "soul making," to making us the full adults God intends us to become.[16]

4. Some process theologians and others propose that there are limits on God's power. God does not prevent all evil because God cannot.[17] Either God is in the nature of things limited in power or else God has freely chosen some form of self-limitation in order to make possible the great adventure of free and independent agents acting in the world.

However Christian theologians explain evil, most have wanted here too to avoid any taint of Manicheanism. There is not an independent, evil deity such as the Manicheans proposed. (If there is a devil, the devil is, as Genesis emphasizes about the tempting serpent, one of the creatures that God made [Gen. 3:1].) Since God created all that is (other than God), Augustine further concluded, as a way of refuting the Manicheans, that nothing that exists, insofar as it exists, is evil. Evil is always an absence or distortion, the lack of some good that might have been. The deformed child is not evil. The evil lies only in the tragedy that it was not born without handicaps, that it lacks perfections it might have had, but the existence of the child is a good. And so, the argument goes, with anything else that exists.

Even when we human beings act for good, theology faces the question of whether and how we act freely. When we turn to evil, as already noted, our freedom sometimes gets offered as an explanation of why God is not responsible.

Many Christian theologians, however, have argued that acting freely is not incompatible with acting under God's direction. The great seventeenth-century American theologian Jonathan Edwards, for instance, maintained that when my will leads me to pursue something I desire, then I *am* acting freely, even if a set of causes determines my action. If you put a gun to my head and order me to give you my money, I am not acting freely; if you offer me a piece of chocolate cake, and I eat it out of my love for chocolate, then I *am* acting freely—even if you knew very well that, given how much I love chocolate, I was bound to eat. No human, of course, can know all the factors at work in my decisions. (Perhaps I have just sworn to go on a diet.) Therefore, no human being can completely determine my behavior without constraining my freedom. But God, Edwards (following earlier theologians, but Edwards made the case with unusual clarity) argues, knows and shapes our every motivation, so that we act as God wills—yet we act freely, since our will guides our action.[18] In her essay here, Kathryn Tanner will develop such an argument that God's power and ours operate not in competition but on completely different levels.

But what about when we turn to evil? Calvin pointed to biblical texts where God seems to be the cause of evil human acts. God hardens Pharaoh's heart, so that he will not let the Hebrew people go from Egypt (Exod. 4:21). God sends the Assyrians and Babylonians to devastate the kingdoms of Israel and Judah, killing women and children.[19] When human beings do evil, God "not only knew what was about to happen, but decreed it."[20] Yet what it means to do evil is precisely to act against God's will. "If anyone object that this is beyond comprehension," Calvin acknowledged, "I confess it."[21]

One could cite similar passages from many other theologians. Does God direct our evil deeds? Or do we act contrary to God's will? There seem good theological reasons for denying either claim, and Christian theology has never produced a definitive answer. Thomas Aquinas concluded, "Whatever takes place in the world proceeds from the plan of the divine intellect: except, *perhaps,* in voluntary agents only, who have it in their power to withdraw themselves from what is so ordained; that is what the evil of sin consists in."[22] A vast quantity of theological debate—and theological wisdom—lies in that *perhaps.*

Does God direct our evil deeds? Or do we act contrary to God's will? There seem good theological reasons for denying either claim.

TWO PROPOSALS

Both the following essays argue that much of our thinking about God goes wrong by thinking of God as one being, standing over against other beings. Once we set up the picture that way, both authors would argue, we inevitably get caught in arguments about who has the most power and who is most responsible for evils.

In contrast, McFague proposes that we think of the world as God's body, so that God is not separate from and over against the world at all. God's incarnation (or embodiment) in Jesus Christ thus turns out to be a special case of what God has always been doing—becoming embodied in the world. Evil arises naturally in the interactions of the different entities within the world. Christians are called to think less about Why questions than about Where questions, less about how we got here than about what we should do to care for the neighborhood in which we find ourselves.

In a very different way of rejecting the model of God as one thing over against the world, Tanner argues that God is not one of the things in the world—not, as she puts it, "a kind of thing at all." Rather, God utterly transcends the categories that define the created world. Therefore, for instance, when we talk about God "creating" things, we should not look for some worldly analogy. Is God's creativity like an egg hatching, or an artist making a drawing, or a carpenter nailing boards together? No, it is altogether different from any of those activities and unique to itself. If God were one of the things in the world, then God's power would be in competition with other powers. Just as it makes sense to ask who has more power, Congress or the president, so we could ask who has more power, God or creatures. But Tanner says that God operates in an altogether different dimension, so that creatures can behave freely in their various ways while *everything* remains at the same time on another level God's doing.

So is God a creator who looks down from heaven and makes a world? Or the one whose body the world is? Or one so unlike any analogy we can imagine as to operate in a completely different dimension of things? What implications would such accounts of God have for how we think about creation, evil, and human freedom? McFague and Tanner offer their own challenging answers to these important questions.

SALLIE MCFAGUE

> *We wake, if we wake at all, to mystery, rumors of death, beauty, violence. . . . "Seem like we're just set down here," a woman said to me recently, "and don't nobody know why." . . . Some unwonted, taught pride diverts us from our original intent, which is to explore the neighborhood, view the landscape, to discover* where *it is that we have been so startlingly set down, even if we can't learn why.*
>
> Annie Dillard, *Pilgrim at Tinker Creek*[1]

When we wake up to the mystery that surrounds us, its beauty and its violence, we ask *why* we are here. "Seem like we're just set down here, and don't nobody know why." Indeed. Most religions are about suggesting answers to that question, which is a fiendishly difficult one. A somewhat easier, more immediate question is the other one: Where are we? As Annie Dillard suggests, "our original intent," as witnessed by a child's interest in and wonder at all things, is "to explore the neighborhood . . . to discover *where* it is that we have been so startling set down, even if we can't learn why."

This is an intriguing suggestion. Should religions be more concerned to learn where we are, what the world is like and where we fit into it, rather than focusing mainly on the Why questions? For instance, on the matter of creation and providence, is it a question of why, when, and how the world was created that is critical, or is it rather discovering the nature, potential, and limitations of the neighborhood where we live? Is talk about creation and providence concerned with intellectual questions of *why* things are the way they are, or is it about *how* we should live in harmony with all the rest of creation? Christianity has traditionally been focused on the Why questions rather than turning our eyes to the beauty, concrete details, processes, and uniqueness of our home, planet Earth. In Christian theology, creation and providence have often been more about God and God's power—evidence that God is in charge—than about human beings living in and caring for the neighborhood in which we have been set down. The Why and Where questions are of course interlinked—we will always wonder about the mystery of why we are where we are—but it may be time, at the beginning of the twenty-first century, for Christian theology to pay more attention to the wonderful, fragile, complex—as well as breathtakingly beautiful and violent—world that we actually inhabit. If creation and providence are not just about God creating and caring for the world but also about us living in it and helping it flourish, then creation and providence are about the most basic relationship between God and the world. How distant, how close, are God and the world? Is God only transcendent over the world or also immanent in it? Is the relationship between God and the world more like a potter and a bowl or a mother and a child? Are we only externally related to God or are we internally related? Is the world more like another subject to God or more like an object? Is God spirit while the world is only matter? Does God have all power over creation, or are human beings also responsible for creation? Are we puppets or partners? These and many more questions dealing with the nature of the relationship between God and the world lie at the heart of different interpretations of creation and providence.

This essay will suggest that the traditional creation-providence story in Christian history has underscored God's power over divine love, God's transcendence over divine immanence, and God's distance from the world rather than involvement in it.

This essay will suggest that the traditional creation-providence story in Christian history has underscored God's power over divine love, God's transcendence over divine immanence, and God's distance from the world rather than involvement in it. This need not, should not, be the case: An interpretation of the God-world relationship based on the basic belief that God is incarnate in the world implies rethinking the issues of creation and providence in light of the world as internally related to God—the world as within God or the world as God's "body"—rather than externally related as an artist is to his or her production. The thesis is, then, that the doctrines of creation and providence are implications drawn from our most basic belief about the God-world relationship, and for Christians this relationship is incarnational: God is with us, here and now, in this world. Our doctrines of creation and providence do not stand alone: They are offshoots of our deepest beliefs about the nature of God's relation to the world. If this belief is that God and the world are wholly other, creation and providence will be seen in that light. If this belief is that God and the world are intrinsically intimate, creation and providence will be understood from within that perspective.

I will unfold this thesis by looking first at the traditional creation myth, then at a range of models of the God-world relationship that have functioned in Christian history, and finally by fleshing out what we mean by an incarnational understanding of creation and providence. We will approach the issues of creation and providence in light of basic models of the God-world relationship, focusing our interest not primarily on why, when, and how God created the world but on the implications of each model for the well-being of all creation and how human beings can be part of that flourishing. I will focus not on the why, but the where: How can we all live justly and sustainably in the neighborhood in which we have so startlingly been set down?

THE TRADITIONAL CREATION MYTH

The First Vatican Council (1870) expressed the God-world relationship in a manner that, with some variations, is common in major creeds of various Christian churches since the Reformation and which lies behind the traditional creation-providence story.

> The holy, Catholic, Apostolic, Roman Church believes and confesses that there is one true, living God, Creator and Lord of Heaven and earth, omnipotent, eternal, immense, incomprehensible, infinite in intellect and will, and in every perfection, who, although He is one, singular, altogether simple and unchangeable spiritual substance, must be pure and distinct in reality and essence from the world, most blessed in Himself and of Himself, and ineffably most high above all things which are or can be conceived outside Himself.[2]

Given this view of the God-world relationship—one of total distance and difference—the story of creation and providence follows. That story, in its simplest form, claims that an absolute, all-powerful, transcendent God created the world (universe) from nothing for entirely gratuitous reasons. God did not need creation, nor is God internally related to it: It was created solely for God's glory. Unfortunately, creation "fell" through the pride of one of its creatures—human beings—making it necessary for God to initiate a reversal of creation's downfall through Jesus Christ, who atones for the sins of all human beings. In this story, creation and providence are part of one coherent, historical, all-inclusive drama in which God is in charge from beginning to end, creating all things and saving them through the atoning blood of his own Son.

This mythic story focuses on God's actions—God is the protagonist of the world drama—and its purpose is to answer Why not, Where questions. The story speaks to our concerns about why the world was made, who is in charge of it, why it is no longer harmonious, and how it is made right again. This story does not speak to our interest in the world or how we should act toward our neighbors. Human beings are, in fact, minor players in the classic Christian story of creation and providence. Moreover, the action does not occur in our physical neighborhoods, the actual spaces and places we inhabit, but over our heads, as it were, in the vast panoramic historical sweep of time, with its beginning (creation), middle (redemption), and end (eschatology). In each of these events, God is totally in charge. We, at most, like good children, are grateful to our all-mighty, all-loving Father and try to follow his will. Even when sin and evil divert the drama from its triumphant course (and cause us to lose faith and hope), the Lord of history will prevail, the King will be victorious.

What is left out of this story of creation is creation itself, that is, "the neighborhood," the lowly, concrete, particular—and fascinating—details of physical reality. In fact, the story does not seem to be about creation at all, but about a God whose "spiritual substance must be pure and distinct in reality and essence from the world." This God does not inhabit creation; in fact, the assumption behind this creation story is that spirit and matter are entirely distinct and in a dualistic, hierarchical relationship. God—and all things spiritual, heavenly, and eternal—are perfect and exalted above all things material, earthly, and mortal, with the latter being entirely different from the former and inferior to it. It is difficult to overstate the importance of this assumption—the dualistic, hierarchical relationship of God and the world—for it encourages not only an understanding of salvation as the escape of individuals to the spiritual world, but also justifies lack of attention to the flourishing of this world. If God is spirit and creation is matter, then God does not occupy the earth and we need not attend to it either. But what if spirit and matter were not entirely different? What if all life—God's and ours, as well as that of all others on earth—was seen to be on a continuum, more like a circle or a recycle symbol than like a dualistic hierarchy? What if spirit and matter were intrinsically related rather than diametrically opposed? Would not this make a difference in how we thought of where God is and where we should be? Would it not turn our eyes to the earth, whether we were searching for God or trying to understand where we belong?

> What if spirit and matter were intrinsically related rather than diametrically opposed? Would not this make a difference in how we thought of where God is and where we should be?

Our present planetary crisis reveals the price we have paid for not paying attention to our earth, the actual neighborhood where we live. When we look at our earth at the beginning of the twenty-first century, we see a planet in increasingly poor health. Moreover, we are not all in the same place on this planet. Some of us are where things are still pretty good while others—most others (including other life-forms)—are where things are falling apart. So when we ask, "Where are we?" or "What is the neighborhood like in which we live?" we have to differentiate between good neighborhoods and poor ones. Where we live is neither just nor sustainable; neglect of the neighborhood is undercutting the possibility of all its inhabitants living well.

Once we lower our eyes from the big heavenly questions—the Why questions that the classic Christian creation story answers—and look around at where we actually live, what our world is like, and how it can support all of us creatures decently, we realize that, while the big Why questions will always interest us, it is the mundane Where questions that may be more pressing. If "creation and providence" has less to do with answering questions of why things are the way they are and more to do with issues of where and how we live, then these issues would have to do not only with God and God's plans, but also and centrally with who we are in the scheme of things and hence how we should behave. If, for instance, the doctrine of creation were principally about our place in nature, then we would need to know a lot about "the natural world," how it functions to stay healthy, what are its limits, how its resources can be justly shared and permanently sustained. If we focused on one piece of the Genesis story, the piece that speaks of Adam and Eve being placed in the garden to care for it, we might have a different creation myth within which to find our place. Could one reason for existence be simply to care for the garden? Were we created not to win salvation in another world but to enjoy this one and help it to flourish? Could the goal of creation be the fulfillment of *all* God's creatures and not just the redemption of a few human creatures?

We will keep these questions in mind as we turn now to a typology of God-world relationships to see which views of creation and providence are both consonant with the Christian tradition and appropriate for the twenty-first century.

MODELS OF GOD AND THE WORLD

The first model we will consider—the deistic one, which arose during the seventeenth-century scientific revolution—is also the simplest. It imagines God as a clockmaker who winds up the clock of the world by creating its laws and then leaves it to run by itself, with the qualification that God intervenes periodically in natural disasters, accidents, and personal crises. The model has the advantage of freeing science to investigate the world apart from divine control, but it essentially banishes God from the world. Of the models we will look at, it separates God and the world most thoroughly; God is externally related to the world as a mechanic is to a machine, who, after getting it going, only tinkers here and there when necessary. Strangely, this model—sterile, distant, and impersonal—is the one assumed by many contemporary Christians as well as nonbelievers. It is a convenient view for those who want "to keep religion out of business and politics," for those who do not wish a God who is immanent within creation and cares about its well-being. The deistic model says God is only minimally creator and caretaker of the world: This God has only to start it up, so to speak, and be present now and then in times of personal and public crisis.

This model is neither Christian, nor is it helpful for our twenty-first-century world. It knows nothing of the great Hebrew and Christian traditions of the compassionate, suffering, and always present Emmanuel, the God with us, the One within whom the beloved creation is both rebuked and held in love. This model sees the world as totally secular, divorced from God and from human beings, except as a "machine" for our use. The relationship between God and the world as well as between human beings and the world is utilitarian: We (and God) are subjects, whereas the world and all its other creatures are objects. It is interesting to note, however, that many scientists, especially biologists such as E. O. Wilson and Stephen Jay Gould, have found that their study of the world ends in wonder and awe, not mere utilitarianism! This suggests, among other things, that the deistic model of God and the world is flat and uninteresting as well as non-Christian.

> Models of God and the world: deistic, dialogic, monarchical, agential, the world as God's body.

A second view of God and the world, the dialogic one, has deep roots in both Hebrew and Christian traditions: God speaks and we respond. It has been a central view within Protestantism and was highlighted in twentieth-century existentialism. In its contemporary form, the relation between God and the world is narrowed to God and the individual: the I-Thou relation between God and a human being. As seen, for instance, in the writings of Søren Kierkegaard and Rudolf Bultmann, this position focuses on sin, guilt, and forgiveness and has the advantage of allowing for a continuous relationship with God, but does so at the expense of indifference to the natural and social worlds. In its still more contemporary form, it embraces both born-again and New Age theologies. For born-again Christians, the God-world relationship is focused on the saved individual, while for the New Age folks, it is limited to what comforts and satisfies the individual.

In the dialogic cases creation does not include the natural and social worlds; rather, the "created" creature is almost exclusively human—and alone. The dialogic position assumes two tracks, religion and culture (the latter including scientific knowledge and all social institutions such as government, the economy, the family), with each left to run its own affairs. God and the human being meet, not in the world (whether of culture or nature) but only in the internal joy and pain of human experiences. Whereas the deistic model kept God and the world totally separate and externally related, the dialogic model allows them to touch, but only at one place—the inner human subject. Liberation theologies have protested the focus on individual alienation and despair—usually white, male, Western, affluent troubles and sorrows—insisting that God's relation to the world must include the political and social dimensions as well. If the individual and the political worlds must be included in a credible doctrine of creation, can we leave out the cosmos itself? What would a doctrine of creation be without nature? The difficulties with

> In the dialogic cases creation does not include the natural and social worlds; rather, the "created" creature is almost exclusively human—and alone.

the dialogic position are only too obvious: It does not allow for a credible contemporary understanding of creation, and it can qualify as Christian in only a narrow sense: in the sense that the incarnation of God—the being of God with us—is limited to human individuals.

A third model—the monarchical one—sees the relation between God and the world as one in which the divine, all-powerful king controls his subjects and they in turn offer him loyal obedience. It is the oldest of the models, the one that lies behind the traditional creation-providence story, and one that is still very popular. It is both a personal and a political model, correcting the impersonalism of the deistic model and the individualism of the dialogic. It also underscores the "godness" of God, for the monarchical imagery calls forth awe and reverence, as well as vocational meaningfulness, since membership in the kingdom entails service to the divine Lord. The continuing power of this model is curious since contemporary members of royalty scarcely call up responses of awe, reverence, and obedience, but its nostalgic appeal, as evidenced in the gusto with which we all sing Christmas carols that are rife with this imagery, cannot be underestimated. Any model that would attempt to criticize it ought to look carefully at the main reason for its attraction: It underscores and dramatizes divine transcendence. In other words, it accomplishes one of the tasks of a model of the God-world relationship: It emphasizes the power and glory of God.

Nonetheless, this model has several problems, the first being that the model of God as king is "domesticated" transcendence, for a king rules only over human beings, a minute fraction of created reality. The king-realm model is neither genuinely transcendent (God is king over one species recently arrived on a minor planet in an ordinary galaxy) nor genuinely immanent (God as king is an external superperson, not the source, power, and goal of the entire universe). Moreover, a king is both distant from the natural world and indifferent to it, for as a political model, monarchy is limited to human beings. At most, nature enters this model only as the king's *realm* or *dominion,* not with all the complexity, richness, and attention-grabbing qualities of the living, mysterious creation of which we are a part. The king-realm model shuts out the earth as earth; that is, because it allows us to imagine the God-world relationship only in terms of a king and his subjects, it (like all models) encourages us to see some things and not others. The king-realm model would not be so harmful if it were not also hegemonic; that is, for many Christians it (along with the father-child model) *describes* the divine-world relationship. It is not "just" a model—that is, one good, useful way of talking about the God-world relationship (while admitting there are other ways)—but *the* way. Whether king-realm or father-child model, both of these favorites exclude the natural world; they exclude the neighborhood we need to pay attention to. Models are dangerous as well as helpful and necessary, for they only allow us to see what they want us to. If the God-world relationship is not expressed in models that include the natural world—God's love for it and our responsibility for it—then we ignore nature: The "world" will mean the human world, either personally or politically.

A fourth model, the agential one, is also old, with strong backing in both the Hebrew and the Christian traditions. Here God is assumed to be an agent, a "person," whose intentions and purposes are realized in history. In its classical form, God is actor and doer, creator and redeemer of the world, as well as its providential caretaker. God the personal agent oversees the world in every way, creating it from nothing; guiding it as father, lord, lover, king, protector; and when it falls away like a wayward child, calling it back through divine sacrifice and compassion. This model obviously has contributed a great deal to the traditional creation-providence story. It, along with the king-realm model, is the backbone of that story, for it is the source of the overarching purposes and goals that are the story's structure. As we recall, in the traditional story, God creates the world for his own glory, apart from any need or desire. Creation is entirely a matter of divine intention; thus, the enduring images of God as willing creation into existence through divine words ("Let there be . . .") and sculpting Adam from the clay, like a potter. These images of creation come from God's "mind" and from God's "hands," from analogies with how human persons make and do things intentionally, with a purpose. In this model, God is "like" us; the model underscores the human-like qualities of God, especially those having to do with our ability to decide, influence, intend, and bring about actions, events, and conclusions.

> The king-realm model would not be so harmful if it were treated as "just" a model—that is, one good, useful way of talking about the God-world relationship (while admitting that there are other ways).

One main difficulty with this model is that, if God is like a personal agent who influences the world and brings it to its fulfillment, how does this take place? In earlier times, most ordinary people had little difficulty imagining God intervening in worldly events to direct and control them. Since the scientific revolution and especially postmodern evolutionary cosmology and biology, this is increasingly problematic. Such a God is an unnecessary intrusion in scientific explanation and has been marginalized to at most starting up the big bang. While there have been efforts on the part of some theologians and scientists to internalize divine action within the cosmic processes and thus retain a notion of divine intention and design in nature, these efforts are mainly aimed at satisfying Why not Where questions; that is, to allow us to believe in both the existence of God and the truth of science. They are not oriented toward helping us learn about and pay attention to the world for its own flourishing; rather, they are meant to suggest that subtle, highly nuanced traces of divine purpose are evident in the world.

Again, it is the "world" that is lacking in this model. The focus is on God and God's intentions for creation—how the divine will conceives, creates, saves, and brings to fulfillment everything that is. But the "everything that is" does not get much attention. Nonetheless, this model is suggestive: What if the model were revised so that God as "person" would not be just mind but also body? What if we did not insist on radical dualism between God and the world, with God being all spirit and the world being all matter or body, but imagined a model with God and the world being both? That is, what if the world were seen to be God's body which is infused by, empowered by, loved by, given life by God? What if the world were seen to be "within" God, not identical with God (as our own bodies are not identical with us, for we can reflect about them, guide them, direct them, etc.), but very, very intimately connected—sort of like a baby in the womb? Would such a model be a way of expressing profound interrelationship between God and the world, a way that might be closer to an incarnational understanding of the God-world relationship than are the other models we have considered?

> What if the world were seen to be "within" God, not identical with God, but very, very intimately connected—sort of like a baby in the womb?

We will shortly consider this possibility in more detail, but before doing so, we need to remember that all models of God and the world are limited, partial, and imperfect. We are trying to get at the most basic expression of that relationship, realizing that there is not just a single right one, that many are needed, and that all have problems. If the most basic relationship for Christians is known in some way or fashion from the story of Jesus Christ, and if one interpretation of that story—perhaps its broadest and deepest interpretation—is that God is with us here and now on our earth, then which of the models we have considered is both Christian and appropriate for our time? Which model is better than the others (all we can aim for) in expressing divine love for and presence in the world we actually inhabit? Is it the model of the clockmaker winding up the clock; the I-Thou model of God and an individual; the model of God as king and the world as his realm; the agential model of God acting in the world; or the model of God as the spirit empowering the universe, the divine body? It is not necessary to choose only one of these models, but it probably is important to give priority to one, for the one we use as our main lens through which to view the God-world relationship will profoundly influence who we think we are in the scheme of things and how we behave in our world, our neighborhood.

CREATION AND PROVIDENCE IN LIGHT OF THE WORLD AS GOD'S BODY

Since nothing that is could exist without You, You must in some way be in all that is: [therefore also in me, since I am]. And if You are already in me, since otherwise I should not be, why do I cry to You to enter into me? . . . I should be nothing, utterly nothing, unless You were in me—or rather unless

> *I were in You "of Whom and by Whom and in Whom are all things." So it is, Lord. So it is. Where do I call You to come to, since I am in You? Or where else are You that You can come to me? Where shall I go, beyond the bounds of heaven and earth, that God may come to me, since He has said: "Heaven and earth do I fill."*
>
> —Augustine, *Confessions*[3]

If God is always incarnate, then Christians should attend to the model of the world as God's body. For Christians, God did not become human on a whim; rather, it is God's nature to be embodied, to be the One in whom we live and move and have our being. In Christianity, the God-world relationship is understood in light of the incarnation; hence, creation is "like" the incarnation. Jesus Christ is the lens, the model, through whom Christians interpret God, world, and themselves. The doctrine of creation for Christians, then, is not different in kind from the doctrine of the incarnation. In both, God is the source of all existence, the One in whom we are born and reborn. In this view, the world is not just matter while God is spirit; rather, there is a continuity (though not an identity) between God and the world. The world is flesh of God's "flesh"; the God who took our flesh in one person, Jesus of Nazareth, has always done so. God is incarnate, not secondarily but primarily. Therefore, an appropriate Christian model for understanding creation is the world as God's body. This is not a description of creation (there are no descriptions); neither is it necessarily the only model. It is, however, one model that is commensurate with the central Christian affirmation that God is with us in the flesh in Jesus Christ, and it is a model that is particularly appropriate for interpreting the Christian doctrine of creation in our time. Its merits and limitations should be considered in relation to other major models of the God-world relationship: God as clockmaker winding up the machine, as king of the realm, as father with wayward children, as personal agent acting in the world, and so forth.

The world as God's body is appropriate for our time (as well as being in continuity with the Christian incarnational tradition) because it encourages us to focus on the neighborhood. It understands the doctrine of creation not to be primarily about God's power but about God's love: how we can live together, all of us, within and for God's body. It focuses attention on the near, on the neighbor, on the earth, on meeting God not later in heaven but here and now. We meet God in the world and especially in the flesh of the world—in feeding the hungry and healing the sick. An incarnational understanding of creation says nothing is too lowly, too physical, too mean

The world as God's body encourages us to focus on the neighborhood. It understands the doctrine of creation not to be primarily about God's power but about God's love: how we can live together, all of us, within and for God's body.

a labor if it helps some creature to flourish. We find God in caring for the garden, in loving the earth well.

The doctrine of creation in this view is a practical affair, not an intellectual one. It is not about God's absolute power (hence, one need not be disturbed by the lack of *ex nihilo* in Genesis!). The point of the doctrine is not to elevate God while demeaning us and the world; rather, it is to focus attention on our home, our garden planet. In Genesis, God not only tells Adam and Eve to care for the garden, but also how good it is: After each act of creation in Genesis 1, God "saw that it was good." After completing the entire creation, "God saw everything that he had made, and indeed, it was very good" (Gen. 1:31a). Interestingly, God does not say that it is good for human beings or even good for me, God, but simply good. This is an aesthetic response expressing appreciation for the intrinsic value of each and every creature, plant, and planetary process (sun, moon, earth, water). As Irenaeus would suggest later: "The glory of God is every creature fully alive."[4]

Hence, this understanding of creation asks us to find out about the neighborhood so we can take care of it. It suggests that human beings are not the only creatures that matter; however, we are special. We are the caretakers, the ones who can help the garden flourish, help the body of God be well fed and healthy—or we can destroy it. We *know* the difference between good and evil; the unique feature of human beings as well as our greatest burden is that we know that we know. We not only know how to do many things (all animals know this), but we *know* that we can do many things, and that some of these things are good and some bad for God's creation, God's body—our planetary garden.

Let us look more carefully at three implications of this model of creation and providence, that is, of how God and the world are related and who cares for the world. The implications of the model of the world as God's body are, first, that we must know our world and where we fit into it; second, that we must acknowledge God as the only source of all life, love, truth, and goodness; and third, that we realize that while God is in charge of the world, so are we.

Knowing the Body, Tending the Garden

In our model, the body of God is the entire universe; it is all matter in its myriad, fantastic, ancient, and modern forms, from quarks to galaxies. More specifically, the body of God needing our attention is planet Earth, a tiny piece of divine embodiment that is our home and garden. In order to care for this garden, we need to know about it; in order to help all creatures who constitute this body flourish, we need to understand how we humans fit into this body.

All understandings of creation and providence rest on assumptions about what the world is like and where humans belong in it. First-century Mediterranean, medieval, and eighteenth-century views of the world and the place of humans differ; the twenty-first-century view does as well. In our evolutionary, ecological view of reality, everything is interrelated and interdependent. "Ecological unity" is both radically individualistic and radically relational. In an organism or body, the whole flourishes *only* when all the different parts function well; in fact, the "whole" is nothing but each and every individual part doing its particular thing successfully. Nothing is more unified than a well-functioning body but, also, nothing relies more on complex, diverse individuality.

Hence, the neighborhood that we have been set down in is one that we must learn to care for in all its diverse parts and needs. We must become "ecologically literate," understanding its most basic law: that there is no way the whole can flourish unless *all parts* are cared for. This means distributive justice is the key to sustainability, or, to phrase it differently, our garden home, the body of God, will only be healthy for the long term if *all* parts of it are cared for appropriately. Before all else, the community, our planet, must survive (sustainability), which it can do only if all members have access to basic necessities (distributive justice). We need to learn "home economics," the basic rules of how our garden home can prosper—and what will destroy it. Most simply, these house rules are: Take only your share, clean up after yourself, and keep the house in good repair for others.

We must do so because, as the self-reflective part of God's body—the part that knows that we know—we have become partners with God in maintaining the health of creation. We are no longer the peak of creation, the one above all the others and for whom the others were made; rather, we are at one and the same time the neediest of all creatures and the most powerful. We cannot exist beyond a few minutes without air, a few days without water, or a few weeks without the plants, but we are also, given our population and high-energy lifestyle, the one species that can undermine the planet's well-being, as global warming, the decline of biodiversity, and the increasing gap between the rich and the poor are illustrating. In a strange paradox, we who have unprecedented power over the planet are at the same time at its mercy. If it does not thrive, neither can we.

> Creation modeled as God's body supports and underscores a radically ecological view of the world. It is entirely opposed to the cult of individualism endorsed by modern religion, government, and economics.

As is evident, this first implication of creation modeled as God's body supports and underscores a radically ecological view of the world. It is entirely opposed to the cult of individualism endorsed by modern religion, government, and economics, all of which claim that human beings are basically separate, isolated individuals who enter into relationships when they wish. This is the view of human beings that underlies both New-Age religion and born-again Christianity, as well as market capitalism and American democracy ("life, liberty, and the pursuit of happiness"). Perhaps the most important implication of creation as God's body is the new anthropology it demands: We are—basically, intrinsically, and always—interrelational, interdependent beings who live in total dependence on the others who compose the body, while at the same time being responsible for the well-being of one tiny part of the body, planet Earth.

God as Source of Life and Love

A second implication of the model of creation as God's body is that it radicalizes both God's transcendence and God's immanence. This model has been criticized by some as pantheistic, as identifying God and the world. I do not believe it is. If God is to the universe as each of us is to our bodies, then God and the world are not identical. They are, however, intimate, close, and internally related in ways that can make Christianity uncomfortable when it forgets its incarnationalism. But we Christians should not shy away from a model that radically underscores both divine transcendence and divine immanence. How does it do so?

In the model of the world as God's body, God is the source, the center, the spring, the spirit of all that lives and loves, all that is beautiful and true. When we say "God," that is what we mean: We mean the power and source of all reality. *We* are not the source of our own being; hence, we acknowledge the radical dependence of all that is on God. This is true transcendence: being the source of everything that is. Our universe, the body of God, is the reflection of God's being, God's glory; it is the sacrament of God's presence with us. The most radically transcendent understanding of God is, then, at the same time the most radically immanent understanding. Because God is always incarnational, always embodied, we can see God's transcendence *immanentally*. Meeting God is not a momentary "spiritual" affair; rather, God is the ether, the reality, the body, the garden in which we live.

God is never absent. God is reality (being), and everything that has being derives it from God (we are born of God and reborn by God). The entire cosmos is born of God, as is each and every creature. We depend on this source of life and renewal absolutely. We could not live a moment without the gifts of God's body—air, food, water, land, and other creatures. To realize this is an overwhelming experience of God's transcendence; it calls forth awe and immense gratitude. Yet at the same time, as Augustine puts it, God is closer to us than we are to ourselves. Where can we go where God is not, since God fills heaven and earth: "I should be nothing unless I were in You." The God whom we meet through the earth is not only the source of my being, but of all being. We see glimmers of God in creation (God's body), and we see the same God more clearly in Jesus Christ, the major model of God for Christians.

> The second implication of our model is that it allows us to meet God in the garden, on the earth, at home. We do not have to go elsewhere, or wait until we die, or even be "religious."

The second implication of our model, then, is that it allows us to meet God in the garden, on the earth, at home. We do not have to go elsewhere, or wait until we die, or even be "religious." We meet God in the nitty-gritty of our regular lives, for God is always present in every here and now. This second implication underscores the first: Since God is here in our world, then surely it is indeed our neighborhood, our planet and its creatures, that we should be caring for. What other vocation could we have but to care for God's body?

Who Is in Charge?

A third implication of our model of the world as God's body is that God alone is not in charge. Our model is not a mechanistic one: God does not control the world as a puppeteer controls puppets or a clockmaker starting a clock or a king commanding his subjects. Divine power is not unilateral—the more one party has, the less there is for the other. Rather, *God shares.* In organisms, power is mutual flourishing, empowerment, symbiosis; the whole does not flourish unless the parts are thriving. But this is messy business and does not result in the well-being of all creatures all the time—how could it? If the body of God is billions of different species and individuals, each one with a desire to live, there will inevitably be many that do not survive or flourish. An evolutionary, ecological picture of reality is not neat, nice, or romantic. It is indifferent, often brutal, and sometime tragic. It is also often serendipitous: The same process that results in the AIDS virus or cancer cells created our brains and our emotions. Hence, so-called natural evil will occur—frequently and for no reason, depending on one's perspective (a flood helps some creatures and devastates others). Add to natural evil what is called moral evil or sin: the perversions of reality (of life, love, goodness, beauty, truth) which we human beings perpetrate, both individually and collectively, and one has an awesome task for providence. A century that has known the Holocaust, Hiroshima, and now global terrorism—not to mention ordinary poverty, discrimination, and greed—does not need to be told how powerful evil is.

But in our model of the world as God's body, even these monstrous examples of evil do not imply "another" reality—an evil power, as it were. There is, in an incarnational creation story, only one reality: The world derives its being from God, lives within and toward God, and is "real" to the extent it reflects the one reality, God. Evil does not "exist"; rather, it is a perversion of good, the absence or distortion of a good that might have been. All that lives depends on God or comes from God; evil does not depend on God or come from God. This does not make it less powerful, less prevalent, or less tragic, but it does suggest that evil is not in charge, all appearances to the contrary. Christians believe that ultimately God is in charge: A doctrine of creation and providence without the resurrection would be a doctrine of despair. There is little in our world that suggests this; in fact, reading a daily newspaper is all one needs to refute it. It is "absurd" to believe it. Perhaps believing in God may be nothing more than trusting that God *is* in charge, no matter what happens. H. Richard Niebuhr says that believing in Jesus Christ means becoming suspicious of one's "own deep suspicion of the Determiner of Destiny."[5] We work this faith out here in our neighborhood. It is figuring out where we are even if we cannot know why we are here. If we see ourselves as within God's body, as tending the garden, as doing home economics for

God's household, we can relax about some things and get busy with others. We can rest in the comfort of God's constant and enveloping presence, knowing that God holds the whole world in her hands. We can, at the same time, get busy learning about our neighbors and how we can all live here justly and sustainably.

CONCLUSION: CREATION OR REDEMPTION CHRISTIANITY?

The model of the world as God's body suggests a creation-oriented Christianity in contrast to the tradition's heavy emphasis on redemption. In the end, there are many similarities between the two perspectives, for in each God is *both* creator and savior. However, the greatest difference between them is where they say we are at home. In creation Christianity we are at home here on the earth, an earth that exists within God. We may not know why we have been placed here, but we know where we are: We live within God. We live within God before we are born, during our time on earth, and after we die. We are always in the same place—within God.

In the other version of the Christian story, we are not at home on the earth. To be sure, God came to earth at one point, in the incarnation of the redeemer Jesus Christ, but otherwise God is only externally related to the world. In both stories we belong to God, but in the redemption-oriented one, we can only find God in and through Jesus Christ and the community founded by him. We are at home in the church, the body of Christ, but not in the world (which is not seen as the body of God). Our final home, where we really belong, is in another time and another place: We reach this world of eternal life through accepting Christ's reconciling death for our sins. Neither God nor we are at home on the earth; it is not where God is or where we (properly) belong.

In the model of the world as God's body, there is only one world, our earth, which we inhabit and of which God is the source, spring, and power. God is primarily and always incarnated, and creation is the witness of that continuous presence with us. In Jesus of Nazareth, Christians believe God's embodied presence reaches its culmination; the implicit becomes explicit; the shadows of divine love and goodness, truth and beauty, move into the light. We see the revelation of God in the face of Jesus Christ. In Jesus' ministry of feeding the hungry, healing the sick, and siding with the poor and oppressed—actions which countered conventional mores and led to his death—we see concretely what living rightly in God's body means. In the story of Jesus, we are brought face to face, as it were,

In the model of the world as God's body, there is only one world, our earth, which we inhabit and of which God is the source, spring, and power. God is primarily and always incarnated, and creation is the witness of that continuous presence with us.

with God's presence, a presence that we have always lived in and at times acknowledged.

In this story we learn two things about where we are: We are in God and we are called to live as disciples of Jesus. We live within God; hence, we can relax and enjoy, for we are at home and there is no other place we want to be. We live also (and at the same time) on the earth; hence, we can get busy caring for our garden home. Moreover, the story of Jesus provides us with a vision of how we should care for this home in the kingdom of God, the eucharistic banquet, to which all are invited to share the feast. The story of ecological economics—home economics for planet Earth—provides us with a way to work toward that vision: through sharing resources with all creatures so earth may prosper (distributive justice for sustainability).

We close with yet another reminder that all models are partial and inadequate. No *one* model is adequate, for each allows us to see some aspects of the God-world relationship, but shuts out others. The model of the world as God's body is meant as a corrective to the tradition, not as a substitute for it. It is offered as one model that is commensurate with Christianity's central incarnational belief and, for our time, helpful for the flourishing of all God's creatures. The final word, however, on this model and on all models is one of caution: "Be careful how you interpret the world; it *is* like that."[6]

KATHRYN TANNER

If Christians know anything about the Old Testament, they know the first few lines in which God is said to have created heaven and earth. Following the early ecumenical creeds in which God's creation of the world is cited first among the acts of salvation history, Christians often express such a belief in the routine course of worship—for example, in the thanksgiving portions of eucharistic services or when renewing baptismal vows.

Providence is another matter. The psalms are a mainstay of Christian worship, and the idea of God's providence does figure centrally in many of them. God's work is alive in nature: God visits the earth with showers and blesses the springs and crowns the year with goodness so that the pastures are full of flocks and the valleys covered in corn (Ps. 65). God is never far from the individual but will find and direct him or her wherever he or she may be—from the womb to the grave, whether in the heights of heaven or the depths of hell (Ps. 139). God is active throughout the history of the particular people Israel, leading them out of Egypt, parting the sea for them to escape their pursuers, providing them with food in the wilderness, giving the laws that define them as a nation, bringing them into the promised land, and so forth (e.g., Ps. 135–136). But direct Christian expression of belief in God's providence is probably more a fixture of popular piety than of formal worship.

In the events of daily life, Christians have occasion to express belief in God's providence where others might appeal to luck. It is providential that, held up by traffic, I missed my flight on a plane that crashed on takeoff. Or Christians may affirm belief in providence as a way of justifying refusal of human responsibility: Whether babies are born with birth defects is a matter of God's will and not a matter for technological intervention. Or Christians may make such an affirmation as an expresssion of resignation before the inevitable, seeking comfort and struggling to regain calm with the thought that God must know what we do not—how the death of a loved one, for example, is something more than simply a tragic loss. When Christians formally confess their belief in God, providence is likely to be simply the unexpressed subtext for the beliefs that really matter. God must have a hand in the world, directing its course according to a plan of God's own devising—that is the least one can say—if what Christians believe about Christ is true: Here, against all the forces of sin and death in the world, God fulfills and completes the covenant that God set up with Israel for all the nations.

If beliefs in creation and providence are clearly important components of the Christian faith, their meaning is not equally clear. The two-thousand-year history of Christian theology can be read as an effort to gain that clarity. Without such clarity, one cannot properly assess the seriousness of contemporary challenges to the faith. Do scientific descriptions of the universe's beginnings compete with the idea that God created it? Do those scientific descriptions tell us how God created the world, as a supplement or alternative to the description the Bible offers? If we can explain how things work in the world in the world's own terms, is appeal to God's providence superfluous? Are some accounts of how the world works incompatible with the idea of God's providence? Isn't, for example, the idea that outcomes in the world are determined by statistical probabilities, by some blind mechanism or chance, incompatible with the idea that God directs the world according to purposes, for ends, of God's own devising? In a world wracked, as ours is, by the havoc caused by the ignorant and sinful acts of men and women, mustn't one lose confidence in God's providence?

Do Christian beliefs about creation and providence provide models of perfectly coercive power for our, unfortunate, imitation? Are these beliefs all about control and about who is in control, God or us?

Without considerable clarity about the meaning of creation and providence, one cannot assess, either, the uses to which these ideas are put. Do Christian beliefs about creation and providence provide models of perfectly coercive power for our, unfortunate, imitation? Are these beliefs all about control and about who is in control, God or us? Is it proper for belief in God's providence to promote submission before the world's injustices and the world's tragedies as if they were an inexorable fate? Or is such a belief properly used in promoting childish hopes: We need not worry, we need not exert ourselves to improve the lot of the world, since God will intervene to save us, at the end, out of the blue? Does the idea of providence support a narrowly self-concerned smugness on the part of those whom the world favors, the sufferings of some serving the well-being of others by God's design? Does my good fortune—my good fortune not to be on that ill-fated plane, for example—suggest that I have an elevated place in God's plan not shared by those who perish?

These are complicated questions, and the present essay can give only hints about how to answer them. What this essay will do is sketch a meaning for creation and providence, culled from the two-thousand-year history of theological discussion of those topics, by means of which the questions may be answered.[1] I hope that, this sketch in hand, the reader will return to these questions and begin to answer them all—in the negative.

My method here of generating a more precise meaning for these beliefs by focusing on the history of theological discussion of them is more controversial and complex in its implications than might appear at first glance. Such a focus in the first place might be thought overly restrictive, since beliefs about creation and providence are not on their face distinctively Christian. Beliefs like these are not limited to Christianity. One can find affirmations at least verbally indistinguishable from the ones Christians make about creation and providence in other world religions and in worldviews of primarily scientific or philosophical derivation (such as Neoplatonism and Stoicism).

Even in Christian use, these beliefs would seem explicable in their meaning apart from beliefs that are distinctively Christian in that they do not make mention of Christ, or seem to depend very directly on what Christians say about him. All this might suggest that there is no distinctively Christian meaning to such beliefs, and that one could therefore fill out their meaning in a freewheeling and eclectic way, providing content for them out of the common creation story or whatever philosophical resources might be currently available for discussing the origins and arrangement of the world. Beliefs about creation and providence would be then a kind of ground floor for explicitly Christian beliefs, specified independently of them and merely subsequently colored by them.

That assumption, and the procedures for determining the meaning of Christian beliefs about creation and providence that go with it, are in my view mistaken. It is true that ideas about creation and providence circulate everywhere, and Christian theologians do indeed work with such ideas—Christian theology is never a self-contained, insular enterprise. If, however, one wants to fill out the meaning that Christians give to those ideas, the trick is to see what Christians do with them, what Christians do with what other people mean by them, and to see what happens to such ideas in Christian use, especially at the time when Christian beliefs in creation and providence developed in the Greco-Roman milieu of the early church. The distinctiveness of that use is apparent, moreover—at the time it developed and, once established (at least in some Christian theological circles), ever after—in the way ideas about creation and providence are systematically shaped in relation to the rest of what Christians believe.

Thus, I do not believe that the meaning of creation in Christian circles is ascertainable apart from Christian beliefs about God, particularly about the transcendence of God as that comes to be developed in Trinitarian terms. This understanding of creation is, in turn, the lynchpin for understanding God's providence; certain ideas about providence follow from it by implication. Furthermore, the Christian interest in both claims—what is at stake for Christians in these affirmations—is only apparent in light of what Christians say about Jesus. Christian beliefs about creation and providence developed, then, at the time Christianity was wracked by controversies over the significance of Christ. The character of God's activity as either creator or providential guide of the world's arrangement and historical course is also concretely specified in much the same way—by what God's dealings with the world in Christ suggest about it. The meaning of both beliefs becomes clear, in short, only when they are set within the whole story of God's dealings with the world, as the nature of those dealings—their gracious beneficence—becomes clear in Christ.

Without this careful specification of the way creation and providence hang together with the whole Christian story, Christian beliefs about creation and providence can mean almost anything, they can be pushed this way and that with impunity, they become a blank screen for the projection of human worries and fantasies—worries, for example, about threatened privilege and fantasies about absolute power. As the often sordid history of Christianity exhibits, even with such efforts of careful specification, such temptations are ineradicable and failure likely.

GOD BEYOND KINDS AND CREATION

Let us start, then, with connections between the doctrine of God and creation. The theologians of the early church who were responsible for developing a Christian account of creation tended to favor one of the ideas about God's transcendence circulating in the Hellenistic philosophical milieu of the day. In Greco-Roman religion and philosophy, divinity is most commonly identified with a general quality or set of qualities—eternality, rationality, order, simplicity, unity—in which a number of things can participate in differing degrees. These qualities might form a particular subset of those constituting the world as we know it, or they might be set off from the world as a whole as just what this disordered world of change, diversity, and division is not. In either case, such ideas about divinity are not easily reconcilable with the monotheism that Christianity shares with Judaism. Contrary to monotheism, in this Greco-Roman view, many things—whether within this world of time and change (e.g., numbers and eternal truths) or outside it (hierarchies of superior and subordinate deities)—are divine to differing degrees. Indeed, certain sorts of things within the world are simply identified with divinity in a fashion that smacks of idolatry.

Christians favor, instead, another understanding of divinity, which has its origins in the surrounding Greco-Roman milieu in what Plato says in the *Republic* about the mysterious "idea of the Good," an idea that seems beyond all forms or kinds of things as some sort of ineffable principle or source of their unity. Divinity is not a kind of thing at all, which might either be like some features of the world or simply opposed to them all, considered as a whole. Christians push this idea of a God beyond kinds in a distinctly monotheist direction. Since divinity is not a generic category in which distinct beings might share to varying degrees, the various deities of Greco-Roman religion and philosophy that lie outside the world of time and change must really only be names for what exists all together and at once in the one and only God. If they are anything at all, these divinities exist in that one and only God, and as such they are all equally God and bear no relations of superiority or subordination with respect to one another.

> Divinity is not a kind of thing at all, which might either be like some features of the world or simply opposed to them all, considered as a whole.

Christians also put this idea of God beyond distinctions of kind to novel use by arguing that there is one God who is directly responsible for the world as a whole—what Christians mean by God's creation of the world. If God is not a kind of thing but beyond identification by kind, it makes sense to say, first of all, that God is responsible, not just for those aspects of the world that are supposedly like God—for example, the world's rational arrangement, mind, and those aspects of the world suitable for rational comprehension according to timeless truths—but for the whole of the world, from the bottom up, so to speak, both the stuff or materials out of which the world takes shape and their organization, both the aspects that change and decay and those that have permanence, both materiality and mind.

> If God is not a kind of thing, then the one God can be directly and intimately involved with the production of the world in all its aspects, without threatening to compromise or dilute either God's divinity or the natures of any of the things in the world.

If God is a kind of thing, then God's responsibility for the world is limited to just those aspects of the world that are most like itself; for example, if God is reason, then God is responsible for only the world's rational arrangement and intelligibility. If God is not a kind of thing, this limitation is removed and God can be responsible for every aspect of the world. And if God is responsible for every aspect of the world, God is not simply giving shape to its parts or arranging them, but producing the world, giving rise to it, as a whole. God is a comprehensive productive principle, in short—the creator of the whole world, both heaven and earth.

If God is beyond kinds, it makes sense to say, in the second place, that the one and only God produces the world directly or immediately. God is not a kind of thing whose nature needs to be protected from compromise and corruption when coming into close contact with things of an opposed nature—the way, say, fire needs to be kept from corruption, the loss of its own nature, through contact by water. Nor, conversely, is divinity a kind of thing that compromises the natures of others when brought into intimate relation with them the way fire compromises the nature of water—dissipating it into the air—by heating it. Kinds of things are essentially defined by not being like other kinds of things, and therefore their borders have to be guarded against those things that they are defined over and against.

A principle of this sort seems to be behind the penchant in religious philosophies of the Hellenistic world (the Greek-speaking world around the eastern Mediterranean in the centuries around the time of Jesus) for multiplying divinities to produce a buffer zone between the highest God and the world. In Hellenistic philosophy, inferior deities are the only ones directly responsible for the properties of the world that most contrast with divinity—matter, for example. Indeed, inferior deities must be the only ones directly responsible for even those properties that most resemble divinity just to the extent they differ from it, by being, say, found in material bodies subject to decay and change. If God is not a kind of thing, then the one God can be directly and intimately involved with the production of the world in all its aspects, without threatening to compromise or dilute either God's divinity or the natures of any of the things in the world.

Interest in both these points—that God produces the whole of the world and that God does so in an immediate way—was fueled by controversies in the early church over the significance of Christ. Take the matter of immediacy. The upshot of these controversies is that Christians want to maintain the closest possible relation between the man Jesus and God: God is identified with Jesus; Jesus is God. And Christians want to say that this God is no inferior or subordinate deity but very God, the one and only highest God. They claim, moreover, that in being so identified, neither the divinity of God nor the humanity of Jesus is compromised. When we are in touch with the man Jesus with the greatest possible physical intimacy (at the time of his existence on earth, grabbing the hem of his garments, receiving his spit on our faces, feeling his touch; or after his death, when drinking and eating of his flesh and blood in a eucharistic meal) we are in touch with God in the highest and with neither a demigod nor a superman.

> The incarnation is therefore the paradigm in a remarkably extreme form of what the Christian doctrine of creation is saying about the immediacy of God's relation to the world, as that follows, we have seen, from the fact that God is beyond kinds.

Although not predictable from the fact of God's creation of the world—the identity between a human being and God is a surprising new level of intimacy between God and the world—the incarnation is therefore the paradigm in a remarkably extreme form of what the Christian doctrine of creation is saying about the immediacy of God's relation to the world, as that follows, we have seen, from the fact that God is beyond kinds. The doctrine of creation when explicated in relation to the doctrine of God helps makes sense of the central Christian affirmations about Christ. If what Christians say about creation makes sense in virtue of God's divinity beyond kinds, then so do the outrageous claims that they make about Christ: Here is God in the flesh! The intimacy of God's relation to a world of suffering, loss, and conflict may not be very apparent. But the most intimate identity of God with the one, Jesus, who saves us out of the world of suffering, violence, and conflict by taking it all on himself, proves God's capacity to be in intimate relations with that sort of world. Christ is the source of our confidence about what we say about God generally: From the very beginning God wishes to be near us, in intimate relation with us. Creation involves an intimate relationship with God on the way to the fulfillment of such relationship in Christ.

The comprehensive character of Christian claims about God's creation of the world is also promoted by Christian interest in making maximal claims for Jesus' significance. Jesus does not come to save a subset of humanity but, in intention if not in fact, to save the whole world—all the nations and the natural world too as it groans, as Paul says, under the powers of affliction and division. And Jesus comes to save the whole world in all its aspects; he brings total liberation, not just spiritual but physical healing, not just the liberation of individuals but of society, starting with the church, not just reconciliation among people but between them and the natural world. There are no irredeemable aspects of the world, which Christians must either flee in order to be saved or simply resign themselves to. God's comprehensive concerns as savior are matched, in short, by God's comprehensive concerns as creator.

The latter, indeed, makes sense of the former: Jesus' range of concern is unlimited because God's range of concern has always been such. As the first few lines of John's Gospel suggest, Jesus does not amount to a *deus ex machina* intervening in a world that is a stranger in most respects to God's designs. God's comprehensive creation of the world—indeed, God the Father's creation of the world through the very Word made flesh in Christ—means that the whole of it has been the object of God's concern from the very beginning. The incarnation simply brings that concern to its culmination and completion in overcoming the forces of sin and death. The sort of divine concern for the world completed in Christ was there from the very beginning when God created a whole world valuable in God's sight, when God looked with love upon all that had been made and declared it very good.

FROM CREATION TO PROVIDENCE

Keeping in mind the comprehensive and immediate character of God's creation of the world and the idea that God is beyond kinds, one can unpack the meaning of God's creation of the world a bit more. Doing so will allow us to draw out the implications of creation for an understanding of God's providence. In fact, explicating the meaning of God's creation of the world is more like excising from that understanding all one's usual presuppositions about productive activity. If God is not a kind of thing, it is not permissible to identify God's creating with any particular kind of agency, operation, or principle of activity to be found in the world. None of those kinds of productive activity, moreover, gives rise to something totally new. The closest that ordinary processes come to this is where a new kind of thing begins to be, in the form of either a new species of thing or a new individual of an existing one. But this kind of production of things as we know it always works on something that already exists, or uses some preexisting stuff in the process, or depends on the cooperation of other productive powers not derived from its own activities.

A productive process employing only the preexisting stuff of its own substance might seem closest to the comprehensive creativeness of God. But what is drawn out of the substance of its cause is similar to it in nature, and the world's relation to a God beyond kinds cannot be like that. Where already existing stuff and cooperative causal agencies have to be presumed, production of something is, moreover, not absolutely immediate, as God's agency is supposed to be; intervening media or processes of production come between a cause and its effect. If the whole of something is brought into existence by God, it is also not appropriate to talk of creation as any sort of change, movement, or process, within what is created. There is nothing to be moved or changed, nothing in which a process could occur, prior to creation, if creation is perfectly comprehensive. Nothing is happening to you in any ordinary sense of the term when you are being created by God. Furthermore, since God's creating is neither instigated by intervening motions (like birth throes or picking up a hammer), nor found within the world of time and change, the temporal progression, the lapse of time, that goes with movement or change is absent from God's creating of the world.

Finally, one should not even think of the creation of the world as a movement or change from a time when nothing existed to a time when everything does (or, for individuals, as a movement from one's nonexistence to existence—for example, at the moment of one's birth). One should think of the world being created by God as it exists, and not in the movement from nothing to something. If the world in its entirety is the creation of God, it is created not simply at its start (assuming it has one) but across the whole time of its existence. Because of the creative activity of God, there never is a time in the world's history when the world does not exist. The movement of the world away from its beginnings does not signal distance from the creative activity of God; it does not mean that the world exists on its own as time goes on, independently of God's action for it as creator.

If the world in its entirety is the creation of God, it is created not simply at its start (assuming it has one) but across the whole time of its existence.

When thinking properly of God's creating the world, one has to exclude, then, all ideas of cooperative agency (in which God would be one among other principles of production), all ideas of intermediate motion or process (God does not do anything to establish a kind of mediating causal bridge between God and the world), all ideas of time and change (nothing is happening in any ordinary sense of the term, as when something is generated or its qualities altered), and all ideas of beginnings in any simple contrast to what comes later. What is left, when all ideas of time, change, and finite process are excised, is the bare idea of a relation of utter dependence on God that holds for the whole world, in every respect, across the whole time of its existence.

What is left, in short, is a very abstract idea, one that might prompt praise and thankfulness—this is certainly a God majestic in giving beyond all comprehension—but one that might seem hardly intelligible. Theologians give the idea of God's creation a more concrete sense through a variety of images—more specifically, by merging in odd ways familiar images of causes of radically different sorts. That odd blending is a way of indicating that God's identity does not abide by the usual contrasts among kinds.

PERSONAL AGENCY OR NATURALISTIC EMANATION

The two images with the widest currency in Christian theology are those of personal agency and naturalistic emanation: God creates the world by intelligence and will as a person would a house, or God creates the world like an overflowing source of water produces a stream or a source of light illumines the air. These images were the most common ones for talking about God's production of the world at the time the Christian doctrine of creation was formulated. Indeed, they were the images favored, respectively, by the two viewpoints Christianity came to oppose: God creates from something—for example, preexisting matter, like a human artificer would create a house from bricks—and the world arises out of the substance of God like heat from a flame or water from a spring; that is, what issues from God becomes progressively less divine the farther it gets from its source. For all their Hellenistic derivations, these are vivid images and rather commonsensical as an exhaustive division of types of causality—intentional agents on the one hand, and natural causes (whether physical or biological) on the other.

> Christian theologians tend to highlight one of these images—personal agency or naturalistic emanation—using the other as a corrective.

Christian theologians tend to highlight one of these images, using the other as a corrective. Thus, one can talk about God as a personal agent creating the world by thinking about what to create and then deciding to do so. This is one model for thinking of the creative action of the Trinity: God the Father creates the world through the Word out of the love that is the Holy Spirit. If one is trying to give concrete expression to the idea of a God beyond kinds who gives rise to the world as a whole, there are several reasons for the appeal of such imagery. First of all, compared with those of natural causes, images of personal agency seem to conform more easily with comprehensiveness. Natural causes seem to have the capacity to give rise to only one sort of thing like themselves (e.g., mares give birth only to horses), while personal agents act according to an intention whose complexity is potentially unlimited: I can choose to build a house, then go to the store, then cook dinner, and so forth.

Second, talking about God's creation of the world in terms of personal agency allows one to display the way in which God is beyond kinds. Unlike talk about natural causes, talk about someone thinking and willing has a peculiar grammatical structure: These verbs have (at least implicitly) clauses for their grammatical objects. Compare "The mare gives birth to a foal" with "I think that John is a rat." "Foal" is the grammatical object in the one case; the clause "that John is a rat" is the other. This grammatical fact brings with it several other odd ones. First, the nouns in the object clause refer to what is being talked about there only under a particular description; and therefore when nouns that describe the same thing differently are substituted, the new sentence may no longer be saying the same thing. So, substituting "the occupant of apartment 2C" for "John," the fact that I think John is a rat does not necessarily mean I think the occupant of apartment 2C is a rat, even if John and that occupant are the same person, since I might not know where John lives. This curiosity brings with it a second. The properties that characterize the thinking and willing need not also characterize what is being talked about in the object clause. So if it is true that I think John is a rat, that does not say anything about whether John is or isn't one—I might be mistaken. Similarly, my thinking him a rat might be necessary because I am such an ill-tempered person, but that suggests nothing about the necessity, or not, of John's being a rat. My thinking so might be petty, but that says nothing about the pettiness of John's being a rat. My act of thinking may be simple and single, without what I am thinking about—the whole complex lot of John's rat-like qualities—being so. And so on.

As the last examples make clear, these grammatical features do not depend on the ignorance of the one doing the thinking (or on the impotence of the one willing, in examples I have not provided) and therefore are not essentially unsuitable for use when talking about God. When so applied to God's creating the world, they display the idea of a God beyond kinds. Following these grammatical features in this new theological use, one sees that the world need not be like or unlike the God who intentionally brings it into existence. The character of God's thinking and willing by which the world is brought to be implies nothing either way about the character of the world, about the character of what God intends to bring into existence.

Other aspects, however, of talk about God's creating the world by acts of thinking and willing have to be severely modified in order to bring that way of speaking into conformity with the comprehensiveness and immediacy of God's creative activity. In doing so, such imagery is brought very close to imagery of natural causes such as fire and light. Thus, contrary to the comprehensiveness of God's creative activity, personal agents always work with materials they do not produce. To build a house, I need bricks and tools. I might make the bricks and tools too, but in order to do so, I require mud for the bricks, and metal and fire to forge the tools, and so on. The agency of fire or light is more serviceable here since fire and light seem (at least to the untutored eye) to be self-sufficient in their activity of heating or illuminating, apparently working even without substantial media to be heated or illumined, or without the need for outside implements.

Moreover, contrary to the immediacy of God's working, personal agents need to take additional steps to bring into existence what they think about and decide to do. If I think about the sort of house I want and decide to build it, the building of it still remains to be done. In order to avoid the suggestion of intervening action, one would have to say that acts of thinking and willing, which have no external effects in the case of humans, have such effects when God is the agent. The closest analogue again would be the way natural processes such as fire and sunlight produce their effects immediately, without needing to do anything and without any intervening process, just by being themselves.

In order to avoid suggesting that God creates through processes involving time and change—by beginning and ending, stopping and starting, in successive acts—one could extend this idea that God does not have to do anything in creating the world to God's even having to make a decision. God creates simply by being what God always is—the God who wants to create the world. If that is God's intention, it always was God's intention; God never came to so decide after a period of indecision. Again, the sun illuminating the air and fire heating things up would seem close analogues: Fire does not come to be what it needs to be in order to heat things up; it is always already in act, throwing off heat.

> God creates simply by being what God always is—the God who wants to create the world—but we need to retain something of the language of deliberation.

Something of the language of deliberation would still have to be retained here, however. Unlike what the cases of fire and light suggest, one should not say that God's intention to create the world is part of God's very nature; God may always intend to create the world, but this is by no necessity of nature. What needs to be retained of the idea of deliberation is the simple idea of a nonnecessary relation between God's being and nature, on the one hand, and God's intention to create the world, on the other. From God's existence and nature one cannot infer with any logical necessity that God intends to create the world. Even if God never doesn't intend to create the world, God didn't have to so intend. Without this free character of intention, the necessity of God bleeds over onto the character of the world, in violation of the idea that God is beyond kinds, neither like nor unlike anything in the world or the world as a whole. If God's nature meant that God had to intend to create the world, then a similar "had to be" must also characterize the existence of the world (assuming that God's intentions cannot be frustrated!).

Finally, personalistic imagery for God's creating might suggest that the world is not equally the creation of God over its whole course, in much the way a house gains independence from its builder once built. Here again a better analogue might be found among natural causes, specifically in the relationship between a natural cause and those of its effects that lack the capacity to retain the properties communicated to them. Air, for example, does not have the ability to remain illuminated apart from the constant shining of a light source.

Other theologians prefer naturalistic imagery. We have already seen some of the positive reasons for its appeal: the way it helps avoid the ideas of creation out of preexisting stuff, of mediating process, temporal change, and narrow associations with the first moment of something's existence. These theologians think the deficits of such language are not very serious and can be remedied through the use, for example, of personal imagery. Thus, images of fire and light need not imply that God's substance is parceled out to created things, or somehow thinned out to make them, like a thin stream from an overflowing basin of water or like a wave of heat from a much hotter stove. It can instead be thought of as a materially discontinuous imitation of the whole in an entirely different medium—less like the rays from the sun and more like a painted picture or photographic image of the sun itself. The world is not, then, quasi-divine; it is the distinctly nondivine reflection of God's own being and beauty. One could argue, moreover, that natural causes are no more limited in the range of their effects than intentional agents are. Fire, for example, can melt bronze or harden mud or make water evaporate.

Finally, natural causes are such because of their superabundance, and this suggests a kind of freedom to their working despite the fact that they must do what they do: Fire must give off heat, and the sun must shine. They do not act out of need; they have in a more perfect form anything that they might achieve by giving rise to light or heat outside themselves. So the triune God has in the divine superabundant life the perfect form of communicated good in the way the three persons of the Trinity give of their own good to one another in perfect equality. God must communicate the goodness of God's own nature outside God in creating a world that is not God; to do so is God's very nature in the way it is fire's nature to give off heat into its surroundings. But this is a free act, since God already has in God's own intra-Trinitarian life the perfect form of self-diffusing good, the perfect form of anything that God might hope to achieve in creating a good but nondivine world. One can talk then of this natural act of creating in personal terms; it is an act of generosity, an unforced demonstration of regard for the other, a gracious exhibition of concern for the good of others.

GOD, PROVIDENCE, AND THE WORLD

With this understanding of creation in hand, one can see how providence is implied by it. Talk of God's providence is just a way of singling out certain features of the world that God creates. If the world is created by God in all its respects, the world is being created by God as things within it act and form arrangements and move toward new ones, by way of natural and human causes. The activity, organization, and historical directionality of the world are all aspects of the world God creates; God gives rise to those aspects of the world as to every other. Since creation is not identified with the beginning of the world (should it have one) but means that the world is being held up into being at all times, the world's processes, and the arrangements of things they produce, are all included in what God creates. The world is the creation of God from start to finish, throughout the whole of natural and human history, and throughout each created cause's course, from its beginning to act through its achievement of effects.

Providence refers to God's plan for the world but also to the way it is executed in a world that has its own powers of activity. By bringing into being a world with such powers, God gives the world a hand in the execution of God's plan; the world is made the partner of that plan, in stronger and weaker senses across the world's history—whether the world's creatures do so by natural instinct or by choice, and whether we do so as Christ does by a will aligned with God or as sinners and those ignorant of God's plans. The doctrines of God and creation reveal certain general features about how the plan is being executed—as that plan comes to fruition in Christ and elsewhere.

Because God is the creator of the world in all its respects, God does not need to replace the activities of creatures with God's own in order to achieve God's ends.

For example, because God is the creator of the world in all its respects, God does not need to replace the activities of creatures with God's own in order to achieve God's ends. God can instead give rise to the very powers and acts of creatures that further those ends. Nor do those actions of creatures replace the need for God's activity as creator; without God's holding of them into existence, such acts would not exist. As everywhere, so in a special way in Christ: God does not save us by replacing the human capacities of Jesus with God's own; God saves in and through the very human acts by which Jesus lives and dies. God works everywhere in and through creatures, while their activities remain their own (for better or worse)—fully finite and fully fallible.

Because God is beyond kinds, God does not carry out God's plans by entering into the world, as one kind of force among others, whether regularly or by spasmodic intervention. God is not the name of one kind of force or principle—say, creativity or a principle of novelty—operating within the world. God is not working alongside us, doing one part of the work that needs to be done while the world does another. Instead, God, as creator, is responsible for the working of the whole. Nor does God enter into the world after the fact, after the workings of the world are done, to coerce or redirect it. Because God brings them to be and holds them up into existence, God doesn't work on or from the outside of causes operating independently of God, in imitation of the way limited creatures have to coerce or redirect matters that preexist their activity.

Nor does God need creatures of any particular sort to achieve God's ends within the world. Remembering the complexities of language of intentional agency helps us to see how the characteristics of God's own planning imply nothing, one way or another, about the world God brings about to execute it. God's plans, for example, are by definition purposeful, but that need not mean that the contents of God's plans for the world include the creation of purposeful agents any more than my plan to hit a bull's-eye requires execution by an arrow with the same end in mind. God may be working in the world for our good out of the goodness of God's heart, but that does not mean that the world is.

The same loose relation with created causes of any particular sort follows from the immediacy of God's agency. Because God's creative powers extend to everything that happens in an equally direct fashion, what God wants to happen is not mediated by the activities of the creatures that carry it out in the strong way that, say, my wanting a submarine to be raised from the ocean bottom is mediated by the workings of heavy lifting equipment. (If that equipment is faulty or its operator has other plans, I'm in trouble!) Unlike the case of creatures bringing about effects through the workings of others, God's creative activity extends directly to everything and not indirectly to some things by way only of their causes. Created causes are not the means by which God brings into existence the effects of those causes, since the whole of those causes, their workings, and effects are the result of God's creative activity. Picture the whole world, in all its complexity of causal process, as a horizontal plane, suspended into existence, at each and every point, by the vertical threads (invisible and infinitesimal) of God's own working, and you will begin to see the sense this all makes.

God's creative activity extends directly to everything that happens, whether or not, therefore, sufficient created causes exist for those happenings or whatever the character of the causes that exist—whether they work purposely or blindly, accidentally or necessarily, and so forth. God can bring about what creatures, of their own powers, cannot, just as, beyond all human capacity, Christ's human powers for living and dying save us from sin and death. God does not have to make creatures the partners of God's plans; God might do without their powers altogether. God does not have to save us, for example, by becoming incarnate—God could, one supposes, simply destroy sin and death by fiat—but

Picture the whole world, in all its complexity of causal process, as a horizontal plane, suspended into existence, at each and every point, by the vertical threads (invisible and infinitesimal) of God's own working, and you will begin to see the sense this all makes.

freely chooses to make human nature in Christ the partner of the process. God can make do with partners in only the weakest sense of that term—with creatures who work not at all, or blindly and without foresight, or with malice of intention. But as shown in Christ, God can also work with the full gamut of created causes, such as with the natural process of dying, willingly entered into by a man whose acts were in knowing conformity with God's, violently achieved through the ignorance and sin of everyone around him—Romans, his own people, and his chosen apostles.

Understanding God's providence in these ways—in light of Christian teachings about God and creation—protects against the idea of a God whose concerns are limited, a God who demands that creatures bend in submission to a tyrannical, inescapable will, a God who must fear frustration by the failure of creatures to match the characteristics of God's own will. But only in Christ is any of this known for sure. In Christ it becomes clear: The plan is one of steadfast, unbreakable love for the whole of what God has created, a plan executed in and through the throes of a life like any other in its humanity, a life that sees the death to which all creatures come, hastened by violent sufferings wrought by the misguided, shortsighted acts of even those closest to him—the self-chosen disciples of his own mission of love. It is by that death, worked in that way, that Jesus saves. If, then, this same God holds up into existence a whole world with these flaws of both finitude and deliberate failing, it must be as an act of beneficent mercy, in which we may trust.

QUESTIONS FOR REFLECTION AND DISCUSSION

1. What do the creation stories in Genesis imply about God's relation to the world? About our relation to the environment?
2. What is the "problem of evil" in theology? What are some traditional responses to it? What are strengths and weaknesses of each?
3. What problems does McFague identify in the traditional creation myth?
4. McFague offers a number of models of the relation of God and world. What are strengths and weaknesses of each?
5. Tanner proposes that God is not a kind of thing at all. What does that mean? What implications does it have for the relation of God and the world?
6. Tanner contrasts personal agency and naturalistic emanation as models of creation. What are strengths and weaknesses of each?
7. How does each of these authors relate creation to Christology?

FOR FURTHER READING

Gilkey, Langdon. *Maker of Heaven and Earth.* Garden City, N.Y.: Doubleday and Co., 1959.

Griffin, David Ray. *God, Power, and Evil: A Process Theodicy.* Philadelphia: Westminster Press, 1976.

Helm, Paul. *The Providence of God.* Leicester: Inter-Varsity, 1993.

Kaiser, Christopher B. *Creation and the History of Science.* Grand Rapids: Wm. B. Eerdmans Publishing Co., 1991.

McFague, Sallie. *The Body of God: An Ecological Theology.* Minneapolis: Fortress Press, 1993.

Moltmann, Jürgen. *God in Creation.* Trans. Margaret Kohl. San Francisco: Harper and Row, 1985.

Overman, Richard. *Evolution and the Christian Doctrine of Creation.* Philadelphia: Westminster Press, 1967.

Soelle, Dorothee. *To Work and to Love.* Philadelphia: Fortress Press, 1984.

Tanner, Kathryn. *God and Creation in Christian Theology.* Oxford: Basil Blackwell, 1988.

Teilhard de Chardin, Pierre. *The Phenomenon of Man.* Trans. Bernard Wall. New York: Harper and Row, 1959.

Ward, Keith. *God, Chance and Necessity.* Oxford: One World, 1996.

Chapter 4

What's Wrong with Us?

Human Nature and Human Sin

CREATURES MADE IN THE IMAGE OF GOD

As the last chapter indicated, Christians believe that *everything* is part of God's good creation and under God's providential care. But human beings are somehow special—special in our relation with God and in our relations with the rest of creation. Theologians have often talked about the distinctive character of human beings by saying that we are "creatures made in the image of God"—*creatures,* and therefore not God, but *made in God's image,* and therefore different from all other creatures. Like many of the ideas central to Christian accounts of human beings, this language comes from the stories in the opening chapters of Genesis. From Origen in the third century to a large number of contemporary theologians, many who have reflected on these stories have not taken them as literal history but have nevertheless found in them profound truths about what it means to be human.

Consider first "the image of God." Genesis 1:26 declares that God made human beings "in our image, according to our likeness." A long tradition sought to distinguish between "image" and "likeness," sometimes arguing that in sin we lose the likeness of God but keep the image. Biblical scholars today, however, mostly think these terms just represent the kind of repetition characteristic of ancient Hebrew style, and we should not try to make distinctions between them.

Uniquely, then, of all the things God created, human beings are made in God's "image and likeness." This surely does not mean that we physically look like God, though Augustine and some others did see a connection between the "image of God" and the fact that we stand upright and can therefore look up to heaven rather than having our heads down facing the earth.[1] More often, however, theologians have identified the "image" with one or more of the following:

1. Human beings have reason and free will. Plants and animals simply live out what they are created to be. We have the capacity to step back, think about our place in the world, and decide what we want to make of our lives. In that capacity to think and decide, we are a bit like God.

2. God put us in charge of the rest of the world, giving us "dominion" over it (Gen. 1:26); in that sense, we are God's representatives and viceroys. God gave us a world "to till it and keep it" (Gen. 2:15; the Hebrew translated as "keep" has connotations of "care for"). Our "dominion" gives us responsibilities to tend and look after a world which, after all, is ultimately God's. The language of "dominion" has sometimes provided the excuse for pillaging the world around us, and some contemporary theologians reject the implication that we humans stand in any sort of superiority to other creatures. Yet today more than ever, human beings do have the power to preserve, damage, or even destroy the whole world in which we live. We might as well be honest about our responsibilities.

3. We have the capacity to be in a conscious relationship with God, and that relationship makes us like God.

4. Our relationships with one another (Karl Barth thought the relations between men and women in particular,[2] though other theologians disagree) are analogous to the relationships of love among the persons of the Trinity.

It is striking that most of these models emphasize an idea also prominent in contemporary philosophy and psychology: that human beings are human only in relationships. The solitary individual—the wolf-raised child, or a Robinson Crusoe who was born on his desert island—cannot be fully human. Just as God is God in the relations among the persons of the Trinity, so humanness involves relatedness—to other humans, to our environment, to God.

> Human beings are made in the image of God, but we are also creatures; we are not God.

However one describes this "image of God" in human beings, Christians believe that we understand it best by looking not to ourselves but to Christ. The rest of us, after all, have failed to be human in the way God meant us to be. Jesus was the only human being who got being human right.

We are made in the image of God, then, but we are also creatures; we are not God:

> Yet you made them a little lower than God,
> and crowned them with glory and honor.
> You have given them dominion over the works of your hands. (Ps. 8:5–6)

And yet:

> As for mortals, their days are like grass;
> they flourish like a flower of the field;
> for the wind passes over it, and it is gone. (Ps. 103:15–16)

God is infinite; we are finite and exist only because God made us.

Does that mean that we are meant to live only a finite time? Christian theologians have long debated whether, in the Genesis story, Adam and Eve were originally made to die, or death came in only as a consequence of sin. The twentieth-century American theologian Reinhold Niebuhr (whose analysis I am following in much of this introduction) was right, I think, to conclude that, while Paul did sometimes understand death as a punishment for sin, the dominant biblical view is that God made us to have a finite span, and there is nothing wrong with death.[3] In the garden of Eden story, God warns Adam, concerning the tree of the knowledge of good and evil, "in the day that you eat of it you shall die" (Gen. 2:17). That makes immediate death sound like a punishment, but it leaves open the question of whether Adam might have died later, even if he had not sinned. And it leaves open the question of whether "death" means physical death or some kind of spiritual self-destruction.

Certainly when the Hebrew patriarchs lived long and rich lives and then died surrounded by their descendants and with every expectation of being long remembered, the Bible does not seem to imply that such a death is an evil. Having a limited time in our lives seems just part of what it means to be human. Because we have finite life spans, our choices matter. I do not have infinite time to try out one career after another, one long-term relationship after another. That seems so much a part of the pattern of our existence that it is hard to imagine humans created to live forever. Perhaps then it is the fear of death, rather than death itself, that sin brings on us.

A generation or two ago, scientists would have dismissed as silly such theological questions about whether humans are meant to die; we are obviously mortal animals, they would have said. Now, however, science raises the possibility of keeping us alive more or less indefinitely, and we have to think seriously about whether this is something we should welcome. To say that we are creatures is certainly to affirm that we are finite in some ways. We owe our very being to God. To pretend that we are infinite, or to say that we are masters of our own fates, is to deny our creatureliness and pretend that we are God.

> Having a limited time in our lives may thus not be a consequence of sin, but part of what it means to be human.

If death seems one of the realities of

being human, another biological fact about human beings, of course, is that we generally come in two sexes. The writers of Genesis knew all about this:

> So God created humankind in his image,
> in the image of God he created them;
> male and female he created them. (Gen. 1:27)

This passage from the first creation story presented in Genesis pictures male and female as created together and equal. The older garden of Eden story which follows has the man created first and the woman made out of one of his ribs, to be "a helper as his partner" (Gen. 2:18). The contrast betweeen "helper" and "partner" raises issues that also come up elsewhere in the text. The woman is not only created later, but is then the first to fall victim to the serpent's temptations. (Of course, one can argue that, in a story where humans are created last, those created later are superior—and that, in the temptation story, the woman is at least active, while the man never takes any initiative at all!)

These and other biblical passages provided the occasion for a long and sad history of the denigration of women in Christian theology. Some theologians held that women were not really human.[4] In all sorts of more subtle ways, theologians have often taken men as the standard model of what it is to be human, with women as somehow an exception to the rule, a deviation from the norm. It is clear enough that we need to get beyond such attitudes, though debates continue about how to do it. Should we affirm that men and women are, in all theologically important ways, really the same? Or should we say that they are different, but not in ways that imply either is superior to the other?

In his essay for this chapter, Clark Williamson argues for the importance of respecting those who are truly different from ourselves and criticizes Christians who think of men as better than women or heterosexuals as better than homosexuals. What should be central to Christian faith, he argues, is our equality before God.

Christians who argue that homosexual activity is a sin usually make either or both of two kinds of arguments. (These arguments for the sinfulness of *activities* do not, it is worth noting, condemn feelings or inclinations.) One sort of argument appeals to a number of biblical texts that seem to condemn sexual intercourse between people of the same sex. The other rests on philosophical claims about what is natural, insisting that same-sex intercourse is unnatural. Williamson reviews the commonly cited biblical texts and argues that their meaning is at least more ambiguous than is often acknowledged. He also raises hard questions about traditional interpretations of human nature.

Debates about these issues, of course, bitterly divide many denominations today. Some thoughtful scholars take positions opposite those of Williamson. The best arguments on both sides do seem to show that issues about homosexuality cannot be settled easily or in isolation; for Christians they relate to questions about how we interpret the Bible and how we understand what it means to be human. Theologians addressing the latter question have described human beings not only as creatures made in God's image but also as combinations of body and soul.

BODY AND SOUL

Some ancient Greek philosophers, such as Plato, thought of the body as something evil from which the soul should struggle to escape. It happened that the Greek words for body (*soma*) and prison (*sema*) were very close, and this encouraged images of the soul's escape.[5] The Bible rejects such a view. It talks about human "bodies," "souls," and "spirits," but it assumes that all these aspects of humanity are created by God, are good, and therefore are not to be discarded or escaped. Today we often think of the soul as some ghostlike substance that lies within us, and we wonder if there is room for souls in a world defined by modern science. Before casting the concept out, however, we need to learn more about how it has actually been used in Christian theology (more of that in a minute). After all, there is a double reality in being human: the chemistry and physics of muscles and brains, and the experience of what it feels like to be in pain, understand the answer, fall in love. The language of *soul* or *spirit* may offer one way of talking about the latter.

In Hebrew the word we translate as *soul* initially meant "throat" or "gullet." *Spirit* relates to words for "wind" or "breath." Roughly speaking, *spirit* was the principle of life that came from God, and *soul* the principle within the individual that was brought to life by spirit—though both terms were used in a variety of ways.

Throughout most of the history of ancient Israel, most people assumed that, when we die, we cease to exist; the breath goes out of us. Toward the end of the Old Testament period, however, in the midst of political and social chaos, Jews grew less confident that a good person could count on a rich life and many children. They began to hope for some sort of life after death, so that those treated unfairly in this life could be appropriately rewarded or punished, but that hope generally took the form of believing in the resurrection of the body, not the soul's escape from it. Paul talks about being raised a "spiritual body" (1 Cor. 15:44)—a notoriously unclear phrase that implies something different from the kind of body we have now—but he is still hoping for *bodily* resurrection at the end of the present age.

Many early Christian theologians, influenced by Plato, began to turn more toward hopes for the soul. In the early third century, Origen even argued that our souls preexist; our bodily birth is simply the entry into this world of a soul which has already existed.[6] Most theologians rejected that point of view, but they could not agree on whether the soul comes into being through sexual intercourse (*traducianism*—from a Latin word meaning "propagate") or is created by God in a special act (*creationism*—not to be confused with the creationism of modern biblical fundamentalists). Tertullian was a traducianist; Ambrose was a creationist.

Augustine seems to have been unable to make up his mind.[7] Whatever their views on the soul's origin, however, theologians were trying to bring together two very real Christian hopes: a hope for bodily resurrection at the time of Christ's return, and a hope of entering God's presence as soon as we die. (Had not Christ promised one of the thieves who shared his crucifixion, "Today you will be with me in Paradise" [Luke 23:43]?)

Theologians were trying to bring together two very real Christian hopes: a hope for bodily resurrection at the time of Christ's return, and a hope of entering God's presence as soon as we die.

When Aquinas, in the thirteenth century, began to base theology on Aristotle rather than Plato, that made a difference for the understanding of souls. Aristotle had been a biologist as well as a philosopher. Unlike his teacher Plato, he thought the body was an essential part of the human being. By *soul* he meant the way the body is organized or put together to make it alive.[8] He thought animals and even plants had souls, and that human souls came to an end at death. After all, if the soul was the way a living body was organized, it could hardly survive the body's death. He did think, however, that one part of the soul, the active intellect, the part which thinks, was not tied to any bodily activity, and so it could survive death.

When we die, Aquinas said, at least this part of our soul goes to be with and to contemplate God; it is that contemplation of the triune God that is our highest blessedness. But a human soul has "a natural aptitude and a natural tendency to embodiment,"[9] and so our souls are incomplete until reunited with bodies in the final resurrection. Thus, he combined these two traditional hopes. The combination, however, generated some interesting debates in the fourteenth century, when people began to wonder what more, if we are already contemplating God, our souls would really require from a body in order to be blessed. If a disembodied soul can perfectly contemplate God, what's the big deal about bodily resurrection?[10] Other debates about these matters continued into the Reformation: Luther thought we simply go to sleep when we die and awake at the resurrection; Calvin believed we begin to experience God's presence as soon as we die. The tension between hoping to be with God at our death and hoping for resurrection when Jesus returns has never disappeared from the Christian tradition; this is a theme to which the final chapter of this book will return.

SIN

So far I have been discussing human beings as we were created and meant to be. One of the important features of the garden of Eden story in Genesis is that it distinguishes *created* humanity from *sinful* humanity. Even if we no longer believe that story as history, it helps to remind us that we should not say, "Well, it is human nature that we are selfish," or "These evils are just part of human nature." Sin comes later in the story; it is not part of human nature as created.

In describing the sin of Adam and Eve, Genesis offers a profound image of the nature of human sin. Given nearly all the riches of the garden to enjoy, they could not resist eating from the one forbidden tree. It was the very fact that it had been forbidden that drew them on. What made their act a sin? Theologians have usually identified its sinfulness as either disobedience or pride. What was wrong with eating the fruit was, first, simply that God had told them not to do it. Second, in disobeying God, they pridefully put themselves in God's place, denying their proper role as God's creatures.

Reinhold Niebuhr developed a helpful analysis of how human nature as created generates the conditions of sin's possibility. If we were simply made in the image of God, he said, then we would be free of temptation. If we were simply finite creatures, we would live out our instincts as animals do. But we are both. Our freedom in the image of God means we can choose among infinite possibilities; our finitude leaves us anxious about the consequences of our choices. If we were truly faithful, we would trust totally in God's love for us, and our anxiety would not lead to sin. But we are not, and so we cannot live comfortably as we are. Either (in the sin Niebuhr called *pride*) we try to deny our finitude and pretend we are all-knowing, all-powerful—in short, God—or (in the sin Niebuhr called *sensuality* and Karl Barth called *sloth*) we deny our freedom and submerge ourselves in finitude, refusing to take charge of our lives.[11] Either way, we sin.

Either (in the sin Niebuhr called *pride*) we try to deny our finitude and pretend we are God, or (in the sin Niebuhr called *sensuality* and Karl Barth called *sloth*) we deny our freedom and submerge ourselves in finitude.

We are responsible for our sin, but at the same time we are somehow victims of the force of sin. In the Genesis story, prior to the sin of the human beings, there is this wily serpent there to tempt them—though the serpent is also identified as a creature and thus made by God. The Christian tradition continued to develop its understanding of the consequences of that first sin. Throughout most of Christian history most theologians believed that Adam and Eve were historical characters and that all their descendants have inherited the penalty of their "original sin." Augustine, who first developed this idea in detail, held that Adam was originally free to sin or not to sin but chose sin.[12] Further, "Through the bad will of that one man all sinned in him."[13] As a result, we no longer have the freedom not to sin. In the shame with which Adam and Eve covered their genitals with fig leaves, Augustine found his explanation: Sin turns love to lust, and thereby the sexual intercourse by which each of us is conceived passes down that inheritance of original sin.[14]

As modern theologians came to doubt the historical reality of Adam and Eve and grew nervous about the negative picture of sexuality implied in the Augustinian account, most still acknowledged something true about the doctrine of original sin. We do all seem trapped in an inability to avoid sinning. It became common, though, to talk about sin as something humans all share without attributing it to biological inheritance. Going further, the eighteenth-century philosopher Immanuel Kant attributed a radical evil to human nature without tying it at all to a historical Adam and Eve.[15] The nineteenth-century liberal German theologian Albrecht Ritschl and American social gospel theologians such as Walter Rauschenbusch said that original sin meant simply the way in which everyone born into a corrupt society would naturally pick up aspects of its corruption.[16] In their essays for this chapter, both Serene Jones and Clark Williamson develop that idea in a direction that takes the reality of the force of sin with full seriousness. Other theologians, however, have moved toward implying that we could avoid sin if we just tried harder.

In recent decades, feminist theologians and others have objected to the traditional focus on the sin of pride. In our society, they argue, men have generally been taught to be too aggressive, too self-centered. They need to be urged to be more selfless. Women, on the other hand, have often been conditioned not to be "selfish" enough—to spend their lives so serving parents, husbands, and children that they fail to develop the gifts God has given them. A sermon denouncing pride leads them even more in the wrong direction they were already heading.[17] Christian theologians had already developed categories for a sin opposite to pride. As already noted, Reinhold Niebuhr wrote of "sensuality," in which we try to escape from our full humanness.[18] Karl Barth spoke of "sloth," the sin of failing to wake up to what God has called us to be.[19] The contemporary American theologian Susan Dunfee and others talk about the "sin of hiding," referring to the moment in the story of the garden when Adam and Eve hide from God—a good metaphor for women (or men) hiding from their own God-given potentials.[20]

Liberation theologians today, writing out of contexts of social oppression, like social gospel theologians several generations ago, have offered another critique of traditional discussions of sin. Too often, they say, those discussions have focused on the sins we commit as individuals, in our private roles, rather than our public, institutional sins. A Christian business executive will in the morning lay off a thousand employees without a qualm to increase profits slightly, and then feel guilty about getting a little drunk that night. Do we not often do far more harm in approving pollution or standing silent in the face of bigotry than in many of the actions in our private lives that first come to mind when we use the word *sin?*[21] To say that is not to deny the seriousness of some personal sins but to expand our thinking about the nature of sin.

Reinhold Niebuhr once remarked that original sin is the only doctrine in Christian theology decisively proven by empirical evidence. Well—maybe not quite. It is only in the light of Christ that we fully understand the extent of our sin. Still, just looking around the world does remind us how badly the wonderful gifts of human nature get misused and distorted. In the end, however, sin is not the most important thing to say about us humans. The renegade Southern

Baptist preacher Will Campbell was once asked to summarize Christian belief in ten words or less. He did it like this: "We're no damn good, but God loves us anyway."[22] The last word about human beings, like the first, is that God loves us.

SERENE JONES

Human nature is one of the most rewarding yet challenging topics I teach theology students year after year. However diverse my students, they all share deep and earnest questions about the meaning of their lives—what Christian faith has to say about human life, its ultimate purpose, and its most fundamental character. Even more pointedly, they want to know what it means to be a human being living in our present day and age, why the world seems so messed up, and how they might learn how to be human in the "right way" as opposed to the harmful ways they see around them and find within them.

I enjoy explaining to these students that not only in Scripture but also in the works of many of the tradition's major theologians they can find insights into their questions. Although they would not initially call it this, my students have stepped squarely into an arena of religious reflection called *theological anthropology.* I explain to them that not only in our church's doctrines, liturgies, and sacraments, but also in the daily patterns and practices of living the church teaches—practices such as praying to and praising God, singing, tithing, caring for others, honoring their bodies, welcoming strangers, and advocating social justice—they can find resources for sorting out their many questions about human nature.[1]

In this essay, I will share some of the themes that have emerged in our conversations. As I hope to make clear in the pages ahead, the doctrine of the human person, or theological anthropology, is a puzzling and ambiguous enterprise, offering few firm answers but more often a series of guiding insights that, if embraced and embodied, will orient one toward God, oneself, and one's neighbor in a particular way—the way of life abundant as revealed in Jesus Christ.[2] In that way of life, human persons know themselves, first and foremost, as those who, along with all of humanity, stand in the light of God's unceasing gracious love.

I have referred to this topic as the "doctrine of the human person." Throughout history, theologians have offered a number of different definitions of *doctrine.* I find it most helpful—and, I hope, faithful—to say that *doctrine* refers to the collection of beliefs that shape how we view a particular topic in Christian theology. When the topic is humanity, those beliefs comprise what we understand to be the deepest truths about what it means to be a person, truths opened to us in Christian Scripture and passed down to us through the living traditions of our communities of faith.[3]

It is easy to think of these beliefs as simply a series of straightforward statements or propositional truth claims that one is required to respond to with either a yes or no. I think it is more complicated than that. Think of your imagination—and by *imagination* I mean not just fantasy but the whole realm of conscious and unconscious thought processes that you use to make sense of your world—as a grand theater, a theater in which you find a variety of props, landscapes, scenery, abstract images, and, of course, a center stage where dramas are enacted and stories unfolded. Now think of *Christian doctrine* as a description of the theater of imagination within which Christians stand as they interpret their world and give shape to their thoughts and actions. This image suggests that our belief systems are not just ideas we espouse but rather spaces in which we live and move. Learning a set of doctrines means more than memorizing a set of statements; it involves receiving a whole array of stage props and scripts that shape how we interpret and participate in the ongoing story of our lives as we see them unfolding in the grand theater of God's continuing relationship with the world.[4]

Think of *Christian doctrine* as a description of the theater of imagination within which Christians stand as they interpret their world and give shape to their thoughts and actions.

As in any dramatic production, we never just repeat the doctrinal scripts we are given. Rather, we inevitably enact our roles with personal flair and create scenery that looks like our familiar surroundings. We improvise and create even as we realize that the scripts we have been given perform us as much as we perform them.[5] It is not difficult to extrapolate from this dramatic metaphor to an understanding of theological anthropology. Take our struggles with questions such as: Who am I? Why is the world so messed up and confusing? How can I become a good person in the midst of the mess? Might we view the Christian doctrine of the human person as a kind of dramatic production we are invited to participate in, to take up its roles and perform its motions as we grapple with these questions?

When we turn to Scripture and tradition and begin exploring the principal features of this "drama of the self," we do not find a single, coherent, monolithic account of humanity. Instead, we encounter several stories, each with its own plotline, stage props, and background scenery. These stories about humanity—I like to think of them as "dramatic portraits"—can be divided roughly into four groups. There is (1) the story of human beings as wondrously earthy creatures of a creator who calls them into covenant relation; (2) the story of a humanity that turns away from the covenant relation with God and falls into sin; (3) the story of humanity as it is redeemed by God who, in Jesus Christ, justifies and sanctifies the sinner; and (4) the story of human beings who anticipate a promised future in which their communion with God is perfected. In the familiar language of our liturgy, these are four portraits of humans as *creatures, sinners, forgiven saints,* and *recipients of life eternal.* A comprehensive picture of our nature is impossible without some reference to all four pictures, but in this essay I will focus on the first two, since other authors will address the last two in the chapters on the Christian life, Christology, and eschatology.[6]

It is tempting to take these four portraits and string them together into a single story that begins with creation, moves on to the fall, and ends with an account of redemption and consummation. I caution against doing this too quickly. I find it more true to the biblical and doctrinal tradition to see these portraits as four dramas that are being enacted, simultaneously and ongoingly, in the life of every person and every community.

> Scripture and tradition offer stories of human beings as creatures, as sinners, as redeemed, and as anticipating a common future.

That may seem frustrating to those who like simple stories and simple answers to complicated questions. I find, however, that many people today have aesthetic sensibilities that are more postmodern than modern and daily encounter a staggering number of enticing media accounts of who they are and what they should become. For them, these four dramatic portraits present a multilayered account of the self that is complex enough to hold their complicated questions and multiple experiences and yet also simple enough to be performed, with varying degrees of mastery, in the course of their everyday lives. What does such a performance look like? Let us turn to each of the stories and explore the theater of faith's imagination into which they invite us.

HUMAN BEINGS AS CREATURES OF GOD

Students look at me with rather puzzled faces when I tell them, "You are beloved creatures of God." The word *creature* conjures up images of animal-like beings crawling around in a teeming, earthy environment. *Of God* adds the figure of a divine creator to the picture. *Beloved* then suggests that these creeping animals are precious to this God to whom they belong. What a strange portrait to have as a grounding image of humanity.

Yet just this picture captures the central features of the first story Christians tell about humanity. Who or what are we? We are embodied, earthbound, material, living creatures who are created by and belong to a God who loves us dearly and seeks to be in relation with us. Embedded in this image of our creatureliness are at least seven claims about how we should understand human nature, each with important implications for how we think about the numerous other stories of the self told by the cultures in which we live.

First, Christians assert that *all of us, as human beings, exist only by virtue of God's decision to call us into being,* a decision that God freely makes. God's will is to give us into life, to create us out of nothing. To be a human being is to be a gift of God; we exist in the space of a continued act of divine giving. Once we recognize the importance of this claim, we can never again imagine humanity without simultaneously seeing the One who actively gives us life. Moreover, once we see our human nature given to us or bestowed upon us, we can no longer imagine that our existence is accidental or that we are rootless, free floating, or radically autonomous. A gracious divine act defines the space in which we live.

> (1) All of us, as human beings, exist only by virtue of God's decision to call us into being. (2) God considers this graciously created humanity to be good just as it is.

Second, the Christian story of human nature claims that *God considers this graciously created humanity to be good, just as it is.* Whatever else we might say about humanity, human beings are, at the most fundamental level, marvelous and wonderful. We often struggle with the feeling that we are basically bad or that our lives have negative value. Even worse, we sometimes feel we simply have no value at all, that life is a "tale told by an idiot, full of sound and fury, signifying nothing."[7] Christian faith tells us to think differently: The founding word about who we are is that we are good.

Intimately tied to the two claims that human existence is both graciously given and good is a third: When God calls humanity into being, *God creates a reality fundamentally different from God, and in this difference, God delights.* As creatures we are distinguishable from our creator. Our goodness does not rest in our being identical with God but in our created differentiation from God. We are not a piece or part of God, like an arm or leg or even a thought of the Divine. Nor are we simply shadows or reflections of God. We are creatures who inhabit our own—albeit given—reality. We exist in an economy of relation marked by the radical difference of the two parties involved. We are not God; we are human beings. And here is the difficult part: This difference is not to be understood as a negative judgment against us. On the contrary, differentiated boundedness is a fundamentally positive feature of our humanity.

> (3) God creates a reality fundamentally different from God. (4) God seeks a relationship with us. (5) To be the wondrous creature to whom God relates is to be an embodied, material, sensual, temporal, social being.

Fourth, however, the God who makes us different from God does not just create us and turn away. Remarkably, God does just the opposite: *God seeks a relationship with us and gives us, in turn, the capacity to be responsive to God.* To be a human being is to be a creature who is profoundly relational, responsive, open, and oriented toward a divinity who is relational, responsive, open, and oriented toward her. This relationality is one of fluid, interactive, effective movement between the two parties, and that fluid openness significantly qualifies my prior image of two parties marked by their bounded differentiation from one another. While we are different from the One who calls us into being, we are creatures with fluid boundaries, profoundly and intimately related to and affected by God. I find it helpful to think of our human nature, in this regard, as one of bounded openness toward God.

It is hard to imagine what this bounded, open creature actually looks like apart from a fifth feature of our human nature: *To be the wondrous creature to whom God relates is to be an embodied, material, sensual, temporal, social being.* We are organic entities that exist in time. We have bodies that change and grow; get sick; reproduce; desire; experience hunger, sorrow, and joy; and need warmth and shelter to survive. There was a time when we were not, and there will be a time when we are no more. We are born, we grow old, and we die, and in between birth and death we are shaped in a vast network of relations. In this regard, our bounded relationality extends not just to the God who creates us but to the world around us and within us as well.

In recent years, the work of biologists, psychologists, and sociologists has prompted us to see that we are in some respects much more determined by our biology and our social environment than we had previously imagined. For example, studies of the human genome and of the ongoing effects of global pollution have shown us, in two very different ways, that both our natural context and our humanly constructed environments exert forceful, shaping pulls on us.

Other studies, however, make it clear that important dimensions of our existence that we previously considered "natural" are, in fact, much more open to human interpretation and change than we had once believed. For example, many people long believed that gender, race, and sexuality were stable features of human existence, with particular, unchanging traits we could measure and define. Today we are increasingly aware that many of these seemingly stable "givens" are negotiable, open-ended, and not as determined—at least biologically—as we had once thought. The character of our embodied relationality thus becomes even more marvelous in its complexity and its possibilities.

(6) God gives human beings the capacity to act in creative ways as they stand held in this weave of determining factors. (7) The God who calls us into being desires that we live our lives in covenant relation with God in a manner that is good for us.

In particular, scholars working in literary and philosophical fields have pushed us to see the role language plays in defining human nature. The language we use to describe our daily experiences is not just a collection of words we have learned to hook onto things we already knew but needed to name. If one takes seriously the degree to which our acquired imaginative theaters—our linguistically structured imaginations—determine how we see the world and act in it, it follows that language is not just an afterthought of experience; rather, it produces experience. Language, like our bodies, is not something we can choose to step in and out of. As in the case of doctrine, language, in its many humanly created forms, provides the imaginative material out of which experience itself emerges.

Our deep language-boundedness is thus not a problem to be avoided but a part of our marvelous, God-given creatureliness.

Having discussed some of the ways in which we are determined, I must now add a sixth feature to my account of human nature: *The God who calls this relational creature into being also gives human beings the capacity to act in creative ways as they stand held in this weave of determining factors*. To be human is thus to be an agent, an actor, a person enabled to improvise as one performs the determinative script of our human givenness. In the language of the Christian tradition, this dimension of our humanness has often been referred to as our "freedom." When human nature is understood in this way, the notion of our bounded openness gains further meaning. Not only are we both different from and yet affected by "the other" (understood very broadly); we are also both bound by the conditions of our material existence and yet, because we are agents, free to determine, creatively, how we are going to "do life" in the context of these boundaries. Who we are and what we are going to become is, to a considerable degree, an open question, and up to us.

Having noted that we are created with such freedom, it is important to add, seventh and finally, that *the God who calls us into being, loves and seeks relation with us, and cherishes our embodied, agentic reality is also a God who desires that we creatures live our lives in a manner that is good for us.* God does not just create humanity and then let it go on its own merry way. Like a parent who wants her child to grow up to be a healthy, flourishing adult, God desires that we make our futures in a manner that will allow us to flourish. Toward this end, God makes a covenant with humanity. God says, "I will be your God, and you will be my people," and then gives us a set of directions for how we might be God's people, a people who flourish.[8]

Christian tradition refers to this set of directions as "the law." At the heart of this law stands a set of divine directives that tells us we shall flourish if we can learn to love God, ourselves, and our neighbors and to care responsibly for the teeming world of which we are a part. The law is, at the most obvious level, a series of rules that suggests a pattern of living most appropriate to us as the given, loved, differentiated, relational, embodied creatures that we are. It is not a burden but a gift—a guide to our flourishing. Different ages and cultures constantly restate it in new ways. The Torah is one articulation. But the same law is written into the fabric of creation itself—the natural law—in the deep rules that govern the universe, the patterns and cycles of existence that compose the contexts of our lives.[9] Even when we are not conscious of its doing so, the law structures the weave of our fundamental relationality as it moves in and through the mysterious order of human existence itself.

These last two features of human nature—that we are free agents and that we are bound by law in covenant—make this portrait of our creaturely reality a drama rather than a static image. Some aspects of our identities are written into the fabric of human nature. We have no choice as to whether our lives are gifts, whether we are loved by God as a good creation, whether we are different from

God and from each other, and whether we are radically relational beings who live in language, have temporal bodies, and are bestowed with agency. I call these stable, given scripts of humanity our *whatness*.[10]

Within the weave of these essential features, however, there is room for us to become selves who are personally unique. I like to refer to this uniquely personal dimension of our humanness as our *whoness*. Who am I? I am not just a generic human being. I am Serene Jones, a person whose life is unfolding in the weave of our shared whatness but who is performing that script with improvised boldness. Out of that performance emerges a Serene who is constituted by her own unique tale of a self.

For example, I was born with a body that our culture defines as "woman" and "white." Both the organic and the constructed dimensions of such features of my personal being are to some degree beyond my immediate control. How I perform this script is, to a certain degree, up to me. How do I become a "woman"? How do I perform "race"? More theologically: Do I accept my life as a gift from God? Do I embrace my difference from God and others but also celebrate my God-given relatedness? Do I struggle to love God, myself, my neighbor, and the teeming world around me? Whether I acknowledge and perform these theological truths about myself is partially under my control and partially not. In this respect, the law lives within me—it determines generally *what* I am and particularly *who* I am, as to a large degree my history and context are given to me—but it also stands outside of me and beckons me toward it as the terms of a covenant with God that I can either move toward or not.

In the Christian tradition, the term used to describe the life path of a person or community that responds to God's desire for covenant relation and attempts to conform their lives to God's will is *faithfulness*. To be faithful to God is to accept and to try to embody the reality of our existence as given, beloved, differentiated, relational, embodied, free covenant partners of God. To be faithful, one need not perform this reality perfectly—an almost impossible task—but one does need to be committed to taking as life's measure the rule of God's will, the law. If one's life is shaped by the law, one will not necessarily be happy all the time. Our creaturely existence has tragic dimensions. We will get sick, we will experience loss, we will have conflicts over our differences. If we are faithful, however, these tragedies will not cause us to reject our covenant relation with the Divine. They will, instead, be experienced as being held in the grasp of a God who gives us into life and calls us beloved, even when times are rough.

In the Christian tradition, the term used to describe the life path of a person or community that responds to God's desire for covenant relation and attempts to conform their lives to God's will is *faithfulness*.

What a compelling picture of the self and the covenant community! A portrait of faithful flourishing! Of life abundant! Of human goodness and wholeness all held in God's wondrous grasp!

But is this portrait alone sufficient to the task of describing the complex character of our lives before God? Christians throughout the ages have answered, sadly, "No, it's not." For reasons unfathomable, human beings constantly follow a different path, the way of life called *sin*. We collectively turn against God and live contrary to God's law. To account for this dimension of human life, the tradition has found it necessary to draw another dramatic portrait of humanity's face, the face of our sin.

HUMAN BEINGS AS SINNERS AGAINST GOD

When my students ask, "Who am I?" and I reply, "You—along with all humanity—are an unfaithful sinner living contrary to God's will, and God is angry," they shift anxiously in their seats. Who wants to hear about a messed-up people and a wrathful God? But I can also tell from their widened eyes that, at a very deep level, this statement rings true to their reality. We live in a world where nations are at war, planes crash into buildings killing thousands, children starve, teenagers commit suicide, and our leaders lie—a world out of kilter, where, even when I want to be good, I seem incapable of doing the right thing. Harsh as this statement about sin and wrath may sound, my students know it speaks to them.

Sin, however, has been interpreted in many ways in the Christian tradition, not all of them good. Talk of sin has been the occasion for debilitating shame or for the social marginalization of whole groups of people, often with devastating results. In cases like this, sin-talk functions as a weapon that harms or divides people. Such ways of talking about sin, indeed, are so common that my students find it hard to believe that understanding ourselves as sinners could have the long-term positive effects of deepening our faith, making us kinder and more open to others, less arrogant and un-self-critical, and more realistic about life and its possibilities. But such goals lie at the heart of a classical Christian account of sin.

Let's consider some central features of that account. First, sin means living against God's will. Because of this, we can never imagine what sin looks like apart from simultaneously imagining the will of the God against whom sin is committed. We live in a world where *sin* is frequently used to name anything that we consider wrong or harmful, be it eating too much chocolate cake, viewing Internet pornography, or selling illegal drugs on the street. Each of these activities may indeed be sinful, but Christians would mean by that not just that the federal government, our neighborhood block watch, or our health advisor disapprove of them, but that they are contrary to the will of God. When God enters the picture, the stakes are raised and the standard of evaluation becomes distinctly theological.

Bringing God into the picture also reminds us that God is angry about sin. In the language of the tradition, sin incurs God's *wrath*. As my students' wide eyes suggest when I tell them this, *wrath* is a strong, potentially frightening word to use to describe the Divine One who gives us life and calls us beloved.

God is not angry with humanity, however, simply because God is a tyrant or a mean, legalistic deity who doesn't like it when divine rules get broken. God's anger is more like the anger a loving parent might exhibit when her teenage child wrecks the car or takes dangerous drugs. God hates our sin because it is harmful to us. It not only prevents us from experiencing the abundant life God offers to us, it threatens to destroy us. Divine wrath thus indicates the depth of God's love for us. God is angry because God wants her beloved creatures to flourish. We suffer from sin. The world becomes a mess when we refuse God's love. The wrecked car and the drug-addicted body are the penalties we incur.

What has made God angry? What exactly is sin? The question is hard to answer not only because sin has been defined in myriad ways but also because at its heart sin doesn't make sense. It doesn't make sense that humanity would turn away from the wondrous offer of covenant relation with God; in this regard, sin is inexplicable.

> Let me offer a definition of *sin* as "unfaithfulness." Recall my earlier discussion of faithfulness as living in conformity to the law of God. Unfaithfulness is the flip side of this picture.

Having acknowledged the problems, let me undertake the impossible and offer a definition of *sin* as "unfaithfulness."[11] Recall my earlier discussion of faithfulness as living in conformity to the law of God. Unfaithfulness is the flip side of this picture. To be in sin is to live in a state that opposes God's will for our flourishing. Sin is thus a state, a general all-encompassing condition, not individual acts—though a state of sinful existence certainly gives rise to acts that can be called "sins" (these are traditionally referred to as the "fruits of sin"). The Christian tradition asserts that this general state of unfaithfulness is universal in scope. Everyone is in it; no one escapes it.

Sin is thus part of our *whatness.* It is simply what we are, regardless of our awareness of it. Just as we are beloved creatures of God, so we are sinful—all of us. But here is the difference: Unlike the universal features of our creaturely nature, this reality is not given to us by God. Humanity has collectively generated it over time. We have conjured it up, imposed it upon ourselves, spread it around, and passed it on to each new generation.[12]

Further, this secondary form of our whatness is parasitically related to our primary created whatness. Our sinful nature lives off of the features that constitute our primary creaturely reality, corrupting and twisting the functioning of our primary nature. But because it is parasitic, sin cannot finally destroy our creaturely goodness without destroying itself. Goodness continues to stand as the baseline truth of our lives.

A similar dynamic is at work in understanding sin in relation to who we are. In describing our *whoness,* I argued that, while we all share the general features of our creatureliness, each one of us performs those features in ways specific to our own culture and language as well as our own chosen life paths. So it is with sin. Each of us performs sin in distinct ways in our individual lives. The way in which sin becomes a part of who we are is a product of human invention. Sin is not God's doing; we each own it in our own peculiar ways. And, like the sinful dimensions of *what* we are, the sin that is manifest in *who* we are is parasitic on the creaturely, good story of who we are.

DISTORTIONS OF THE SEVEN FEATURES OF CREATURELINESS

Sin distorts each of the seven characteristics of being creatures I discussed earlier. *The first feature is that our lives are gifts of God.* In this context, sin sometimes wears the face of a human pride that believes that we ultimately create ourselves, that we are masters of our own universes, and that the world around us is there to be used and controlled by us according to our own desires and needs. We start to worship ourselves as gods.

> Our lives are gifts of God. In this context, sin sometimes wears the face of human pride.

This pride may also take the form of our will to master and dominate other people, or to treat our environment as if it is a commodity we may use and dispose of as we see fit. It may also take the burdensome form of assuming a God-like responsibility for bearing the weight of the world's problems. In each of these contexts we meet the face of a humanity that lives under the illusion that life is not, first and foremost, dependent on the loving will of the Divine.

> The second form of our creatureliness is our belovedness of God. Sin can take the form of the belief that human beings are fundamentally bad or that some lives are more valuable than others. The third form is that as creatures we are different from God and each other. Sin can take the form of idolatry, an obsessive valorization of sameness, or disrespect of the boundaries that mark off one life from another.

The second feature of our creatureliness is our belovedness to God. God loves us and values each of our lives as a precious, good gift. What does a sinful distortion of this reality look like? It can take the form of the belief that human beings are fundamentally bad, that our bodies are bad, that sex is bad, that the use of our minds is bad, and that because of this, life itself, in all its teeming wonder, is something we should try to escape rather than embrace. Another form that sin can take in this context is the belief that some lives are more valuable than others, and that we can calculate these values according to some culturally generated standard. We find an example of this in the gradations of health care that most employers in North America use when constructing their health benefit plans, so that some lives are judged worthy of receiving more health care than others. From a Christian perspective, this is a mark of our sin because it contradicts the universal scope of God's love for *all* of humanity.

The third feature of our creatureliness is that our difference from God and the differences among human beings are good. Sinful distortion of our creaturely differences can take several forms. We see it in communities where an individual person (a charismatic leader) or group (a political party) or object (a flag, a cross, the stock market) is imbued with special divine qualities. The tradition refers to this form of sin as *idolatry*, the divinization of the creaturely. Idolatry loses the distinction between God and creatures.

Our refusal to celebrate difference at a human level takes the form of an obsessive valorization of sameness.[13] We posit a standard of what we consider normal (with respect to race, usually some version of "whiteness") and evaluate, often quite unconsciously, different racial configurations according to the degree to which they deviate from that norm. Similar dynamics play into our thinking about gender, sexuality, religion . . . and the list goes on as far as our differences extend.

Another form that sin takes in the context of our thinking about difference is the human tendency to disrespect the boundaries that mark off one life from another. Think of the desire we often have when we love someone dearly to get inside their skin, as it were, and somehow possess them. When this happens, lives are unhealthily enmeshed as one loses the capacity to see where one ends and another begins. The autonomy and integrity of both parties' differentiated reality is threatened by the unbounded character of their relating.

The fourth feature of our creatureliness is our fundamental openness to God and to the world, our radical relationality. The sinful distortion of this relationality can take at least two forms. The first is the easiest to grasp. When I live unfaithfully and sin against God, I am relating wrongly to God. So too with my neighbors and the world: In my sin I relate wrongly and, most often, destructively to others (and myself). The second kind of distortion of relationality is harder to understand. If I am a creature whose reality is constituted by the weave of relations in which I find myself, and if sin happens in those relations, then sin is something that happens to me by virtue of my constitutive openness to the reality in which I live. To use the language of the tradition, sin is passed on to me through my commerce with the world in which I live. In this sense, sin is something I inherit; it is given to me by virtue of my relationship to an expansive environment of relations shot through with unfaithful modes of being.

> The fourth feature of our creatureliness is our fundamental openness to God and to the world. In my sin, I relate wrongly to God, others, and myself, and sin is passed on to me through my commerce with the world in which I live. Fifth, I am an embodied, organic, time-bound, socially constituted, and hence deeply linguistic being. Sins such as pride, despair, abhorring difference, and desiring to possess or use another person all take different forms as social sin.

To give more substance to this idea that sin lives in relations and is thus passed on, let us turn to the fifth feature of our creatureliness. Recall my claim that *to be a creature of God is to be essentially an embodied, organic, time-bound, socially constituted, and hence deeply linguistic being.* Distortions of this feature of creatureliness transform forms of sin we have already discussed.

Take the sin of pride. In its *collective* pride, humanity constructs institutions—forms of government, economic systems, and structures of domestic life—that seek to take the place of God in our lives, to control and dominate not only whole groups of people but the environment as well. Take the case of global capitalism and its gross exploitation of labor in poor countries, its often unfettered extraction of natural resources for profit, and its production of commodities unnecessary and even harmful to those who become the consumers of capital's output. Since I am a middle-class person living in North America, this institution affects everything I see and do; it carries sin into every corner of my life and my being, often in ways beyond my conscious control.[14]

As another example, take the sin of despair, the belief that life is meaningless and expendable or that one's being is fundamentally bad and shameful. Drugs, alcohol, food, sex, pornography, work—any number of things can be used as coping mechanisms for dealing with this reality. Sociologists and psychologists have made us all increasingly aware that these forms of addictive behavior are not just products of individual sin; they are passed down from generation to generation. The addicted mother passes her addiction down to the children to whom she gives birth. Family systems pass down destructive patterns of life often encouraged by industries that benefit from the consumption they require.

The list of examples goes on. Consider the sin that seeks sameness and abhors difference and recall my previous discussion of language and its power to shape our perceptions and actions. In recent years, feminist, race, and queer theorists have pressed us to see that embedded in our linguistic systems are assumptions about gender, race, and sexuality so deeply entrenched we are often unable to name their presence. Because of the way our language system works, we identify persons, without even thinking about it, as "men" and "women," assume what counts as "appropriate" behavior, and name deviations from such norms as perversions. We make analogous assumptions when it comes to race or sexual orientation.

As a final example, consider the sin of desiring to possess or use another person so that even the other's bodily integrity is violated in incest, emotional abuse, domestic violence, or sexual misconduct. These forms of abuse damage the whole being of the person abused (as well, I might add, as the being of the abuser). Victims often think of themselves as "bad" and the world as an untrustworthy place and act accordingly, particularly in their understanding of their relation with God. The consequences of such sin become a prison that holds them, sometimes for an entire lifetime, and that get passed down from one generation to another.

Theologians refer to all the examples I have been discussing as *social sin,* the sin that lives in the structures of our corporate life and the linguistic patterns of our culture. When we are implicated in these social dynamics, sin becomes so normalized and so seemingly natural that we are unable to see it as sin. It can corrupt us totally, and central to this total corruption is sin's power to disable our capacity to know we are sinners in the first place.

Recall that I described human freedom as the sixth feature of our creaturely lives. Juxtapose that feature of our creatureliness with the power of sin just discussed and we must ask: Are we actively responsible for sin, or are we simply victims of unconscious forces that cause us to sin despite ourselves? Do we sin freely, or is sin forced upon us?

> Human freedom is the sixth feature of our creaturely lives. The tradition asserts that we are both responsible for sin and yet also victims of it.

The tradition asserts that we are both responsible for sin and yet also victims of it. To understand this claim, let us first look at what it means to say we are responsible for sin. Central to this assertion is the theological contention that God is not the author of the evil in this world. If God does not create sin, it stands to reason that we do. We collectively create and pass on patterns of life contrary to God's will. This sinful creativity originates in the strange mystery of our freedom and lives in the institutions and cultural worlds we invent.

In addition to affirming this social character of sin, however, Christians also recognize our individual responsibility for it. Each of us, as we live the stories of our lives, bears the guilt for the sin we daily enact, both instances when we are aware of the harm we do and also instances when we sin without knowing it.

But how can we be responsible for something we can't even see? When grappling with this question, the tradition has invoked the concept of *the bondage of the will.*[15] When the social reality of sin seeps deep into our being, it profoundly affects our will. It takes over our desires, and we start actively wanting to sin. As a consumer in a capitalist system, for instance, I want to buy products that are unhealthy for me (I even convince myself that I need them). My will is, as it were, imprisoned—not disabled, because I am still "choosing," but locked into a prison house from which it cannot escape. Thus, in sin I am simultaneously responsible for and not responsible for the unfaithfulness of my responses to God, myself, and my neighbors.

As Christians, we have to affirm both sides of this paradox. If we were not at all responsible for sin, then God would have to be, and we would start believing we could just enjoy the free ride of sin, since resistance is futile. If we assert that each of us is solely responsible for our sin, on the other hand, we will almost certainly collapse under the weight of a burden that we cannot bear. We cannot fix the world; we cannot even fix ourselves. Indeed, if we try to save ourselves, then we begin to assume the prideful position of God.

> The last feature of our creatureliness is our call to covenant relation, and thus to obedience to the law. But the law itself can become the occasion of sin.

The last feature of our creatureliness is

our call to covenant relation. Each of the dimensions of sin I have already described constitutes a facet of humanity's state of broken covenant. Sin is something we do, both collectively and individually, in conscious and unconscious ways, when we live against God. Sin is also something that happens to us, what we suffer, when other people and institutions harm us. Our breaking of our covenant relation with God can happen both in our most intimate one-on-one relation and in the depths of our own soul's conversations with itself and God as well as in the midst of our nation's foreign policy initiatives and our most grandiose economic patterns of engagement.

Recall that an important feature of our call to live in covenant relation with God is the call to follow the law, to live according to God's will. We can sin by breaking the law, but the law itself can become the occasion of sin. The law itself can "kill." We all know self-righteous people of faith who become so zealous and certain of their ability to embody the law that they become prideful, arrogant, dismissive of difference, and relationally dominating in the name of covenant relation. We all know, as well, people for whom their inability to live perfect lives becomes the occasion for despair and depression; they feel helpless and alone precisely because they hold the law so dear and feel miserably judged by their failures. In both instances, the law seems a burden rather than the gift that it is.

Such misunderstandings of the law make it hard to think of the doctrine of sin as the herald of good news, as I earlier claimed. Let me end this section with two more positive notes, however, that may make this claim easier to accept. First, a realistic view of human sin has, over the years, been incorporated into the basic principles of pluralistic democracy. Central to democratic values is the belief that people are fundamentally guided by self-interest, and that we need to create state structures which ensure that our differences are protected and that we are prevented from either dominating or destroying one another. This vision of democracy reflects a distrust of autocratic authority and a concomitant commitment to spreading political power around as widely as possible: one voice, one vote. Democracy is the form of government that sinners need; it makes us more tolerant by checking our distorted will to power and requiring internal standards of self-criticism. For those of us who value such a system, this seems like good news.

My second answer is much more theological. If all I have said about sin is true, then I should not be able to know anything about it. My knowledge of sin should be impossible, given that the totality of sin's hold on me prevents me from knowing my creaturely relation to God and, hence, from knowing God's will, the law. So how have I been able to write this chapter? In the Christian tradition, the answer is that I only know sin because I have come to know Jesus Christ, by the intervention of grace, and in him my sin is revealed to me. When I look at him, I see by contrast how far I, along with the rest of humanity, have fallen. He reveals sin to me because, in faith, he steps into the imaginative world of my sin-clouded mind and shows me what abundant life looks like.

Ideally, then, a discussion of Christology should come before a discussion of sin. But Christ and the law are not two distinct realities; they both embody God's will. Thus, the reality of Christ has been implied every time I have invoked the divine will in my previous discussions of creation and sin. Moreover, as I said at the outset, the four portraits of humanity that compose my overarching account of human nature are to be viewed simultaneously, not sequentially. I do not come to know about Jesus only after I know about creation and sin. It is Jesus Christ who fully reveals my sin. But in Christ not only do we see that humanity has broken covenant with God, we also see that God has done something about it. In Jesus Christ, we see that God constantly recreates sinful humanity by forgiving us and offering us the possibility of renewed covenant life with God. God meets our sin with grace, and in this meeting a new visage of human nature comes into view. To this third portrait let us now turn.

HUMAN BEINGS AS JUSTIFIED AND SANCTIFIED

When my students ask me, "Who am I?" and I respond with the third answer that the tradition offers, "You are sinners who are justified and sanctified in Christ," I often get blank stares. The terms *justified* and *sanctified* sound strange to our modern ears. Yet they tell us a story of humanity that carries profoundly good news about our lives and God's relation to us. They remind us that even though we are caught in sin, grace abounds and new life is ours. Later chapters on Christology and the Christian life will elaborate this story of redemption and grace with much more detail than I can offer here, but without saying something about these themes, the portrait of humanity I have been sketching would remain incomplete.

The central word used in this third portrait to describe how God relates to us as sinners in need of redemption is *grace*. The term *grace* means "unmerited love"; it emphasizes the fact that God seeks to redeem us not out of any externally imposed necessity but solely because God decides to do so. In this regard, God's decision to save is similar to God's decision to create. It comes to us as a gift, and there is nothing we can do to earn or deserve it.

> *Justification* and *sanctification* clarify how God relates to us in grace.

Justification and *sanctification* clarify how God relates to us in grace. To proclaim that God justifies sinners involves using a term from the ancient world of Latin law courts.[16] When people were justified, they were "made just" or "made righteous" by virtue of the court's decision that they were not guilty and therefore should not be punished and could be set free. In Roman courts, even knowing a person was guilty, a judge would sometimes use his power to pronounce the defendant free anyway, thereby imputing a sentence of innocence. People who received an imputed sentence were made righteous even if they could not in fact claim to be innocent of their crimes.

Christians make a similar claim in saying that we are justified through God's grace. God pronounces us not guilty even though we have done nothing to deserve such a sentence. In this portrait, the face of humanity has not ceased to be sinful, but superimposed upon (or imputed to) its sinful visage is a picture of a forgiven humanity loved by God and set free from the prisons that hold us. In a traditional phrase, we are *simul iustus et peccator* ("simultaneously justified and sinner")—a wandering, broken humanity enveloped by the love of a God who refuses to let our sin cause her to turn away, a God who, by forgiving this fallen humanity, continually offers to us anew the possibility of knowing the life abundant that God has promised.

Sanctification is the other word used to describe the working of God's grace in us. When God saves us, God not only forgives our sins (justification) but makes us "holy" (*sanctus*), giving us the power actually to live differently in the light of that forgiveness.[17] In the context of sanctification, the law no longer stands before us only as a mark of our created goodness and a standard that we fail to live up to in sin. The law now stands before us as a new possibility, a reality that we are free to try to fulfill, knowing that we will be forgiven for our failures to do so.

Christ serves as a model of that new possibility, but he is more than a role model. In him a truth about human reality is actively enacted, made real, accomplished. His reality fundamentally changes us, even when we are not able to live as his example suggests. In the person of Jesus Christ, God becomes flesh and shares our lot, puts on our created nature as well as the whole mess of our sinful reality, and thereby is revealed as a God who does not let our fallenness be the occasion for turning away from us. On the cross we meet a God who takes on the power of sin and bears it in God's body; in the resurrection, we meet a God who announces to us that new life is ours, constantly, in the abiding grace of God's love.

In Christ we do not see just a picture of something we may or may not be able to make true in our own lives. We rather see a picture of the way things actually are with respect to this God who remains faithful to us. We are forgiven and made holy by God. This picture of our redeemed humanity in Christ overlies our created and sinful humanity as a third-tier account of our *whatness,* something true about us even if we do not recognize it. As with the other portraits of humanity, however, we each embody this reality in specific ways. At the level of our *whoness,* each of us has the opportunity to climb into this given script of redemption and to wear, actively and consciously, the grace in which we are enveloped.

In Christ we do not see just a picture of something we may or may not be able to make true in our own lives. We rather see a picture of the way things actually are with respect to this God who remains faithful to us.

The Christian tradition refers to this process of taking up and embracing the reality of our graced nature as "coming to faith." Faith is true and certain knowledge of God's redeeming love for us; it is deep and abiding trust that the benefits of grace have been poured out in Christ for us.[18] When we come to this knowledge and it begins to transform the way we actually live, we enter the realm of existence known as the Christian life. In one widely used image, "We put on Christ and his benefits." We wear the garb of forgiveness and new life that Christ embodies for us. Unfortunately, this does not mean that we stop performing sinful roles at the same time that we are acting as if we are forgiven; the reality of *simul iustus et peccator* still holds. When we stand in the light of Christ's saving benefits, however, we recognize that our sinful performances are not the final word about who we are before God. God remains committed to us; we are beloved and redeemed.

HUMAN BEINGS AS PARTICIPANTS IN ETERNAL LIFE

It is not until the end of the academic year that I have a chance to offer my theology students yet a fourth answer to their question, "Who am I?" When we reach the last topic of systematic theology, eschatology (the study of the last things), I explain to them that in the Christian tradition one final portrait of humanity, superimposed on the others, completes the picture.

Who are we? We are people to whom God has promised eternal life; we are created, sinful, redeemed human beings who await the final fulfillment of God's gift of life abundant. Having listened to me all semester lifting up the image of "life abundant" as the goal of human existence, it is with relief that they receive the news: God has promised you and all of humanity this; it awaits you! But in their relief, I also find looks of perplexity crossing their faces. What exactly is the thing called eternal life abundant, and what on earth (or in heaven) does it mean to say it awaits us?

Answering these questions is perhaps the hardest task I have as a professor of theology. It is hard because I do not have firm answers for them. Unlike the other portraits, I cannot sketch in the details of this one with strong lines and bold colors. All I can do is say to them, in concert with theologians who have spoken across the ages, "Whatever awaits us, in the end, it will be good. We will all dwell with God and all things will be made right. Life abundant."

They immediately want to know: Am I talking about the end that awaits us when we die, each as individuals, or am I talking about the end of time, when life as we know it draws to a conclusion? Or am I talking about humanity as it appears to God in each moment of our living—life abundant in every minute of our lives? The answer I offer to all these possibilities is "Yes," followed by, "but I can't pin it down for you." As they wrestle with this, I also point out to them that, if they truly grasp and live into the humanity portrayed in the other pictures I have drawn, and if they truly affirm the reality of God that attends each portrait, then what they are called to do with respect to this last picture is to trust in God's goodness and power, and to live in hope.

Living in hope does not mean living in utter ignorance with respect to the form of our end; our hope has content to it. This last portrait is of a humanity that is still "under construction," but the materials and blueprint for the project of this grand tale of human life should be familiar to us from our previous portraits.

Recall the features of creation and redemption. Whatever awaits us, we know that we will be with the God who gives us life and calls us beloved. We will dwell with this God and one another in a manner that celebrates our differences—we will not be blended into some amorphous oversoul—and fills out relationships with goodness and a richness of spirit. We will participate in life abundant as particular people; our bodies, minds, history, our unique modes of time and space, our multiple modes of existence—all these particular features of our *whoness* will be part of that fulfillment. In the world to come, we will still be agents as well, but there, we hope, our choices will be forever life giving and life sustaining. And our abundance will reside in the fullness of the covenant community these choices create—a place where we eternally respond to God's welcoming, "I am your God," with a joyful, "And we are your people." And in that place, as forgiven and recreated sinners, we will abide with God in a manner that, most amazingly, delights the One who gives us life.

CLARK M. WILLIAMSON

THE HUMAN QUESTION

We human beings are a question to ourselves. Who are we? What is the meaning and destiny of our lives? What are we to do? How are we to understand ourselves in relation to this world in which we live? How are we to understand the world, in which we have to decide who we are and what it is that we are given and called to be and do? How are we to understand ultimate reality, God, and ourselves in relationship to God? Who are these other people, how are we to relate to them, and what are we to do about and with them?

To the community of faith, given and called to work the way of life in service of God and neighbor, the question that human beings are and ask of themselves presents itself in at least two ways. How are we to understand ourselves, we who are given and called to be a blessing to each other, to serve each other's well-being? And how are we to understand these other people, these strangers, who do not participate in our way of being human but who may be participants in another religious tradition or in no religious tradition whatsoever? We will look first at this second question.

Neighbors God Has Given Us to Love

As the community of faith seeks to walk the way of life in an increasingly crowded world, it encounters other people—strangers to it and its way of life. Who are these people? How are we to understand them? What should be our characteristic attitudes and actions toward them? The thesis of this essay is simple: All these strangers are our neighbors on planet Earth, neighbors whom God has given us to love, whose well-being is given to us to guard and protect, those toward whom we are to see that justice is done. Strangers are different from us, alien, foreign. In the parlance of postmodern thought, they represent *otherness.* They think and act differently; they bring their questions with them. To love strangers is to love questions, and to love questions is to love strangers. Yet we are commanded: "You shall love the alien as yourself, for you were aliens in the land of Egypt: I am the LORD your God" (Lev. 19:34). We are freed by God to love these strangers, knowing that as we have been freely loved we are freed to love.

All these strangers are our neighbors on planet Earth, neighbors whom God has given us to love, whose well-being is given to us to guard and protect, those toward whom we are to see that justice is done.

This thesis denies that all those who are different from us are to be understood as an "alienated other." Historically, all religious traditions have failed to understand others on their own terms. This failing is hardly unique to Christianity, but as this is a theology for Christians, we are obligated to address our own problems. There is no honest way to evade the fact that we have had a strong tendency to project onto other groups traits, characteristics, and faults that we find reprehensible. Projecting these faults onto others neatly allows us to avoid the self-criticism, repentance, and openness to the transformation graciously offered us by God that is at the heart of biblical faith. In the history of the church, women, Jews, heretics, members of other religions, and minorities have all been victimized by our tendency to define them as less than fully human or to demonize them. Today, homosexuals are similarly vilified.

Doing theology without any alienated other is necessary if the purpose of our way of life is to be a blessing to our planetary neighbors. But it is a goal more easily stated than achieved. We will look later at some contemporary indications that this remains a problem for much contemporary theology.

Understanding Ourselves Appropriately

It is not only the case that we have difficulty understanding and acting appropriately toward our neighbors who are different from us. We also have had a terrible difficulty understanding and acting appropriately with each other within the church. Sexism, racism, and anti-Judaism have created a deeper rupture within the church than has any other source of division (anti-Judaism signaled the first great ecumenical rupture). We must take this into account in our developing understanding of human beings, of who we are in relationship to God and neighbor and what God gives and calls us to be and do. Sexism, heterosexism, racism, anti-Judaism, attitudes toward "pagans," heretics, and "infidels" do not exhaust our difficulties with understanding what we as Christians should understand about ourselves and our neighbors as human beings. Another challenge is that in our postmodern, consumerist economy there are many proposals for how we should understand ourselves. Often we buy into them because they are simply part of the fabric of our society. These cultural forces work hard to convince us that they know best what it means to be a human being.

AN ALTERNATIVE UNDERSTANDING OF HUMANITY

Where we take our definition of humanity from is a critical matter. According to the understanding of human beings found in the economist's understanding of liberal capitalism, human beings are naturally aggressive competitors. Each person is a threat to all others. My neighbors are my competitors. It is our nature to fear one another. We live with the anxiety that at any moment we may be attacked and robbed of our property or deprived of it by some trick. Our prevailing concern is to survive, to maximize our possessions, and to chase after our interests.

We may have once believed that all human beings are essentially good, that together we constitute a family of sisters and brothers, that our destiny is to live in reconciliation with one another, or that we are watched after by a God who is graciously disposed toward us. But the insight of capitalism has been that only when we cease being mystified by fairy tales and let ourselves be guided by enlightened self-interest can we assure our safety by a government that protects the rights of all by limiting the power of each.

In such a worldview, it is irrational and utopian to be concerned about peace, social justice, fresh air, clean water, disarmament, a sustainable society, and a living wage. The rule of life is competition, curbed only by the competitiveness involved in the war of each against all. Loving your neighbor as yourself results in neurosis, or worse, failure to compete efficiently, which is capitalism's definition of sin.

Contrary to this, Christians are given to believe that human beings are created for relationships of love and justice, that God not only watches graciously over us but is engaged in travail with us, that matters of compassion and solidarity (the social name for love) are, far from being utopian, the only realistic alternative to the way of death represented in the war of each against all, and that our destiny is intended by God to be one in which the war of each against all will finally be overcome (Rev. 21:4). Christian faith is an alternative possibility, and sometimes in its conversations with the situation, its answer is no. However gentle, it is nonetheless a resolute no. The market does not determine the world and

> Christians are given to believe that human beings are created for relationships of love and justice.

value of any human being. The "bottom line" is not the only norm, nor is it a moral norm.

Humanity in the Bible

What does the biblical witness have to tell us with regard to what it means to be a human being? We begin at the beginning, first with the Hebrew Bible, then with the New Testament.

First, the Hebrew Bible knows nothing about autonomous humanity in the modern sense not only of freedom but of self-sufficiency.[1] Human nature is determined entirely by our relation to God, to nature, and to other people (which includes the relationships of well-being that God wants us to have with God and each other), a relation that preserves the distinction between God and humanity, between the Creator and the creature. The belief that human beings are created in God's image (the *imago dei*) defines our relation to God and to the rest of nature. We are not divine or descended from God. We are created for and called to a unique companionship with God, one another, and the world. This companionship involves responsiveness to God's freeing us to love and loving us into freedom. Covenant is a controlling metaphor for the Bible: We are created to be the kinds of beings with whom God can enter into covenant and who live in covenantal responsibility with one another and the environment.

Because God transcends nature, our duty is not defined in terms of a mystical identification of ourselves with nature so as to achieve harmony with it. Humanity is a psychophysical organism that, as a whole, is related to God. There is in human beings no immortal part that can survive death on its own account. Human beings are good, indeed "very good," because we are cherished by God. But all human beings, not only our kind, are so treasured, and so are all of God's other creatures, whom God also pronounces "very good." We are created for a covenant relationship of life and blessing with one another and with God.

The Ugly Word: Sin

Sin is revealed for what it is by what it opposes: Sin is our opposition against life, against well-being, against the freedom to love God with all our selves and our neighbors as ourselves, against the love that frees us to do so, against being loved, against God, and against God's gift to us of abundant life. Apart from the revelation of God's gracious love, the nature and character of our sin are not clear. God's self-disclosure, and therefore the disclosure of the nature of sin, occur throughout Scripture and with decisive clarity in Jesus Christ. We see sin clearly when we clearly see what it opposes and the depth and virulence of its opposition. We see sin clearly when we see it in ourselves first and know that we are *simul iustus et peccator*, at one and the same time justified and sinners. It is idolatrous to project sin onto others and regard them judgmentally as if we had the status to make such judgments. This is the sin of arrogance, committed by the self-righteous.

Because of our creatureliness and in the absence of faith, we are in a state of anxiety. Human beings are sinful, but being sinful is not part of the definition of human beings. It is not necessary that we sin. Sin is something we freely do—even when, as in the case of systemic sins, we are not quite aware of our complicity—and something from which we can be freed. We are all "recovering sinners," precisely because we are not necessarily sinners. God is not a cosmic prankster who creates us as sinners in order to give us the pointless injunction not to be so.

The Hebrew Bible does not theorize about sinfulness and knows nothing about the loss of our likeness to God (the image of God). It knows a lot about sinfulness. Its most remarkable analysis of the human situation is Genesis 3–11. We sin because we wish vainly to assert our autonomy over against God. Adam, Eve, Cain, Lamech, the builders of the tower of Babel all exhibit this. In Genesis 3–11, sin (murder, violence, and injustice) so pollutes the earth that God sends a flood and makes a new start with Noah, Noah's children, and all the "living creatures" who are included in the Noachite covenant. Psalm 143 petitions God not to judge the psalmist, because "no one living is righteous before you." Psalm 51, a confession of sin and plea for mercy is radical: "Indeed, I was born guilty, a sinner when my mother conceived me." This psalm articulates the Augustinian motifs of biblical faith: "Create in me a clean heart, O God, and put a new and right spirit within me" (51:10).

The prophets provided a searching analysis of sin as estrangement from and rebellion against God. This corresponded to their convictions about God's holy, loving, and righteous will. Our creaturely weakness is not the direct cause of sin so much as the temptation that can occasion sin. The sin of Adam and Eve was the effort to be "like God"; the sin of the builders of the tower of Babel was that there was no limit to their ambition. The prophets criticize kings, in one case a Babylonian, for saying, "I will ascend to heaven. . . . I will make myself like the Most High" (Isa. 14:13–14).

> In contrast to the humility of Christ, sin is pride (which I prefer to call arrogance); in contrast to the majesty of Christ, it is sloth; and in contrast to the truth of Christ, it is a lie.

Sin takes several forms. It is self-centeredness, manifesting itself as arrogance (arrogating to ourselves a status that is God's, regarding ourselves as the ground and end of our own being and meaning). It is sloth, not thinking highly enough of ourselves as loved by God and given and called to the possibility of a life of blessing and well-being (sloth amounts to a rejection of oneself as created in the *imago dei*). It is avarice, envy, lust, and anger—those sins against the neighbor that destroy the neighbor's well-being and refuse the possibility of a life of blessing and reconciliation with our actual human associates. Karl Barth's view of sin is extraordinarily helpful: In contrast to the humility of Christ, sin is pride (which I prefer to call arrogance); in contrast to the majesty of Christ, it is sloth;

and in contrast to the truth of Christ it is a lie. "Epigrammatically," Barth says, "and to be taken with a grain of salt, we might say that falsehood is the specifically Christian form of sin." These are not three separate forms of sin: "Proud and slothful, he [meaning any human being] is necessarily false as well."[2] That sin is a lie is a particularly important insight. We cannot lie unless we know the truth. The truth that Christians have been given and called to know has to do with the unfathomable love and grace of God that have disclosed to us the conditions of life and well-being and done so throughout the history of the God of Israel with the Israel of God and with manifest clarity in Jesus Christ. Only those to whom this has been given to know can lie about it. And we let ourselves believe the lies that the systemic sins of our world drum into our heads. We will return to this point in our following discussion of original sin.

The Unity of Humanity

The Scriptures think of humanity as one whole; all human beings have the same parents. Israel's privilege and responsibility are because of God's grace and on behalf of "all the Gentiles" and because of no superiority on Israel's part. It is a particular election within a universal inclusiveness. Israel is called to be a representative human community and, as such, experiences to the full the responsibility of being involved in historical existence.

This insistence denies all racism. Jewish legends about the creation of Adam illustrate this point. According to one, God took dirt "from all four corners of the earth," so that a human being, whether from east or west, north or south, would be at home anywhere. The legend continues that the dirt was of different colors—red clay, black loam, white sand, and yellow soil—so that no race of human beings could ever be told "you do not belong here."[3]

The Scriptures think of humanity as one whole; all human beings have the same parents.

Paul agreed when he declared at Athens that God had "from one ancestor made all nations to inhabit the whole earth" (Acts 17:26). In the table of the peoples in Genesis 10, the Hebrew people take their place among all the others. When Abraham is summoned to his special destiny by God, God promises that by him "all the families of the earth shall be blessed."

God is equally concerned with Ethiopians, Philistines, and Syrians as well as with Israel (Amos 9:7). Said Isaiah on behalf of God: "Blessed be Egypt my people, and Assyria the work of my hands, and Israel my heritage" (Isa. 19:25). This inclusive outlook reaches its pinnacle in the picture of the Servant of the Lord in Second Isaiah (42:6) who is to be a "light to the nations"; in the vision of a unified humanity with its religious center in Jerusalem (Isa. 2:2–4; Mic. 4:1–3); and in the books of Jonah and Ruth. Gentiles (and Gentile women) are listed in the genealogies of the Messiah, and in Genesis 9 God makes a covenant not only with all humanity but with all the "living things." Israel was unaware of the kinds of distinctions with which the Greeks divided humanity into Greeks and barbarians. If Israel was chosen from among the nations, this was not because of any merit but because of the unfathomable will of God.

HUMAN WORTH

Human beings have several characteristics, of which the first is worth. This is not a value that we expropriate for ourselves, but a gift from God. It is a blessing, part of our well-being, to think well of ourselves; but it is only so as a gift, not as a form of self-congratulation. As made in the image and likeness of God, we have worth both as God's gift and because we matter to God. In a number of places in Scripture, the self is designated by the words for *honor* and *glory,* notably so in Psalm 8:3–5:

> When I look at your heavens, the work of your fingers,
> the moon and the stars that you have established;
> what are human beings that you are mindful of them,
> mortals that you care for them?
> Yet you have made them a little lower than God,
> and crowned them with glory and honor.

In themselves, human beings are fragile. The classic affirmation of the value and worth of fragile, breakable, irreplaceable people is in Psalm 103:13–17:

> As a father has compassion for his children,
> so the LORD has compassion for those who fear him.
> For he knows how we were made;
> he remembers that we are dust.
> As for mortals, their days are like grass;
> they flourish like a flower of the field;
> for the wind passes over it, and it is gone,
> and its place knows it no more.
> But the steadfast love of the LORD is from everlasting to everlasting.

The same comparison of human beings to grass or to dust and ashes is found is Isaiah, Jeremiah, 2 Chronicles, the Psalms, and Genesis. Paul the apostle talks in several places about human weakness, a Pauline theme too often overlooked. Human frailty is reflected in our liability to disease, in the fact that our strength diminishes with age, and in our mortality. We are the beings who have to die and know it. As a result of our vulnerability and mortality, we experience anxiety and fear; the fear of death (Paul Tillich's "anxiety of nonbeing") is a major factor to be confronted in coming to terms with a biblical understanding of human being and human sinfulness. Do we sin out of sheer malevolence, or are there objective factors in the human condition (the snake already in the garden) that are the occasions of temptation?

In the New Testament, the person, male or female, is the creature whose body is made alive by God's breath, whose divine image can be defaced (but not effaced) by sin and redeemed by Christ through the Holy Spirit, and whose historical destiny is defined from birth to death by relationships. The legacy of the Hebrew Bible is generally carried over into the New Testament in that humanity is viewed as a totality, with terms such as *heart, soul, flesh,* or *spirit* denoting the entire person from a particular point of view. Human beings are sexual, and flesh is intrinsically good, so long as one does not boast about it.

In the New Testament, the person, male or female, is the creature whose body is made alive by God's breath, whose divine image can be defaced (but not effaced) by sin and redeemed by Christ through the Holy Spirit, and whose historical destiny is defined from birth to death by relationships.

Since all New Testament writers assume the human dilemma lies in disobedience rather than in materiality, the crucial differences among them arise in conceptualizing sin and its cure. There is a tendency to divide the world between saints and sinners along moralistic lines; this is found in Revelation and the Pastoral Epistles. There is another tendency toward moral gradualism through obedience to moral norms; this is found in Luke, Matthew, and James. There is a doctrine of relationship, according to which the line between saint and sinner is marked by faith in God or lack of faith. Typically, for the historical Jesus (on most reconstructions) and the Pauline and Johannine traditions, this line runs down the middle of every person.

Each approach to sin implies a different sense of human destiny and a different meaning of salvation. Since the last option has the strongest claim to originality, consistency with the event of Jesus Christ, and appropriateness to the gospel of God's gracious love, it will be developed more fully here.

Discipleship and Servanthood

That "no one can serve two masters" (Matt. 6:24) presupposes that human beings are created for covenantal relationship with one another, with God, and with the rest of creation. We are determined by whom or what we serve, whether God or mammon (or something else). *Serve* here has the meaning of "love." You are what you love. You are what you love because in deciding what to love you constitute yourself as such a person with such a love. Freedom is not absolute autonomy, but release from idolatrous forces that distort life. Paul's attack on justification by works of the law (he means "ritual works") would apply to any attempt to seek justification by any kind of works. His critique, and the struggle in the letters to the Hebrews and Colossians against the veneration of cosmic forces, all aim at restoring humanity to proper servanthood. The images of stewardship (Matt. 25:14–30; Luke 17:10), discipleship (Mark 6:8–11), sonship (Gal. 4, "adulthood"), and being begotten by God (John 3) imply high levels of independent initiative for those who know God's will.

To stand fast in freedom (Gal. 5:1) is to fulfill one's destiny through service in love and to reject continuously all conformity to the world, while being impelled by grace to render service to the world (Rom. 12:1–2). For those set free by Christ, socially imposed subservience is no longer determinative, and equality is the result:

> There is no longer Jew or Greek, there is no longer slave or free, there is no longer male and female; for all of you are one in Christ Jesus. And if you belong to Christ, then you are Abraham's offspring, heirs according to the promise. (Gal. 3:28–29)

Paul makes clear in Galatians 4 that these "heirs" are not "minors," but mature children of God ready for grown-up responsibility and freedom.[4]

Finitude and Ethics

Freedom does not include release from the essential conditions of bodily historical existence. We remain "body"; our life is "in the flesh." Paul did not think of a real self in contrast with fallen flesh, for these were categories borrowed from his opponents and hence redefined in the context of Pauline theology. So constitutive is bodily existence that each person must find an appropriate way to express sexual inclinations (1 Cor. 7). Each must work for daily bread (1 Thess. 4:11–12). The alienation that these relationships produce is overcome by Christ, but we remain finite. Thus, although there are remarkable efforts to overcome inequalities, Paul once found it necessary to reimpose traditional sex roles temporarily in the face of gnostic demands to eradicate such finite factors from Christian self-identity (1 Cor. 11:2–16). Each person's sexual gift must be exercised in "holiness" and display the love of Christ (1 Cor. 7:4).

The love ethic (John 13:34–35) requires the full use of our sagacity. The gift of the Spirit unleashes, rather than subordinates, the use of the intellect (1 Cor. 14). Human beings are the creatures who move toward God's future (Phil. 3; Heb. 13), whose deeds and values face judgment and whose virtues can never be an occasion for boasting (Eph. 2:9). Even the most exalted spiritual or theological insights are finite and need eschatological fulfillment (1 Cor. 13:12). To be human requires faith rather than perfect certainty, hope rather than present fulfillment. As pilgrims, we are to "[go] out, not knowing where [we are] going" (Heb. 11:8). With adversity our expected lot, we remain vulnerable until the eschaton.

Reconciliation and Resurrection

Salvation involves reconciliation in, rather than release from, finitude. Each person repeats the choice of Adam to sin by disregarding individual limits (Rom. 5:12–21). The essence of sin is not rule breaking but alienation—the refusal of the creature to acknowledge the Creator and to love the neighbor. Alienation is a matter of what Augustine termed the self that was *incurvatus in se ipsum*—curved in upon itself. One can be curved in upon oneself in more than one way—in arrogance and *hubris* (self-elevation), or in self-pity, sloth, self-disparagement. *Flesh* in this context denotes the tendency to mistake one's accomplishments for the good or to make oneself the center of reality (*concupiscence,* in the tradition). The human dilemma is not weakness per se but mistaken strength, which is related closely with Paul's critique of misguided zeal (Rom. 10:1–4) and Jesus' opposition to unbridled anger (Matt. 5:21–26). The cross reveals the depth of this alienation, and the resurrection gives the power that we need to break free from it (Rom. 3:21–26).

When people receive this gospel and are reconciled with God, the righteousness of God is restored (Rom. 1:17–18), and we regain our rightful role in the creation (Rom. 8:12–23; 12:1–2; 1 Cor. 6:3). We take up responsibility in the world and extend reconciling love into our economic, family, and political obligations (Eph. 5:21–6:9; 1 Pet. 2:13–25; 1 Cor. 7; Rom. 13:1–7). We are set free to enjoy creaturely existence (Matt. 11:19; Phil. 4:8) and to find "rest" in our encounter with God's word (Heb. 3:7–4:13). Thus restored, we exhibit an alert, resourceful vitality as we move in hope toward the fulfillment that only God can provide (Matt. 24; Phil. 3:8–16; Heb. 11–12). We are reconciled to the exigencies of historical life and can face death with courage, expecting the resurrection. Yet we live on this side of God's final judgment, as justified sinners dependent on God's grace and, at best, we only fragmentarily and occasionally manifest the newness of life by which we are called and claimed.

> The essence of sin is not rule breaking but alienation—the refusal of the creature to acknowledge the Creator and to love the neighbor.

In short, human beings are created, sustained, called, and claimed for God's future by God's gracious love. They are those beings who can understand themselves in any ultimate sense in terms of, and only in terms of, God's love freely given to them and, in turn, as called to love God with their whole being and their neighbors as themselves.

SOME CONTEMPORARY ISSUES

The question of what constitutes an appropriate Christian theological understanding of what it means to be a human being is a theological theme that shifts and develops over time. The issues and possibilities presented by the context in which we live have to be addressed by Christian teaching. Feminist and African American theologians call into radical question traditional Christian understandings of what it means to be human. They do so from their experience of inherited doctrines as oppressive or manifestly inadequate to their experience. Women theologians correctly claim that there is a gender bias in traditional anthropology, and African American theologians note that racist assumptions have too often shaped Christian thought.

The dualistic model of traditional theological ways of thinking about human beings, in which the soul was regarded as of more value than the body, and the body as a "seducer" of the soul, has been tremendously injurious for women. When males are regarded as more "rational," and females more "carnal," women are viewed as potentially seductive of men, causing them to sin. Such a view regards women as more to be feared morally than men. Females are not intrinsically evil, but morally more dangerous. Thomas Aquinas argued that women are hierarchically subordinate to men in status and that they deficiently exhibit human nature.[5] Women participate less in the image of God, he contended. He was guided by Aristotle's biological understandings of the role of women and men in procreation and concluded from them that women should not be ordained because they were defective males. If we are called to love our neighbors as ourselves, such understandings need revision. The appropriate direction for change is to argue that it is human beings as created for covenantal love and mutual respect, for being a blessing to each other, that are meant by saying that we are created in God's image.[6]

Understanding what it means to be a human being is related to other major Christian doctrines. How we understand God, the world (creation, providence, and evil), salvation, and so on, is part of the picture. Also, our theological understanding of human existence must be in conversation with understandings of human beings in such sciences as psychology and sociology. The philosophical perspective we bring to the discussion (tacitly or explicitly) plays its own role: What do we assume about reality and, hence, human reality that colors the way we construe the Christian witness? Our unexamined Stoicism, individualism, consumerism, and culture-bound visions of the good life need to be looked at critically.

Because of the conversational character of theology, we cannot think about human beings by proof-texting the Bible, mining it for "what the Bible says" about women or homosexuals, and then using the result of such proof-texting in an authoritarian manner to settle contemporary issues. We have to think theologically in our context, as the writers of Scripture did in theirs. The deeper insights of Scripture, that all human beings are loved by God, that God calls the creation of human beings "good," that we are given and called to serve the well-being of each other, that we are embodied and sexed and that this, too, is "good," that the one thing God said was "not good" was that Adam was alone (Gen. 2:18), that Jesus Christ is God's gracious gift to the ungodly who are without a judgmental leg to stand on—all these will guide our thinking.

Because of the conversational character of theology, we cannot think about human beings by proof-texting the Bible and then using the result in an authoritarian manner to settle contemporary issues. We have to think theologically in our context, as the writers of Scripture did in theirs.

Some Propositions about Human Beings

Human beings are created. Human life is limited (subject to weakness, ignorance, illness, and mortality), but not reducible to the result of inscrutable fate or change (a mere accident of evolution, although we are evolved creatures). Creation is not the corrupted or emanated form of an ideal world, but the object of God's communicative love—and it is good by God's creating of it. Human beings are not ultimately tragic figures (as in classic Greek tragedy), not ultimately pathetic (as in much twentieth-century drama—e.g., Willy Loman). Human beings are good, are sinful, and are redeemable. Still, human existence, as finite, is dependent on God as the ground and end of all being and is also subject to all manner of causes operating efficaciously upon it in the world—bacteria, viruses, weather, and so on.

Human beings come equipped with libidos, sweat glands, metabolism, sometimes grow bald, get flat feet, and are found in all shapes and sizes. They are capable of incredible acts of love and self-transcendence, as well as unspeakable evil.

> Human beings are created. Human beings are social and political. Human beings are created for covenant. Human beings are sexual. Not all human beings are heterosexual.

Human beings are social and political. Far too many Christians, especially in America, think of human beings individualistically. One gets the impression that all the social roles we play, all the relationships in which we participate, are like the sides of a banana that can be peeled off, enabling us to get to the "real person" beneath the roles and relations that make up our being. As a result, often we are unaware of all the many ways in which we are inherently related to one another, to nature, to God, and to the societies, cultures, and institutions that do so much to shape our understandings of who we are and how we are to relate to each other.

This has not always been so in the Christian tradition. For many earlier thinkers, human life was social and corporate (this is radically so for the Bible), exemplified more in the public sphere than in "private" religion. In America we have experienced the privatizing of religion, which goes along with certain political assumptions about the individual as the aim or end of the body politic and its organizations. In contrast, Whitehead once remarked, "The topic of religion is individuality in community," not individuality by itself.[7] We need to deprivatize our understanding of human beings in order to do justice to the political and communal character of life. The communally worshiping church reflects its faith in a covenantally related God. Zeal for the unity of the church is a hope for the unity of humanity. Christian unity as usually treated is so trivialized as to be malicious. Responsibility for public, communal life is not an occasional theme in Christian theology, but a constant melody.

Human beings are created for covenant. Human beings are essentially related to God, one another, and the rest of the created order (the natural environment).

The God of Israel breaks with all culturally accepted definitions of deity in Canaanite society (gods who are preoccupied with their "rule") and opts for faithful interrelatedness, steadfast solidarity. Yahweh identifies a faithful covenant partner, responding to the groans of an oppressed people (Exod. 2:24–25). This is an irreversible move, one that is definitional for God and for God's covenant partners. Covenant is possible not because the covenant partner is worthy, but because God commits God-self to new kinds of solidarity with that partner. Walter Brueggemann states, "This God has given up power in the certainty that real saving power is found in uncompromising faithfulness, the very posture the other gods in heaven could not countenance."[8] Hence, covenant is never properly understood as enforced legality with dangerous power coercing our agreement. Covenant is definitional for human beings: We are created for proper relationships with God, ourselves, one another, and nature. Covenant is a social prescription for hope—what human life might yet be like ("your will be done on earth, as it is in heaven") and a subversion of all present worldly ways of organizing life that oppress, subjugate, and enslave the *imago dei.*

Human beings are sexual. In some parts of the Christian tradition, sexuality per se is viewed as evil. Does *agape* stand in final opposition to *eros?* Is *agape* best defined as "self-sacrificial love"? Does it oppose *eros,* or can it transform *eros* and libido? Is it "regard for the other as other," respectful of the personhood and dignity of the other, so that *agape* can redeem relationships of *eros,* libido, and *philia?*[9] Laboring under the weight of a profoundly negative tradition, Christian thought has to forge new meanings in sexuality and, in overcoming heterosexism, understand anew what it means to be human beings as males and as females. The tradition has had a hard time overcoming its acceptance of Aristotle's definition of woman as a "misbegotten male" and its own preference for Genesis 2 and Eve's being "second" over Genesis 1, according to which men and women are both created in the image of God in their cohumanity. The tradition has had such a difficult time talking credibly about sexuality at all that one wonders how it can discuss sanely any controversial issues related to sexuality.

Not all human beings are heterosexual. The question of the status of gay men and lesbians in the church today is a controversial issue. We discuss it in light of the conviction that human beings are created by God for covenant relationship with God and one another, that all human beings are justified and ultimately reconciled with God and one another by the act of God in Christ, that we are given and called to be transformed by Christ and not conformed to the world, and that God made us who we are, as we are, embodied persons enlivened by God's spirit.

Some Favorite Proof Texts from the Hebrew Bible

Many churches today refuse to ordain gay men and lesbians who are "open and practicing," requiring of their clergy "fidelity in marriage and celibacy in singleness." Typically this practice is justified by proof-texting a few verses from disparate parts of the Bible, with the added assumption that it is clear that these texts condemn homosexuality. Defenders of this practice frequently claim that the sin of Sodom was homosexuality, but "the test of Sodom," says J. Gerald Jantzen, "turns on the question of hospitality."[10] "Gang rape of guests," comments Marti Steussy, is offensive regardless of sexual orientation. She points out that Ezekiel 16:49 does not see Sodom's sin as homosexuality: "This was the guilt of your sister Sodom: She and her daughters had pride, excess of food, and prosperous ease, but did not aid the poor and needy."[11] The Sodom story (Gen. 19) is not helpful to the discussion because it describes an activity, gang rape, that everybody agrees is wrong.

Here is a good place to make an important point: The Scriptures do not have a concept of homosexuality as an orientation. Whenever they talk about homosexuality or about what some interpreters have taken to be homosexuality, the reference is always to behavior, as in the story we just considered.

Those who regard homosexuality as a sin and support fidelity in marriage and celibacy in singleness do not tell certain biblical stories. They do not tell of Solomon's seven hundred wives and three hundred concubines, nor of the fact that the Scriptures do not criticize him for this. He is censured, rather, because some of his wives led him to fail to be "true to the LORD his God" (1 Kgs. 11:4). Nor is David criticized for loving Jonathan. Jonathan loved David, we are told, "as he loved his own life," and at Jonathan's death David sobbed, "Greatly loved were you to me; your love to me was wonderful, passing the love of women" (2 Sam. 1:26).

Were David a contemporary Christian, he could not be ordained.[12]

Where the Scriptures differ from the practice of the contemporary church, as Christopher Morse makes plain, is in this: A practice constitutes sexual infidelity when it violates faithfulness to the covenant with God.[13]

The legal codes in Scripture assume patriarchy—the rule of the fathers—and are concerned with matters of purity and property. For example, Leviticus 18:6–18 spells out forbidden relations. Marti Steussy points out that the operative principle in the list, however, is that of violation of privilege. The list does not forbid fathers to "uncover the nakedness" of their daughters. Leviticus 18:19–24 includes a prohibition of homosexual activity: "You shall not lie with a male as with a woman." But, according to Walter Brueggemann, here the operative principle in the whole list of banned practices is that the male "seed" shall not be wasted.[14]

The following sexual relations are banned for men: with a menstruating women (the seed cannot sprout), with a kinsman's wife (the field is being seeded by someone else), by sacrifice to Molech (a waste), with another man (pointless if seed is not to be wasted), with an animal (equally pointless). In this list, lesbian relations are not banned; they do not waste male seed. Judith Plaskow notes that while the Talmudic rabbis condemned male homosexuality, they "indicate no knowledge of homosexual orientation in the modern sense." Also, the Talmudic rabbis regarded lesbianism less seriously "because it involves no intercourse and no 'wasting of seed,'" and therefore "brought no legal penality."[15]

Jon Berquist points out that such passages make assumptions having to do with the nature of the household in ancient Israel. A household had one adult male and other people including women and children, some older adults who needed to be cared for, slaves, and servants. Each household was economically self-sufficient. "The key to understanding sexual behavior," he says, "is that the male head of the household owned the sexuality of those inside the household, but was forbidden to have sex with members of another man's household."[16] This explains why father-daughter and father-son incest shine by their absence from the list of prohibited behaviors. This does not mean that ancient Israelites regularly practiced such incest; it does mean that the relations that are forbidden are those with women whose sexual function is the legal property of another man.

Marti Steussy asks this question: "We tend to regard the Bible as a collection of morals (statements about what you should/shouldn't do), but there are demonstrable ethics (underlying reasons) associated with those morals. Does a moral still apply if its ethics has been rejected?"[17] Jon Berquist claims that the kind of sexual ethics just described is "unhelpful in thinking about contemporary sexuality."[18]

Some Favorite Proof Texts from the New Testament

Fred Craddock proposes that we take seriously an often overlooked question in dealing with the New Testament's statements about homosexual behavior. We should look, he proposes, at how the earliest Christian communities discussed the topic, and learn again to hear biblical texts conversing about the topic within their particular religious, cultural, and political contexts.[19] We should note first, he points out, what the New Testament does not do. It does not use as instructions for Christians any passage from the Hebrew Bible that bears directly upon homosexuality. It never refers to the life of Jesus as providing a model for how to deal with or relate to homosexuals. It never quotes a saying of Jesus concerning homosexual behavior. It cites no early Christian prophet as giving a "word from the Lord" on the topic. It contains no list of household duties (such as that in Eph. 5:22–6:9, for example) that "offers any advice, warning or command related to homosexual conduct."[20]

The New Testament does contain lists of vices, lists developed to denounce and, hence, use as a moral bulwark against the surrounding culture. Such lists are found in Mark 7:21–22; 1 Timothy 6:4–5; 2 Timothy 3:2–4; 1 Corinthians 6:9–10; Romans 1:24–31; and 1 Timothy 1:9–10. The last three contain "the only clear references to homosexual behavior in the New Testament."[21] Since Craddock wrote his article in 1979, the clarity of some of these references has been called into question. Yet we need to attend to them because proof-texters appeal to all of them.

What does Paul make of these vice lists, once he has quoted them? Of the vices listed in 1 Corinthians 6:9–10, he says to his readers: "And this is what some of you used to be. But you were washed, you were sanctified, you were justified in the name of the Lord Jesus Christ and in the Spirit of our God" (v. 11). The list serves to provide a contrast with what the church is given and called to be. Also, the list contains ten vices; it is far from clear that Paul meant that the Corinthians had been guilty of all ten. Paul does not use the list to discuss homosexual behavior. A further difficulty is that the term often translated "homosexuals," *arsenokoitai,* literally the "soft ones," was widely used to refer to men who decked themselves out in order to attract women![22] Greek culture apparently regarded homosexual encounters as evidence of being macho, not soft. In this light, 1 Corinthians 6:9 seems less clear than it once did.

Another vice list is found in Romans 1:24–31:

> For this reason God gave them up to degrading passions. Their women exchanged natural intercourse for unnatural, and in the same way also the men, giving up natural intercourse with women, were consumed with passion for one another. Men committed shameless acts with men and received in their own persons the due penalty for their error. (vv. 26–27)

To interpret these verses as condemning homosexuality overlooks the introduction and the conclusion of the passage. The introduction makes it clear that the long list of bad behavior that follows happened because people turned away from God and exchanged the glory of God for images (Rom. 1:20–23). The conclusion contradicts the proof-texting use of the passage: "Therefore you have no excuse, whoever you are, when you judge others" (Rom. 2:1). "All the world is indicted," says Craddock, "every mouth is stopped from boasting, and the word of grace is awaited."[23] Beverly Gaventa comments that this passage affirms that homosexual behavior is no more or less sinful than self-righteousness; hence, we cannot use it as a basis for calling homosexual persons sinners.[24]

Romans 1:24–31 is the only New Testament text that clearly mentions homosexual behavior, and the conclusion that it draws from its list of vices is simply this: "Therefore you have no excuse, whoever you are, when you judge others; for in passing judgment on another you condemn yourself."

First Timothy 1:9–10 uses the same term, *arsenokoitai*, as does 1 Corinthians 6:9–10, and hence is subject to the same difficulty of interpretation. But even if one takes it as clearly referring to homosexual behavior, Craddock's observation is to the point: All we have is a list. "There is no charge, no counter charge, no discussion, no instruction to a congregation, no discipline, no embrace, no affirmation of love, no call to obedience."[25]

The result is that Romans 1:24–31 is the only New Testament text that clearly mentions homosexual behavior, and the conclusion that it draws from its list of vices is simply this: "Therefore you have no excuse, whoever you are, when you judge others; for in passing judgment on another you condemn yourself" (Rom. 2:1). Using any of these texts to draw any other conclusion than Paul himself draws is unscriptural.

A CONSTRUCTIVE ALTERNATIVE

Where does all this leave us? Just here: "What the Bible says" about sexuality and sexual practice is much less clear than generally supposed. The proof texts cited in defense of an anti-gay and lesbian stance have lost their obviousness, and the only clear case in the New Testament contradicts such usage. The ethical reasoning lying behind some passages from ancient Israel (preservation of the male seed, the father's ownership of the sexuality of members of the household) is no longer convincing. The one thing clearly condemned—violation of fidelity to the covenant with God and one another—is a point on which there should be no disagreement within Christian circles (except for supersessionists who think that God violates covenants!). Lastly, all parties to the discussion should be clear that they reject behavior, whether heterosexual or homosexual, that violates the integrity and well-being of another person.

The current practice of the church in denying ordination to persons whose sexual orientation is gay or lesbian is incoherent, contradicting the gospel of Jesus Christ, and immoral, because it is destructive of the well-being of those who are made in the image of God.

Earlier we pointed out that the Scriptures do not have the concept of homosexuality as an orientation. It is now time to pick up this point. Being gay or lesbian, as best we can know, is not a choice, preference, or decision. The best argument for this claim comes from the experience reported by heterosexuals. Neither I nor any of my male heterosexual friends can recall ever having decided to be heterosexual. Since having fallen in love with our sixth-grade sweethearts, all we know is that we have just "been" this way. Each of us has also always been either right- or left-handed. Being right-handed is not a choice, or a decision for which I can be held morally accountable. It is just the way I am, more like the color of my eyes, for which I am also not responsible, than like deciding to go into the ministry. So is my heterosexuality; it is just the way I am created.

There is the rub, or part of it. "In what amounts to a tragic cruel joke," says Christopher Morse of gay men and lesbians, "their being human as God has made them and their being faithful as God calls them are presented as antithetical."[26] The other part of the rub is that the only alternative the church offers to gay men and lesbians is "celibacy in singleness." Here the church directly contradicts the spirit of the remark made by God about Adam before Eve was created in Genesis 2:18: "It is not good that the man should be alone." How does the church require what God declares "not good"?

> If our sexuality indeed is a given, not something that we choose, then is it not one of those gifts that we have from God?

Christian faith denies, says Morse, "that the way God makes us, in creation, including our sexuality, is ever a cruel joke." It also denies that God calls us to "a life of lonely repression," devoid of affection and relationship to others, and denies that who we are called to be in salvation contradicts what we are given to be in creation.[27]

The promise and challenge held out to the church today is to come to see sexuality in a way it has hardly ever seen it before: as a part of who we are and of what enables us to reach out beyond ourselves to others, as a primary component of the new and transformed lives that we are given and called to live as Christians. Can the church be mature enough to place the issue of homosexuality in this framework? If our sexuality indeed is a given, not something that we choose, then is it not one of those gifts that we have from God (via whatever genetic or otherwise biological means that are yet to be determined) and hence neither something about which to boast nor to refuse? We should raise for the church the question Judith Plaskow asks of Judaism: Are we willing to affirm the values "of each of us being able to find that place within ourselves where sexuality and spirituality come together?"[28] Or will we continue to see to it that the only available paths to the Christian life systematically exclude some from following them?

Gay men and lesbians are human beings, made in the *imago dei*. It is past time to say so. Part of what that means is involved, along with other matters, in the following propositions.

Human Beings Are Equal

The Scriptures go a long way toward overcoming ethnocentrism and the various dualisms into which Hellenistic culture divided human beings (Greeks and barbarians, slaves and free, male and female, with the latter of each pair "less" than the former). The Christian message proclaims that in Jesus Christ, God accepts all persons as potential heirs of God or "fellow citizens of the kingdom." Hence, all inherited theological doctrines that argued that some people contain in themselves more of the *imago dei* than do others are rejected. Any claim or implication that any human beings, because of race, gender, ethnicity, skin color, culture, sexual orientation, religious tradition, or whatever, are less than fully human is hereby denied.

Human Beings Are Part of Nature

Christian tradition has tended to cut off human beings from the natural order. This has given us too great a sense of our importance over the rest of nature and has assumed that God values us at its expense. Part of our sin of arrogance has been the brazen denial that we are dependent on a matrix of relations without which we would not even have air to breathe. It has also contributed, more indirectly than directly but quite really,

> Human beings are equal. Human beings are part of nature. Human beings are moral. Human beings are fallen.

to the rapaciousness displayed toward nature in what Tillich calls the "Protestant-bourgeois" era.[29] Ecological awareness has helped to restore this more unified biblical picture of humankind-in-and-of-nature. It prompts us to look at sin as an arrogant refusal to admit that we are a dependent part of an interdependent ecological system.

Human Beings Are Moral

Created for covenantal relationship, we receive from God the ability to esteem God's moral attributes (love, mercy, justice, holiness, etc.) and to make decisions and develop a moral sense or conscience. This moral capacity is part of our real, limited freedom. Christian existentialists stress the ever renewed decisions of faith and love as the quintessential precondition for authentic life. Maturing in the Christian life, however, as in any committed relationship, means not having to decide anew every day whether to love God or one's spouse. Theology needs to reclaim the stress that the creation story in Genesis articulates the conditions for the covenant, as well as the understanding that because of God's steadfastness, human beings can also be steadfast.

Human Beings Are Fallen

In putting it this way, we deliberately avoid saying that "human nature is fallen." That way of speaking brings with it two unfortunate implications. One is that there is something called "human nature," some Platonic essence we all have in common. I would like to suggest that as made in the image of the God who is free to be whomever/whatever God will be, we need a "negative anthropology." It is not yet clear what we might become. This Platonic assumption is also radically questioned by the observation that all the different cultures and religions of the world are alternative ways of being human. It is further questioned by the additional observation that it is human beings who construct these cultures and religions. (That human beings construct religions does not deny that God discloses God's self to us in revelation, unless one chooses to argue that religion is nothing but a social construction.)

The other unfortunate implication of saying that "human nature is fallen" is that it is our very nature to sin. Salvation, consequently, would require the annihilation of human nature. Like the tragic Vietnamese village, it would have to be destroyed in order to be saved. Some salvation! Sin is not definitional of human beings. It is not necessary that we sin. We are free not to sin, even though we fail to avoid doing so. Christian theology must deny determinism in its understanding of human beings. It is not unknown, even in these narcissistic days, that sometimes people appropriately feel guilty for having sinned. Were determinism true, both the sin and the feeling of guilt would be determined, mistaken though the latter would be.

It is more helpful to think of the fall in this way: All human beings are born into a fallen world and, unless we are open to the transforming grace of God, we become sinners. How is this so, how does it work? A post-Holocaust theology, like a feminist theology, takes sin with radical seriousness and understands it as historically and socially originated. We are born into and shaped by a sociocultural world whose beliefs, values, institutions, and practices make us who we are long before we can even begin to think critically about them. Yet we can come to see it for what it is and become responsible for trying to change it.

As an autobiographical example, I was born in the mid-South, into a world where segregation and Jim Crow laws were as thorough as was the apartheid system in South Africa. Blacks and whites used separate water fountains, attended separate schools and churches, sat in separate parts of a bus, visited the zoo on different days, and faced markedly different economic prospects. We did nothing together and were denied almost all possibility of getting to know each other. The theory supporting this social system and practice held that blacks were naturally inferior to whites (being less fully human), like children, except that, unlike children, blacks could not grow up. Their comparatively greater poverty and lack of economic attainment, assured by the system of segregation, was taken as evidence of their inferiority. All this shaped our values, our psyches, and our self-understanding. Born as human babies made in God's image, we became sinners.

We are not born carrying a load of original sin, but we pick it up with remarkable quickness.

We are not born carrying a load of original sin, but we pick it up with remarkable quickness. A racist society, made by people who were racists, in turn makes people into racists. To grow up in such a society and, by the grace of having had a few faithful Christian teachers (as well as some excellent non-Christian teachers!), to learn to see it as a lie, is to learn what it means to be lonely. Sin in this sense, original or inherited sin, is not something for which we are guilty, but something whose victims we are because of our human vulnerabilities. We are damaged not only by racism, but by all the other systemic sins that make up our world and go into the making of us. This is why Rita Brock says that "sin is not something to be punished, but something to be healed."[30] It is precisely because of our relationality, our openness not only to other persons but to the influences of institutions, cultures, and ingrained attitudes, that we can be deeply harmed.

Marjorie Suchocki reminds us of the contributions to the understanding of original sin made by the work of Walter Rauschenbusch and Reinhold Niebuhr. Rauschenbusch argued that sin is transmitted to us by our immersion in a social system that is either sinful or capable of great sin: "We draw our ideas, our moral standards, and our spiritual ideals from the social body into which we are born; these are mediated to us by the public and personal institutions that make up the society."[31] The most powerful institutions of the society are driven by economics, by greed. As Rauschenbusch argued: The problem of sin is that it is profitable. There is money to be made in the marketing of cancer-causing cigarettes, of death-dealing instruments of war, in selling handguns, in slum housing. The value system of such a society exalts evil, justifies it, provides it with an ethics. "Each generation corrupts the next."[32]

What Reinhold Niebuhr added to Rauschenbusch was a more deeply realistic view of groups and institutions as profoundly hypocritical and only rarely capable of self-criticism and self-transformation. He does not spare churches, as institutions, from this same criticism; the only difference there is that the hypocrisy is more blatant. Both contend that sin is mediated to society and to persons by the very mechanisms of society.

As such, it is profoundly personal and deeply structural. The powers and principalities, now understood as the magnitudes that govern our lives in so many dimensions, tempt us to believe the lie (e.g., the lie that the meaning of life is to be found in the possession of material goods and that our moral responsibility is to shop till we drop) and to be slothful, not to resist the injustices or challenge the lies.

The tendency of middle-class American churches is to treat sin, when it is talked about at all (and we are cautioned that talking about it is not conducive to church growth, because it is not a happy topic), as an individualistic, privatized matter. Sin is individual peccadilloes and sexual straying. Contrary to this, for the Bible and the greater part of the Christian tradition, sin is not only profoundly personal (persons are not unrelated individuals), but deeply structural. The great insight of the social gospel movement in liberal Protestantism and of various liberation theologies is that personal sins alone do not build the prison in which so much of humanity is caught. The crimes of the poor in the ghetto are, indeed, crimes, but so is the ghetto. And the crimes of the poor cannot be understood apart from the structures of consistent and often violent marginalization inflicted upon them.

The death-dealing ways of our civilization that result in the deaths worldwide of eighteen hundred children per hour for lack of simple nutrition and elementary medical care cannot be blamed simply on individual sins. It is related to the powerful impact of economic and political realities and forces that can be named. The kind of ecological disaster represented by destruction of whole swaths of rain forest is similar. The impact of such forces could be resisted, but it is not. Personal sin figures into this discussion as the reason why we do not resist the powerful and destructive forces of the world. The sin of the churches is their almost unanimous silence on what one rabbi, Yeshua ha Notsri (Jesus of Nazareth), called "the weightier matters of the law" (Matt. 23:23).

The great insight of the social gospel movement in liberal Protestantism and of various liberation theologies is that personal sins alone do not build the prison in which so much of humanity is caught.

According to the doctrine of original sin, everyone participates in this fallen world, though whether each is "guilty" has been a debatable point. Theologians have disagreed about the cause, locus, and degree of this disorder. They have disagreed about its effect upon the *imago dei,* which characterizes human beings as created by God. But all agree that the central theme of Christian anthropology is the fact of, and the remedy for, this disordered reality and broken image.

It is appropriate to describe human existence, in its contradictions and ambiguities, as irreducibly mysterious, as dignified and miserable, as human but less than human. To refer to "mystery" is not to plead for theological silence; it is to warn of the dangers of excessive confidence and precision in theological anthropology.

How we assess the human situation is the most critical part of our theological anthropology. If we see the human situation before God and with one another as serious but not perilous, we will see human beings as only in need of moral correction and education, and little more. That we do need correction and education is not disputed. The more we see the human situation as in deep crisis, the greater and deeper is the divine response of grace and forgiveness required. In the latter case, our Christology will have to make of Jesus Christ more than an example or symbol of God's goodwill toward us. Jesus Christ will have to be seen as the one in whom God declares God's acceptance of humanity in its lack of humanness, thus making it possible for us in our estrangement to appropriate the gift of a new and transformed life.

ALL THOSE STRANGERS ALONG THE WAY

Traditionally, Christians have only, with difficulty and all too rarely, been able to look upon all those "other, different" people in the world as neighbors whom God has given us to love. The closed-off, ethnocentric self-understanding of historical Christianity was often able to tolerate the stranger, if at all, only as a potential candidate for conversion. The stranger was permissible as long as we could sustain the assumption that, one day, she would become one of us, like us, and in no significant way any longer a stranger. In the political structure of Christendom, for example, Jews were the only religious minority that had any rights or protections. Ironically, they might have been better off without such protections had they emigrated (as did the Church of the East—the Nestorians) to a less threatening environment. When Jews were seen to be resistant to conversion, Chrysostom in the fifth century declared them "fit only to be slaughtered," and Luther in the sixteenth advocated burning their houses, synagogues, and holy books, putting them to work at forced labor, and, if necessary, expelling them from the country.[33]

> The moral measure of Christian theology will increasingly be taken by its capacity to welcome strangers and to guard their dignity and well-being.

The closed-off, absolutist, ethnocentric theology of Christendom cannot finally permit others to be in the world. One of the biggest challenges to contemporary Christians is to learn to welcome strangers. Their ways of being human, by sheer contrast with ours, will cause us self-doubt and self-questioning. Openness to strangers requires openness to questioning and a willingness to be questioned, because strangers are questions to us and bring their questions with them. Nonetheless, the moral measure of Christian theology will increasingly be taken by its capacity to welcome strangers and to guard their dignity and well-being.

QUESTIONS FOR REFLECTION AND DISCUSSION

1. What are the implications of saying that human beings are "creatures made in the image of God"? What does it mean to say that we are both "body" and "soul"?
2. What are the four stories Serene Jones uses to think about humanity? Why not just combine them into one story?
3. What are the seven characteristics she finds in human beings as creatures of God? How does sin distort each of those characteristics?
4. What does it mean to define sin as "unfaithfulness"?
5. What is added to the portrait of human beings by saying we are "justified and sanctified in Christ"? What is added by saying that we are "people to whom God has promised eternal life"?
6. What does Williamson take to be our society's dominant view of humanity? How does he think the Christian view is different?
7. What does he identify as important characteristics of human beings?
8. Do you find persuasive his interpretations of biblical passages often cited as condemning homosexuality?
9. How does he understand "the stranger" as a critical category for understanding how human beings ought to live?

FOR FURTHER READING

Berkouwer, G. C. *Sin*. Trans. Philip C. Holtrop. Grand Rapids: Wm. B. Eerdmans Publishing Co., 1971.

Brunner, Emil. *Man in Revolt.* Trans. Olive Wyon. Philadelphia: Westminster Press, 1957.

Hoekema, Anthony A. *Created in God's Image.* Grand Rapids: Wm. B. Eerdmans Publishing Co., 1986.

Jones, Serene. *Feminist Theory and Christian Theology: Cartographies of Grace.* Minneapolis: Fortress Press, 2000.

McFadyen, Alastair. *Bound to Sin.* Cambridge: Cambridge University Press, 2000.

Niebuhr, Reinhold. *The Nature of Destiny of Man,* vol. 1. New York: Charles Scribner's Sons, 1941.

Pannenberg, Wolfhart. *What Is Man?* Trans. Duane A. Priebe. Philadelphia: Fortress Press, 1970.

Plantinga, Cornelius, Jr. *Not the Way It's Supposed to Be: A Breviary of Sin.* Grand Rapids: Wm. B. Eerdmans Publishing Co., 1995.

Ricoeur, Paul. *The Symbolism of Evil.* Trans. Emerson Buchanan. Boston: Beacon Press, 1967.

Ruether, Rosemary Radford. *Women and Redemption.* Minneapolis: Fortress Press, 1998.

Segundo, Juan Luis. *Grace and the Human Condition.* Trans. John Drury. Dublin: Gill and Macmillan, 1980.

Wilson-Kastner, Patricia. *Faith, Feminism, and the Christ.* Philadelphia: Fortress Press, 1983.

Chapter 5

How Does Jesus Make a Difference?

The Person and Work of Jesus Christ

As already noted in chapter 2, Christians early came to insist that Jesus Christ was not just a wise person or a great prophet or even an angel, but truly God. In the fourth century, against the Arians, the Nicene Creed affirmed that Christ was not even just a lesser divine being but "God of very God, begotten, not made, being of one substance with the Father." In every way they could, the authors of the creed affirmed that, whatever we mean by "God," Jesus Christ cannot be less.

In those first centuries, Christians also came to insist that Christ was truly human. Docetists (whose name comes from a Greek word meaning "to seem") argued that Jesus only seemed to be human. God could surely, they thought, not have gotten so involved in this dirty, evil world of matter as to take on a human body! He just seemed to have a body, seemed to suffer, seemed to die. The majority of Christians, reacting against this, said that Docetism would turn the incarnation (literally, "becoming bodily") into a fake. It sounded as if Jesus were just pretending, putting on an act.

By the beginning of the fourth century, then, most Christians were affirming that Christ was indeed fully human and fully divine. But how were this divinity and humanity related to one another?

THE ROAD TO CHALCEDON

Theologians in the city of Alexandria in Egypt began their efforts to understand the incarnation with the words from John's Gospel: "The Word became flesh and lived among us" (John 1:14). As Athanasius, one of the greatest Alexandrian theologians, put it in the early fourth century, "The Word of God took a human body to save and help human beings, so that having shared our human birth, he might make human beings partakers of the divine and spiritual nature."[1] This model kept clear that there was one agent, the Word of God, at work. As other Alexandrians sought to explain how the Word became flesh, however, they got into trouble. Apollinaris, a younger friend of Athanasius, explained that the Word took the place of a human mind or soul in Christ. I have a human body and a human mind; Christ had a human body but a divine mind.[2]

Theologians soon realized that this "Apollinarianism" posed problems for Christian theology. For one thing, was Christ "truly human" if he lacked a human mind or soul? Could he really suffer? Could he really empathize with us? Moreover, Christians generally believed (more of this shortly) that Christ saved us by uniting us with God and thereby transforming us. But if Christ did not have a human mind, then the human mind had never been united with God, and accordingly had not been saved. "What he has not assumed," Gregory of Nazianzus insisted in the fourth century, "he has not healed."[3] This is particularly a problem since it is presumably our mind or soul that really sins. If Christ only united the *body* with divinity to cure it, Gregory said, that would be like taking someone with an injured eye and bandaging her foot![4]

The theologians of Antioch, one of Alexandria's competitors as a great city of the eastern Mediterranean, proposed a different way of thinking about the human and divine in Christ. They said that Christ had "two natures"—human and divine—in "one person." If Christ had a full human nature, then he had a human mind as well as a human body, so this position avoided Apollinarianism. But at least some of the Antiochene theologians separated the two natures so much that they seemed to threaten the unity of the one person. The Bible's stories about Jesus Christ, after all, clearly describe him as one agent, doing and suffering what he does, not as a divine one and a human one living together in the same body as some odd sort of split personality.

Matters came to a head in the early fifth century when Nestorius, bishop of Constantinople and an advocate of Antiochene theology, opposed calling Mary "the Mother of God" (or *theo-tokos,* "God-bearer"). She was just the mother of the human nature, he insisted; he was willing to compromise and accept calling her "the Mother of Christ," but not "the Mother of God." Nestorius soon discovered that theologians get into real trouble when they start threatening popular piety. His opponents attacked him as a defamer of the Virgin Mary, and a majority of Christians turned sharply against him.

Cyril of Alexandria, the ambitious patriarch of Alexandria in the early fifth century, continued the Alexandrian side of the fight. He first preferred to say that

Christ had only one nature, but eventually accepted the language of "two natures," as long as one made very clear that there was only one person or one individual in Christ. In practice, that meant saying that human and divine were so united in Christ that one could apply predicates that belonged to one nature to the other. The Latin term for this interchange of properties is *communicatio idiomatum*. So one could say that the divinity suffered or that the humanity worked miracles—or that Mary was the Mother of God.

The Council of Chalcedon in 451 affirmed that Christ was "truly God and truly human [thus refuting Arians and Docetists] . . . consisting of a reasonable soul and a body [having a 'reasonable soul' refuting the Apollinarians] . . . born of the Virgin Mary, the Mother of God [thus refuting the Nestorians] . . . to be acknowledged in two natures, without confusion, without change, without division, without separation."

> Chalcedon affirmed Christ as "truly God and truly human . . . consisting of a reasonable soul and body . . . born of the Virgin Mary, the Mother of God . . . to be acknowledged in two natures, without confusion, without change, without division, without separation."

Debates about finding a middle ground between Alexandria and Antioch continued among Eastern Christians, arguably with major consequences that reached beyond theology. Those most committed to Antiochene views, the "Nestorians" or "Church of the East," split off from "Chalcedonian" Christians and spread all the way to China. Those most committed to the conclusions of Alexandria continued to insist that Christ had only one nature and were therefore called "Monophysites" (*mono-physis,* "one nature"); they were particularly strong in the Middle East and North Africa. When Islam began to expand from Arabia, the first Christians it encountered were often Monophysites or Nestorians who felt alienated from the Chalcedonian Christians of the eastern Roman Empire and were unlikely to get help or support from them. Who knows if parts of the world now dominated by Islam might have remained Christian had it not been for these theological divisions?

Long before these debates settled down in the East, Western Christians generally accepted Chalcedon—particularly as interpreted by a letter written by the pope of the time, Leo I—as the final word on issues about Christ. In his essay for this chapter, Robert Jenson will argue, among other things, that Leo led his fellow Latin-speaking Christians astray in important ways. In most ways, Jenson supports the traditional Christology of the church as the logical outcome of what the Bible requires us to say about Jesus. But he thinks that Western Christians (both Catholic and Protestant) especially have virtually become secret Nestorians: We think of Christ's "two natures" as so separate that we lose the oneness of the person Jesus is. Talking about what the divine nature does and what the human nature does, we stop talking about what Jesus Christ does. Jenson offers his own solution to the problem.

THE HISTORICAL JESUS

Beginning in the nineteenth century, with the rise of the modern historical-critical method, some theologians began to insist that, if Christ were truly human, then we ought to be able to study him the way historians would study any other human being who lived in the past. More liberal theologians in particular, who wanted to criticize many of the church's traditional doctrines, sometimes hoped that, if they could get back to the "historical Jesus," they would find beliefs more compatible with their own.

Debates have continued about how much theology needs to know concerning what historical research can tell us about Jesus, and the fact that different historians keep coming up with different pictures of Jesus has not clarified the issues. In the 1940s and '50s, the German Lutheran New Testament scholar and theologian Rudolf Bultmann said that all we really needed to know was that Jesus existed and died on a cross. Influenced by existentialist philosophy and also by Luther's theology of faith, Bultmann believed that faith confronts us with the need for a decision for or against the claim that God loves us in Christ; we are "suspended in mid-air and cannot demand a proof of the Word."[5] Trying to establish evidence to settle the question misunderstands the commitment that faith requires.

Bultmann's contemporaries Karl Barth and Paul Tillich both argued, in quite different ways, that we need more content in our picture of Jesus but that that content will not take the form of historical facts accurate in detail. Tillich thought that the Bible gives us an "expressionist portrait" of Jesus,[6] capturing the essence of who he was in the way that a painting can do better than a photograph. Barth said we cannot penetrate behind the biblical stories; we have to retell them in the faith that they capture Jesus' identity in a narrative form. Others keep hoping for clearer historical results, and the library of historical portraits of Jesus grows ever larger, but many of the "historical" accounts seem to reveal more about their authors than they do about Jesus.

Even among those suspicious of trying to ground Christian faith in historical evidence, recent theologians have often paid more attention to the Gospels' accounts of Jesus' life and teaching. The classic creeds and much earlier theology tend to jump straight from his birth to his death and resurrection. That leaves out all the stories in the Gospels about what Jesus did and said. A new attention to Jesus' teaching and ministry has drawn attention to a number of features, four of which I will mention here.

First, understanding Jesus in his historical context has made it clearer how much he had in common with many other Jewish teachers of his time. The Pharisees were the party in his society devoted to religious reform; some were obsessively worried about following Jewish law, but others were more open and tolerant. Jesus' contemporaries might in many ways have classified him as a "liberal Pharisee." Certainly we cannot, as Christians too often have in the past, treat the Pharisees as the villains of the story or contrast Jesus' teaching about love with

"Jewish legalism," for almost every statement he made about love and forgiveness has a parallel in Jewish texts.

Second, his talk about the "kingdom of God" or (as Matthew usually has it) "kingdom of heaven" seems to have been central to Jesus' teaching. This book's final chapter, on eschatology, will return to the question of what that talk meant. For now, suffice it to say that any account of Jesus that makes him an ethical teacher and leaves out his hopes for God's actions in the future seems unfaithful to both Bible and history.

> Jesus identified with the oppressed, the poor, the outsiders of his society. Unlike the "Zealots" of his time, he did not propose a violent revolution, but he *was* a revolutionary.

Third, Jesus identified with the oppressed, the poor, the outsiders of his society. Unlike the "Zealots" of his time, he did not propose a violent revolution, but he *was* a revolutionary. He proposed the ideal of a radically different sort of society. The African American theologian James Cone proposes that, since Jesus was on the side of the oppressed in his society, he stands on the side of the oppressed in our society—and in modern North America that means above all African Americans.[7] Latin American theologians such as Gustavo Gutiérrez say the same thing to the impoverished peasants of their societies[8] about the significance of this Jesus who condemned the rich and was executed by those in power. Jesus also ate with tax collectors and Pharisees as well, of course, and cured the daughter of a Roman centurion. Even as he cared about the outsiders of his society, he never identified with any one class or cause.

Fourth, Jesus did live a life of poverty, but he was a man. Denying the particularity of his sex leads to denying his humanity. The poor can say, "He was like us," but in one important respect women cannot. It has been pointed out that in the Gospels, remarkably for his time, he never says anything demeaning about women, he has women traveling with him as his disciples, and he uses female imagery to describe both himself and God.[9] Even in the Middle Ages, prominent Christian theologians male and female prayed to Jesus as "Mother."[10] And of course he was not just a man, but a Jew, a person of the first century, and so on. It is not simply that men are like Jesus and women are not: each of us is like him in some ways and unlike him in others. Feminist theologians continue to struggle with the impact of his maleness on women; Leanne Van Dyk will address the topic in her essay.

THE WORK OF CHRIST

Another issue of concern to some feminist theologians is the way we talk about Christ's work of salvation. Leanne Van Dyk's essay attempts to retrieve important elements of the tradition on this issue while hearing the challenges of some contemporary critiques. As I will be noting below, classic accounts of how Christ saves us often put an emphasis on his suffering. As Joanne Carlson Brown and Rebecca Parker have written, "The central image of Christ on the cross as the savior of the world communicates the message that suffering is redemptive. If the best person who ever lived gave his life for others, then, to be of value we should likewise sacrifice ourselves. Any sense that we have a right to care for our own needs is in conflict with being a faithful follower of Jesus."[11] And that, they argue, is precisely the message that women in particular do not need to hear. Even more, for women who were victims of abuse as children, the idea of the Christ who dies to appease the angry Father gives exactly the wrong message—an image of child abuse at the heart of the gospel. On the other hand, theologians male and female argue that such a picture misinterprets the traditional doctrines, and that the gospel may sometimes be right to challenge us to risk suffering in the midst of our often comfortable lives.

The part of Christian theology that concerns Jesus Christ needs to discuss who he is and what he does—his person and his work, or *Christology* and *soteriology* (the study of how he acts as *soter,* or Savior). As already noted, the early church worked out beliefs about his person in some detail. By contrast, one of the odd features of the Christian tradition is that, while the notion *that* Christ saves us lies at its heart, the church has never developed an official position on just *how* that salvation is accomplished. This is a useful reminder that the church usually draws sharp lines only when faced with beliefs that seem to lead away from what it needs to affirm to secure the reality of its faith. Somehow, that never happened concerning what theologians have traditionally called "the work of Christ."

From early on, though, several motifs from Paul's letters seemed important to any account:

Recapitulation. Irenaeus, bishop of Lyons in France in the second century, picked up Paul's theme of Christ as "second Adam" (1 Cor. 15:45). Christ, he said, repeated or recapitulated what Adam had done wrong, getting it right this time. Thus, although Adam had been disobedient to God, Christ was perfectly obedient.[12]

The transformation of humanity. Paul elaborated the Adam/Christ contrast in this way: "Just as one man's trespass led to condemnation for all, so one man's act of righteousness leads to justification and life for all" (Rom. 5:18). Plato had taught that individual objects have their reality by participating in eternal and unchanging forms. Fido is a dog and Socrates is a human being because they participate, respectively, in the forms of "dogness" and "humanity." The forms are ultimately "more real" than the particulars that participate in them.

Under the influence of such ideas, early Christian theologians found it easy to speak of how humanity had been transformed since Christ united it with divinity. "Having become what we are," Gregory of Nyssa wrote, "He . . . again united humanity to God."[13] Even apart from Plato's philosophy, however, the idea of a transformation of all human beings remained. Eastern Christians generally spoke of how we had thus been "deified"; in the West, where many theologians were nervous about "deification," it was more common to say that, while Christ was Son of God "by nature," he made us children of God "by adoption."

The blessed exchange. "For our sake," Paul wrote the Corinthians, God made Christ "to be sin who knew no sin, so that in him we might become the righteousness of God" (2 Cor. 5:21). Somehow Christ took on the burden that was rightfully ours, in what has traditionally been called "vicarious atonement"—Christ made us "at one" with God "vicariously," by doing or suffering what it was properly ours to do or suffer. "This is our acquittal," as Calvin explained, "that guilt that held us liable for punishment has been transferred to the head of the Son of God."[14]

Given these basic motifs, as already noted, one could explain Christ's work in a number of ways:

Christ the Victor. In the early centuries of Christianity (from Origen in the second century to Augustine in the fourth), again with Luther, and then again in an important book called *Christus Victor* published by the Swedish theologian Gustaf Aulén in 1931, the idea came to the fore that Christ saved us by freeing us from the power of the devil. By sin, we had voluntarily put ourselves under the devil's sway. In some versions of this account, Christ pays the devil a ransom which frees us. In others, he defeats the devil in some sort of spiritual combat. In still others, he tricks the devil. Since the devil has authority over all human beings, he sees Christ, looking like just a human being, and seizes him. Since Christ is also God, however, the devil thereby overreaches his proper claims, and the arrangement by which he held sway over all of us is abrogated. Christ's humanity becomes the bait disguising the fishhook of his divinity. In Augustine's words, "The cross of the Lord became a trap for the Devil; the death of the Lord was the food by which he was ensnared."[15] This image of winning our salvation through trickery, and even the idea of making deals with the devil,[16] makes many people nervous, but the power of this account is that it captures the sense every addict knows, in which, though we freely enter into sin, it comes to hold power over us. Moreover, many who use this model emphasize that Christ triumphs over the devil without the use of violence, thereby offering a nonviolent model of struggle with evil, which has important ethical implications.

> Three versions of the work of Christ: Christ the victor who defeats the powers of evil, Anselm's account of the Christ who pays the debt we owe to God's honor, Abelard's moral influence theory.

Paying our debt. Around 1100, Anselm, the archbishop of Canterbury, articulated another theory in classic form. As Van Dyk notes in her essay for this chapter, this "substituted punishment view" has become the dominant theory of salvation or soteriology for most Catholics and Protestants. We owe all possible honor and obedience to God, Anselm said. "He who violates another's honor does not enough by merely rendering honor again, but must, according to the extent of the injury done, make restoration in some way satisfactory to the person whom he has dishonored."[17] Even God cannot simply ignore injustice. In sin we fall short of giving what we owe, but we cannot pay up this debt by running up a future surplus since we owe God everything, and we cannot give God more than everything.[18] We thus seem to owe God an unpayable debt in honor. Since it is humanity that owes that debt, only a human being could fairly pay it. But only God could make the payment, as Christ does by voluntarily taking on suffering and death—and therefore only one who was both human and God could accomplish our salvation by reconciling us with God.

Anselm drew on medieval ideas of honor, lords, and vassals. In a later age, Calvin and others used the imagery of law courts or business transactions to express roughly the same idea: We owe a debt to God, and Christ alone can pay it. The risk of this account is that, if distorted, it can make "God" or "God the Father" seem like the villain of the story, with Christ the hero who wins our freedom. It does capture the seriousness of our sin and the cost which Christ pays to redeem us. (The language of "redemption" is also related to ideas of ransom and can be connected to the image of Christ as our liberating victor.) Van Dyk's essay seeks to preserve what is of value in such imagery, while freeing it from problematic associations.

Moral influence. Anselm's near contemporary Peter Abelard argued that it seemed "cruel and wicked . . . that anyone should demand the blood of an innocent person as the price for anything . . . still less that God should consider the death of his Son so agreeable that by it he should be reconciled to the whole world."[19] Abelard preferred saying that Christ's suffering shows us how much God loves us and therefore inspires us to be more loving and lead better lives. I suppose liberals ever since (from Abelard in the twelfth century to Faustus Socinius, a seventeenth-century theologian who denied the Trinity and Anselm's theory of the atonement, to the great nineteenth-century German theologian Friedrich Schleiermacher), nervous about the implications of the other two models, have favored this one. It avoids images of a vengeful God, but it does have the danger of making Christ seem merely a model, an example, who shows us how to accomplish our own salvation rather than himself doing it.

THE REST OF JESUS' STORY

The Apostles' Creed affirms belief in Jesus Christ, God's "only Son our Lord, who was conceived by the Holy Ghost, born of the Virgin Mary, suffered under Pontius Pilate, was crucified, dead, and buried; he descended into Hell. The third day he rose again from the dead; he ascended into heaven, and sitteth on the right hand of God the Father Almighty; from thence he shall come to judge the quick and the dead." So far, this discussion of Christ's person and work has focused on his life, death, and resurrection; it remains to make some brief notes about some of the concluding phrases.

As early as the third century, Christians affirmed that, between his death and resurrection, Christ went to hell to rescue the virtuous people of ancient Israel and take them to heaven with him.[20] Aquinas and Luther both agreed with this picture of the "descent into hell" as a postmortem rescue mission. Calvin, however, thought that it referred to the agonies Christ experienced on the cross before he died, especially his sense of abandonment by God.[21] In the late twentieth century, the Catholic theologian Hans Urs von Balthasar combined the two ideas. Yes, he said, the descent into hell did come after Christ's death, but it was not a victory march but a movement into radical loneliness and darkness in solidarity with those who have rejected God.[22] Because the dead Christ enters even the state of hell, we can be sure that no place is so dark as to be utterly apart from God's love.

The image of Christ seated "on the right hand of the Father" offers another sort of comfort. At whatever level of decision making or authority there is in the universe, this phrase implies that Christ is present, the same Christ who came to this world, even to the cross, from love of us and who "himself was tested by what he suffered" (Heb. 2:18). Therefore, the news that Christ will return to judge the living and the dead is good news: When we face our judge, we will not face a stranger.

ROBERT W. JENSON

It began in this way: Events compelled certain first-century Jews to believe that the rabbi, prophet, and healer they had followed during a few years' ministry in Galilee and Judea, Jesus of Nazareth, whom the authorities had executed as a threat to religious and civil order, had been raised from that death, and in his complete humanity, soul and body.[1] Moreover, their experience of the risen Jesus did not conform to the supposition that he had merely come *back* from the dead; rather, if their meetings with him rightly displayed the risen Jesus' location in reality, death had been *undone* with him, so that it was left *behind* him.

As worshipers of Israel's God and familiars of its Scriptures, they knew what such an event had to mean if—incalculably!—it had happened:[2] that resurrection of the dead, the undoing of death and evil promised by Israel's prophets,[3] had happened "proleptically" (as the foretaste of a coming future); that in anticipating the resurrection with this one person, the God of Israel had confirmed Jesus' words and deeds, and indeed installed him as Israel's Messiah, as the agent of such liberation for others. Moreover and most disorienting, all this together had to mean that the God of Israel is *identified* by and so with this one Israelite. As the New Testament regularly has it, God just *is* "he who raised our Lord Jesus from the dead."[4]

After some argument, most of them came to think also that if these things were true, the way was now open for the gathering of the Gentiles to Israel's God, which according to its prophets was one defining goal of its calling. Thus, they set out to bring their news to Jews first but to Gentiles also, and found everywhere some of both who believed and so became messengers in turn.

This message, called "the gospel" by its initial messengers, themselves called "apostles" (those sent out), is therefore primally a truth claim, that "Jesus is risen." Christian theology is the continuing labor of thought internal to understanding and formulating this claim. It is the reflective effort to make the news about Jesus' resurrection communicable in the religious and intellectual milieus of the always new places or times to which the mission comes or which come to it, to find the concepts and structures of thought that will let it be spoken intelligibly to the new questions new historical situations pose.

In the nature of the case, this thinking will have two tasks, corresponding to the subject and predicate of the claim "Jesus is risen." So long as the messengers could suppose that their hearers knew who Jesus is, and were sufficiently at home in Israel's Scriptures to realize what "is risen" entails, the message needed little unpacking.

But when the message reaches those who have not heard of Jesus or are badly informed about him, the name has to be expanded descriptively in order to identify *who* is risen: "Jesus, that is, the one who died . . . and suffered . . . and said . . . , is risen." For while "Jesus, that is, the rabbi who ate with publicans and sinners, is risen" can be good news, "Hitler, that is, the one who instituted the Shoah, is risen" would not be. The biblical outcome of this need is a literary genre, the Gospels, each of which is effectively a long proposition of the form, "Jesus, the one who . . . and who . . . and who . . . , is risen."

When the mission reaches Gentiles,[5] who are not at home in the Old Testament and so do not immediately understand "is risen,"[6] conceptual explication is required. The course of this clarification will vary with the previous convictions and conceptual stock of each new set of hearers. The New Testament letters are—among other things—samples of apostolic response to the early appearance of this second need.

The Christian church, with her liturgy, her polity (the ways the church is organized), her ethos and social mission, and her reflections on these things, is the community through time of this gospel mission, of those who believe that the God of Israel has indeed raised Jesus and that this means what Israel's Scriptures say such an event must mean. Christianity is primally a specific shared conviction about a specific human person, and only attendantly thereon a religion or cult or morality or metaphysics or social enterprise.

> The Christian church is the community through time of those who believe that the God of Israel has indeed raised Jesus.

Therefore, Christian theology cannot make our antecedent religious or moral commitments or, in recent jargon, a "theory" of whatever kind, foundational, in order then to inquire how Christ fits with them; Christian theology goes the other way around. And communities that are not communities of witness to Jesus' resurrection, or theologies that have a different program, may be fine moral or spiritual communities or religious systems, and some may even be sustained by certain memories of Jesus, but they are not the community or theology which can with honesty be called "the Christian church" or "Christian theology," or with which we are here to be concerned.

CHRIST AND THE TRINITY

Thus, all Christian doctrine and practice somehow concern the person and work of Christ. The assignment of this chapter, however, is not the whole of Christian theology, but Christology as a specific topic thereof, that is, a particular nest of questions and accepted or proposed answers that has historically developed within the structure of the Western church's thinking.[7] Very roughly, we may say that Christology comprises the question, "What sort of being must this one be, who has death behind him?" and proposed answers to it.

Within this topic, as within a few others, there is a small body of theological propositions that the church has in its history formally decided are so necessary to understanding and speaking the gospel that they define its own faithfulness to the gospel; such teaching is technically called *dogma.*[8] It may be helpful to summarize—very drastically—existing christological dogma at the start: The one Lord Jesus Christ is at once one of the Trinity, in God the Father's identification with him, and one of the human community, in his identification with us. In that he is one of the Trinity, he can have death *behind* him; were he not one of us, he would not have *death* behind him.

Assigning Christology to one chapter and the doctrine of God to another, written by different persons, thus poses a certain difficulty. I have just needed to refer to the Trinity; both historically and conceptually, Christology depends upon the antecedently developed doctrine of God as triune. But any attempt to present the latter as foundation would take this chapter's whole space. To lay the basis of Christology, we are thus forced to proceed in a perhaps unsatisfactory fashion, making assertions without always developing supporting arguments.

Finally, on this line of preliminaries, there is a methodological dead end to warn against. The church ecumenically supposes that the New Testament's witness to Jesus must somehow be the norm of its Christology. The question is how the two are related. Much scholarship, including what is often found in textbooks, assumes that the church's Christology derives from New Testament witness by a historical development of "ideas" about Jesus, especially of the connotations and associations of christological titles such as *Son* or *Savior* or *Lord.*[9] The assumption is made both by many who regard the development discovered in the New Testament and early church teaching as appropriate, and by many who regard it as unfortunate or even as falsification.

Any scholar of linguistics, however, will tell us that this whole notion betrays a fatal naïveté about how language works. No discourse consists of concepts or images, but rather of sentences, of which the sort here relevant state judgments, that such and such is the case. And judgments usually can be equivalently stated using a wide variety of concepts or images.

Thus, the question is not, for example, what Peter had in mind when at Pentecost he used the title *Lord* for Jesus, or what stage in its development the title had then reached, but what judgments Peter made about Jesus—indeed, with sentences that use this word among others. The real question about the relation of church doctrine to the biblical witness is not about the development of ideas, but about whether the church's Trinity doctrine and Christology make—and then develop and analyze—the same[10] judgments about Jesus that Scripture does.[11]

It is easy to show on any of the more relevant passages that this is in fact the case. We will take space for just one example. In Peter's sermon just mentioned, presented by Luke as the paradigm of Christian preaching for repentance, Peter proclaims the risen Christ as the "Lord" who from heaven "pours out" the Spirit on his disciples (Acts 2:33–34). But in Israel's Scriptures, and in the very passage Peter cites from them (Joel 2:9), it is "*the* Lord," the one God of Israel, who gives the Spirit from heaven. Are there then "*two* lords in the heavens"?[12] That would be a polytheistic horror for any faithful Jew, such as Peter himself of course was. Or does Peter think the risen Jesus is simply identical with the Lord of Israel? Clearly not, since he has just said that God did something *to* Jesus, that is, raised him from the dead.

Both Peter and Athanasius make the same judgment as the prologue of John's Gospel: The Word—that is, the protagonist of The Gospel that follows—*is* God just in that he is eternally *with* God, and vice versa.

Peter's claim, it appears, is that the risen Christ, without violation of God's singularity, does what only the God of Israel *himself* does, and that he does this precisely by virtue of his situation *with* the God of Israel. Peter cites Psalm 110 to the effect that Christ *is* the one Lord in that he is addressed as Lord *by* the one Lord. We need not suppose that Peter had thought through the provocative implications of such a proposition to determine that Peter's judgment is thus in exact agreement with what the fourth-century prime architect of the church's Trinitarian doctrine, Athanasius of Alexandria—who had indeed painstakingly worked through the implications—would teach. The Council of Nicaea (325) had laid it down that the Christ is *homoousios to patri* (of one being with the Father). According to Athanasius, this means that the Christ is the self-same God *as* God the Father precisely in and by his relation *to* God the Father.[13] And so both Peter and Athanasius make the same judgment as the prologue of John's Gospel: The Word—that is, the protagonist of the Gospel that follows—*is* God just in that he is eternally *with* God, and vice versa (John 1:1).

THE TRIUNE GOD-STORY

I will not proceed further by such analysis of individual openly christological or Trinitarian passages, which unless it were developed into an entire biblical theology could lead back to the very error just warned against. I will from here on pursue a more general line of reflection. I will begin by remembering that the church—that is, the community of interpretation that for its specific purpose put the Bible together in the first place—intends this book, for all the diversity of documents collected in it, as one continuous story of Israel's God with his people and his creation. The two great plot-determining events of this metanarrative are the Lord's raising of Israel from Egypt and of the one Israelite, Jesus, from the tomb.

Through the Bible, this story is in inescapably observable fact carried by three *dramatis dei personae* (divine characters in the drama). There is the God of Israel in person, whom Jesus distinctively addressed and referred to as "my Father," just so making himself out to be his distinctive Son. There is this Son, the protagonist of the Gospels, who, according to the New Testament, appears also throughout the Old Testament in such figures as "the angel of the Lord" or "the glory of the Lord" or the mysterious "servant" of Second Isaiah or, indeed, as Israel itself, the "Son" whom the Lord called from Egypt.[14] As the aggressively human Jesus of John's Gospel puts it, "Before Abraham was, I am."[15] There is the Spirit of God, who is the agent of life and history throughout Scripture.[16] The story of which these three are the *dramatis personae* is the story about the one and only God. It all comes together most stringently in the command of the risen Christ by which he launches the church's mission. A formula specifying the three in their mutual relations,[17] and so constituting a tight summary of the whole Bible's plot, is mandated as a personal name of the God to whom the mission brings hearers: They are to be baptized "into the name 'the Father, the Son, and the Holy Spirit.'"[18]

Through the Bible, the story is carried by three *dramatis dei personae*. There is the God of Israel in person, whom Jesus addressed as "my Father." There is this Son, the protagonist of the Gospels. And there is the Spirit of God, who is the agent of life and history throughout Scripture.

The great question that agitated the church's thinking for centuries is then: Is the triune story the Bible tells about God-with-us truly God's own story, or is it only the story of divine adaptation to our temporal situation?[19] Is the baptismal triune name God's proper personal name, or a nickname believers once gave him, which we can then of course change? Is the Father's relation to the Son and the Spirit determinative of the Father's own reality as God, or only of his relation to us? And similarly for the other two persons? Indeed, is the just used distinction between "for himself" and "for others" a meaningful distinction with the God of the gospel, as it indeed was with the gods of those to whom the gospel came on its way to us, that is, the conceptually hellenized religionists of late Mediterranean antiquity?

The Bible surely tells its triune God-story as God's own, and all original Christian liturgy inhabits it that way.[20] But it was a dogma of the pagan religion of the Mediterranean world—as of its survivals or revivals in our descendent culture—that God can have no story because deity's defining character is sheer timelessness, exemption from time and its successions of events. Deity, Mediterranean paganism thought, is defined as immunity to the possibilities and threats with which time presents finite beings. Confronted with the gospel, this culture therefore had to ask, skeptically: Can God really be identified with one to whom things happen and who works at things, who even suffers birth and execution?

> The Bible tells its triune God-story as God's own. But it was a dogma of the previous religion of the Mediterranean world that God can have no story, because deity's defining character is sheer timelessness. Converts from that world therefore tried to modify the Bible's story by turning it into modalism or subordinationism.

Thus, converts coming from Mediterranean paganism experienced severe cognitive dissonance between the Scriptures' storytelling about God and the theology they brought with them from their previous religion, which defined deity precisely as immunity to stories. Naturally, they looked first for ways to compromise the dissonance.

Two ways are logically possible, and theologians quickly concocted both. Historians call the one *modalism.* This is the explanation—which remains the Sunday-school explanation to this day—that the *dramatis personae* of the biblical story about God, *Father, Son,* and *Holy Spirit,* are successive modes of God's presence in time, roles that deity takes on for us while itself[21] abiding untouched above them. Historians call the other *subordinationism.* This proposes that it is just one of the three, the Father, who is God above time, while the Son and the Spirit are almost-gods as his subordinate agents in time. This remains in various guises the favorite of merely academic theology.

But in the course of the theologically and politically strenuous fourth century, the church's pastors and other teachers were finally driven to see that these evasions would not do, that in this matter—but by no means in all—Christian conviction and the theology inherited from their previous culture-religion were simply incompatible.[22] The eternity of the Bible's specific God—of Father, Son, and Spirit—could not be thought as mere timelessness, as immunity to temporal doings, for the gospel and all Scripture tell of things *going on* with this God that are real for him and not just for us. Father and Son have a life together in the Spirit; this Son is in fact the nation of Israel and the one Israelite, the crucified and risen Jesus of Nazareth; and this Spirit is in fact the Spirit who moves history and enlivens the church. And the *life* so specified *is* God; in a favorite formula of the present author, God is what happens between Jesus and his Father in their Spirit. At the Councils of Nicaea (325) and of Constantinople (381), the church was therefore brought to confess that the same "one Lord, Jesus Christ" who suffered the definitive temporalities of birth and death, is "true God from true God," and that the Spirit is equally "Lord and giver of life."

ANTIOCH, ALEXANDRIA, AND CHALCEDON

The cognitive dissonance suffered by culturally Gentile Christians was not thereby alleviated—indeed, it was perhaps aggravated. It remained that Jesus suffers and acts in time and that the common theology of Mediterranean antiquity's previous religions did not want deity contaminated by time in this way.[23] One compromise seemingly was still possible. It had been settled at Nicaea and Constantinople that Father, Son, and Spirit are, each by his relation to the others, mutually the one and only God, so that we must confess the Son who is Jesus as God the Son with no attenuation of "God." But perhaps one could nevertheless rescue this God the Son from the supposed pollution of time and the body by instead attenuating the "is" in "the Son who is Jesus," by positing a distinction between God the Son and the man Jesus[24] such that the Son can remain temporally inviolate, as the culture said God must be, while Jesus suffers the temporal indignities that the Gospels in fact attribute to their protagonist.

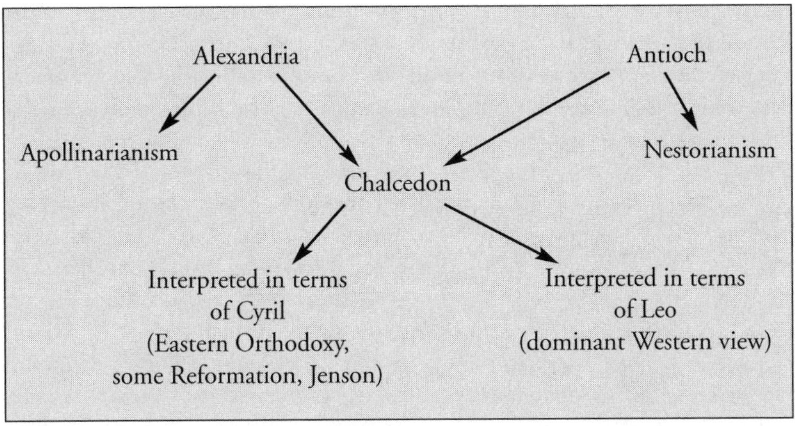

Fourth- and fifth-century theologians known as "the school of Antioch" proposed two "natures" in Christ, that is, two realities shaped and moved each by its own inner purposiveness, one divine and the other human, which are indeed united in Christ but are *so*[25] united that while it is right to worship and invoke them together as one Lord, the divine nature nevertheless remains immune to the birth, death, and other temporalities[26] suffered by the human nature.[27] Early in the discussion, the Antiochenes had the more powerful thinkers,[28] who succeeded in setting the terms of argument. Thus were born the questions thereafter determining Christology: What is the status of each of Jesus' divine and human natures? And just how are they one?

It is important to see that putting the question the Antiochene way drastically shifted the perspective. Earlier it had been the general assumption that any term that can serve as the subject of sentences about Christ, whether *Christ* or *Son of God* or *Jesus* or whatever, refers to the same entity, the protagonist of the story told by the Gospels; and that this person is God the Son by virtue of his unique filial relation to the Father, the God of Israel. Now, however, *Son of God* and similar terms are taken to refer initially to one (divine) entity, and *Jesus* or similar terms to refer initially to another (human) entity. Jesus is now thought to be Son of God not by his relation to the Father but by the relation of his human nature, according to which he is the human individual named Jesus, to his divine nature, that of *the* Son of God.

Readers will perceive that I regard this shift as a disastrous misstep, but history cannot simply be canceled out. The notion of one Christ in "two natures" continues to set the problems for Christology—perhaps most treacherously for those who think they must reject the church's teaching yet wish somehow to be Christian, and are likely to be taken in by the traditional question's unbaptized underlying assumptions.

The school of Antioch was opposed by the school of Alexandria, of which the eventual great representative was the clear-sighted and unpleasantly polemical Archbishop Cyril of Alexandria.[29] Cyril saw that the Antiochene position would, if consistently carried through, break up the Gospels' story, assigning the God-things Jesus does, such as restoring the dead or expounding the Old Testament as its author, to one agent, the divine nature, and human things, such as emerging from a womb or praying or dying, to another agent, the human nature. On the contrary, insisted Cyril, the Gospels tell one story of one Lord and Savior: We must confess that "one and the same" agent stills storms and is crucified, forgives sin as only the Father can do, yet prays to the Father for his help. And if this offends the culture's definition of deity, because consistently carried through it must mean also that somehow God, as the person of the Son, must be the one who is born of a woman and is crucified, the Alexandrians were willing—if sometimes with a little hemming and hawing—to endure the offense.

> Cyril insisted the Gospels tell one story of one Lord and Savior: We must confess that "one and the same" agent stills storms and is crucified, forgives sin as only the Father can do, yet prays to the Father for his help.

The issue between Antioch and Alexandria split the church;[30] indeed, the schisms between Alexandria's and Antioch's most devoted followers, and between each of these groups and what became the mainline church, remain to the time of this writing.[31] A council was called at Chalcedon in 451 to discuss the dispute. The council failed at reconciliation, but for the mainline church it established certain limits of christological teaching and the concepts with which christological discussion has since mostly been conducted.

A first part of the decree of Chalcedon is narrative in form, and follows Cyril. "The same" one Lord is the protagonist of the saving story told by the Gospels in all its acts and connections, whether divine or human; as one and the same, he is born in God and is born of Mary. A second section then adopts a more conceptual-analytic mode. Here the council lays down that Christ is one *hypostasis,*[32] in two *ousiai* ("natures"),[33] which latter are neither mixed together nor in themselves attenuated.

No doubt these propositions are fine so far as they go. But it is then this *hypostasis* that has now to be Cyril's single protagonist of the gospel story and the "one Lord" of Nicaea's creed. Chalcedon's text, however, says nothing at all about what a *hypostasis* is, or can then do; and, in the context of what it says about the natures, does not in fact seem to talk about the *hypostasis* as something that could do anything at all, much less be the protagonist of such a history as the Gospels tell. At the conceptual center of the question posed to it, Chalcedon thus left a blank. In the mainline churches, much of subsequent christological reflection has been devoted to repairing or maneuvering around this lack.

In Eastern Orthodoxy and in some Reformation theology, the effort has been to fill out Chalcedon in ways that will bring it fully in line with Cyril—that is, so to explicate the notion of *hypostasis* as to make "one *hypostasis*" denote a plausible active protagonist of the Gospels' total narrative.[34] According to this Christology, there is in Christ's case one "synthetic" *hypostasis* of divine and human character, and this one *hypostasis* is what actually exists.[35] The phrases "Christ's divine nature" and "Christ's human nature" are then understood to be analytic: It is the one *hypostasis* of Christ that we see acting and suffering in the gospel, and that he "has" these "two natures" means that he lacks nothing to be fully one of the Trinity and that he lacks nothing to be fully one of us—that is, that he is indeed able to do and suffer all the different things the Gospels say he does.

In most Western theology, there has instead been the attempt to live with Chalcedon as written. To make matters yet more difficult, the council had affixed to its decrees a letter of the pope in office at the time—the *Tome* of Leo, as it is called—as an authorized interpretation, and this document has perhaps determined Western Christology more than the decrees themselves. Leo seems to make the natures the exclusive agents of the Gospels' narrative and to attribute no active reality to the *hypostasis:* "Each nature is agent of what is proper to it, working in fellowship with the other: the Word doing what belongs to the Word and the flesh what belongs to the flesh."[36] Struggle with the legacy of this hyper-Antiochene[37] proposition has resulted in a Western history of marvelously ingenious and sophisticated, but in my judgment finally impotent, christological systematics, whose basic structure has carried through high-medieval scholasticism, most lines of Reformation theology, standard post-Reformation Catholic theology, and most lines of nineteenth- and early twentieth-century Neo-Protestant theology.

Amalgamating these otherwise very different theologies to the point of caricature, typical Western Christology has construed the "human nature" of Christ as the personal agent of salvation, which is said to be uniquely empowered to this work by the divine Son with whom it is "hypostatically" united. This "hypostatic union" has no material consequences in itself; it does not itself bring it about that the man Jesus as man actually shares in divine agency or that God the Son as God actually shares in the suffering of the man. That the human Jesus can save is accomplished rather by a grant to the human nature of abilities that while unique are nevertheless creaturely; the hypostatic union merely marks Jesus as the one to whom these are appropriate. And propositions like "Jesus rules" or "the Son suffered," are true as stated, but their form does not mirror the facts they state; the propositions that do this would be "God the Son—who is the *hypostasis* of the man Jesus—rules," and "The man Jesus—whose *hypostasis* is God the Son—suffered."

Thus, to mention just one religiously central matter, the risen Christ's fully human and so embodied presence in the Eucharist cannot according to this Christology be enabled by any participation of his human nature in the Son's transcendence of space and time; Christology itself does not account for the truth of "This is my body." This must then be otherwise accounted for. In Catholic theology, this is usually done by reference to powers granted the church; in most Protestant theology, the "real presence" is accounted for by the irrelevance for faith of spatial and temporal separation—or may just be denied.

When we speak of "one *hypostasis*" and "two natures," it must be the one *hypostasis* to which we attribute the story of salvation, and this *hypostasis* must simply be the one the Gospel tells of and says is risen. *He* is born of Mary and is "one of the Trinity"; *he* prays and rules nature, suffers and rises.

Insofar as we must continue to work with the tradition's language, we should in my judgment follow the "Neo-Chalcedonian" East; Leo's kind of Christology is not up to carrying faith's actual message and practices.[38] When we speak of "one *hypostasis*" and "two natures," it must be the one *hypostasis* to which we attribute the story of salvation, and this *hypostasis* must simply be the one the gospel tells of and says is risen: *He* is born of Mary and is "one of the Trinity"; *he* prays and rules nature, suffers and rises. We should in consequence entertain a strong version of what has been called *communicatio idiomatum,* "the fellowship of attributes," the way in which in the being and work of the one *hypostasis,* each nature brings not only what is proper to it but also what is proper to the other, so that by Christ—and by him alone—divine things are done humanly and human things divinely. "Jesus rules" and "God the Son is crucified" are not just notionally or verbally true, but state facts about the one concrete person of Christ, and have the appropriate form for so doing.

THE IDENTITY OF JESUS CHRIST

It is time to turn from rehearsing the tradition, with its triumphs and tribulations, to a form of teaching that seeks to get behind the missteps which make the tradition so tortured. The gospel, I said at the beginning, is the message, "Jesus, the one who . . . , is risen," with the ellipsis filled in by descriptions of this man's life and death. The canonical Gospels once in place, and the doctrine of Trinity once in place, we can make this read, "Jesus, the human protagonist of the Gospels, is the second identity of the Trinity." Proper Christology would be clarification of this form of the gospel claim.

The first and fundamental christological teaching should then be: When you talk of Christ, always remember that you are talking about a single figure, the one protagonist of the Gospels' narrative, of whom the gospel message claims that he is risen. Say nothing that in any way suggests that any one of "Jesus" or "the Christ" or "the man from Nazareth" or "the Son of God" or "the Christ-principle," or whatever other christological name, title, or description, inherited or made up, refers to a different entity from any other.

The second and decisive teaching should then be: It is precisely this one who is an identity—or "person" or *hypostasis*—of God. The first-century male Galilean Jew, Jesus of Nazareth, prophet and rabbi and healer,[39] is one of the three whose life together *is* God.

A third teaching then follows: When you talk of Christ, be prepared to attribute to him anything and everything the Scriptures attribute to the triune God, and anything and everything the Scriptures attribute to Jesus as one of the human community. Say nothing that in any way suggests that he is not fully one of us or that he is not fully one of the Trinity.

Who or what is it that undergoes birth from Mary, or crucifixion, or questioning by the religious authorities, or the struggle in Gethsemane? It is the person of whom the Gospels tell these things—our brother in humanity, Jesus of Nazareth. And this very one is God, by and in his relations to the one he called Father and to the Spirit that rested on him.

Who or what is it that undergoes birth from Mary, or crucifixion, or questioning by the religious authorities, or the struggle in Gethsemane? It is the person of whom the Gospels tell these things—our brother in humanity, Jesus of Nazareth. And this very one is God, by and in his relations to the one he called Father and to the Spirit that rested on him.

Does this mean that God suffered and died on the cross? Not if by *God* we mean a divine essence or monadic first cause, as does the side of our thinking inherited from pagan Mediterranean antiquity. The proposition "God died," abstracted from a radically Trinitarian understanding of God, was tried early in the history of the church and rejected as obviously oxymoronic.[40] Indeed, God the Father does not die, since he is the source of all reality including death; nor does the Spirit, who *is* life. But the one who is the Son does die, and this death belongs to his relations to the Father and the Spirit, that is, to some of the very relations in which the three are mutually God.[41] Thus, this one death indeed belongs to the life that is God.

Does the man Jesus rule the universe? Not if by the man Jesus we mean a religious guru, or a historical object of religious regard, or our great exemplar, or any other of the stock figures of decadent modernity's ex-Christian religiosity. But the actual rabbi and prophet and healer Jesus in his unique relation to the Father and the Spirit is indeed the defining identity of the life that is God—that is, he is the person in whom the Father hears and sees himself and so determines who and what God is. And this Life, thus determined in its content by Jesus' history and character, does indeed rule the universe. To understand what is behind the vast spaces, whether of the cosmos or of the human heart, the only thing we can do is what God the Father himself does as he rules them: Consider his Son Jesus.

The person of the Son is identified by the Gospels' narrative of the man Jesus. Our address to the Father in the Son's name, or directly to the Son, is therefore that of human persons in the name of or to a human person, and precisely so and not otherwise is prayer to God.

Jesus, to be sure, has died and therefore even as risen can now be invoked or addressed only as an inhabitant of that future beyond death into which he is risen. Therefore, he is available to our addresses from within this present age only in the special way called *sacramental*. What we can see or touch or hear is never something that sounds or looks like Jesus; it is always some other human reading Scripture or preaching or otherwise speaking the gospel claim, or is a loaf and cup or a basin of water, or hands making the sign of a cross, or an icon of Mary with her son, or any of the church's multitude of signs of Christ's presence. But if the gospel claim of his resurrection is true, when we encounter these things we do indeed meet the living human person Jesus.

This human personality is then an identity of God: Toward the Father in the Spirit he lives the mutual self-giving that God is. And vice versa, this "second" identity of the Trinity is simultaneously a human identity: With his mother and his executioner and you and me he has his place in the converse of human community. Thus, he is born in created time of the Virgin and in God's time of the Father, is condemned by Pilate, and is delivered over by the Father.

It will be seen that the notions of "divine nature" or "human nature," if we now use these phrases, have in the just previous paragraphs become labels for communities. To have "human nature" in the christologically relevant sense is not to instantiate an essence shared by all humans—though doubtless there are characteristics without which we would not call an entity human—but is rather to have a role in the one community through time of those who together make that history in which Jesus, and Napoleon, and the writer and readers of this essay, and the writer's great-aunt all participate. To have the "divine nature" is not to instantiate an essence shared by all putative gods—though doubtless there are characteristics without which we would not think of something as divine—but is rather to be one of the three whose mutuality is the life that creates all that is not one of those three, the life that therefore is God.

The relation between these two memberships is asymmetrical. Christ's human history happens because his triune history happens and not vice versa, which is simply to say that God is Creator and we are creatures, so that Christ, who is both, is both in that order.

THE WORK OF CHRIST

Finally, we must consider the doctrine of Christ's work, of the difference he makes for others and how it is that he makes any difference at all. How do his death and resurrection "redeem," or "reconcile," or "atone for," or "save" others?

That Christ has *work* to do on our behalf, that requires him to be both one of God and one of us, supposes of course that our relation to God requires some working on, that we and God are somehow alienated and need to be brought back together. Indeed, that is how Scripture tells the story. It has been debated whether the incarnation would have occurred had humankind not sinned,[42] but for the immediate purposes of this chapter we may prescind from this question and simply take it that humankind is in fact alienated from God and that the work of the incarnation, as it in fact occurs, is to reconcile us to him.

Notoriously, the history of theology has been rich in theories of atonement, and explanations of this reconciliation, none of which has been fully persuasive or has in fact persuaded the church as a whole. The most widely taught construct, powerfully formulated by Anselm of Canterbury in the twelfth century and varied by many theologians since, has been that the death of Christ fulfills the demands of justice, without which our sin would separate us from God.

It is easy to caricature this teaching, making it picture God the Father as a hanging judge who can only be appeased by his own Son's death, and some proponents and most opponents have done so. In Anselm's own teaching, however, what must be "satisfied" is not God directly but the structure of justice he has built into creation, without which life as a creature would be meaningless, and which God, therefore, precisely for the sake of creatures, cannot allow us simply to undo.

In Scripture it is never God who is reconciled to us; it is always God who reconciles us to himself.

Nevertheless, the Anselmian atonement theory is indeed flawed, if not for the reasons usually advanced. It pictures the reconciliation between God and creatures as accomplished from the creature's side: The man Jesus pays the debt owed by all human beings—which he can do because he is also God the Son—and so reconciles God to us. But in Scripture it is never God who is reconciled to us; it is always God who reconciles us to himself.

Recognition of this error has led to the creation of theories that rightly make *us* the object of what God does in Christ. If Anselmian theories describe the difference Christ's death is supposed to make in God's attitude to us, these describe the difference Christ's death makes in our attitude to God. Thus, they consist in analysis of the moral and religious impact of the life, death, and resurrection of Christ. Doubtless the profoundest such construct is that of Friedrich Schleiermacher, the early nineteenth-century founder of "neo-Protestant" theology, which may be quickly identified to readers, as it remains the dominant if often unacknowledged theology of the mainline American Protestant churches. According to Schleiermacher, Christ is the Son of God in that his existential relation to God was perfect and unbroken, surviving even the test of death; and he shares his perfect religiosity with us, through the normal processes of a community's continuing fellowship, in this case, those of the church.

Yet nor are such theories sufficient to the burden an interpretation of Christ's work must carry. For since according to them the efficacy of Christ's life, death, and resurrection consists in the effects it has in us, preaching, pedagogy, and pastoral care shaped by such theories threaten to be useless precisely when most needed. It is just when I do *not* fear and love God, when Christ's person and death have *not* had recognizable impact on me, that a theory of atonement should have its spiritual office by describing a new situation between God and me that Christ's life, death, and resurrection have created, a situation that obtains independently of my subjective state toward it, and that just so can enable or encourage my fear and love of God.

As it seems to the present author, a right doctrine of atonement has two parts. The first is simply the telling of the Gospels' story, that is, an identification of the one who is risen. In utmost concentration: Jesus is a prophet of the coming of God's kingdom, who taught that the kingdom is so close that his hearers' relation to it is determined by their reception or rejection of his message of its coming; a rabbi, who interpreted Israel's Scriptures as if he had written them, radicalizing their moral demands and at the same time—or rather just so—teaching a fruit-basket-upset of moral judgment, so that the righteous are offended and the declassé and sinners find a friend; and a healer and wonder worker whose deeds were parables of the overcoming of sin, death, and suffering in the kingdom. This one died rather than mitigate the love which was the inner secret of his prophesying and teaching and healing.

Jesus died rather than mitigate the love which was the inner secret of his prophesying and teaching and healing. If now this one is risen and so is identified as the second identity of God, then what we may hope for from God is utterly different from what we could otherwise have supposed.

If now this one is risen and so is identified as the second identity of God, the Word in converse with whom the Father knows himself, the Son whose subsistence enables the fatherhood of the Father so that the two are in fact but one God mutually, then what we may hope for from God is utterly different from what we could otherwise have supposed. Then the final future of all things is the world prefigured in Jesus' verbal and acted-out parables, then entry into this kingdom is effected by fellowship with Jesus, and then it is we publicans and sinners who are thus blessed.

In a formula: *Who* and *what* is the God of Scripture is settled by the life and death of Jesus. The Father determines what it means to be God by looking to the one identified by this particular life and by his particular death. *That* this God is in fact God is settled by Jesus' resurrection.

Is this a "theory" of atonement? Not if by that is meant explanation in either the way of Anselm or the way of Schleiermacher. Both sorts of explanation suppose a *causal* relation between God and humanity: Either Christ as human reconciles God or Christ as God reconciles us humans. But there is and can be no such causal relation between the Creator God of Scripture and his creatures. Just this, I suggest, is an inevitable flaw of all "theories" of atonement, and it derives from the Christology of Pope Leo's *Tome,* which posits two active "natures" doing things to each other and suggests we look for something like a natural law of these actions.

Neither God in Christ nor humanity in Christ works our reconciliation. The one person, who is simply as himself both, works reconciliation. Or better, he just *is* our reconciliation, for finally, with respect to persons, what one is and what one does are the same. As we are imperfectly personal, there may in our case be a necessary distinction between being and acting, but Christ is perfectly personal. Christ's person and Christ's work can, for certain purposes, be separately discussed. But at bottom, if we ask who Christ is, the answer is that he is the one who does what the gospel tells of him; and if we ask what he does, the answer is that he enacts that unity of God with us, that is his person.

LEANNE VAN DYK

The cross of Jesus Christ has been a prism for Christian belief for more than twenty centuries. Like the spectrum of colors in a ray of light, a wide variety of understandings and assumptions about the cross have reflected through this prism and have powerfully influenced prayer, devotion, ethics, and piety. The practices of Christian devotion and piety are deeply connected to all the particularities of culture, time, place, and a myriad of other contextual factors. How Christian believers have appropriated the death of Christ is a key factor in the variety of Christian practices over time. Implicit or explicit understandings of the necessity of the cross, the efficacy of the cross, what the cross saves human beings from and for, how human beings receive the benefits of salvation—all these issues have shaped belief and practice in each particular Christian tradition.

In his fourth-century treatise, *On the Incarnation of the Word,* Athanasius presents the problem of human rebellion against God's original intent for human flourishing. Repeatedly, he asks the rhetorical question, "What was God to do?"[1]

His answer skillfully employs a number of themes related to the cross, including creation, the incarnation, and the resurrection. His understanding of the cross as the decisive victory against evil, ignorance, and death leads to his confident statement that "the darkness of the idols prevails no more, and all parts of the world in every direction are illumined by [Christ's] teaching."[2]

Around the year 1100, Anselm and his questioner, Boso, famously puzzled through the logic of the cross and developed a position many of whose features have come to dominate Western theology. They concluded that the Father allowed the Son to be treated with such cruelty on the cross because this is precisely what was required; only this produces praise and honor to God and salvation to humanity.[3] This particular refraction of the wide variety of options in the tradition was to have momentous consequences. More than any other theological reflection on the cross, this account, in traditions which trace their roots to the Latin West, has shaped the piety of Christian believers, the sermons of pastors, and the curricula of church education programs.

In recent years, some theologians have asked hard questions about the most commonly assumed understandings of the cross, especially those with roots in the Anselmian tradition.[4] They have observed deep problems in classic atonement accounts and wish to engage carefully the difficult task of assessing the inherited theological tradition, to examine again the biblical witness, to face up to unintended—perhaps sometimes intended—consequences of atonement doctrine in human social structures.

> More than any other theological reflection on the cross, Anselm's account, in traditions which trace their roots to the Latin West, has shaped the piety of Christian believers, the sermons of pastors, and the curricula of church education programs.

As a result of this inquiry, there is some modest consensus among these writers on Christian atonement theology. The consensus clusters around the problems of violence, punishment, and forgiveness. These problems arise due to deep links between punishment and forgiveness in the classic Western atonement tradition. Because of these deep links, there is a corresponding connection between violence and forgiveness. This essay will present and acknowledge persistent problems in classic atonement theology and suggest certain reformulations in an effort to highlight the love and mercy of God revealed in the cross and resurrection of Christ.

THE DOMINANT WESTERN VIEW

The cross of Jesus Christ is the center of the Christian faith. Yet the precise saving effect of the cross is by no means clear. It is often remarked by historians of doctrine that while the orthodox contours of Christology and Trinitarian doctrine were settled by the early church in ecumenical councils after long and vigorous debate, no such settled doctrine developed with respect to the cross. The various reformations of the church—including the sixteenth-century Reformation—likewise often arose over issues of sacramental theology and ecclesiology, not interpretations of the cross.

Many students of theology find it somewhat surprising that the very wide variety of interpretations of the cross of Christ in the tradition has never promoted the kind of controversy that, say, the struggle over the Trinity did in the fourth century. To be sure, there have been pointed debates on how to understand the saving effects of the death and resurrection of Christ. For example, the reaction against substitutionary atonement in the seventeeth century by the Socinians—the followers of Faustus Socinius, who rejected many traditional views about the Trinity and the atonement—centered on interpretations of the cross. But the attitude of the church, an attitude which parallels that of the New Testament, has been remarkably hospitable to rather generously drawn boundaries on Christian understandings of the cross.

It would be a good thing to explore these generous boundaries. The interesting differences of emphasis in the Gospel of John, Paul's Letter to the Romans, the book of Hebrews, and the book of Revelation on the saving effects of Christ's death and resurrection would be one place to begin. Early Christian writers offer important and influential variations as well, including Irenaeus's concept of recapitulation (Christ's obedience recapitulates, and thereby undoes, Adam's disobedience), Athanasius's connection between the incarnation and the cross (by becoming human Christ restores the divine image in us; by dying he frees us from sin), and the fascinating use of the image of the fishhook in Gregory of Nyssa. (Our sin has made us subject to the devil, Gregory says, but Christ's humanity tricks the devil into thinking of Christ as part of his legitimate prey, as bait covers a fishhook. In seizing Christ, however, the devil tries to capture divinity, and thereby overreaches his just entitlement; he has broken the rules, and we are freed from his power.) And on it goes—to Augustine, Gregory the Great, Anselm, Abelard, and the early Protestant scholastics, to name just a few.

In spite of the chorus of voices in the tradition concerning the cross, however, a single voice has dominated in the Latin West. A particular atonement understanding has, since Anselm, reigned supreme in the Western Christian tradition—Catholic and Protestant—such that the elasticity of the broader classic tradition has been lost.

> The dominant Western view has several troubling problems, including the question of whether, and to what extent, it masks, even legitimates, the violence which is such a painful characteristic of our society.

This dominant Western view has obscured other understandings of the saving effects of the cross. Some might consider this a good thing. One primary theological understanding of such a central doctrine might look like cause for celebration in a church otherwise so divided. Yet the dominant Western view has several troubling problems, including the question of whether, and to what extent, it masks, even legitimates, through its approach to punishment and forgiveness, the violence which is such a painful characteristic of our society.[5]

The Heidelberg Catechism, a question-and-answer summary of the faith written by German Reformed Christians in 1563, offers a clear presentation of the dominant Western view. The very first answer states, "Jesus Christ has fully paid for all my sins with his precious blood, and has set me free from the tyranny of the devil." The tenth answer says, "As a just judge, God punishes sinners now and in eternity." The next answer adds, "God's justice demands that sin, committed against supreme majesty, be punished with the supreme penalty." Again, the next answer clearly echoes Anselm by saying, "God requires that his justice be satisfied. Therefore the claims of his justice must be paid in full, either by ourselves or by another." Answer 17 completes the logic: "By the power of his divinity, Christ bears the weight of God's anger."[6]

The dominant Western view states that human sinners have seriously violated the law of God, a law that carries with it the penalty of condemnation and death. Because God is a just and righteous God, the penalty cannot simply be set aside. It must be exacted. But because of God's great love for humanity, God is unwilling to exact this penalty. Instead, in a gracious Trinitarian decision, Jesus Christ—fully God, fully human—takes on the responsibility of humanity's disobedience and the punishment human beings deserve. This punishment includes torment, death, and God-forsakenness.[7]

John Calvin, too, is a primary source for this view, although his presentation is much more nuanced than that of the Heidelberg Catechism. Some of the nuances in Calvin's account will be noted below, in the section on certain reformulations of atonement theology. But in large part, Calvin affirms and transmits the dominant Western view. In book 2 of his *Institutes of the Christian Religion,* Calvin says,

> But here we must earnestly ponder how God accomplishes salvation for us. . . . No one can descend into himself and seriously consider what he is without feeling God's wrath and hostility toward him. Accordingly, he must anxiously seek ways and means to appease God—and this demands a satisfaction. No common assurance is required, for God's wrath and curse always lie upon sinners until they are absolved of guilt. Since God is a righteous Judge, God does not allow the divine law to be broken without punishment, but is equipped to avenge it.[8]

A bit further on, he says, "Hence, when Christ is hanged upon the cross, he makes himself subject to the whole curse. It had to happen in this way in order that the whole curse—which on account of our sins awaited us, or rather lay upon us—might be lifted from us, while it was transferred to him." Calvin clarifies further, "Therefore, to perform a perfect expiation, he gave his own life, upon which our stain and punishment might somehow be cast."[9]

Calvin is often accused of holding a particularly harsh penal substitutionary account. He does occasionally say things that might lead to this conclusion. For example, he says that "God's righteous curse bars our access to him, and God in his capacity as judge is angry toward us."[10] Yet Calvin also took pains to state clearly that God's love is the foundation and the motivation of the atonement. He says, "It was not after we were reconciled to him through the blood of his Son that he began to love us. Rather, he has loved us before the world was created."[11] A little further in the *Institutes,* Calvin remarks on how obvious this understanding of the atonement was in his day: "I take it to be a commonplace that if Christ made satisfaction for our sins, if he paid the penalty owed by us . . . then he acquired salvation for us by his righteousness."[12] This was simply the assumed theory.

Calvin is often accused of holding a particularly harsh penal substitutionary account. Yet Calvin also took pains to state clearly that God's love is the foundation and the motivation of the atonement.

It must be recognized that, in developing the themes of satisfaction and substitution, Calvin was taking his cue not only from the Anselmian-Catholic tradition he inherited but also from key passages of Scripture. In support of the notion of substitution, Calvin refers to Hebrews 9:26: "Christ has appeared once for all . . . to wipe out sin by the sacrifice of himself." Again, he cites Paul's analogy in Galatians 3:13: "Christ . . . became a curse for us." The classic verse 2 Corinthians 5:22 was enormously important to Calvin: "For our sake, [God] made him to be sin who knew no sin, so that in him we might become the righteousness of God."

These verses, and others like them, led Calvin to the conclusion that Christ's death substituted for us, that Christ took upon himself the penalty of our sins. Furthermore, that substitution *satisfied* God. Christ's death, then, righted a terrible wrong. It balanced an unbalanced world. It rescued stranded humanity. It saved us.

Many Christians, if someone asked them how we are saved through the death of Christ, might stammer out an explanation that bears a resemblance to Calvin's. They might say, "We are saved because Jesus died for us. You know, Jesus took the punishment that we deserved. That's how salvation happens." There is no question that this particular understanding of the cross has been enormously influential, not only in North America but in many Christian communities around the world. Many Christians simply assume that this version of the cross, which sounds so familiar to them, is the best—perhaps even the only—understanding of the cross.

The Suffering Servant passages of Isaiah have been interpreted in a way that buttresses the dominant Western account. Isaiah 53 is especially influential for hymn writers, theologians, preachers, and countless Christian believers:

Surely he has borne our infirmities
  and carried our diseases;
yet we accounted him stricken,
  struck down by God, and afflicted.
But he was wounded for our transgressions,
  crushed for our iniquities;
upon him was the punishment that made us whole,
  and by his bruises we are healed.
All we like sheep have gone astray;
  we have all turned to our own way,
and the LORD has laid on him
  the iniquity of us all. (Isa. 53:4–6)

This is a powerful text, one that speaks directly to the terrible dilemma of humanity, burdened by transgressions too heavy to carry off. Only the Suffering Servant, read by Christian eyes as a direct reference to Jesus, could bear this punishment. The tragedy and drama of this text has deeply connected with the imaginations and piety of many Christians. There is no question that the received interpretation of several key biblical texts, especially Isaiah 53, has encouraged the tilt toward the dominant Western view.

The dominant Western view is very prominent in American evangelicalism and fundamentalism as well. Some Christian colleges, Bible colleges, and seminaries in North America require their faculty to sign a statement of doctrinal orthodoxy that goes beyond an affirmation of Jesus Christ as Lord and Savior to an insistence that the mechanism of salvation is substituted punishment. Parachurch organizations also typically use language drawn from the dominant Western view. Nationwide college ministry organizations often strongly emphasize themes of substituted punishment in their worship services. The impact of this imagery on the spiritual development of children, teenagers, and college students is largely unexamined. Given the complexity and individuality of spiritual growth and development, it is very hard to imagine how the impact of substituted punishment imagery could be measured or interpreted in any church culture or group. Yet it is an issue of considerable importance. The proclamation of the faith has always demanded of Christian educators, pastors, and theologians a high level of care and commitment in finding the right words to say. This challenge includes also, perhaps especially, the claims of the faith about the saving effects of the cross of Christ.

CRITIQUES OF THE DOMINANT WESTERN VIEW

In recent years, the doctrine of the atonement—particularly what I have called the dominant Western view—has been the focus of pointed criticism, renewed scrutiny, and a wide variety of constructive revisionings. Some of the critique is angry.[13] Some is impressively interdisciplinary—incorporating anthropological, linguistic, and philosophical resources.[14] Some displays an effort to come to a fresh understanding of the key biblical texts.[15]

Not every Christian today is as confident as Calvin was about images of substitution and satisfaction. For some contemporary Christians, this view of atonement sometimes feels contrived, even mechanical. Robert Farrar Capon particularly dislikes the concept of satisfaction that Calvin inherited from Anselm because it coughs up "a tough little ball of fur"—the idea that forgiveness and punishment are inseparably linked.[16] Capon and others think that the notion that God *had* to exact a penalty in order to forgive is profoundly confusing to the believer. It brings down a thick fog of fear rather than joy and gratitude for God's grace.

It strikes some thoughtful people that this theory casts God as a cold and heartless judge, demanding punishment for infraction of the divine law, even at the cost of the life of the beloved Son. Some women have seen this classic understanding of the atonement as a tacit legitimization of the abuse of women. There is no doubt that abusers use the Bible, or their perverse understanding of the Bible, to justify battering their wives or partners. It is, perhaps, no wonder that some feminist theologians have utterly rejected any traditional understanding of salvation through the death and resurrection of Jesus Christ. They point out the depressing history of Christian legitimization of violence, of denial that violence exists, of ways that violence subtly has been endorsed. The victims of violence are usually the powerless—women, children, and other marginalized groups. Thus, the critique is sharp and unambiguous of any theory of the cross that itself seems to justify violence.[17]

It strikes some thoughtful people that this theory casts God as a cold and heartless judge, demanding punishment for infraction of the divine law, even at the cost of the life of the beloved Son. Some women have seen this classic understanding of the atonement as a tacit legitimization of the abuse of women.

Social psychologists, political philosophers, and theologians have produced a diverse literature in the past twenty-five years that explores the connections between religion and violence. Some studies focus on family relationships and probe for the possible links between religion and domestic abuse.[18] Other works question the conceptual and political connections between atonement theology and penal criminal theories.[19] The corpus of work by René Girard asks even more fundamental questions regarding the cultural foundations of societies and the roots of violence.[20] The scope of this literature is very broad, but the shared interest in the connections between cultural forms and violence is important to Christian constructive theologians. Theological formulations which may contribute, in complex and submerged ways, to violence must receive tough criticism from theologians and pastors who are convinced the Christian gospel must be articulated in ways that promote life, not deal death.

The angry, passionate criticisms of traditional forms of Christian doctrine are often difficult for comfortable, privileged Christian people to hear. "Surely the gospel doesn't legitimate abuse—these arguments are nonsense," they might say.

But the hurt and anger of people long oppressed, trivialized, or demeaned must be heard. Often it is these voices of pain and frustration that alert those in the church to their own cozy, comfortable ways of understanding the gospel. Certainly, when the gospel has been twisted to prop up abusive power structures, Christians must resolve to reclaim the genuine good news of the gospel and to reject all understandings of the faith that deal death rather than life.

> Certainly, when the gospel has been twisted to prop up abusive power structures, Christians must resolve to reclaim the genuine good news of the gospel and to reject all understandings of the faith that deal death rather than life.

Michael Welker states that the dominant Western view is "nothing less than destructive of faith."[21] He explains the logic of this traditional view:

> God requires a compensation for human beings' deficiency. Since no sinful human being is in a position to produce this atoning compensation, the sinless Son of God, the Lamb of God, must be sacrificed. Only this sacrifice can pacify God's anger. . . . This has propagated a latent image of God that is deeply unchristian, indeed demonic: This God is always seeking compensation; it takes a sacrificial victim to calm and pacify this ultimately merciless and vengeful God.[22]

It is important to note that Welker thinks that the substituted punishment view does not take sin seriously enough, that a more radical notion of sin is required—one that overturns the equation of sin and compensation.

The complaints against the dominant Western view in recent atonement theology are extensive. Anselm is criticized for constructing an atonement theology *remoto Christo,* apart from Christ.[23] Calvin is criticized for an account overly weighted on the priestly role of Christ, neglecting the prophetic and kingly. Hymnody, liturgy, and popular Christian literature—all heavily influenced by the dominant Western view—are criticized as well. Thus, according to this multifaceted critique, all are inadequate truly to express the gospel. The criticisms charge that the real light of the gospel is dimmed by these images, which trail behind them unhealthy social consequences.

At the core of all the criticisms is the problem of violence—specifically, the presumed link between the violence of the cross and the saving effects for the world. The key assumption in the dominant Western view is that justice is accomplished by inflicting punishment. Reconciliation requires punishment and is not attained unless and until the punishment is carried out.

This key assumption also operates in the criminal justice system in the United States, England, and other Western countries. The theory of retributive criminal justice rests precisely on this assumption. The challenge for the courts and the prisons is simply to determine what the *quid pro quo* formula is. What prison sentence should accompany any given crime?

Likewise, in the dominant Western view of the atonement, a similar question is asked: What punishment should accompany this crime of human sin? The answer is, the death of the beloved Son is the substituted punishment for the accumulated total of human sin. Notice the logic here: Punishment is rooted in the divine economy. It is an equation. Christ's death is a negotiation with sacred order. Anthony Bartlett notes that the common denominator of the multiple variations on the dominant Western view is "the brutal violence inflicted on Jesus and the way this violence always functions to bring about the desired goal of human redemption."[24]

Anselm gets the blame in all of these critiques. However, there are deeper roots in the early church for the notions of substituted punishment and the logical necessity of violence in atonement theology. Substituted punishment motifs appear in some form in Ambrose, Athanasius, Eusebius, Augustine, the Cappadocians, and Gregory the Great. But it is Anselm who takes the biggest hit. Anselm's influence on both Catholic and Protestant theology is unmistakable. Certainly, the story is complex and nuanced—Thomas Aquinas modifies Anselm, as do Calvin, Hugo Grotius, and the Protestant scholastics. But the shadow of Anselm falls long on the dominant Western view.

Anselm stated that because God is a just God, the dishonoring of God by human sin cannot be overlooked. The only possible way for humanity to be saved is for Jesus Christ, fully God and fully human, to offer his life as a gift of infinite value to the offended honor of God.

Anselm stated that because God is a just God, the dishonoring of God by human sin cannot be overlooked. God cannot turn a blind eye to human sin. Justice requires either punishment for sin or a satisfaction for the offended honor. Punishment would require death for sinners. But God, in great mercy, does not will to destroy all humanity. Instead, God seeks a way to restore the balance of divine honor by the alternative of satisfaction of divine honor.

The only possible way for humanity to be saved is for Jesus Christ, fully God and fully human, to offer his life as a gift of infinite value to the offended honor of God. Jesus *can* render satisfaction because his life is of infinite worth. So when Jesus takes our place, satisfaction is truly accomplished. We were the ones who should have made payment for God's offended honor. But Jesus is the one who did it, and therefore order is restored.

An interesting feature of Anselm's theory of the atonement is often overlooked in descriptions of his account. Because the life of Jesus Christ was of such great value, it deserves a reward from God. Jesus gave a gift of infinite value. This satisfies God's honor, but there is an enormous "surplus." The gift is so large that it is only right that God reward Jesus. But what could Jesus possibly need? Being fully divine, he lacks for nothing. So in gracious generosity, Jesus transfers to humanity the surplus that he earned. He gives us the promise of eternal life and fellowship with God.

Many critics point out the mechanical feel of this account. It portrays God as a litigant in a grudge lawsuit, who requires compensatory damages for lost honor. It suggests that forgiveness is like math—it all has to add up. It focuses so much on Jesus' death on the cross that his life of ministry, teaching, and healing is passed over. The resurrection as well seems an unnecessary appendix to the drama of salvation.

Another criticism of Anselm points out that this theory is blind to the problems of social disorder and big systemic sins. Salvation seems to occur outside of history or above history, rather than in the actual mess and muck of history. The classic Christian doctrine of the incarnation emphasizes that Jesus entered our history, our earthly, bodily, gritty history.

Anthony Bartlett says, of the logic of Anselm's *Cur Deus Homo,* "Violence is its beating heart, and it either creates a sophisticated system of honor and satisfaction within which individuals are saved, or unleashes itself with unchecked fury."[25] In short, "We can hear the screeching of gears" in Anselm—the gears of divine wrath being compensated. The equation is balanced. The wrath has been appeased. And from this, salvation, restoration, reconciliation is won.

J. Denny Weaver is another theologian who critiques that fatal link between punishment and justice in the dominant Western account. In his recent book, *The Nonviolent Atonement,* Weaver wishes to develop a Christian atonement theology that rejects all violence. From his Mennonite tradition he wishes to develop "an understanding shaped by nonviolence that lays bare the extent to which satisfaction atonement is founded on violent assumptions."[26]

One insight that thinkers such as Weaver and Bartlett bring to the discussion is an insistence that the penal substitutionary account of the atonement—the dominant Western view—has had its own unique context and social location in the history of Christian doctrine. It is not only feminists and liberation theologians and various global theologies that have context and particularity. The classic theologies of the Latin West—and the reigning theological assumptions of North America—also have context and social location. Similarly, our regnant interpretations of such passages of Isaiah 53 have their own histories, assumptions, and sociopolitical context. Nothing is exempt from honest questions about power, privilege, and particular cultural blind spots. Weaver expresses gratitude to womanist theologians because they "shone a bright light on the fact that the received theology of Christendom in general and satisfaction atonement in particular also have a context. . . . [I]t became evident that the dominant tradition of Anselmian atonement was not general theology, not a universally recognizable, uncontestable foundation of common truth that all right-thinking Christians were bound to accept."[27]

This simple acknowledgment—that the dominant Western theory has its own particular social location—gives theologians with deep commitments to the Christian faith not only the freedom but the obligation to examine these dominant views, to critique them, to correct them, if necessary, and to find more faithful ways to express the faith.

REVISIONING ATONEMENT THEOLOGY

Although the "dominant Western view" was identified above as the most influential form of atonement theology in all the church traditions that find root in the Latin West, it must be emphasized that there are many important variations within that dominant tradition. Calvin is often identified as a prime example of a penal substitutionary view, yet, in key texts in the *Institutes,* he adjusts and nuances the substituted punishment model. Clearly, Calvin thought that Christ's death was a penal substitutionary act—that Christ took on our punishment and released us from its consequences. But, in a remarkable passage in the *Institutes,* Calvin points out that this atonement explanation has enormous effectiveness for increasing our gratitude to God. Calvin believed this view is pastorally helpful to people. Such a view in no way portrays a harsh and judgmental God, Calvin thought.

In fact, Calvin suggests that the biblical passages about the anger and wrath of God are crutches for our own limited understanding. He explains, "Expressions of this sort have been accommodated to our capacity that we may better understand how miserable and ruinous our condition is apart from Christ." Without them "we would have underestimated the benefit of liberation."[28] Calvin's goal in this section of the *Institutes,* as always, is to highlight the free grace of God.

In fact, Calvin suggests that the biblical passages about the anger and wrath of God are crutches for our own limited understanding.

He further defends his use of the language of punishment and wrath by imagining the reaction of a person hearing a sort of "general" explanation about salvation through Jesus Christ. In this imaginary scene, a person is told that human sin is a rebellion against God, that people are all terribly estranged from God, but that God has put it all right, bringing us once again into relationship with God. Calvin remarks, "[The person] will surely experience and feel *something* of what he owes to God's mercy."[29]

But consider, continues Calvin in his imagination, how that person's gratitude would be increased if he or she thought about mercy as freeing us from God's wrath:

> On the other hand, suppose he learns, as Scripture teaches,
> that he was estranged from God through sin,
> is an heir of wrath,
> subject to the curse of eternal death,
> excluded from all hope of salvation,
> beyond every blessing of God,
> the slave of Satan,
> captive under the yoke of sin,
> destined finally for a dreadful destruction and already involved in it;
> And that at this point Christ interceded as his advocate,

> took upon himself and suffered the punishment that, from
> God's righteous judgement, threatened all sinners;
> that he purged with his blood those evils which had rendered
> sinners hateful to God;
> that by this expiation he made satisfaction and sacrifice duly to
> God the Father;
> that as intercessor he appeased God's wrath;
> that on this foundation rests the peace of God with people;
> that by this bond his benevolence is maintained toward them.

> *Will [the person] not then be even more moved by all these things* which so vividly portray the greatness of the calamity from which he has been rescued?[30]

This passage reveals an important insight into the way Calvin thought about the faith and how to find the right words to express the faith. As a scholar trained in the classic disciplines, Calvin cared about the rhetorical impact of his words on his readers and hearers. A theological articulation must go beyond mere statement or report. It must raise the awe, wonder, and joy of believers. It must shed the brightest light on the glory of God. This principle of rhetorical fittingness applied to Calvin's understanding of the cross as well. He remarked that "trembling consciences find repose only in sacrifice and cleansing by which sins are expiated."[31] He addressed his readers with the hope that their trembling, shaky consciences would be calmed, comforted, and rooted in the assurance of God's love from before the foundations of the world.

But what if the consciences of twenty-first-century Christians are not comforted by these images of punishment and sacrifice? Are the resources of our theological traditions flexible and resilient enough to discover other biblically rooted images, ones that comfort contemporary people and arouse their hearts to gratitude for God's boundless mercy?

This question calls for careful reformulation in atonement theology, especially to the end that the fateful mechanism between forgiveness and punishment be mitigated. First, an adjusted concept of satisfaction is a possible move to break the link between God's justice and punishment. The Son is the satisfaction for our sin—this much is affirmed. But not in a penal sense. Nor in the classic Anselmian sense of a satisfaction of God's offended honor, so evocative of a feudal social system. Rather, the whole life, death, and resurrection of Christ satisfies God. Such an approach would offer a broader, more narrative, and less mathematical understanding of satisfaction. By the incarnation itself, Jesus Christ satisfied God—satisfied God's determination to be a God-for-us in full human form. Jesus continued to satisfy God by his obedient life and his willingness to drink the cup of death as an inevitable

> But what if the consciences of twenty-first-century Christians are not comforted by these images of punishment and sacrifice?

consequence of that obedience. Jesus satisfied God in his bearing the sins of the world in his body and spirit on the cross. Jesus Christ was the bearer of our sins in the sense of his absorbing the burden of our sins, not in the sense of bearing substituted punishment for us.

If this adjustment to the notion of satisfaction is made, that fateful link between punishment and forgiveness is broken. The notion of satisfaction I am suggesting is actually a reclaiming of a broader traditional voice. For Athanasius, Jesus Christ satisfied God's primal decision to be known by human beings. God created humans for fellowship with God. Humans broke their fellowship through sin. Jesus Christ restored that fellowship by renewing us and revealing himself to be the Word of God. God's original self-determination to be related to us is satisfied in Jesus Christ.

Even Anselm, much maligned, brings to the issue of satisfaction a theme worth considering. Christ's death restores a certain divine order or fittingness. The shedding of blood for the sins of the world is somehow fitting.[32] As noted already, Anselm himself avoids the language of punishment. I am not suggesting that we keep the full Anselmian theory with its mechanical, artificial feel. But his notion of satisfaction as restoring God's original order and harmony is worth reclaiming.

Perhaps we can incorporate as well a thought well attested in nineteenth- and twentieth-century British theology, beginning with the work of the nineteenth-century Scottish theologian John McLeod Campbell. The passion and death of Jesus Christ in some ways satisfied the love of God. In this dramatic divine self-surrender, God's love finds its fullest satisfaction and expression.[33]

Other more contemporary ideas suggest that Christ's death satisfied the compassion of God, the mercy of God, and the forgiveness of God. Reclaiming a broader notion of satisfaction does not "solve" the problem of violence and the cross. The cross was a violent act. But it does cut the knot between punishment and satisfaction. Anthony Bartlett suggests the term "abyssal compassion" as a construction that captures the core divine grace of the cross—a divine compassion that is offered by Christ on the cross and answered in the experience of forgiveness and love on the part of the believer.[34] This insight on satisfaction avoids the mechanism of legal theories of punishment and reaches for an understanding that is uniquely and particularly divine, one that finds its source in the Gospel narratives themselves.

Anthony Bartlett suggests the term "abyssal compassion" as a construction that captures the core divine grace of the cross—a divine compassion that is offered by Christ on the cross and answered in the experience of forgiveness and love on the part of the believer.

In addition, a broader notion of substitution may be considered. Again, this broader notion is well attested in the tradition, but it tends to be muted in the dominant Western view. Jesus Christ does not substitute for us only on the cross. Rather, Christ substitutes for us and we participate in Christ in the birth of Christ, in his life of obedience and communion with the Father, in his passion and death, in his victorious resurrection, in his ascension, reign, and promised second coming. Calvin includes the whole of Jesus' life, teachings, healings, and interactions with people as part of the pattern of Christ's obedience to the Father: "The remainder of the obedience that he manifested in his life is not excluded" in a consideration of our salvation.[35] All these moments of the broad salvation event include us in him and he for us.

A much more expansive understanding of substitution might then include our own participation in the life of Christ. Substitution concepts of the atonement are markedly individualistic and detached from community. But if the boundaries of this classic formulation are enlarged, the shape of a uniquely sacramental and ecclesial reality begins to emerge. Through the waters of baptism, each member of the community is cleansed, united with Christ, and incorporated into the community. In the shared meal of communion, the community is nourished by the living Christ, who is made present through the Spirit. In the practices of the faith, reconciliation is enacted again and again, in a profound pulse of divine grace that restores life.

The contemporary English theologian Timothy Gorringe echoes such an ecclesial vision in his constructive reflections on the saving effects of the cross, proposing that attention shift from theories of satisfaction and retribution to the biblical roots of redemption and reconciliation. These biblical roots reveal that "Christ 'redeems' us from the principalities and powers, from the social structures which warp human behavior and produce violence and crime, partly by laying bare the way in which they scapegoat and exclude, but also, correlatively, by inaugurating a continuing practice of reconciliation."[36] Only when the community joins in concrete practices of forgiveness, reconciliation, seeking justice, bearing one another's burdens, and waiting expectantly for the full flowering of God's kingdom is salvation comprehensible, visible, and fruitful.

Both provisional suggestions in this final section need fuller biblical and theological clarification. It is important to note that they are both in significant continuity with the tradition. Yet they also call into question social consequences of the tradition that need our committed theological examination. The first proposal sketched in this final section was an expanded conception of satisfaction, drawing in the full range of metaphors from the Christian tradition. Such an expansion would avoid a conception of the atonement heavily dependent on retributive justice theories or suggesting mechanistic divine strategies. The second proposal similarly expands the theme of substitution in such a way that the practices of the church in corporate worship and service are a participation in Christ such that he is for us and we are in him.

Only when the community joins in concrete practices of forgiveness, reconciliation, seeking justice, bearing one another's burdens, and waiting expectantly for the full flowering of God's kingdom is salvation comprehensible, visible, and fruitful.

QUESTIONS FOR REFLECTION AND DISCUSSION

1. What were the views of the Apollinarians and Nestorians? What problems did each position create? How did Chalcedon address those problems?

2. What models of the work of Christ have been used in the Christian tradition? What are the strengths and weaknesses of each?

3. Jenson admits that the New Testament does not state "the doctrine of the Trinity," but he insists that the Trinitarian way of thinking about God is already present there. How so?

4. Jenson says that Eastern Orthodox and some Reformation theologies have filled out Chalcedon in ways that bring it in line with Cyril of Alexandria. Why does he think this approach is much better than the theology, common in the West, based on the *Tome* of Leo?

5. Jenson does not propose a theory of the atonement in a traditional sense. What does he offer instead?

6. What problems does Van Dyk see with the dominant Western view of the atonement? Does this view in fact foster violence and abuse?

7. How does Van Dyk think that elements of the tradition can be rescued from its problems? What does she think has to go?

FOR FURTHER READING

Aulén, Gustaf. *Christus Victor.* Trans. A. G. Herbert. New York: Macmillan, 1969.

Bartlett, Anthony. *Cross Purposes.* Harrisburg, Pa.: Trinity Press International, 2001.

Boff, Leonardo. *Jesus Christ Liberator.* Trans. Patrick Hughes. Maryknoll, N.Y.: Orbis Books, 1978.

Bonhoeffer, Dietrich. *Christ the Center.* Trans. E. H. Robertson. New York: Harper & Row, 1978.

Bonino, José Miguez. *Faces of Jesus.* Trans. Robert R. Barr. Maryknoll, N.Y.: Orbis Books, 1984.

Brunner, Emil. *The Mediator.* Trans. Olive Wyon. Philadelphia: Westminster Press, 1947.

Cobb, John B., Jr. *Christ in a Pluralistic Age.* Philadelphia: Westminster Press, 1975.

Franks, R. S. *The Work of Christ.* New York: Thomas Nelson & Sons, 1962.

Frei, Hans W. *The Identity of Jesus Christ.* Philadelphia: Fortress Press, 1975.

Grant, Jacquelyn. *White Women's Christ and Black Women's Jesus.* Atlanta: Scholars Press, 1989.

Griffin, David Ray. *Process Christology.* Philadelphia: Westminster Press, 1973.

Hellwig, Monica K. *Jesus, the Compassion of God.* Collegeville, Minn.: Liturgical Press, 1983.

Johnson, Elizabeth A. *Consider Jesus.* New York: Crossroad, 1990.

Meyendorff, John. *Christ in Eastern Christian Thought.* Crestwood, N.Y.: St. Vladimir's Seminary Press, 1987.

Moltmann, Jürgen. *The Crucified God.* Trans. R. A. Wilson and John Bowden. New York: Harper & Row, 1974.

———. *The Way of Jesus Christ.* Trans. Margaret Kohl. San Francisco: Harper, 1990.

Pannenberg, Wolfhart. *Jesus—God and Man.* Trans. Lewis L. Wilkins and Duane A. Priebe. Philadelphia: Westminster Press, 1968.

Pelikan, Jaroslav. *Jesus through the Centuries.* New Haven, Conn.: Yale University Press, 1985.

Placher, William C. *Jesus the Savior.* Louisville, Ky.: Westminster John Knox Press, 2001.

Soelle, Dorothee. *Christ the Representative*. Trans. David Lewis. London: SCM Press, 1967.

Weaver, J. Denny. *The Nonviolent Atonement.* Grand Rapids: Wm. B. Eerdmans Publishing Co., 2001.

Yoder, John Howard. *The Politics of Jesus.* Grand Rapids: Wm. B. Eerdmans Publishing Co., 1972.

Young, Frances M. *Sacrifice and the Death of Christ.* Philadelphia: Westminster Press, 1975.

Chapter 6

Why Bother with Church?

The Church and Its Worship

All of us have heard the phrases, and maybe some of us have said them: "I'm spiritual . . ." or "I'm religious . . ." or "I'm a Christian . . . ," ". . . but I'm not really involved in the church." Sometimes it gets said sheepishly, with the implication that active church membership would be a good idea if only one had more time. Sometimes the tone is aggressive, and further conversation makes it clear that the speaker thinks institutional churches are fraudulent and have betrayed what was best in the spirit of Jesus.

Claiming to be a Christian, or perhaps a "follower of Jesus," while distancing oneself from the church is a relatively new phenomenon in Christian history. It is probably still mostly a North American phenomenon. Through the centuries, and still in many parts of the world, people just assumed that following Jesus implied belonging to one version or another of his church. Indeed, until the seventeenth century, the Christians in a given territory generally all belonged to the same Christian body. The idea of "shopping around" for a congregation you like is as new as the idea of being a Christian without any connection to the church.

Why has the church been so important to so many Christians? What do we mean by "the church"? How did it develop? How might we generate more enthusiasm for it?

DEVELOPING INSTITUTIONS

The very first Christians probably gave little thought to institutions and their organization. Caught up in the excitement of proclaiming the resurrection, they likely expected that little time would pass before Jesus' return. So why bother about structures?

Reasons for bothering soon emerged. As time passed, it became clear that Christians would be around for a while. Preaching, teaching, feeding the hungry—there was work to be done, and they needed some form of organization to do it. Moreover, challenges from inside and outside threatened their community and its faith, and they needed ways of assuring some degree of stability and integrity.

In Rome in about 150, for instance, a Christian named Marcion proposed dropping the Old Testament and using only an edited version of the New Testament that would fit his view that the God who created the world and spoke through the Jewish prophets was a different deity (a rather incompetent one) from the wholly good God now revealed in Christ. Until that time, Christians had been fairly casual about what counted as "Scripture," but now they needed to develop a *canon* (meaning a "rule") of the books that would be included in the Bible. Our canon emerged only gradually and was not completely settled until the fourth century, though most of the decisions over what and what not to include had been made well before then.

> Over time, Christians developed a canon, creeds, and a hierarchy of officials.

As noted in previous chapters, Christians also began to write creeds summarizing the essence of their faith in the face of those they thought were getting it wrong. They also decided they needed officials. The Gospels report that Jesus appointed twelve apostles to continue his work of preaching, teaching, and healing. Acts 6 tells of the first deacons, whose job was to administer the food made available to the needy and therefore free the apostles up to preach and teach.

Further challenges came after the New Testament period. By the second century groups of *gnostic* Christians were claiming to have a special wisdom passed down in secret about the true meaning of Christianity (*gnosis* means "wisdom"). No, their critics answered, Jesus taught the twelve apostles, and they taught their successors, the bishops (*episcopoi,* literally "overseers"). If there were any secret wisdom, the bishops would know it. "We should regard the bishop as the Lord himself," Ignatius, bishop of Antioch, wrote about 110.[1] "As many as are God's and Jesus Christ's, they are on the bishop's side."[2]

Some early Christian communities were led by a group of elders (*presbyteroi*);

others by a single bishop. The model of one ruling bishop per city, however, soon became the dominant pattern. The bishops of the greatest cities—Jerusalem, Antioch, Alexandria, Constantinople, and Rome—came to have particular authority, and Greek-speaking Christians thought of these five "patriarchs" as the leaders of the church. Among the five cities, Rome had a special place. Its church (at least in legend) had had Peter, first among the apostles, as its first head. Rome was the traditional capital of the empire, and the only one of the five great cities in the Latin-speaking West. In the West, the bishop of Rome (the *pope,* originally an informal term meaning "father" or "priest") came to be recognized as the head of the whole church. Though an official break came only in 1054, by the fourth century, Greek-speaking Christians in the East (Orthodox) and Latin-speaking Christians in the West (Catholic) were already drifting apart.

Many early Christians probably thought of deacons, elders, and bishops simply as people fulfilling particular jobs within the church. As early as 96, however, Clement of Rome, writing a letter of advice to the church at Corinth—note the authority already assumed by the Roman church—speaks of the difference between "priests" and "laypeople."[3] On an analogy with the priests of the Old Testament, he thinks of priests as a separate class, uniquely ordained to administer the sacraments. Women, who clearly had positions of real if informal authority in the communities Paul was visiting, were excluded from the start from "priesthood," and therefore, as the sense of a priestly class developed, rather quickly came to have far less power in the church.[4]

As the church grew in size, the number and power of church officials inevitably grew too. A hierarchical model of the church dominated the Middle Ages. Most aspects of society were hierarchical, from kings and their nobles, to lords and their vassals, to masters, journeymen, and apprentices in the craft guilds. It seemed natural that the church should have the pope or the great patriarchs at the top, then bishops, priests, and laypeople.

ONE, HOLY, CATHOLIC, AND APOSTOLIC

The Nicene Creed (originally adopted at the Council of Nicaea in 325 but edited into roughly its current form at the Council of Constantinople in 381) had defined the church as "one, holy, catholic, and apostolic." In the essays in this chapter, both Hughes Old and Letty Russell will analyze the importance of those four adjectives, though the implications they draw from them will differ. (Even their terminology is different, and there are no standard terms here: Old calls these the four "marks" of the church; Russell calls them "signs" and reserves "marks" for the Reformation's identification of the true church as the place where the Word is purely preached and the sacraments properly administered.)

Paul had written that the church is the "body of Christ," and therefore, if divided or corrupt, could not really be the church—thus, it had to be both "one" and "holy." *Catholic* meant "universal." Christians anywhere were part of the same "church" as Christians anywhere else; a Christian group confined to one particular territory could not define itself as "the church." *Apostolic* implied, among other things, that the church preserved the original faith of the apostles, in particular through an "apostolic succession" which passed that tradition down through the line of bishops.[5]

Problems arose when one of these criteria came into conflict with another. In fourth-century North Africa, for instance, debates arose in the aftermath of the last great Roman persecution of Christians. Some bishops had caved in under threat of torture, denounced Christ, and given up copies of the Bible to be burned. The Donatists (named after one of their heroes, a man named Donatus) argued that, if the church is holy, then these traitors could no longer be bishops. The people they ordained were not bishops, and the children they baptized were not truly baptized.

Augustine and others who opposed the Donatists argued, first of all, that there were Donatists only in North Africa, and therefore their church was not universal. Moreover, they said, if the validity of my ordination or baptism depends on the holiness of the priest who baptized me, and the bishop who ordained him, and so on, then I can never be sure of its validity. One could never know if the church was truly apostolic. If the act of a sacrament is performed properly by an appropriate official, they insisted against the Donatists, then it is valid *ex opere operato* ("by the having been done of the thing done"), never mind the sinful past (or present) of the person performing it. Secret sins in the priesthood do not destroy the validity of the church's sacraments.

> If a sacrament is performed properly by an appropriate official, Augustine insisted against the Donatists, then it is valid *ex opere operato,* never mind the sinful past (or present) of the person performing it.

Augustine's views brought into particular focus some tensions embedded in what many theologians taught about the church. On the one hand, in God's eyes the real church (it came to be called the "invisible church") was made up of those God had chosen or elected. The "visible church"—the people who actually turned up on Sunday morning—presumably did not correspond to the invisible church. Yet almost no one suggested that we should, on that account, give up on the visible church. In the visible church, as Calvin admitted, "are mingled many hypocrites who have nothing of Christ but the name and outward appearance." Nevertheless, "Just as we must believe . . . that the former church, invisible to us, is visible to the eyes of God alone, so we are commanded to revere and keep communion with the latter, which is called 'church' in respect to men."[6] Christians could acknowledge the corruption of the visible church while nevertheless recognizing their obligations to it.

In the sixteenth-century Reformation, of course, tensions about such issues led to breaking points. Luther believed that the church of his time had diverged from the teachings of the gospel and had become corrupt. Thus, it was no longer apostolic or holy. His Catholic opponents protested that he was ignoring the teachings of the pope and the bishops and breaking off from the church, with the result that the community of his followers was no longer apostolic or part of the one church. Luther, who started with no intention of dividing the church but only a hope of purifying it, found himself having led a split. But he and other Reformers insisted that they had not left the church. The true "marks of the church," Protestants said, were that the gospel be properly preached and the sacraments properly administered, not that there be some tie to the pope.

But how far would change go? Luther and other Reformers proclaimed the "priesthood of all believers"—there were different jobs to be done in the church, but not a fundamental distinction between priests and laypeople. Yet the pattern of excluding women from ordination, historically one of the characteristic features of priesthood, remained in place in most Protestant groups until the middle of the twentieth century. German peasants in revolt appealed to Luther's precedent—they were overthrowing secular lords just as he had overthrown the lords of the church. But Luther reacted in genuine horror—whatever he had begun, it was not a political revolution.

Luther, as well as the founders of the Reformed tradition, John Calvin and Ulrich Zwingli (based in the Swiss cities of Geneva and Zurich), and the leaders of the Church of England, were willing to divide the church for the sake of reforming it. Within a particular territory, however, these leaders of the *magisterial* Reformation (the part of the Reformation that worked with the magistrates) continued to assume that all Christians would belong to the same church. It was hard for sixteenth-century folk to imagine, for one thing, how people could be loyal to a ruler who did not share their beliefs about God, so they assumed that a given political territory would have to have a common religion. As parts of Germany became "Lutheran" and various Swiss cities became "Reformed," they were willing to make some compromises and move only gradually for the sake of keeping at least their local community united.

> As parts of Germany became "Lutheran" and various Swiss cities became "Reformed," people were willing to make some compromises and move only gradually for the sake of keeping at least their local community religiously united. For the followers of the "radical Reformation," however, holiness was all important.

For the followers of what historians call the "radical Reformation," however, holiness was all important. Beginning in Switzerland as early as the 1520s, communities of Anabaptists ("rebaptizers") deliberately separated from their neighbors into communities attempting to live pure Christian lives. They required that their members be rebaptized as adults as a sign of their new birth and clear commitment to this community and its life. They suffered persecution for their beliefs and their pacifism; their most direct descendants survive today in the Mennonites and Amish.

In the 1640s, amid the chaos of the English Civil War, many of the same issues arose again. The Parliamentary forces fighting against the king generally opposed what they considered the moral corruption and excessive ritual of the Church of England, but they disagreed on what to do about it. Moderate "Puritans" simply wanted to purify the church. "Presbyterians" sought to replace bishops with regional gatherings, called "presbyteries," of pastors and elders on the model of Calvin's churches in Geneva. "Congregationalists" favored independence for each local congregation. "Baptists," like the Anabaptists on the continent, affirmed membership in their purified communities by adult baptism. When the monarchy was restored in 1660, the Church of England became again its country's official church, and these other groups remained as minorities or fled to North America, where many rapidly grew in number.

Our contemporary American model of many competing denominations would have seemed utterly strange throughout most of Christian history. There is something fundamentally wrong about a divided church. Some Christians claim that those who do not belong to their own body are not part of the church at all; others discern a hidden unity even in the divided churches; others work in the ecumenical movement for church reunion. Some efforts to heal divisions in the church, like the Disciples of Christ, founded by Presbyterians and Baptists in West Virginia in the 1820s, have ended up just creating one more denomination, but Christians cannot give up exploring ways to end their divisions.

SACRAMENTS AND PREACHING

Divisions among Christians often become most problematic in relation to the sacraments. Do *we* accept *their* baptism? Can I take Communion in your church at the wedding? In the face of such questions, we become painfully aware of the church's splits.

A sacrament is, in a phrase from the Episcopal Book of Common Prayer, "an outward and visible sign of an inward and spiritual grace"—some visible action that becomes the manifestation of God's grace. For centuries, Christians used the term without much precision; anything from the church itself to the saying of the Lord's Prayer could count as a sacrament. Only in 1438 did the Council of Florence identify the Catholic list of seven sacraments: baptism, confirmation, the Eucharist, penance, the last rites, marriage, and ordination.

Luther initially reduced the list to three—baptism, confirmation, and the Eucharist. Later he shifted to the two—baptism and the Eucharist—usually counted as sacraments in Protestant churches that talk about sacraments at all.

The New Testament describes Christians as baptizing new members from the very beginning of the church (Acts 2:41, for instance). Only adults are specifically identified as receiving baptism, but several are baptized together with their households (Acts 16:16; 18:8), and the households may have included children.

By the time we are clear about baptismal practices—about 200—infants as well as adults were being baptized. Before that, we simply do not know.

Adult baptism was a dramatic event in the early church. After a lengthy period of study and fasting, the new Christian would be, in the darkness of Easter morning, stripped naked and fully immersed before being reclothed in new white garments—a symbol of death to the old life and birth to the new.

Critics of infant baptism argue that it is contrary to the practice of the earliest church, that it trivializes what ought to be a moment of decision to commit one's life to Christ, and that it imposes on babies a decision that they ought to have the right to make for themselves when they are adults. Defenders cite the parallel of circumcision, the Jewish analogue to baptism, which was and is nearly always performed on infants, and argue that infant baptism is a marvelous symbol of God's grace, which takes hold of us before we are even aware of it.

The main debate about baptism, then, concerns infant baptism; disputes about the Eucharist (or *Communion* or the *Lord's Supper—Eucharist* means "thanksgiving") have proven more complex. On the night before he died, three of the Gospels report, Jesus shared bread and wine with his disciples, identifying it as his body and blood. (The Fourth Gospel presupposes this last supper, but the ritual it describes that last night is Jesus washing his disciples' feet. Foot washing remains a regular practice in the Church of the Brethren, one of the groups that emerged from the radical Reformation.) Paul, who also reports this last supper, describes how it was often repeated as part of a communal meal, in which, ideally, the rich would bring extra food and the poor would share in it. He is scandalized to note that in Corinth some Christians ate too much and got drunk.

The Eastern Church early on affirmed the "real presence" of Christ's body and blood in the sacrament, but that phrase and its meaning continued to be debated in the West, in part because Augustine, who was so influential in the West, on some occasions referred to a "spiritual presence" of the body and blood in what remained physically ordinary bread and wine.[7] A minority of medieval theologians (Ratramnus in the ninth century, Berengar of Tours in the eleventh) insisted that the bread and wine become Christ's body and blood, "not materially but spiritually."[8] In contrast, some popular piety in the Middle Ages passed down very literalistic stories of a little baby appearing in place of the bread during the Eucharist.

> In the Eucharist, Aquinas said, the *properties* of the bread and wine remain the same, but their *substance* changes.

Official teaching finally took a middle ground, most clearly expressed by Aquinas, drawing on the philosophy of Aristotle. Aristotle distinguished between a "substance" and its "properties." In the normal course of things, properties change, but the underlying substance remains the same. I paint a red box blue, and its color has changed from red to blue, but it remains a box. In the Eucharist, Aquinas said, the properties remain the same, but the substance changes. The elements still look and taste like bread and wine, but the bread and wine have been *transubstantiated* into the body and blood of Christ. In 1215, the Fourth Lateran Council affirmed transubstantiation as a doctrine of the church.

Practice as well as theory was changing in the Middle Ages. The idea that in each Eucharist a sacrifice of Christ's body and blood was again offered to God made the priest's saying of the Mass more important than the participation or even presence of the laity. To avoid dangers of spilling, only the priest drank the wine become blood; laypeople shared only in the bread. Medieval eucharistic theology, one recent Catholic author has said, "is a theology of and for the priest rather than a theology for the baptized,"[9] though recent scholarship has shown how powerfully it still shaped the life and faith of ordinary people.[10]

In practice, the Reformation sought to engage the whole congregation more in the sacrament. Everyone both ate the bread and drank the wine. Since Christ had been sacrificed once for all on the cross, the Reformers said, the sacrifice was not repeated, and the Eucharist should take place only as the shared activity of a Christian community. Luther and Calvin both affirmed the real presence of Christ but rejected transubstantiation as a particular philosophical theory that tried to explain what we should be willing to leave as a mystery. Luther put more emphasis on the objective presence of Christ in the body and blood; Calvin emphasized the faith of those taking the elements, but their theories are not incompatible. (Luther spoke of *consubstantiation*—the bread and wine remained bread and wine while also becoming Christ's body and blood. Calvin preferred the term "real presence.") Calvin's fellow Swiss Reformer Ulrich Zwingli (along with many of the more radical Reformers) thought of the meal simply as a memorial in which we remember what Christ has done for us, but in which Christ is not really present. The Reformed tradition has struggled to reconcile its Calvinist and Zwinglian heritages on this matter ever since.

Preaching became more central to the worship of most Protestant communities. Though recent scholarship has reminded us of the greatness of many medieval preachers,[11] the standard of preaching in the average church was clearly low. Protestant *and* Catholic preaching after the Reformation improved dramatically. Luther emphasized with characteristic vividness that the Word of God was in the mouth of the preacher, and Calvin too said that Christ has promised that in preaching "it was he himself who would speak and promise all things through their lips as his instruments."[12]

The church itself, of course, not just its Eucharist or its preaching, is "the body of Christ" (Rom. 12:4–5). As the representative of Christ in the world, it is at once the community of the people of God, the witness of the gospel, and the servant of all the world's poor and rejected. It keeps alive the dangerous memory of the gospel even as it anticipates the reign of God. Both the essayists in this chapter believe that churches are not doing a very good job these days of being what they ought to be, though both their diagnoses of the problem and the solutions they would propose are very different.

HUGHES OLIPHANT OLD

Millions of us today have a sense of being alienated. We have a feeling of being left alone in this world, orphaned, divorced, or abandoned. The extended family is a relic of the past. We don't even know who our neighbors are anymore. That is the way it is in the city, at least. The best we can hope for is a nuclear family or a close community of friends, but more and more our social life has degenerated into living in isolation. That there might be a real church, somehow, somewhere, is to so many of us very good news. Yes, implicit in the gospel is the message that we are welcomed in the church. That there really is a communion of the saints is part of the Christian hope.[1] It is a transcendent reality into which even now we can enter.

It was in the pouring out of the Holy Spirit on the day of Pentecost that the risen and ascended Jesus established the church. He established the church as he had promised when he had commissioned the apostles to preach the gospel to all peoples. There was nothing surprising or unexpected about this. What Jesus did in establishing the church had been envisioned by the prophets of Israel for centuries.[2] In the founding of the church, the covenant made with Abraham was fulfilled (Gen. 12:3) as well as the covenant made with David (2 Sam. 7:4–17). Founding the church was simply the unfolding of the messianic ministry which Jesus claimed had been bestowed upon him and which he had come to fulfill (Luke 4:21). The shepherd had come to gather his flock.

Very early in his ministry Jesus began to gather around himself a group of disciples. We hear of two disciples of John the Baptist, John and Andrew, the brother of Simon Peter. Then came Philip and Nathanael (John 1:35–51). Jesus took these men into his fellowship. They became his friends and took part in his ministry of preaching and healing. We hear of Matthew the tax collector, with all his talents and abilities, being brought into this fellowship. Mary Magdalene, in spite of her sordid reputation, and Simon the Zealot, apparently an experienced counterculture revolutionary, were included as well. Then there were Mary and Martha, women of such differing gifts. They too were part of the fellowship.

Jesus was quite clear about the ministry the church was to maintain. He was to bring all of us into communion with God: men, women, and children of all sorts and conditions were to be brought into the communion of God's people. At the Last Supper, Jesus instituted the sacrament of Communion before he went to the cross in order to establish a covenantal union between himself and his disciples. On that night in the Upper Room he prayed for the Church, for its unity, its sanctity, and its continuity (John 17). Having joined himself to his disciples at the Last Supper, having prayed with them and for them through the night, he went to the cross and offered himself up to the Father for the sin of the world, for our sin, all of it, from beginning to end. His sacrifice was obedient, complete, and sufficient, and was received in heaven as atonement for all our sin—the whole obscene, corrupt, and accursed mess. As a sign that the sacrifice was accepted, God raised up Jesus from the dead. It was then the risen Jesus who, once more in the Upper Room, bestowed the Holy Spirit on the apostles that they might be ministers of God's forgiving mercy. As Jesus had been sent to preach God's forgiveness of sin, so now Jesus sent the Twelve to continue his ministry. They became apostles.[3]

At the time of his ascension, Jesus commissioned the apostles to preach the gospel to all peoples and to make disciples of all nations, baptizing them and teaching them everything Jesus had taught. With this the sacrament of baptism was instituted as a means of bringing people into the church and promising them the washing away of sin and the bestowing of the Holy Spirit. Baptism became the divinely given sign of our being received into the household of God and our growing up into eternal life.

NEW TESTAMENT IMAGES OF THE CHURCH

On the day of Pentecost, that which Jesus had promised was fulfilled. The Holy Spirit was poured out on a great variety of people from distant lands, from Egypt and Persia, from Rome and Arabia, from Asia Minor and Libya, as well as on Judeans and Galileans (Acts 2:7–11). On that day the church was established and about three thousand people were baptized. Through that baptism they became part of the church.

It was Jesus who founded the church, and he established it quite intentionally, giving it a particular ministry to perform. The New Testament Scriptures unfold at some length what this church is which Jesus established and just what ministry it is to perform.[4]

First, the church is to be the *people of God.* Just as God had called Abraham out of Ur of the Chaldees that he and his descendants might be God's chosen people, and just as God had called Moses and the children of Israel to leave Egypt and its slavery behind and enter a new and promised land to serve God in righteousness and justice, so now God sent his own Son to gather the whole people of God from every land and every people. God sent Jesus to be the Good Shepherd and gather about himself the flock of God's people. Jesus himself often spoke about this, both directly (John 10:1–18) and in his parables (Luke 15:3–7).

> The New Testament speaks of the church as the people of God, a spiritual temple, the body of Christ, and the bride of Christ.

This figure of the church as the people of God, the new Israel, or the household of faith is developed at several points in the New Testament. A particularly important passage is found in 1 Peter 2:9–10: "But you are a chosen race, a royal priesthood, a holy nation, God's own people. . . . Once you were not a people, but now you are God's people."

Second, in the same passage from 1 Peter, for example, we find the church spoken of as a *spiritual temple*—in this text described as built on the rock of our salvation, Jesus Christ himself. We like living stones are built up into this spiritual house "to be a holy priesthood, to offer spiritual sacrifices" (1 Pet. 2:5).[5] To be sure, here is a classic case of mixed metaphors, but the sense is clear. The church is a temple because it is a priestly people, a holy nation which lives for nothing quite so much as to worship God. We are a "chosen race, a royal priesthood, a holy nation, God's own people," that we may bear witness to God's mighty acts of creation and redemption. This image of the church as a spiritual temple makes clear the priority of worship in the life of the church as well as making equally clear that that worship involves the proclamation of the gospel.

We find this same image developed by the apostle Paul in the Epistle to the Ephesians: "So then you are no longer strangers and aliens, but you are citizens with the saints and also members of the household of God, built upon the foundation of the apostles and prophets, with Christ Jesus himself as the cornerstone. In him the whole structure is joined together and grows into a holy temple in the Lord" (Eph. 2:19–21).[6] Here the apostle underlines the continuity between the ministry of the church and the ministry of Israel. It is Christ who is the cornerstone, chosen and precious, who is the pattern of our service to God the Father. It is in preaching Christ that the church opens up the mystery, hidden for ages (Eph. 3:9), and invites all people to enter into the fellowship of the household of God and by faith to know the love of Christ (Eph. 3:19).

It is through faith that each of us is built into this living temple. Just as the temple in Jerusalem was built on a great rock, so the church is built on the rock that is Christ. Each of us, when we come to know Jesus as the Christ, the Son of the living God, is thereby built squarely on the foundation of the apostles and prophets. It is by faith in Christ that we become part of the church. So it is that Christ himself is the rock on which he builds his church (Matt. 16:13–18).[7]

Third, the apostle Paul adds to the image of the spiritual temple the image of the church as the *body of Christ.* The significance of this figure of the church has been much discussed in recent times.[8] This image of the church underlines the unity of the church. It also makes especially clear the dependence of the different members on one another. The apostle exhorts the Ephesians "to maintain the unity of the Spirit in the bond of peace" (Eph. 4:3). The apostle Paul goes on to explain: "There is one body and one Spirit, just as you were called to the one hope of your calling, one Lord, one faith, one baptism, one God and Father of all, who is above all and through all and in all" (Eph. 4:4–6). But if the body has unity, it has diversity as well. The different members of the one body allow the body to perform a variety of functions.

If the body has unity, it has diversity as well. The different members of the one body allow the body to perform a variety of functions.

God seems to cherish diversity. It was God himself who seems to have taken the initiative in bringing very different kinds of people into the church. Philip's ministry to the Samaritans (Acts 8:4–25) and Peter's baptism of Cornelius, the Roman centurion in Caesarea (Acts 10:1–48), would seem to indicate that there was great variety in the Church from the earliest times. This variety was not just a matter of race or nationality. From all that we can gather, it would appear that Peter and Paul were very different personalities. The one was a fisherman, the other an academic theologian. Lydia was a businesswoman (Acts 16:14–15), while Dionysius the Areopagite was a philosopher (Acts 17:34). There were plenty of slaves in the early church, plenty of widows, and, yes, there were soldiers, jailers, and artisans of all kinds. There were even members of Caesar's household (Phil. 4:22).

Because different members have different spiritual gifts, the church can perform a variety of ministries. Among the most prominent are the apostolic ministry, the prophetic ministry, the evangelistic ministry, the pastoral ministry, and the teaching ministry (Eph. 4:11).[9] These spiritual gifts, as John Mackay, former president of Princeton Theological Seminary, used to insist, were to equip the saints for the work of ministry.[10] Spiritual gifts have a strong ministerial function. The ministers of the church are set apart not to be served, but to serve (Mark 10:43–45).

Fourth, an image of the Church which we find frequently in the New Testament is the *bride of Christ.* This image is implied in a number of the parables of Jesus, such as the Wedding Feast of the King's Son (Matt. 22:1–14) and the Wise and Foolish Virgins (Matt. 25:1–13), but also in the story of the wedding at Cana where Jesus shows himself to be the bridegroom (John 2:1–11). This image holds up the ideal of purity, holiness, and single-hearted devotion to the Lord to which the church should aspire. But not only is the bride obedient to her husband, the bridegroom is faithful to his bride and loves her to the point of giving his life for her (Eph. 5:25). Just as the love which unites a bride and bridegroom in marriage can lead to children, the bride of Christ becomes the mother of the faithful (Gal. 4:26).

THE CHURCH IN THE EARLY CREEDS

Down through the centuries these passages of Scripture have shaped the way Christians have understood the church and its ministry. Sometimes these basic biblical passages have been understood in one way, sometimes in another. The church has carried out its ministry in a variety of cultures. Sometimes it has performed its basic ministry rather well, but sometimes it has not done as well. Let us look at just a few of these interpretations.

One of the first attempts of the church to understand its ministry is expressed in the Apostles' Creed.[11] The core of this text comes to us from about the year 200.[12] The creed confesses, "I believe in the Holy Spirit, the holy catholic church, the communion of saints, the forgiveness of sins. . . . " The first thing we notice about this is that the belief in the church and its ministry is developed out of belief in the Holy Spirit. A Trinitarian understanding of God makes clear that the unity of God is not some dead, monolithic uniformity, but that in the unity of God there is communion. God is a God who reaches out. God is a communicating God, not a static, silent entity. God is a Spirit, an outpouring, inspiring, creating, and anointing Spirit, a strengthening, confirming, and comforting Spirit.

We should also notice that the affirmation of the church as it issues from our belief in the Holy Spirit leads to the affirmation of the communion of saints and the forgiveness of sin.[13] That the church is a communion, or fellowship, is an important dimension of the reality of the church and, even more, the reality of God. There is, of course, nothing which visualizes what the church really is so much as the actual celebration of the sacrament of Communion. The sacrament is a God-given sign of the reality of the church and even more a covenantal promise that this sign will be fulfilled among us.

The Nicene Creed gives four marks which identify the church: It is one, holy, catholic, and apostolic.

A particularly important statement on the nature of the church comes from the Nicene Creed, formulated in the fourth century. The Nicene Creed gives four marks which identify the church: It is one, holy, catholic, and apostolic.[14] We have already mentioned the importance the apostle Paul gave to the unity or oneness of the church. The same importance we find in the high priestly prayer of Jesus in the Gospel of John (John 17:1–26). There Jesus prays for the church that the church "may be one, as we are one, I in them and you in me, that they may become completely one" (John 17:22–23).

The second mark of the true church proposed by the Nicene Creed is that it be holy. In the same high priestly prayer in the Gospel of John, Jesus prays for the holiness of the church: "Holy Father, . . . sanctify them in the truth" (John 17:11, 17). That the church is to be pure is implicit in the image of the church as the bride of Christ. Christ gave his life for the bride "in order to make her holy by cleansing her with the washing of water by the word, so as to present the church to himself in splendor, without a spot or wrinkle or anything of the kind—yes, so that she may be holy and without blemish" (Eph. 5:26–27). In the sacrament of baptism we receive a sign and a promise of the cleansing power of God's Spirit. By the blood of Christ and the power of the Holy Spirit, all our sins are washed away. Baptism brings us into the church, and in the fellowship of the church we are more and more transformed into the image of Christ (Rom. 6:1–23).

The church should also be catholic, according to the creed. This word can be taken all kinds of ways, but for us today it should probably be understood as urging us to maintain the historic faith of the church as it has been maintained over the centuries in one land and another, from one culture to another, century after century. To believe in the catholicity of the church is to believe that the truth of the Gospel transcends our nationalistic ideologies and cultural predispositions (cf. 1 Cor. 1:10–25 and Col. 2:8–23).

To speak of the catholicity of the church is very important today, even among the most conservative evangelicals. The ideologies of our day find it hard to talk about any kind of faith "once for all entrusted to the saints" (Jude 3). Yet that is what catholicity means. Historians of Christian doctrine, indeed, find it difficult to identify just exactly what that faith is which has been believed by all Christians, in all places, and at all times. Perhaps it is because true faith is somehow above attempts to arrive at a precise statement. Truth somehow resists being corked up in a bottle. The true church should be generous in its understanding of the truth. And yet Jesus himself, as the Gospel of John reports it, taught that he himself is the way, the truth, and the life (John 14:5). For the church to give up its catholicity is in the end a form of self-destruction.

The catholicity of the church, not unlike the unity of the church or its sanctity, is a matter of faith. It really is there even if we cannot exactly grab it, hold it in our hands, or package it. The creeds of the ancient church, the confessions of faith of the Reformation, the writings of classic theologians, the sermons of many a preacher witness to it, even if we all too often quibble over one issue or another.

Finally, the Nicene Creed teaches us that the church should be apostolic. It should, following the Great Commission, go out to every land and every people to make disciples (cf. Matt. 28:16–20). The true Christian faith is essentially a missionary faith. Unlike Hinduism, Shintoism, Confucianism, and Judaism, it is not the religion of a particular culture or ethnic community. Rather, it claims now, as it always has, the allegiance of all the peoples of the world. About this, Scripture is abundantly clear.

Syncretism (the combination of elements from different religions or philosophies) has often been a temptation to genuine Christianity. In the Roman Empire there were many religious societies and schools of philosophy. Christians were constantly pressured to understand Christ as one more god in the pantheon, one more prophet or philosopher who established yet another school of philosophical thought. Ever since Alexander the Great in the fourth century before Christ tried to enlist all the priests, all the seers, and all the wise men from the Ganges to the Nile into a system of religious sanctions for his Hellenistic empire, syncretism has been pushed on God's people. Syncretism is nothing new.

Syncretism (the combination of elements from different religions or philosophies) has often been a temptation to genuine Christianity.

The problem with syncretism is that it tries to understand the Church as an expression of a particular culture. Yet, from very early times we find that God's people have insisted that the true God is not a tribal divinity but the one eternal God whose reign embraces all the earth and all its peoples. God chose Abraham and his descendants that all the peoples of the earth might be blessed (Gen. 12). The Psalms call all nations, even the Gentiles, to praise the Lord (Ps. 96). The prophets particularly had made the point that the one true God is to be worshiped on every shore, from the rising of the sun to its setting (Mal. 1:11). In the same way, Jesus sent out the apostles to preach the gospel to all nations, to make disciples in all lands, to baptize them into the church, and to teach those people everything he himself had taught (Matt. 28:18–20). They were to start in Jerusalem, then go through all Judea and Samaria, and from there to the ends of the earth (Acts 1:8).

During the Middle Ages the church crossed the Alps and won Northern Europe, from the British Isles to the forests of Russia, and yet in many respects it began to lose its focus. Its basic faith remained intact, but it often confused its role with that of the state. It became secularized and politicized. It became a hierarchy more than a fellowship.

THE CHURCH IN THE REFORMATION

The Protestant Reformation aimed at recovering the original vision of the nature and mission of the church. One might say that the Reformers reemphasized its existence rather than its essence, or, one might say, the Reformers focused on its function. The Augsburg Confession, the classic statement of Lutheran faith, understood the church as being where the Word is truly preached and the sacraments rightly administered. For Luther, as for Protestantism in general, the priority of worship was reasserted. The ministry of preaching and teaching, evangelizing and discipling, was seen as fundamental to the life of the church, rather than its hierarchical structure or institutional shape.[15] Luther's greatest contribution was the example he set of what it means to preach the gospel. Luther took the Bible and explained its meaning, declaring God's love for us and inviting us to put our faith in Christ. He refocused preaching; to preach was to preach the gospel. For Luther, preaching was a matter of presenting the gracious promises of God and encouraging us to receive these promises by faith. Luther's preaching invites us into the household of faith. This kind of preaching gathers the church, builds the church, and equips the church to perform the ministry to which God has called it.

> Bucer insisted that the life of the church should be centered in four things: preaching and teaching, sharing, the breaking of bread, and prayer.

The basic insight of Luther was elaborated by a number of the Reformers, but of particular interest is the work of Martin Bucer, the reformer of Strasbourg. Starting with the text of Acts 2:42, which tells of how after the sign of Pentecost the primitive church devoted itself to "the apostles' teaching and fellowship, to the breaking of bread and the prayers," Bucer insisted that the life of the church should be centered in four things. The first is the ministry of preaching and teaching. The second is the ministry of sharing, which includes the giving of alms and works of mercy. The third is the breaking of bread, that is, the Eucharist. The fourth is the prayers in which the members of the church join together in a ministry of supplication and intercession, thanksgiving and praise.

Several of the South German and Swiss Reformers, such as John Oecolampadius in Basel and Ulrich Zwingli in Zurich, joined the reformers of Strasbourg in reorganizing the ministerial offices of the church. The hierarchical principle was replaced with an emphasis on the parity of ministers. Zwingli's essay "Der Hirt" ("The Shepherd") emphasized the pastoral office. In Strasbourg much attention was given to the revival of church discipline. To this end the office of elder was reestablished. The primary ministry of the elder was the pastoral ministry. Another major concern of the Reformation was a recovery of the office of deacon.[16] As the Reformers interpreted Acts 6:1–6, it was the responsibility of the deacons to lead the church in its charitable concerns. Before long the Reformers began to speak of four dimensions of the ministry of the church: the preaching ministry, the teaching ministry, the pastoral ministry, and the diaconal or charitable ministry. Yet, as all the Reformers understood it, the ministry was above all the ministry of the Word. To be sure, there are varieties of ministerial service, but in the New Testament church there seemed to be a preeminence given to the ministry of preaching and teaching. As the apostle Paul put it, "God has appointed in the church first apostles, second prophets, third teachers; then deeds of power, then gifts of healing, forms of assistance, forms of leadership, various kinds of tongues" (1 Cor. 12:28; cf. 1 Tim. 5:17). If the church was to be understood in terms of its function, the maintaining of these various ministries was essential.

Among the Reformers, Calvin was one who gave most attention to the doctrine of the church.[17] No one could have made more clear than Calvin that the Protestant reemphasis on the ministry of Word, prayer, and sacrament was in no way a rejection of the traditional teaching on the unity, holiness, catholicity, and apostolicity of the church.[18] A number of Roman Catholic scholars have come to recognize this in the last generation.[19] At the same time, Calvin was very much in agreement with the Augsburg Confession in affirming that the true church is where the Word is truly preached and the sacraments rightly administered.[20]

For Calvin, the church has authority. It has the power to forgive sins and the responsibility to maintain discipline. This power is exercised both in the public preaching of the gospel and in private pastoral admonitions. But it is also exercised in the councils and courts of the church as long as it is exercised according to Scripture. The church is far more than a human institution. It has a transcendent reality. It is indeed the mother of the faithful.[21] Even from the first edition of Calvin's great work, *Institutes of the Christian Religion,* the *Ecclesia mater* ("mother church") plays a role.

For Calvin, the church has authority. It has the power to forgive sins and the responsibility to maintain discipline.

Calvin carefully affirms the catholicity of the church.[22] All God's people are united in Christ. We may be gathered together in different congregations, but by the fact that we have one head we are one; we are joined and knit together as are the limbs of a human body. We are made truly one since we live together in one faith, hope, and love. This is the work of the Holy Spirit. We are, through the work of the Holy Spirit, one in the body of Christ. In this world and at this time it may not seem that way, but it is true nevertheless.

For Calvin, the catholicity of the church very particularly implies that the true church has one and the same faith through every age and in every land: "The church universal is a multitude gathered from all nations; it is divided and dispersed in separate places, but agrees on the one truth of divine doctrine."[23] This agreement, to be sure, is not in every detail, but, rather, in the fundamental teachings of the faith.

Calvin also affirms that the church is a communion of saints.[24] As Calvin sees it, each of us should keep in fraternal agreement with all God's children. Christians should gather together in "the society of Christ." We should unite in fellowship with Christ. This fellowship should be benevolent; we should share with one another both spiritual and material goods. This practice should be based on the principle that whatever benefits God confers on us, we should in turn share with one another. The gifts of the Holy Spirit are variously distributed. For Calvin, sharing with one another is of the essence of the church. If we really believe God is our Father, then we ought to be united in fraternal love to the point of sharing God's gifts with one another.

Calvin paid particular attention to the biblical image of the church as the elect people of God, the holy commonwealth, the New Israel. Again following Augustine, Calvin sees the church as the people whom in every age God has called out from the world to serve him. His doctrine of election leads him to a very strong doctrine of the Church. As it is found, once again, in 1 Peter 2:9–10, "But you are a chosen race, a royal priesthood, a holy nation, God's own people, in order that you may proclaim the mighty acts of him who called you out of darkness into his marvelous light. Once you were not a people, but now you are God's people." For Calvin, the church was the elect people of God called out of this world to proclaim God's Word.

> For Calvin, the high calling of the church goes hand in hand with the humility of the church. We have these treasures in earthen vessels.

The church is, in spite of all appearances, holy. This is surely one of the marks of the church. Its holiness, however, is not yet complete. The church is called to holiness. It is engaged to be the bride of Christ, without spot or wrinkle. As a sign and seal of this purity, we have been given baptism to assure us of God's promise that we shall day by day, more and more, be washed of our sins.[25]

For Calvin, the high calling of the church, however, goes hand in hand with the humility of the church. The church is a human institution at the same time it is a holy communion. We have these treasures in earthen vessels, as the apostle Paul made so clear (2 Cor. 4:7).[26] The leaders of the church can and often do err. The church is a field of grain in which tares all too often have been sown, but this is no excuse to separate ourselves from the church, for it is God's field.[27] Beside that, we need each other. To none of us has God given all the spiritual gifts. The church is a means of grace because God has seen fit to bless us through each other. In the wisdom of God, it is in this way that the Christian commonwealth is bound together. God's blessings come through the hands of our brothers and sisters in Christ. We need each other, both in material things and in spiritual things.

As Protestantism developed in seventeenth-century England, the Puritans also gave attention to the doctrine of the church. The Westminster Confession of Faith, written in 1647, provides us with a well-balanced statement of the traditional doctrines of the church. Chapter 25, "Of the Church," starts out by affirming, "The catholic or universal church, which is invisible, consists of the whole number of the elect, that have been, are, or shall be gathered into one, under Christ the Head thereof; and is the spouse, the body, the fulness of Him that filleth all in all."[28] One notices how tenaciously the Westminster Confession holds on to the term *catholic,* not only in regard to the invisible but also the visible church.

> One of the strengths of the Westminster Confession's doctrine of the church is its recognition of the difference between the church visible and the church invisible.

One of the strengths of the Westminster Confession's doctrine of the church is its recognition of the difference between the church visible and the church invisible. Typically Augustinian, Westminster wants to emphasize that while the church is called to holiness, and must ever strive for holiness, none in this life can claim to have attained it: "The purest churches under heaven are subject both to mixture and error."[29] As an institution, the visible church should cultivate humility. It should be dedicated to mercy, justice, and holiness in all that it does, and yet the church should be mindful that sanctification is by faith. Sanctification is by faith as much as justification.[30]

The ministerial nature of the church is characteristic of the teaching of Westminster: "Unto this catholic, visible church Christ hath given the ministry, oracles, and ordinances of God, for the gathering and perfecting of the saints, in this life, to the end of the world: and doth, by His own presence and Spirit, according to His promise, make them effectual thereto."[31] Just as in the Augsburg Confession, the church is understood in terms of the ministry it has been given to perform: its maintaining of worship, its preaching and teaching, its pastoral care, its works of mercy, its fellowship, its service of prayer, and its observance of the sacraments.

Particularly important for understanding the teaching of the church found in the Westminster Confession is that the chapter on the church is followed by a chapter on the communion of the saints. This phrase goes back to the Apostles' Creed. The point of this chapter seems to be a concern to emphasize the personal dimension of the church over and above the institutional form of the church. It focuses on the church as fellowship, or, to use the original Greek word, *koinonia.* This word refers to the sharing of material goods as well as the sharing of faith. It means joining together with others in mutual support: "All saints that are united to Jesus Christ their Head, by His Spirit, and by faith, have fellowship with Him in His grace, sufferings, death, resurrection, and glory: and being united to one another in love, they have communion in each other's gifts and graces."[32] It is just this, of course, which is demonstrated in the sacrament of Communion, as we have already intimated. We as Christians receive the bread and wine sitting around the Lord's Table. We are served the gifts of God by others, and in turn we serve others. The very meal is a sign of our fellowship: "The cup of blessing that we bless, is it not a sharing of the blood of Christ? The bread which we break, is it not a sharing in the body of Christ?" (1 Cor. 10:16) There is nothing which illustrates the true nature of the church quite so well as a celebration of the sacrament of the Lord's Supper. The sacrament of Communion is a sign and a promise of true community, the fellowship of the people of God in the household of faith. As we so often find it in the communion sermons of the Puritans, the Lord's Supper is a foretaste of the wedding feast of the Lamb.

THE CHURCH TODAY

The question now seems to be how we are to function as members of a divided church. Catholic and Protestant, Eastern and Western, high church and low church, old school and new school—the church is in schism, and it will probably be that way for some time. Maybe we are just going to have to think of the unity of the church as an eschatological reality.[33]

One of the biggest questions the American church has to face right now is how we are going to understand the apostolic function of the church. Once again the prevalent culture of our day is pressing syncretism on us. Are we to abandon evangelism, especially evangelism in foreign countries? Strangely enough, at the same time the liberal churches of the West are beginning to drop the missionary responsibility, the young churches in Africa and Asia are taking it up with amazing success. It is almost as though what the older "mainline" churches have lost, the younger churches have found. One wonders, seeing the decline of the "mainline" churches, if, in God's sight, we have become fig trees that no longer bear fruit.

That the church is the bride of Christ, without spot or wrinkle, seems to be a faded vision. The purity of the church is an increasing problem. Many of us find ourselves belonging to churches that countenance practices quite contrary to historic Christian teaching. Many Christians are scandalized by the immorality of their ministers. One tries to be patient. One does not want to fall into the errors of the Donatists, the fourth-century heretics who maintained that immoral priests could not perform valid sacraments. The sin of the ministers does not invalidate their ministry, and yet a corrupt ministry weakens the faith of even the most faithful Christians.

In times such as these, it seems to me, one has to lay a firm hold on the invisible church. In times like these, we have to continue praying the high priestly intercession of Jesus. We have to pray for the unity, the sanctity, and the continuity of the church. When we do that, we actually begin to experience its reality.

The worst of all our problems with being a true church is our awkwardness in preaching the Word. We have forgotten how to do it. We may claim to be the heirs of Luther and Calvin, Jonathan Edwards and Charles Haddon Spurgeon, but we are just plain clumsy in the pulpit. No one listens to us anymore. We have shortened our sermons, we have filled them with jokes, we have cut them loose from all that tedious exegesis. We have made them relevant to the problems of our day, but no one comes to hear us anymore. We have supplemented the Word with slide shows, devotional skits, and coffee hours, but none of it seems to work. Are we really sure the true church is where the Word is truly preached and the sacraments rightly administered?

> The worst of all our problems with being a true church is our awkwardness in preaching the Word. We have forgotten how to do it.

As I see it, at least, it is the Word that gathers the church, purifies the church, and nourishes the church. The preaching of the Word is the primary ministry of the church (1 Cor. 12:2f.), and, even more than that, it is the seed of the church (1 Pet. 1:23). In the preaching of the Word the promises of God are proclaimed, and with the sacraments they are sealed and delivered to us. In this Word is life, "and the life was the light of all people. The light shines in the darkness, and the darkness did not overcome it" (John 1:4).

Yes! When the Word of God is heard, the church begins to take shape. That is the way community happens. We come together to hear the Word and we discover true community; it is from the Word that we are "born anew, not of perishable but of imperishable seed, through the living and enduring word of God" (1 Pet. 1:23).

For the present, at least, our first job has to be to listen to the Word. For times like these we probably need to do nothing, just sit down and listen. Then when the true church has listened long enough and carefully enough, it will know what to do next.

Luther was almost right when he said that the true church is where the Word is truly preached and the sacraments rightly administered, but, if one might be allowed a maverick comment, the church of today is going to have to listen awhile before it can preach again. In times like these, the true church is the one that *listens* to the Word. And this is gospel: When we listen to the Word of God and receive the Word of God, the church will be the church, as my teacher, the

Swiss theologian Jean-Jacques von Allmen, used to put it. True community will be ours. We will have together what God promised to us in our baptism and what we have begun to taste in Communion.

LETTY M. RUSSELL

Recently I went to Nicaragua to attend an ecumenical consultation with Latin American women theologians and pastors entitled "Women's Voices and Visions: Being Church."[1] What the women had to say was very challenging. In situations of poverty and struggle for survival like those in Nicaragua, the church is a strong presence. However, that presence is not always one of advocacy. Sometimes the church takes the side of those who would dominate others through political and economic power. Other times the church reinforces prejudices that prevent women's full participation in the church. In preparation for their ecumenical discussion of these problems, the conference planners had hung up a huge banner with the words, *Siendo Iglesia.* The English on the banner read, "Been Church"!

This mistake in translation was more accurate than we might suppose. It reminds us that a lot of what happens in the church belongs to a past and present that are not necessarily life giving. Often it seems that, in the name of tradition, people use the church as a way to avoid the needs of the world around them and to exclude those who do not share the same set of beliefs, language, race, or culture. This problem of "been church" confronts us all as we seek to understand ways communities of faith describe themselves as "church," and what that would mean in our own life of faith. Often we are ambivalent about how we should relate to the churches, and a good place to begin to sort out some of that ambivalence is in trying to understand the nature and calling of the church.

My contribution to the discussion will not be exhaustive, nor will the answers make any claims to be the only way to look at the church. They describe how I have come to understand the church as a white, Protestant, lesbian theologian who has spent many years teaching feminist and liberation theologies at Yale Divinity School. As a theologian I work to transform the theology of the church so that it is life giving and welcoming for *all* persons, especially women, lesbians, and marginalized men and women in this country and abroad.

I would describe the church as a community of Christ, bought with a price, where everyone is welcome.

I would describe the church as a community of Christ, bought with a price, where everyone is welcome.[2] It is a *community of Christ,* because here Christ, through the power of the Spirit, constitutes people as a community gathered in Christ's name (Matt. 18:20; 1 Cor. 12:4–6). This community is *bought with a price,* because the struggle of Jesus to overcome the structures of sin and death constitutes both the source of new life in the community and its own mandate to continue the same struggle for life on behalf of others (1 Cor. 6:20; Phil. 2:1–11). It is a community *where everyone is welcome,* because it gathers around the table of God's hospitality. Its welcome table is a sign of the coming feast of God's mended creation, with the guest list derived from the announcements of the jubilee year in ancient Israel (Luke 4:18–19; 14:12–14).

In his book *God of the Oppressed,* James Cone addresses the question "Who is Jesus for us today?" by talking about the "was-ness," "is-ness," and "shall-be-ness" of Jesus Christ. I will use this way of discussing our theological traditions to address the same question.[3] The first section, *the church is what it was,* will discuss biblical and theological traditions of the meaning of the church as a community of faith. The middle section, *the church is what it is,* will present the plurality of contemporary church structures and traditions, and the calling of the church to become a community of faith and struggle. The final section, *the church is what it shall become,* will look at the church as a sign of new creation and a community of Word and sacrament.

THE CHURCH IS WHAT IT WAS

For every person who is alienated by the churches and their many shortcomings, there are other persons who find that the traditions of the churches are a source of security and assurance that God is with them in their lives. Regardless of whether we feel alienated, secure, or just mixed up, we all acknowledge that the church is what it was because it has a story that is rooted in God's action in the life, death, and resurrection of Jesus Christ. The church's history is also the history of Jesus of Nazareth. It shares the same ancestors and the same hopes of those who came to believe that God's victory over death in Jesus Christ was the beginning of a new and mended creation. It is the presence of this resurrected Christ that constitutes the community of Christ that we call the church and provides its signs or marks of identity.

> The church is what it was because it has a story that is rooted in God's action in the life, death, and resurrection of Jesus Christ.

Tradition

As in other aspects of Christian theology, there are many ways of understanding tradition and the church. Yet it is possible to say that all tradition is derived from the tradition of God handing over (*paradosis*) Jesus Christ to the world (Matt. 17:22; Rom. 8:31–32). Through the power of the Spirit, God continues to inspire us with Christ's presence, by which the Christian community is constituted as it responds through proclamation, liturgy, community, and service.[4]

Of the ninety-six images or analogies for church in the New Testament, Paul Minear identifies four clusters of meaning: "body of Christ," "people of God," "communion of faith, hope, and love," and "creation of the Spirit."[5] The word "church" or *ekklesia* (assembly) occurs only three times in the New Testament and was not the only word used to describe the early Christians (Matt. 6:18; 18:17).[6] An earlier term seems to have been "people of the Way," and the word *koinonia,* or community, was often used to refer to the gathering of Christians in each place (Acts 2:42; 24:14).[7] Within a few years, however, the local churches were being described as *ekklesia tou theou* ("*ekklesia* of God"), gathered in the name of Christ (1 Thess. 2:14).[8] *Ekklesia* had been used in the Septuagint, the translation into Greek of the Hebrew Scriptures, to translate the Hebrew word, *qahal,* meaning "assembly, meeting, or gathering." With the exception of James 2:2, the New Testament does not use the word *synagogue* except to refer to Jewish congregations, so it is often assumed that *ekklesia* was to be understood in terms of *qahal* with its overtones of a holy, set-apart assembly of Israel (Deut. 23:1–14). Yet it is more likely that a new meaning had been attached to the Greek word which conveyed its particular Christian usage to the Greek-speaking world.[9]

The usage of the word *ekklesia* reflects its functional character. It is used as a description of the totality of Christians living in any one place, such as a city or a house (1 Cor. 1:2; 16:19). It is also used to describe the church universal to which all believers belong as part of the eschatological people of God (1 Cor. 12:28). These communities were defined simply by the reality of Christ in their midst, and viewed their task as that of proclamation of the gospel (Matt. 18:20).

Community of Christ

The church has no nature of its own because its existence is derivative from Christ's presence. Yet over the centuries it has claimed that that presence is manifest in particular signs that make it possible to identify where the true church is located. Although they are part of a long tradition concerning the identity of the church, the signs are always in need of testing to see if they actually do make clear the mandate of the church to be where Christ is and to share in God's work of new creation.[10]

As Robert Schreiter has pointed out, these defining characteristics of the church that are clearly evident for all to see are usually drawn from "the addition made to the Nicene Creed by the Council of Constantinople in 381: 'and in one, holy, catholic and apostolic church.'"[11] Discussion begins here with a common creed recognized by Orthodox, Roman Catholic, and Protestant traditions, but it moves to other signs as well, and it becomes controversial as one confessional body considers the marks of another to be invalid. Thus, at the time of the Protestant Reformation, the discussion of whether the Protestant or the Roman Catholic church had the true marks and was truly church was very much part of the persecution and religious wars of the sixteenth and seventeenth centuries in Europe. Unity among churches, based on mutual recognition of one another as communities of faith in Jesus Christ, still involves us in the question of the identity of the church of Christ.

As we explore the self-understanding of the church, we find that historical descriptions are helpful for locating ourselves within the Christian tradition and discerning indicators of faithfulness, even though they are clearly *not* helpful as rules used to exclude others. We also find that these traditional signs are not nearly as self-evident as they were once considered to be, for they themselves require considerable explanation and verification even among churches who continue to accept the four signs spelled out in the Nicene-Constantinopolitan Creed. For instance, the World Council of Churches Faith and Order Commission studied this creed for ten years as part of its program on "Towards a Common Expression of the Apostolic Faith Today." It has taken many consultations and volumes to try to establish that this creed is, in fact, a common basis for "confessing one faith."[12]

The understanding of the church shifts when we interpret "one, holy, catholic, and apostolic" from the point of view of those at the periphery of life, society, and the church.

The understanding of the church shifts when we interpret "one, holy, catholic, and apostolic" from the point of view of those at the periphery of life, society, and the church. As with the other identifying marks, what is of most importance is not the presence of certain characteristics, but their use and practice. According to Hans Küng, "Unity, holiness, catholicity and apostolicity are therefore not only gifts, granted to the Church by God's grace, but at the same time tasks which it is vital for the Church to fulfil in a responsible way."[13] The signs themselves cannot make the authenticity of the church clear if they do not show forth God's grace in service to the poor and as a sign of a mended creation, as well as in the witness, liturgy, and gathering of the community.

The *unity of the church* is a gift of the Spirit or presence of Christ. The church is one because all who call on Christ's name discover Christ in their midst. As God in Christ and the Spirit are one, the many parts of the church are gathered together through one divine action as the sign of the coming household of God (Eph. 4:4–6). The unity of God with humankind brought about by God's reconciling action in Jesus Christ is imaged by the unity of the church across barriers of diversity.

In actuality, churches live out neither their unity in Christ with one another nor with the world. In the face of the differences caused by confessional splits and the deep differences caused by racism, heterosexism, and all the other forms of oppression, it is perhaps best to emphasize the need for diversity rather than unity, for it is at this point that the churches are unable to live out their calling to unity. The church cannot be a sign of unity if it achieves unity by marginalizing those who do not fit. Unity at the expense of the weak is not a sign of Christ's hospitality welcoming all into God's household. As Mary Tanner has put it, "A united Church in which ecclesial divisions were overcome but in which divisions based upon race, class, sex, or wealth remained would not be a church truly united. The church must be renewed into unity."[14]

The *holiness of the church* is also derived from Christ's presence and from the power of the Spirit to transform the church so that it can live in a relationship of righteousness and justice with God. In the biblical tradition, holiness is a fulfillment of covenant relationship with God. The community of faith lives out what Paul Hanson calls a biblical "triad of justice and mercy and faith."[15] In the Sermon on the Mount, the directive to be perfect as God is perfect is a way of expressing this need to respond to God's putting things right, by living that way ourselves (Matt. 5:48). This intention of holiness extends far beyond the church itself, for, in the words of Marjorie Suchocki, it is part of God's purpose in mending creation by "weaving creation together in a bond of love."[16]

> The church cannot be a sign of unity if it achieves unity by marginalizing those who do not fit.

Again, as we look at the actions of local, national, and international church bodies, we are struck by dualism in the interpretation of the sign of holiness. The church is to be holy by being apart from the world, persons are to be holy by being apart from their bodily selves, and holiness is an individual practice of Christian virtue apart from a community that shares in the suffering of those who oppose injustice. The gift of holiness in the church should lead to a spirituality of connection to our whole selves, to a community of faith and justice, and to those on the margin of society.

Christ's gift of *catholicity in the church* refers both to the universality of Christ's presence in all the world and to the orthodoxy of the church as it witnesses to the story and teachings of Jesus Christ. If God has acted in Jesus Christ to renew the whole earth, then it is important for the church's self-understanding to recognize Christ as present in the whole of creation. In this sense, to be catholic is to be connected to all of the creation in all of its groaning parts and to take responsibility for the needs of the many different churches and peoples of the world. In sharing the one story of God's liberating love in Jesus Christ, the church is also catholic as it witnesses to that story in ways that are faithful to the biblical and church traditions yet continually works to reinterpret them in new contexts.

> Catholicity in the church refers both to the universality of Christ's presence in all the world and to the orthodoxy of the church as it witnesses to the story and teachings of Jesus Christ.

This tradition of catholicity has often been honored in ways that have denied the true universality of God's message of love and replaced it with an assertion that one particularity includes all of what God's message might be about. In a traditional patriarchal paradigm of domination, universality is understood as a mandate for the church to dominate all religions and all people and require them to live according to its teachings. In the same way, the patriarchal paradigm of *orthodoxy* ("right belief") has led to the idea that right doctrine is to be defined by those who rule over a particular community and is more important than *orthopraxy,* the "right practice" of communities of faith and struggle as they seek to be connected to the world around them. Catholicity should be expressed, however, in the responsibility of churches for one another as well as for their neighbors in all parts of the world, living out a story of faith that witnesses to God's love for that world.

The *apostolicity of the church* is a sign of Christ's presence in the life of the church as the true witness to Christ's own story. By the inspiration of the Spirit of God in Christ, the church continues to share in the witness to that story both in word and action. The continuity of the continuing story of salvation is assured in the view of Roman Catholic, Orthodox, and Anglican churches through the passing on of ordination or commissioning of the apostles through each generation of leadership. For others, the apostolic witness is understood in terms of the quality of life of those who continue to live out the biblical story of Christ and the apostles in their own time.[17]

Unfortunately, the patriarchal paradigm of domination has played an important part in the idea of apostolicity as authoritative witness and the guarantee of that authority through chosen male leaders. But it is important to remember that an apostle, in the earlier Pauline sense of the word, is a witness or missionary—someone sent to tell the good news (Rom. 1:1; 1 Cor. 12:28). In this sense it is possible to invite all the community of faith to become part of the apostolic tradition and not just those who are set apart by clerical ordination. For the church, a sign of Christ's apostolate is the sign of participation in God's mission: traditioning, sending, and liberating action in the world.

In our present society, it would seem that the concern for Christ's presence among the poor and outcast would lead us to stress the importance of a sign of justice, as part of the four creedal signs or in addition to them.

The signs of the church as a community of Christ continue to be interpreted in new ways because they are a description of the ever unfolding relationship between Christ and the church. Over the centuries there have been many interpretations and many other signs suggested. According to Robert Schreiter, there never has been a set number of signs, and a widespread consensus on the four signs was achieved only in the nineteenth century.[18] In our present society, it would seem that the concern for Christ's presence among the poor and outcast would lead us to stress the importance of a sign of justice, as part of the four creedal signs or in addition to them. As Delores Williams has put it, "Along with the original distinguishing marks of apostolicity, catholicity, unity and holiness, the church needs to add another mark, namely, opposition to all forms of violence against humanity, nature, the environment and the land."[19]

However we name it, we know that the gift of Christ's presence allows us to describe that presence in continuity with the church that was, as well as in connection with the challenges of the world in which each and every church finds itself today.

THE CHURCH IS WHAT IT IS

Our own everyday experiences of church life and of the many ways churches do and do not live up to their calling to serve in Christ's name keep reminding us that the church is what it is. The nature of the church rests not only on its source but also on the lived reality of Christian communities that struggle to live out their faith day by day. The church is an expression of God's presence in the world through Jesus Christ, but it is also the expression of the life and history of countless human beings and human frailties. Often, instead of "handing over Christ" to new generations, the church "hands Christ over" by betraying Christ's story and ministry through its unfaithfulness (Matt. 17:22).

The original grammar of the Apostles' Creed declares that we "believe the holy catholic church." This formulation of the creed reminds us that we *believe the church* and not *in the church.* We believe in God, and the church is not God. We remember this as we recognize that the church and its teachings, worship, and ministry are important for the continuing nurture of faith even in its many inadequate and human forms.[20] To believe the church is to risk believing that the particular communities of faith and struggle where we are members partake in some way in the one church of Jesus Christ.

Traditions

The church is a community of people who believe in God in Jesus Christ and, as such, is full of the variety and differences that make up the human condition. In each particular faith tradition and context, the gospel takes root in different ways. Different forms of worship, theology, and service are recognizably Christian, not because they are alike but because they are formed out of an interpretation of Scripture and church teaching through reason and experience. The theology of the church serves to give an account of its faith and how it is in touch with Scripture and church tradition. The ongoing practice of a church includes this theology, but also includes many ways the church orders its life and work together through patterns in such things as what clergy wear, when church is held, what language is used in the service, and much more. These various traditions not only connect to the Scripture and teaching of the church; they also give people a sense of their own particular identity and worth as Anglicans, Roman Catholics, Baptists, and so forth. In a real sense they help to constitute *the church that is* as it seeks to open itself to the presence of the Spirit of God in Christ in its midst.

Although these traditions matter a great deal to many of us because they have shaped our Christian faith and practice, they do not matter ultimately in our relationship to Christ. What matters is how well they guide us in living out a life of justice and love as seen in the lifestyle of the One we are called to follow. If they come between us and our relation to God and neighbor, then they have to be reevaluated and questioned. Thus, in the life of the churches there is constant discussion of the ways in which traditions of polity and practice need to be reshaped to speak the gospel more clearly in each time and place. Three very important issues for churches in this regard that might occur to us right away have been the need to question interpretations of slavery, the role of women in the church, and the inclusion of lesbian, gay, bisexual, and transgendered persons in the life and ministry of the church.

Community of Faith and Struggle

The church is constantly struggling to live up to its mandate to participate with God in the mending of creation through the works of justice and love. In this regard, one can say that the church is called to order the traditions of its life so that it becomes a community of faith in Jesus Christ and struggle for God's justice and wholeness. One metaphor that emphasizes this is *church in the round.* A metaphor is an imaginative way of describing what is unknown by using an example from present concrete reality. To speak of "church in the round" is to provide a metaphorical description of a church struggling to become a community of faith and service, working to anticipate God's new creation by becoming partners with those who are at the margins of church and society.[21] The metaphor emphasizes the need to move away from structures of hierarchy and exclusion toward structures of community life that are participatory and welcoming of those who gather round to share God's hospitality and love for the world.

> To speak of "church in the round" is to provide a metaphorical description of a church struggling to become a community of faith and service, working to anticipate God's new creation by becoming partners with those who are at the margins of church and society.

For centuries the church has seen itself as a community of faith in Jesus Christ and has developed traditions that reflect the way the community lives out its faith in a particular time, place, and culture. In our time, we recognize that we live in a world of great disparity between those who can eat and live with ease and those who cannot. The need for God's justice in putting things right and mending creation is so pressing that there is no way a Christian church can ignore the call to struggle for justice and an end to oppression. We remember the ancient call of the Prophet Amos: "let justice roll down like waters, and righteousness like an everflowing stream" (Amos 5:24). But this call for putting things right in society and for right living is everywhere in the Scriptures, so much so that Robert McAfee Brown has said that "justice appears to be God's middle name!" (Isa. 58:6–9; Luke 4:8–19)[22] *The church that is* needs to strive to be a community of faith in Christ and to struggle for God's justice so that the present reality of the church can express God's love and care for the world.

THE CHURCH IS WHAT IT SHALL BE

There is no way to understand how the churches can continue to fail to live up to their gospel calling and still be a place that is open to God's Spirit unless we also remember that the church is what it shall be. The church is constantly moving toward God's future as a sign of new creation. The church itself is not God's kin-dom, nor is it the one who brings the kin-dom.[23] Its calling is to point to God's intention for new creation by sharing in God's action in mending the creation or putting things right. It already is connected to that future because it is connected to the resurrected Christ. And it celebrates that future and participates in its anticipation through the sharing of Word, sacrament, and service in Christ's name.

Traditioning

In interpreting the church in the past, present, and future tense, we should not forget that these tenses are interwoven in the life and work of the church. The church lives from *tradition* as God continues to hand over Jesus Christ into our hearts and lives. The church struggles to live out its calling to be a community of faith and struggle that is expressed in various *traditions* as they reflect Scripture and church teaching. And the church is also being transformed as it participates in a *traditioning* process that keeps unfolding the meaning of God's future intention for new creation.

Understanding tradition as a process of God continuing to hand over Jesus Christ helps us to remember that it is not only about the past or the present but also about the still living and evolving past that is shaping the future of the church. In a way we can say that the church is a memory of the future!

> The church is Christ's body because each and every person who is baptized in Christ's name is joined to Christ, because Christ promises to be present in the gifts of ministry, and because it continues to be nurtured by Christ as it joins in the breaking of bread and the sharing of wine in Christ's memory.

The metaphor which best describes this traditioning action in the churches is the *body of Christ*. First, the church is Christ's resurrected body because each and every person who is baptized in Christ's name is joined to Christ and, through the cleansing of the water, shares in his death and resurrection. Women and men alike share in his resurrected body and are already part of God's new creation. Thus, Paul says, "So if anyone is in Christ, there is a new creation," and reminds the Corinthians that Christ is the "first fruits" of the resurrection (2 Cor. 5:17; 1 Cor. 15:23). Second, the church is Christ's body because Christ promises to be present in the gifts of ministry (1 Cor. 12:12). Its calling is to become the hands and feet of Christ in serving those in need and witnessing to God's love. Third, the church is Christ's body because it continues to be nurtured by Christ as it joins in the breaking of bread and sharing of wine in Christ's memory. In the act of Eucharist or giving thanks, the church also proclaims "the Lord's death until he comes" in a continual traditioning action in which past and present become a sign of God's kindom (1 Cor. 11:26).

The church lives by the promises of God's future and celebrates those promises in its worship and its actions of justice and love in the world. According to Jürgen Moltmann, there are three different groups of assurances of Christ's presence in the New Testament and these are connected to the church that will be—to the future of God's kindom.[24]

The first set of promises is related to Jesus' promise to be present in the witness to the gospel, in Word and sacrament, and in the gathered community.[25] For instance, Matthew 28:18–20 declares the promise of Christ's presence in witness, baptism, and teaching. In fact, the traditional signs of Christ's presence in the church are all anticipated in this text as it speaks of baptism in the *one* name, *holiness* through the continuing presence of the Spirit, *catholicity* as an invitation to all the nations, and *apostolicity* through faithful preaching. First Corinthians 11:23–26 declares the gift of Christ's presence in the Lord's Supper, and Matthew 18:20 promises, "Where two or three are gathered in my name, I am there among them."

The second set of promises is related to the presence of Christ among the poor and marginalized. In Matthew 25:31–46, Jesus seems to be telling his own story of identification with the poor and outcast so that, together with the Messiah, all who hunger and thirst, all who are naked, sick, or in prison, become the real presence of God's mending work. In solidarity with the least of Jesus' brothers and sisters we find a social biography of struggle that continues Jesus' own story. Just as the Christians of faith and struggle call out "*Presente!*" when the lists of the martyrs in Central America are read at the Eucharist, Christians everywhere can call out "*Presente!*" and know that Jesus lives through the continuing actions of solidarity with the poor and oppressed.

The third set of promises, related to Christ's future coming and the fulfillment of the household of God, is also linked to the parable of the Last Judgment in Matthew 25. Jesus promises to be present wherever God's will is done, until the time comes when that will for justice and peace is done on earth as in heaven (Matt. 6:10). Moltmann underlines this justice connection: "The one who is to come is then already present in an anticipatory sense in history in the Spirit and the word, and in the miserable and helpless. His future ends the world's history of suffering and completes the fragments and anticipations of his kingdom which are called the church."[26]

Community of Word and Sacrament

In the Reformation of the sixteenth century and beyond, there was a long period of controversial theology in which the Protestant reformers and their descendants argued against the Roman Catholic reformers and their descendants about what made the church truly church.[27] The Protestants claimed that the true church was not only recognized by the visible signs (*signa*) of Christ's presence in oneness, holiness, catholicity, and apostolicity, but also by what they called the marks (*nota*), or distinguishing characteristics or functions of the church. These marks of the church were claimed to be what obviously constituted it as true church, namely, the Word truly preached and the sacraments rightly administered. Thus, John Calvin says, "For whenever we find the word of God purely preached and heard, and the sacraments administered according to the institution of Christ, there, it is not to be doubted, is a Church of God."[28]

> For the Protestant reformers, the marks of the church were that the Word is truly preached and the sacraments rightly administered.

The Protestant reformers did not deny the importance of the Nicene formula—one, holy, catholic, and apostolic—but they wanted to build their reformation on the Scriptures. For this reason they tried to discern in the biblical tradition how the church might be faithful in its preaching and sacramental life. Today it is generally recognized by Roman Catholics and Protestants alike that the witness of the Scriptures to Jesus Christ is the basis of the life of the church.[29] The *marks* of the church do not finally point to a different definition than those four *signs* of the church. As Jürgen Moltmann says, a "church in which the gospel is purely preached and the sacraments are rightly used is the one, holy, catholic and apostolic church."[30] The marks of Word and sacrament indicate the heart of what the church is called to do, while the signs of the church indicate the way in which the presence of Christ shapes its life.

For the Protestant reformers, the Word was understood as pure and the sacraments rightly used if they were administered by the duly ordained clergy, according to the scriptural promises, and conveyed the gospel to believers through preaching or signs of bread and water. Ecclesiastical discipline or the fencing of the table (allowing only approved people to come to the common table) became for some a third mark, in that it made sure that God's word was truly preached and celebrated. Today there are many different interpretations of the proper way to share in the preaching of the Word and in the sacraments. Critical voices are heard, not only from different confessional groups but also from those who have been excluded from the altar because of gender or sexual orientation, as well as from those who seek a community that lives out the promise of these acts of worship by doing justice, loving kindness, and walking humbly with God, as Micah 6:8 commands.

At the center of Christian life is the gathering in community to worship God, to give God praise, honor, and thanksgiving for the presence of God's love in our lives. In Greek, this action of worship is called *liturgy*, or public work (*leitourgia*), for it is the work of the people of God as they gather to praise God in Jesus Christ, and as they scatter again to work as God's people in the world living out the message of the good news of God's love through the power of the Holy Spirit. In liturgies of adoration, confession, thanksgiving, and intercession, the community gathers to hear God's word read in the Scriptures and preached through the power of the Holy Spirit. The Bible is not literally the words of God, for it is written and interpreted by human beings, but it is the record of the story of Christ and of God's action in history. The preaching is not literally the word of God, for it is the words of women or men who seek to interpret biblical and church tradition. Yet, in the reading, study, and preaching, the Holy Spirit is able to enliven that word so that it opens our hearts to God.

In the same way, the community shares in the sacraments of the church with the confident expectation of Christ's presence in forgiving our sins and transforming our lives. The word *sacramentum* literally means an "oath of allegiance," like that taken by a Roman soldier. It does not appear in the New Testament, but by the third century it was used to describe baptism and Eucharist as sacred actions of Christian worship. By the thirteenth century the Roman Catholic Church numbered seven sacraments: baptism, confirmation, penance, Eucharist, holy orders, matrimony, and extreme unction. Most Protestant churches have followed the Reformers in celebrating only baptism and Eucharist because of their biblical importance (Matt. 28:19; Acts 2:38; Matt. 26:26–29).[31] They often use the terms *Communion* or the *Lord's Supper* for the Eucharist, although *Eucharist* simply means "giving thanks," and refers to Jesus' words in giving thanks before offering the bread and cup: "Then he took a cup, and after giving thanks he gave it to them, and all of them drank from it" (Mark 14:23).

The sacraments have a long tradition and many meanings as the churches have combined biblical tradition, the elements such as water, bread, and wine, and the actions of each liturgy. Baptism can represent conversion, rebirth, death and resurrection, messianic anointing, incorporation into a priestly people, and more.[32] It recalls the baptism of Jesus and the descent of the Holy Spirit, and then moves on to speak of death and rebirth as part of Christ's body (Mark 1:9–11). Whether as infants or adults, whether by pouring, sprinking, or immersion, baptism affirms the beginning of new life in Christ for both women and men: "For just as the body is one and has many members, and all the members of the body, though many, are one body, so it is with Christ. For in the one Spirit we were all baptized into one body—Jews or Greeks, slaves or free—and we were all made to drink of one Spirit" (1 Cor. 12:12–13).

There are many contradictions between the teachings about baptism and its practice in church tradition. Although all are anointed with the Spirit, not all are allowed to serve as ministers or priests in the church. The baptism of women or homosexual persons is often not honored when it comes to ordination. Persons of color frequently find that they are not as welcome as white persons in many churches. In addition to this, the tradition of baptism as a time of cleansing and new life has reinforced traditions that the entrance of a child through the breaking of the birth water of the mother somehow renders the child unclean, conveying sin to the child which must be removed by the male clergy. There is still a lot of traditioning that needs to be done with baptism so that it clearly shows the connection of *all* people to the risen Christ.

While baptism is imaged as birth and new life, Eucharist is the ongoing nourishment of the life in Christ.

While baptism is imaged as birth and new life, Eucharist is the ongoing nourishment of the life in Christ. It shares with baptism a long tradition of accumulated meanings. According to Marjorie Procter-Smith, there are seven New Testament motifs of Eucharist: thanksgiving, remembering, community, "sacrifice, the presence of Christ, the action of the Holy Spirit, and the eschatological banquet."[33] We *give thanks* to God for God's work in all creation, in our lives, and in the life, death, and resurrection of Jesus Christ. We *remember* the night and actions of sharing bread and wine at the Last Supper, and *celebrate our connection to one another* and the communion of saints through the ages. The *sacrifice* of Christ is enacted, recognizing Jesus' opposition to the religious and political powers and the price he paid for that opposition. The way in which Christ is *present* in the bread and wine is explained in a variety of ways in the different traditions, yet all point to the power and possibility of unity with Christ through the sacrament by the *power of the Holy Spirit.*

The eucharistic tradition, however, shares with baptism in the many contradictions between the theological traditions and their practice. This meal of unity is the meal at which Christians are badly separated due to lack of recognition of one another's practices of ordination or Communion. It is also a meal in which there is usually division by race, class, nationality, and language. Frequently it has been used as a powerful tool by churches who deny the sacraments as a means of God's grace or salvation to those who do not conform to their teachings. The idea of sacrifice has too often been used not to speak of the once and for all sacrifice of love, but of sacrifice as a style of Christian life especially important for women and marginalized persons. The refusal to allow women to represent Christ at the altar has also carried with it the implication that women are not able to be instruments of God's forgiveness and grace.

The list of contradictions and difficulties that churches face as they try to make sense of their traditions and actions can go on and on. It is especially important, therefore, to remember that the church is what it will be. At the

Lord's Supper we also celebrate the *eschatological banquet,* or the memory of God's future—a future in which there is to be no more suffering and pain, a future in which creation is mended. For that reason, we break bread and drink the cup using the words from 1 Corinthians 11:26: "For as often as you eat this bread and drink the cup, you proclaim the Lord's death until [Christ] comes." At this feast of the future, we celebrate the promise of a still living and evolving past, which shapes our future with God.

In his letters to the churches, Paul often writes about salvation using different tenses to express the many ways that we are reconciled to God in Jesus Christ. Working to express the way that salvation is a gift of God in Jesus Christ and yet a continuing journey, Paul says that we are saved through the death and resurrection of Jesus Christ in which God has reached out to reconcile the world to God's self. At the same time, however, we are in the process of being saved in our daily struggles to live in love and faithfulness. And we live by faith that someday we will all be saved as part of the new creation.[34]

What we have been learning about the church can also be described in the past, present, and future tenses. *Being church* and *been church* are just two of these descriptive tenses. We are the church, and the *church is what it always was:* a gift of God in Christ. We are always struggling to be the church, for *what the church is* includes collective and personal actions that constantly fall short of our calling. Nevertheless, we are living in the hope that one day *we shall be the church* that God intends. And then, perhaps as Revelation 21:22 indicates, there will be no need for the church because everyone will walk in the light of God's glory!

QUESTIONS FOR REFLECTION AND DISCUSSION

1. Why did the early church develop a canon of Scripture, creeds, and a hierarchy of officials? How did these developments change the church?

2. The Reformation arguably made the church more holy (it led to reforms among Catholics as well as Protestants), but the church ceased to be one. How does one balance the need for a holy church against the need for unity?

3. The New Testament offers a variety of images of the church. How do different images lead us to think differently about the church?

4. Both Old and Russell analyze the Nicene Creed's list of the four signs of the church (one, holy, catholic, and apostolic). How does each author interpret them?

5. What do Old and Russell each identify as the central problems of the church today?

6. Against the Donatists, Augustine argued that the moral purity of a priest was irrelevant to the efficacy of the sacraments the priest performed. How important is the character of its leaders to the church? Can the church become so corrupt that it stops being the church?

7. The Reformers identified the Word purely preached and the sacraments

properly administered as the marks of the church. Why are these marks important for the integrity of the church?

8. Russell defines the church as what it was, what it is, and what it will be. Why is each element important in defining the church?

FOR FURTHER READING

Alston, Wallace M., Jr. *The Church of the Living God: A Reformed Perspective.* Louisville, Ky.: Westminster John Knox Press, 2002.

Dulles, Avery. *Models of the Church.* Garden City, N.Y.: Doubleday, 1974.

Gustafson, James M. *Treasure in Earthen Vessels.* Chicago: University of Chicago Press, 1961.

Hodgson, Peter C. *Revisioning the Church.* Philadelphia: Fortress Press, 1988.

Küng, Hans. *The Church.* Trans. Ray and Rosaleen Ockenden. New York: Sheed & Ward, 1968.

Minear, Paul. *Images of the Church in the New Testament.* Philadelphia: Westminster Press, 1950.

Moltmann, Jürgen. *The Church in the Power of the Spirit.* Trans. Margaret Kohl. San Francisco: Harper, 1991.

Niebuhr, H. Richard. *The Purpose of the Church and Its Ministry.* New York: Harper & Brothers, 1956.

Old, Hughes Oliphant. *The Reading and Preaching of the Scriptures in the Worship of the Christian Church.* 7 vols. planned. Grand Rapids: Wm. B. Eerdmans Publishing Co., 1998–.

Russell, Letty M. *Church in the Round.* Louisville, Ky.: Westminster/John Knox Press, 1993.

Segundo, Juan Luis. *The Community Called Church.* Trans. John Drury. Maryknoll, N.Y.: Orbis Books, 1973.

Chapter 7

How Should We Live?

The Christian Life

As both this chapter and the previous one emphasize, being a Christian is not a solitary activity. Christians live out their faith in the context of a Christian community, the church. Therefore, the previous chapter's discussion of the church and its worship had much to say about the forms of Christian life. Still, Christians face the challenge of filling out those forms with content, actually living in a way that shows the difference our faith makes for our lives. It ought to make a big difference: Christianity and our competitive, consumerist culture offer very different models of what counts as a good life.

Ellen Charry and Michael Battle have each written essays for this chapter that emphasize the importance of belonging to a community, denying oneself, cultivating a spiritual life, and standing against the dominant values of our culture. Charry's essay takes the form of a kind of commentary on one of the first and greatest discussions of the Christian life, Paul's First Letter to the Corinthians. She shows how Paul redefines wisdom and strength in Christian terms and then draws concrete implications from his redefinitions for everything from sexuality to shared meals before concluding with an account of Christian love and its place among other spiritual gifts.

Battle challenges the values and assumptions of our Western culture by looking, not back to Paul but to South Africa, where he has studied with Bishop Desmond Tutu, and to traditions of spirituality particularly important in Eastern Orthodox churches. He emphasizes the dangers of individualism and the values of community, spiritual direction, and Christian discernment.

Neither Battle nor Charry thinks that we *earn* salvation by the kind of life we live; both recognize that salvation comes only as grace, as gift. The Christian life is about showing gratitude for what we have been given, not about anxiously struggling for what we hope to deserve. Nevertheless, their essays emphasize that the life of appropriate gratitude to which we are called is not an easy one. This introduction will set a context for those essays by tracing how Christian theologians have come to think about the relation between God's grace and our works, and between justification (being saved) and sanctification (becoming holy).

GRACE AND WORKS

In A.D. 386, a thirty-four-year-old North African teacher of rhetoric named Augustine was struggling with the possibility of becoming a Christian. Intellectually, he found Christian faith attractive, and he admired the lives of Christian martyrs and monks. But he could not quite take the plunge, in part because he could not face giving up his active sexual life. He later wrote that it was as if his prayer had been, "Make me chaste and continent—but not yet."[1] Then one August afternoon in a garden in Milan, he heard a voice like that of a child chanting, "Take it and read." He snatched up a Bible

> and read in silence the passage upon which my eyes first fell: "not in reveling and drunkenness, not in debauchery and licentiousness, not in quarreling and jealousy. Instead, put on the Lord Jesus Christ, and make no provision for the flesh, to gratify its desires" [Rom. 13:13–14]. I had no wish to read further; there was no need to. For immediately I had reached the end of this sentence it was as though my heart was filled with a light of confidence and all the shadows of my doubt were swept away.[2]

Augustine had not, he admitted, been struggling toward faith with his own best efforts. On the contrary, he had been resisting God with all his might, until God saved him anyway, by pure grace—by God's unmerited love.

One of Augustine's contemporaries, a British monk named Pelagius, read Augustine's account with horror. Augustine, he said, would encourage people to lie back and relax, just waiting for God's grace. Yes, we need grace in order to be saved, but God will give grace to those who have been working hard on their own. Augustine replied that God had given him grace when he was not working for it, that apart from grace sinners are so trapped by sin that they cannot on their own break free of it—and anyway, grace earned, even partly, is not really grace. God does not just help those who help themselves, but those unable to do the first thing to start helping themselves.

Pelagius said that God will give grace to those who have been working hard on their own. Augustine replied that God had given him grace when he was not working for it, and that apart from grace sinners are so trapped by sin that they cannot on their own break free of it.

In various forms, the debate between Augustine and Pelagius has continued down through the centuries. Almost no one has wanted to be identified as a "Pelagian," but many have sought to avoid the full force of Augustine's radical conclusions. The late medieval theologian Gabriel Biel, for instance, whose theology Martin Luther learned as a student, taught that God would give us grace only as a reward for our own best efforts. Even our best would be inadequate, so we would still need grace, but, in order to get it, we would first have to do the best we could.

Trying to live out this theology nearly drove the young Luther mad. How could he ever be sure, he wondered, that he was really doing his best? Perhaps he could have confessed one more sin, concentrated a bit harder at prayer. But then, after reading Paul, he realized that grace could not and need not be earned: "To trust in works . . . is equivalent to giving oneself the honor and taking it from God."[3] We need only turn to God in faith and, like Abraham, who "believed God, and it was reckoned to him as righteousness" (Rom. 4:3), we can be justified by grace through faith.

Calvin and other Reformers very much agreed with Luther that works could play no role in our justification. Yet even committed Protestants kept qualifying the claim that the reception of grace has *nothing* to do with our virtues. Around 1600 (a generation after Calvin's death) a Dutch Calvinist pastor named Jacob Arminius argued that, while it is true that no one can earn grace, our justification does partly depend on ourselves, since, when we are offered grace, we can either accept it or turn it down.[4] In response, the Synod of Dort in 1619 defined five basic principles of Dutch Reformed orthodoxy:

> *Total depravity:* In sin no one has the power to choose grace.
>
> *Unconditional election:* Justification and damnation rest only on God's free decision.
>
> *Limited atonement.* Christ's saving work applies only to the elect.
>
> *Irresistible grace.* One cannot turn down grace if it is offered.
>
> *Perseverance of the saints.* God so preserves the elect that they do not fall away.[5]

(Notice that the first letters of these five principles spell out the name of the most famous of Dutch flowers.)

These "Canons of Dort" affirmed in strongest form the doctrine of *election* or *predestination* Calvin had already developed in a more cautious and qualified way. (Calvin was in particular ambiguous about limited atonement.) Grace comes without regard for merit, Calvin said. But not everyone receives grace: Scripture refers to those on the left hand as well as those on the right, goats as well as sheep. Indeed, we can see for ourselves that "in actual fact, the covenant of life is not preached equally among all, and among those to whom it is preached, it does not gain the same acceptance either constantly or in equal degree."[6] Arminius said that grace is offered to everyone, but some turn it down. But that makes the difference between justification and damnation depend on *us*, and denies the glory which we should give to *God alone* for predestining the elect to salvation. Calvin insisted, "We call predestination God's eternal decree, by which is compacted with himself what he willed to become of each man. For all are not created in equal condition; rather, eternal life is foreordained for some, eternal damnation for others."[7]

"We call predestination God's eternal decree, by which is compacted with himself what he willed to become of each man. For all are not created in equal condition; rather, eternal life is foreordained for some, eternal damnation for others." —John Calvin

Calvin did not invent predestination. Passages in Paul seem to imply it, and Augustine, Aquinas, Luther, and many others state something like it. But Calvin did state *double predestination* (the claim that people are predestined to damnation as well as to salvation) with unusual bluntness. For him, it was simply logical that if one side was predestined the other must be too, but that was a step previous theologians had rarely taken, at least so explicitly. The results caused many to rebel, among them Arminius in the seventeenth century and John Wesley, the founder of Methodism, in the eighteenth. He would rather be "a Turk, a Deist, yea an atheist," Wesley wrote, than believe "the *horrible decree* of predestination."[8] Arminius was right; grace is not irresistible. Indeed, at some time "every child of God" has the opportunity to accept or reject grace and "has in himself the casting voice."[9] Otherwise, God would be a monster, and preachers, who called all to salvation when they knew some were predestined to damnation, would all be hypocrites.

Already in the sixteenth century, at the Council of Trent, Catholics had rejected the Reformers' accounts of justification. They agreed that salvation cannot be achieved without grace, but they rejected the claim that justification comes from grace alone. An awakening and assisting grace, Trent said, begins the process of justification, but then the person involved must consent to and cooperate with that grace. Justification, therefore, "is not only a remission of sins but also the sanctification and renewal of the inward man through the voluntary reception of the grace and gifts whereby an unjust man becomes just and from being an enemy becomes a friend."[10] Someone who is not getting better (achieving sanctification) cannot be really justified.

JUSTIFICATION AND SANCTIFICATION

The Council of Trent thus taught that justification and sanctification went hand in hand. Both Luther and Calvin kept the two more distinct. Of course, they both expected that justified Christians would struggle to transform their lives. "Ours is a holy calling," Calvin wrote. "It demands purity of life and nothing less; we have been freed from sin to this end, that we may obey righteousness."[11] Our moral efforts, however, come only in gratitude for what God has already given us; they have nothing to do with our justification. Thus, Protestants usually talked about "imputed righteousness"—God simply *declared* that we were justified—while Catholics spoke of "infused righteousness"—God actually began transforming us with the love planted in our hearts.

Luther and his fellow Reformers held that Christians were always *simul justus et peccator* ("at once justified and sinners"). John Bunyan's classic Protestant allegory, *Pilgrim's Progress,* beautifully captures the point. The pilgrim, Christian, faces one temptation after another, sometimes falling, sometimes sufficiently sustained by grace as to overcome them. Eventually, thanks to grace, he makes it to heaven. But before then, he does not seem much to improve or to learn from past mistakes. He just continues to live as one at once saved by God and still a sinner. By contrast, in Dante's *Divine Comedy,* perhaps the greatest literary presentation of the Catholic point of view, Dante the pilgrim gradually improves and becomes more worthy as the story progresses. These two great literary works thus present very different models of Christian life.

> If Catholicism traditionally thought of Christians as steadily morally progressing, and Luther and Calvin saw a steady tension between sin and justification, John Wesley pushed the Catholic position one step further. Wesley thought we could keep improving until we arrived at a state of "Christian perfection."

If Catholicism traditionally thought of Christians as steadily morally progressing, and Luther and Calvin saw a steady tension between sin and justification, John Wesley pushed the Catholic position one step further. Wesley thought that we could keep improving until we arrived at a state of "Christian perfection" or "full sanctification," in which we would "feel all faith and love; no pride, no self-will, or anger" and "have continual fellowship with God."[12] In such a state, the fully sanctified "cannot voluntarily transgress any command of God."[13] If one doubted such claims, Wesley could cite evidence from among his converts: "The habitual drunkard, that was, is now temperate in all things. The whoremonger now flees fornication. He that stole, steals no more. . . . These are demonstrable facts. I can name the men, and their several places of abode."[14]

Wesley and the Methodist movement he began have thought of the process of achieving perfect sanctification as a gradual one. The Holiness churches, beginning in the nineteenth century, believed that, after their baptism, some

Christians receive a "second blessing," in which they experience full sanctification all at once in a moment. Pentecostal churches, begun in their modern form in the early twentieth century, go one step further. They hold that after justification and the experience of sanctification some Christians experience a third crucial moment in their lives, a baptism in the Holy Spirit, after which they experience a variety of special gifts, particularly the ability to "speak in tongues" (*glossolalia*). This seems to have been an important feature of Christian life in New Testament times (see Acts 2 and 1 Cor. 12–14), which Pentecostals and other charismatic Christians have recovered.

ORGANIZING THE CHRISTIAN LIFE

However one thinks of the Christian life as developing, the sacraments have provided many Christians, particularly Catholics and Orthodox (who believe in seven sacraments), with a way of organizing it. One enters the Christian community through *baptism,* takes on new responsibilities at *confirmation,* is sustained by the *Eucharist,* accepts particular callings and their associated responsibilities in *marriage* or *ordination,* and prepares for death by the *last rites* (or extreme unction). Above all, *penance* structures the Christian life.

In the earliest church, baptism freed one from previous sins, but there was an assumption that the good Christian would not sin after baptism.[15] Thus many Christians, like the emperor Constantine, were baptized only on their deathbeds, so as to save the cleansing power of baptism as long as possible. As Christians began to accept the inevitability of sin after baptism, penance emerged as the way to deal with it. One felt truly sorry for one's sin (contrition) and confessed it to a priest. He assigned an appropriate penance and then declared one absolved.[16] The sacrament offered an ordered way for sinners to continue their growth in Christian life.

Protestants rejected the ideas that one needed to confess to anyone but God, and that anyone but God could absolve the sinner. Too often, as a result, Protestants have "gone it alone," and not taken advantage of pastors and spiritual directors, though Luther at least urged that they do so.[17] (Michael Battle's essay urges rethinking the value of spiritual directors.) Still, one should not think of the classic Protestant spiritual life as an isolated, individual one, for shared Bible reading and family prayers often played a key role in it. Moreover, the idea of *vocation* or *calling,* which for Catholics had traditionally referred only to the special calling of priests, monks, and nuns, was expanded by Protestants to include the calling of one's job and one's family responsibilities. Every Christian had a vocation, and that vocation played an important role in shaping his or her life. In Calvin's words, "lest through our stupidity and rashness everything be turned topsy-turvy, [God] has appointed duties for every man in his particular way of life. And . . . he has named these various kinds of living 'callings.' Therefore each individual has his own kind of living assigned to him by the Lord as a sort of sentry post so that he may not heedlessly wander about throughout life."[18]

Another way of organizing the Christian life would be around the virtues. Medieval theologians developed a classic list of seven virtues. Prudence (or wisdom), courage, moderation, and justice—the four virtues Plato identified in his *Republic*—were accessible to Christians and non-Christians alike. Thus, medieval Christians were not surprised if Muslims proved wise in interpreting Aristotle or brave in battle. But they believed that the three "theological virtues" Paul mentions in 1 Corinthians 13—faith, hope, and love (or charity)—were available only to Christians.[19] Only through revelation can we know what to believe, what we can hope for, and how we should love in order to obtain our "supernatural end" of communion with God. A good many recent Christian ethicists, Catholic and Protestant alike, have been putting more emphasis on the importance of developing the virtues. Ethics is not, they say, primarily a matter of making the right decision at a particular moment, but of becoming over time a virtuous person—who will be, among other things, the sort of person who will make the right decision. Such "virtue ethics" calls greater attention to the shape of a whole Christian life.

> Cardinal virtues (available to everyone): prudence, courage, moderation, justice.
> Theological virtues (unique to Christians): faith, hope, and love.

Contemporary theologians, however, sometimes want to modify the traditional lists of virtues (and parallel lists of vices). As noted in an earlier chapter, for instance, many feminists believe that in our culture women have been less apt to be guilty of self-assertive pride than of an opposite sin in which they do not sufficiently manifest the abilities God has given them but live their lives too exclusively through husband and children. Self-affirmation may be a more important virtue for them to cultivate than humility.[20] Similarly, liberation theologians, having noted that the sins we commit as citizens or businesspeople may be more significant than the sins of our private lives, would emphasize the importance of public, political virtues.[21]

Whatever lists of virtues and vices they work with, however, Christians do not cultivate virtues or overcome vices without a strong prayer life. No account of Christian life can be complete without reference to prayer. One traditional classificatory scheme divides prayer into *adoration, confession, thanksgiving,* and *supplication*. In prayer we adore God's wondrous mystery, confess our sins, give thanks for God's benefits, and pray for those who need God's help. Though all good things come from God, prayers of supplication assume that God may graciously allow our prayers to serve as one of the means through which God does good to others.

In public prayer, some traditions (Orthodox, Catholic, Episcopal, Lutheran) usually use set, liturgical prayers. Others pray spontaneously, as guided by the Spirit. In private prayer, those most advanced in their prayer lives often turn to the simplest of prayers, such as the Lord's Prayer or the so-called Jesus prayer of such influence in the Eastern church ("Jesus Christ, Son of God, Savior, have mercy on me, a sinner"). Perhaps the deepest of all prayers occur in silence, "for we do not know how to pray as we ought," but the Spirit "intercedes in sighs too deep for words" (Rom. 8:26). Mystics describe experiencing a union with God in the midst of silent contemplative prayer, and Michael Battle's essay will discuss the way in which Christian knowledge of God must always take the form of acknowledging the mystery we cannot know. However profound such experiences or other special gifts of the Spirit may be, however, Paul reminds us that the greatest of God's gifts are faith, hope, and love, "and the greatest of these is love" (1 Cor. 13:13). It is in loving God and loving neighbor that we most perfect the Christian life—a theme to which Ellen Charry's essay will return.

But what does it mean, in more concrete terms, to love God and love my neighbor? How do I go about getting better at it? Where should I turn for help? In reflections on Paul, and ideas drawn from South Africa and Eastern Europe, Ellen Charry and Michael Battle provide Christian answers that challenge our society's most common beliefs about what "success" or a "good life" means.

ELLEN T. CHARRY

We are not our own: let not our reason nor our will, therefore, sway our plans and deeds. We are not our own: let us therefore not set it as our goal to seek what is expedient for us according to the flesh. We are not our own: in so far as we can, let us therefore forget ourselves and all that is ours.

Conversely, we are God's: let us therefore live for him and die for him. We are God's: let his wisdom and will therefore rule all our actions. We are God's: let all the parts of our life accordingly strive toward him as our only lawful goal.

- John Calvin[1]

Christianity is more than a set of beliefs and more than a set of practices. It is a window on the world that comes from beyond the world and reaches beyond the world as we know it. Christianity cannot be understood or lived out apart from a community; it is a way of life that embodies a common mind shared among trusting friends. Christians make their way in the world by growing into this common mind in ways refined over many centuries. They need spiritual friends, both those who have gone before and those now present, who accompany them and whom they in turn accompany as they wend their way through worlds that do not necessarily share, or even understand, their common mind. A Christian phalanx, marching in tight formation, shields in place, is sometimes appropriate.

Some particularly inspired and articulate Christians have written down their experience and their advice regarding this common mind for Christian living, establishing patterns for the less imaginative among us. The first such document, still as important as any, is the long first letter Paul wrote to the church at Corinth about 54 or 55. This letter remains a classic statement of Christian self-understanding. Corinth has become a byword for Christian congregations that repeatedly fail to understand and therefore live up to their calling.

Paul writes to newly baptized Christians who only dimly grasp the faith he taught them, the faith they embraced at their baptism. This is not surprising. Christianity is only at the very earliest stage of taking shape. There is as yet no definitive understanding of who Jesus is or what he promises them. Nor is it clear how people are different as Christians from how they were as Jews or pagans. No wonder they disagree with one another about how they should live. It is not surprising that the Corinthian Christians need help from their spiritual father, a more seasoned Christian, and one who is not immediately a member of the local body. The opinion of an authority who stands at a slight remove from the immediacy of a situation is often likely to have more credibility than the views of one who is a party to the dispute.

In his capacity as mentor to this congregation, Paul proves himself a wise guide. His letter responds in part to a letter he has received from them requesting his help. They are quarreling divisively and not happy about it, since they are unable to resolve the problems they face by themselves. Rather than moving in and telling them what to do right away, Paul believes that they can only maintain a harmonious and godly community if they understand who they are in Christ and act out of the hope and confidence that he gives.

THE WISDOM OF THE CROSS

Paul begins his letter by reassuring the Corinthian Christians that they already possess everything they need in order to be a happy and righteous community—only they haven't grown into it yet. They have, he says, every spiritual gift that they need, because these come from the grace of God that they have received through Christ Jesus; they are living in the fellowship of God's Son. Paul teaches them what this fellowship is by framing his letter to them around the two events in Christ's life that shape the identity of the community and each of its members: his ignominious death on the cross (chap. 1) and his glorious resurrection that is the hope of all who die (chap. 15).

The Corinthians' problem is that they do not know how to use this identity for the welfare of the community. In teaching them to understand better what it means to belong to God, Paul helps them learn the mind of Christ (2:16) that is now the source of their life together (1:30).

Paul further reassures them that it is not surprising that they have now only a superficial grasp of the Christian sensibility. He starts out by saying that the Christian mind-set begins at the cross of Christ, which is, on the face of it, ridiculous. It makes no sense to organize one's life around a man executed for treason and blasphemy by his political and religious opponents. Hardly anybody who heard about it accepted the idea that this ignominious death was the work of the God of Israel, the maker of heaven and earth. Only a few hardy (or gullible) Jews and Gentiles ventured into this tiny fledgling group of Jesus' followers. There were good reasons for most people to look askance at these odd people.

After assuring them that they can master the problems that beset them, Paul explains to them the saving wisdom of God on which they have decided to base their lives from here on, but need to grasp more richly (1:18–31). The message of the cross of Christ, Paul acknowledges, does not accord with the wisdom of the world. Few "get it." Scripture itself prepares us for this. Isaiah 29:14, a passage Paul cites (1:19), is part of a judgment on people who worship God with their lips only, by rote rather than from the heart. God threatens to destroy their wisdom. Similarly, the truth and wisdom of God, revealed in the cross of Christ, will overthrow what the world takes to be wisdom. The unlikely and perhaps unsuspecting Corinthian Christians are the vanguard of God's minions.

Isaiah's condemnation is not to be taken lightly. Paul teaches that in light of the truth revealed by the execution of this ignorant Jewish artisan, the great moral-philosophical teachings of ancient Greece, the cults of Roman religion, as well as the law of God interpreted by the authorities in Jerusalem, miss the point. It is the equivalent of saying that university education is useless, or that the honorable way of life of one's family is for naught. Rather, Christ crucified reveals divine wisdom and strength in God that are of a different order from anything Jews and pagans know.

On the face of it, Christ on the cross looks ridiculous. It is a shame that he was so naive or foolish as to disturb the authorities so much that they had to get rid of him. He looks like a man who did not have either the smarts or the following to elude or overpower his enemies, and so he succumbed under their strength. Paul teaches that to see the Jesus story this way is to look with human eyes. Christians, even baby ones, have been given spiritual eyes—through baptism, which purifies and rectifies them, filling them with the Spirit of God. Christian vision sees something totally different in the cross, in fact, the exact opposite of what it looks like to the casual viewer.

What no Greek wisdom, Roman power, or even God's law can grasp is that weakness voluntarily assumed to rescue others is spiritual nobility and strength, and that military and political power reveal spiritual weakness.

The craftiness to outwit—or the power to overcome—enemies, which Jesus either lacked or refused to employ, is strength or wisdom in human perspective. But it is precisely foolishness in God's view. God's wisdom and strength are seen in Jesus' helplessness and apparent weakness. It was his refusal to be crafty, his insistence on acting naively that is his wisdom and strength. What no Greek wisdom, Roman power, or even God's law can grasp is that weakness voluntarily assumed to rescue others is spiritual nobility and strength, and that military and political power reveal spiritual weakness. Greece and Rome, like the great economic and military capitals of our world, found security and strength in political authority, military strategy, economic prowess, and public authority. Caesar appeared powerful when he returned from war parading his foreign captives and booty before Rome. And from a "worldly" point of view, of course, he is powerful and to be feared. Paul, however, says that this is an utterly wrong view of the matter. True strength and power lie hidden in an executed has-been. This wisdom is to be loved, not feared.

How is this weakness power, and how is this ignominy wisdom? How are the Corinthians to grasp what God has done in the death of this man that makes them truly wise? The point is that there has been a great reversal of power. In God's own time, it will conquer the world. Those who gird themselves with the accoutrements of worldly power actually reveal themselves to be fearful of loss and so always vulnerable. That is why they put on a great show of outward strength. The catch is that the more they acquire and the harder they scheme, the more insecure and fearful they actually show themselves to be. Those who have no outward forms of protection, authority, or power actually reveal themselves to be spiritually strong. Jesus did not run from his fate. He did not urge his disciples to plan an escape for him, nor did he organize them as a military unit to meet the police. He did not even defend himself when accused. Rather, he accepted his fate with grace and dignity, even though he was frightened. In this, he showed himself to be stronger and wiser than his accusers.

God has not chosen the power brokers, those well born, or the skilled technocrats, but a simple person like many of the Corinthian Christians, of no background, training, or importance. He has become the power of God that says that strength, wisdom, and power are spiritual gifts, not the equivalent of the latest guns and planes, the best mutual funds, or the latest e-commerce strategy. True power and wisdom are spiritual commodities that cannot be learned because they are gifts. The leaders of the world cannot even fathom this. They do not, cannot, craft foreign or domestic policy from the Christian conviction that political weakness may disclose spiritual and moral power. Their responsibility is at best the national interest, at worst, their personal power and authority.

With this explanation, perhaps the Corinthians begin to droop as they see why they are having trouble getting along. Although they have publicly agreed to it, holding this death of a nobody as the viewfinder for their own wisdom and strength is no easy feat, because it requires them to rid themselves of the natural desire for personal power and authority. Paul realized that our normal ability to interpret what we see does not equip us to grasp that weakness and strength have changed places. The Corinthians' problem is that they are still working out of their natural desires and not out of the new identity of the crucifixion. They do not yet have the mind of Christ that empowered him to do what he did. They are still scheming to gain advantage over one another. Of course they are at odds with one another. They have not yet been saved from strength and wisdom as the human eye sees them. They do not get the Christian notion of salvation.

Paul divides the world into those who "get it" and those who do not. Only those gifted by God grasp this hidden wisdom (2:6–16). Only God can teach it. Who can look directly at the cross and see the truth, the righteousness, the redemption, the holiness, and the wisdom that reside there? Only those taught by the Spirit of God can see the wisdom of the crucified one and come to have the mind of Christ.

> Only those taught by the Spirit of God can see the wisdom of the crucified one and come to have the mind of Christ.

Perhaps to their amazement, Paul expects the Corinthian Christians to have the mind of Christ and to live according to it. Still, they cannot. Paul must treat them like babies (3:1), for although they have what they need for spiritual maturity, jealousy that leads to quarreling besets them. As Paul portrays it here, jealousy is the symptom of an immature self that resorts to scheming and politicking to have its own way. This contrasts with having the mind of Christ.

While Paul seems to draw a line in the sand between Christians and non-Christians, in truth, whether he realized it or not, he has brought Greek philosophical wisdom with him in interpreting the cross. Greek philosophies were spiritual ways of life that sought truth beyond military and economic power, just as Paul did. They, however, often phrased their spiritual knowledge as a means toward happiness. For example, Plato taught that truth is connected to goodness, and the Stoics believed that complaining is the main roadblock to happiness. Giving up complaining is no trivial pursuit. One can hear echoes of these philosophical schools in Paul's understanding of the cross and his commendation of the Christian life. One important difference between Paul and the Greek philosophers is that according to the philosophers, one has to work out a way of life that stills unhappiness. According to Paul, the God of Israel, acting in Christ Jesus, has already set forth the way—a radically different one than even Plato or the Stoics could imagine.

HAVING THE MIND OF CHRIST

One of Paul's most striking teachings is that God has not only broken into history in Jesus but has taken up residence in the bodies of the baptized. Christianity is not simply a set of ideas that one agrees, either enthusiastically or reluctantly, are true, and thereby is "saved." One is not saved by ideas but by knowing that God no longer dwells in the temple in Jerusalem and demands animal sacrifices. Rather, in the person Jesus of Nazareth, God has made us his own. By baptism into Christ, God now dwells in us. In chapter 6, Paul pushes the envelope on this notion: Because God resides in your body, it does not belong to you. It belongs to God.

Nothing is more foreign or threatening to our modern way of life than the idea that our bodies do not belong to us but are indwelt by and therefore belong to someone else, especially if that someone else is God. Our age believes firmly that our bodies and our minds belong fully to ourselves, and that we have or ought to have complete control over them. Giving over one's mind or body to another is a sign of moral weakness or ignominy. This notion that modern society prizes so highly as a sign of autonomy, freedom, and maturity is precisely the false wisdom, the worldly understanding of power, that the message of the cross turns on its head. It is only the wise who have the strength to give their mind and body to God. The foolish believe that they own themselves.

For the Christian, Paul teaches, living as if we belong to ourselves is a sign of spiritual weakness and immaturity. Living out the realization that we are not our own but wholly God's has come at a price. Christ's death confuses us and makes us uncomfortable. It threatens us to think that our identity comes from a crucified God. We must let go of the notion that we are in control of our destiny and can control that of others.

Parents who present their children for baptism assign the identity of God crucified to them. Christianity is not for the blasé. This is another example of what Paul intends by the great reversal of strength and weakness. The bulk of his letter moves among various themes explaining what having the mind of Christ entails for daily life.

Perhaps at this point the reader is becoming weary. There seems to be no fun here. So much righteousness sounds downright dreary—and it is so hard. If we turn to another great treatise on the Christian life, the Sermon on the Mount in Matthew, we find a different rendition of similar themes. Does God give us no relief? What about the good news of failure, the forgiveness of sins, and Christian freedom from the law? Why would anyone volunteer for this life? How does one respond to having been captured for it by one's parents in cahoots with the clergy?

Oddly enough, the fact is that Christianity spread rapidly throughout the Greek and Latin-speaking world, although it never caught on among Jews in a big way. Indeed, in some important ways, expectations for the Christian life became even higher just two generations after Paul. The desire to imitate Christ, for example, led to an eagerness for martyrdom under persecution that is quite alien to our way of thinking. Yet Christian martyrs believed that in suffering for Christ they demonstrated having his mind.

Paul reminds the Corinthians that some of them were criminals and big-time sinners before they were washed, purified, and restored to righteousness in the name of Christ and the Spirit of God (6:11). Why would such people voluntarily embrace such a rigorous way of life? Why would they want to embrace not only self-discipline but a set of enforceable moral and social standards?

One answer to these questions might be, of course, that they did not realize quite what they had let themselves in for. Maybe their friends were doing it, and some went along for the adventure. Yet stumbling into Christianity does not account for why people stayed, especially after they encountered Paul's explanations of just what it was really about. The great reversal of worldly notions of power and weakness, dramatically promised in the resurrection of the dead Christ, meant that an old world was dying and a new one coming to birth. It was a world for which Roman civilization unknowingly longed.

Despite its great philosophies, buildings, and literature, the ancient world was harsh. Slavery dominated the social and economic structure. Most people did not have control over their own lives. But Christian freedom involved a liberating surrender of one's mind and body to purity and goodness. Such freedom implied a control over one's life that appealed to the lower classes. At the same time, Christian faith appealed to wealthy citizens, especially wealthy and powerful women. They too were looking for freedom from the violence of gladiatorial shows, ostentatious living, sexual promiscuousness, and military prowess. Christians like Tertullian reached a point of disgust with pagan culture and with their own participation in it that drove them to this other way, a way that escaped the whole rat race.

The church was a true counterculture. Although Christians did not at first withdraw from their place in the wider culture, they took to living by an altogether alternative set of values and ideals embodied in small communities of friends. Gentile and Jew, male and female, slave and free equally gave their minds and bodies over to divine guidance following Paul's vision of crucifixion and resurrection.

> Christians reached a point of disgust with pagan culture and with their own participation in it. The church was a true counterculture.

While from a "worldly" point of view the cruciform life appears strenuous, those who have the mind of Christ realize that they are participating in the turn of the ages. Christ's death and resurrection herald the transformation of the world that God is beginning to bring about even in this fractious little Christian community.

Wanting to march to a different drummer is one thing; actually marching is another thing entirely. Paul saw that internalizing the mind of Christ was not easy and did not happen spontaneously. Some things are not to be tolerated. Incest within the church has been reported to Paul (5:1). He is disturbed not only that this has happened but also that the offender was not disciplined by the community. Leadership is needed. Perhaps he singles out sexual behavior for special treatment because sex is the most destabilizing area of our lives. Still, Paul does not harp on sexual matters. He repeatedly lists financial misconduct, drunkenness, theft, and idolatry as requiring similar discipline (5:9, 11). The community's identity and calling are expressed through the lives of its members, both what they understand to be public and what they may pretend to themselves is their private business. Those who lack the strength to live as the dwelling of God that they are must be helped, as Paul says, to glorify and not embarrass God in their bodies (6:20). Here the wisdom and trust of the community prove their strength.

Paul not only attends to the potential for pollution within the church. He also attends to the face of the community in the wider culture. It shames the community to have Christians suing one another in pagan law courts (6:2–6). How can pagan judges judge Christian litigants who claim to live by spiritual standards that the pagan judge does not understand? Recourse to pagan courts, rather than abiding by ecclesiastical judgement to settle civil disputes, belies one's Christian identity. Those who truly have the mind of Christ will have no need to seek legal advantage over another member of the church and have no need of external judges, because they can rise above self-interest. If one truly grasps that Christ's death expresses spiritual power, one should even allow oneself to be defrauded or financially wronged and not seek redress (6:7). Ethical dilemmas arise only when members of the community cannot live out of their Christlike identity and instead slip back into their instinctive desire for self-advantage. Paul's teaching enabled people to see and even taste the powerful beauty of this new way inaugurated by God in the death and resurrection of Christ.

SEX, IDOLATRY, AND TABLE MANNERS

Although the Corinthians reading this letter may have been psychologically exhausted by this time, it is only when Paul reaches chapter 7 that the letter begins to treat the issues they have asked him about. Apparently, it did not occur to the Corinthians to write about the case of incest. The first two issues they seek guidance on that Paul addresses are whether Christians may marry (chap. 7) and whether they may purchase and eat meat sacrificed to pagan gods (chap. 8). According to the Jewish tradition, sexual immorality and idolatry are two of the three most heinous sins (the third being murder). Christians accepted this judgment, so the questions on which they seek guidance are of paramount importance. If the community is divided on these central features of its life, and different members of the community go their own way, they jeopardize the very identity of the church.

Paul's teaching on marriage has both aspects that we can readily understand and aspects that sound strange to modern ears. This may be because he believed that the world would soon end, a vision he shares toward the end of the letter. It was not until the fifth century that Christians relinquished the hope that Christ was going to return imminently and definitively faced the fact that the church had to prepare for a long life on earth. Still, plans for the long haul already began to take shape in the New Testament. Marriage of course is one of them, since it is the chief guarantor of social stability and the primary means for rearing healthy children who will carry on the Christian way of faith and life.

Chastity in marriage and celibacy in singleness are the only patterns for sexual behavior that Paul condones. Sex is good and necessary, but Paul realized that it is unstable, and must be guarded to protect the community as well as individuals from harm. Here he deals with marriage. Marriage, he realizes, can be as spiritually stressful as it is spiritually rewarding. It is stressful because living tranquilly with another person for a long period of time is difficult; spouses argue, even become hurtful and sometimes violent against one another. Some people prefer living alone so that they do not have to take responsibility for another person's well-being, which is the basic obligation of marriage. Yet many people find the loneliness and the sexual temptation of not being married too much to bear. Marriage provides an opportunity for husband and wife to sanctify one another in the Lord, both spiritually and sexually. It is an opportunity for evangelism.

> Sex is good and necessary, but Paul realized that it is unstable, and must be guarded to protect the community as well as individuals from harm.

Christian marriage is demanding. Paul himself, not thinking about the distant future, prefers celibacy to marriage because being married presses one to become more involved with worldly affairs, where it is tempting to be lured by the understandings of wisdom, strength, and power that operate there. He thinks it is more difficult to follow the teaching of the cross when married than when celibate, because married couples want to satisfy one another's and their children's needs, and this often requires money, a nice house, servants (in that culture), business entanglements, and so forth.

Paul does not consider here the opposite possibility—that it is more difficult to focus one's life on God without a partner to sanctify and be sanctified by, another mind to think things through with, and a person close at hand to offer gentle correction when one's own spiritual life begins to fray. Paul himself, apparently, was not married and so did not taste marriage's joys and benefit from its strengths. Neither was Jesus. The Gospels' accounts of Jesus' radical call to follow him urge people to abandon their families, another indication that the evangelists, if not Jesus himself, also thought that time was short.

In short, both options, marriage and celibacy, allow for different temperaments and different sexual needs. Both ways of life can nourish the Christian life and build up society honorably.

Paul develops one of the most important principles of Christian ethics when he responds to the question of whether Christians may eat meat sacrificed to idols. In the Greco-Roman world, the meat for sale at the local market had often come from a temple, where it had first been used as part of a sacrifice to one of the gods. The honor of the community required that recent pagan converts to Christianity do all that they could to separate themselves from any hint of idolatry. Since they had been joined to the God of Israel, and, from their point of view, to the people of God, all traces of idolatry must be repudiated so that everyone who sees them knows for certain that they worship the God of Israel and not the gods of Rome or Egypt.

Paul knows that, if they have completely rejected idolatry, then they will no longer experience eating sacrificial meat as an act of worship. If the Greek and Roman gods do not exist, then nothing really happens in the rituals at their temples, and meat used in the sacrifices is no different from ordinary meat. Yet he also knows that gossip is difficult to bear. Some members of the community, being sensitive to public opinion, fear being misinterpreted if they are seen doing something that may arouse suspicion that they are still pagans at heart. Even having one member of the church be seen in such a compromising position could shed doubt upon the other members. Paul thinks that the scrupulous persons who worry about such matters are weak in conscience. Instead of criticizing them, however, he puts the burden of the public image of the church on all its members. For the sake of the scrupulous or "weak" in conscience, it is better for all to abstain from everything having to do with idols. Christian freedom is voluntarily restrained by the spiritual vulnerabilities of the church's weakest members. The community is strengthened when the stronger cater to the needs of the weak. At the heart of Pauline ethics is the notion of self-restraint in order to strengthen others.

Christian freedom is voluntarily restrained by the spiritual vulnerabilities of the church's weakest members. The community is strengthened when the stronger cater to the needs of the weak.

To live on such a high moral plane requires paying careful attention to the sensibilities of others, perhaps even understanding what they need before they recognize it themselves. In the Christian life, no one is on his or her own. Everyone is cared for by all the members of the community, even when they do not know they are being protected, cared for, or corrected. Here is yet another example of the great reversal in which what looks like weakness is really strength—the strength to set aside one's prerogatives for the sake of others who, for whatever reasons, cannot make it alone.

Paul applies a similar line of reasoning to behavior at the Lord's Supper. The custom in Paul's churches was quite different from ours. They may have eaten a whole meal together in church, each bringing their own food, to commemorate the last supper of Jesus with his friends. Here Paul is concerned that the divisions within the church are also showing up at the Lord's Table. People are failing to attend to one another's needs, as symbolized by not waiting to eat and drink together.

This may sound like a small, even trivial item of etiquette. Etiquette is not, however, a trivial matter at the Lord's Table. Paul complains that without a communal rule for sharing and regulating what they eat, some eat whenever they want to, while others go hungry or get drunk. This is no kind of behavior for a Christian community. Decorum at the Lord's Table reinforces and recollects the mind of Christ that is the foundation of the community's life. One cannot claim to be in Christ and disgrace the Lord in the gathered body.

LOVE AND OTHER SPIRITUAL GIFTS

The Christian ethic of self-restraint for the sake of the "weak" that Paul works out in chapter 8, is, I suspect, his response to the threat of jealousy that he takes to be the great enemy of the church. His teaching on spiritual gifts, especially his famous teaching on Christian love, in 1 Corinthians 12 and 13 respectively, indicates the power of God to transform personalities as they grow into the mind of Christ.

In his teaching on spiritual gifts, alluded to early in the letter, Paul creates the powerfully binding metaphor of the members of the church as members of a body that turns out to be Christ's body. We know that the Christian body is the dwelling place of God and that the Christian life pertains especially to how we use our bodies. Now he shifts the image a bit to suggest that all Christians together form one body, the mystical body of Christ himself, carried forward in time and space as the institutional church. With this theological understanding of the church, all the spiritual gifts given to individual members are gifts of God. Like our bodies, our "natural aptitudes" no longer belong to us. All gifts and talents are God's, to be used for the common good rather than for personal advancement.

Here is another point at which the message of the cross grates heavily against the modern sensibility. Among the wealthy, attentive parents heed any sign of special abilities or aptitudes in their children, so that these may be developed as early and as thoroughly as possible. Parents who see athletic ability in their child may start dreaming of the Olympics. Parents who recognize intellectual skills may dream of Harvard. Children with musical talent may be groomed for performance, and so on. Following their parents' lead, children who sense that they have special gifts or abilities may become the focus of jealousy or competition from their peers, or experience the special spiritual danger of being taken with themselves.

> All Christians form one body, the mystical body of Christ himself.

Those who find themselves lacking in highly prized abilities, in contrast, will suffer when comparing themselves to the front-runners. Natural aptitudes can distort both those who have them and those who lack them. Jealousy again rears its ugly head when gifts are used for personal advantage. When they are used to build up the body of Christ, however, their holder gains everyone's respect.

Paul seems presciently to have grasped our own predicament about jealousy and competition. He places all gifts under one umbrella. Gifts do not belong to their holders but to the one Spirit, the one Lord who gives them. Each is needed by, and is to be used for, the good of the entire body. When one suffers, all suffer; when one is honored, all share the honor. Or, to put it more pointedly, when one suffers, Christ suffers; when one is honored, Christ is honored. Diverse gifts build up the new way of life when they are used for the common good and not to glorify their holders.

Moving from a mentality in which we own our gifts to a mentality in which God owns our gifts for the sake of Christ's body is another quite strenuous spiritual claim on the Christian. It demands a practice of selflessness at a highly sophisticated psychological level. The point here is that one's gifts are to be developed and honed to the degree possible and feasible, yet that in growing in strength from our gifts we may never think that they belong to us. Thus, the spiritual gifts of God provide double strength. When used rightly they both strengthen and provide proper self-esteem to the one to whom they have been given, and strengthen and empower the community on whose behalf they are given. Perhaps knowing how difficult this is, Paul explains that it is only possible when we have the greatest gift of all: love.

First Corinthians 13 is one of the most famous chapters in the Bible. It was once read regularly in public schools and is often read at weddings. Paul's teaching on Christian love is notably separated from his discussion of marriage. Christian love certainly applies to the married, but is by no means limited to them. Indeed, sometimes those closest to us are the hardest to love. The teaching on love continues the teaching on spiritual gifts. Christian love is a divine gift. It is the key to the new world that Christ's death and resurrection intimate.

Paul begins the brief chapter by admonishing that unless all of the gifts enumerated above (and some not mentioned) are motivated by the spirit of love, they amount to nothing. Love is the antidote to the spiritual dangers that plague the Corinthians. The jealousies, divisions, boasting, and arrogance that are bringing shame upon the church all stem from a want of true love that is long-suffering, hopeful, trusting, humble, and does not insist on its own way. Although Paul does not refer back to it, perhaps this is another way of understanding the message of the cross, the great reversal of power and weakness displayed by Christ Jesus. God's self-giving was an act of true love in the sense that Paul articulates it in Romans 5:8: "But God proves his love for us in that while we still were sinners Christ died for us."

Love is different in that it never ends, it never ceases giving. It is never depleted or used up.

All other gifts will eventually end. If we are fortunate, they will have fulfilled their God-given purpose through us. Love is different in that it never ends, it never ceases giving. It is never depleted or used up. We do not fully understand this now, Paul warns. And here, finally, Paul seems to empathize with rather than chastise the Corinthians who understand Christian faith and life so poorly. He too fails fully to understand the love that is the gift of God. Yet perhaps in our future—when the last trumpet sounds and the dead are raised and the living are transformed into immortal bodies—perhaps then the gift of love will be fulfilled. Until then, Paul counsels the bumbling Corinthians to hold fast to the portals of the reign of God: faith, hope, and love—with the greatest being love.

The context for the Christian life is, of course, the whole of one's life, but it is especially visible in the worship life of the gathered community of Christians. Here they build one another up with songs, lessons, and encouragement. Some of the practices Paul commends seem strange. It is difficult for most Christians today to see how speaking in tongues (14:2ff.) and silencing women in public

(14:34–36) build up the church, since they have the immediate effect of dividing people from one another and creating resentments and injustice.

Although the whole letter presupposes the transformation of the ages in which the baptized now participate, Paul clarifies the dramatic and even violent revelation of the good news that he anticipates only in chapter 15: "that Christ died for our sins in accordance with the scriptures, and that he was buried, and that he was raised on the third day in accordance with the scriptures, and that he appeared to Cephas [Peter], then to the twelve [disciples]. Then he appeared to more than five hundred brothers and sisters at one time" (15:3–6).

The good news is that Christ's story is the story of those who die to the ways of the world, take on the mind of Christ, and liken themselves to him. Together the new Christians become the body of Christ in the world and are the beginning of a new possibility in which the pain of sin and death will be stilled.

PAUL FOR TODAY?

Paul's letter to the Corinthian Christians was written long ago and far away, in a culture and amidst sensibilities and moral standards quite different from our own. It envisions a radically transformed society being ushered in by God that will culminate in the overcoming of mortality, sin, and dissension. While all of this is the work of God, it requires intentional commitment on the part of those who join the community. After seeing the world plod sinfully on for two thousand years, it is difficult to hold to the heightened anticipation that fills Paul's vision of radical transformation. Yet because of his venerable place in the Christian tradition and, one might add, the sublime insights into human nature and the fragility of community that he brings us, Paul is not easy to dismiss as out of date. Let us then ask the question bluntly: Can we take this normative prescription for the Christian life as a guide for the Christian congregations in which we live, indeed for our own lives?

If we answer flatly no, we must ask what grounds Christians have for rejecting Paul. To say that Paul's is merely one opinion among many, or that our modern values and preferences are morally superior to those of the early church, will not do. Paul is not just any Christian. He is the apostle who gave Christian theology its basic shape and direction. It may be possible to argue with Paul in good faith, but to dismiss him out of hand is to set oneself outside the Christian community that canonized his letters as Scripture.

Simply to say that God's call is too hard, or old-fashioned, will not do either. Fashion is of no interest to truth. If we try to hedge our bets, intending to elect the parts that comfort us and reject the parts that seem to us too strenuous or patriarchal for modern taste, we must render an account of the authority we have to cut and paste to our taste. Yet if, on the other hand, we think we want to embrace Paul's theology fully, perhaps we flatter ourselves that we are somehow more mature than the petulant Corinthians.

Yet perhaps there is a way forward. If Paul truly has glimpsed the reign of God, even imperfectly, perhaps he really can help us. Perhaps we really need him to help us. If we may summarize the themes we have covered, it seems that Paul's basic ecclesiology is that the church's members must be socialized into the mind of Christ and out of the mind-set of the world so that they can help one another grow more deeply into the reign of God that has begun in them at baptism. Such community takes spiritual strength. It requires joining the group with a humble spirit, ready to be led. Members of Christ's body do not vie for power in an ordinary space; they share common ground. That ground is the mind of Christ and the task of growing one another into it. This requires Christian love. It means living in the already begun kingdom of God.

There will be times when one is unable to share the common mind of the body of Christ, and one or several may decide to leave the community, to protect both its honor and integrity and their own consciences. This should not been taken as a failure of hospitality, but the result of honest soul-searching in the name of Christ. In such cases, remaining members of the community would want to inquire after the reasons some must take their leave, for only so can the concerns at the heart of this rupture become constructive criticism for the health of the church.

The demands of the Christian life may, in truth, require that some may have to be expelled or set apart from the community until they can be reconciled to its standards. Such moments are painful, and must be undertaken most carefully and through duly authorized procedures. Still, those who truly seek life with God in a humble spirit may themselves see the wisdom of such discipline when necessary to protect both themselves and the community's integrity. Pastoral care cannot always afford to be only comforting if it is for the common good as well as the good of the individual. Perhaps the older term "cure of souls" is a more apt term for pastoral leadership.

Another demanding aspect of Paul's version of the Christian life is that our minds, our bodies, and our talents belong to God and are not ours to dispose of as we see fit. This not only contradicts our modern notion of autonomy; it also calls for submission to one whom we trust more than ourselves. Contemporary cynicism argues that we should trust ourselves more than anyone else. If we have been hurt or damaged by someone who has had some sort of power over us, it is understandable that we would build a defense system around ourselves so that it cannot happen again. Or we seek revenge or recompense. Anyone who wants our trust must earn it, and we are often suspicious of people who volunteer for this office. We assume that everyone is out for their own advantage. This is to say that our world operates precisely on the principles that Paul diametrically opposes to Christian ones. This is the mentality that the spiritual gifts of

According to Paul, our minds, our bodies, and our talents belong to God and are not ours to dispose of as we see fit.

faith, hope, and love rob of its power. The ability to celebrate this foundation of new life in Christ is the wisdom of God.

Since we seem to be wired, or at least warned, not to trust others until they demonstrate their trustworthiness, why should we trust God enough to surrender ourselves to his reign? Paul's answer to this is that God has already proven his trustworthiness in the cross and resurrection of Christ that is our hope of forgiveness of sin and resurrection of our bodies when sin once controlled us. Christ's obedience of mind, body, and talents unto death to serve God's purpose on earth is finally not the whole story of God's purpose. Jesus may have been willing to die for his friends, but God raised him from the dead. He is both the giver and the given of God's gifts. Paul begins his treatise on the Christian life with the message of the cross, but he ends it with the promise of resurrection seen first in Jesus. Only when we see the unity of the cross and the resurrection and the ascension of Christ to the Father's right hand do we see the full purpose of God: forgiveness, purification of life, and the glorification of our bodies in the hope of the resurrection are the gifts of God in Christ, for they save us from lesser hopes and dreams.

Even if God has demonstrated his trustworthiness to us by proving that his goal is our glorification, even if suffering may be entailed in having the mind of Christ, there are still other impediments to embracing Paul's interpretation of the cross. One, of course, is that it is unnatural. The world's way comes more easily to us; that is the reason it is so widespread. The wisdom of the cross seems to betray the goals of leadership, which are efficiency and profit. The CEO is expected to make decisions to these ends, and it is accepted that some decisions will hurt some people. Indeed, perhaps the most tragic aspect of the worldly understanding of power and strength is that we are often unaware of just how strong and powerful we are. Sometimes the exercise of power is callous, but, unfortunately, sometimes exercising power for virtuous goals has negative consequences for some people. Jesus sacrificed himself for these sins too.

Another impediment to adopting Paul's message of the cross is that unlearning what comes naturally to us, and relearning a completely opposite orientation, is an enormous undertaking, and we do not know if we can pull it off. It takes constant vigilance. Beyond this, however, lies another fear—really a further lack of trust or faith. Not only do we not trust ourselves to have the mind of Christ, but also we suspect that others will scoff at it. If we operate in faith, while others operate according to business-as-usual, they are likely to crush us, just the way they crushed Jesus. There are simply too few Christians willing to take this on to make a difference. When we look at the church itself, we do not always find a helpful

We fear that, if we operate in faith, according to the mind of Christ, while others operate according to business-as-usual, they are likely to crush us, just the way they crushed Jesus.

role model either. Holding on to the promises of God—that is, faith—is one of the three great spiritual gifts Paul highlights in chapter 13.

Perhaps we have reached the point where we finally understand Paul's self-description as a spectacle and a fool for Christ (4:9–10). It does not mean dressing up in clown costumes to make the congregation laugh. It means a willingness to be ridiculed for living by the radically counterintuitive vision of the strength, power, and wisdom of the cross. It means not seeking one's own interests in order to preserve peace in the community. It means protecting others from us. It means using one's body, mind, and talents for the common good. It means helping others take on the mind of Christ, and asking others to do the same for you.

Perhaps the Christian orientation to life does not require us to be martyred as Jesus was. He literally died for friends who, fearing for their own lives, abandoned him in the pinch. After all, he accepted death because he knew he could prevent a Roman-sponsored bloodbath in Israel. Yet, as his followers, are we not called to continuous little deaths when they promote the well-being of others? When seen in this light, opportunities for living out the Christian orientation are everywhere.

The reward for living by the message of the cross is an inner sense of purity and well-being, a security, or truly godly self-esteem that comes when we use our bodies, minds, and talents to the greater glory of God in building up the church and the culture. Christian self-esteem is very powerful, but it stands on a completely different foundation than secular self-esteem, which is nourished by accomplishments recognized and honored by worldly standards. Paul's teaching is the basis of Christian vocation—that claim that God has upon us by virtue of having first loved us enough to reconcile us to himself and call us to holiness. Holiness is living from the mind of Christ, acting out the message of the cross—the wisdom of God in the promise of glorification.

> To live by faith is to trust in what is not self-evident. To live in hope is to defeat the satanic forces that would render us cynical, suspicious, or filled with despair, fear, or anger. To act out of love is to take everyone at their best, their most sincere, their most vulnerable, and to refuse to be moved from the faith and hope that all can be knit together in harmony and peace.

Living as a Christian takes a certain kind of energy, but not the energy of entrepreneurship or of playing politics. Energy for Paul's vision of the Christian life takes what Thomas Aquinas called the "supernatural virtues" of faith, hope, and love. Paul mentions these three at the end of chapter 13 of the letter we have reflected upon here. These are gifts of the Holy Spirit of God, not our natural aptitudes. To the degree that we have them, we have the holiness of God. Living by faith, in hope, and through love means seeing more than what lies on the surface. To live by faith, as Paul says in 2 Corinthians 5:7, is to trust in what is not self-evident, for example, our final glorification in the midst of suffering. To live in hope is to defeat the satanic forces that would render us cynical, suspicious, or filled with despair, fear, or anger. To act out of love, the greatest of the supernatural or theological virtues, is to take everyone at their best, their most sincere, their most vulnerable, and to refuse to be moved from the faith and hope that all can be knit together in harmony and peace.

These virtues cannot be forced; they must be given. If we believe that the power of the Holy Spirit is given in baptism, then perhaps we can also believe that these virtues are the fruit of this great gift of God's own holiness. Perhaps we cannot see them operating in friends, family, or colleagues just now. That does not prove that they are not present, only that they lie neglected, unmined, or not yet understood.

The Christian life, according to Paul, is life lived in the reign of God inaugurated with the death and resurrection of Christ. It continues in the life of the baptized, who participate in it by dying and rising with Christ to new and unending life in him. This reign of God rests on a foundation entirely different from that of the empires and nations of the world, which understand power in economic, military, and political terms. The reign of God overturns all this through the wisdom of God disclosed in the death and resurrection of Christ. All who participate in it are raised to new life based on the mind of Christ. Those who have the mind of Christ live in testimony to the transforming power of the self-sacrificing love that is God's wisdom. They offer hope to a world that groans in sin and pain, aching for the gospel that will release it from the reign of military and political self-interest.

Christians then witness to a new world and to a wisdom that seems foolish to most. They live from faith rather than fear, hope rather than despair, love rather than ambition. Christ, Paul says at the beginning of his letter, is the power and the wisdom of God. As he concludes, he exhorts, "Therefore, my beloved, be steadfast, immovable, always excelling in the work of the Lord, because you know that in the Lord your labor is not in vain" (15:58).

MICHAEL BATTLE

I must preface this essay with a brief discussion of two difficulties. The first concerns how one defines Christian life. We cannot simply say that "Christian life" means the kind of life led by Christians. For example, some may argue that Mahatma Gandhi, a Hindu, exemplifies the Christian life more than does Jerry Falwell, a Baptist minister. This problem of naming the Christian life is like a Garrison Keillor joke:

> A grasshopper hops into a bar and sits down, waiting for a drink. The bartender says, "We haven't had many grasshoppers come into this bar. Despite what people may think, that's surprising because we have a drink named after you."
>
> The grasshopper responds, "Well, that *is* unusual because I have never heard of a drink named Bob."[1]

The ridiculous idea of a grasshopper having a name is similar to the outrageous occupation of defining one particular kind of human life as "Christian life."

The second difficulty concerns how one moves beyond a simple taxonomy of what it means or looks like to be a Christian to the more important task of identifying practices and disciplines to facilitate more examples of a flourishing Christian life. The challenge is that a Christian lifestyle is so extraordinary that, even when we begin to understand it, we still find it very hard to follow. There is no such thing as ordinary Christian life. Archbishop Desmond Tutu states:

> The last mark of the operation of the Spirit seems to be that those who are chosen to be special instruments are destined for suffering. . . . Those who are God's friends are distinguished by the fact that they suffer. . . . There is an unbroken link in the mystery of service and suffering, witness and persecution, stretching from the Old Testament to the New Testament. . . . A church that does not suffer cannot be the Church of Jesus Christ, the suffering servant of the Lord.[2]

Because of these two difficulties of defining Christian life and then identifying the extraordinary practices that can form it, I will ask us to imagine, as Aristotle sometimes did, how to define a thing by what it is not. I will ask us to imagine how Christians should *not* live. For even as we attempt this description of something called life, even more particularly Christian life, we find ourselves bringing our cognitive, categorizing faculty of knowing into operation. This is distinct from affective ways of knowing by heart, the heart as defined by the core of one's being where one is most truly one's self.

> "Those who are God's friends are distinguished by the fact that they suffer." —Desmond Tutu

The seventeenth-century philosopher Descartes proposed that I can understand my self as a thinking being simply by looking inward, focusing on my own existence as an individual. To try to understand Christian life that way, however, would be like the dog who thinks itself born to turn in circles to chase its own tail. Christian life carries with it the daily need of habits and skills given to Christian individuals through the communal life of the church.[3] *Christian life is necessarily communal life.* There can be no experience of God solely as an individual's experience, as if God's presence resides only in the personal realm. Human beings become conscious of Christian life through the meaningful practices of God's presence in the world. Individual Christians, made in the image of God, learn the meaning of what is personal and unique as the Christian life is practiced and tested against other worldviews that make outrageous and transcendent claims on reality.

Doubtless you have heard the saying that, in order to be a Christian, you must have a personal relationship with your Lord and Savior Jesus Christ. And surely you have it heard preached that, if you were the only one alive, God would still come and die for you. You have heard these things—but these ways of naming Christian life are individualistic and unintelligible to the way that Jesus taught his disciples how to live. Jesus taught that the Christian life is modeled by the image of God existing as diverse persons in a unified nature—the Trinity. Jesus taught that the Christian life should not resemble a special-interest group of self-interested individuals. In other words, we learn both from Jesus' relation to the Godhead and Jesus' model of discipleship that *community* is the image of God. Christian life reflects this communal image of the triune God.

Given this preface, and the two difficulties of defining Christian life and displaying its extraordinary lifestyle, in what follows I propose the concept of community as the organizing meaning for how to understand the Christian life. Christian life implies maturation, a constancy of new life not just for the individual but also for the community. Community implies life because life is not any one person's possession. Life is, always, new life—that is to say, a new world of possibilities, a new future which is to be constructed day by day.

> We learn both from Jesus' relation to the Godhead and from Jesus' model of discipleship that *community* is the image of God.

Archbishop Desmond Tutu is a master at articulating how community implies new life for all and not just for some. Through such communal practices as confession, repentance, and forgiveness, Tutu believes human communities are doing no less than practicing a future that is better than the present. Not to engage such practices is to give way to decay and regression.[4] It is worth noting how much stress Scripture lays upon the themes of new life and the call to maturity and the risks of regression: Salvation is to be realized in growth, and not to grow is to fall away.[5] Life, after all, implies movement and growth toward new life. This implication that life moves toward life leads me to believe that community is the organizing meaning for Christian life. Perhaps this obvious point that life implies community is an indicator of what must be central for any adequate understanding of Christian life.

WHAT CHRISTIAN LIFE IS NOT

I noted earlier the difficulty in naming Christian life; indeed, we need more of a concerted effort to display the distinguishing characteristics of Christian life that can move western Christendom beyond thinking of one person's heart's experience as the sole criterion of Christian life. When I lecture to my students at Duke Divinity School, I call this way of characterizing the Christian life "baseball spirituality." Just as you score a run if you touch every base and slide home safe, so "baseball spirituality" holds that, as long as you can verbalize the formula of Christian salvation, then all requirements of the Christian life are accomplished. The western, Enlightenment notion of self-contained piety has come to define the Christian life. Such a description of the Christian life (as simply a matter of cognitive display or verbal articulation), however, does not adequately name it. In many senses, this baseball spirituality is derived from European Enlightenment formularies that define the essential reality of the individual as a thinking agent. As a result, the Christian life has come to be defined through self-avowed Christians who, in Descartes's phrase, think, therefore, they exist.

The Christian life, however, is not about personal journeys of faith, as if the locus of authority of knowing God in Christ and how one should live in such reality is given to the individual alone. In other words, we do not know the Christian life privately as if to maintain individual autonomy. We cannot know life this way (much less "Christian" life) because life is not something disconnected from everything else. Scientists and medical practitioners can tell you more powerfully than I that life is a deeply connected system. In light of our knowledge that Christian life cannot be known apart from the context of relationships, most notably our relationship in the atoning work of Christ to God the Father and Spirit, we come to the point of discerning how one is able to describe the mystery of Christian life.

Most of our images of God are inherited through communal ways of knowing, and these communal ways of knowing are, in fact, how Jesus teaches his followers how to live. Another way of describing this communal practice of knowing is Christian discipleship. But this communal way of knowing does not come easy, as Tutu explained earlier: "Those who are God's friends are distinguished by the fact that they suffer." In some sense, we are taught in Christian mystical literature that in order to know Christian life, a living death (martyrdom or, to translate the meaning of that Greek word, "witness") is required of us to know even ourselves. In our egalitarian milieu, however, this language of discipleship and martyrdom may seem incommensurate with our understanding of individual wholeness and well-being. We find it strange if not masochistic when Tutu asks, "Who says that death is the worst thing that could happen to a Christian?"[6]

> Christian life cannot be known apart from the context of relationships.

So far, my argument has been that Christian life is not about an aggregate of individuals in pursuit of their experience of God, but a communal way of being in which Christian pilgrims and disciples display relationships and behaviors akin to how Christ displayed relationships and behaviors. Now I want to discuss the primary agency of Christian life—the church. In the Christian life, we begin with the mystery of the church's deepest experience; it is a mystery because the church's origin is deeper than our minds can take us. The church had an experience of God long before it could articulate that experience. In other words, what we know at the deepest place of the church, we know not with the clarity of our cognitive minds but through something more obscure and more particular to the church. I call this "knowing through obscurity" because the church, since its beginning, has had to seek God in unknowing.[7] Only a few in the church have claimed an immediate awareness of God through contemplative intuition.[8]

In the kingdom of heaven, we will discover a great mystery. Because of our reliance on others, both in knowing God and our own experience of God, there are certain assumptions that the church gives us to deepen how one lives the Christian life in the divine mystery of the church. The contemporary Orthodox theologian Vladimir Lossky explains that the Holy Spirit is now unknown due to the absence of a reciprocal image; for example, the Son is the image of the Father and the Holy Spirit the image of the Son, but as of yet there is no image of the Holy Spirit. Here Lossky displays the beautiful insight that the Holy Spirit's presence simultaneously diversifies and unifies, as in the biblical account of Acts 2:1–13. This natural tendency of the Holy Spirit should also reflect the mystery of the church in its diversity and unity. Lossky concludes that the multitude of the saints in the church will be the Spirit's reciprocal image. In other words, the church will be the reciprocal image of the Holy Spirit.[9]

The Holy Spirit's presence simultaneously diversifies and unifies.

Through the coming of the Holy Spirit, the Trinity dwells within us and deifies us, conferring upon the church the uncreated energies of which the church must partake to have Christian life. The Holy Spirit mysteriously identifies herself with human persons while remaining incommunicable. She substitutes herself for ourselves and cries on our behalf (Rom. 8:1–17). In the Holy Spirit, the will of God is no longer external to the church: She confers grace inwardly and outwardly at the same time, manifesting grace within our very person and external to our person in others insofar as our human will remains in accord with the divine will and cooperates with it in making grace exist as the community called the church. This is the way of deification, of becoming like God. But deification (the Greek term is *theosis*) is impossible to explain to Western sensibilities apart from the initiatives of the Holy Spirit, the Spirit who is no longer external to the church. In short, the church is the image of the Holy Spirit.

This is good and bad news, however. This is good news as the church basks in the image of Holy Spirit who through Pentecost helps the church celebrate diversity as unity and unity as diversity. This is bad news in the sense that the church betrays the image of God by being other than God is. In other words, we make God look atrocious through our practices of greed, disunity, and victimization. The Western church further risks blasphemy against the Holy Spirit as it locates the spiritual life in a private, separate sphere of existence. It is because of these difficulties that we now turn to clearer examples of Christian life for those of us with more Western sensibilities of the church.

SPIRITUAL DIRECTION, SPIRITUAL THEOLOGY, AND DISCERNMENT

One of the predominant traditions in the church by which to seek clearer examples of Christian life is the tradition of spiritual direction. Spiritual direction has always been a vital part of the Christian tradition. Spiritual direction serves as an aid to the discernment of God's presence in one's life and as a means of accountability for one's faithful response in all of life. Spiritual direction serves as a reality check, a preservation from the myopia of narrow, self-centered vision. It also sharpens one's awareness of solidarity with all God's people and challenges one toward communal choices. Spiritual directors are responsible to direct persons outside of personal boundaries so that the focus of our spiritual life becomes our love for God, which concurrently shows our love for neighbor. Spiritual direction enables a person to do a better job of contributing healthy solutions to sociopolitical problems of everyday life, which is being constantly bombarded by social ills that can easily paralyze any one individual's soul. So, in light of these characteristics of spiritual direction, in what framework do I assume the Christian life is most intelligible?

The category that helps us answer this question is called spiritual theology, better known in Roman Catholic theological education than among mainline Protestant Christians. As the category of spiritual theology becomes better known among Protestants as Christian spirituality, an opportunity is given to us all to think more deeply about the nature of the Christian life. One advantage of spiritual theology is that we become a little less tempted toward a "baseball spirituality" (simply the right words and answers to things with our cognitive minds), while still valuing those minds for what can come through them. Through spiritual theology, God's active presence is realized to pervade both our knowing and our unknowing, and we do not have to press our knowing beyond its limits at a given time. Spiritual theology (as opposed to systematic, foundational, or speculative theology) seeks to interpret the particular ways God seems to move directly within and among Christians, inviting those of us who call ourselves by this name into deeper communion, and into compassionate, creative lifestyles through a life of prayer.

Spiritual theology seeks to interpret the particular ways God seems to move directly within and among Christians, inviting those of us who call ourselves by this name into deeper communion, and into compassionate, creative lifestyles through a life of prayer.

Because a life of prayer is the ordering principle, spiritual theology also deals with the intentional spiritual disciplines that help us notice and freely respond to these invitations and in the process help us notice and deal with counterinvitations: those that emanate from insular egos and destructive societal forces and from forces of evil. Spiritual theology as a category is helpful because, as I have argued in the beginning, the Christian life is not known simply through propositional statements or cognitive ideas. So what is the Christian life in the light of the communal experience of the church and this helpful category of spiritual theology? Spiritual theology helps us answer this question through the following methodology. Before there can be an interpretive level of knowledge of the Christian life, there must be the level of simple description of the Christian life—that is, a simple, childlike lifestyle of prayer and optimism in a world often seen as hostile and limited. Thomas Kelly, a well-known Quaker, states,

> Under the silent, watchful eye of the Holy One we are all standing, whether we know it or not. And in that Center, in that holy Abyss where the Eternal dwells at the base of our being, our programs, our gifts to God, our offerings of duties performed are again and again revised in their values. . . . If we center down, and live in that holy Silence which is dearer than life, and take our life program into the silent places of the heart, with complete openness, ready to do, ready to renounce according to God's leading, then many of the things we are doing lose their vitality for us.

At this simple, stripping level of the spiritual life, we sense a quality of desire, presence, trust, love, and willingness that carries an obscure knowledge of life into a larger caring reality of life defined by God in Christ.

In other words, the Christian life is known first in its simplest formation of behavior informed by the life of Christ. Just as Jesus taught through stories, so too does one know the Christian life through simple connections between faith and behavior. This notion of the simplicity of knowing is given to us through contemplative traditions in Christianity which say that there is an even more direct way of knowing that is not conditioned by our cognitive theological categories, our symbols, our heart senses, or our past experience. Before one approaches any of these sources of knowledge, there is made available, because of the atoning work of Christ, a direct awareness of what is that carries its own unconditioned immediate knowledge. As one continues through this way of knowing, there is no experience of a sensation at this level, no content of knowledge. Rather, this direct knowledge involves unitive awareness, a quality of innocent, naked presence. This contemplative way of knowing is called discernment.

> Christian life comes to mean a *communal* habit of discernment: that ongoing availability and sensitivity to God.

The problem with Christian discernment is that too many people have quoted Augustine, "Love God and do what you will," to rationalize and excuse inappropriate behavior. Even the axiom of the twentieth-century Trappist monk Thomas Merton, "Whatever is demanded by truth, by justice, by mercy or by love must surely be taken to be willed by God," can lead many to nebulous definitions of the Christian life if there is no interpretive framework by which to distinguish what we mean by Christian life.

Perhaps, in its most useful sense, Christian life comes to mean a *communal* habit of discernment: that ongoing availability and sensitivity to God. This habit permeates all of life and determines choices. The questions involved for the habit of discernment are:

- Am I becoming more present to the triune God in all of life?
- What is my sense of attentiveness to God?
- What is my sense of distraction from God?
- What is my belief about God's active involvement in the present moment?

Discernment as a spiritual act involves actively and consciously seeking God in a particular circumstance. From such seeking, the Christian life actively turns to the Holy Spirit within and without to confirm our choices. The Holy Spirit naturally leads the seeker to Christian community (the church) to verify such judgments. Questions around a specific choice might be:

- Can I maintain the overall direction of my life with this choice?
- Is there a sense of conformity with the mind and heart of Christ in this choice?
- Is there a growing sense of authenticity, wholeness, and integration with this choice?
- Is there a sense of congruence with who I am in God and how God has been active in my life and other lives with this choice?
- Is there a sense of eternal life, of what is permanent over what is transient, in this choice?
- How does my decision fit as I imagine myself with all else stripped away but my desire for God in this choice?
- Does the choice fit within the overall tradition of the Christian community?
- Am I willing to test this out within my various communities?

Discernment of what is the Christian life in its fullness takes a practiced heart, truly a gift of God, but not one a person is given dropped from the skies fully formed. I would say the same about Christian life, namely, that in essence it is a gift from others, cultivated and brought to perfection by a prayerful life. The Christian life, I conclude, is the habit of viewing all of life through the eyes of faith, and in that faith-stance noticing the movements of the heart to determine which of these movements is leading to greater community and discipleship in Christ, and which of them is turning one toward insular egos and destructive societal forces. Christian life, in the end, is the habit of discernment rooted in the conversion of individuals to form the multitude of saints.

In short, in order to answer the question "What is the Christian life?" one must be willing to enter a circular argument, believing even at the start that God will be the conclusion of one's search for wisdom. One must be willingly present for God's answer in Christ—an orientation, a stance of our whole being, which encompasses whatever way we are knowing at a given time. This open, nakedly trusting, willing presence for God's loving truth can be lost when we lean forward to grasp for individualistic interpretive knowledge; then our knowing loses its immediate openness to God and becomes more insular. We need our thoughts to grow out of and feed into our immediate givenness to God. This means that since our interpretive theologizing is relative to a mystery that transcends our capacity to understand fully, we can have honest differences of interpretation on what in fact constitutes the Christian life. Mahatma Gandhi should make us pause and wonder whether Christians are living the Christian life. When we gather together to probe this deep mystery of the character of the Christian life that we sense is at work in us, we can trust the mystery of the church, that where two or three are gathered together in true willingness for God, Christ's Spirit will guide us, even if our probing leaves us at different places of understanding or uncertainty at a given time.

HOW THEN SHOULD WE NOT LIVE?

If the reader has followed my inductive reasoning so far and accepts the destination of my argument that the Christian life is a habit of ongoing discernment practiced in Christian community, then we may proceed to the conclusion of this chapter by asking this question: How should a Christian not live? In the kingdom of heaven, we will discover the great mystery that we need others to know God and ourselves. Even now, we recognize that we need others to discover the concepts of beauty, language, and faith. I need someone else to know if I am handsome or ugly, to know if I have intelligence. I need a community to make sense of myself. I also need to know saints to make sense of how God exists in a world such as this. Because of our reliance on others, both in knowing God and our own experience of God, Christian life becomes the communal practice of staying awake in the presence of God. In other words, Christian life looks like a community of saints who know themselves through the deep awareness of each other's presence. And such a community is knowledgeable of itself as Christian through the awareness of the greatest other, God, revealed in Jesus Christ. Such Christian communal awareness is not static, however; it is an ongoing, dynamic knowledge that depends upon spiritual habits and practices of the triune God's revelation in Jesus. Since Jesus' own immediate disciples had trouble practicing Jesus' ways, and most of all had trouble staying awake with Christ, we all the more need to be aware of a practiced Christian spirituality of community. In order to practice a Christian spirituality of community, I want us to look at two bad habits of westernized Christians.

The Bad Habit of Personal Religion

The church gives us certain assumptions for understanding spirituality as a practiced revelation. These assumptions facilitate our training in the divine mystery of the church that I mentioned before—that we know the self through the other. Such divine knowledge comes only through practice. For example, the late Alexander Schmemann, a distinguished Orthodox priest and teacher, once told a group of students why he believed Christians have to practice sensitivity to the presence of angels. When he was a young man living in Paris, he was traveling on the Metro one day with his fiancée. They were very much in love and bound up only in each other. The train stopped and an elderly and very ugly woman got on. She was dressed in the uniform of the Salvation Army and, to their disgust, she sat near them. The young lovers in Paris began to whisper to each other in Russian, exclaiming to each other about the grossness and ugliness of the old woman in a language they assumed she would not understand. The train came to a stop. The old woman got up and, as she passed the two young people, she said to them in perfect Russian, "I wasn't always ugly!" That person, insisted Father Schmemann, was an angel of God. She brought the shock of revelation, the shock that was needed for him to see that what was here was much, much more than an ugly old woman. Next time he would be able to look at an unattractive person in a self-effacing, uninterfering way. It takes practice, however, to spot angelic presences, just as it takes practice to recognize God. But practice alone is not enough, unless one has a great threshold for living in the paradox of practicing being surprised.[10] We need both spiritual practices and community in order to have a vibrant Christian spirituality.

> I want us to look at two bad habits of westernized Christians: the bad habit of personal religion, and the bad habit of thinking of self as God.

As Schmemann learned, what is needed in contemporary forms of Christian spirituality are communal practices of God's presence that inform how a person moves beyond Western definitions of spirituality that are often self-contained with little understanding of relationality. To move spiritual discourse beyond a Western infatuation with self is a most difficult task because the impetus to be spiritual in Western cultures comes from the so-called personal, erotic, or subjective sphere. For example, the dominant question in the region of the United States known as the Bible Belt is, "Do you have a personal relationship with Jesus?" But how many times does someone ask us, "Do you have a communal relationship with Jesus?" Moreover, how many times are we asked this communal question as if it had the same soteriological or salvific importance as the personal salvation question? In other words, does a communal relationship with Jesus matter just as much as a personal relationship with Jesus in matters of salvation? For most people in our culture, I suspect, the answer is no. Western Christian conceptions of salvation are normally confined to one's own personal relationship with Jesus. Therefore, Western understandings of the Christian life are usually about one's own personal journey.

> What is needed in contemporary forms of Christian spirituality are communal practices that lead beyond Western definitions of spirituality that are often self-contained with little understanding of relationality.

My task, however, is to show how the Christian life is personal only to the extent that it is practiced communally. Personal spirituality is recognizable and intelligible only to the extent that it is relational and relates fully to one's neighbor. And who is one's neighbor? The answer to this question is only discovered, as taught by Jesus, through practices of hospitality and sacrifice. In other words, Jesus teaches a specific kind of spirituality through the story of the Good Samaritan—that one cannot know who is neighborly unless such a relationship is demonstrated through practices such as rescuing and feeding the dying (Luke 10:29–37; Matt. 22:34–40; Mark 12:28–34). In the same way that we must practice being good neighbors, so too must we discover the obvious definition of Christian life through spiritual practices such as prayer, fasting, confession, and reconciliation, in which we recognize God's presence on earth as it is in heaven. Through such practices, Christian life affects the world politically, as seen for example through the spiritual work of Archbishop Tutu on the Truth and Reconciliation Commission in South Africa. In other words, Christian life is obvious in its practices. One sees it in its demonstration in the same way that one understands the truth of the joke: What do you get when you cross a river?—Wet feet.

The Bad Habit of Thinking of Self as God

The problem of practicing the Christian life, however, is that God is not always obvious. We often even see our own misinformed actions as providential and part of divine justice. By doing so, we create a scandal of the cross and stumble over God, nailing God to a cross and thinking that we are doing good. Unfortunately, we still mistake God in our midst for an enemy. This lack of discernment of God's presence correlates to a lack of ongoing spiritual practices that prepare us to meet and recognize our Maker. What these ongoing spiritual practices entail are the tasks of prayer in which trust and faithfulness build a Christian character able to withstand the truth of God. In a Western cultural definition of spirituality, however, many people practice a form of spirituality in which there is no conceptual space to confess that there is someone who is and should be greater than one's self. As a result, the truth of God that scared most biblical characters rarely frightens Western Christians who easily define God through a personal relationship.

Further still, in Western Christian spirituality there seems to be only space enough for the fulfillment of personal salvation. For example, the concept of heaven in the Western world is only intelligible as some form of individual, existential bliss. If one thinks hard, however, how could anyone be content in heaven, fully cognizant of others in hell? This question is not often asked in the Western world with its disconnect between personal salvation and communal salvation. Traditions such as the Eastern Orthodox and the Anglican Church in Africa are much more in touch with how complete bliss, joy, and heaven are only intelligible through communal awareness. With the kind of Christian spirituality that most of us practice in the Western world, I would dare say that we worship ourselves more than God. What we often call a personal relationship with God is shorthand for my own version of God. Instead of seeing ourselves made in the image of God, we, like the great sociologist Emil Durkheim, see that God is made in our image. Someone described such a God as an individualistic deity contemplating suicide at the edge of the universe.

In the West, especially from the time of the Enlightenment, the self has been understood as a distinct individual, with unique value and distinct rights. Persons have the right to make something of their lives, to take responsibility for their life direction, to use their talents and gifts to the full. Such emphasis puts supreme value on the right of self-determination, self-achievement, self-satisfaction. Such personal responsibility for the shaping of one's life is a good, and flows from the Judeo-Christian understanding of the dignity and worth of each human being. What is weak in this worldview is the bonding of the person with the community. Especially in this century and particularly in North American culture, individual self-determination has been exalted over the needs of the community, giving rise to individualism, which found its most skewed expression in the "Me Generation"—my needs above all else. This cultural value has profoundly influenced all facets of life, including politics, economics, and religion.

When a Western person, formed in this worldview of the importance of the person and her or his rights and responsibilities, meets, for example, an African person in the Christian life, they meet someone whose experience of the self is distinctly different. The African individual does not exist apart from the community. The classic phrasing of this intrinsic relationship was started by John Mbiti and carried on by Desmond Tutu; I call it an *ubuntu* sensibility, an African concept meaning that we form our own identities only in relation to others. In contrast to the philosopher Descartes's characteristically Western assertion, "I think, therefore I am," Africans would say, "I am, because we are; and since we are, therefore I am." The person is part of the whole, and one's identity flows from the corporate experience and never in isolation from it, since it is the community

> The African individual does not exist apart from the community.

which defines who one is and who one can become. The uniqueness of each person is affirmed and acknowledged, but one's own individuality and freedom are always balanced by the destiny of the community.[11]

Understanding the world is also distinctly different in Western and African worldviews. Much has been written recently about Western abuse of the environment as stemming from a perversion of the biblical mandate to "fill the earth and subdue it" (Gen. 1:28) and about the need for a spirituality that will form persons and communities in care and concern for our earth. The person stands over and against creation in all its dimensions, using and abusing it for one's own ends. Key to this Western worldview is the separation of the person and the community from the world of nature. Domination best describes this stance in which nature is made the servant of human needs, wants, and desires. The exaltation of the uniqueness and goodness of humanity is seen in discontinuity with the goodness and value of all the other facets of creation. Humanity and the rest of creation are in a relationship of ruler to servant, rather than of interdependence which acknowledges the truth that the earth provides humanity its basic sustenance—air, water, food, and so forth—and thus the human community is called to steward it faithfully and carefully.

The African experience is again decidedly and strikingly different. In the same way as we have seen that the person is vitally and organically bonded in community with others, so also is this union extended to all of creation. The African worldview shares with the Judeo-Christian tradition the understanding of God as creator of the material universe. Nature in all its dimensions is alive with the presence of God, and communities and their members experience God in and through creation. In contrast to the Western mode of domination, the African strives to live in harmony with nature. The various facets of creation—the sky, the sun and moon, mountains, forests and trees, rivers and water, plants and animals—all have at least implicit religious meaning and often explicit significance. All of these elements of the African view of the world and creation thus are distinctly different in many ways from the Western perspective. The African person in the situation of Christian life brings to this sacred relationship the experience of harmony with nature, a lack of domineering attitude toward it, a sense of the invisible world alive in the visible, and a strong conviction that various spirits can communicate with the person and the community. These challenge Western perceptions of the secularity of the universe, a sense of control over it, and great skepticism about the existence of any kind of spirits or similar beings with power to influence human behavior (notwithstanding the contributions of modern psychology, which has shown us that we are far more complex than we had dreamed).

Different also are Western and African understandings of religion and its relation to life. During the past several hundred years, religious belief, practice, and experience have become for Western persons one option among others and not a core way to organize life experience. For those who remain believers, too often religion is a separate compartment of life, with various religious duties to be "done" but with little influence on ordinary life other than the vague desire to do good and respect the rights of others. One attends church on Sunday and then gives little thought to religious commitment the rest of the week. Organized religion in the West has seen its influence decline in many ways as this dichotomy between the religious and the secular has become more pronounced. Even the rise of various fundamentalist groups has not challenged this approach, since personal faith is seen as operative in a fairly narrow, restricted sphere with little social or political implication for the wider setting.

The Western person brings much of this perspective to the understanding of the Christian life when the matter to be discussed is only that which is "religious." Prayer experience is important, but one's involvement with a local political party is not. Any approach or suggestion that reinforces this dichotomy in Western experience between "religion" and "life" widens the gap. Africans who become Christian or Muslim or followers of any other world religion look for an experience of religion that also encompasses their whole life: language, thought patterns, social relationships, attitudes, values, desires, fears. It is not enough to "do religious things" regularly, since their desire is for a religious worldview that will fill the world with meaning and be especially sustaining in times of fear and crisis.

In the Christian life, the African person brings her or his desire that experience of God be found in every facet of life without exception. Western persons, formed in the pattern of religion as one part of life, can be disconcerted by the wholistic view presented by their African brothers or sisters, but they have much to gain from it. It is clear, then, what misunderstandings can easily occur in the Christian life when Western persons urge Africans to assume a degree of self-consciousness and self-assertion for which their cultural experience has not prepared them. At the same time, the distinct values of both worldviews can enrich each other, the Western person learning the value of community experience as formative of the person, and the African coming to a deeper awareness of her or his unique personal goodness and worth.

In the Christian life, the African person brings her or his desire that experience of God be found in every facet of life without exception.

In the desert tradition of early Christian monks, the African desert father Abba Moses tells the story of a disciple who wanted salvation that he could achieve on his own through asceticism. Abba Moses instructed the disciple first to go and curse the dead. The disciple did as he was told. "You are the most vile of souls!" the disciple proclaimed in a graveyard. Upon the disciple's return, Abba Moses asked, "What did they say back to you?" The disciple said, "There was no reply." Abba Moses then instructed the disciple to return, this time to praise the dead. "You are the most beatific of souls!" the disciple proclaimed in the graveyard. Upon the disciple's return, Abba Moses asked, "What did they say back to you?" The disciple said, "Not a word. They were as silent as before." Abba Moses said to the disciple, "In order to be saved, you must be like the dead, beyond cursing and praise."

Abba Moses teaches us Christian disciples that our pursuit of the meaning of the Christian life that disregards the living, that disregards the other, is not life. In order to be like the Christian image Abba Moses leaves us with, the Christian disciple must mature beyond the infantile conceptualization of "me" and "mine" into the contemplation of the communal ways of knowing God. There is an African proverb: The reason that two antelopes walk together is so that one might blow the dust from the other's eyes. The antelopes can see clearly only because, in community, they help each other. From this communal understanding of spirituality we can better understand the following assumptions of the Christian spiritual life.

1. Christian life makes real the revelation that life is a gift.
2. Christian life eventually reveals the mystery that God is the one praying in us.
3. Christian life makes real the axiom that all manner of things will be made well.
4. Christian life informs us of the truth that all that is concealed will be revealed, that nothing can be hidden from God.
5. Christian life reveals that all of life contains the possibility of meeting God.
6. Christian life reveals that Scripture and tradition are privileged mediators of God's presence; however, God is not contained by any single word, image, idea, or experience.
7. Christian life reveals that as one's relationship with God changes, so will its expression in prayer. Persons need to continue to grow in the presence of God.
8. Christian life reveals how God turns us into friends through the mystery of mutuality between the Creator and the creature.
9. Christian life reveals that any form of spirituality must always serve relationality and be reflective of it.
10. Ultimately, the Christian life reveals that the one who prays is a symphonic voice, a voice that cannot be heard without the relation of other voices.

QUESTIONS FOR REFLECTION AND DISCUSSION

1. What divided Augustine and Pelagius? The Arminians and the Synod of Dort? What were the arguments on each side?

2. How would traditional Catholicism, Reformers like Luther or Calvin, and Wesley each think about the relation of justification and sanctification? Again, what are the arguments for each position?

3. Charry argues that early Christianity turned the values of Greco-Roman culture upside down. Is that true for our culture as well?

4. Given the challenge of being a Christian, why did it so grow in popularity? Do those reasons still work today?

5. What does it mean to say that we are "not our own"?

6. What are the advantages and disadvantages of marriage and singleness for Christians?

7. Why is love the virtue that never ends?

8. Battle quotes Bishop Tutu: "God's friends are distinguished by the fact that they suffer." Is that true?

9. Why is community essential to being a Christian?

10. How might a spiritual director be helpful in cultivating discernment?

11. Are the "bad habits" Battle lists particularly characteristic of the modern West? Are those of us who live in this culture just stuck with them, or can we work to overcome them?

FOR FURTHER READING

Bass, Dorothy C., ed. *Practicing Our Faith.* San Francisco: Jossey-Bass, 1998.

Battle, Michael. *Reconciliation: The Ubuntu Theology of Desmond Tutu.* Cleveland: Pilgrim Press, 1997.

Boff, Leonardo. *Liberating Grace.* Trans. John Drury. Maryknoll, N.Y.: Orbis Books, 1979.

Bondi, Roberta C. *Memories of God.* Nashville: Abingdon Press, 1995.

Bonhoeffer, Dietrich. *The Cost of Discipleship.* Rev. ed. Trans. Reginald H. Fuller. New York: Macmillan, 1966.

Brown, Robert McAfee. *Spirituality and Liberation.* Philadelphia: Westminster Press, 1988.

Carter, Harold A. *The Prayer Tradition of Black People.* Valley Forge, Pa.: Judson Press, 1976.

Charry, Ellen T. *By the Renewing of Your Minds.* New York: Oxford University Press, 1997.

Glaser, Chris. *Come Home! Realizing Spirituality and Community as Gay Men and Lesbians.* San Francisco: Harper and Row, 1990.

Jones, L. Gregory. *Embodying Forgiveness.* Grand Rapids: Wm. B. Eerdmans, 1995.

Lossky, Vladimir. *The Mystical Theology of the Eastern Church.* Trans. members of the Fellowship of St. Alban and St. Sergius. London: James Clarke, 1957.

Miles, Margaret R. *Practicing Christianity.* New York: Crossroads, 1988.

Pannenberg, Wolfhart. *Christian Spirituality.* Philadelphia: Westminster Press, 1983.

Rice, Howard L. *Reformed Spirituality.* Louisville, Ky.: Westminster/John Knox Press, 1991.

Thompson, Marjorie J. *Soul Feast.* Louisville, Ky.: Westminster John Knox Press, 1995.

Thurman, Howard. *Disciplines of the Heart.* New York: Harper & Row, 1963.

Chapter 8

What About *Them?*

Christians and Non-Christians

Throughout most of Christian history, most Christians gave little thought to the status or fate of non-Christians. Christians lived surrounded almost entirely by other Christians, and news from other parts of the world arrived very late if at all. Buddhism or Hinduism were just not topics they considered.

There were of course exceptions to this generalization. In the church's first few centuries, it moved as a minority into a world of diverse religions and philosophies. Christians generally labeled the gods of pagan religions as "demons" (the word *daimon* had previously just meant "spirit," without any negative connotations) and ridiculed their squabbles and love affairs. But they often quite boldly appropriated the categories of classical philosophies and identified their favorite philosophers as precursors of Christian faith. "Those who have lived by reason are Christians," Justin Martyr declared in the second century, "even though they have been considered atheists."[1]

Once Christianity became the dominant religion of Europe, however, the occasions for talking with with non-Christians inevitably decreased. Christians sometimes had conversations with Jews in their midst, and there was sometimes religious discussion as well as violence and tension across the shifting boundary between the Christian and Islamic worlds. Thomas Aquinas again and again quotes not only the pagan philosopher Aristotle but "Rabbi Moses" (the Jewish philosopher Moses Maimonides) and the famous Islamic commentators on Aristotle's philosophy with admiration and respect.

Still, the experience of having a Muslim mosque down the street, a Hindu doctor, or a Buddhist son-in-law, common enough for Christians even in American small towns and suburbs these days, is unparalleled in most of Christian history. Many European Christians live in the midst of even greater diversity, and Christians in Asia and parts of Africa find themselves a minority in the midst of adherents of other religions. As a result, our attitudes to non-Christians are on the theological agenda in new ways. It is harder simply to write non-Christians off as destined to hell or think of them purely as the objects of distant missionary work if they live next door and we have known them all our lives, but Christians are still sorting through alternative beliefs.

CHRISTIANS AND JEWS

Of course, the one exception to the past distance between Christians and non-Christians concerns the Jews, and there the record is dreadful. For centuries, Jews were identified as the killers of Christ, suspected of spreading the plague, and accused of killing Christian children for use in Jewish rituals. In 305 the Council of Elvira, in Spain, prohibited marriage between Christians and Jews and forbade Christians from eating with Jews. Other councils ordered Jews not to appear in public during Holy Week and permitted Christians to kidnap Jewish children in order to raise them as Christians. In 1215 the Fourth Lateran Council directed Jews to dress in distinctive fashion so that they could be easily recognized.[2]

Early in his career, Luther thought that the Jews had failed to convert only because of the corruption of the church. Once Christians had reformed, the Jews would see the truth of the gospel. When this failed to happen, and as he grew older and more embittered on any number of topics, he spoke ever more negatively of the Jews, culminating in a quite horrible pamphlet, "On the Jews and Their Lies," in which he advises

> First, to set fire to their synagogues or schools and to bury and cover with dirt whatever will not burn, so that no man will ever again see a stone or cinder of them. . . . Second, I advise that their houses also be razed and destroyed. . . . Third, I advise that all their prayer books and Talmudic writings, in which such idolatry, lies, cursing, and blasphemy are taught, be taken from them. Fourth, I advise that their rabbis be forbidden to teach henceforth on pain of loss of life and limb.[3]

Some factors qualify or partially explain such horrors. In the first century, Christians were a small minority threatened with persecution. Judaism was an officially approved religion in the Roman Empire; Christianity was not. If Christians claimed to be Jews, or even claimed to represent the true strand of Judaism, and Jews (understandably) rejected this view, they left the Christians open to arrest. The New Testament preserves the fears and defensiveness of that time, and its polemics were often applied unreflectively in very different times when Christians held most of the power rather than being a persecuted minority. At least through most of the Middle Ages, moreover, the worst of anti-Jewish feeling and the murdering of Jews seems to have risen up from the lower class; the church hierarchy, if anything, usually tried to keep it in check. The worst form of anti-Semitism, Nazism, had religious roots in neopaganism and was finally opposed to Christianity as well as Judaism. Nevertheless, it is deeply distressing to see that nearly every Nazi action had a Christian precedent.

> Some factors qualify or partially explain the horrors of Christian anti-Semitism. Nevertheless, it is deeply distressing to see that nearly every Nazi action had a Christian precedent.

Partly in reaction to the horrors of the Holocaust, Christian communities at least since the 1960s have condemned anti-Semitism. The Second Vatican Council deplored "the hatred, persecutions, and displays of anti-Semitism directed against the Jews at any time and from any source," and, citing a metaphor from Romans 11, insisted that the church cannot forget "that she draws sustenance from the root of that good olive tree onto which have been grafted the wild olive branches of the Gentiles."[4] In 1987 the Presbyterian Church (U.S.A.) acknowledged "in repentence the church's long and deep complicity in the proliferation of anti-Jewish attitudes," repudiated such teaching, and affirmed "that the church elected in Jesus Christ has been engrafted into the people of God established by the covenant with Abraham, Isaac and Jacob. Therefore, Christians have not replaced Jews."[5]

The idea that Christians have replaced Jews as God's chosen people is called *supersessionism,* and a good bit of recent theology is determined to avoid it. After all, God made promises to the descendants of Abraham, and God does not break promises. Thus, God remains in covenant with the Jewish people. Christian theologians therefore need to explain the role of Christ in salvation in a way compatible with God's ongoing relation with Jews.

Another issue with which theologians continue to struggle concerns the New Testament. As already noted, much of it was written in a time when Christians felt threatened by Judaism, and it reflects that situation in passages that do seem to be anti-Jewish. Can we write such passages off as the unfortunate products of their particular historical circumstances, or do we have to find a different way of interpreting them? What implications do the way we interpret these texts have for Christian understanding of biblical authority generally? Thus, questions about Christian-Jewish relations lead back to issues about authority discussed in chapter 1.

THEOLOGY OF RELIGIONS

The special relations between Christianity and Judaism, as well as the shadow of the Holocaust, make Christian understanding of Judaism a special case. But an analogous pattern of increased openness has emerged in Christian attitudes to other religions, and it is this issue that the two essays in this chapter address.[6]

The classic position of Christian theology, now often called *exclusivism,* was that those who remained non-Christians would all end up in hell. "No one remaining outside the Catholic Church, not just pagans, but also Jews or heretics or schismatics, can become partakers of eternal life," the Council of Florence declared in the fifteenth century, "but they will go to the 'everlasting fire which was prepared for the devil and his angels' [Matt. 25:41] unless before the end of life they are joined to the Church."[7] Meeting in Chicago in 1960, a group of evangelical Protestants, the Congress on World Missions, lamented that, "In the years since the war [World War II], more than a billion souls have passed into eternity, and more than half of these went to the torment of hell fire without ever learning of Jesus Christ."[8] Non-Christians, the assumption went, cannot be saved.

Attitudes toward non-Christians	Knitter's terminology
Exclusivism	Replacement model
Inclusivism	Fulfillment model
Pluralism	Multiplicity model

An alternative view, *inclusivism,* holds that non-Christians can achieve salvation by somehow believing and acting as Christians without realizing it, or by converting to faith in Christ at the moment of death or even after death. In his *Divine Comedy,* written in the early fourteenth century, Dante has the Trojan hero Ripheus and the Roman emperor Trajan both miraculously converted to Christianity—Ripheus by angelic intervention centuries before Christ, and Trajan by being raised in order to hear the gospel and be converted. If this can happen for one or two, Dante writes, how can any human being judge whether more?[9] Dante thus left the door to heaven open just a crack for non-Christians.

More recently, it has opened further. The non-Christian who has not heard of the gospel but is longing for something like it can be considered, in the term made popular by the Catholic theologian Karl Rahner, an "anonymous Christian," someone who is in important ways a Christian, and therefore saved, without knowing it.[10] In a letter to the archbishop of Boston, the Holy Office wrote from Rome in 1949:

> To gain eternal salvation it is not always required that a person be incorporated in fact as a member of the Church, but it is required that he belong to it at least in desire and longing. It is not always necessary that this desire be explicit. . . . When a man is invincibly ignorant [that is, ignorant through no fault of one's own] God also accepts an implicit desire so called because

> it is contained in the good disposition of soul by which a man wants his will to be conformed to God's will.[11]

Inclusivists who want to preserve the need for explicit Christian faith in order to be saved sometimes introduce the possibility of a mysterious confrontation with the gospel at the moment of death, in which people who have until then been non-Christians can hear, believe, and be saved.

Other theologians, like the Protestant John Hick and the Catholic Paul Knitter, have taken a further step from inclusivism to *pluralism.* They maintain that there is more than one way to achieve the goal to which human life should aim. Hindus or Buddhists or Muslims can achieve salvation or some equivalent goal, not by turning out to be anonymous Christians, but simply by being good Hindus, Buddhists, or Muslims.

In his essay for this chapter, J. A. DiNoia argues that pluralism papers over the important differences among the world's religions. Pluralists, DiNoia argues, are apt to claim that all religions are following different paths to the same goal and using different terms to point to the same reality. Therefore, the path one chooses does not ultimately matter, since one can reach the same place by multiple routes. But different religions are not, DiNoia insists, trying to get to the same place. Buddhists seek nirvana—the extinction of desires and attachments. Christians hope for communion with the triune God. By no stretch of the imagination are these different names for the same thing. DiNoia maintains, therefore, that Christians should unapologetically offer to everyone the hope they know in Christ and not assume that others already have the same hope via a different route.

Conscious of critics like DiNoia, Knitter offers in his essay a more sophisticated version of pluralism, one which acknowledges that Christianity has a unique contribution to make to the conversation among the world's religions. Knitter is clearly not claiming that all religions say more or less the same thing. On the other hand, he leaves open the question of whether "what constitutes Jesus' distinctiveness is also found in others" and claims that Jesus' work is to reveal the "universal active presence of God" which was already there had we been able to see it or trust in it. DiNoia would suspect that the problems of pluralism remain: Universal religiousness continues to lie behind what is presented as distinctively Christian.

Knitter, at the same time, criticizes positions like DiNoia's (which he labels "the acceptance model") for cutting off the possibility of real dialogue among religions. On the acceptance model, he says, different religions are simply pursuing different goals, about different things, as unlikely to come into conflict (or learn from each other) as the study of birds and the study of Hungarian. It is a challenge DiNoia would have to answer by elaborating what he means by saying that different religions, with their different goals, nevertheless all offer "comprehensive patterns of life." If offered as the ultimate goals for our existence, maybe they do come into conflict; at least it seems we would have to choose among them.

Both these authors want to encourage interreligious dialogue. Neither wants to consign all non-Christians to hell. Neither thinks that all religions are saying the same thing. They are both operating on the cutting edge of complex debates in which it is not easy to maintain a variety of potentially conflicting concerns. Christian theologians have recognized those conflicts for a long time. Christians, John Calvin once remarked, ought to pray for all "who dwell on earth. For what God has determined concerning them is beyond our knowing except that it is no less godly than humane to wish and hope the best for them."[12]

PAUL F. KNITTER

Over the past decades, for many Christians (particularly Western Christianity), there has been a slow but marked shift in the way Christians view the "them" in the title of this chapter. Especially in mainline churches, pastors are noting a change in the attitudes of their congregations toward persons of other religions: The "alien others," we might say, are becoming the "neighborly others."

A SHIFT FROM ALIEN TO NEIGHBOR

Throughout most of church history, "religious others" have been for Christians "alien others." Those who walked Hindu, Buddhist, Confucian, Taoist, even Jewish, and especially Islamic paths were generally felt to be strangers, often enemies, or competitors. They were aliens—feared, perhaps hated, always dangerous or suspect. If there was a more positive Christian relationship with them, it was based on the desire to try to convert them, for on their own paths, Christians assumed, they were moving away from God and toward eternal damnation. So to help them, one had to convert them.

Especially since the second half of the past century, such attitudes, both pastorally and theologically, have been changing. The theological shift occurred explicitly in the Second Vatican Council (1962–1965), but that was perhaps more an effect than a cause of what was already going on within the Christian communities.[1] Gradually, more and more Christians felt the need to get along with, respect, learn about, maybe even learn from Hindus and Buddhists and Muslims. What may have been the scowl Christians saw on the face of the religious other was turning to a smile. The question Christians began to ask themselves was not, "How do we get them into heaven?" but "How do we talk with them?"

Many factors contributed to this shift. Primarily, the world has become smaller. Not only do ideas move around more quickly and more clearly, but so do people. We live in an age of greater, smoother communication, information, migration. What has been happening religiously within our world and communities was captured way back in the 1960s by Wilfred Cantwell Smith, a pioneer of interfaith exploration, when he observed that now we no longer just read about Hindus or Muslims, but "we drink coffee with them personally as well." They live down the street, work in the same office, play with (maybe even marry!) our kids.[2]

Furthermore, centuries of missionary labors may have planted the Christian church on every continent, but these labors have not changed the basic contours of the religious map of the world. Some theologians, therefore, are drawing the tentative but unsettling conclusion that the many religions of the world are not "a matter of fact" but a "matter of principle." They just don't *happen* to be there—as the result of the vagaries or aberrations of history; they are *intended* to be there—intended by the one God of history. In some way, the religions are playing a role in what Christians call the history of salvation.[3] God seems to love diversity, not only among plants and animals and peoples, but also among religions. If this is so, Christians have to figure out what the role of these other religions is. That is a theological question. It is a question that can be answered not only by consulting the Bible but also through knowing more about these religions. One of the best ways to understand them is by talking with their followers. Dialogue becomes a theological requirement.

> We no longer just read about Hindus or Muslims, observed Wilfred Cantwell Smith, but "we drink coffee with them personally as well."

From the Age of Monologue to the Age of Dialogue

The necessity of interreligious dialogue becomes all the more pressing when we consider, and feel overwhelmed by, the state of our world. What I am trying to get at is best expressed in the well-known announcement of Hans Küng: There will be no peace among nations unless there is peace among religions. And there will be no peace among religions unless there is greater, more effective dialogue among them.[4] What Küng is urging goes beyond tolerance between the religions. Certainly there can be no doubt that the religious communities need to tolerate each other—that is, respect each other, let each other be. But tolerance, as urgent as it is, is not enough. Religious people also have to talk with each other, and in a way that will lead not only to greater understanding and respect but also to cooperation. Küng is calling for an interreligious dialogue that will facilitate not only interreligious tolerance but interreligious action—not only the ability to live together but the ability to work together in order to change this world.

For Christians, as well as for other religious believers, dialogue is thus becoming an ethical imperative. Humanity today faces a broad, menacing array of ethical problems that threaten us all, and that therefore can be resolved only through the collaboration of all nations and cultures. These include the violence of material poverty, the violence of economic injustice, the violence of some people taking advantage of other people on the basis of race or of gender, and especially the violence that touches everyone everywhere—the depletion and destruction of the life-sustaining ability of the ecosystem. And looming over (or under) this list is the violence and warfare and terrorism that is justified and fortified in the name of religions. The analysis and resolution of such life-threatening ethical challenges cannot come piecemeal, from any one nation or culture; rather, they require shared concern and shared action among all peoples based on some kind of shared ethical values.

Thus, the growing discussion about the need for a global ethic—fundamental, shared values, principles, and commitments that have to be elaborated by all peoples and cultures in order to be acted on by all peoples and cultures. Such a global ethic, if it is to be realized at all, will be the work of politicians, economists, political scientists, philosophers, grassroots organizations. Many are claiming, however, that it must also involve the work and contribution of religious communities. For great numbers of the world's population, the values that will ground a global ethic and the energy and resolve actually to live by it will come from their religious faith and traditions. So the religions of the world must make their contribution to addressing the common ethical challenges facing humanity, and they must do so individually by looking into the treasures of their own tradition and collectively through dialogue and cooperation with other traditions.

> The religions of the world must make their contribution to addressing the common ethical challenges facing humanity, and they must do so individually by looking into the treasures of their own tradition and collectively through dialogue and cooperation with other traditions.

Though the phrasing may sound somewhat grandiose, we can say that Christians, as well as all religious persons, are today being called to move from an age of monologue to an age of dialogue. *Age of monologue* describes most of the religious history of humankind—the centuries when for the most part religions were born in their own cultural neighborhood and felt they could do perfectly well by staying there and talking only among themselves. Good fences made for good neighbors; when those fences were not well maintained or well observed, problems resulted, even warfare. This age of monologue is, as I have suggested, starting to crumble, or at least come under questioning. Yes, religious fundamentalism is growing among various traditions; and a synonym for *fundamentalist* might well be *monologuer.* But this growth of fundamentalism, and the excesses of intolerance and violence to which it can lead, is itself becoming one of the strongest motives behind the call for dialogue.

Whether it is because of the dangers of a fundamentalist exploitation of religion, or because our religious neighbors are moving closer to our neighborhood and we are getting to know and even to like them, or because the kinds of problems facing our broader city or world require the cooperation of all the neighborhoods—for a variety of reasons Christians, with other believers, feel that the new millennium needs to be the threshold of a new age of dialogue. In an age of dialogue, one must be religious interreligiously. That brings us to the real challenge of interreligious dialogue.

The Challenge of Dialogue: Commitment and Openness

Real interreligious dialogue is not easy. And it can be dangerous. If we understand dialogue to be more than just chit-chat in which we talk mainly to be nice to each other, and more than just an exchange of information so that we can understand each other better—if dialogue is going to be a real conversation in which we both talk and listen, in which we both speak our mind and open our mind, in which we both try to persuade the other of the truth and value of what we believe and at the same time are ready to be so persuaded by what our partner holds to be true and valuable—then dialogue is going to make both difficult and risky demands. Dialogue is a complex movement of "both-and"—both speaking and listening, both teaching and learning, both clarity and questioning, both firmness and suppleness.

All these duets can be summarized in the polarity of commitment and openness. In a genuine religious dialogue (really, in any conversation where people speak out of different viewpoints), one has to be firm in what one believes, persuaded that what has been true and good for oneself might be the same for others. This enables one to have something to contribute to the dialogue. And yet, if the conversation is going to be two-way, if there are going to be equal rights for all the participants in the dialogue, then one has also to be open to listening to and possibly learning from the commitments of the dialogue partner. And "learning from" can mean changing one's mind and admitting mistakes.

For Christians, this means that we have to be fully committed to Christ and his gospel and at the same time genuinely open to what God may be trying to tell us through other religions. But for most Christians, this is something new, maybe something bewildering or threatening. Just how does one balance such commitment to Christ and openness to others? Is it even possible? Wouldn't it be something like asking married people to be committed to their spouses and at the same time open to other potential spouses? For Christians in the dialogue, openness to other religions might lead them to lessen or even lose their own allegiance to Jesus and the gospel.

> Right now, we Christians do not have the equipment to manage such a balancing of commitment and openness in an authentic religious dialogue.

Just because something is difficult or dangerous does not mean that it is not necessary. Indeed, for many—a growing number it seems—dialogue with persons of other faiths, despite the complexities and risks, has become an ethical imperative. One might even say that one of the most urgent and daunting challenges (though certainly not the only one) facing Christians as they step into the new millennium is how to carry on a dialogue with other religions that will, first of all, help all religions to work together in, as Küng puts it, "global responsibility" for the ethical challenges facing humankind. Such a dialogue will also enable Christians to understand themselves and their own convictions better in the light of so many other thriving religious faiths. Such a dialogue will require the complex balancing of commitment and openness. Can Christians do it?

Right now, it seems to me, we Christians do not have the equipment to manage such a balancing of commitment and openness in an authentic religious dialogue. That is, we do not have the theological tools. We are in a situation with analogies throughout church history where our practice (or the need for practice) has outstripped our theory.[5] (That is really the way Christian understanding or theology grows—by trying to accompany, help, or catch up with Christian living.) We do not have the theological clarity and guidance for carrying out an interreligious dialogue that would balance commitment and openness. In the words of Jacques Dupuis, one of the most knowledgeable and careful Christian theologians of religions, such a dialogue-sustaining theology will require a qualitative shift in the way Christians understand other religions.[6] That shift has not yet happened. Therefore, a Christian theology of religions that is informed by and can support a Christian dialogue with religions is a work in progress. A brief, hasty review of contemporary theologies of religions will, I think, indicate progress made and still needed.

CURRENT THEOLOGIES OF RELIGION DO NOT MEET THE CHALLENGE OF COMMITMENT AND OPENNESS

Classifying is always risky. Fitting things into neat categories often means stuffing them into boxes where they do not quite fit (or leaving any misfits on the floor). Still, in an effort to bring some order into the array of current Christian attitudes toward other religions, let me offer a lineup of categories or models that, I think, covers most of the theological terrain. Most Christian theologians writing about other religions may move between these models, but each of them, I venture to say, spends more time in one than in the others.[7] I will give a thumbnail sketch of each and then comment on how well it balances the commitment and openness needed for dialogue.

The Replacement Model

For Christians who follow this model, the best way to relate to persons of other religious paths is to share the good news of Jesus with them and hope that this will bring them into the community of Jesus' followers. This attitude is found especially among the fundamentalist and evangelical churches, though much of its theology was laid out, powerfully and prophetically, by Karl Barth. For these

Christians there are certain beliefs, given in God's revelation through Jesus, that are simply nonnegotiable. Among these are the announcement to all the world that God has given hope and the possibility of well-being (salvation) through the life, death, and resurrection of Jesus the Christ—here and nowhere else. As stated so clearly in 1 Timothy 2:4–5, God does not discriminate in God's love and "desires everyone to be saved," but God offers this saving love through the "one mediator between God and humankind, Christ Jesus." In other religions we may find many worthwhile, even necessary, questions as to how humans can get their act together, but the only real, effective answer is given in the message and the person of Jesus. While Christians will always love persons of other religions and try to talk with them, they will show their love by attempting to replace their previous religious beliefs and practices with baptism into Christian life and practice.

Clearly this model meets all the requirements of the commitment necessary for dialogue, but it lags in openness. How can one be open to the possibility of learning from others when one already has the fullness of God's truth? How can one really cooperate with other religions in trying to solve the ethical, global issues of the day when one is convinced that the one and only solution has already been given in Jesus? Admittedly, Christians who hold to this replacement model see no need for dialogue and feel no uneasiness in announcing to Buddhists or Muslims that without embracing Jesus they cannot be saved.[8] But for those followers of Jesus who feel the imperative of dialogue, this model, though it offers a good example of commitment, does not work.

The Fulfillment Model

This model came into clear focus, especially for Catholics but also for Protestants, when the Second Vatican Council tried to lay the theological groundwork for a more positive attitude toward, and therefore a real dialogue with, members of other religions. For the first time, in formal, official statements of a Christian church, Christians publicly recognized that there is much that is "true and holy" in other religions, that they contain "truth and grace . . . as a sort of secret presence of God," that God is revealing, perhaps saving, through them, and that therefore Christians are "exhorted . . . prudently and lovingly . . . to dialogue and collaborate" with these religions.[9] What, as it were, burst onto the Christian world in Vatican II has to a great extent been endorsed and developed and become a consensus among many members and theologians of the so-called mainline churches—that the God revealed by Jesus cannot be confined to the Christian churches.

For the fulfillment model, what is the ultimate purpose of dialogue? The answer is determined by the same nonnegotiable belief that guides the replacement model—Jesus as the one and only savior.

But what, for this model, is the ultimate purpose of dialogue? The answer is determined by the same nonnegotiable belief that guides the replacement model—Jesus as the one and only savior. Though representatives of this fulfillment model allow the effects of Jesus' death and resurrection to work outside the church, within and through other religions (cosmically or anonymously), they insist that it is only in Jesus that God's gift of saving love is actually offered or constituted, and therefore only in Jesus that God's truth is fully, finally, unsurpassably revealed. The final end of dialogue, therefore, must be fulfillment. In Jesus and in his church, all the truth and value and beauty of other religions are to find their completion. As the Second Vatican Council put it, "Whatever goodness or truth is found among them [the religions], it is considered by the Church as a preparation for the Gospel."[10]

With this model, how do commitment and openness balance out? Like the replacement model, this attitude weighs in heavily with commitment; at the same time, it provides possibilities of greater openness by strongly affirming the active presence of God in other religions. But is this openness sufficient to sustain a conversation in which both sides are really able not only to speak but to learn? If the value of Buddha is actually made possible by Jesus, if we Christians have the full and final Word of God, if therefore whatever truth might be found in Hinduism has to be already given in Christian revelation—how much can Christians really learn in the dialogue? How much can be added to what is already "full and final"?

The Mutuality Model

Spokespersons for this model try to make up for the deficiencies of openness that they find in the other models. For them, what is nonnegotiable is still open to new interpretations. And so they press their case that the witness of the New Testament and Christian tradition can, in this age of pressing dialogue, be so understood that Christians can proclaim Jesus to be *truly* Savior of the world (that is the nonnegotiable piece), but not the *only* Savior of the world. In other words, the saving role of Jesus remains universal—that is, meant for all peoples and not just for Christians—but this role is not exhaustive of what God is up to in the world. Therefore, just as Christians must continue to announce that Jesus and his message are necessary for humanity to understand and live what God intends for creation, so might other religious figures or revelations be equally necessary. (They say *might,* for it is only through dialogue that they can find out.) This is not to say that therefore there are no differences between the religions, or that they are all essentially saying the same thing, or that every religious belief is equally valid or effective in revealing God's

> Clearly there is greater openness in the mutuality model. But has it just tipped the scales in the opposite direction? Openness seems to outweigh commitment.

truth. The differences between the religions are real, they are often stark, and they matter. Differences constitute the stuff of dialogue.[11]

Clearly there is greater openness in this model. But has it just tipped the scales in the opposite direction? Openness seems to outweigh commitment. If many religious figures can have universally relevant and equally valid messages, then doesn't Jesus end up as "one of the boys," one of many saviors? Is this really consistent with all the New Testament language that attributes to Jesus a specialness not found elsewhere? Is it consistent with the belief, in the New Testament and throughout Christian history, that Jesus was "Son of God" in a way that differs from how we are all sons and daughters of God? And if God saves in many ways, why should I choose one way over another? Why be a Christian rather than a Buddhist?

One can also ask advocates of the mutuality model whether they are as open to other religions as they think they are. If we really hold something to be true, if that truth colors our whole life, won't it also color what we see in other religions? Won't we always be viewing and understanding and evaluating the other religious person from the perspective of our own commitments? We will judge something to be true and good in another religion because it reflects or relates to our own truth and good. If it does not, we will judge it to be false or evil. How open is that, really?

The Acceptance Model

This model seeks to recognize and live with the complexity, even the well-nigh impossibility, of neatly balancing commitment and openness. Influenced by what is called postmodern consciousness (that is why this model is also termed a *postliberal* perspective), its proponents accept the reality that we are all living in our own cultural worlds, that the world we live in, like a pair of glasses, affects how we look at everything else, and that the many cultural-religious worlds that make up humanity are very, very different. In fact, they are so different that you really cannot "measure" one from the perspective of the other; each world or religion is incommensurable with the others.[12] Some advocates of this model suggest that each religion has its own goal, or ultimate end, that is different from the others. The religions are seeking, not *salvation* but *salvations*, each, as it were, going its own way to its own final destination, both in this world and in the next.[13] This means, more clearly and practically, that we all have our nonnegotiables; we all have our absolutes or full and final truths, and you really cannot judge one in the light of another. To try to do so will lead either to distorting the other so that it will fit yours, or reducing yours so it will make room for the other.

This model calls upon Christians, and all religious persons, simply to accept the other religions. Let them be. Be good neighbors to each other, but stay in your own backyard. Yes, talk to each other as much as you can, but let it be over your backyard fences. And if there is going to be any kind of a dialogue in which the partners search for deeper truth or a solution to common problems, know that it will really be a conversation in which each participant, for the most part, will be making an apology for, or promoting, his or her own truth. Dialogue is, and should be, a kind of holy competition, in which everyone lays out his or her own nonnegotiable truths as clearly and courteously as possible, in the hope that the deeper or higher truth will prevail.[14]

In the acceptance model, religions are actually confined to their own backyards. Each is securely committed to its own truth—but maybe too securely. Does this model really allow for any kind of real challenge to religious truth from the outside?

It seems that this acceptance model does achieve a neat balance of commitment and openness, recognizing that all religions make their own absolute or nonnegotiable truth claims and urging them all to respect each other for doing that. But, one may ask, does this understanding of religious pluralism, even when it urges dialogue as apologetics, go anywhere? It appears that the religions are actually confined to their own backyards. Each is securely committed to its own truth—but maybe too securely. Does this model really allow for any kind of real challenge to religious truth from the outside? Also, while each religion is open to and accepts the differences and the absolute claims of other religions, does this acceptance really end up as tolerance rather than as a dialogue in which both sides are ready not only to defend but to criticize their own positions? Can religions really search for truth and cooperation together when they are going in different directions, toward different salvations?

So where do we go from here? It seems that none of these models, by itself, does the job of aiding Christians to achieve the convergence of commitment and openness necessary to respond to the imperative of dialogue. As I said, the theology of religions and dialogue is a work in progress. To push along the progress, I would like to outline in the remainder of this chapter some helpful ingredients for a more dialogical Christian theology of religions. My intent is not to propose a new model but to identify the components of a more dialogical attitude toward other religions. These components or ingredients are drawn from traditional Christian beliefs. But these beliefs will be, I hope, reviewed, refurbished, reappropriated under the pressure of the dialogical imperative, of the need for a more balanced commitment to Christ and openness to others. What we are doing is carrying on the age-old job of theology—linking the signs of the times or the questions of the day with the original and ongoing witness of Scripture and tradition—and in the process, we hope, understanding both the questions and witness more deeply.

A theology that will promote openness without jeopardizing commitment needs to be confessional, kenotic, sacramental, and kingdom centered. A theology that will promote commitment without jeopardizing openness needs to be Christocentric, prophetic, and reconciliatory.

A THEOLOGY THAT WILL PROMOTE OPENNESS WITHOUT JEOPARDIZING COMMITMENT

Confessional

A theology of religions that can enable greater openness toward them (and greater openness on their part toward us) would do well to follow the advice of H. Richard Niebuhr, given in 1941. In relation to outsiders, he urged Christians to confess and state clearly what had been their experience of Jesus and the church, what they believed—without trying to "justify it as superior to all other faiths." Niebuhr felt that such claims of superiority "become more destructive of religion, Christianity, and the soul than any foe's attack can possibly be." So he counseled his fellow Christians to enter the conversation with others "by stating in simple, confessional form what has happened to us in our community, how we came to believe, how we reason about things, and what we see from our point of view."[15] Without any further talk of "only" or "superior," he continued, let the dialogue move forward. In this scenario, we would take seriously the recommendations of both the replacement and (especially) the acceptance model: Confess boldly what Jesus means for us, but leave out the comparisons or condemnations.

Such an approach will help Christians interpret and make better dialogical use of the abundance of exclusive language in the New Testament ("no other name," Acts. 4:12; "only begotten Son," John 1:18; "one mediator," 1 Tim. 2:5). This is confessional language, or, as one exegete puts it, love language. It is poetic, affective language, meant primarily to express the early community's excitement about, commitment to, and love for Jesus, as well as their conviction that he and his message could arouse the same feelings in all peoples. It is not philosophical or theological language, meant to define in clear, rock-hard concepts Jesus' ontological place in the scheme of things. Its purpose is to stir love for and commitment to Jesus, not to put down Buddha or Confucius. It is, one might say, meant for internal consumption only—to be used in our liturgies and prayers to express the knowledge and hope of our hearts, not to be flaunted in the face of those who find their hopes rooted in other stories.[16]

Kenotic

Ever since Paul, in Philippians 2:5–11, quoted and expanded a hymn already circulating in the Christian communities, *kenōsis,* or "self-emptying," has been at the heart of Christian understandings of Jesus. Jesus is who he was and is through *kenōsis.* Incarnation and redemption take place through a divine self-emptying in and through and as Jesus. Without *kenōsis,* there is no incarnation or redemption. But it is only recently that theologians, again under the pressure and guidance of their encounter with other religions, have begun to unpack the dialogical insights and demands of *kenōsis.* Self-emptying, we are realizing, is self-opening to, self-relating with others. Without others, without those who are different (as different as creatures are from the Creator), *kenōsis* is meaningless and, ultimately, impossible. Perhaps we can say that *kenōsis* is practically synonymous with dialogue. In other words, Jesus would not be the Christ and Christians would not be his followers without openness to and dialogue with those who are "other" to Christ and Christians. From such a kenotic Christology, we see that, indeed, commitment to Christ requires openness to others, for, as John B. Cobb, Jr., puts it, the kenotic Christ is "the way open to other ways."[17]

Kenōsis calls Christians to a greater openness than they have practiced in the past, for it requires an openness that, as proponents of the acceptance model admonish, truly respects the otherness of the other.

Kenōsis calls Christians to a greater openness than they have practiced in the past, for it requires an openness that, as proponents of the acceptance model admonish, truly respects the otherness of the other. That means that Christians will be wary of too hastily replacing, or including, or subsuming into their own understanding the differences that constitute the otherness of a Hindu or Buddhist or Muslim. For it is precisely in and through the ineradicable—yes, incommensurable—differences of the other that God preserves, reveals, and seeks to surprise us with God's own otherness. The mystery of God's otherness is contained and protected in the utter mystery of the face of the one who speaks a different language, practices a different culture, follows a different religion. To deny, or capture, or too hastily convert the otherness of the human other is to capture or control the otherness of God. That is idolatry.

A kenotic theology of religions still allows Christians to believe, as the replacement and fulfillment models insist, that Jesus brings the *fullness* of God's truth. But Jesus does this kenotically or dialogically, which means that we cannot grasp or unpack that fullness unless we are opening and emptying ourselves to others. We need others in order to understand who Jesus is and to delve ever more deeply (but never totally) into the depth of the riches that God offers in him. This means that the uniqueness of Jesus needs the uniqueness of others. But it also means that, as the mutuality model warns, we have to be very careful of privileging or ranking Jesus' uniqueness above all the others. *Kenōsis* and ranking are uncomfortable bedfellows. David Jensen, a pioneer in showing how the kenotic Christ is the dialogical Christ, makes this point strongly:

> The movement of *kenosis* is to de-center the 'self'—and anything else—from a privileged place of permanence. . . . The confession of the kenotic Christ cannot rest in pointing to the *figura* of Jesus Christ alone, above all others. . . . Christomonism—the proclamation of Jesus Christ at the expense of everything else—is a distortion of the life of discipleship and not its faithful execution. Indeed, conformity to Christ involves being claimed by others, and not claiming others as our own.[18]

Sacramental

The openness to others that the dialogical imperative requires of Christians (and that, as we just saw, a kenotic Christology makes possible) calls on Christians to recognize the real possibility that God saves in and through other religions. But such a recognition ricochets back on to traditional theology: If God saves through others, how does that fit with the way God saves through Jesus? That is the soteriological question that Christians have been trying to answer through the ages. In our present, religiously plural age, I would suggest we can achieve a dialogical understanding of Jesus' salvific role by drawing more on the Johannine writings of the New Testament and not just on Paul. This will enable us to develop a *sacramental* soteriology (Protestants prefer the term *representative*) in order to balance the traditional *constitutive* soteriology. To summarize (without, I hope, trivializing) the difference: As a sacramental cause, Jesus saves by *revealing;* as a constitutive cause, he saves by *fixing.*

As a sacramental cause of salvation, Jesus is understood along the lines of traditional sacramental theology: In his life, death, and resurrection he reveals what is already there in the world but not really available to us because we do not see it, or are not aware of it, or do not trust it.

As the constitutive cause of salvation, Jesus is generally understood to have effected something or done something which in some way repaired or bridged the rift between God and humanity. His death and resurrection are basically what he did, or underwent, and they were the act that opened the gates of heaven, or reconnected humans and God, and so constitute the possibility of salvation for everyone. As a sacramental cause of salvation, Jesus is understood along the lines of traditional sacramental theology: In his life, death, and resurrection he reveals what is already there in the world but not really available to us because we do not see it, or are not aware of it, or do not trust it—namely, the ever present, affirming, accepting, forgiving love of God. Jesus re-presents, embodies, symbolizes the universal, active presence of God—but he does so in a way through which that Divine Presence or Spirit can transform our lives in a manner that was not possible without Jesus.

I do not think that a constitutive and a sacramental Christology or soteriology are necessarily contradictory.[19] Yet the differences between them are stark when we apply them to the question of openness to other religions. A constitutive cause is intrinsically singular. Once something is fixed, it does not need to be, or it cannot be, fixed again. But a sacramental cause is at least potentially open to being multiple. What is revealed at one point in history, or in one culture, or in one set of particular human needs, can be revealed very differently, but just as appropriately, in another culture or historical context. And when what is being revealed is the incomprehensible, ever rich, and creative mystery of God, then a variety of revelations, or sacraments, of this divine mystery not only makes sense but would be expected. A theology that understands *Jesus the Savior* as *Jesus the Sacrament* is open to other sacraments.

Kingdom Centered

If we try to be more specific about what Jesus the Sacrament reveals, one answer would have to be the kingdom or reign of God. New Testament scholars may not be able to agree on much about the historical Jesus, but on one issue they arrive at something like consensus: that his message was centered on the reign of God. This is what he wanted people to believe in, and to hope and work for. Yes, he wanted them to believe in God, but if this God did not call and inspire them to love each other, to treat each other justly, to respond to the needs of each other, and to work for a society in which people would really live this way, then it was not the God of Jesus. A God without the reign of God was for Jesus a false God.[20]

> Followers of Jesus will also know that "those who are not against us are for us" (Mark 9:40), and that therefore non-Christians may have much to teach Christians about God's kingdom.

A theology that is as kingdom centered as Jesus was would also be a more dialogical theology. Following the example of Jesus, the primary (which does not mean the only) motivation, goal, and guideline in the Christian dialogue with other religions is not to convert non-Christians to the Christian church, not even, we can add, to bring them to accept Jesus as their only Savior. Rather, Christians engage other believers first of all in order to work with them to further God's Kingdom on earth, to contribute to a world of greater love, peace, and justice. The scene of the Last Judgment in Matthew 25 seems to tell us that to be so engaged in doing God's work on earth does not require knowing or believing in Jesus. Certainly Christians will want to, and will need to, bear witness to other believers about how Jesus and his God can make this reign of love and justice possible and workable. But followers of Jesus will also know that "those who are not against us are for us" (Mark 9:40), and that therefore non-Christians may have much to teach Christians about God's kingdom. Even Roman Catholic theology is recognizing that God's kingdom is larger than, even more important than, the Christian church.[21] Therefore, there may be much to learn about that kingdom from those who live outside the Christian community.

A THEOLOGY THAT WILL PROMOTE COMMITMENT WITHOUT JEOPARDIZING OPENNESS

A real dialogue with others, as we have stressed, requires of Christians just as much a resolute commitment to Jesus and his message as it does a bold openness to other religions. In a sense, Christian belief, with its insistence on Jesus as the only way to God, has always fostered that commitment. So our question now is: What would be some of the qualities of a theology that, without insisting on *only*, could still inspire commitment? Again, I can only sketch some suggestions.

Christocentric

To bracket confessionally the "one and only" language of Christian claims (as Niebuhr suggests) is not to deny the uniqueness or the universal (missionary) outreach of Jesus and the gospel. Advocates of the mutuality model stress this, and so they insist that both in their own lives and in their dialogue with others, they remain thoroughly Christocentric.[22] To be a Christian means that one's life is informed and formed by God-as-Jesus, by the Christ continuing to live in the community. And this centeredness is founded on the conviction, which cannot be watered down in the dialogue, that in Jesus the Christ, God has done something that God has not done elsewhere. This something is particular, unrepeatable, distinctive; it cannot be subsumed under, or boiled down to, a universal truth or principle. It is unique. And what's more, it is *universally* unique—that is, its meaning and power are to touch and transform all peoples. It is a particularity that overflows with universality. Christians proclaim that without Jesus, salvation or human well-being—as God intends it to be realized—is not really and fully possible. Without Jesus, no matter how advanced and deep and beautiful other understandings of the Ultimate and of human well-being may be, something will be missing. This is why to be a Christian is to be a missionary.

Such convictions about the uniqueness and universality of Christ can be sustained in a relationship with Jesus as Sacrament. But this is a relationship that, as we noted, is not threatened by being open to the possibility of other, different but effective, sacraments of saving power and truth, other manifestations of the Divine that are also unique and universally relevant.

Prophetic

A theology of religions that will sustain commitment will have to face a further question: What is it that makes Jesus unique? Why are he and his message universally urgent? Two clarifications or precautions are necessary before taking up this unavoidable question. First, by *uniqueness* I do not mean that Jesus has something that absolutely no one else does. (Such a view of uniqueness defines identity negatively: I am who I am because you are not.) Rather, by *uniqueness* I mean that which makes Jesus who he is, that without which he would not be Jesus, that without which his message and life would not be universally relevant and urgent. Maybe a better word is *distinctive*. Whether what constitutes Jesus' distinctiveness is also found in others is an important but secondary question. My second precaution is just as important: The question about what makes Jesus unique or distinctive can never really be answered—that is, it can never be answered fully or finally or in only one way. It is the same question that Jesus asked of his followers: "Who do you say I am?" (Mark 8:27) It has to be answered, again and again, in different ages, in different historical contexts, in response to different signs of the times.

By *uniqueness* I mean that which makes Jesus who he is, that without which he would not be Jesus, that without which his message and life would not be universally relevant and urgent.

In *our* age and historical context, trying to connect the New Testament witness to the signs of our times, how can we describe what makes Jesus unique? Taking up the insights especially of Asian theologians, who are trying to follow and proclaim Jesus in a world of both many religions and much poverty, I would suggest that one of the most faithful (to the New Testament) and most relevant (to the needs of our world) approaches is to locate Jesus' uniqueness in his role of *prophet*. This relates back to the centrality of the reign of God in his message: Jesus was a prophet announcing the coming kingdom. But he did so in a very distinctive way: with a preferential (that does not mean exclusive) concern for the poor, for the marginalized, for those who were being taken advantage of by others, for victims. Writing from Sri Lanka, Aloysius Pieris, S.J., puts it this way: "Jesus is the covenant between YHWH and the non-persons of the world." Jesus embodies and announces "the irrevocable covenant between God and the poor." Here Jesus echoes with intensity the message of his fellow Jewish prophets. But he seems to go even further when the cross becomes part of this covenant with the marginalized: "[T]he kind of God revealed in Christ on Calvary has crossed the threshold of propriety."[23] God not only covenants with victims and slaves; God identifies with them, to the point of suffering with them. In Jesus, God dies *with* victims in order to die *for* victims. The cross, followed by the resurrection, contains the distinctiveness of Jesus' revelation of who God is:

> This God has foolishly and scandalously (1 Cor 1:23) exposed the true Divine Self as Love that gets hurt and even breaks down before human ingratitude, a God who weeps, sweats, and bleeds, sharing the pain and the fear and the despair of Her co-victims on earth, a God who does not live on others but dies that others may have life in abundance, a God who opts not just to be human but to associate with the socially degraded persons in the manner of living and dying.[24]

From his broad knowledge of Asian religions, Pieris does not think that this image of the Divine identifying with, to the point of suffering with, the outcasts of the world is found as clearly or centrally, or at all, in nonbiblical religions as it is in the life and message of Jesus. Be that as it may, "Our specifically Christian mission is to share the Crucified God's solidarity or friendship with the poor, a friendship which led him to lay down his life for them (Jn. 15:13)."[25] This is the message we are committed to and make bold to lay before others: If people who call themselves religious are not in some way concerned about and reaching out to the victims of this world, something essential is missing in their religious experience. No matter how deep or inspiring or assuring their vision of the Divine may be, no matter how much they feel at-oned with the Ultimate, if a concern for the marginalized is missing, then something essential is missing in their religious experience or in their claims to have attained salvation or enlightenment. Christians may have much to learn from other religions, other sacraments of the Divine, but this is what they have to contribute and stand for in the dialogue.

> This is the message we are committed to and make bold to lay before others: If people who call themselves religious are not in some way concerned about and reaching out to the victims of this world, something essential is missing in their religious experience.

Such a commitment to Jesus, Pieris continues, not only allows for openness to what our religious brothers and sisters may have to tell us, but it also fosters openness on their part to us. Jesus' invitation to all religious people to hear the cry of the poor and to act with the hope of moving the world closer to what he called the reign of God—this can be heard by other believers as good news. For Pieris's Buddhist, Hindu, and Muslim friends in Sri Lanka, "the God he presents who lives and dies in Jesus is not a threat to them as the Colonial Christ was." The Colonial Christ had come insisting on the superiority of Christianity (and of Europe), on we-have-it-and-you-don't, on Jesus as the only Savior. Jesus as the divine prophet, embodying the kenotic God who invites us to follow his example of giving oneself for others, especially for the poor and the victims, is perceived as the Dialogical Christ, challenging yet open.

Reconciliatory

Jesus the prophet remains Jesus the self-emptying servant. He joined bold prophecy with self-giving, other-embracing love. This too is part of his uniqueness, to which Christians, especially in our present conflict-ridden and violent world, must be committed. This means that if Christians who follow the prophetic Jesus must denounce those who are exploiting others, this denunciation will always have to be kenotic—loving, self-giving, embracing. In loving the victims of injustice, Jesus' followers can never hate or exclude the perpetrators of injustice. The preferential option for the poor can never be disconnected from the self-emptying embrace of all.

Stated more positively: Jesus calls all to pursue justice *and* reconciliation. In fact, if we follow the imagery of Philippians 2:7, the Divine in Jesus had to first empty itself (*eauton ekenosen*) in order to "take the form of a slave" (*labon morphen doulou*) and become a servant of the poor. This suggests that we are to pursue justice *through* reconciliation, or that reconciliation is a means to, not simply the result of justice. The first steps toward a more just society, then, would not be to insist on a change of political or economic structures (though that is essential), but to work toward the reconciliation of relationships. To the principle "If you want peace, work for justice," Christians will add, "And if you want justice, work toward reconciliation." This is why recently Christian theologians and missiologists have been urging that the primary, central purpose of Christian mission today is to promote the reconciliation of peoples and nations.[26]

In interreligious dialogue, Christian witness will therefore always include a commitment to and call for reconciliation—a reconciliation that can be achieved only through a self-emptying love for and embrace of the other, even the "enemy."[27] Such a Christian voice within the dialogue will certainly challenge the other, but it also stands a good chance of being heard, perhaps embraced. And it allows, even requires, Christians to be open to what the other religions might have to contribute to achieving such reconciliation.

In interreligious dialogue, Christian witness will therefore always include a commitment to and call for reconciliation—a reconciliation that can be achieved only through a self-emptying love for and embrace of the other, even the "enemy."

All these suggestions indicate that our work in progress—an adequate Christian theology of religions—calls for more work. Christian theologians, from whatever model, need to keep talking with each other. If they can do so using these two "hermeneutical flashlights"—searching for a theology of religions that would facilitate both commitment to Christ and openness to others—they can, I trust, achieve a theology that will make for a more satisfying Christian spirituality, a more effective dialogue with others, and a greater healing for our world.

J. A. DiNoia, O.P.

Is Jesus Christ the unique mediator of salvation? I was one of five panelists assigned to address this question at a recent meeting of Catholic theologians. I was the first to speak and, as it turned out, the only panelist prepared to advance an unqualified affirmative response to the question. Why is this? Why would a group of Catholic theologians decline to affirm what, until recently, would have been considered an unquestionable tenet of ecumenical Christian faith?[1]

As the session unfolded, it became clear that their reluctance to do so was motivated at least in part by a desire to avoid giving offense to religious people of other traditions. The underlying premise of their remarks, and of the ensuing discussion, seemed to be this: To ascribe a uniquely salvific role to Jesus Christ would constitute a denial of the salvific role of other religious founders (like the Buddha and Muhammad) and thus would be an affront to their communities.

The way that many theologians think about this issue has been influenced by the pluralistic theology of religions popularized by John Hick, Paul Knitter, and others.[2] Indeed, Paul Knitter was one of the panelists at the session I mentioned above. In a nutshell, pluralists claim that in one way or another all religions aim at salvation. In John Hick's influential definition, salvation is the movement from self-centeredness to "Reality-centeredness." Since, according to pluralists, ultimate reality is incomprehensible and ineffable, no one religious description can claim primacy over rival descriptions, and no tradition can claim exclusive rights to the means of salvation.

In the pluralist perspective, therefore, each religious founder must be regarded as in some sense a savior. Exclusive or unique status, with respect to the knowledge of, provision for, or access to, salvation can no more be claimed for Jesus of Nazareth than it can be claimed for Gautama the Buddha or for Muhammad. Naturally, pluralists do not deny that these founders were unique historical personalities. What they deny is that any one of them could provide a uniquely privileged or exclusive access to salvation.

It follows for pluralists that Christian theologians cannot give a simple affirmative answer to the question, "Is Jesus Christ the unique mediator of salvation?" On the basis of their study of religious traditions, pluralist philosophers and theologians contend that salvation, though diversely mediated, is nonetheless universally accessible. It is not just in order to avoid giving offense to other religious people that pluralists have championed this view. Pluralists argue on empirical and philosophical grounds that a structure of salvation underlies all religious traditions and thus variously orients their adherents to "Reality" as it is diversely figured in these traditions. Only in this way can Christian theologians affirm the universality of salvation and of religious truth, as least as possibilities, without giving offense to other religious people.

Pluralists argue on empirical and philosophical grounds that a structure of salvation underlies all religious traditions and thus variously orients their adherents to "Reality" as it is diversely figured in these traditions.

To be sure, pluralists are not the only theologians who have been concerned with the salvation of persons who are not Christians. According to the typology prevailing in current theology of religions, the chief alternative positions on this issue are represented by exclusivism and inclusivism. In contrast to pluralists, both exclusivists and inclusivists would have no difficulty in giving an affirmative answer to the question, "Is Jesus Christ the unique mediator of salvation?" For all their sharp differences, exclusivists and inclusivists concur in their avowal of the uniquely salvific role of Christ. But exclusivists deny the possibility of salvation for non-Christians who do not before death explicitly profess faith in Christ. Inclusivists, on the other hand, allow for the possibility of salvation chiefly on the ground of some form of implicit faith in Christ, combined with a morally upright life, on the part of non-Christians.[3]

The Christian concern not to give offense to other religious people is a praiseworthy one, while the concern to allow for the possibility of their salvation is a doctrinally crucial one. But suppose that, far from being an affront to other religious traditions, a strong Christian affirmation of the uniqueness of Christ's salvific role were fundamental to traditional Christian universalism. Suppose, in other words, that the particularity of salvation in Christ were nonexclusive. Suppose, further, that an affirmation of this nonexclusive particularity of salvation in Christ were not an obstacle to but a condition for genuine respect for other religious people.

> Even where other religious communities employ the term *salvation,* their conceptions of the aim of life differ from one another and from that espoused by Christian communities.

I have argued this position at length elsewhere.[4] It rests not only on central Christian doctrines but also on the suggestion that *salvation* is not a term that encompasses what all religions seek, but is a properly Christian designation for that which should be sought above all else in life. Salvation has a distinctively Christian content: transformation in Christ with a view to ultimate community with the triune God. Even where other religious communities employ the term *salvation,* their conceptions of the aim of life differ from one another and from that espoused by Christian communities. By framing the agenda of theology of religions primarily in terms of the possibility of extra-Christian salvation, pluralists and inclusivists often fail to give enough weight to the specificity and distinctiveness of religious aims. Inclusivists fail to notice their distinctiveness because they tend to reinterpret non-Christian patterns and aims in Christian terms. More at the center of my attention in this essay, however, are pluralists who make salvation an all-encompassing designation for the variety of aims that religious traditions espouse and commend.

If the issues here were framed differently, it might turn out that to affirm Christ's unique role in salvation is not to exclude persons who are not Christians but to embrace them. In other words, it might turn out that we could give a strong affirmative answer to the question, "Is Jesus Christ the unique mediator of salvation?" and still both show respect for other religious people and include them in the final consummation of all things for which we have reason, only in Christ, to hope.

A HYPOTHETICAL CONVERSATION WITH A BUDDHIST

In order to reframe these issues, and at the same time to identify what seems to be the weakness especially of typical pluralist approaches to them, I want to engage in an experiment. I will compare the question, "Is Jesus Christ the unique mediator of salvation?" with the question, "Is the Buddha the unique revealer of the dharma?"

Suppose that I pose this second question to a Buddhist friend. Along with most Buddhists, she will answer it affirmatively. The dharma—the "way" or "path" Buddhists seek to follow—comprises all that concerns nirvana and its attainment. Even though Buddhists commonly insist that knowledge of the dharma is in principle accessible to anyone, still they regard the discovery and teaching of the dharma by Gautama, the historical Buddha, as unique in this era.[5]

Consider how the conversation might proceed at this point. If my Buddhist friend should caution me that I will never attain nirvana by following the course of life laid out for me by the Christian community, I do not feel anxious about this. I have not been persuaded that seeking nirvana is what I should be doing. If I did begin to be persuaded of this, then I should undertake to discover the path and try to make my way along it. I would, in other words, have begun to be a follower of the Buddha. I might then even join a Buddhist community, or at least become an inquirer. Some Catholics I know have done this very thing. But if I continue to be convinced that it is salvation that I should be seeking and that Christ is the unique mediator of this salvation, then I would continue on the Christian path.

One thing to notice about this hypothetical encounter between me and my Buddhist friend is that I have not felt affronted by her warning that I shall not attain nirvana unless I follow the Excellent Eightfold Path (right views, right resolution, right speech, right conduct, right livelihood, right effort, right mindfulness, right concentration) taught uniquely by the Buddha. On the contrary, my initial reaction is that what she has said to me makes perfect sense. If the Excellent Eightfold Path is the way to nirvana, and if I do not choose to pursue this path, then it follows that I may not reach nirvana. But, since I have as yet no desire to attain and enjoy nirvana, I am not offended by this reasoning. I have not been persuaded that nirvana is what I should be seeking.

> If the assertion "The Buddha is the unique revealer of the dharma" is not offensive to me, then why should the assertion "Jesus Christ is the unique mediator of salvation" be offensive to Buddhists?

Without trying to field a "definition" of religion—something that has proven notoriously difficult to do—I could say that the Christian community and the Buddhist community (with their various subcommunities) both seem to have some conception of an ultimate aim of life and have developed a pattern of life geared toward attaining it. Other major religious communities share this tendency as well.[6] What is ultimate, whether it be a transcendent agent or as yet unrealized state of being, invades life at every moment, and summons the community's members to order and shape their lives in view of this aim. The world's religious communities differ in their descriptions of the aims that are ultimate in this sense (e.g., the extinction of the self, or communion with the triune God) as well as in their provision for the cultivation of the patterns of life ordered to the attainment and enjoyment of such aims (e.g., the dharma or the gospel). But they seem to agree in espousing and commending comprehensive aims of life, and in striving to shape the lives of their members with a view to those aims.

I can now formulate a preliminary result of the consideration of the hypothetical conversation between me and my Buddhist friend. If the assertion "The Buddha is the unique revealer of the dharma" is not offensive to me, then why should the assertion "Jesus Christ is the unique mediator of salvation" be offensive to Buddhists, or, for that matter, to Muslims, Vedantists, or Jews? A Jewish rabbi once said to me, revealingly, "Jesus Christ is the answer to a question I have never asked." This remark suggests that we might be on the right track in our reflections. Salvation in the Christian sense, it implies, is not what the rabbi is seeking. Asking the question to which Jesus Christ is the answer commits oneself to an inquiry (logically speaking) that may lead to the adoption of a Christian way of life. At least in part, this will mean that what Christians aim for, as expressed by the umbrella term *salvation,* has begun to look appealing or even ultimately important. One might conclude: *This* is what I should be aiming for in my life. But what would this be?

WHAT SALVATION MEANS TO CHRISTIANS

When Christians try to answer this question, we find ourselves becoming quite specific. When we try to say what salvation comprises, we find ourselves talking about the triune God; the incarnation, passion, death, and resurrection of Jesus Christ; grace, sin, and justification; transfiguration and divinization; faith, hope, and charity; the commandments and the moral virtues; and many other characteristically Christian things as well. We should not be surprised if, in trying to answer a cognate question, a member of another religious community, say a Buddhist, should also become very specific about nirvana and all that bears on its attainment. We should not be surprised, furthermore, if the descriptions of salvation and nirvana do not coincide. But, for the moment, let us continue the experiment by sketching some of the things that a Christian description of salvation might have to include.

Allowing for variations across its various subcommunities, we can understand the ecumenical Christian community to teach that the ultimate aim of life is a communion of life—a communion of life with the Father, through the Son, and in the Holy Spirit. According to ecumenical Christian faith, this is a truth proclaimed by Christ and a destiny made possible for us by his passion, death, and resurrection; this is what Christians mean by salvation; the term embraces both the goal of ultimate communion and the empowerment to attain and enjoy it.

Human persons are called to nothing less than communion with the Father, Son, and Holy Spirit, and with each other in them. Indeed, Christianity affirms that the triune God could not bring about a more intimate union with created persons than that which has already been initiated in baptism and will be fulfilled for us in Christ. Ultimate communion involves nothing less than becoming part of the Trinitarian family.

But if we are destined to enjoy this ultimate communion, then we must change. We must become fit for it. Interpersonal communion with God is only "natural" to uncreated persons; for created persons, who are also sinners, such communion is possible only through justification and grace. Through the redeeming grace of Christ and, specifically, through the transformation that this grace makes possible, we are rendered "fit" participants in the communion of the Father, Son, and Holy Spirit. Our transformation will be a conformation: The more we become like Christ, the more surely do we discover our true selves, the unique persons created by the triune God to share in the divine life and to enjoy the personal life of the Trinity. As Catholics pray in one of the Sunday prefaces: "Father . . . you sent him as one like ourselves, though free from sin, that you might see and love in us what you see and love in him."[7]

The more we become like Christ, the more surely do we discover our true selves, the unique persons created by the triune God to share in the divine life and to enjoy the personal life of the Trinity.

However, this conformation does not amount to a mere conformity. The conformation to Christ that is the principle of our transformation is not a mere cloning but the realization of our distinctive and unique personal identities. This must be so, for otherwise the communion to which this transformation is directed could not be consummated. The image of God in us consists precisely in the spiritual capacities for knowing and loving that make interpersonal communion possible. But authentic interpersonal communion presupposes the full realization of the individual persons who enter into it. Thus, if Christ is to be the principle and pattern of our transformation, in being conformed to him we must each discover and realize our own unique identities as persons, and be healed of the sinful dispositions that obstruct the flourishing of our true selves.

This is the force of the astonishing saying of Christ:

> If any want to become followers, let them deny themselves and take up their cross and follow me. For those who want to save their life will lose it, and those who lose their life for my sake will find it. For what will it profit them if they gain the whole world but forfeit their life? Or what will they give in return for their life? (Matt. 16:24–26)

None of us, whether as teachers, parents, or pastors—no matter how inflated our conceptions of ourselves or how confident our sense of our abilities—would ever dare to say to anybody in our charge that they will find their true selves by imitating *us.* In effect, Christ asserts that an indefinite number of human persons will find their distinctive identities by being conformed to *him.* A moment's reflection shows us that only the Son of God could make such an assertion. No mere human could do so. Only the inexhaustibly rich, perfect image of God who is the person of the Son in human nature could constitute the principle and pattern for the transformation and fulfillment of every human person who has ever lived.

When Christians affirm that Jesus Christ is the unique mediator of salvation, something like the above can stand as a summary of what they mean. Leave aside for a moment the question whether such a description includes or excludes persons who are not Christians. What we need to consider first, as we continue to reflect on my hypothetical conversation with a Buddhist friend, is whether such a description of what Christians mean by salvation is offensive to persons who are not Christians—Buddhists, for example. Informed of what a Christian means by salvation, would there be reason for a Buddhist to feel excluded by the assertion that Jesus Christ is the unique mediator of salvation?

We have seen that salvation has a specific content for Christians: It entails an interpersonal communion, made possible by Christ, between human persons and the Father, Son, and Holy Spirit. At least at first sight, this seems to be something very different from what Buddhists can be supposed to be seeking when they follow the Excellent Eightfold Path that leads them on the way to realizing enlightenment and the extinction of self in nirvana.[8] At least on the face of things, what Buddhists mean by *nirvana* and what Christians mean by *salvation* do not seem to coincide.

> At least on the face of things, what Buddhists mean by *nirvana* and what Christians mean by *salvation* do not seem to coincide.

This does not mean that they are opposed. It remains to be seen whether seeking salvation and seeking nirvana are complementary to each other or related in some as yet unspecified manner.[9] However, it seems clear that interpersonal communion is a very different thing from the extinction of the self entailed in nirvana. Many forms of Buddhism are concerned to cultivate dispositions that increasingly unmask the illusoriness of personal identity. As I noted above in my sketch of what most Christians mean by salvation, Christians understand personal identity to be of permanent, indeed eternal, significance because eternity centrally involves interpersonal communion.

THE PROBLEM WITH PLURALIST THEOLOGY OF RELIGIONS

Let us return to my hypothetical conversation with a Buddhist friend. You will recall that we left the conversation at the point when she cautioned me that I would not reach nirvana unless I followed the Excellent Eightfold Path. This warning was not disturbing to me, for I do not want to attain nirvana. Suppose that when the conversation resumes I offer a description of what Christians mean by salvation, a description not unlike the one presented above. Would we be surprised to find that my Buddhist friend wants no part of this? It is difficult for us to understand and accept that what we regard as most important—more so than anything else, absolutely speaking—other religious people challenge or repudiate.

Buddhist communities in all their variety possess highly ramified teachings about the true aim of life and about the means to attain it. These teachings do not, at least on the surface, coincide with what Christians teach about these very matters. Buddhists do not want ultimate communion; they do not seek it, and, insofar as they think about it, they may regard us as misguided for wanting and seeking it. For, by wanting and seeking ultimate communion, we remain, from a Buddhist point of view, incorrigibly attached to the very conceptions of personal identity that constitute the chief obstacle on the way to nirvana.

Gautama the Buddha is the authority on these matters. He discovered and taught the dharma, and through it attained enlightenment. His role in revealing the dharma to others is regarded by most of his followers as something original, at least in the present epoch. Hence, while it makes good sense for Buddhists to affirm that the Buddha is the unique revealer of the dharma, it makes little sense for them to be offended when Christians describe Jesus Christ as the unique mediator of salvation. Buddhists regard Christian beliefs about this as misguided and perhaps only partially true, but they will not be anxious or offended by such a Christian affirmation. They are not interested in seeking and attaining salvation as Christians understand it.

> Buddhists are not interested in seeking and attaining salvation as Christians understand it. Pluralists want to define *salvation* so broadly that it includes both what Christians mean by it and what Buddhists mean by *nirvana.*

To be sure, some people—pluralists in particular—want to define *salvation* so broadly that it includes both what Christians mean by it and what Buddhists mean by *nirvana.* On this account of things, my hypothetical encounter with a Buddhist friend would not present either of us with a choice between seeking nirvana and seeking salvation. Some would say that to think that there is a serious choice here is, religiously speaking, overly literalistic and even simpleminded. Indeed, pluralists contend, precisely at this juncture the superiority of pluralist theology of religions is displayed. Pluralists argue that all religious communities advance their members toward specific aims—communion or enlightenment, as the case may be—that are surpassed or transcended by a more ultimate, but indescribable, aim. All religious communities seek this yet more ultimate aim with varying degrees of clarity and success. Not only is this conception closer to the truth of the matter, it also provides the basis for the sympathetic understanding, fruitful dialogue, and mutual respect that are desperately needed today.

In fact, however, this basic premise of pluralist theology of religions will not stand up under close scrutiny. Even if religious communities were prepared to accept some such description of what they are about—something few of them show any inclination to do—it still remains true that they espouse and commend specific aims that differ from one another. Furthermore, these specific aims call forth distinctive patterns of life in each of the major religious traditions and in local traditions as well. Certain kinds of life are understood to foster the enjoyment of certain kinds of ends of life, and others to obstruct this enjoyment. This seems to be an ineradicable feature of the characteristic discourse and ethos of most religious communities. Individual lives come to be shaped by the ultimate aims that are sought. So even if the true aim of life were one that transcended the particular aims of all religious traditions—something stipulated by pluralists—no one could seek it. No one could undertake to order life in such a way as to attain and enjoy an ultimate aim of life of which no description could be given.

But this goes directly against the grain of characteristic religious affirmation and conviction. Religious people, by and large, believe themselves to be in possession of understandings, incomplete though they may be, of what is ultimately important in life and how to orient life in its direction. Significant disagreements obtain among the major and local religious traditions about these matters. Pluralist theology of religion does not so much explain these disagreements as explain them away. In this way, pluralism seems to offer a massive redescription, rather than an interpretation, of religious beliefs and practices, and of the arresting differences among them.

Thus, the following statements are not problematic in the way that many people, like those I joined on the theological panel, seem to think: "Jesus Christ is the unique mediator of salvation," and "The Buddha is the unique revealer of the dharma." Were representatives of Christian or Buddhist communities to retreat from advancing such claims, it is not clear what they would have to offer to the world. There would be no compelling, or even interesting, reasons to persevere in membership in these communities, or indeed to seek it.

> The great challenge facing present-day Christian theology of religions and interreligious conversation is to avoid minimizing the distinctive features of the major religious traditions through a well-intentioned universalism.

The great challenge facing present-day Christian theology of religions and interreligious conversation is to avoid minimizing the distinctive features of the major religious traditions through a well-intentioned universalism. Christian confidence in the universal scope of salvation rests on convictions about the historical career and perduring agency of Jesus Christ. Only if his identity is affirmed in its fullness—in accord with Scripture, the great councils, and the church's liturgy—as the Son of God who became human and died for us, can the hope of Christians for themselves and for others be sustained. "For in him all the fullness of God was pleased to dwell, and through him God was pleased to reconcile to himself all things, whether on earth or in heaven, by making peace through the blood of his cross" (Col. 1:19–20).

If the salvation that the triune God wills for the entire human race entails ultimate communion with the three persons of the Trinity, then the creaturely and sinful obstacles to this communion must be overcome. It has never been claimed that anyone but Jesus Christ could overcome these obstacles. Through him we are both healed and raised to an adoptive participation in the life of the Trinity. The obstacles to this participation are either overcome or not. If they are not overcome, then Christians have nothing for which to hope, for themselves or for others. In that case, they will hawk an empty universalism on the highways of the world. When Christians abandon the proclamation of Christ's unique mediatorship, they have no other mediatorship with which to replace it.

How persons who are not now explicit believers in Christ are to share in the salvation he alone makes possible is a large topic that I have not addressed in this essay. But if Christians no longer confess Christ's unique mediatorship in making ultimate communion a real possibility for created persons, then the problem of how non-Christians can share in it is not resolved. It simply evaporates. True Christian universalism depends on the affirmation of the nonexclusive particularity of salvation in Jesus Christ.

QUESTIONS FOR REFLECTION AND DISCUSSION

1. What is supersessionism and why do so many contemporary Christian theologians try to avoid it? Do such attempts create problems?
2. What questions does the history of Christian anti-Semitism raise about the authority of the Bible and tradition?
3. What attitudes do exclusivism, inclusivism, and pluralism (Knitter's replacement, fulfillment, and mutuality models) take toward adherents of non-Christian religions? What are the strengths and problems in each position?
4. Why is interreligious dialogue important?
5. Knitter identifies his own position as confessional, kenotic, sacramental, kingdom centered, Christocentric, prophetic, and reconciliatory. What does he mean by each of those terms, and why is each important to him?
6. What conclusions does DiNoia draw from his hypothetical conversation with a Buddhist?
7. Acording to DiNoia, what are the implications of saying "Jesus Christ is the only mediator of salvation" for adherents of religions other than Christianity?
8. How would Knitter and DiNoia each criticize the other? What common ground would they have?

FOR FURTHER READING

Braaten, Carl E. *No Other Gospel.* Minneapolis: Fortress Press, 1992.

Cobb, John B., Jr. *Transforming Christianity and the World.* Maryknoll, N.Y.: Orbis Books, 1999.

Cragg, Kenneth. *The Christ and the Faiths.* London: SPCK, 1986.

D'Costa, Gavin, ed. *Christian Uniqueness Reconsidered.* Maryknoll, N.Y.: Orbis Books, 1990.

———. *The Meeting of Religions and the Trinity.* Maryknoll, N.Y.: Orbis Books, 2000.

DiNoia, J. A. *The Diversity of Religions.* Washington: Catholic University of America Press, 1992.
Dupuis, Jacques. *Toward a Christian Theology of Religious Pluralism.* Maryknoll, N.Y.: Orbis Books, 1997.
Fackre, Gabriel. *What about Those Who Have Never Heard?* Downers Grove, Ill.: Inter-Varsity Press, 1995.
Griffiths, Paul. *An Apology for Apologetics.* Maryknoll, N.Y.: Orbis Books, 1991.
Heim, S. Mark. *Salvations: Truth and Difference in Religion.* Maryknoll, N.Y.: Orbis Books, 1995.
Hick, John. *A Christian Theology of Religions.* Louisville, Ky.: Westminster John Knox Press, 1995.
Hick, John, and Brian Hebblethwaite, eds. *Christianity and Other Religions.* Philadelphia: Fortress Press, 1980.
Hick, John, and Paul F. Knitter, eds. *The Myth of Christian Uniqueness.* Maryknoll, N.Y.: Orbis Books, 1986.
Jensen, David H. *In the Company of Others.* Cleveland: Pilgrim Press, 2001.
Knitter, Paul F. *Introducing Theology of Religions.* Maryknoll, N.Y.: Orbis Books, 2002.
———. *Jesus and the Other Names.* Maryknoll, N.Y.: Orbis Books, 1996.
———, *No Other Name?* Maryknoll, N.Y.: Orbis Books, 1985.
Panikkar, Raimundo. *The Interreligious Dialogue.* New York: Paulist Press, 1999.
Pinnock, Clark. *A Wideness in God's Mercy.* Grand Rapids: Zondervan Publishing House, 1992.

Chapter 9

Where Are We Going?

Eschatology

Eschatology comes from a Greek word (*eschatos*) meaning "final" or "last." Thus, it is the part of theology that deals with the "last things." Such matters are not just a casual afterthought. We all want to know what happens to us after we die. As discussed in chapter 3, we live in a world full of suffering and evil that often does not look as if God is in charge of it and therefore poses the question of theodicy—whether or not God is just. One way to affirm God's ultimate lordship and justice is to say that injustices will be repaired and things will generally improve at some time in the future. That leads to what Ted Peters's essay for this chapter calls "eschatological theodicy." Most scientists, however, tell us that eventually the universe itself will either collapse in on itself or slowly dissipate into utter randomness. If that is true, what becomes of any kind of ultimate hope? Will God's rule over all things ever become clear? If so, how?

The Old Testament for the most part reflects little concern over such matters. In contrast with the preoccupation with existence after death characteristic of neighboring cultures like Egypt, the ancient Hebrews focused mostly on this life. Pious Israelites hoped for a long and rich life with many descendants to keep their memory alive, but death brought the important part of personal existence to an end. Perhaps there was some shadowy underworld of the dead called Sheol, but "there is no work or thought or knowledge or wisdom in Sheol" (Eccl. 9:10), and it is certainly not a place to which one would look forward.

Toward the end of the Old Testament period, however, discouragement about present life led Jews to think more about what might come after it. Israel faced one defeat after another. People died young and tragically, and in the chaos of the time could not trust that their children would remember them or even manage to survive. *Apocalyptic* writings (from a Greek word meaning "disclose" or "reveal") addressed such concerns. The prophets of Israel had often focused their discussions of the future on concrete threats or hopes—to punish us for our sins, the Assyrians will defeat us; or, soon we will return from exile. Apocalyptic texts, by contrast, usually held out little if any hope for the short term. Things will just keep getting worse, they declared, until God brings the whole present age of history to an end and establishes God's own reign over the world. In dramatic, symbolic language they described the destruction of the present order and the establishment of an entirely different one.

But what good would that do those who died in the meantime? Apocalyptic writers such as the author of Daniel began to suggest that at least some of the dead would be raised to receive appropriate rewards and punishments: "Many of those who sleep in the dust of the earth shall awake, some to everlasting life, and some to shame and everlasting contempt" (Dan. 12:2).

In some Gospel passages, Jesus speaks in the language of apocalyptic, describing a future cosmic catastrophe when

> the sun will be darkened,
>   and the moon will not give its light,
> and the stars will be falling from heaven,
>   and the powers in the heavens will be shaken.
>
> Then they will see 'the Son of Man coming in clouds' with great power and glory. Then he will send out the angels, and gather his elect from the four winds, from the ends of the earth to the ends of heaven. (Mark 13:24–27)

> In contrast to *futuristic eschatology,* which makes Jesus' return a future public event, other Gospel passages seem to present a *realized eschatology*—God's reign is already being secretly established in Jesus' ministry. Many of Jesus' parables combine elements of these two accounts. A future, public manifestation of God has already begun in secret, like a tiny seed germinating in the earth.

In contrast to this *futuristic eschatology,* which makes Jesus' return as the "Son of Man" a future public event, other Gospel passages seem to present what scholars have called *realized eschatology*—God's reign is already being secretly established (made real) in Jesus' ministry.[1] In Luke, for instance, Jesus tells the Pharisees, "The reign of God is not coming with things that can be observed; nor will they say, 'Look, here it is!' or 'There it is!' For, in fact, the reign of God is among you" (Luke 17:21).

Many of Jesus' parables combine elements of these two accounts. The reign of God, Jesus says, "is like a mustard seed that someone took and sowed in the garden; it grew and became a tree, and the birds of the air made nests in its branches" (Luke 13:19). According to Jewish tradition, the mustard seed was the smallest of all seeds, indeed, the very smallest thing the human eye can perceive, but it grows into a bush nearly as large as a tree.[2] This parable thus implies that there will be a dramatic, future, public manifestation of the reign of God, but it has already begun in secret, like a tiny seed germinating in the earth, in Jesus' ministry and the response to it.

HOPES FOR INDIVIDUALS

Not all the Jews of Jesus' time believed in resurrection, but those who did expected a *general* resurrection at the end of the present age. Jesus' resurrection thus unexpectedly anticipated the end of history in the midst of history and therefore, his followers thought, provided a clue to how history will turn out. The earliest Christian hope for existence after death focused on resurrection. But as Christianity spread out into the Mediterranean world, it increasingly encountered the belief that human beings consist of a body and a soul, and that the soul is immortal. Many Greek and Roman philosophers even thought of the soul as entrapped in the body, so that death would come as its liberation.[3] Many early Christian writers opposed such talk. The body, they insisted, is part of God's good creation and part of what it is to be human, not something to be discarded, and thus our hope lies in *bodily* resurrection.[4]

On the other hand, when martyrs died for their faith, their fellow Christians often hoped, not that their bodies would *eventually* be raised but that their souls would go *at once* to be with God—Jesus' promise to one of the thieves crucified with him, "Today you will be with me in Paradise" (Luke 23:43) was often cited as the basis for such a hope. The most common medieval Christian view, then, was that, when we die, our souls go immediately to heaven for reward, hell for punishment, or purgatory for purification, but that eventually, when Christ returns, our bodies will be raised and joined with our souls. The human soul, Aquinas said, has "an aptitude and a natural inclination to be united to the body,"[5] and therefore remains incomplete until the resurrection.

During the medieval period, the church gradually began to teach the existence of purgatory (a place where those not good enough to go directly to heaven could do penance for their earthly sins until they were prepared for heaven) and limbo (a place for morally upright but unbaptized pagans and unbaptized infants). By the Council of Florence in 1438–1439, purgatory had become one of the key differences between Western Catholicism and Eastern Orthodoxy. Many of the Orthodox believed in purgatory, but they were not willing to follow the Catholic pattern and include its existence among the official teachings of the church.

Catholic theologians today would concede that the doctrine of purgatory had led to abuses by the time of the Reformation. During the Middle Ages, it gradually became possible to avoid some penances by purchasing an indulgence. One still had to feel genuine contrition and confess, but it seemed to make more sense that a repentant sinner should sacrifice some money the church could use for good works rather than going through a penance that would benefit no one else. After 1476, one could purchase indulgences for friends or relatives in purgatory, and the immediate impetus of the Reformation came from the young Luther's sense that people were being invited, not even to *earn* salvation but to *buy* it. What had happened to grace?

Luther believed that we go to sleep at death and wake up only at the resurrection. Calvin thought that we are joyously in the presence of God or else beginning our eternal punishment as soon as we die. But both argued that heaven and hell are the only alternatives, that there was no purgatory.

THE FUTURE OF THE WORLD

The emphasis on all these teachings concerning the fate of individual souls after their deaths had the effect, however unintentionally, of downplaying the hope for the end of the present age and the inauguration of God's reign, which were so central to biblical eschatology. Christians' hopes focused more on what awaited them as individuals after death than on the future of the earth or the cosmos.

Even in the Middle Ages, however, Christian reflection about history and its end had continued. In the twelfth century, an Italian monk named Joachim of Fiore proposed that history could be divided into three ages: the Age of the Father, described in the Old Testament; the Age of the Son, which began with Jesus; and a still to come Age of the Spirit. Some of the more radical followers of St. Francis, critical of the institutional church and its wealth, believed Francis to be the founder of the Third Age, with Joachim as his John the Baptist. Similar anticipations of the imminent end of the present age appeared throughout the Middle Ages, among some Anabaptists at the time of the Reformation, and among some radicals during the English Civil War of the 1640s.[6] People who felt themselves to be outsiders, at odds with the dominant values of their culture, repeatedly found their imaginations set afire by reading the apocalyptic texts of Scripture, above all the book of

People who felt themselves to be outsiders, at odds with the dominant values of their culture, repeatedly found their imaginations set afire by reading the apocalyptic texts of Scripture, above all the book of Revelation.

Revelation. Even today, those disaffected with their society often turn to apocalyptic texts for hope.

By the eighteenth century, however, most Christians who thought about such issues believed that the reign of God on earth would come gradually, through the steady improvement of society. After all, missionaries were spreading Christianity around the world, and humankind seemed to be getting beyond the worst sins of barbarism. If things kept getting better, eventually the kind of world God wanted would gradually emerge. Again, a minority view emerged from the fringes of society. In the nineteenth century, an Irish clergyman named John Nelson Darby developed what came to be called *premillennial dispensationalism.*

Like Joachim of Fiore centuries before, Darby believed in different stages (dispensations) of history, and he thought that God has a differently ordered relationship with the world during each dispensation. The current age, he thought, will get steadily worse until Jesus' return. Then the *rapture* will lift particularly faithful people straight to heaven,[7] sparing them a horrible three-and-a-half-year period of *tribulation,* after which Jesus will reign on earth for the thousand years described in Revelation 20 as coming before the last judgment. (Jesus will return *before* the thousand-year reign—thus Darby was a *premillennialist* in contrast to *postmillennialists,* who believe that Jesus will return *after* the thousand-years reign, and *amillennialists,* who do not believe in a literal thousand-year reign at all.)

Darby's followers, the Plymouth Brethren, remained a small group in Britain and North America, just as the Seventh-Day Adventists, followers of William Miller, who in upstate New York initially predicted the end of the world in 1843 or 1844, remained relatively small in number. (The Seventh-Day Adventists drew their name because they anticipated Christ's coming or *advent* and returned to the Old Testament practice of celebrating the Sabbath on the seventh day of the week, Saturday, rather than Sunday.) But Darby came to have wide indirect influence among more conservative Christians. He was a biblical literalist, and dispensationalism provided a way to interpret the Bible literally by explaining apparently contradictory passages as referring to different dispensations. In 1909 an American lawyer named Cyrus Scofield published the *Scofield Reference Bible,* with detailed notes explaining passages in dispensationalist terms, and it became one of the standard texts of many American fundamentalists. Debates about the rapture and the thousand-year reign, topics generally unknown to other Christians, became central in this branch of Christianity.

Interest in the end of the present age was also growing in very different circles. At the beginning of the twentieth century, German scholars such as Johannes Weiss and Albert Schweitzer insisted on the importance of apocalyptic in Jesus' teaching.[8] The church, they said, had downplayed eschatology too long and made Jesus into primarily an ethical teacher. On the contrary, the expectation of the imminent end of the present age and the inauguration of God's reign stood at the center of his teaching (see, for instance, Matt. 10:28). A good many theologians conceded the point: We could reinterpret Jesus' teaching on this point, or even conclude that he had been wrong and figure out what to do about that, but we could not ignore its importance.

Another reason for academic theologians to think more about eschatology came from conversations with science. Particularly when some scientists wrote more popular books describing the ultimate fate of the universe as destruction or descent into complete chaos, some theologians felt a need to respond with an alternative cosmology. In the first half of the twentieth century, the French Jesuit paleontologist Pierre Teilhard de Chardin achieved particular note with his arguments that evolution (contrary to Darwin) was in fact a process developing toward a goal. Just as the development of the universe had led up to the development of human beings, so human development would eventually lead to a spiritual "Omega point."[9]

More recently, a number of Christian physicists have argued that a whole series of factors in the universe, if only very slightly different, would have made the existence of human beings impossible. Thus, they conclude, things are not random, but an "anthropic [human-directed] principle" is guiding development to some good end.[10]

CURRENT DEBATES

Christians today continue to discuss one very old debate—whether some people will end up lost or punished eternally. The dominant view among Orthodox, Catholics, and Protestants has been that all human beings are sinners who deserve to go to hell but that God graciously rescues some—but only some. In the words of the Athanasian Creed (written not by Athanasius but probably in the early fifth century), "Those who have done evil will go into everlasting fire."[11] Yet some theologians throughout history, most notably Origen in the early third century, have affirmed the doctrine of *apocatastasis*—the final restoration of all things. "To the Almighty nothing is impossible," Origen wrote, "nor is anything beyond the reach of cure by its Maker."[12] Therefore, "there is punishment, but not everlasting. For when the body is punished the soul is gradually purified and so is restored to its ancient rank."[13]

> Some theologians throughout history have affirmed the doctrine of *apocatastasis*—the final restoration of all things.

It is certainly possible to find passages from the New Testament supporting both positions.[14] Three of the greatest theologians of the twentieth century, the Protestant Karl Barth and the Catholics Hans Urs von Balthasar and Karl Rahner, refuse to limit God's grace and yet conclude that we cannot simply assume that all will be saved. They cautiously hope that in the end no one will be lost.[15] Perhaps here, as so often elsewhere in theology, we need to be humble and admit how much we do not know.

Both authors in this chapter seek a balance between the individual eschatology that addresses our individual fate after death and the alternative—what Richard Mouw calls *general eschatology* and what Ted Peters divides into *collective* and *cosmic* eschatology—considering, respectively, the ultimate fate of humankind and of the physical universe. Mouw, one of America's most prominent evangelical scholars, is himself an amillennialist, not persuaded that Revelation's references to a thousand-year reign should be taken literally. But he thinks premillennialists and postmillennialists have important points to make, and that debates on such matters have been too much neglected in academic theology. He urges theologians to think more seriously about the kind of eschatological questions ordinary Christians really ask. Peters writes as a theologian who has been very much engaged in conversations between theology and science, trying to think of what meaning traditional symbols about the "last things" can have for contemporary Christians.

RICHARD J. MOUW

One of the most memorable—although certainly not one of the most edifying—sermons that I heard in my youth was preached by a traveling evangelist who held a week-long crusade at a local church. For several nights he had encouraged his hearers to be sure to be present for his "prophecy night" service, when he would preach on the topic "Are Hitler and Roosevelt Really Dead?" I was there for the big night. This was in the mid-1950s, and both figures featured in his title—the much-hated Nazi dictator and the highly popular American president—had disappeared from the scene a decade earlier. But this young evangelist insisted that both were still alive. He pointed out that Hitler's body had never actually been identified in the rubble of the building where he had reportedly taken his own life, and that, in the ceremonies following the announcement of Roosevelt's death, the president's coffin had always remained closed. This preacher was convinced that not only was each of them still alive but that they were actually in hiding together somewhere in South America, plotting the takeover of the world. And he was convinced that when they reappeared on the international scene, the reign of the antichrist would begin.

I do not recall too much else about the sermon. But I do remember clearly that, while he made brief reference to the facts surrounding these alleged deaths, he spent most of his time that evening expounding some "prophetic truths" that he drew from the Scriptures. Like others who propagated these ideas, he was convinced that the events associated with the "last days" were beginning to unfold, and that the Bible provides us with solid information, especially in the books of Daniel, Ezekiel, and Revelation, regarding the end-time scenario. Once we properly

> Many candidates for the antichrist role have come and gone in the accounts offered by Bible prophecy speculators.

decode these biblical materials—understanding, for example, that the reference to "Gog and Magog" in both Ezekiel 38 and Revelation 20 is about present-day Russia (just as "Gomer" and "Meschech" in the same Ezekiel passage refer to Germany and Moscow, respectively)[1]—we can go on to identify key figures, such as Hitler and Roosevelt, and to grasp their nefarious schemes before they begin to unfold.

It is safe to assume by now that this young evangelist had it wrong. But predictive failures have done little to deter people like him. The formal plot of their prophetic speculations has remained the same throughout the decades (even centuries), even though different specific individuals have been inserted into the relevant villain roles. Take, for example, the warnings issued in John's epistles (see 1 John 2:18, 22; 4:3; and 2 John 7) regarding the appearance of the antichrist as the end of human history draws near. Many candidates for the antichrist role have come and gone in the accounts offered by Bible prophecy speculators: Catholic popes have been regularly featured, as have especially evil political leaders—during President Nixon's administration, several Bible prophecy teachers even insisted that Secretary of State Henry Kissinger was the antichrist. And the basic plotline, with somewhat different villains, is set forth in the *Left Behind* novels—best-sellers in the early years of the twenty-first century—even as it was a few decades earlier in Hal Lindsey's highly popular *The Late Great Planet Earth.*

This sort of apocalyptic interpretation of current events is not confined to Protestant fundamentalism. It shows up regularly in Roman Catholicism as well, especially in connection with Marian devotion. For example, the Virgin Mary is claimed to have appeared in 1917 to three shepherd children in Fatima, Portugal, whom she entrusted with three secrets about the end time. The children turned this information over to the pope, and one by one over the course of many decades, the three secrets of Fatima have been made public. For a long time, however, the fact that their message was not revealed to the larger world stimulated periodic speculation about the last days.[2] Some Catholic splinter groups are convinced even now that the true content of the Virgin's revelations has not really been disclosed by the hierarchy to the larger world. They tell stories of impostor popes and secret alliances between the Vatican and various anti-Christian forces in recent times—a grand conspiracy that will be brought to naught, they confidently affirm, as the events prophesied at Fatima come to pass.[3]

This sort of Christian interest in prophecies about the last days has its parallels in secular popular culture as well. New Age devotees jog while listening to tapes of *The Celestine Prophecies,* and a quick tour of the cable channels at two o'clock on any morning is quite likely to turn up an infomercial for the reading of tarot cards. The quatrains (four-line poems) of the sixteenth-century writer Nostradamus are widely believed—especially by the folks who read the supermarket tabloids—to contain coded accurate predictions about contemporary political events and natural disasters.

PASTORAL ESCHATOLOGY

What should theology—the sort of theology we study in academic settings—have to say about these matters? Anyone familiar with contemporary theologians will know that most of them have little sympathy for the kinds of interests I have been briefly describing. Most of them want nothing to do with conspiracy theories—nor are they given to the kind of specificity that characterizes grassroots thinking about prophetic topics.

None of that, however, provides a good excuse for simply ignoring these patterns in our theologizing. Theology, if it is going to serve the larger Christian community, must address the real concerns of ordinary believers. Not that theological inquiry should limit its scope to dealing with felt needs, but neither can it refuse to address those needs. Rightly understood, Christian theology has a pastoral dimension to its task. The agenda to be addressed by a well-formed theology is a broad one, but it certainly includes the deepest hopes and fears that arise out of the day-to-day concerns of the community of faith.

Indeed, it is difficult to think of a branch of academic theology that has more direct relevance to the lives of ordinary believers than eschatology. Many Christians can make it nicely through their lives as obedient servants of Jesus Christ without ever raising questions about the nature of the Trinity, or about the proper way of understanding the relationship of Christ's divinity to his humanity. But we all worry about the future. Questions about what God is doing in the world are some of the most urgent issues that we wrestle with in our lives. And none of us can avoid thinking about death and the possibility of life beyond the grave. The sorts of popular obsessions that show up so regularly in popular culture—prophecies about world events, secrets revealed by heavenly messengers, tarot cards, astrology, and the like—can all be seen as having their connections to these existential concerns.

I have been helped in understanding these connections by some observations from the missionary anthropologist Paul Hiebert regarding a lesson that he learned while working in rural villages in India. His theological education had provided him, he reports, with a broad and biblically grounded understanding of "the origin and purpose of the destiny of the self, society and universe." His training in the social sciences had given him both an empirical orientation to the study of the human condition and a set of theoretical models for interpreting his findings. But in the villages in which he worked, he quickly became aware of a gap in his understanding of the religious habits of the people whom he was attempting to serve as a representative of the church. He discovered that when converts to Christianity wrestled with very complex personal "questions of the uncertainty of the future, the crises of the present life and the unknowns of the past"—concerns about sick family members, worries about finances, fears about the destructive forces of nature—they would typically not turn to the church for answers. Instead, they would return, Hiebert observed, to the local diviner, an authority whom they saw as capable of giving them specific answers for "the problems that loom large in their everyday life." This experience convinced Hiebert of the need for Christians to develop "a holistic theology" that would deal with the ways of "God in human history: in the affairs of nations, of peoples and of individuals." Such a perspective would develop a "theology of divine guidance, provision and healing; of ancestors, spirits, invisible powers of this world; and of suffering misfortune and death."[4]

Theology needs to help us understand better the ways of God in human affairs—both the big patterns of our collective existence and the specifics of our own individual lives.

Hiebert's agenda is a complex one, but it obviously includes eschatological topics. And the concerns he is asking us to address in this regard are not limited to the residents of villages in India. They are the stuff of everyday human life as such. Theology needs to help us understand better the ways of God in human affairs—both the big patterns of our collective existence and the specifics of our own individual lives.

It should be obvious, of course, that Christian theology should not even try to compete with the diviners and astrologers at their own game. From a Christian way of viewing things, they are offering the kinds of answers that we should not expect to receive. But this is precisely the kind of topic theologians need to explore. We can address the underlying human concerns that drive human beings to seek out the "expertise" of the shamans—whether they practice in Asian villages or advertise their services in our local newpapers—by clarifying the differences between the magical worldview and a mature Christian faith. Magic seeks to control reality by formulaic power; if we perform the right rituals or utter the right words or tap into the right sources, we can make things happen in accordance with our own desires. The desire to know precise details about the future is related to this way of viewing reality; if we only know where to look, we can discover secrets that are hidden to the rest of humankind, or we can decodify crucial "prophetic" information about the future.

To be sure, the Christian message does contain themes that at first glance resemble those of the magical worldview. For example, the apostle tells the Colossians that "the mystery that has been hidden throughout the ages and generations . . . has now been revealed to the saints" (Col. 1:26). And this mystery does give the believing community "inside" information about the future. But the mystery that is revealed is not so much about specific events as it is about a person and his mission. The mystery, the apostle tells us, is this: "Christ in you, the hope of glory" (Col. 1:27). We can face the future with a basic confidence, not because we have been provided with a special collection of secret facts about what is to come, but because we have been allowed by grace to enter into a relationship with the Lord of the future.

The Christian life is all about *trust* in the promises of a personal God, a sovereign Ruler who assures us of the ultimate victory over all that oppresses us.

Pastoral eschatology must develop the resources for guiding Christian people toward a spiritual maturity that features this sort of trust. And this will include paying attention to the proper ways for understanding how the Bible addresses questions about the future course of history.

NINETEENTH-CENTURY PREDICTIONS

The final years of the nineteenth century offer us a fascinating case study in contrasting Christian views about the kind of thing we can expect in the course of human history. Many liberal Protestants were quite hopeful about what the new century would bring. In their thinking, they combined the idea of progress—quite popular in some intellectual circles at the time—with a growing interest in "the social gospel." They were convinced that through the efforts of Christians who opposed poverty, warfare, and other human ills, considerable gains would be made in establishing a social order that would embody the peace and justice that is associated with the kingdom of God. Some of them even expressed the conviction that the world was about to enter into "the Christian century"—thus the name of a still-popular Christian magazine, which was founded at the time.

This outlook differed greatly from the views of the Protestant movement that would soon come to be known as *fundamentalism.* These Christians were busy organizing "Bible prophecy conferences," in which a decidedly pessimistic view of the future was set forth. The speakers at these gatherings taught that the world was entering "the last days," where the events would come to pass that Jesus spoke about as immediately preceding the end time: "wars and rumors of wars . . . nation will rise against nation, and kingdom against kingdom . . . famines and earthquakes in various places" (Matt. 24:6–7).

> In retrospect, the Bible prophecy people were much closer to the truth. The new century not only failed to bring the just and peaceful social order that the liberal Protestants hoped for, but it was a period of horrendous evils. For all of that, of course, the Bible prophecy people were wrong about many things too.

In retrospect, the Bible prophecy people were much closer to the truth. The new century not only failed to bring the just and peaceful social order that the liberal Protestants hoped for, but it was a period of horrendous evils: the Holocaust, nuclear destruction, the spread of totalitarian communism, political corruption in Western democracies, apartheid. There were indeed many wars and rumors of wars, nations did rise up against nations, and famines and earthquakes did devastate many populations.

But for all of that, of course, the Bible prophecy people were wrong about many things. The battle of Armageddon did not take place in the twentieth century. Every proposed identification of some particular tyrant as *the* antichrist turned out to be mistaken. Many of their favorite scenarios fell apart with the collapse of the Soviet Union.

The fact that both late nineteenth-century perspectives—liberalism and fundamentalism—were seriously mistaken in their specific predictions about the twentieth century does not mean, though, that they are not worthy of our theological attention. They represent two very prominent Christian views about how history "goes"—views that influence in fundamental ways Christian expectations about the future. We need to take views of this sort seriously, because not only do they have important implications for other theological topics, but they also are crucial factors in shaping our spiritual outlooks.

THINKING ABOUT THE MILLENNIUM

One helpful way of understanding the theological options here is to examine the three major schools of thought in the Christian tradition regarding the reference to the thousand-year reign of Christ in Revelation 20:1–6. Actually, these labels are most familiar to evangelicals. (We evangelical types not only spend much effort mapping out the future—we also put in more time than other Christians do in mapping out *views* about the future!) But while the distinctions marked out by these three labels may not be common currency in the larger theological world, they do help to clarify matters that are important for other theological systems.

The three labels refer to how the schools of thought understand the relationship of Christ's return to the millennial period.[5] *Premillennialists* believe that Christ will return from heaven before the millennium. *Postmillennialists* believe he will return after the millennium. *Amillennialists* do not believe that there is a literal millennium that will take place in the future.

Premillennialists believe that Christ will return from heaven before the millennium. Postmillennialists believe he will return after the millennium. Amillennialists do not believe that there is a literal millennium that will take place in the future.

The premillennialists are the most literal in their interpretation of Revelation 20 and other texts that have an end-time feel. After the bad things prophesied in Matthew 24 occur, they say, the scenario sketched out in Revelation 20 will unfold as described there. Christ will return and "bind" Satan, putting the evil one out of commission for a thousand years. During this time, Christ—along with those who have been martyred for the faith throughout history—will bring a worldwide millennial reign of peace and righteousness. When the millennium comes to an end, Satan will be released and will deceive a vast majority of the human race. A mighty conflict will then take place—the great battle of Armageddon (see Rev. 16:15–16). Here Satan will be decisively defeated and will be cast into "the lake of fire and sulfur," where he will be "tormented day and night forever and ever" (Rev. 20:10).

The postmillennialists take less of a "blow-by-blow" approach in their interpretation of Revelation 20. The actual one-thousand-year number, they say, does not need to be understood literally; it may be only a symbol. But it does point, they insist, to an extended reign of peace and righteousness that will occur in the last stages of human history, prior to Christ's triumphant return. During this period, the Christian church will make great gains in its influence. Many will be brought into the church, and the influence of Christian teaching will have a positive influence throughout the world, even where people do not convert to the Christian faith. Peace and righteousness will prevail, with a significant alleviation of the problems that have long plagued humankind.

Amillennialists do not interpret the reference to the millennium to be a prophecy about a future period of time. They argue that this is a highly symbolic way of pointing to the establishment of the church. In his redemptive work on the cross, and in his victorious resurrection, Christ "bound" Satan—he guaranteed the inevitable defeat of the evil one. The founding of the church at Pentecost is the beginning of the "millennium"; the one-thousand-year reign is a symbol for the perfection of God's reign as it has been realized in the life and mission of the Christian community. To be sure, the struggle with Satan's power continues, but his doom is already sealed. When Christ returns, "making all things new" (Rev. 21:5), Satan and his legions will finally be banished from the transformed creation.

THE DIRECTION OF HISTORY

As Stanley Grenz has observed, each of these schools of thought about the millennium "illustrates a deeper conviction concerning the flow of history." Premillennialism has often fostered a rather pessimistic view of how things will unfold as we move toward the culmination of human history, while postmillennialism has generated a more optimistic outlook. Amillennialism, which Grenz associates with a "realistic" perspective, does not necessarily commit to either a pessimistic or an optimistic viewpoint. It insists that "victory and defeat, success and failure, good and evil will coexist until the end."[6]

To be sure, there are also important questions at stake here in biblical interpretation, issues that we will not be able to attend to in this discussion. But the very question of the relationship of one's interpretation of specific texts to one's views about the overall direction of history is itself an interesting topic to consider. For example, while postmillennialism was very popular in the nineteenth century, when the ideology of progress was a dominant motif in the larger culture, today it is a much less attractive perspective. This is not simply because people became less convinced of postmillennialism's interpretation of biblical texts. One obvious factor in the demise of postmillennial eschatology is the developments we have already mentioned: The past one hundred years or so have produced events that make it difficult to believe that the church's message of peace and righteousness has been influential in bettering the general condition of humankind. Another factor has been the emergence of religious and irreligious perspectives that are openly hostile to Christian belief and practice, such as militant Islam and a secularist ideology.

It is interesting to note also the parallels between the apocalyptic outlook that shows up so often in fundamentalist Protestantism and the viewpoints of Christian groups who pay much less attention to the specifics of "Bible prophecy." Consider, for example, the attitudes that are sometimes associated with the strong Catholic interest, mentioned earlier, in Marian apparitions. For Roman Catholicism, with its robust understanding of "the development of dogma" and its long tradition of openness to visions and miraculous intercessions, the notion that God would reveal some new secrets about the course of history through the Blessed Virgin is not an outrageous one. But when sensational information about the future is delivered directly to ordinary Catholics by the Blessed Virgin herself, this sometimes gives rise to a grassroots theology that is out of step with official teaching—a danger that takes shape in its starkest form in the thinking of the Catholic dissident groups that I mentioned earlier. The dissidents see the hostility of the hierarchy toward their teachings as itself a part of the prophecies' fulfillment. They are convinced that official Catholicism is a part of an evil conspiracy that looms large in their pessimistic outlook on the course of human history. The result is the emergence of a sectarian version of Catholicism that has strong formal similarities to certain versions of Protestant fundamentalism. Each of them espouses an apocalyptic eschatology in which for both groups, ironically, the Vatican is seen as a force for evil! Their pessimistic outlook on the immediate future is tied to a "remnant" ecclesiology in which the "true church" is identified with a small group of faithful believers who have been entrusted with the secrets about the bad things that will happen prior to Christ's return.

In dealing with this sort of apocalyptic outlook, whether in its Protestant or Catholic varieties, it will probably do no good simply to offer alternative interpretations of either biblical texts or the church's teachings. The underlying issues here are likely tied to a sense of cultural marginalization and a distrust of the more "official" versions of Christian thought. People who accept the apocalyptic scenarios often do so because they feel a lack of control over their personal and collective destinies.

WHAT WE *CAN* SAY ABOUT THE FUTURE

An effective pastoral eschatology must address this question of control, and our pastoral approach must give expression to this very basic biblical truth: that the business of controlling is not something that is up to us as human beings. Our responsibility is to trust in God's control. The old slogan put it well: "I know not what the future holds, but I know who holds the future."

But we must also be clear about the fact that the God who is in control of the future has not left us completely ignorant about what will inevitably come to pass. While we are right to approach the futuristic dimensions of eschatology with much caution, our caution ought not to inhibit us from affirming those things that we *can* be confident about, as people who have received a word from the Lord on how things will turn out in the end.

The world has not seen the last of Jesus of Nazareth. He is coming again. And when the final act of human history is completed, people—all the human beings who have ever lived—will appear before the divine Judge. Those who are "in Christ" will be raised up to eternal life.

Basic to what we firmly believe about the future are the eschatological convictions expressed in the Apostles' Creed: We believe that the One who presently sits at the right hand of the Father will come from heaven "to judge the living and the dead"; and we believe in "the resurrection of the body, and the life everlasting." These teachings, accepted by faith by the believing community, set forth the basic plot of the end time. The world has not seen the last of Jesus of Nazareth. He is coming again. And when the final act of human history is completed, people—all the human beings who have ever lived—will appear before the divine Judge. Those who are "in Christ" will be raised up to eternal life. These convictions are essential components of the biblical narrative. To believe these things is to face the future with a fundamental confidence in God's wise purposes.

I am also convinced that there is other revealed information about the end time that we must take seriously. My own views about biblical interpretation lead me to question many of the "Bible prophecy" scenarios that are based on highly symbolic passages, such as those found in the book of Revelation. But there are passages in, for example, the Pauline epistles that do clearly urge us to be on guard about events that are yet to occur. An important case in point is the warning spelled out in 2 Thessalonians 2:1–12. There the apostle tells us that the day of the Lord "will not come unless the rebellion comes first and the lawless one is revealed." This person will make himself known some time before the return of Christ, "declaring himself to be God."

Is this a prophecy about someone who has already appeared in history? Perhaps—but I am not convinced that this fits the sense of the passage. Is it a graphic way of warning the believing community of the ever present threat of a spirit of lawlessness that threatens to wreak havoc in the good creation? Perhaps—but I am not satisfied with this interpretation either. The apostle seems to me to be telling us something rather specific, namely, that when the last days approach, a highly influential person will appear on the scene who embodies in a special way the spirit of lawlessness that stands over against God's creating and redeeming purposes. This warning, which has important links to other references to the antichrist in the epistles, strikes me as something we must take seriously as we look to the future.

I am convinced that it is *healthy* for us to take a warning of this sort seriously. Whether I am right or wrong in suspecting that this is information about a specific person who is yet to appear in history, it is certainly a good thing for Christians to be on the lookout for special signs of of lawlessness, of rebellion—overt or subtle—against God's creating and redeeming purposes in the world. As long as we prepare ourselves to oppose this lawlessness wherever and whenever it appears, this sensitivity to warnings about the future can serve to strengthen us for faithfulness to the gospel.

There are two important defects that have characterized much of the "Bible prophecy" approach to eschatology when dealing with a biblical passage like the one just discussed. One is that the typical response has been to focus on the identity of "the lawless *one*"—engaging in endless speculation about who the specific individual might be—rather than cultivating sensitivities to the ongoing *patterns* of lawlessness that afflict humankind. The other is that when attention *has* been given to the phenomenon of lawlessness, it has often been with a rather myopic focus, often with an emphasis on rising crime rates and the like. To be sure, this kind of lawlessness deserves to be criticized. But the Christian community must also address the broader patterns of lawlessness that show a disregard for that which God deeply cares about: racial justice, the plight of the poor, fidelity in human relationships, the dignity of the nonhuman created order.

A VISIBLE REIGN

While my own sympathies lie with the amillennial position, there are some features of the *pre-* and *post-* perspectives that I admire. I especially appreciate the way in which both perspectives place a strong emphasis on the need for the reign of Christ to be manifest as a concrete reality. Here is how George Ladd, a premillennialist theologian, made the point: "Christ is now reigning as Lord and King, but his reign is veiled, unseen and unrecognized by the world. . . . His reign must become public in power and glory and his Lordship universally recognized."[7]

> Amillennialists tend to miss out on the motivating force for Christian action that is generated by the other two perspectives.

The core insight here is an important one, and it is sometimes missed by amillennialists, who—in reaction to the literal interpretations of the other two schools of thought—tend to spiritualize the idea of the reign of Christ, locating this reality primarily in the "hearts" of believers. In so doing, they tend also to miss out on the motivating force for Christian action that is generated by the two other perspectives. This motivation is obvious in the case of postmillennialism, which encourages Christians to see themselves as agents of an expansive Christian "kingdom building" in fulfillment of prophecy. Since premillennialists are not known for their social activism, it may seem that they do not draw on similar motivational resources. But while premillennialists have traditionally been weak in their understanding of the corporate dimensions of the gospel, they have in fact been extremely diligent in evangelistic-missionary type of activities. This is because they believe that the millennial reign—which will be ushered in by the return of Christ—can only happen after the gospel has been preached to all of the nations of the earth.

The *pre-* and *post-* positions, then, have each in their own way encouraged an activism that is clearly linked to their understanding of prophecy. Any perspective that rejects their ways of interpreting the Bible's scenario for the future must be sure to find other ways of motivating the Christian community actively to make visible the present reign of Christ in the midst of our broken world.

FORETELLING AND FORTHTELLING

There is an old distinction that has been used to distinguish between two dimensions of the prophetic task: Prophesying includes both *foretelling* and *forthtelling*. The biblical prophets were allowed, by the illumination of God's Spirit, to look into the future—they *foretold* what was to come. But they also spoke boldly about God's concerns concerning what was happening in the present—they *forthtold* God's message for contemporary life, calling human beings, in both individual and collective settings, to conform to divine standards of righteousness.

These two tasks are also assigned to the church. We too can foretell some features about what the end of history will be like. But we also must speak forth a message about God's will for present-day life. The contours of this twofold mission were made clear to the disciples at the time of Jesus' ascension to heaven. After their Lord had disappeared into the clouds, his followers received an important message of assurance from the angels: "This Jesus, who has been taken up from you into heaven, will come in the same way as you saw him go into heaven" (Acts 1:11). But this word about the future came only after an important conversation between the disciples and their Lord, just before he departed from their midst. When they asked him whether he would now "restore the kingdom to Israel," he replied by warning them that "it is not for you to know the times or periods that the Father has set by his own authority." But this they *could* know, he quickly added: "You will receive power when the Holy Spirit has come upon you; and you will be my witnesses" (Acts 1:7–8).

We cannot separate the foretelling from the forthtelling function. This is the mistake that is often made by Christians who spend a lot of time thinking about "prophetic truths." They act as if they are passive observers of an unfolding divine plan—as people who stand on the sidelines of history calmly checking off events on a prophetic scorecard. But this is not the way the biblical prophets engaged in their task. They were very concerned to call people in their own cultural surroundings to turn from their wicked ways and live in obedience to the divine will.

To be sure, they also talked about what God would bring about in the future. But in doing so they were not crystal ball–gazers who "read" the future in a dispassionate manner, using a "historical" mode of discourse to describe events that had not yet come to pass. Rather, as persons who were intensely involved in the agonies of their own historical situation, they discerned—usually in terms of images and types, but always with a consciousness of God's mighty acts in the past—the shape of the fulfillment that the Lord of history would bring about by sovereign power. And this is also the way the church is called to respond to Jesus' mandate: "You will be my witnesses"—as foretellers *and* forthtellers.

GENERAL ESCHATOLOGY AND INDIVIDUAL ESCHATOLOGY

If we were to provide a comprehensive discussion of "last things" here, we would have to honor the traditional distinction between *general eschatology* and *individual eschatology*. Our focus here has been on the general. Given the complexity of topics relating to the eternal destiny of individuals—"intermediate state," purgatory, resurrection of the body, heaven and hell—it might seem arbitrary to turn to some very brief comments on that aspect of the subject in these concluding paragraphs.

We must at least note, however, that an effective pastoral eschatology will pay close attention to the relationships between the two areas of concern. I observed earlier that Christians often buy into apocalyptic schemes about the future of the human race—and a corresponding view of the church as a "remnant" that stands on the margins of culture—because they sense that things are out of control. The appropriate pastoral response to this syndrome, I insisted, is not so much to convince them that *they* can control things, but to nurture in them an abiding trust in *God's* sovereign rule over all of reality.

> "What is thy only comfort in life and in death?"
> "That I, with body and soul, both in life and in death, am not my own, but belong to my faithful Savior Jesus Christ."
> — Heidelberg Catechism

But this surely also includes a trust in God's control over our *individual* destinies. We all need to be reassured that the One who charts the paths of history in general also cares deeply about each of us in our individual uniqueness. Our efforts to "tell forth" a message of healing for the large wounds that inflict our present collective existence must draw on the deep assurance that our own very personal wounds are being healed by the power that has been made available to each of us through the Savior's atoning work.

There are many helpful resources to draw upon in developing a model for the kind of pastoral eschatology that integrates the general and the personal. My own favorite is the sixteenth-century Reformed confessional document, the Heidelberg

Catechism. Unlike its British counterpart, the Westminster Shorter Catechism, which begins with a question about generic humanity—"What is the chief end of man?"—the Heidelberger employs a very personal voice. Its first question and answer speak in warmly spiritual tones of both the assurance of Christ's loving care and our responsibility to serve God's purposes in the world:

> What is thy only comfort in life and in death?
>
> That I, with body and soul, both in life and in death, am not my own, but belong to my faithful Savior Jesus Christ, who with his precious blood has fully satisfied for all my sins, and redeemed me from all the power of the devil; and so preserves me that without the will of my Father in heaven not a hair can fall from my head; yea, that all things must work together for my salvation. Wherefore, by his Holy Spirit, he also assures me of eternal life, and makes me heartily willing and ready henceforth to live unto him.[8]

As the catechism goes on to deal with major Christian teachings, it regularly focuses on the meaning of those teachings for the individual Christian life. Especially helpful for our present discussion is the treatment of the rule of the ascended Christ. Having confessed that Christ presently "governs all things" and "defends and preserves us against all enemies,"[9] the catechized is then asked, "What comfort is it to thee that Christ *shall come again to judge the quick and the dead?*" The answer begins, "That in all my sorrows and persecutions, with uplifted head, I look for the self-same One who has before offered himself for me to the judgment of God, and removed from me all curse, to come again as Judge from heaven. . . ."[10]

This is a powerful affirmation, and not only for what it means regarding "all *my* sorrows and persecutions." In a world in which so many people are experiencing such horrendous forms of oppression, it is important to know that there is indeed a divine Judge who will bring about a just solution in the end. But it is also important to draw on the comfort that the catechism describes. This Judge is "the self-same One" who has stood in our place, taking all of our sufferings upon himself at Calvary, and thereby securing the means of the final victory over sin and death.

The Lord of history is both Savior and Judge. The One who controls the broad paths of humankind in general is "the self-same One" who holds each of our personal destinies in hands that were pierced by the nails at Calvary. This crucial message, along with the call to bear active witness to the reign of God, must be at the heart of a theology that speaks to our deepest concerns—both general and individual—about "last things."

Ted Peters

To ask "Where are we going?" assumes change. Most simply, "going" means changing locations in space over time. Yet, even if we remain in one space, we are "going" in the sense that time changes our state of being. Nothing remains static. All of creation is in movement. Theologically speaking, this movement is toward fulfillment, consummation, the attainment of God's purposes and goals. Key here is the concept of the end, end as both completion (*finis*) and goal (*telos*).

Eschatology is the part of Christian theology that focuses on what is ultimate, final, definitive. Yet, because the word *eschatology* means "study of last things," it is also like a laundry basket into which we toss a variety of conceptual garments to dress our vision of the future. These garments include: new creation, the everlasting kingdom of God, the second advent of Christ, death, resurrection, judgment, heaven, hell, purgatory, and related concerns. Out of the eschatological basket, this essay will draw three ensembles concerned with: the future of the individual (individual eschatology), the future of humanity (collective or universal eschatology), and the future of the world (cosmic eschatology).

INDIVIDUAL ESCHATOLOGY: ANXIETY OVER TIME

To be is to have a future. As soon as our future is eliminated, we cease to exist. When we sense that our future is about to be taken away from us or even constricted, we become anxious. Will I be forever constricted to the cold black box of my own past? Will I be buried below while the world above lives on beyond me? Will I be dropped into the dark abyss while reality moves on without me? Will I cease to exist? Will the cumulative meaning of my tradition, my life story, my relationships, my achievements, my unfulfilled dreams, all simply dribble away like sand through my fingers?

Time is both friend and thief. As friend, time allots to each of us the years that make up our life story; or it allots to our people centuries to construct meaningful traditions that permit cumulative creativity to build monuments of achievement and identity. As thief, time is constantly passing, ever eroding, ever destroying, ever forgetting. Time is merciless. Time steals from every entity its future; everything is subject to its relentless rusting, corroding, weakening, dissipating, and dissolving. The Christian hymn "O God, Our Help in Ages Past" by Isaac Watts (1674–1748) reflects our anxiety over time:

> Time, like an ever-rolling stream,
> Soon bears us all away,
> We fly forgotten, as a dream
> Dies at the op'ning day.

Am I only a dream, scheduled to die at the opening of the next day? Is this cosmos scheduled for the same fate?

These are existential questions, because they cut to the depth of our very existence. Hamlet's "To be, or not to be?" is an existential question. It is a question to which Christian eschatology is poised to offer an answer. We may not have the power of our own future in our own hands, but God has a future. And God promises that we will be part of that divine future. God comforts our anxiety over time by offering us eternity. This divine promise is the ground of Christian hope.

Although the Christian hope is specific to the followers of Jesus, the existential questions it addresses are universal. People in virtually all cultural contexts ask these questions, and they propose answers. In our contemporary pluralistic context, we are confronted by a diversity of competing views on nearly a daily basis. It can be helpful in pursuing Christian theology to compare and contrast distinctively Christian commitments with alternative religious and secular views. Not only does this method help clarify what commitments Christians are willing to make, it compels the theologian to say why we believe what we do. It responds to the biblical admonition to be ever ready to provide "an accounting for the hope that is in you" (1 Pet. 3:15).

> Options concerning existence after death: scientific naturalism, immortality of the soul, reincarnation and absorption into the infinite, astral projection, ancestral presence as the living dead, out-of-body experiences, and bodily resurrection.

In what follows immediately I will ask: What does Christian theology affirm about life beyond death? The Christian answer to the question of what lies beyond death is only one among a plurality of options. What we in the modern West call *scientific naturalism,* for example, simply accepts death as the final end to life. Nature is the only reality. This atheistic position denies that anything happens to the individual after he or she dies. At the other extreme we find the classic belief in the *immortal soul.* Coming into the West from ancient Greek philosophy, this belief holds that the essence of each person is found in the immaterial soul or mind, and once we have died and shed the body, our immortal soul will go on to live disembodied in eternity. The vocabulary of the immortal soul can be found in the New Testament, but the emphasis on resurrection of the body distinguishes the Christian position from the Greek position.

A third option grows out of ancient India, namely, reincarnation and absorption into the infinite. The Indian equivalent of the soul or self is the Atman. Each of us as Atman is essentially at one with the whole of reality, with the All, with the infinite reality of Brahman. Our spiritual task, accordingly, is to realize consciously that we are one with Brahman, that our finite selves are in fact infinite. If we fail to attain this realization during our lifespan, then the law of karma will have an effect on us, and we will be subject to rebirth. After we die, we will be reincarnated and live another finite life. Only when in one of our incarnations we realize the truth that our Atman is at one with Brahman will we be able to jump off the wheel of rebirth and enter eternal rest, *moksha,* or bliss, *ananda.*

A fourth option is *astral projection*. The concept of the astral body is found in occult and New Age spirituality. The word *astral* has to do with the stars, and our essence here is found in our "star body," which has form but no substance. Upon death the astral body is released from our physical body to climb the seven planes of spiritual existence and pursue absorption into the infinite oneness of all things.

The fifth on our list of options comes from traditional African culture—*ancestral presence as the living dead.* Among East African tribal cultures, we find belief in the spiritual presence of deceased ancestors who influence the course of a family's activities. After a period of five generations or so, when no one can remember their names, they begin to fade into nonexistence.

Sixth, returning to the modern West, we find *life-after-life,* or *out-of-body experiences.* These are typically clinical deaths in the operating room where a person feels he or she departs from the body and views the body remotely. This may involve seeing and hearing events in remote sites. Symbolism of a dark tunnel with a light at the end of it frequently accompanies reports of such dramatic experiences. Some claim to visit heaven or hell and then return. These reports seem to repudiate naturalism, but it is not yet clear whether they retrieve immortality of the soul or astral projection.

What Christian eschatology teaches conforms to none of these options. What each of the last five options share in common is an individual eschatology with a *soulechtomy* ("soul-removing operation")—that is, they tend toward extracting a nonmaterial essence or soul from a person and slating this soul to live on without the body and without the physical world. In contrast, it appears quite clear that followers of Jesus affirm a future resurrection of the body; and our bodies in the resurrection require an accompanying renewed world, the new creation or kingdom of God.

What follows will first proceed along the trail of individual eschatology, looking at the theology of death, the significance of the death of Jesus, and the relation of Jesus' Easter resurrection to cosmic eschatology. We will turn then to understanding heaven and hell, and take up collective eschatology by asking about the debate between double destiny and universal salvation.

Death as the Destruction of Evil

What about death? Is death just a blemish on God's otherwise good creation? Or does death have positive theological significance?

The biblical story of the garden of Eden in Genesis 2–3 introduces us to the tension between knowing that we must die yet imagining life without dying. The fall into sin that subjects us to mortality was precipitated by the violation of God's command to avoid the knowledge of good and evil. Reacting to this disobedience, God threw Adam and Eve out of the garden and placed the cherubim at the gate with a flaming sword, preventing the man and woman from returning. Why did God react with such force? Was it due to a divine temper tantrum? Could God plead temporary insanity, claiming that it was blind rage that drove him to pull the trigger that led to the death of Adam and Eve? No, the expulsion from the garden expresses the same abiding love of God that leads to redemption and salvation.

The reason for the expulsion from the garden of Eden has to do with the second special tree. Although Adam and Eve had eaten the fruit from the tree of the knowledge of good and evil, they had not yet tasted fruit from the tree of life. This is theologically important. Had they eaten fruit from the tree of life, then they would "live forever" (Gen. 3:22). What we now call *the fall* introduced into God's otherwise good creation such things as enmity between humans and wild beasts, the sweat of the brow by which a living must be wrested from nature, pain in childbirth, and all manner of suffering. None of us, not even God, wants the items on this list to continue forever. It is redemptive love, then, that motivates God to separate Adam and Eve from the tree of life. In its own way death becomes a gift of divine grace; it marks the point at which the consequences for sin come to an end. There is no suffering in the grave. Death is the door that God slams shut on evil and suffering within his creation.

"The wages of sin is death," writes Paul (Rom. 6:23). What does this mean? We may interpret this negatively to mean that death is the appropriate penalty for disobedience. Yet we might consider another interpretation as well. Might we say, in light of Genesis 3 and in light of Easter, that death plays an important role in the divine plan of salvation? Could we think of death as a necessary step down the path toward resurrection to new life, to a new life immune from the sufferings of this fallen world?

The Bible severely affirms that we humans are mortal. We really do die and cease to exist.

If this interpretation holds, then we need to emphasize the totality of death. The Bible severely affirms that we humans are mortal. We really do die and cease to exist. There is no salvation by heroic soulechtomy. The understanding of sin with which we work is that sin is a virus which eats away at the totality of human existence, leaving no organ, whether physical or spiritual, uninfected. The resulting death means full extinction.

Curiously, this appears to come close to the model of scientific naturalism. Death, theologically understood, puts an end to all that we are and have on this side of mortality. It puts an end to all evil. It also puts an end to all that is good, mortally good. We do not possess an intrinsically good, immortal soul that is somehow exempt from the disease of sin so that it can simply shed the body like a shelled oyster and go on to a heavenly plane of disembodied souls. And certainly there is no room for an evil, immortal soul that similarly sheds the body so that its evil existence will continue on everlastingly. Whoever and whatever we are dies totally and completely. Death symbolizes that end, the termination.

The Death and Resurrection of Jesus

The result of the Adam and Eve story applies to Jesus. The messiah is born a mortal and dies a mortal, and he knows it. Death for Jesus is the end. In Gethsemane he is "greatly distressed and troubled," saying to his disciples, "my soul is sorrowful, even to death" (Mark 14:33–34). In agony Jesus prays "with loud cries and tears" (Heb. 5:7), and his sweat becomes like great drops of blood falling down upon the ground" (Luke 22:44). Jesus petitions God, "Remove this cup from me" (Mark 14:36). "Jesus is afraid," writes Oscar Cullmann. "He is afraid in the face of death itself. Death for him is not something divine; it is something dreadful."[1] Jesus cries from the cross, "My God, my God, why have you forsaken me?" (Mark 15:34). This is death in all its frightful horror. It is what Paul calls the "last enemy" of God (1 Cor. 15:26).

Does this suggest that Jesus is cowardly? By no means. His courage is stalwart. Despite his petition in the Gethsemane prayer that he not have to drink the cup of death, he still concludes his prayer, "Yet not what I want, but what you want" (Mark 14:36). And despite his agonizing sense of abandonment on the cross, he still cries out, "Father, into your hands I commend my spirit" (Luke 23:46). Death is terrible, but Jesus' faith is strong.

The death Jesus dies on Good Friday is the death of Adam, the death of us all. Yet this is not the end of the story. On Easter, God raises the dead Jesus to new and everlasting life. Jesus dies a mortal, but God the creator of the old creation acts with the power of the new creation. God bestows new life.

This new life—the life of the new creation—is different from the old life which Jesus gave up. The new life is no longer subject to sin, suffering, or death. It is this that makes Jesus' resurrection salvific. In this regard we see a contrast between Jesus' Easter resurrection and other resurrection miracles, such as the widow's son at Nain (Luke 7:11–17), Jairus's daughter (Mark 5:21–43), and Lazarus (John 11:38–44). In these miracles we find the resuscitation of a corpse. Three persons were raised, but they were not raised to immortality. They were simply returned to mortal life. They would all have to face death again just like the rest of us. But Jesus' corpse was not merely resuscitated, not merely restored to ordinary life. No one expected Jesus to return to Nazareth to resume his duties as a carpenter. Jesus' resurrected existence had become eschatological. Jesus will not have to die again. When those who enjoyed fellowship with the risen Jesus reported what they saw, they did not say, "Wow, the Nazarene is back!" Rather, they reported that they had seen "the Lord" (Luke 24:34; John 20:18).[2]

Easter opens the gate so that as we share in Jesus' resurrection we pass through to a new and everlasting life. Jesus is the "first fruits" of those who have fallen "asleep" in their graves (1 Cor. 15:20). Jesus is the anticipation, the prefiguration, the prolepsis of what we will become in our resurrection. As he rose on Easter, so will we rise into the new creation. As we turn and look backward, we see Jesus' death standing like the angel with the fiery sword at the garden of Eden, preventing suffering and death from following us into the new creation.

The Spiritual Body

At this point we will turn to more detail regarding the nature of the resurrected body. As we proceed, it will become clear that we are working with a new model, one quite different from those discussed earlier.

The image Paul employs is that of a seed planted in the ground. The flower or tree that grows up looks quite different from what had been planted. However, in order to guard against any possible misinterpretation in terms of soulechtomy, he exploits the deadlike appearance of the typical seed to say, "What you sow does not come to life unless it dies" (1 Cor. 15:36). This analogy is delicate. Paul wishes to affirm continuity and discontinuity between the present and future realities. Resurrection is not exactly creation out of nothing, but creation of something out of something else. In contrast to the creation of the world out of nothing, *creatio ex nihilo,* resurrection is transformation or *creatio ex vetera* ("creation out of something old"); yet the power of God's creation is at work in both instances. This is the point Paul is making: A dead seed is sown, but what is harvested is new life.

Paul describes this eschatological harvest in terms of four complementary contrasts:

> So it is with the resurrection of the dead. What is sown is perishable [corrupt, *phthora*], what is raised is imperishable [incorrupt, *aphtharsia*]. It is sown in dishonor [*atimia*], it is raised in glory [*doxa*]. It is sown in weakness [*astheneia*], it is raised in power [*dynamei*]. It is sown a physical body [*soma psychikon*], it is raised a spiritual body [*soma pneumatikon*]. (1 Cor. 15:42–44)

To be raised "imperishable," whether applicable to Jesus or to us, is to be raised to everlasting life. One's body would not be resuscitated for the purpose of simply returning to one's daily toil. *Doxa,* which in reference to the heavenly bodies usually means "luster," here means we are raised in "honor." The "power" into which we will be raised, *dynamis,* is the same power by which miracles of healing are performed (1 Cor. 12:28).

"So it is with the resurrection of the dead. What is sown is perishable, what is raised is imperishable. It is sown in dishonor, it is raised in glory. It is sown in weakness, it is raised in power. It is sown a physical body, it is raised a spiritual body." —1 Cor. 15:42–44

It is theologically important, I think, to give special attention to the contrast between the earthly and the spiritual bodies. Paul does not describe the dead earthly body as a "body of flesh" (*soma sarkikon*), as one might have expected. Rather, Paul describes it as a "psychic body" (*soma psychikon*). Literally, this is the ensouled body which we would associate with the Greek philosophical tradition. This notion of a human being was commonly known among Greek-speaking Jews such as Paul. The import is this: For Paul, the soul dies. And as if to rub it in, Paul says it is not the *psyche* which we find in the resurrection, it is the *soma.* The resurrected body is a "spiritual body" that rises into the new creation, into God's kingdom.[3]

THE COMING NEW CREATION: COSMIC ESCHATOLOGY

As I have been suggesting, human destiny is inseparable from cosmic destiny. One element in common among the various models of immortality—scientific naturalism, immortality of the soul, reincarnation with absorption into the infinite, astral projection, ancestral presence, and life after life—is this: They all deal with the question of human destiny in isolation from that of cosmic destiny. All assume the natural world will remain basically what it is. Not so with the Christian vision. What happens to us depends on what happens to the universe. The resurrection to a spiritual body can only occur at the advent of the *eschaton*, the "end time." If there is no cosmic transformation, then there is no resurrection, and if there is no resurrection, then our faith is in vain and we of all people are most to be pitied (1 Cor. 15:14, 19).

This means that your resurrection and my resurrection are indispensably tied to the eschatological *parousia,* the second coming of Christ. Paul suggests an order to things. First comes Christ, the first fruits (1 Cor. 15:23). This probably refers to Easter. Then at his coming, "the dead in Christ will rise first, then we who are alive" (1 Thess. 4:16–17). He "will transform the body of our humiliation that it may be conformed to the body of his glory" (Phil. 3:21; see Rom. 8:29). "Then comes the end, when he hands over the kingdom to God the Father, after he has destroyed every ruler and every authority and power. . . . The last enemy to be destroyed is death" (1 Cor. 15:24, 26). To understand the resurrected body, we need to place it within the broader horizon of God's promised new creation. As the creation is transformed, so are we.

The Conflict between Entropy and Eschatology

Yet contemporary theologians are confronted with an immense challenge at this point, a challenge coming from physical cosmology in the natural sciences.[4] The reigning theory of the origin of the universe is the big bang theory. According to this theory, the universe is drenched in temporality; it has a finite past with a beginning perhaps 13.7 billion years ago. At the beginning point, an unfathomably dense singularity exploded. The big bang sent matter and energy hurling outward, and we on earth now find ourselves flying outward and away from the original cosmic bang. This scientific theory looks consonant with the fundamental biblical commitments to a divine creation out of nothing. It appears that science provides an indirect testimony to what Christians claim to be the character of God's creation.

Theologians may cheer about what science tells us about the past. Not so about the future, however. The second law of thermodynamics, otherwise known as entropy, raises questions for Christian eschatology. This law states that energy flows in only one direction, from hot to cold, not the reverse. Entropy is the level of disorder in the universe, and the second law declares that entropy, overall, is always increasing. If the big bang back at the beginning was the hottest moment in the history of the cosmos, then the future we look forward to is one of increased entropy, of dissipation into equilibrium. What this means is that the universe is destined to freeze itself out of existence. Even if along the way gravity causes it to collapse into another dense fireball and explode again, the present cosmos will still come to an end. Whether freeze or fry, the future of life in our world is not endless. Like individuals, the cosmos as a whole is destined for death. At least, this is the scientific prophecy of physical cosmologists.

Whether freeze or fry, the future of life in our world is not endless. Like individuals, the cosmos as a whole is destined for death. At least, this is the scientific prophecy of physical cosmologists.

Does this prophecy look like the one announced by Christian eschatology? No. Entropy and eschatology appear to be locked in conflict. Christian eschatology does not prophesy a far future at equilibrium which has forgotten its past. Rather, it looks now through a mirror dimly at a bright shining future, the future of the new creation promised by God in the Easter resurrection of Jesus. The present creation is marked for transformation, and Jesus' Easter resurrection is the microcosm of the promised macrocosmic transformation. "But in fact Christ has been raised from the dead," writes Paul, "the first fruits of those who have died" (1 Cor. 15:20). As he rose, so will we. And what we rise into is the new creation.

We would like to see consonance, but instead we see dissonance between physical cosmology and Christian eschatology. In principle, then, physical cosmology as scientists pursue it has the potential for falsifying Christian belief in the resurrection. For Christians, the very notion of the Easter resurrection implies the divine promise for the renewal of the whole of creation. The failure of the creation to undergo transformation would invalidate the Christian claim. If scientific naturalism wins—meaning that Jesus remained dead and so will we—then the Christian faith is in vain.

Theologians need not rush to the unemployment window. Even though we may say that the Christian claim is falsifiable in principle, this is not empirically achievable. Any final disproof of the Christian claim would require observing the actual dissipation of the universe in 65 billion years or so in the far distant future. No laboratory of the present generation is expected to last that long, and no scientist will live long enough to see it.

Nevertheless, this challenge has a message for theological methodology. Eschatological forecasting, so it appears, ought not rely upon the present state of natural science for conceptual support. If a future new creation actually arrives as God has promised, then its arrival will have to be due to a divine intervention. God will have to act. The natural world will not evolve into a new creation on its own. If such a transformation is to take place, it will have to come as a gift from our creative God. No one can predict a creative act of God; hence, it will remain unforeseeable by scientific investigation.

Judgment, Heaven, and Hell

The divinely promised new creation will not be like that which appeared following Noah's flood, a return to the old laws of nature and the old patterns of human divisiveness and sinfulness. The new creation will be genuinely new in at least one significant respect, namely, all the laws of nature and all the willful actions of redeemed humanity will conspire with God's holy will to sustain a realm of blessed fulfillment. Because we now see only through a mirror dimly, our speech about this transformed reality must consist in exercises of imagination, of creative interpretations of the biblical symbols. Rather than aiming at targets, we must fire arrows of conjecture. Rather than knowing our destinations, we must point in felicitous directions. Rather than asserting dogmatic conclusions, we must propose conceptually tentative yet faithfully confident hypotheses. This will be our approach to eschatological subtopics such as judgment, heaven, and hell.

Judgment. Judgment is a biblical symbol that gives rise to theological thought.[5] The Westminster Shorter Catechism thinks about judgment this way when it answers question 38: "At the resurrection, believers' being raised up in glory, shall be openly acknowledged and acquitted in the day of judgment, and made perfectly blessed in the full enjoying of God to all eternity."[6] Where does this notion of a future and final judgment come from?

The concept of a final judgment became nearly universal in civil society for two millennia prior to Jesus, and it played a vivid role in the apocalyptic mindset so widespread on the eve of the New Testament. Already in the prophecy of the book of Daniel, we find a new aeon being brought in by Michael—whom the book of Revelation later identifies with Jesus Christ—at which point the resurrection takes place. "Many of those who sleep in the dust of the earth shall awake, some to everlasting life, and some to shame and everlasting contempt" (Dan. 12:2). In the New Testament, the final judgment is located at the point where this parting of the destinies occurs, and this is followed by everlasting life in heaven or unending perdition in hell.

We might ask: Is this final judgment for us in the future or past? Let us try the past on for size. Consider our justification by faith as stressed by Paul. We are "*now* justified by his grace as a gift, through the redemption that is in Christ Jesus" (Rom. 3:24). We are rendered just before God by an act of divine grace; our justness is not the product of our acts, deeds, works, accomplishments, or merits. The cosmic court has already heard our case. We have been found guilty. The punishment in the form of a sentence to death has already been meted out, although it was administered to Christ, not us. The trial and execution are over. Because of Christ our sins have been forgiven. Before God we stand justified. There is no double jeopardy. "Very truly, I tell you," are the words we hear from Jesus, "anyone who hears my word and believes him who sent me has eternal life, and does not come under judgment, but has passed from death to life" (John 5:24).

On the one hand, it would seem, especially from the point of view of the Gospel of John, that the final judgment is a thing of the past, having occurred already on Calvary (John 12:31). On the other hand, the same Johannine tradition produced 1 John 4:17, where we find a sense of the still outstanding future: "We may have boldness on the day of judgment, because as he is, so are we in this world." So the day of judgment is yet to come as well. Might we think of the final judgment as a single act of God which begins on Calvary and concludes on the last day? Then our entire existence would be found amidst this one inclusive act of God.

What will be the purpose of a future final judgment? To determine each individual's final destiny? No. That will have already been determined prior to physical death. The purpose is rather to reveal the justice and sovereignty of God. Until judgment time the truth of God's justice will have been hidden under the ambiguities of history. The wheat and the tares have been growing together and within history, and one can only catch occasional glimpses of the difference between them. A final sifting needs to take place so that one can see clearly what has been the case all along. In short, the final judgment is an act of revelation more than it is an act of salvation.

What will be the purpose of a future final judgment? To determine each individual's final destiny? No. That will have already been determined prior to physical death. The purpose is rather to reveal the justice and sovereignty of God.

Heaven. Heaven is also a symbol rising up into thought. Heaven is associated with a place, with what is up. Yet we do not literally think of it as up. In both the Old Testament and the New Testament, the words for heaven (*shemayim, ouranos*) refer to what is geographically located up in the sky where the clouds are. The sky is where God and the angels dwell (Gen. 28:12; Ps. 11:4; Matt. 6:9), although the "heaven and the highest heaven cannot contain" God (1 Kgs. 8:27), who is omnipresent (Ps. 139:8–10). Gnostics and others in the ancient world assumed there was a hierarchy of heavens (2 Cor. 12:2–3), some planes of which were ruled by demonic powers (Eph. 6:12) and beyond which Christ was raised when he "ascended far above all the heavens" (Eph. 4:10). When early in the space program a Russian astronaut mocked the religious people of the world by saying he had gone to heaven but could not find God, he was making the false assumption that the religious mind takes such things literally. Some people do, of course. But even in ancient and medieval times it was the symbolic—not the literal—power of the heavens which communicated things divine.

There are four dominant images through which the meaning of heaven has been communicated in Christian tradition: the ecstasy of worship, the vision of God, the garden of paradise, and the new Jerusalem.

The symbol of heaven points us toward the future transformed reality promised by the Easter resurrection of Jesus Christ. Heaven is not a region in the sky to which disembodied souls fly when released from their anchor on earth. Heaven is present here and now amidst bodily life in a *proleptic* (anticipatory) way. It will be present here fully when the ultimate future—the kingdom of God—is finally established.[7]

Symbols come with images. There are four dominant images through which the meaning of heaven has been communicated in Christian tradition: the ecstasy of worship, the vision of God, the garden of paradise, and the new Jerusalem. Let us look at them in turn. The first is the ecstasy of worship. There is no need to have a temple in heaven because the worship of the almighty God explodes spontaneously from every quarter of creation (Rev. 21:22). Living creatures never cease to sing, "Holy! Holy! Holy!" And the twenty-four elders cast their crowns before the throne of grace intoning, "You are worthy, our Lord and God" (Rev. 4:10–11).

There is ecstasy in such music. There is also ecstasy in the second significant image of heaven, the beatific vision of the Godhead known as the *visio dei.* In the Beatitudes, Jesus says that the pure in heart will "see God" (Matt. 5:8). Paul contrasts present and future by saying, "For now we see in a mirror, dimly, but then we will see face to face" (1 Cor. 13:12). Apprehending the full truth of God is an exciting prospect, but by no means is this a dominant motif in the New Testament.

The third and fourth images are a pair, both depicting a healed community. One is rural, and the other is urban. What we are calling the rural image here is that of paradise, usually depicted as a great garden in which all the animals and plants and spiritual realities exist together in natural harmony. In the New Testament we find the word *paradise,* coming from an old Persian term meaning "park" or "garden." When used to designate heaven (Luke 23:43; 2 Cor. 12:3; Rev. 2:7), it frequently connotes a return to the garden of Eden prior to the fall, to a state of pristine innocence. What we experience today as alienation from nature resulting from mechanized farming and factories for milk production will be healed in heaven. Inherent in Christian appreciation of creation is a love of the natural World; and heaven can be conceived of only as a reintegration of what is human with what is natural. Heaven will result from a new creation.

Fourth in our list is the urban image of heaven, the new Jerusalem. The Holy City is a variant on the kingdom of God theme. In Matthew, *kingdom of heaven* and *kingdom of God* are used interchangeably, leading to the surmise that all these images belong together in a single family of symbols. Perhaps we should call this the "heavenly *polis*" (*polis* is the Greek word for "city-state"), because it derives from a vision of God's intention to establish an eschatological body politic. It is the capital city of God's new creation. Its descent is described amidst the crescendo at the end of Christian Scripture, the Apocalypse.

> Then I saw a new heaven and a new earth; for the first heaven and the first earth had passed away, and the sea was no more. And I saw the holy city, the

> new Jerusalem, coming down out of heaven from God, prepared as a bride adorned for her husband. And I heard a loud voice from the throne saying,
>
> "See, the home of God is among mortals.
> He will dwell with them as their God;
> they will be his peoples,
> and God himself will be with them;
> he will wipe away every tear from their eyes.
> Death will be no more;
> mourning and crying and pain will be no more,
> for the first things have passed away." (Rev. 21:1–4)

A tour guide to the new Jerusalem would point out a number of features. The Holy City does not just stay up in heaven. Following the battle between the children of light and the children of darkness, it descends to take up its abode where we are. We do not go to it; it comes to us. When it comes it brings salvation, the healing of sorrow, the drying of tears, the forgetting of suffering, the dwelling in safety with God forever.

Note that the kingdom of God and the new Jerusalem are political symbols. They imply a community of interacting individuals, not simply a sublime knowledge present to the individual soul. Instead of a mystical union, they imply a political communion. Heaven is made up of transformed men and women who continue their personal identity and mutual recognition into the resurrection, and yet they transcend most of the other categories of this finite and time-bound world. Heavenly salvation is not for the individual alone; it belongs to the community that is made up of humanity and the natural world. It belongs to the new creation.

Hell. Hell is the abode of the reprobate, the damned. There are two overlapping concepts of hell in the New Testament. *Hades* is the Septuagint translation of the Hebrew *Sheol*, referring to the shadowy realm of the underworld where it was originally thought that all the dead went, both good and bad (Ps. 89:48; Matt. 11:23). The second concept is *Gehenna,* where only the bad go. Both John the Baptist and Jesus warn of the menaces of Gehenna as a place where an everlasting and unquenchable fire burns (Matt. 5:22; 13:42), and, perhaps contradictorily, where there is darkness and gnashing of teeth (Matt. 8:12; 22:13). A bit more abstract in tone, Paul describes hell in terms of destruction, perishing, and loss of relationship with God (Rom. 9:22; 2 Thess. 1:9; 2:10). Hell is like prison, a punishment meted out to the devil and his angels and to those of us who persist in our reluctance to show love to the needy or who refuse to repent and accept God's offer of newness of life (Matt. 5:29; 25:41).

As the symbol of hell gives rise to theological reflection, let us ask: Is there literally an everlasting fire, or are we to think of hell metaphorically? Thomas Aquinas does not shrink from literalism: "The fire of hell is not called so metaphorically, nor an imaginary fire, but a real corporeal fire."[8] The twentieth-century Catholic theologian Karl Rahner deviates from Thomas, warning us against such literalization. What the Bible says about hell should be interpreted in keeping with "its literary character of 'threat-discourse' and hence not . . . be read as a preview of something which will exist some day." Rahner elects the metaphorical in preference to the literal on the grounds that the reference to hell's fire is "something radically not of this world."[9] Regardless of whether we take hell literally or metaphorically, its function is clearly that of a warning and a challenge for us to make a decision in the face of the possibility of being everlastingly separated from God. What hell signifies is that our rejection of God can result in everlasting estrangement.

DOUBLE DESTINY VERSUS UNIVERSAL SALVATION: COLLECTIVE ESCHATOLOGY

Over the last two centuries, liberal minds have been bitten by a moral conscience that finds such threat-discourse undignified and revolting. We modern people with more gentle standards of morality are appalled at the thought that God might punish for eternity someone who committed a temporal sin. Theologians wrestle with questions such as: How could the very concept of hell with its everlasting punishment fit coherently with the concept of a loving God? Does it make moral sense to think of the God of love, perhaps together with the saints in heaven, watching for all eternity hopeless, pitiless, cruel, and apparently loveless suffering? Could a God of love be so hardhearted? Even apart from love, could our God be so unjust? Is it just to mete out an infinite punishment for a finite sin? Even the crimes of an Adolf Hitler or a Joseph Stalin are not bad enough to warrant all that hell exacts. Thus, in our time hell is more and more thought to be incompatible with the idea of God as infinite love, because it lodges the existence of suffering right into the creation for all eternity. A God of both love and power would put an end to suffering, is this not the case?[10]

This is the theodicy problem—the problem of understanding, in the face of evil, how God is just—in its eschatological form. How could our God, who loves us, justify inflicting infinite suffering and pain? Addressing such thoughts has led many in our time to an outright rejection of the doctrine of hell in favor of universal salvation. Yet, we might ask: Is it sufficient reason to reject a Christian doctrine simply because it rubs against the grain of modern sensibilities? This question is especially relevant when an argument that appeals to modern sensibilities can be raised in defense of the doctrine of hell: Hell affirms an important modern value, namely, freedom. "Since we have free will," argues Timothy Kallistos Ware, "it is possible for us to reject God. Since free will exists, Hell exists; for Hell is nothing else than the

> According to the double destiny position, when we die we enter one of two everlasting realms, heaven or hell. According to belief in universal salvation, only one destiny awaits us beyond death, namely, salvation in heaven.

rejection of God."[11] Curiously, the affirmation of human freedom seems to require the affirmation of a possible realm which eternally rejects the love and grace of God.

Perhaps we should turn here directly to the theological battle between double destiny and universal salvation. According to the double destiny position, when we die we enter one of two everlasting realms, heaven or hell. According to belief in universal salvation, only one destiny awaits us beyond death, namely, salvation in heaven.

Advocates of universal salvation are frequently critical of the narrow-mindedness of the church when it asserts, *extra ecclesiam nulla salus* ("no salvation outside the church"). The ecclesial logic seems to be that pagans and heathens need to join the church to get a ticket to heaven. If this is what the phrase means, then we have here a case of religious arrogance. Critics say this is demeaning to non-Christian religions, and it ascribes authority to church leadership that is unwarranted. Yet this criticism risks missing the point. The criticism tries to solve a problem within eschatology by appeal to ecclesiology (the doctrine of the church). It would be better to tease out the internal logic of the eschatological issue itself.

If we are to tease out the internal logic of the eschatological discussion, we must begin by noting that our difficulty begins already with the New Testament. It appears that the New Testament may be saying three different—and perhaps even incompatible—things.

The New Testament contains a number of passages that appear to presume double destiny. These double destiny passages can be divided into two subsets. The first subset seems to say that everlasting salvation will apply to some of us on the grounds that we have *faith*. In Paul we find that salvation is for "everyone who has faith" (Rom. 1:16), and the oft-quoted John 3:16 says eternal life is given for those who believe in him. So we must ask: What happens to those who do not have faith? Do such passages require that those without faith are condemned to everlasting perdition? If so, then salvation is by no means universal.

The second subset of double destiny passages changes the criterion from faith to *works*. Here everlasting salvation is dependent upon the virtuous works we perform. Perhaps the most forceful example of this position is Jesus' parable of the Last Judgment in Matthew 25. Here the sheep are separated from the goats. What is Jesus' criterion? Love of neighbor. The saved sheep go to the right hand of the Son of Man because they visited the sick and imprisoned, gave food and drink to the hungry and clothes to the destitute. The goats, who failed to love their neighbors in this way, follow the direction the left hand is pointing. It points to everlasting hell. Faith or belief are not mentioned in this passage. Only good works determine if a person goes to heaven or not. Does such a parable require adherence to a doctrine of double destiny?

The third set of New Testament passages tends to support the position of universal salvation. Here salvation is so dependent upon God's grace over against human works that all conditions are precluded. Salvation is a gift, not a reward.

Paul repeatedly emphasizes that it is by grace that we are saved. "It is the gift of God" (Eph. 2:8; Rom. 3:24). And God's grace is universal; it knows no bounds. Christ "died for all" (2 Cor. 5:15), "so all will be made alive in Christ" (1 Cor. 15:22). How should we interpret this "all"? Does it refer to everybody? To those without faith as well as the faithful? To non-Christians as well as Christians? It would seem to. "The act of righteousness of one leads to acquittal and life for all" (Rom. 5:18). According to these passages, a doctrine of double destiny would appear to show lack of gratitude for God's universal gift.

Systematic theologians lie awake at night wrestling with seemingly irreconcilable positions within the New Testament. Whether we are granted everlasting salvation apparently depends on (1) whether or not we have faith, (2) whether or not we perform loving works on behalf of our neighbor, or (3) neither of the above, because salvation is totally a free gift of God's grace and hence cannot be earned by anything we do. Are these three positions just three different ways of saying the same thing, or is there a real incompatibility here? Unfortunately for the theologian, the differences seem to run deep. What the theologian needs to do is elect one or the other position and then ferret out the implications in an attitude of tentativeness. Tentativeness, as opposed to dogmatic swagger, can be a virtue in theological situations such as this.

> Tentativeness, as opposed to dogmatic swagger, can be a virtue in theological situations such as this.

In this attitude of tentativeness, let us formulate some corollaries to the universal salvation position and see how they cohere with other theological commitments. If we focus on divine love and grace, this would lead us to offer two corollary hypotheses. First, salvation will be universal—that is, it has been given in Christ and will be applied to all of God's creatures regardless of their sinful behavior on earth. Second, hell, if it does exist now, cannot last forever. Only God's kingdom is everlasting. Why does the argument go this direction?

The theodicy problem back in the doctrine of creation—namely, how do we justify a creator God who is all-powerful and all-loving if evil exists in the creation?—returns in eschatology. If God is all-powerful (omnipotent) and all-loving (omnibenevolent), then the forces of evil cannot have ultimate or final power. If hell or Hades represents the domain of the devil, and if this domain is understood as the kingdom of evil, then it cannot be as enduring as the kingdom of God. If hell were to last forever, it would provide a constant reminder that God's will is not completely done, that God's power is less than complete. Unless God's kingdom is universal and all-inclusive, then God is not all-powerful. It follows then that hell, if it exists, must be temporary, and once it passes out of existence then all will be taken into the consummate kingdom of God.

A double destiny advocate might counter: Suppose we think of hell not as the domain of the devil which exists contrary to the will of God, but rather as existing under the domain of divine power itself? Suppose we think of hell as God's means for executing retributive justice? Responding to this counter, we would ask just what it means to say that God is all-loving. Divine love as understood by the Christian gospel applies even to sinful people, even to those who have not loved God. "Christ died for the ungodly" (Rom. 5:6). Hence, this love is expressed in terms of mercy, grace, and forgiveness. We are justified by God's grace in Christ, not by exacting retributive justice. If God's love is capable of extending grace and forgiveness even to those most detestable to him, then it seems that this love would effect the elimination of a hell understood as justifiable punishment. Thus, to posit that God uses omnipotent power to establish the existence of a place of everlasting torment and suffering as retribution for sin would appear to draw a limit to God's gracious loving.

Emphasis on divine love leads to another much more delicate argument in behalf of the concept of universal salvation. Key here is that "we love because he first loved us" (1 John 4:19). What is love like? One of the significant characteristics of love is sympathy. Combining *syn* ("with") with *pathos* ("feeling"), the word *sympathy* means feeling someone else's pain with him or her. The precedent begins with God. Yahweh, the God of Israel, saw the sufferings of the chosen people in Egypt and "heard their cry" (Exod. 3:7). God then responded with the exodus deliverance. Christians also believe God has responded to the sufferings of the whole world by sharing in them through Jesus' sufferings, and by using such sufferings as a means of deliverance. To love is to feel the pain of the other. To feel someone else's pain is to be pained in oneself. One who genuinely feels sympathy cannot be released from pain until healing for the other has occurred. Just as God so loved this world (John 3:16), so also do those who love God groan in travail (Rom. 8:22) in behalf of the healing of all things. Sympathetic love brings to expression an underlying interconnectedness and wholeness to all creation. Love will not rest from sympathetic suffering until all things are made whole.

What this implies is universal salvation and a finite end to hell. How? Let us try a thought experiment. Suppose heaven would be populated with persons who genuinely love others just as God first loved us. And further suppose these loving souls (actually resurrected bodies) would become aware that somewhere beyond the walls of heaven there exists another place, hell, where the souls of the damned undergo continuous and everlasting suffering from the incessant hot flames which neither consume them nor let them lose consciousness. How would those people in heaven feel? If they love sympathetically, they too would feel the pain of the damned. So anxious would they be to see the sufferings of the damned stopped and their souls released from agony that they would find heaven a miserable place. And if heaven is miserable, then it is not truly heaven. It is intrinsic to the nature of love that it be complete and whole. Partial fulfillment—fulfillment for oneself while others remain unfulfilled—runs contrary to the very nature of the love that Christians

> In sum, heaven could not be heaven if there existed a hell alongside it.

believe we have inherited from God. In sum, heaven could not be heaven if there existed a hell alongside it.

Note the kind of argument this is. It is not strict biblical exegesis. Rather, it is an attempt to interpret the Bible by teasing out the logical implications of fundamental biblical commitments to God's power, love, and grace. What it leads to is the doctrine of *apocatastasis,* that is, the belief that finally all of creation including even the devil and the devil's angels will be incorporated into God's kingdom. Apocatastasis has been thought to be heresy in certain periods of church history, but its logic returns on occasion as a lively theological option.

When Protestant or Roman Catholic theologians see thoughts about universal salvation appearing on the horizon, they shrink from pressing on too far. Karl Barth, for example, argues for the universal saving work of Jesus Christ for all persons; yet Barth will not permit us to say that God's salvific intention will "finally be coincident with the world."[12] Similarly, Karl Rahner shifts nervously here. On the one hand, Rahner universalizes God's grace while, on the other hand, he shrinks from positively endorsing apocatastasis, saying that "the existence of the possibility that freedom will end in eternal loss stands alongside the doctrine that the history of the world as a whole will in fact enter into eternal life with God."[13] Commitment to earthly freedom translates into openness toward eternal damnation. This nervous shifting, as we have seen, might be expected because an ambiguity lies in the biblical symbols themselves. This ambiguity continues to be reflected in the systematic yet faithful explication of those symbols.

CONCLUSION

> *For now we see in a mirror, dimly, but then we will see face to face. Now I know only in part; then I will know fully, even as I have been fully known. And now faith, hope, and love abide, these three; and the greatest of these is love.—1 Cor. 13:12–13*

QUESTIONS FOR REFLECTION AND DISCUSSION

1. What is the difference between *futuristic* and *realized* eschatology? Are they incompatible?

2. What are the differences between premillennialism, postmillennialism, and amillennialism? What are the strengths and weaknesses of each position?

3. The Christian tradition uses a great many symbols to convey its hopes. Is it possible to define a nonsymbolic core of Christian beliefs about the future?

4. Our culture offers a variety of hopes for existence after death—Peters provides a list of them. How is the Christian hope for resurrection different from these others?

5. Should Christians think of death as an evil?

6. Most contemporary scientists believe that the universe is running down, that entropy just keeps increasing. Is such a view incompatible with Christian hope?

7. What are the arguments for and against *apocatastasis* (universal salvation)?

8. At different times Christians have put more emphasis on individual eschatology or on cosmic eschatology. Do these two sorts of hope fit together into one picture?

FOR FURTHER READING

Balthasar, Hans Urs von. *Dare We Hope "That All Men Be Saved"?* Trans. David Kipp and Lothar Krauth. San Francisco: Ignatius Press, 1988.

Berkouwer, G. C. *The Return of Christ.* Grand Rapids: Wm. B. Eerdmans Publishing Co., 1972.

Bultmann, Rudolf. *History and Eschatology.* Edinburgh: Edinburgh University Press, 1957.

Fiddes, Paul. *The Promised End.* Oxford: Basil Blackwell, 2000.

Moltmann, Jürgen. *The Coming of God.* Trans. Margaret Kohl. Minneapolis: Fortress Press, 1996.

———. *Theology of Hope.* Trans. J. W. Leitch. New York: Harper & Row, 1967.

Peters, Ted. *Futures—Human and Divine.* Atlanta: John Knox Press, 1978.

Pittenger, Norman. *After Death.* New York: Seabury Press, 1980.

Polkinghorne, John, and Michael Welker, eds., *The End of the World and the Ends of God.* Harrisburg, Pa.: Trinity Press International, 2000.

Rahner, Karl. *On the Theology of Death.* Trans. C. H. Henley. New York: Herder & Herder, 1961.

Sauter, Gerhard. *What Dare We Hope?* Harrisburg, Pa.: Trinity Press International, 1999.

Schwartz, Hans. *Eschatology.* Grand Rapids: Wm. B. Eerdmans Publishing Co., 2000.

Williams, Rowan. *Resurrection.* Harrisburg, Pa.: Morehouse Publishing, 1994.

THE FIRST NINETEEN CENTURIES

0	Jesus c. 4 B.C.–c. 30		
	Paul c. 10–c. 62		
	Ignatius of Antioch c. 35–c. 107		
100	Clement of Rome active 96		
	Irenaeus c. 130–c. 200		The Early Church
	Tertullian c. 160–c. 225		(The Patrisic Era)
200	Origen c. 185–c. 254		50–450
	Eusebius c. 260–c. 340		
	Athanasius c. 296–373		
300	Basil c. 330–379	Council of Nicaea 325	
	Gregory of Nazianzus 329/30–389/90		
	Gregory of Nyssa c. 330–c. 395	Council of Constantinople 381	
400	Augustine 354–430		
	Theodore of Mopsuestia c. 350–428	Council of Chalcedon 451	
	Cyril of Alexandria d. 444		
500	Leo I d. 462		
	Gregory the Great c. 540–604		
	Maximus Confessor 580–662		
600			
	John of Damascus c. 655–c. 750		
700			
			The Middle Ages
800	Ratramnus c. 800–c. 870		500–1500
900			
1000			
	Anselm c. 1033–1109		
	Peter Abelard 1079–1142/43		
1100	Peter Lombard 1100–1160		
	Joachim of Fiore c. 1135–1202		
	Francis of Assisi 1181/2–1226		
1200		Fourth Lateran Council 1215	
	Bonaventure 1217–1274		
	Thomas Aquinas c. 1225–1274		
1300	Gregory Palamas c. 1296–1359		
	Julian of Norwich c. 1342–1416 or later		
1400	Gabriel Biel c. 1420–1495		
		Council of Florence 1438–1439	
	Martin Luther 1483–1546		
1500	Ulrich Zwingli 1484–1531	Augsburg Confession 1530	
	John Calvin 1509–1564	Council of Trent 1545–1563	The Reformation
	Teresa of Avila 1515–1582	Heidelberg Catechism 1562	1520–1570
1600	René Descartes 1596–1650		
	George Fox 1624–1691	Synod of Dort 1619	
		Westminster Confession 1647	
1700	John Locke 1632–1704		
	Jonathan Edwards 1703–1758		The Enlightenment
	John Wesley 1703–1791		1640–1790
1800	Immanuel Kant 1724–1804		
	Friedrich Schleiermacher 1768–1834		
	John Henry Newman 1801–1890		
	Søren Kierkegaard 1813–1855		

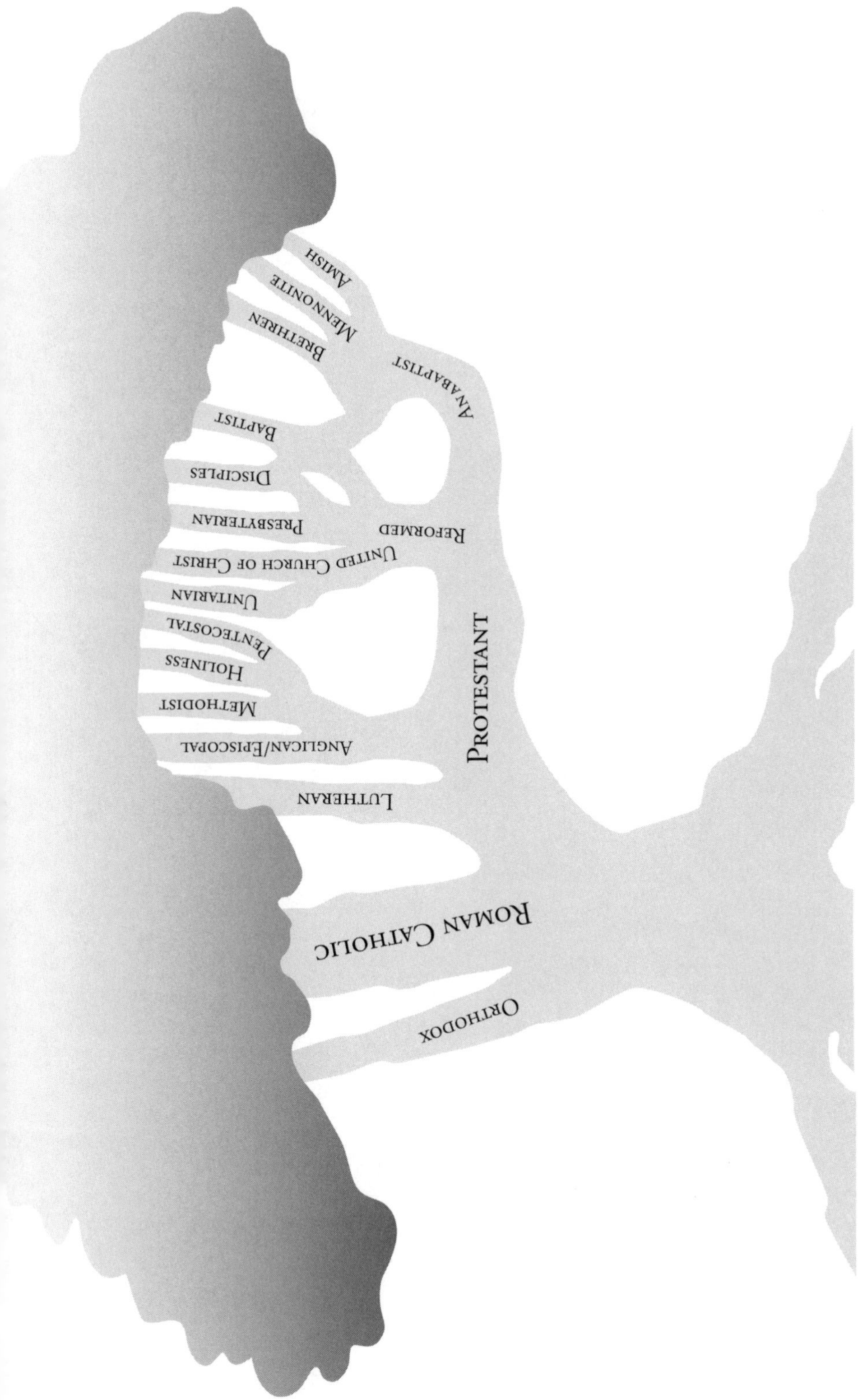

Protestant
Anabaptist
Amish
Mennonite
Brethren
Baptist
Disciples
Reformed
Presbyterian
United Church of Christ
Unitarian
Pentecostal
Holiness
Methodist
Anglican/Episcopal
Lutheran
Roman Catholic
Orthodox

Glossary of Names and Terms

Abba Term some scholars think Jesus used as an informal way of addressing God, meaning something like "Daddy" (see Mark 14:36; Rom. 8:15; Gal. 4:6).

Abelard, Peter (1079–1142/43) Theologian who criticized Anselm and proposed a "moral influence" theory of the atonement: Christ's death inspires us by showing us how much God loves us.

agape The New Testament's most common word for "love," meaning a love purely interested in helping the one loved, in contrast to *eros,* which always seeks some benefit for the person loving.

allegorical sense The meaning of a biblical passage (particularly in Old Testament) that alludes to Christ, in contrast to the literal sense. Can also refer more generally to any hidden, spiritual meaning.

Ambrose (340–397) Bishop of Milan and important influence on the young Augustine.

amillennialists Those who reject any literal interpretation of the "thousand-year reign" described in Revelation 20.

Amish Conservative Anabaptist group that split off from the Swiss Brethren in the early 1700s under the leadership of Jakob Ammann.

Anabaptists Radical groups in the Reformation who believed in rebaptizing (*ana-* means "re-") committed adult believers who had been baptized as infants.

anagogical sense The meaning of a biblical passage that refers to eschatology.

analogy Language about God that is between literal (where two uses mean exactly the same thing) and equivocal (where two uses have completely different meanings). *Healthy* is used analogously in "healthy person" and "healthy diet."

anhypostatic Doctrine that there is no human *hypostasis* in Christ; therefore, it makes no sense to ask about the human being Jesus would have been if he had not been the Son of God.

annunciation The angel's announcement to Mary that she was pregnant with the Son of God (see Luke 1:28–38).

anthropic principle View held by some contemporary scientist-theologians that the universe was designed from the start eventually to produce human beings.

apocalyptic Jewish writings in the centuries before the time of Jesus which expected history to continue getting worse until God intervened to end the present age.

apocatastasis Eventual salvation of everyone, also known as *universalism.*

Apollinarians Heretical followers of Apollinaris (c. 310–c. 390) who held that Christ had a human body but not a human mind.

Apostles' Creed Early summary of Christian faith, in legend written by the apostles, but in fact probably developed in Rome in the late fourth century.

apostolic succession Belief that bishops have their authority as passed down a line of succession from the original apostles.

Aquinas, Thomas (c. 1225–1274) Theologian who combined Christian thought with the philosophy of Aristotle.

Arians Heretics named after Arius (c. 270–336), who taught that Christ was divine, but a lesser divine being than the Father, a position refuted by the Nicene Creed.

Aristotle (384–322 B.C.) Greek philosopher, student of Plato, influence on Thomas Aquinas.

Armageddon Great battle at the end of history, referred to in Revelation 16:16.

Arminius, Jacob (1560–1609) Dutch Calvinist who rejected the doctrine of predestination and whose views were opposed by the Synod of Dort. Those who agree with Arminius (who include John Wesley, the founder of Methodism) are known as Arminians.

Athanasius (c. 296–373) Patriarch of Alexandria, great opponent of the Arians and defender of the Nicene Creed.

Atman In Hinduism, the essential self.

atonement From "at-one-ment," the way in which Christ makes us at one with God, above all in Christ's death on the cross.

Augsburg Confession (1530) Classic early statement of Lutheran beliefs.

Augustine (354–430) North African theologian who developed the idea of grace into belief in predestination and worked out a Western view of the Trinity.

Aulén, Gustaf (1879–1977) Swedish theologian who reintroduced the *Christus victor* motif, the idea that Christ saved us by defeating the power of evil.

Austin, J. L. (1911–1960) English philosopher, who developed speech-act theory.

Balthasar, Hans Urs von (1905–1988) Swiss Catholic theologian who thought about theology in terms of drama and developed an account of Christ's "descent into Hell" as the point at which Christ identifies even with those who have rejected God.

Baptists Christian group that practices adult or "believers'" baptism; originated with German and Swiss Anabaptists and with radical groups from the time of the English Civil War in the 1640s.

Barth, Karl (1886–1968) Swiss Reformed theologian who opposed the Nazis and developed a theology based on a critique of all natural theology.

Basil (c. 330–379) Cappadocian theologian who established a rule for Eastern monasticism and helped develop the doctrine of the Trinity.

beatific vision The saints' vision of God after death.

begetting In traditional Trinitarian terminology, the way the Son comes from the Father.

Belgic Confession (1561) Statement of Calvinist faith in the Netherlands.

Berengar of Tours (c. 1010–c. 1088) Theologian who denied any material change in the bread and wine in the Eucharist.

biblical theology movement Campaign by mostly American theologians in the 1950s and '60s who argued that the Bible is a history book in which we learn of God's great deeds.

Biel, Gabriel (c. 1420–1495) Late medieval theologian against whom Luther reacted, who taught that God gives grace only to those who have done their best.

Bonhoeffer, Dietrich (1906–1945) German Lutheran theologian, martyred by the Nazis.

bishop (in Greek, *episcopos* or "overseer"). Leader of the church in a given community.

Brahman In Hinduism, ultimate reality.

Brethren, Church of the Baptist group founded in Germany in 1708.

Brunner, Emil (1889–1966) Swiss theologian influenced by Martin Buber, who tried, in opposition to Karl Barth, to preserve a "point of contact" between revelation and human experience.

Buber, Martin (1878–1965) Jewish philosopher who contrasted "I-Thou" and "I-It" relations.

Bucer, Martin (1491–1551) Leader of the Reformation in Strassburg, influence on Calvin.

Bultmann, Rudolf (1884–1976) German theologian and New Testament scholar, influenced by existentialism, who taught that we should "demythologize" the New Testament.

Bunyan, John (1628–1688) English Baptist, author of *Pilgrim's Progress*.

calling Vocation; the job or life to which God calls us.

Calvin, John (1509–1564) Leader of the Reformation in Geneva, one of the theological founders of the Reformed tradition.

Campbell, John McLeod (1800–1872) Scottish pastor and theologian, tried for heresy because of his controversial views on the atonement.

canon The books identified as part of Scripture.

Cappadocians Fourth-century theologians from what is now Turkey who helped shaped the doctrine of the Trinity: Basil, his brother Gregory of Nyssa, and his friend Gregory of Nazianzus.

catholic Literally "universal"; in the Nicene Creed, one of the defining characteristics of the church.

Chalcedon, Council of (451) Ecumenical council that defined the relation of the human and divine in Christ.

charismatic Filled with the gifts of the Spirit; used for Christian groups that manifest distinctive signs of the Spirit, particularly speaking in tongues.

Christian perfection Methodist teaching that we can overcome sin in this life.

Christus victor Theory of the atonement taught in the twentieth century by Gustaf Aulén that Christ saves us by defeating the powers of evil.

Clement of Rome (active 96) Wrote letter to church at Corinth making recommendations; assumed distinction between priests and laypeople.

communicatio idiomatum ("exchange of distinctive features") Belief that human and divine are so united in Christ that the properties of one can be applied to the other. So, for instance, Mary gave birth to the human Jesus but can be called "the Mother of God."

Communion The sacrament of bread and wine; also Eucharist, Lord's Supper.

communion of the saints Phrase in the Apostles' Creed which refers to the community of all Christians with the dead who are already with God.

concurrence The aspect of providence whereby each act of a creature is also God's act.

Cone, James (1938–) African Methodist Episcopal theologian, founder of black theology movement.

confirmation One of the seven Catholic sacraments, in which a person who has already been baptized receives a laying on of hands and anointing from a bishop.

Congregationalists Group that split off from the Church of England in the 1640s and favored the independence of local congregations; one of the origins of today's United Church of Christ.

Constantine (d. 337) First Roman emperor to convert to Christianity.

Constantinople, First Council of (381) Ecumenical council that formulated the Nicene Creed in roughly its present form.

consubstantiation Lutheran view that, in the Eucharist, the bread and wine become Christ's body and blood while (in contrast to the Catholic theory of transubstantiation) still also remaining bread and wine.

contrition Being truly sorry for one's sin; part of the process of penance.

cosmogony Theory of the origin of the universe.

creationism (1) Belief that the world was recently created by God and that the theory of evolution is false; (2) belief that each human soul is created by a special act of God.

Cyril of Alexandria (d. 444) Patriarch of Alexandria who argued for the unity of Christ against the Nestorians.

Daimon Greek word for "spirit," originally used to refer to all sorts of spiritual beings and only gradually specifically for evil ones ("demons").

Dante Alighieri (1265–1321) Author of *The Divine Comedy*, the great poetic expression of medieval Catholicism.

Darby, John Nelson (1800–1882) English premillennial dispensationalist and founder of the Plymouth Brethren.

deacons (from *diakonos,* "servant") Church officials charged with distribution of charity; also, any lesser church official (see Acts 6:1–6).

deification Doctrine that, just as Christ became human, so we are saved by becoming divine.

Deism Seventeenth- and eighteenth-century movement of people, mostly English, who believed that God had created the universe but was not further involved in it.

Descartes, René (1596–1650) French philosopher and mathematician who proposed "I exist as a thinking thing" as the first thing one can know for certain, distinguished soul and body as two separate substances, and believed that animals, who lacked thinking souls, could not experience pain or other emotions.

descent into hell Phrase in the Apostles' Creed, possibly based on 1 Peter 3:19, that supposed that Christ rescued people from hell between his crucifixion and his resurrection.

Deus ex machina ("God from the machine") Reference to an operation in Greek plays, where an actor playing God could appear from the stage machinery, sometimes to rescue the playwright from a dead end with no other solution.

dharma In Buddhism, the proper rules or norms for behavior.

discernment In spiritual theology, the ability to make good judgments in one's spiritual life.

Disciples of Christ Group founded in the United States in the early nineteenth century by Presbyterians and Baptists, led by Alexander Campbell and Barton W. Stone, in an effort to foster church unity.

dispensationalism Teaching common among fundamentalists that different passages in Scripture refer to different "dispensations" or periods in history.
Docetism Early heresy which held that Christ only *seemed* to have a human body.
Donatism Fourth-century heresy, mostly in North Africa, named after Donatus, one of its leaders, which held that sinful priests could not perform valid sacraments.
Dort, Synod of (1619) Calvinist gathering in Holland which affirmed five points (total depravity, unconditional election, limited atonement, irresistible grace, perseverance of the saints) against the Arminians.
Durkheim, Emile (1858–1917) French anthropologist who taught that religion began with totems (sacred animals) which symbolically bound communities together.

ecclesiology The part of theology that deals with the church (*ekklesia*).
ecumenical Involving the whole Christian church or relations among different Christian groups.
Edwards, Jonathan (1703–1758) New England preacher and theologian who defended the doctrine of predestination and led a famous revival movement.
Ekklesia ("community") The church.
election The doctrine that people are saved (or not) without regard for their good works or other merits.
Elvira, Council of (305) Spanish church council which passed anti-Jewish regulations.
emanation View held in Neoplatonism and other philosophies that goodness simply flows out of, or emanates from, God.
empiricism The philosophical school which teaches that knowledge begins with experience. *Radical empiricism* (a term coined by the American philosopher William James) teaches that our sources of experience are more varied than the senses.
enhypostatic The belief that the humanity of Christ exists only in the divine *hypostasis*.
entropy The level of disorder in the universe. The Second Law of Thermodynamics teaches that entropy is always increasing.
Enuma Elish Babylonian creation story.
episcopus ("overseer") Bishop; the head of the Christian community in a city or area.
eros The kind of love which always seeks something for itself (whether sexual fulfillment or greater wisdom), in contrast to *agape*.
eschatology The part of theology which deals with "last things."
Eucharist ("thanksgiving") Communion or Lord's Supper.
Eusebius (c. 260–c. 340) Bishop of Caesarea and early church historian.
ex nihilo ("out of nothing") *Creatio ex nihilo* teaches that God created the universe out of nothing, rather than from some preexisting matter.

ex opere operato ("from the doing of the thing done") Doctrine (developed against the Donatists) that sacraments are valid regardless of the moral state of the priest performing them.

Excellent Eightfold Path Buddhist rules on how to live: right views, right resolution, right speech, right conduct, right livelihood, right effort, right mindfulness, right concentration.

existentialism Philosophical school which teaches that human nature is not determined in advance, but each of us decides what being human will mean for us.

exclusivism Belief that only Christians can be saved.

extra ecclesiam nulla salus ("outside the church, no salvation") Belief that one cannot be saved apart from belonging to the church.

extreme unction Last rites; the sacrament administered to the dying.

filioque ("and the Son") Word added to the Nicene Creed in the West to say that the Spirit "proceeds from the Father and the Son"; still a major source of division between Eastern and Western Christians.

Florence, Council of (1438–1439) Church council which tried unsuccessfully to negotiate unity between Catholic West and Orthodox East, seeking compromises on *filioque* and purgatory.

foundationalism Philosophical theory that our knowledge rests on a foundation of self-evident first truths (whether logical principles or sense data).

free will defense Argument that God allows human beings to do evil because a world without any freedom would be worse than a world in which some people choose evil.

full sanctification Methodist teaching that we can free ourselves from sin in this life.

futuristic eschatology Idea reflected in some New Testament texts that the kingdom of God Jesus promises will be a dramatic public event in the future.

Gehenna Hell; named after the valley (*ge*) of Hinnom southwest of Jerusalem, where human sacrifices by burning were performed.

general revelation The knowledge of God available to everyone, as opposed to *special revelation* known only through the Bible or other particular source.

glossolalia Speaking in tongues; practice described in Acts 2 and 1 Corinthians 12–14.

Gnosticism (*gnosis,* "wisdom") Movement that reached its peak in the second and third centuries, partly a Christian heresy, partly independent of Christianity, which taught that many levels of spiritual beings exist and that salvation lies in knowledge of secret truths.

governance The aspect of providence which has to do with God's directing all things toward a purpose.

grace God's unmerited love for us.

Gregory of Nazianzus (329/330–389/390) Cappadocian theologian and preacher who helped develop the doctrine of the Trinity; friend of Basil.

Gregory of Nyssa (c. 330–c. 395) Cappadocian theologian and mystic who helped develop the doctrine of the Trinity; younger brother of Basil.

Gregory the Great (c. 540–604) Pope who strengthened the papacy, reformed the church, and developed the idea of purgatory and multiple senses of reading Scripture.

Grotius, Hugo (1583–1645) Dutch theologian and legal philosopher who taught that Christ saves us by offering inspiring evidence of God's love and by being a model for us.

Gutiérrez, Gustavo (1928–) Peruvian theologian, founder of Latin American liberation theology.

Hades The Greek underworld; used in Greek as a translation of the Hebrew *Sheol.*

Hartshorne, Charles (1897–2000) American philosopher and theologian, influential figure in process theology.

Hegel, G. W. F. (1770–1831) German idealist philosopher. Argued that history exhibits a rational pattern and that Christianity, the "absolute religion," represents a simplified version of his own "absolute philosophy."

Heidelberg Catechism (1562) Statement of German Reformed faith written by Zacharius Ursinus and Caspar Olevianus.

Hellenistic Period of Greek history from the death of Alexander the Great (323 B.C.) to the Roman conquest of Egypt (30 B.C.), in which Greek culture spread throughout the Middle East.

Henry, Carl F. H. (1913–) Founding editor of *Christianity Today* and important American evangelical theologian.

heresy (from *hairesis,* "choice") Unorthodox teaching.

hermeneutics The theory of how to interpret.

Holiness movement The campaign by Holiness churches, Churches of God, and Nazarenes, who broke off from Methodists in nineteenth-century America to emphasize full sanctification, thought to come all at once in a "second blessing."

holy orders Ordination; one of the seven Catholic sacraments.

homoiousios ("of similar substance") View of Arians and others that Christ was like God, but not really God (not *homoousios* with the Father).

homoousios ("of the same substance") Doctrine affirmed in the Nicene Creed that the Son was not just similar to the Father but was fully God.

Hume, David (1711–1776) Scottish philosopher and religious skeptic who argued that no sense observation can rationally justify our belief in causation.

hypostasis ("particular substance") What there are three of in the Greek version of the doctrine of the Trinity.

idealism Philosophy which holds that things exist only as ideas in someone's mind.

Ignatius of Antioch (c. 35–c. 107) Bishop of Antioch and theologian who emphasized the authority of the bishop and taught the real humanity of Christ against Docetism.

illocution In speech-act theory, the intent of a speech act. The illocution of "John, close the door" is that I want John to close the door.

imago Dei Doctrine that human beings are created in the image of God (see Gen. 1:26).

immanence Presence in things; God is immanent in the world by being present here; contrasts with transcendence.

impassibility Doctrine that God cannot be affected by other things.

imputed righteousness Reformation doctrine that Christ's righteousness is imputed to believers, so that they are counted as righteous even while they remain sinners.

incarnation ("being embodied") Doctrine that God became human, specifically in Jesus Christ.

inclusivism Belief (in contrast to exclusivism) that non-Christians can be saved but (in contrast to pluralism) that they can be saved only through Christ.

infused righteousness Catholic doctrine that Christ's righteousness infuses believers, so that they gradually become sanctified.

invisible church The community of those who are saved, whose boundaries are known only to God.

Irenaeus (c. 130–c. 200) Bishop of Lyons and theologian who refuted heresies and developed the doctrine of "recapitulation": Christ undid Adam's disobedience by recapitulating or repeating it, but this time obediently.

J Ancient source of some of the material in the first five books of the Bible (for instance, the garden of Eden story beginning at Genesis 2:4b); uses "YHWH" (or "Jahweh"—hence J) as the name of God.

Joachim of Fiore (c. 1135–1202) Italian theologian who envisioned three ages in world history. Some radical Franciscans later thought that St. Francis had begun the third, the Age of the Spirit.

Johnson, Elizabeth (1941–) American Catholic feminist theologian.

Julian of Norwich (c. 1342–1416 or later) English mystic who used feminine language of God.

justification Salvation; reconciliation with God.

Kant, Immanuel (1724–1804) German philosopher who distinguished between the world of "phenomena" we experience and the world of "things in themselves" we cannot know.

kenōsis ("emptying") Belief that Christ gave up his divinity or at least its attributes to become human (see Phil. 2:7).

Kierkegaard, Søren (1813–1855) Danish Lutheran writer, influence on existentialism, critic of Hegel. He attacked the cultural compromises of the Danish church and emphasized the importance of taking the risk of faith.

koinonia ("commmunity") The community of the church.

last rites Sacrament administered to the dying, also called *extreme unction.*

Lateran Council, Fourth (1215) Church council that adopted transubstantiation as the official explanation of what happens in the Eucharist.

Leibniz, Gottfried (1646–1716) German philosopher and mathematician who argued that all knowledge could ideally be derived from logical first principles.

Leo I (d. 461) Pope and author of the *Tome* of Leo, which stated (and arguably oversimplified) the doctrine of the Trinity in Latin terminology.

liberation theology Theology which grows out of the situation of oppressed people, emphasizing the sins of their oppressors and salvation as liberation.

limbo In Catholic theology, the fate after death of virtuous non-Christians and unbaptized infants. They are cut off from salvation but otherwise unpunished.

liturgy (from *leitourgia*, "public work") The ritual of a church service.

locution In speech-act theory, the actual words spoken.

Lord's Supper The sacrament of bread and wine; also, Communion, Eucharist.

Lossky, Vladimir (1903–1958) Russian Orthodox theologian who lived most of his life in Paris and did much to introduce Byzantine theology to the West.

Luther, Martin (1483–1546) German theologian and biblical scholar, first leader of the Reformation.

Maimonides, Moses (1135–1204) Jewish philosopher, born in Spain but had to flee to Cairo; argued for philosophical interpretation of Judaism that minimized the importance of revelation.

Manicheanism Religion founded by Mani (c. 216–276) in what is now Iraq, which saw the world as a place of conflict between good and evil deities and was for a time a serious competitor of Christianity.

Marcion (died c. 160) Heretic who came from Asia Minor to Rome and taught that the Old and New Testaments referred to different Gods. He tried to get rid of the Old Testament and edit out references to the God of Israel from the New Testament.

Marduk In Babylonian religion, the God who made the universe.

marks of the church In both Lutheran and Reformed teaching, that the Word is truly preached and the sacraments properly administered.

Mennonites Anabaptist group founded by Menno Simons (1496–1561) in the Netherlands; related to the Swiss Brethren.

Merton, Thomas (1915–1965) Trappist monk, poet, and essayist.

metaphysics The part of philosophy which deals with first principles and the most basic questions.

Methodism Denomination which grew out of the work of John Wesley, gradually separating from the Church of England; teaches full sanctification and opposes predestination.

Miller, William (1782–1849) Founder (in upstate New York) of the Seventh-Day Adventists.

mission One of the "sendings out" (of the Son or the Holy Spirit) in the Trinity.

Moltmann, Jürgen (1926–) German Reformed theologian who has connected the tradition of German academic theology with many of the concerns of liberation theology.

Monophysites Radical followers of Cyril of Alexandria who broke off after the Council of Chalcedon, insisting that Christ has only one nature (*monophysis*). The Coptic Church in Egypt today is Monophysite.

Montanus (active c. 160) Heretic in Asia Minor who taught that the Holy Spirit spoke directly through him and his followers.

moral evil Evil caused by human actions, in contrast with natural evil.

Müntzer, Thomas (c. 1489–1525) German radical Reformer who fought with Luther and joined the Peasants' Rebellion.

natural evil In contrast to moral evil, evil in the world (volcanoes, diseases, etc.) not caused by human actions.

natural theology Theological conclusions reached by reason apart from revelation.

nature (*physis*) The two realities, human and divine, in Christ.

negative theology Theology, often associated with mysticism, which teaches that we can only say what God is not, and not make positive statements about God.

Neoplatonism School of philosophers like Plotinus (c. 205–270) who emphasized the mystical, religious side of Plato's thought.

Nestorians Heretical group, named after Nestorius (died c. 451), who emphasized the two natures of Christ, at the expense of Christ's unity, in particular claiming that Mary could be called the bearer of the human being but not the bearer of God (*theotokos*).

Nicaea, Council of (325) First ecumenical council of the church; adopted the Nicene Creed against the Arians, affirming that the Son was *homoousios* with the Father.

Niebuhr, H. Richard (1894–1962) Theologian and ethicist, brother of Reinhold Niebuhr.

Niebuhr, Reinhold (1892–1971) Theologian and political activist, developed a serious modern interpretation of original sin.

nirvana ("extinction") In Hinduism and Buddhism, the goal of life, to be achieved by the extinction of all drives and attachments.

objective immortality In contrast to *subjective immortality*, the idea that people will continue to exist after death in the memory of God, but not as experiencing subjects.

Oecolampadius, John (1482–1531) Reformer in the Swiss city of Basel.

Omega point In the theology of Pierre Teilhard de Chardin, the spiritual end point toward which history is evolving.

ontology The part of philosophy which has to do with the nature of being.

Origen (c. 185–c. 254) Great theologian of Alexandria, who encourged allegorical interpretation and taught *apocatastasis* (the eventual salvation of all).

orthodoxy (1) "Straight teaching," in contrast to heresy; (2) generic term for the churches of Eastern Christianity.

orthopraxy ("straight practice") Particularly for liberation theologians, the idea that true Christians should be judged by proper action as well as proper belief.

ousia ("substance or essence"). In Greek, what there is one of in the Trinity.

panentheism Doctrine that God is not identical with the universe (which would be pantheism) but also not separate from it; characteristic of process theology.

Pannenberg, Wolfhart (1928–) German Lutheran theologian, known for his theory of revelation as history and affirmation of the literal historicity of Jesus' resurrection.

pantheism Doctrine that God is identical with the universe.

paradosis ("handing over") Teaching that the Father "handed over" the Son to suffering and death in order to accomplish human salvation.

parousia ("coming") The second coming of Christ at the end of history.

patriarchs Bishops of the five greatest cities of early Christianity.

Patripassionism Heresy which holds that, since there is one God, the Father suffers on the cross.

Pelagianism Heresy named after Pelagius (active c. 400), opponent of Augustine, who insisted that grace comes to only those who have earned it.

penal substitution Belief that Christ substitutes for sinners who had been found guilty and condemned, freeing them from condemnation by taking their sin on himself.

penance Catholic sacrament in which one is genuinely sorry for one's sin, confesses to a priest, gets an assigned obligation to perform, and receives absolution or forgiveness.

Pentecost On this Jewish festival (fifty days after Passover), the Holy Spirit descended on the assembled apostles, and the church began (see Acts 2).

perlocution In speech-act theory, the action one wants to generate by speaking. To say, "John, shut the door" is to want to make John shut the door.

persona In Latin, literally the mask an actor wears to play a given character; what there are three of in the Trinity.

Pharisees Jewish party in Jesus' time committed to strict observance of the law.

Plato (427–347 B.C.) Greek philosopher who taught that particular objects have reality only insofar as they participate in eternal forms.

pluralism View that non-Christians can be saved by other paths than Christianity.

Plymouth Brethren Premillennial dispensationalist group with strict moral code founded in England by John Nelson Darby in 1830.

pneuma Greek for "spirit," related to words for "breath" and "wind."

polis In classical Greece, an independent city-state.

polity The organizational structure of a particular denomination.

postmillennialism Belief that Christ will return after the thousand-year reign described in Revelation 20.

predestination Teaching that people are predetermined to be saved (or damned) without regard for their merit.

premillennialism Belief that Christ will return before the thousand-year reign described in Revelation 20.

Presbyterians Denomination in the Reformed tradition with principal origins in Scotland, organized with neither bishops nor independent local congregations but with power resting in regional assemblies called presbyteries.

presbyters ("elders") In the early church, leaders of individual congregations, below the level of bishops; in the Reformed tradition, elders who share governance with pastors.

preservation The aspect of the doctrine of providence which holds that it requires a continuing action on God's part to keep the universe from ceasing to exist.

priest (same origin as *presbyter*, meaning "elder") Church officials set apart, on analogy to priests in Israel (and in pagan religions), with special powers to perform the sacraments. The Reformation challenged this radical distinction by affirming "the priesthood of all believers."

Priestly account One of the traditions behind parts of the first five books of the Bible, represented by the "seven days of creation" story beginning in Genesis 1:1.

process theology Twentieth-century theological movement influenced principally by the English philosopher Alfred North Whitehead, which teaches that the world is made up of interrelated processes rather than isolated substances and that God is the most related rather than the most independent of all beings.

procession In Eastern theology, the way the Holy Spirit comes from the Father. In Western theology, a more general term for the ways the Son comes from the Father and the Holy Spirit comes from the Father and the Son.

prolepsis Anticipation. Theologians such as Wolfhart Pannenberg see Jesus' resurrection as a prolepsis of the end of history.

prosopon In Greek, literally an actor's mask; what there are three of in the Trinity.

Protestant scholastics Theologians, mostly in the seventeenth century, who reintroduced into Protestant theology some of the technical philosophical terminology the Reformers had rejected.

providence Doctrine concerning how God watches over all of creation.

psyche ("soul") In Greek thought, the living principle (often thought to be immortal) which is joined with a body to make a human being (or, sometimes, any living thing).

purgatory In Catholic doctrine, the place where people who are saved but still have penance to do for their sins go after death before they can go to heaven. Many Orthodox theologians accept purgatory, but they have resisted making it an official doctrine. Protestants reject it altogether.

Puritans Party in the Church of England in the seventeenth century who wanted to purify the church of moral corruption and excessive ritual.

qahal Hebrew for "assembly, meeting, or gathering"; translated in Greek as *ekklesia*, the word usually used for "church."

Rahner, Karl (1904–1984) German Catholic theologian, influenced by existentialism, one of the important advisors at the Second Vatican Council; taught that non-Christians could be saved by being "anonymous Christians."

Ratramnus (c. 800–c. 870) French theologian who taught that the body and blood of Christ were spiritually but not physically present in the Eucharist.

Rauschenbusch, Walter (1861–1918) American Baptist, influential leader of the social gospel movement.

real presence Calvin's way of affirming that the body and blood of Christ are "really present" in the Lord's Supper without insisting on any particular philosophical theory about how this happens.

realized eschatology The idea, suggested in some New Testament texts, that the *eschaton* or end of the present age has already happened in Christ's ministry, so that we need not wait for a future eschaton.

recapitulation Irenaeus's idea that Christ accomplishes our salvation by repeating Adam, this time with obedience rather than disobedience.

reconciliation Salvation, atonement; what Christ does to restore our relationship with God.

redemption Christ's freeing us from the forces of evil to accomplish our salvation.

Reformed The Protestant tradition founded by Calvin and Zwingli and represented today in churches such as the Presbyterians and the United Church of Christ.

Ricoeur, Paul (1913–) French Reformed philosopher who has written of the role of symbol and myth, particularly in understanding evil.

Ritschl, Albrecht (1822–1889) Liberal German theologian who emphasized the ethical elements of Christianity.

Ruether, Rosemary Radford (1936–) Leading American feminist theologian.

sacrament An outward sign of God's grace. Catholics and Orthodox recognize seven sacraments; most Protestants two.

saga A term Karl Barth borrowed from Martin Buber to refer to poetic narratives such as the beginning of Genesis which are not, he believed, to be taken as literal history.

sanctification Becoming holy; that which follows justification in the Christian life.

satisfaction The idea that Christ saves us by repaying obligations we incurred by our sin.

schism Split or division in the church.

Schleiermacher, Friedrich (1768–1834) Liberal German Protestant theologian who emphasized the role of feeling in Christian faith.

Schmemann, Alexander (1921–1983) Russian Orthodox theologian who taught most of his life in the United States and introduced the Russian tradition to American theologians.

Scofield Reference Bible Bible edition published in 1909 (edited by the American Cyrus Scofield) with notes offering a dispensationalist interpretation; influential among many fundamentalists.

second blessing Teaching in Holiness churches that one receives full sanctification all at once.

Second Law of Thermodynamics Theory in modern physics that entropy (disorder) always increases in the universe.

Seventh-Day Adventists Group founded by William Miller in the 1840s in upstate New York that originally anticipated the imminent end of the world. Later it emphasized temperance, encouraged vegetarianism, and held worship on Saturdays.

Sheol The Hebrew term for the underworld.

signs of the church In the Nicene Creed, that the church is one, holy, catholic, and apostolic.

simul justus et peccator ("simultaneously justified and a sinner") Reformation view, particularly clear in Luther, that we remain sinners all our lives, even though Christ has justified us.

social gospel Nineteenth-century American theology that held that human beings could bring in God's kingdom by working for social justice in the world.

Socinians Group led by the Italian theologian Faustus Socinius (1539–1604) which, like later Unitarians, denied Christ's divinity and believed that he saved us by offering us a moral example.

sola Scriptura Reformation doctrine, articulated by Luther, that only the Bible and not church tradition can function as authority for theology.

soma Greek for "body."

soteriology (*soter*, "savior") Part of theology dealing with the work of Christ and how Christ saves us.

speaking in tongues (*glossolalia*) Practice in the early church and Pentecostal and charismatic groups today of praying under the guidance of the Holy Spirit in no known language.

special revelation The revelation given in Scripture or other particular sources, in contrast to *general revelation,* which is available to all people.

speech-act theory Philosophy developed by J. L. Austin and others which analyzes the way acts of speech function.

Spinoza, Baruch (1632–1677) Dutch Jewish pantheist philosopher.

spiritual director Person who guides one in one's spiritual life.

Spurgeon, Charles Haddon (1834–1892) Famous English Baptist preacher.

Stoicism Greek and Roman philosophy which taught that we should accept providence and learn not to mind the apparently bad things that happen to us.

subjective immortality The view that we survive death as experiencing subjects, in contrast to objective immortality, where we survive only in the memory of others.

subordinationism Doctrine that the Son is subordinate to the Father; denies the equality of the persons of the Trinity.

substantia ("substance or essence," Greek, *ousia*) What there is one of in the Trinity.

Suffering Servant Servant of God described in Isaiah 53 and identified with Christ in Christian thought.

supersessionism Belief that Christianity has superseded or replaced Judaism, so that God's covenant with Judaism no longer applies.

Teilhard de Chardin, Pierre (1881–1955) French Catholic paleontologist and theologian who thought that all things were evolving toward a spiritual "Omega point."

Tertullian (c. 160–c. 225) North African theologian who introduced one *substantia* and three *personae* as the standard Latin terminology in the Trinity.

theodicy (*theos,* "God"; *dike,* "justice") Accounts which attempt to explain why God allows evil.

Theodore of Mopsuestia (c. 350–428) Theologian from Antioch who emphasized the two natures which form one person in Christ.

theosis Deification. Theory that we are saved by becoming godlike.

Theotokos ("God-bearer") Name given the Virgin Mary, which Nestorius rejected because he thought Mary bore only the humanity, not the divinity, of Christ.

Tiamat In Babylonian myth, the monster from whose body the universe was made.

Tillich, Paul (1886–1965) German Lutheran theologian who fled to the United States to escape the Nazis, and who was influenced by existentialism.

***Tome* of Leo** Letter written by Pope Leo I defining Latin terminology for the Trinity.

traducianism Belief that the soul comes into being through sexual intercourse rather than being directly created by God.

transcendence God's independence beyond the universe.

transubstantiation Catholic doctrine concerning the Eucharist. In terms borrowed from Aristotle's philosophy, the properties of the bread and wine remain the same, but their substance changes into the body and blood of Christ.

Trent, Council of (1545–1563) Catholic council which defined the church's response to the Reformation.

Trinity, economic The Trinity as it appears to the world.

Trinity, immanent The Trinity as it is in God's essence.

tropological sense The sense of a biblical text which applies to the reader's moral life; also called the *moral sense.*

Tutu, Desmond (1931–) Anglican archbishop of South Africa, president of the Truth and Reconciliation Commission.

Ubuntu African concept that persons' identities are formed by their relationships with others.

Vatican Council, First (1869–1870) Catholic council which opposed modernism and affirmed the infallibility of the pope.

Vatican Council, Second (1962–1965) Catholic council which directed that the Mass would no longer be in Latin and opened relations to non-Catholics and even non-Christians.

vicarious atonement Doctrine that Christ saves us, making us at one with God, by suffering in our place the consequences of our sins.

virtue ethics Ethical theory (influenced by Aristotle and Aquinas) which emphasizes the development of moral virtues rather than making the right decision in individual cases.

visible church The people who belong to the church and show up on Sundays, as opposed to the "invisible church," whose membership is known only to God.

visio Dei ("vision of God") The vision of God which awaits the saved after death and is the goal of human existence.

vocation The occupation or activity in life to which God has called a person.

Watts, Isaac (1674–1748) English hymn writer.

Wesley, John (1703–1791) Preacher, theologian, and founder of Methodism.

Westminster Confession of Faith (1647) Classic statement of British Reformed faith, designed (during a time of Puritan rule) as a statement of faith for the English church but in fact adopted among Presbyterians, initially in Scotland.

Westminster Shorter Catechism Question-and-answer presentation of faith which accompanies the Westminster Confession.

Whitehead, Alfred North (1861–1947) English philosopher and mathematician who came late in life to the United States and developed a philosophy which has shaped process theology.

Wittgenstein, Ludwig (1889–1951) Austrian philosopher who spent his teaching career in England; a key figure in the contemporary philosophy of language.

womanist Term for African American theologians which distinguishes them from white *feminist* theologians.

Zealots Jewish party in the time of Jesus that worked for a violent revolution against the Romans.

Zwingli, Ulrich (1484–1531) Reformer of Zurich and (with John Calvin) one of the founders of the Reformed tradition.

Notes

Why Bother with Theology? An Introduction

1. "Theological reflection—that is, the understanding of our faith—arises spontaneously and inevitably in the believer. . . . There is present in *all believers* a rough outline of a theology." Gustavo Gutiérrez, *A Theology of Liberation*, trans. Caridad Inda and John Eagleson (Maryknoll, N.Y.: Orbis Books, 1973), 3.
2. Thomas Oden, *The Living God* (San Francisco: HarperCollins, 1992), 1.
3. See Robert J. Wuthnow, *The Restructuring of American Religion* (Princeton, N.J.: Princeton University Press, 1988).

Chapter 1: How Do We Know What to Believe?

1. Karl Barth, *Church Dogmatics* II/1, trans. T. H. L. Parker et al. (Edinburgh: T. & T. Clark, 1957), 172–74.
2. Martin Luther, *Luther at the Diet of Worms*, trans. Roger Hornsby, in *Luther's Works*, ed. Helmut T. Lehmann, vol. 32 (Philadelphia: Muhlenberg Press, 1958), 112–13.
3. "Decree concerning Canonical Scriptures," in *Canons and Decrees of the Council of Trent*, H. J. Schroeder (St. Louis: B. Herder Book Co., 1941), 17.
4. See, for instance, Origen, *On First Principles* 4.2.5, trans. G. W. Butterworth (New York: Harper & Row, 1966), 277–78.

5. Karlfried Froehlich, *Biblical Interpretation in the Early Church* (Philadelphia: Fortress Press, 1984), 28.
6. Martin Luther, *Table Talk* no. 5443, trans. Theodore G. Tappert, in *Luther's Works*, ed. Helmut T. Lehmann, vol. 54 (Philadelphia: Fortress Press, 1967), 424.
7. John Calvin, *Commentary on a Harmony of the Evangelists* (on Luke 8:19), trans. William Pringle, vol. 16 of *Calvin's Commentaries* (Grand Rapids: Baker Book House, 1989), 89.
8. Westminster Confession of Faith 1.6, in *Book of Confessions* (Presbyterian Church U.S.A.) 6.006.
9. Carl F. H. Henry, *God, Revelation, and Authority* (Waco, Tex.: Word, 1976), 2:87.
10. Ibid., 3:456.
11. Avery Dulles, *Models of Revelation* (Maryknoll, N.Y.: Orbis Press, 1992), 40. See Henry, *God, Revelation, and Authority*, 4:201–10, 220–42.
12. Wolfhart Pannenberg, *Theology as History* (New York: Macmillan, 1968), 135, 137.
13. Wolfhart Pannenberg, *Systematic Theology*, vol. 1, trans. Geoffrey Bromiley (Grand Rapids: Wm. B. Eerdmans Publishing Co., 1991), 191.
14. See Langdon Gilkey, "Cosmology, Ontology, and the Travail of Biblical Language," *Journal of Religion* 41 (1961): 194–205.
15. William James, *The Varieties of Religious Experience* (Cambridge, Mass.: Harvard University Press, 1985), 66–67.
16. "So we may say that the particular mental image which the mystic forms of his objective, the traditional theology he accepts, is not essential. Since it is never adequate, the degree of its inadequacy is of secondary importance. . . . We cannot honestly say that there is any wide difference between the Brahman, Sufi, or Christian mystic at their best." Evelyn Underhill, *The Essentials of Mysticism* (New York: E. P. Dutton, 1960), 4.
17. Eusebius, *The History of the Church* 5.16, trans. G. A. Williamson (New York: New York University Press, 1966), 218–19.
18. Quoted in Roland H. Bainton, *Here I Stand* (Nashville: Abingdon-Cokesbury Press, 1950), 261.
19. See, for instance, the passage from Margaret Fell, quoted in Hugh Barbour, *The Quakers in Puritan England* (New Haven, Conn.: Yale University Press, 1964), 98.
20. Quoted in Geoffrey F. Nuttall, *The Holy Spirit in Puritan Thought and Experience* (Oxford: Basil Blackwell, 1947), 35.
21. Friedrich Schleiermacher, *The Christian Faith*, trans. H. R. Mackintosh and J. S. Stewart (Edinburgh: T. & T. Clark, 1928), 50.
22. Ibid., 16.
23. George A. Lindbeck, *The Nature of Doctrine* (Philadelphia: Westminster Press, 1984), 31–35.
24. See, for instance, Phyllis Trible, *God and the Rhetoric of Sexuality* (Philadelphia: Fortress Press, 1978).
25. See, for instance, James H. Cone, *God of the Oppressed* (San Francisco: Harper & Row, 1975). For a general survey of contemporary approaches to the Bible, see Donald K. McKim, *The Bible in Theology and Preaching* (1994; reprint, Eugene, Ore.: Wipf & Stock Publisher, 1999).
26. René Descartes, *Discourse on Method and the Meditations*, trans. F. E. Sutcliffe (Harmondsworth, England: Penguin Books, 1968), 95.
27. Ludwig Wittgenstein, *On Certainty* #248, trans. Denis Paul and G. E. M. Anscombe (New York: Harper & Row, 1969), 33.

Stanley J. Grenz's Essay

1. This essay is an update and adaptation of sections from chaps. 3–5 of Stanley J. Grenz and John R. Franke, *Beyond Foundationalism: Shaping Theology in a Postmodern Context* (Louisville, Ky.: Westminster John Knox Press, 2001). The author expresses gratitude to the press for permission to use previously published material.
2. For an example, note the table of contents in Millard Erickson, *Christian Theology* (Grand Rapids: Baker Book House, 1983), 1:8–9. See also Harold Lindsell, "Inspiration," in the *Zondervan Pictorial Encyclopedia of the Bible*, ed. Merrill C. Tenny (Grand Rapids: Zondervan, 1976), 3:289.
3. Bernard Ramm, *The Pattern of Religious Authority* (Grand Rapids: Wm. B. Eerdmans Publishing Co., 1959), 28.
4. The Westminster Confession of Faith 1.10, in *Creeds of the Churches: A Reader in Christian Doctrine from the Bible to the Present,* ed. John H. Leith, 3rd ed. (Atlanta: John Knox Press, 1982), 196.
5. See, especially, J. L. Austin, *How to Do Things with Words*, ed. J. O. Urmson and Marian Sbisa, 2nd ed. (Cambridge, Mass.: Harvard University Press, 1975).
6. For a helpful summary of speech-act theory, see Kevin J. Vanhoozer, "The Semantics of Biblical Literature: Truth and Scripture's Diverse Literary Forms," in *Hermeneutics, Authority, and Canon*, ed. D. A. Carson and John D. Woodbridge (Grand Rapids: Zondervan, 1986), 85–92.
7. Peter L. Berger, *The Sacred Canopy: Elements of a Sociological Theory of Religion* (Garden City, N.Y.: Doubleday, 1969), 20.
8. Peter L. Berger and Thomas Luckmann, "Sociology of Religion and Sociology of Knowledge," *Sociology and Social Research* 47 (1963): 421.
9. Berger, *Sacred Canopy*, 32–36.
10. Wesley A. Kort, *Take, Read: Scripture, Textuality, and Cultural Practice* (University Park, Pa.: Pennsylvania State University Press, 1996), 10–14.
11. Paul Ricoeur, *Interpretation Theory: Discourse and the Surplus of Meaning* (Fort Worth, Tex.: Texas Christian University Press, 1976), 87. See also Paul Ricoeur, *Hermeneutics and the Human Sciences: Essays on Language, Action, and Interpretation*, ed. and trans. John B. Thompson (Cambridge: Cambridge University Press, 1981), 176–81.
12. This marks a reformulation of Barth's christologically informed bibliology. See Karl Barth, *Church Dogmatics,* I/1, 2nd ed., trans. G. W. Bromiley (Edinburgh: T. & T. Clark, 1975), 88–124. See also G. C. Berkouwer, *Holy Scripture* (Grand Rapids: Wm. B. Eerdmans Publishing Co., 1975), 166.
13. For a somewhat similar idea, see James Barr, *The Scope and Authority of the Bible* (Philadelphia: Westminster Press, 1980), 126–27.
14. David H. Kelsey, *The Uses of Scripture in Recent Theology* (Philadelphia: Fortress Press, 1975), 89.
15. See, for example, George Herbert Mead, *Mind, Self, and Society*, ed. Charles W. Morris (Chicago: University of Chicago Press, 1934), 138–58.
16. Robert N. Bellah et al., *Habits of the Heart: Individualism and Commitment in American Life* (Berkeley, Calif.: University of California Press, 1985), 81.
17. See, for example, Alisdair MacIntyre, *After Virtue,* 2nd ed. (Notre Dame, Ind.: University of Notre Dame Press, 1984), 221.
18. Roger E. Olson, *The Story of Christian Theology: Twenty Centuries of Tradition and Reform* (Downers Grove, Ill.: InterVarsity Press, 1999), 21.
19. For a compilation of such "milestones" in the history of the church in its various expressions, see John H. Leith, ed., *Creeds of the Churches: A Reader in Christian Doctrine from the Bible to the Present* (Atlanta: John Knox Press, 1982).

20. See, for example, John W. Bennett and Melvin M. Tumin, *Social Life* (New York: Alfred A. Knopf, 1948), 208–9.
21. Anthony Cohen, *Self Consciousness: An Alternative Anthropology of Identity* (London: Routledge & Kegan Paul, 1994), 96.
22. Ibid., 118–19.

Noel Leo Erskine's Essay

1. William Hordern, *Speaking of God* (New York: Macmillan, 1966), 123.
2. John Macquarrie, *Principles of Christian Theology* (New York: Charles Scribner's Sons, 1966), 7.
3. Ibid., 6.
4. Paul Tillich, *Systematic Theology* (Chicago: University of Chicago Press, 1967), 1:111.
5. Martin Buber, *I and Thou*, trans. Ronald Gregor Smith (New York: Charles Scribner's Sons, 1958). In his important text *Models of Revelation* (Garden City, N.Y.: Doubleday, 1983), 86, Avery Dulles suggests that the theologian Emil Brunner, drawing on Buber's work, collapses the subject-object relationship in his talk about God as absolute subject: "Brunner likewise maintains that God, as absolute subject, makes himself known as absolute mystery and hence as nonobjectifiable. The truth of revelation he writes 'is neither subjective nor objective, but it is both at once: it is the truth which may be described, in other words, as the encounter of the human "I" with God's "Thou" in Jesus Christ.'"
6. Tillich, *Systematic Theology*, 1:111.
7. This remembrance is still practiced throughout Jamaica. For a full accounting of this practice, see Noel Leo Erskine, *Decolonizing Theology* (Trenton, N.J.: Africa World Press, 1998), 66–75.
8. Erskine, *Decolonizing Theology*, 35.
9. See Paul King Jewett, *Emil Brunner's Concept of Revelation* (London: James Clarke & Co., 1954). See also Gabriel Fackre, *The Doctrine of Revelation* (Grand Rapids: Wm. B. Eerdmans Publishing Co., 1997), for an excellent attempt to relate revelation to Christian doctrine.
10. Emil Brunner, *Revelation and Reason*, trans. Olive Wyon (Philadelphia: Westminster Press, 1946), 23.
11. See Jewett, *Emil Brunner's Concept*, 73. Here and elsewhere, I am simply quoting Brunner's masculine language, problematic though it is.
12. Brunner, *Revelation and Reason*, 26.
13. Ibid., 26–27.
14. Ibid., 27.
15. Ibid.
16. Ibid., 28.
17. *Eros*, the most common Greek word for love, implies seeking for something one does not have (whether a sexual object or wisdom or virtue). The gods, some Greek philosophers taught, could not have *eros*, since they already possessed everything they could desire. In contrast, the New Testament word for love is nearly always *agape*, a way of loving purely for the sake of the one you love, without regard to any benefits for yourself. God has this love in pure form, and we can only hope to approximate it.
18. Brunner, *Revelation and Reason*, 29–30.
19. Ibid., 31.
20. Ibid., 32.
21. Elizabeth Johnson, *She Who Is: The Mystery of God in Feminist Theological Discourse* (New York: Crossroad, 1998), 105.

22. Ibid., 107.
23. Ibid., 112.
24. Ontology, literally the "study of being," is the part of philosophy that deals with the nature of what exists or is real. Thus, Johnson's "ontology of participation" says that things exist only in participating in "the very dynamism of existing which God in essence is."
25. Johnson, *She Who Is,* 114.
26. Ibid., 119.
27. Ibid., 76.
28. Ibid., 27.
29. Ibid., 78.
30. Jewett, *Emil Brunner's Concept,* 80–81.
31. Dulles, *Models of Revelation,* 30.

Chapter 2: What Do We Mean by "God"?

1. Some editions use the title *Summa Theologica* ("theological summation"), but most scholars today think *Summa Theologiae* ("summation of theology") is the authentic title.
2. Thomas Aquinas, *Summa Theologica* 1a.2.3, trans. Fathers of the English Dominican Province (Westminster, Md.: Christian Classics, 1981), 13–14.
3. See Friedrich Schleiermacher, *The Christian Faith*, trans. H. R. Mackintosh and J. S. Stewart (Edinburgh: T. & T. Clark, 1928), 738–51.
4. See Karl Barth, *Church Dogmatics* I/1, trans. G. T. Thomson (Edinburgh: T. & T. Clark, 1936), 339–560.
5. Gregory of Nyssa, *The Life of Moses,* trans. Abraham J. Malherbe and Everett Ferguson (New York: Paulist Press, 1978), 95.
6. Westminster Confession of Faith, in *The Creeds of Christendom*, ed. Philip Schaff (New York: Harper & Brothers, 1877), 3:606.
7. Aquinas, *Summa Theologica* 1a.3.pref, 14.
8. Ibid., 1a.13.5, 64.
9. Aristotle, *Metaphysics* 12.9.1074b, trans. Richard Hope (Ann Arbor, Mich.: University of Michigan Press, 1960), 266.
10. Aquinas, *Summa Theologica* 1a.13.7, 66.
11. See Charles Hartshorne, *The Divine Relativity* (New Haven, Conn.: Yale University Press, 1948).
12. Alfred North Whitehead, *Process and Reality* (New York: Macmillan, 1929), 526.
13. Ibid., 413.
14. Elizabeth A. Johnson, *She Who Is: The Mystery of God in Feminist Theological Discourse* (New York: Crossroad, 1992), 250–53.
15. "The So-called Second Letter of Clement," in *The Apostolic Fathers*, trans. Edgar J. Goodspeed (New York: Harper & Brothers, 1950), 85.
16. Pliny the Younger, *Letters* 10.96, in, *A New Eusebius*, ed. J. Stevenson (London: SPCK, 1968), 14.
17. John Cobb's essay emphasizes the New Testament passages that use the term *Abba* (Mark 14:36; Rom. 8:15: Gal. 4:6), which many scholars, like Cobb, think was an informal form of reference to one's father—something like our "Daddy"—whose use shows the special intimacy of Jesus' relation with his *Abba*. Other scholars dispute both that *Abba* had that informal meaning and that we have good reason to think Jesus used the term. See Mary Rose D'Angelo, "*Abba* and 'Father': Imperial Theology and the Jesus Traditions," *Journal of Biblical Literature* 111 (1992): 611–30; and James Barr, "*Abba* Isn't 'Daddy,'" *Journal of Theological Studies* 39 (1988): 28–47.

18. Gregory Nazianzus, Oration 42.15, trans. Charles Gordon Browne and James Edward Swallow, in *Nicene and Post-Nicene Fathers*, 2nd series (Peabody, Mass.: Hendrickson Publishers, 1994), 7:390.
19. Augustine, *On the Trinity* 7.4.7, in *Nicene and Post-Nicene Fathers*, 1st series, 3:109; for clarity's sake, I have used the Greek and Latin.
20. Karl Barth, *Church Dogmatics* I/1, 2nd ed., trans. G. W. Bromiley (Edinburgh: T. & T. Clark, 1975), 355.
21. Karl Rahner, *The Trinity*, trans. Joseph Donceel (New York: Crossroad, 1997), 103–15.
22. Gregory of Nyssa, *Address on Religious Instruction*, trans. Cyril C. Richardson, in *Christology of the Later Fathers*, ed. E. R. Hardy (Philadelphia: Westminster Press, 1954), 301.
23. Catherine Mowry LaCugna, "The Baptismal Formula, Feminist Objections, and Trinitarian Theology," *Journal of Ecumenical Studies* 26 (Spring 1989): 243.

David S. Cunningham's Essay

1. Rowan Williams, "Trinity and Revelation," *Modern Theology*, 2 (1986): 3, reprinted in *On Christian Theology* (Oxford: Basil Blackwell, 2000), 131. Many of Williams's essays in this volume will be useful in explicating further the themes outlined in this chapter.
2. Augustine, *The Trinity* 1.1.5, my translation. See Augustine, *The Trinity*, trans. Edmund Hill (Brooklyn, N.Y.: New City Press, 1991), 68.
3. For a detailed investigation of this point, see Douglas Farrow, *Ascension and Ecclesia* (Grand Rapids: Wm. B. Eerdmans Publishing Co., 1999).
4. This phrase is taken from the title of Nicholas Lash's fine book *Believing Three Ways in One God* (Notre Dame, Ind.: University of Notre Dame Press, 1992). This book is an excellent "next step" for students seeking to improve their understanding of the doctrine of the Trinity.
5. Thomas Aquinas, *Summa Theologica* 1a.27.1, trans. Fathers of the English Dominican Province (Westminster, Md.: Christian Classics, 1981), 147.
6. Aquinas's account of why there are four real relations, but only three subsistent relations, is very complex and related to his defense of the word *filioque* ("and the Son") in the Western form of the Nicene Creed. For more information, see David S. Cunningham, *These Three Are One* (Oxford: Basil Blackwell, 1998), 62–63.
7. Lash, *Believing Three Ways*, 32.
8. For some interesting commentary on the placenta as illustrating the "necessary third" in human relationships, see the work of Luce Irigaray, for example, *je, tu, nous: Toward a Culture of Difference*, trans. Alison Martin (New York: Routledge, 1993), 37–44.
9. Even the "Fathers" of the Church objected to the claim that God was male. See Gregory of Nazianzus, "Fifth Theological Oration: On the Holy Spirit," trans. Charles Gordon Browne and James Edward Swallow, in *Nicene and Post-Nicene Fathers*, 2nd series (Peabody, Mass.: Hendrickson Publishers, 1994), 7:320; and Athanasius, "On the Councils," trans. A. Robertson, in *Nicene and Post-Nicene Fathers*, 2nd series (Peabody, Mass.: Hendrickson Publishers, 1994), 4:472.
10. Elizabeth Johnson, *She Who Is: The Mystery of God in Feminist Theological Discourse* (New York: Crossroad, 1998), 82.
11. Vladimir Lossky, *The Mystical Theology of the Eastern Church*, trans. members of the Fellowship of St. Alban and St. Sergius (Crestwood, N.Y.: St. Vladimir's Seminary Press, 1957), 35; see also Pseudo-Dionysius, *On the Divine Names* (a good English edition is in Pseudo-Dionysius, *The Complete Works*, trans. Colm Luibheid [New York: Paulist Press, 1987]).

12. A good stimulus to further thinking on these questions is Ruth C. Duck and Patricia Wilson-Kastner, *Praising God: The Trinity in Christian Worship* (Louisville, Ky.: Westminster John Knox Press, 1999).
13. The development of this language owes much to my ongoing conversations with The Y Group, and particularly to Margaret Adam.
14. This was a central theme in Rowan Williams's 1997 Hale Lectures at Seabury-Western Theological Seminary, and will be central in his forthcoming book on the Trinity.
15. For a good discussion of the contrast between Christian thought and modern economic theory on matters such as scarcity and force, see D. Stephen Long, *Divine Economy: Theology and the Market* (London: Routledge, 1999).
16. This point is made with clarity and precision in Bruce D. Marshall, *Trinity and Truth* (Cambridge: Cambridge University Press, 1999).
17. For more on this point, see my essay, "Interpretation: Toward a Rehabilitation of the Vestigia Tradition," in *Knowing the Triune God: The Work of the Spirit in the Practices of the Church,* ed. James J. Buckley and David Yeago (Grand Rapids: Wm. B. Eerdmans Publishing Co., 2001), 179–202.
18. See Hans Urs von Balthasar, *Theo-Drama: Theological Dramatic Theory,* trans. Graham Harrison, 4 parts in 5 vols. (San Francisco: Ignatius Press, 1988–2000).
19. Balthasar, *Theo-Drama,* 1:279.
20. Many thanks to my students at Seabury-Western Theological Seminary; their feedback and friendship have made me a better theologian. Particular thanks to those who commented on earlier drafts of this chapter: Margaret Adam, Russ Bohner, Richard Easterling, Tripp Hudgins, Deb Seles, Karl Stevens, Heather Voss, Kara Wagner Sherer, and Lisa Walters.

Chapter 3: Is God in Charge?

1. Walter Brueggemann, *Theology of the Old Testament* (Minneapolis: Fortress Press, 1997), 153.
2. James Weldon Johnson, "The Creation," *Complete Poems* (New York: Penguin Books, 2000), 15.
3. Karl Barth, *Church Dogmatics* II/1, trans. T. H. L. Parker et al. (Edinburgh: T. & T. Clark, 1957), 257.
4. Baruch Spinoza, *Ethics,* in *The Collected Works of Spinoza,* trans. Edwin Curley (Princeton, N.J.: Princeton University Press, 1985), 420.
5. Alfred North Whitehead, *Process and Reality* (New York: Macmillan, 1929), 524, 530.
6. See Sallie McFague, *The Body of God* (Minneapolis: Fortress Press, 1993), 131–58.
7. Karl Barth, *Church Dogmatics* III/1, trans. J. W. Edwards et al. (Edinburgh: T. & T. Clark, 1958), 81.
8. See David and Eileen Spring, *Ecology and Religion in History* (New York: Harper & Row, 1974).
9. Jürgen Moltmann, *God in Creation,* trans. Margaret Kohl (San Francisco: Harper & Row, 1985), 3.
10. John Calvin, *Institutes of the Christian Religion* 1.16.4, trans. Ford Lewis Battles (Philadelphia: Westminster Press, 1960), 201–2.
11. "Sir Isaac Newton, and his followers, have also a very odd opinion concerning the work of God. . . . [T]he machine of God's making, is so imperfect, according to these gentlemen, that he is obliged to clean it now and then by an extraordinary concourse, and even to mend it." Gottfried Leibniz, "Mr. Leibnitz's First Paper," in *The Leibniz-Clarke Correspondence,* ed. H. G. Alexander (Manchester: Manchester University Press, 1956), 11.

12. The Belgic Confession, in *The Creeds of Christendom*, ed. Philip Schaff (New York: Harper & Brothers, 1919), 3:397.
13. See Heinrich Heppe, *Reformed Dogmatics*, trans. G. T. Thomson (London: George Allen & Unwin, 1950), 251–65; William Stacy Johnson and John H. Leith, *Reformed Reader*, vol. 1 (Louisville, Ky.: Westminster/John Knox Press, 1993), 174–83.
14. Thomas Aquinas, *Summa Theologica* 1.22.2 ad 2, trans. Fathers of the English Dominican Province (Westminster, Md.: Christian Classics, 1981), 123.
15. Alvin Plantinga, "The Free Will Defense," in *The Analytic Theist* (Grand Rapids: Wm. B. Eerdmans Publishing Co., 1998), 48.
16. John Hick, *Evil and the God of Love* (San Francisco: Harper & Row, 1966), 385.
17. See David Ray Griffin, *God, Power, and Evil* (Philadelphia: Westminster Press, 1976).
18. See Jonathan Edwards, *Freedom of the Will* (New Haven, Conn.: Yale University Press, 1957), 225–38.
19. Calvin, *Institutes* 4.20.30, 1517.
20. John Calvin, "Brief Reply in Refutation of the Calumnies of a Certain Worthless Person," *Theological Treatises*, trans. J. K. S. Reid (Philadelphia: Westminster Press, 1954), 339.
21. John Calvin, *Concerning the Eternal Predestination of God*, trans. J. K. S. Reid (London: James Clarke, 1961), 123.
22. Aquinas, *Summa Theologica* 1a.17.1, 96, translation altered, emphasis added.

Sallie McFague's Essay

1. Annie Dillard, *Pilgrim at Tinker Creek* (New York: Bantam Books, 1974), 2, 12.
2. First Vatican Council, "Dogmatic Constitution concerning Catholic Faith," in *The Sources of Catholic Dogma*, ed. Heinrich Denzinger, trans. Roy J. Defarrari (St. Louis: B. Herder, 1957), 443.
3. Augustine, *Confessions* 1.2, trans. F. J. Sheed (Indianapolis: Hackett Publishing, 1993), 3–4.
4. Irenaeus, *Against Heresies* 4.20.7, in *Irenaeus of Lyons*, ed. Robert M. Grant (Routledge: London, 1997), 153, translation modified.
5. H. Richard Niebuhr, *The Responsible Self* (New York: Harper & Row, 1963), 175.
6. Erich Heller, *The Disinherited Mind* (New York: World, 1961), 211.

Kathryn Tanner's Essay

1. Readers seeking examples and further details should consult my *God and Creation in Christian Theology* (Oxford: Basil Blackwell, 1988).

Chapter 4: What's Wrong with Us?

1. Augustine, *The Literal Meaning of Genesis,* trans. John Hammon Taylor (New York: Newman Press, 1982), 1:193.
2. Karl Barth, *Church Dogmatics*, III/4, trans. A. T. Mackay et al. (Edinburgh: T. & T. Clark, 1961), 117.
3. Reinhold Niebuhr, *The Nature and Destiny of Man* (New York: Charles Scribner's Sons, 1941), 1:173–74.
4. See Mary Aquin O'Neill, "The Mystery of Being Human Together," in *Freeing Theology*, ed. Catherine Mowry LaCugna (San Francisco: Harper, 1993), 148.
5. Plato, *Gorgias* 493a, trans. Terence Irwin (Oxford: Clarendon Press, 1979), 67.
6. Origen, *Contra Celsum* 3.81, trans. Henry Chadwick (Cambridge: Cambridge University Press, 1965), 182.

7. Augustine, *The Retractations* 1.1.3, trans. Mary Inez Bogan (Washington: Catholic University of America Press, 1968), 10.
8. Aristotle, *On the Soul* 2.412a, in *The Basic Works of Aristotle*, trans. Richard McKeon (New York: Random House, 1941), 555. See also Thomas Aquinas, *Summa Theologica* 1a.75.1, trans. Fathers of the English Dominican Province (Westminster, Md.: Christian Classics, 1981), 363.
9. Aquinas, *Summa Theologica* 1a.76.1 ad 6, 372.
10. Caroline Walker Bynum, *The Resurrection of the Body in Western Christianity 200–1336* (New York: Columbia University Press, 1995), 283–90.
11. Niebuhr, *Nature and Destiny of Man*, 1:178–85.
12. Augustine, *The City of God* 14.13, trans. Gerald G. Walsh and Grace Monahan (New York: Fathers of the Church, 1952), 380.
13. Augustine, *Marriage and Desire* 2.5.15, in *The Works of Saint Augustine*, 1/24, trans. Roland J. Teske (Hyde Park, N.Y.: New City Press, 1998), 61.
14. Augustine, Sermon 151.5, in *The Works of Saint Augustine*, 3/5, trans. Edmund Hill (New Rochelle, N.Y.: New City Press, 1992), 43–44.
15. Immanuel Kant, *Religion within the Limits of Reason Alone*, trans. T. W. Greene (Chicago: Open Court Publishing Co., 1934), 27.
16. Albrecht Ritschl, "Instruction in the Christian Religion," in *Three Essays*, trans. Philip Hefner (Philadelphia: Fortress Press, 1972), 233; Walter Rauschenbusch, *A Theology for the Social Gospel* (New York: Macmillan, 1922), 58.
17. See Valerie Saiving, "The Human Situation: A Feminine View," *Journal of Religion* 40 (1960): 100–112.
18. Niebuhr, *Nature and Destiny of Man*, 1:228–40.
19. "The sinner is not merely Prometheus or Lucifer . . . [but also] a lazy-bones, a sluggard, a good-for-nothing" who stands as bitterly in need of exaltation as pride stands in need of humiliation. Karl Barth, *Church Dogmatics*, IV/2, trans. G. W. Bromiley (Edinburgh: T. & T. Clark, 1958), 404.
20. Susan Dunfee Nelson, "The Sin of Hiding: A Feminist Critique of Reinhold Niebuhr's Account of the Sin of Pride," *Soundings* 65 (1982): 316–27.
21. Gustavo Gutiérrez, *A Theology of Liberation*, trans. Caridad Inda and John Eagleson (Maryknoll, N.Y.: Orbis Books, 1973), 175.
22. Will D. Campbell, *Brother to a Dragonfly* (New York: Continuum, 1994), 220.

Serene Jones's Essay

1. See Dorothy C. Bass, ed., *Practicing Our Faith* (San Francisco: Jossey-Bass, 1997), and Miroslav Volf and Dorothy C. Bass, eds., *Practicing Theology* (Grand Rapids: Wm. B. Eerdmans Publishing Co., 2002).
2. My own orientation as a constructive theologian is in the Reformed tradition. I also approach these topics as a theologian whose perspective has been influenced by the ongoing work of feminist theologians and theorists, race theorists, and a variety of other contemporary social theorists, philosophers, and theologians.
3. The view I develop here is broadly ecumenical in scope but has distinct roots in the Reformed tradition, particularly in Calvin and Edwards. See Amy Plantinga Pauw, *"The Supreme Harmony of All": The Trinitarian Theology of Jonathan Edwards* (Grand Rapids: Wm. B. Eerdmans Publishing Co., 2002).
4. Note that I am expanding Lindbeck's cultural-linguistic account of doctrine. See George A. Lindbeck, *The Nature of Doctrine* (Philadelphia: Westminster Press, 1984).
5. For a contemporary discussion of this "performative" metaphor, see Judith Butler, *Gender Trouble* (New York: Routledge, 1990). I also want to make it clear that

calling doctrines "imaginative" does not mean that they are imagined or illusory. It points to the fact that doctrines function to shape the mental apparatus we use to apprehend the world.

6. Here I am indebted to David Kelsey, whose forthcoming work in theological anthropology has encouraged me to see these stories as independent and yet mutually implicating accounts of humanity and not as progressive stages in a single story of human nature and its fall, redemption, and eventual consummation. I should note that Kelsey's analysis includes only three stories. He appropriately incorporates sinful humanity into his story of redeemed humanity. For heuristic purposes, I am dividing the two.
7. William Shakespeare, *Macbeth*, Act 5, scene 5.
8. See Exod. 6:7; Jer. 7:23; 11:4; 30:22; Ezek. 36:28, among others. Also see Heb. 8:10: "This is the covenant that I will make with the house of Israel after those days, says the Lord: I will put my laws in their minds, and write them on their hearts, and I will be their God, and they shall be my people."
9. See Isa. 51:7; Jer. 31:33. For a discussion of natural law in the tradition, see Thomas Aquinas, *Summa Theologiae* 1a2ae.94, ed. Thomas Gilby, vol. 28 (New York: McGraw-Hill, 1964), 75–98.
10. For a more developed discussion of this point, see my treatment of strategic essentialism in Serene Jones, *Feminist Theory and Christian Theology* (Minneapolis: Fortress Press, 2000).
11. Other words frequently used to describe this breech in the covenant relation are *alienation, disobedience,* and *exile.*
12. The word *imputed*, discussed more fully in the next section, captures something of the illusory yet real character of the false performative reality that sin imposes upon us.
13. For an extended discussion of this dynamic in language, see Jacques Derrida, *Of Grammatology*, trans. Gayatri Chakravorty Spivak (Baltimore: Johns Hopkins University Press, 1976), and Luce Irigaray, *Speculum of the Other Woman*, trans. Gillian C. Gill (Ithaca, N.Y.: Cornell University Press, 1985).
14. Karl Rahner discusses a similar situation in his *Foundations of Christian Faith*, trans. William V. Dych (New York: Crossroad, 1978), 110–11. He depicts the dilemma of a European purchasing a banana at a price that could not fairly pay the growers, pickers, and transporters of that banana, a situation which reinforces and perpetuates unfair, sinful structures.
15. This theme pervades Augustine's anti-Pelagian writings. See, among others, his "Treatise on Rebuke and Grace," in *Nicene and Post-Nicene Fathers*, 2nd series (Peabody, Mass.: Hendrickson Publishers, 1994), 5:487. Luther devotes an entire treatise to the question in his debate with Erasmus. See "The Bondage of the Will," trans. Philip S. Watson, *Luther's Works,* ed. Helmut T. Lehmann, vol. 33 (Philadelphia: Fortress Press, 1972).
16. For Paul's use of *justification*, see Acts 13:39, Rom. 3:24; 4:25; 5:16–18.
17. See John 17:19; Rom. 6:22; 1 Cor. 6:11; Heb. 10:10.
18. John Calvin, *Institutes of the Christian Religion* 3.2.7, trans. Ford Lewis Battles (Philadelphia: Westminster Press, 1960), 551.

Clark M. Williamson's Essay

1. See G. Ernest Wright, *The Biblical Doctrine of Man in Society* (London: SCM Press, 1954).
2. Karl Barth, *Church Dogmatics* 3/1, trans. G. W. Bromiley (Edinburgh: T. & T. Clark, 1961), 368–69, 372.

3. Louis Ginzberg, *The Legends of the Jews*, vol. 1, *From the Creation to Jacob* (Philadelphia: Jewish Publication Society, 1909), 54–55.
4. See Martin Luther, *The Freedom of a Christian*, in *Martin Luther: Selections from His Writings*, ed. John Dillenberger (Garden City, N.J.: Anchor Books, 1961), 42–85.
5. See Thomas Aquinas, *Summa Theologica*, 1a.92.1 ad 1, trans. Fathers of the English Dominican Province (Westminster, Md.: Christian Classics, 1981), 466.
6. Some important feminist theologies are Rosemary Radford Ruether, *Sexism and God Talk* (Boston: Beacon Press, 1983); Letty M. Russell, *Human Liberation in a Feminist Perspective—A Theology* (Philadelphia: Westminster Press, 1974); and Anne E. Carr, *Transforming Grace* (San Francisco: Harper & Row, 1988).
7. Alfred North Whitehead, *Religion in the Making* (New York: Living Age Books, 1960), 86.
8. Walter Brueggemann, *A Social Reading of the Old Testament*, ed. Patrick Miller (Minneapolis: Fortress Press, 1994), 45.
9. Chapter 2 of Paul Tillich, *Love, Power, and Justice* (New York: Oxford University Press, 1954), is a groundbreaking reflection on the relation of *agape* and *eros*, one that does not see them as inherently conflictual. Sallie McFague, *Models of God* (Philadelphia: Fortress Press, 1987), builds on such developments to use *eros* and *philia* as metaphors for God's love: "*Agape*, the love that gives with no thought of return, *eros*, the love that finds the beloved valuable, and *philia*, the love that shares and works for the vision of the good . . . all of them in different ways attest to the oneness of love, so evident in sexual union, as 'that which drives everything that is towards everything else that is'" (131).
10. J. Gerald Jantzen, *Abraham and All the Families of the Earth* (Grand Rapids: Wm. B. Eerdmans Publishing Co., 1993), 61.
11. Marti Steussy, class lecture on "Sex and the Bible," for Introduction to the Hebrew Bible, Oct. 23, 1997.
12. Obviously, the relationship between David and Jonathan need not have been homosexual; it has, however, long been so interpreted.
13. Christopher Morse, *Not Every Spirit* (Valley Forge, Pa.: Trinity Press International, 1994), 276.
14. Cited in Steussy, "Sex and the Bible."
15. Judith Plaskow, *Standing again at Sinai* (San Francisco: Harper & Row, 1989), 182.
16. Jon Berquist, April 14, 1998, correspondence with the author. Judith Romney Wegner agrees with Berquist on this point; see her "Leviticus," in *The Women's Bible Commentary* (Louisville, Ky.: Westminster/John Knox Press, 1992), 41.
17. Steussy, "Sex and the Bible."
18. Berquist, correspondence.
19. Fred Craddock, "How Does the New Testament Deal with the Issue of Homosexuality?" *Encounter* 40, no. 3 (1979): 197.
20. Ibid., 199–202.
21. Ibid., 203.
22. Berquist, correspondence; he refers to Robert Brawley, ed., *Biblical Ethics and Homosexuality: Listening to Scripture* (Louisville, Ky.: Westminster John Knox Press, 1996).
23. Craddock, "How Does the New Testament Deal?" 206.
24. Beverly Gaventa, "Romans," in *Women's Bible Commentary* (Louisville, Ky.: Westminster/John Knox Press, 1992), 316–17.
25. Craddock, "How Does the New Testament Deal?" 207.
26. Morse, *Not Every Spirit*, 280.

27. Ibid., 281–82.
28. Plaskow, *Standing again at Sinai,* 208.
29. See James Luther Adams, "Tillich's Concept of the Protestant Era," in Paul Tillich, *The Protestant Era,* ed. James Luther Adams (Chicago: University of Chicago Press, 1948), 273–316.
30. Rita Nakashima Brock, *Journeys by Heart* (New York: Crossroad, 1988), 7.
31. Marjorie Suchocki, *The Fall to Violence* (New York: Continuum, 1995), 114.
32. Quoted in Suchocki, *Fall to Violence,* 114–15.
33. On Chrysostom, see "Homily 1 Against the Jews," in *Christians and Jews in Antioch,* ed. Wayne A. Meeks and Robert L. Wilken (Missoula, Mont.: Society of Biblical Literature, 1978), 89. As for Luther, see his "Concerning the Jews and Their Lies, in *Disputation and Dialogue,* ed. Frank E. Talmage (New York: KTAV, 1975), 34–36.

Chapter 5: How Does Jesus Make a Difference?

1. Athanasius, *Life of Antony* 74, in *Nicene and Post-Nicene Fathers,* 2nd series (Peabody, Mass.: Hendrickson Publishers, 1994), 4:215.
2. Apollinaris, "Letter to the Bishops Exiled at Diocaersarea," quoted in G. L. Prestige, *Fathers and Heretics* (London: SPCK, 1940), 111.
3. Gregory of Nazianzus, Letter 101, to Cledonius the priest, in *Nicene and Post-Nicene Fathers,* 2nd series 7:440.
4. Ibid., 441.
5. Rudolf Bultmann, "Bultmann Replies to His Critics," in Hans W. Bartsch, *Kerygma and Myth,*, trans. Reginald H. Fuller (New York: Harper & Row, 1961), 211.
6. Paul Tillich, *Systematic Theology* (Chicago: University of Chicago Press, 1967), 2:116.
7. James Cone, *Black Theology and Black Power* (New York: Seabury Press, 1969), 151.
8. Gustavo Gutiérrez, *A Theology of Liberation,* trans. Caridad Inda and John Eagleson (Maryknoll, N.Y.: Orbis Books, 1973), 226–31.
9. Patricia Wilson-Kastner, *Faith, Feminism, and the Christ* (Philadelphia: Fortress Press, 1983), 72.
10. Anselm, "Prayer to St. Paul," in *The Prayers and Meditations of St. Anselm,* trans. Benedicta Ward (Harmondsworth, England: Penguin Books, 1973), 153; Julian of Norwich, *Showings* (long text) 58, trans. Edmund Colledge and James Walsh (New York: Paulist Press, 1978), 293–94. See Caroline Walker Bynum, *Jesus as Mother* (Berkeley, Calif.: University of California Press, 1982).
11. Joanne Carlson Brown and Rebecca Parker, "For God So Loved the World?" in *Christianity, Patriarchy, and Abuse,* ed. Joanne Carlson Brown and Carole R. Bohn (New York: Pilgrim Press, 1989), 2.
12. Irenaeus, *Against Heresies* 3.21.10, in *Ante-Nicene Fathers* (Peabody, Mass.: Hendrickson Publishers, 1994), 1:454.
13. Gregory of Nyssa, *Against Eunomius* 12.1, in *Nicene and Post-Nicene Fathers,* 5:241.
14. John Calvin, *Commentary on the Gospel according to John* (on John 12:27), trans. William Pringle, vol. 18 of *Calvin's Commentaries* (Grand Rapids: Baker Book House, 1989), 32.
15. Augustine, Sermon 263.1, in *Sermons on the Liturgical Seasons,* trans. Mary Sarah Muldowney (New York: Fathers of the Church, 1959), 392.
16. "How shameful that that robber should receive not only a ransom, but a ransom consisting of God Himself." Gregory of Nazianzus, Oration 45.22, *Nicene and Post-Nicene Fathers,* 7:431.

17. Anselm of Canterbury, *Why God Became Man*, in *Basic Writings*, trans. S. N. Deane (LaSalle, Ill.: Open Court, 1966), 202.
18. Ibid., 227.
19. Peter Abailard, *Exposition of the Epistle to the Romans*, in *A Scholastic Miscellany*, ed. Eugene R. Fairweather (Philadelphia: Westminster Press, 1956), 283.
20. Clement of Alexandria, *Miscellanies*, in *Ante-Nicene Fathers*, 2:491.
21. John Calvin, *Institutes of the Christian Religion* 2.16.11, trans. Ford Lewis Battles (Philadelphia: Westminster Press, 1960), 516.
22. Hans Urs von Balthasar, *The Von Balthasar Reader*, ed. Medard Kehl and Werner Loser, trans. Robert J. Daly and Fred Lawrence (Edinburgh: T. & T. Clark, 1985), 183.

Robert W. Jenson's Essay

1. Or, if one objects to this anthropology, in whatever content one wishes to describe.
2. The foundational modern discussion of what was entailed in the Judaism of the time by the assertion of a "resurrection" is by Wolfhart Pannenberg, *Jesus—God and Man*, trans. Lewis L. Wilkens and Duane A. Priebe (Philadelphia: Westminster Press, 1968), 53–88.
3. Perhaps the most remarkable example is the famous "dry bones" passage in Ezekiel 37.
4. For full discussion of the latter point, and the necessary scholarly apparatus, see my *Systematic Theology*, vol. 1 (New York: Oxford University Press, 1997), 42–89.
5. This, of course, is us, the writer and the great majority of possible readers.
6. Thus, the archetypical Gentiles of Luke's story about Paul in Athens apparently thought that *resurrection* was the name of a goddess; see Acts 17:18.
7. The Eastern church's theology does not typically have such a standard sequence of topics.
8. The church's formally deciding something obviously presupposes an authority able to speak for the whole church, as were the ecumenical councils of the ancient church. In the circumstance of a divided church, the promulgation of dogma becomes problematic.
9. This has been crushingly rebuked by David Yeago, "The New Testament and Nicene Dogma," *Pro Ecclesia* 3 (1994): 152–64.
10. That is, identifying the same logical subject and making predications with equivalent truth-conditions.
11. Yeago, "New Testament," 160–62.
12. This is a phrase of the rabbis, for what they thought the Christians might think.
13. Jenson, *Sysematic Theology*, 1:102–3.
14. Thus, the logic noted above appears throughout the Old Testament: For example, in Gen. 22, the story of the so-called sacrifice of Isaac, the "angel *of* the Lord" speaks to Abraham and refers to himself in the first person *as* the Lord. For the "Son" in the Old Testament, see Jenson, *Systematic Theology*, 1:75–86.
15. See Jenson, *Systematic Theology*, 1:75–80.
16. See ibid., 1:86–89.
17. Thus, the formula has nothing whatever to do either with metaphors or with psychological projections of fatherhood.
18. Matt. 28:19. "Father, Son, and Holy Spirit" is not optional for baptism, or therefore Christian liturgy generally, as it is the personal name identifying the particular God into whom the person is baptized. Such a formula as "Creator, Redeemer, and Sanctifier" identifies no one; all putative gods somehow have these functions.

19. On the following, see Jenson, *Systematic Theology,* 1:90–114.
20. For example, classic Christian prayer is *to* the Father, *with* the Son, and *in* the Spirit.
21. In this scheme, the pronoun must indeed be *itself.*
22. Leonard Hodgson, *The Doctrine of the Trinity* (New York: Charles Scribner's Sons, 1944), 103, has the precise aphorism: "Christianity began as a trinitarian religion with a unitarian theology. The question at issue in the age of the Fathers was whether the religion would transform the theology or the theology stifle the religion."
23. Sundry late modern "theories" still do not.
24. And eventually between the Spirit himself and his gifts.
25. The nature of that *so* has remained impossible to clarify from that day to this.
26. Such as, in modern versions of the old evasions, the human person's ethnicity (the "German Christians" who under Hitler excluded those with "Jewish blood" from the ministry), gender (much "feminist" theology), or class (the Protestant mainline).
27. Antioch was a major Christian center in Syria. The Antiochene school got a good reputation with an earlier generation of historians of doctrine for its supposed concern for the humanity of Jesus. In fact, they feared humanity, and their concern was to protect his deity from contamination by it.
28. Who included one very great one, Theodore of Mopsuestia.
29. Alexandria was the great cultural and intellectual center of the eastern Mediterranean.
30. Lest readers think the division was for trivial cause, let them think about the difference between a God who can truly be a human doer and sufferer and one whose deity consists in aloofness from such things.
31. The Antiochenes who left fellowship with the imperial church are usually called *Nestorians,* after Nestorius, a fifth-century patriarch of Constantinople who emphaszied the twoness of the "two natures," though they called themselves the Church of the East. Those Alexandrians who left for opposite reasons are known as *Monophysites,* since they believed that Christ had only "one nature" (*monophysis*). Ecumenical dialogues are currently in process of repairing some of these schisms.
32. This term is taken over from previously developed Trinitarian teaching, in which Father, Son, and Spirit are three *hypostases* in and of one God. By itself, the term is almost meaningless, deriving its content from use in context.
33. The language was taken from a consensus-formula once proposed by Cyril.
34. Scholars refer to the development in the East as "neo-Chalcedonian." Within the Reformation, it was the Lutherans who shared this concern.
35. The human nature is *anhypostatic* (*an-* means "not," so *anhypostatic,* applied to the human nature, means there is not a separate human *hypostasis,* some human individual Jesus would have been if he had not been also divine) and *enhypostatic* (the human being that is Jesus exists *in* the divine *hypostasis*).
36. "Epistola Papae Leonis ad Flavianum," in *Decrees of the Ecumenical Councils,* ed. Norman Tanner (Washington, D.C.: Georgetown University Press, 1990), 1:79,3–7.
37. If its author were not a great pope, and a great teacher, one would simply say "heretical."
38. Candor requires that at this point I confess my confessional bias: I am denominationally a Lutheran, and it is the Lutheran emphases in Christology that continue to interest me about my confession.
39. If this description is offensive, it is an equal-opportunity stone of stumbling; there is in it something to put anyone off.

40. This heresy is called *patripassionism.*
41. "My God, my God, why have you forsaken me?" (Matt. 27:46; Mark 15:34).
42. *Si Christus venisset si Adam non pecasset?* ("Would Christ have come if Adam had not sinned?"). For the classical Western debates on this matter, see J. M. Bissen, "La tradition sur la prédestination absolue de Jésus-Christ du VIIe au XIIIe siècle," *France Franciscaine* 22 (1939): 9–34.

Leanne Van Dyk's Essay

1. Athanasius, *On the Incarnation of the Word,* in *Christology of the Later Fathers,* ed. E. R. Hardy (Philadelphia: Westminster Press, 1954), 55–110.
2. Ibid., 109.
3. See Anselm, *Why God Became Man,* in *A Scholastic Miscellany,* ed. E. R. Fairweather (Philadelphia: Westminster Press, 1956), 100–183.
4. These writers include J. Denny Weaver, Anthony Bartlett, Robert Hamerton-Kelly, Raymund Schwäger, Michael Welker, Elizabeth A. Johnson, and Timothy Gorringe.
5. Violence has scarred every human society, as the biblical account of Abel's murder by his brother, Cain, attests. No facile attempt to attribute blame to atonement theology for the epidemic of violence is intended. But the possibility of deep cultural links of particular formulations of atonement theology to destructive social effects is crucially important for Christian theologians to examine.
6. Heidelberg Catechism, in *The Creeds of Christendom,* ed. Philip Schaff (New York: Harper & Brothers, 1877), 307–12.
7. The dominant Western view is frequently called the "Anselmian theory" or the "penal substitutionary view" or, sometimes, the "substituted punishment view." The first term, "Anselmian theory," however, is regularly used inaccurately. Anselm's view of the atonement, although including some troublesome concepts that will be identified below, does not require the punishment of Jesus Christ by a just Father in heaven. In fact, Anselm expressly denies that Christ suffered punishment on the cross, proposing instead a theory of the cross as an infinite act of divine honoring. Thus, Anselm does not have a "penal substitutionary" view of the atonement, although the dominant Western view owes much to him in the structure and logic of a penal substitutionary view. I consider the "dominant Western view" to be a close synonym to "penal substitutionary" atonement.
8. John Calvin, *Institutes of the Christian Religion* 2.16.1, trans. Ford Lewis Battles (Philadelphia: Westminster Press, 1960), 504.
9. Ibid., 2.16.6, 510.
10. Ibid., 2.15.6, 501.
11. Ibid., 2.16.4, 506.
12. Ibid., 2.17.3, 531.
13. See, for example, the work of Rebecca Parker or Delores Williams.
14. René Girard or Michael Welker are examples of this kind of interdisciplinarity.
15. N. T. Wright and Alan Lewis are just two of a much larger group.
16. Robert Farrar Capon, *The Fingerprints of God: Tracking the Divine Suspect through a History of Images* (Grand Rapids: Wm. B. Eerdmans Publishing Co., 2000), 117.
17. Abusers, of course, do not have a carefully articulated theology that legitimates their violence based on the cross of Christ. The influences of religion on behavior, attitudes, and actions are, no doubt, profoundly complex. But the witness of abused women lends considerable credence to the notion that violence is often religiously defended.

18. See Philip Greven, *Spare the Child: The Religious Roots of Punishment and Psychological Impact of Physical Abuse* (New York: Alfred A. Knopf, 1991).
19. See Timothy Gorringe, *God's Just Vengeance: Crime, Violence, and the Rhetoric of Salvation* (Cambridge: Cambridge University Press, 1996).
20. See René Girard, *Violence and the Sacred*, trans. Patrick Gregory (Baltimore and London: Johns Hopkins University Press, 1977); and René Girard, Jean-Michel Oughourlian, and Guy Lefort, *Things Hidden since the Foundation of the World*, trans. Stephen Bann and Michael Metter (Stanford, Calif.: Stanford University Press, 1987).
21. Michael Welker, *What Happens in Holy Communion?* trans. J. Hoffmeyer (Grand Rapids: Wm. B. Eerdmans Publishing Co., 2000), 109.
22. Ibid.
23. Anselm claimed to work out "apart from Christ" the logic of why it would be necessary for God to become human and only then to add the specifics of Christ's story.
24. Anthony Bartlett, *Cross Purposes: The Violent Grammar of Christian Atonement* (Harrisburg, Pa.: Trinity Press International, 2001), 5.
25. Ibid., 83–84.
26. J. Denny Weaver, *The Nonviolent Atonement* (Grand Rapids: Wm. B. Eerdmans Publishing Co., 2001), 7.
27. Ibid., 6.
28. Calvin, *Institutes* 2.16.2, 505.
29. Ibid., emphasis added.
30. Ibid., emphasis and line divisions added.
31. Ibid., 2.16.5, 508.
32. Timothy Gorringe expressly rejects any use of the shedding of blood as a means to restored order. He allows that "a messianic image of the work of Christ contributing to the *eventual establishment* of order might be more appropriate. It is not in the least clear, however, that Christ's *death* would do that." Gorringe, *God's Just Vengeance,* 234.
33. See John McLeod Campbell, *The Nature of the Atonement* (Grand Rapids: Wm. B. Eerdmans Publishing Co., 1999). The original publication of this influential book was in 1834. Campbell's influence has reached beyond his contemporaries (F. D. Maurice, Edward Irving, Samuel Taylor Coleridge) to later British thinkers (R. C. Moberly, T. F. Torrance, James Torrance) to twentieth-century American theologians (Michael Jinkins, James Goodloe).
34. Bartlett, *Cross Purposes,* 39.
35. Calvin, *Institutes* 2.16.5, 508.
36. Gorringe, *God's Just Vengeance,* 269.

Chapter 6: Why Bother with Church?

1. Ignatius of Antioch, "To the Ephesians," in *Early Christian Fathers*, trans. Cyril C. Richardson (New York: Macmillan, 1970), 89.
2. Ignatius of Antioch, "To the Philadelphians" in *Early Christian Fathers*, 108.
3. Clement of Rome, "Clement's First Letter," in *Early Christian Fathers*, 62.
4. See Elisabeth Schüssler Fiorenza, *In Memory of Her* (New York: Crossroad, 1983), 285–315.
5. Irenaeus, *Against Heresies* 3.2.2, in *Ante-Nicene Fathers* (Peabody, Mass.: Hendrickson Publishers, 1994), 1:415.
6. John Calvin, *Institutes of the Christian Religion* 4.1.7, trans. Ford Lewis Battles (Philadelphia: Westminster Press, 1960), 1021–22.
7. Augustine, Sermon 112.5, in *The Works of Saint Augustine* 3/4, trans. Edmund Hill, (Brooklyn: New City Press, 1992), 150.

8. Berengar of Tours, *Epistle to Adelman*, quoted in A. J. Macdonald, *Berengar and the Reform of Sacramental Doctrine* (Merrick, N.Y.: Richwood Publishing Co., 1977), 240.
9. David N. Power, "Eucharist," in *Systematic Theology*, ed. Francis Schüssler Fiorenza and John P. Galvin (Minneapolis: Fortress Press, 1991), 2:278.
10. Eamon Duffy, *The Stripping of the Altars* (New Haven, Conn.: Yale University Press, 1992).
11. See Hughes Oliphant Old, *The Reading and Preaching of the Scriptures in the Worship of the Christian Church*, vol. 3 (Grand Rapids: Wm. B. Eerdmans Publishing Co., 1999).
12. Calvin, *Institutes* 4.11.1, 1213.

Hughes Oliphant Old's Essay

1. This has been expressed in a variety of ways. See, for example, John Alexander Mackay, *God's Order* (New York: Macmillan, 1956); H. Richard Niebuhr, *The Purpose of the Church and Its Ministry* (New York: Harper & Brothers, 1956); Eduard Schweizer, *Lordship and Discipleship* (London: SCM Press, 1960); Karl Rahner, *The Church and the Sacraments*, trans. W. J. O'Hara (New York: Herder & Herder, 1963); Hans Küng, *The Church*, trans. Ray and Rosaleen Ockenden (Garden City, N.Y.: Image Books, 1976); John H. Leith, *The Church, a Believing Fellowship* (Atlanta: John Knox Press, 1981); Wallace M. Alston, Jr. *The Church* (Atlanta: John Knox Press, 1984); and Christian Link, Ulrich Luz, and Lukas Vischer, *Sie aber hielten fest an die Gemeinschaft* (Zurich: Benzinger, 1988).
2. Particularly helpful on the place of the church in the messianic expectation is Yves Congar, *The Mystery of the Temple* (London: Burns & Oates, 1962).
3. On the ministry of the apostles, see Philippe-Henri Menoud, *L'Église et les ministères selon le Nouveau Testament* (Neuchâtel and Paris: Delachaux et Niestlé, 1949), 25–34.
4. On the New Testament imagery for the church, see Lesslie Newbigin, *The Household of God* (New York: Friendship Press, 1953); and Mackay, *God's Order*. Formative for much recent thought on the nature of the church in the New Testament is K. L. Schmidt, "*ekklesia*," in *Theological Dictionary of the New Testament*, ed. Gerhard Kittel, trans. Geoffrey W. Bromiley (Grand Rapids: Wm. B. Eerdmans Publishing Co., 1965), 3:501–36. For an important Catholic point of view, see Rudolf Schnackenburg, *The Church in the New Testament*, trans. W. J. O'Hara (London: Burns & Oates, 1974); and Lucien Cerfaux, *The Church in the Theology of St. Paul*, trans. Geoffrey Webb and Adrian Walker (New York: Herder & Herder, 1959).
5. On the sacerdotal function of the church, see Menoud, *L'Église et les ministères*, 17–24.
6. On the Pauline use of the word *church*, see Schmidt, "*ekklesia*," 506–13.
7. On the interpretation of the passage, see Schmidt, "*ekklesia*," 518–26.
8. See Mackay, *God's Order*, 123–29; Eduard Schweizer, "*soma*," in *Theological Dictionary of the New Testament*, ed. Gerhard Kittel, trans. Geoffrey W. Bromiley (Grand Rapids: Wm. B. Eerdmans Publishing Co., 1965), 7:1024–94; Cerfaux, *Church in the Theology of St. Paul*, 267–86.
9. On the priority of these ministries of preaching and teaching, see Menoud, *L'Église et les ministères*, 35–54.
10. See Karl Barth on the task and ministry of the Christian community. Karl Barth, *Church Dogmatics*, IV/3, trans. G. W. Bromiley (Edinburgh: T. & T. Clark, 1962), 681–901.
11. On the ecclesiology of the ancient church, see Hans von Campenhausen, *Ecclesiastical Authority and Spiritual Power in the Church of the First Three Centuries*,

trans. J. A. Baker (London: Black, 1969). For a Roman Catholic interpretation of the ecclesiology of the ancient church, see Gustave Bardy, *La théologie de l'Église de saint Clément de Rome à saint Irénée* (Paris: Les Éditions du Cerf, 1945); and Gustave Bardy, *La Théologie de l'Église, de saint Irénée au Concile de Nicée* (Paris: Les Éditions du Cerf, 1947).

12. See J. N. D. Kelly, *Early Christian Creeds* (New York: D. McKay, 1972).
13. Of particular interest on the subject is Karl Barth, *Church Dogmatics,* IV/2, trans. G. W. Bromiley (Edinburgh: T. & T. Clark, 1958), 614–726.
14. For a thorough exposition of this, see Karl Barth, *Church Dogmatics*, IV/1, trans. G. W. Bromiley (Edinburgh: T. & T. Clark, 1956), 643–739.
15. On Luther's view of the church, see Paul Althaus, *The Theology of Martin Luther*, trans. Robert C. Schultz (Philadelphia: Fortress Press, 1966), 287–344; Eugene F. Klug, "Luther on the Church," *Concordia Theological Quarterly* 47 (1983): 193–207; and Vilmos Vajta, "Die Kirche als geistlich-sacramentale communio mit Christus und seinen Heiligen bei Luther," *Lutherjahrbuch* 51 (1984): 10–62.
16. See Elsie Anne McKee, *John Calvin on the Diaconate and Liturgical Almsgiving* (Geneva: Librairie Droz, 1984).
17. See John T. McNeill, "The Church in Sixteenth Century Reformed Theology," in *Major Themes in the Reformed Tradition*, ed. Donald K. McKim (Grand Rapids: Wm. B. Eerdmans Publishing Co., 1992).
18. On Calvin's role in the development of a Reformed ecclesiology, see Alasdair I. C. Heron et al., "Church," in *Encyclopedia of Christianity*, ed. Erwin Fahlbusch et al. (Grand Rapids: Wm. B. Eerdmans Publishing Co., 1999), 1:477–502.
19. See Alexandre Ganoczy, *Calvin, théologien de l'église et du ministère* (Paris: Les Éditions du Cerf, 1964); and Kilian McDonnell, *John Calvin, the Church, and the Eucharist* (Princeton, N.J.: Princeton University Press, 1967).
20. John Calvin, *Institutes of the Christian Religion* 4.1.9, trans. Ford Lewis Battles (Philadelphia: Westminster Press, 1960), 1023.
21. Ibid. 4.1.4, 1016.
22. Ibid. 4.1.2, 1014.
23. Ibid. 4.1.9, 1023.
24. Ibid. 4.1.3, 1014.
25. Ibid. 4.1.17, 1031–32.
26. Ibid. 4.3.1, 1054.
27. Ibid. 4.1.17–22, 1031–36.
28. Westminster Confession of Faith, in *The Creeds of Christendom,* ed. Philip Schaff (New York: Harper & Brothers, 1877), 2:657.
29. Ibid., 2:658.
30. See the introduction to the following chapter for a discussion of sanctification and justification.
31. Westminster Confession, in Schaff, *Creeds,* 3:658
32. Ibid.
33. See Barth, *Church Dogmatics* IV/1, 725–39.

Letty M. Russell's Essay

1. The consultation was part of a study process being conducted by the World Council of Churches, 2000–2003. See "On Being Church: Women's Voices and Visions," *Ecumenical Review* 53, no. 1 (January 2001)
2. Letty M. Russell, *Church in the Round: Feminist Interpretation of the Church* (Louisville, Ky.: Westminster/John Knox Press, 1993), 14.

3. James H. Cone, *God of the Oppressed,* rev. ed. (Maryknoll, N.Y.: Orbis Books, 1997), 110, 116.
4. Russell, *Church in the Round,* 42–43.
5. Paul Minear, *Images of the Church in the New Testament* (Philadelphia: Westminster Press, 1960), 268–69. For a discussion of predominant images, see Peter C. Hodgson, *Revisioning the Church: Ecclesial Freedom in the New Paradigm* (Philadelphia: Fortress Press, 1988), 28–35.
6. Russell, *Church in the Round,* 42–43.
7. Raymond E. Brown, *Biblical Exegesis and Church Doctrine* (New York: Paulist Press, 1985), 114–19.
8. Hodgson, *Revisioning the Church,* 25.
9. Paul S. Minear, "Church, Idea of," *The Interpreter's Bible Dictionary* (Nashville: Abingdon Press, 1962), 1:608.
10. Russell, *Church in the Round,* 131–36.
11. Robert J. Schreiter, "Marks of the Church in Times of Transition," in *The Church with AIDS: Renewal in the Midst of Crisis,* ed. Letty M. Russell, (Louisville, Ky.: Westminster/John Knox Press, 1990), 122. The Nicene Creed in the form we usually recite today is not the creed adopted at Nicaea in 325 (which concluded simply, "and in the Holy Spirit") but essentially the revised version adopted at Constantinople in 381.
12. See *Confessing the One Faith: An Ecumenical Explication of the Apostolic Faith as It Is Confessed in the Nicene-Constantinopolitan Creed (381),* Faith and Order Paper no. 153 (Geneva: WCC Publications, 1991).
13. Hans Küng, *The Church,* trans. Ray and Rosaleen Ockenden (New York: Sheed & Ward, 1967), 268–69.
14. Mary Tanner, "Toward a Common Confession of the Apostolic Faith Today," in *Women and Church,* ed. Melanie May (Grand Rapids: Wm. B. Eerdmans Publishing Co., 1991), 179–80.
15. Paul D. Hanson, *The People Called: The Growth of Community in the Bible* (San Francisco: Harper & Row, 1990), 426.
16. Marjorie Suchocki, "Holiness and a Renewed Church," in *The Church with AIDS: Renewal in the Midst of Crisis* ed. Letty M. Russell (Louisville, Ky.: Westminster/John Knox Press, 1990), 117.
17. Schreiter, "Marks of the Church," 131–32.
18. Ibid., 124.
19. Delores S. Williams, "Straight Talk, Plain Talk: Womanist Words about Salvation in a Social Context," in *Embracing the Spirit: Womanist Perspectives on Hope, Salvation, and Transformation,* ed. Emilie M. Townes (Maryknoll, N.Y.: Orbis Books, 1997), 118.
20. Karl Barth, *The Faith of the Church: A Commentary on the Apostles' Creed according to Calvin's Catechism,* ed. Jean-Louis Leuba, trans. Gabriel Vahanian (New York: Meridian Books, 1958), 148–49.
21. Russell, *Church in the Round,* 12.
22. Robert McAfee Brown, "The 'Preferential Option for the Poor' and Renewal of Faith," in *Churches in Struggle: Liberation Theologies and Social Change in North America,* ed. William K. Tabb (New York: Monthly Review Press, 1986), 10.
23. In this sentence a hyphen is used for emphasis: *kin-dom.* The term *kindom* is widely used of God's reign in order to move us beyond hierarchical imagery to one of community and welcome. See Ada Maria Isasi-Diaz, *En la Lucha: (In the Struggle): Elaborating a Mujerista Theology* (Minneapolis: Fortress Press, 1993), xi.
24. See Jürgen Moltmann, *The Church in the Power of the Spirit,* trans. Margaret Kohl (San Francisco: Harper & Row, 1977), 121–32.

25. Russell, *Church in the Round*, 130–31.
26. Moltmann, *Church in the Power*, 132.
27. Russell, *Church in the Round*, 137–38.
28. John Calvin, *Institutes of the Christian Religion* 4.1.9, trans. Ford Lewis Battles (Philadelphia: Westminster Press, 1960), 1023.
29. Küng, *Church*, 267.
30. Moltmann, *Church in the Power*, 341.
31. Fredrica Harris Thomsett, "Sacraments," in *Dictionary of Feminist Theologies*, ed. Letty M. Russell and J. Shannon Clarkson (Louisville, Ky.: Westminster John Knox Press, 1996), 251.
32. Marjorie Procter-Smith, *In Her Own Rite: Constructing Feminist Liturgical Tradition* (Nashville: Abingdon Press, 1990), 141.
33. Procter-Smith, *In Her Own Rite*, 160, citing James F. White, *Sacraments as God's Self Giving* (Nashville: Abingdon Press, 1983), 54–61.
34. Alan Richardson, "Salvation, Savior," *The Interpreter's Dictionary of the Bible*, ed. George Arthur Buttrick (New York: Abingdon Press, 1962), 168–81.

Chapter 7: How Should We Live?

1. Augustine, *Confessions* 8.7, trans. Rex Warner (New York: New American Library, Mentor-Omega Books, 1963), 174.
2. Ibid. 8.12, 182–83, biblical passage revised in accord with NRSV.
3. Martin Luther, "Heidelberg Disputation," trans. Harold J. Grimm, in *Luther's Works*, ed. Helmut T. Lehmann, vol. 31 (Philadelphia: Muhlenberg Press, 1957), 46.
4. See Carl Bangs, *Arminius* (Nashville: Abingdon Press, 1971), 216.
5. See John T. McNeill, *The History and Character of Calvinism* (Oxford: Oxford University Press, 1967), 265.
6. John Calvin, *Institutes of the Christian Religion* 3.21.1, trans. Ford Lewis Battles (Philadelphia: Westminster Press, 1960), 920–21, translation altered.
7. Ibid. 3.21.5, 926.
8. Quoted in V. H. H. Green, *John Wesley* (London: Thomas Nelson & Sons, 1964), 51.
9. Quoted in William Ragsdale Cannon, *The Theology of John Wesley* (Nashville: Abingdon-Cokesbury Press, 1946), 107.
10. "Decree concerning Justification," in *Canons and Decrees of the Council of Trent*, ed. H. J. Schroeder (St. Louis: B. Herder Book Co., 1941), 33.
11. Calvin, *Institutes* 3.16.2, 800.
12. John Wesley, *The Journal of John Wesley*, Nov. 29, 1761, in *The Works of John Wesley* (Grand Rapids: Zondervan Publishing House, 1958), 3:75.
13. John Wesley, Sermon 19, *Sermons on Several Occasions* (London: Henry G. Bohn, 1845), 95.
14. John Wesley, "An Answer to the Rev. Mr. Church's Remarks," in *The Works of John Wesley* (Grand Rapids: Zondervan Publishing House, 1958), 8:402.
15. See Tertullian, "On Penitence," in *Treatises on Penance*, trans. William Le Saint (Westminster, Md.: Newman Press, 1959), 23, 29, for the beginnings of a transition.
16. Thomas Aquinas, *Summa Theologica* 3a.84.5, trans. Fathers of the English Dominican Province (Westminster, Md.: Christian Classics, 1981), 2527.
17. "I refuse to go to confession simply because the pope has commanded it and insists upon it. For I wish him to keep his hands off the confession and not make of it compulsion or command, which he has not the power to do. Nevertheless I will allow no man to take private confession away from me, and I would not give

it up for all the treasures in the world, since I know what comfort and strength it has given me." Martin Luther, Sermon at Wittenberg, March 15, in 1522, *Basic Theological Writings*, ed. Timothy Lull (Minneapolis: Fortress Press, 1989), 442.

18. Calvin, *Institutes* 3.10.6, 724.
19. Aquinas, *Summa Theologica* 1a2ae.62.3, 852.
20. See Margaret A. Farley, *Personal Commitments* (San Francisco: Harper & Row, 1986).
21. See Jurgen Moltmann, *The Crucified God*, trans. R. A. Wilson and John Bowden (New York: Harper & Row, 1974), 332–35.

Ellen T. Charry's Essay

1. John Calvin, *Institutes of the Christian Religion* 3.7.1, trans. Ford Lewis Battles (Philadelphia: Westminster Press, 1960), 690.

Michael Battle's Essay

1. Garrison Keillor, *A Prairie Home Companion,* The Annual Joke Show, April 2000.
2. Desmond Tutu, "The Holy Spirit and South Africa," from his handwritten lecture notes. For further reference to Tutu's communal theology, see my previous work, Michael Battle, *Reconciliation: The Ubuntu Theology of Desmond Tutu* (Cleveland: Pilgrim Press, 1997).
3. One of the best and most prolific Christian minds on this subject of Christian community is Stanley Hauerwas. See Stanley Hauerwas, *A Community of Character: Toward a Constructive Christian Social Ethic* (Notre Dame, Ind.: University of Notre Dame Press, 1981); and *The Hauerwas Reader,* ed. John Berkman and Michael Cartwright (Durham, N.C.: Duke University Press, 2001).
4. Desmond Tutu, *No Future without Forgiveness* (New York: Doubleday, 1999). Also see Greg Jones's excellent work on forgiveness: L. Gregory Jones, *Embodying Forgiveness: A Theological Analysis* (Grand Rapids: Wm. B. Eerdmans Publishing Co., 1995).
5. For example, see Jesus' parables about the fragility of seeds (Mark 4:1–9, 13–20; Luke 8:4–8, 11–15; Matt. 13).
6. Tutu, handwritten notes, Undated.
7. Pauline biblical work is especially important here in that Paul's theory of knowledge is based upon his claim of not knowing fully. See 1 Cor. 13:12, 13.
8. For further work on this theme on the immediacy of knowing in Christian mystical literature, see Pseudo-Dionysius, the Areopagite, *The Divine Names and Mystical Theology*, trans. John D. Jones (Milwaukee: Marquette University Press, 1980), and *The Cloud of Unknowing,* ed. James Walsh (New York: Paulist Press, 1981).
9. Vladimir Lossky, *Orthodox Theology: An Introduction*, trans. Ian and Ihita Kesarcodi-Watson (Crestwood, N.Y.: St. Vladimir's Seminary Press, 1978), 173ff.
10. See Alan Jones's astute discussion of Alexander Schmemann in Alan Jones, *Soul Making: The Desert Way of Spirituality* (San Francisco: Harper & Row, 1985), 53–54.
11. See Battle, *Reconciliation.*

Chapter 8: What about *Them?*

1. Justin Martyr, *First Apology* 46, in *Saint Justin Martyr,* trans. Thomas B. Falls (New York: Christian Heritage, 1948), 83.
2. Clark M. Williamson, *A Guest in the House of Israel* (Louisville, Ky.: Wesminster/John Knox Press, 1993), 27–28.

3. Martin Luther, "On the Jews and Their Lies," trans. Martin H. Bertram, in *Luther's Works,* ed. Helmut T Lehman, vol. 47 (Philadelphia: Fortress Press, 1971), 268–69.
4. "Declaration on the Relationship of the Church to Non-Christian Religions," in *The Documents of Vatican II,* ed. Walter M. Abbott, S.J. (New York: Herder & Herder, 1966), 662.
5. Statement of the 1987 General Assembly, Presbyterian Church (U.S.A.), quoted in Williamson, *Guest in the House,* 34, 37. See also Gabriel Fackre, "The Place of Israel in Christian Faith," *Ecumenical Faith in Christian Perspective* (Grand Rapids: Wm. B. Eerdmans Publishing Co., 1993), 147–67.
6. For a lengthier survey of differing views, see S. Mark Heim, *Salvations: Truth and Difference in Religion* (Maryknoll, N.Y.: Orbis Books, 1995).
7. *The Church Teaches,* no. 165 (Denzinger, no. 714), trans. John F. Clarkson et al. (Rockford, Ill.: Tan Books & Publishers, 1973), 78.
8. Statement of the Congress on World Missions, in *Facing the Unfinished Task,* ed. J. O. Percy (Grand Rapids: Wm. B. Eerdmans Publishing Co., 1961), 9.
9. Dante Alighieri, *Paradise* 20.133–35, trans. Dorothy L. Sayers and Barbara Reynolds (Harmondsworth, England: Penguin Books, 1962), 236.
10. Karl Rahner, *Theological Investigations,* vol. 5, trans. Karl-H. Kruger (New York: Seabury Press, 1966), 131.
11. *Church Teaches,* nos. 274–75, p. 120.
12. John Calvin, *Institutes of the Christian Religion* 3.20.38, trans. Ford Lewis Battles (Philadelphia: Westminster Press, 1960), 901.

Paul F. Knitter's Essay

1. See "Declaration on the Relationship of the Church to Non-Christian Religions," in *The Documents of Vatican II,* ed. Walter M. Abbott, S.J. (New York: Herder & Herder, 1966), 660–68.
2. Wilfred Cantwell Smith, *The Faith of Other Men* (New York: Harper & Row, 1962), 11.
3. Edward Schillebeeckx, *The Church: The Human Story of God* (New York: Crossroad, 1990), 163, 167; Jacques Dupuis, *Toward a Christian Theology of Religious Pluralism* (Maryknoll, N.Y.: Orbis Books, 1997), 11.
4. Hans Küng, *Global Responsibility: In Search of a New World Ethic* (New York: Crossroad, 1991), xv.
5. I have tried to lay out this creative tension between practice and theory, especially for Roman Catholics, in "Catholics and Other Religions: Bridging the Gap between Dialogue and Theology," *Louvain Studies* 24 (1999): 319–54.
6. Jacques Dupuis, "Christianity and Other Religions: From Confrontation to Encounter," *The Tablet,* October 2001, 1484–85 (see also 1520–21, 2001–2).
7. I have tried to describe these models in a broader and balanced manner in *Introducing Theology of Religions* (Maryknoll, N.Y.: Orbis Books, 2002).
8. There are some exceptions. Recently, evangelical theologians have been laboring to devise theological theories that would enable "pagans" who have not heard of Jesus actually to be saved—through special revelations at the moment of death, or postmortem, or through God's "middle knowledge," or "by exception" in anticipation of Jesus' death. There have even been some evangelical thinkers who would allow for God, in the divine "wider mercy," actually to act and save through other traditions. Such views would probably blend into the next model. See Clark Pinnock, *A Wideness in God's Mercy* (Grand Rapids: Zondervan Publishing House, 1992).

9. "Declaration on the Relationship," 662; "The Decree on the Church's Missionary Activity," in *The Documents of Vatican II,* ed. Walter M. Abbott, S.J. (New York: Herder & Herder, 1966), 595–96; and "Pastoral Constitution on the Church in the Modern World," in the same volume, 306.
10. "Dogmatic Constitution on the Church" in *Documents of Vatican II,* 35 (misprint in this edition). For representatives of this fulfillment model, see Dupuis, *Toward a Christian Theology*; Gavin D'Costa, *The Meeting of Religions and the Trinity* (Maryknoll, N.Y.: Orbis Books, 2000); and Pope John Paul II, *Redemptoris Missio* (Washington: United States Catholic Conference, 1990).
11. Representatives of this mutuality model can be found in *The Myth of Christian Uniqueness: Toward a Pluralistic Theology of Religions*, ed. John Hick and Paul F. Knitter (Maryknoll, N.Y.: Orbis Books, 1986).
12. Spokespersons for this acceptance model would include George Lindbeck, *The Nature of Doctrine: Religion and Theology in a Postliberal Age* (Philadelphia: Westminster Press, 1984); and J. A. DiNoia, *The Diversity of Religions* (Washington, D.C.: Catholic University Press of America, 1992).
13. See S. Mark Heim, *Salvations: Truth and Difference in Religions* (Maryknoll, N.Y.: Orbis Books, 1995); and S. Mark Heim, *The Depth of Riches: A Trinitarian Theology of Religious Ends* (Grand Rapids: Wm. B. Eerdmans Publishing Co., 2001).
14. See Paul Griffiths, *An Apology for Apologetics: A Study in the Logic of Interreligious Dialogue* (Maryknoll, N.Y.: Orbis Books, 1991). See also William C. Placher, *Unapologetic Theology: A Christian Voice in a Pluralistic Conversation* (Louisville, Ky.: Westminster/John Knox Press, 1989).
15. H. Richard Niebuhr, *The Meaning of Revelation* (New York: Macmillan, 1962), 39, 41.
16. For more on reinterpreting New Testament exclusive language as confessional language, see Krister Stendahl, "Notes on Three Bible Studies," in *Christ's Lordship and Religious Pluralism*, ed. Gerald H. Anderson and Thomas F. Stransky (Maryknoll, N.Y.: Orbis Books, 1981), 7–18; Paul F. Knitter, *No Other Name? A Critical Survey of Christian Attitudes toward World Religions* (Maryknoll, N.Y.: Orbis Books, 1985), 182–86; and Paul F. Kritter, *Jesus and the Other Names: Christian Mission and Global Responsibility* (Maryknoll, N.Y.: Orbis Books, 1996), 67–71.
17. John B. Cobb, Jr., "Beyond Pluralism," in *Christian Uniqueness Reconsidered: The Myth of a Pluralistic Theology of Religions,* ed. Gavin D'Costa (Maryknoll, N.Y.: Orbis Books, 1990), 91.
18. David H. Jensen, *In the Company of Others: A Dialogical Christology* (Cleveland: Pilgrim Press, 2001), 190, 87, xii.
19. In fact, when we consider the fundamental adage in Catholic sacramental theology, *symbolizando causant* ("causing by symbolizing"), we can also say that Jesus as sacrament "constitutes" salvation—but he does so by symbolizing or representing rather than by "fixing."
20. Such an understanding of Jesus and the kingdom is contained in the images of the historical Jesus of Dominic Crossan, Marcus Borg, and even Geza Vermes and N. T. Wright. See especially Jon Sobrino, *Jesus the Liberator: A Historical-Theological Reading of Jesus of Nazareth*, trans. Paul Burns and Francis McDonagh (Maryknoll, N.Y.: Orbis Books, 1993).
21. Dupuis, *Toward a Christian Theology,* 336–42.
22. Or, as David Tracy prefers, "christomorphic": "There is no serious form of Christian theology that is not christomorphic. This is a more accurate designation of the christological issue, I believe, than the more familiar but confusing word 'christocentric.' For theology is not christocentric but theocentric, although it is

so only by means of its christomorphism." David Tracy, "Theology and the Many Faces of Postmodernity," *Theology Today* 51 (1994): 111.

23. Aloysius Pieris, *Fire and Water: Basic Issues in Asian Buddhism and Christianity* (Maryknoll, N.Y.: Orbis Books, 1996), 150–51.
24. Aloysius Pieris, "Christ beyond Dogma: Doing Christology in the Context of the Religions and the Poor," *Louvain Studies* 25 (2000): 220; and Aloysius Pieris, *God's Reign for God's Poor: A Return to the Jesus Formula* (Kelania, Sri Lanka: Tulana Research Centre, 1998), 71–72.
25. Pieris, *God's Reign for God's Poor*, 71–72.
26. Robert J. Schreiter, "Reconciliation as a Model for Mission," *New Theology Review* 10 (1997): 6–15.
27. It would seem that such a self-emptying embrace of others is not possible without nonviolence toward them. *Kenōsis* and nonviolence are, it seems, inseparable. Controversial though it be, one could also make the case that nonviolence constitutes another essential ingredient in the distinctiveness of Jesus and therefore a necessary Christian contribution to the dialogue.

J. A. DiNoia's Essay

1. This essay is a slightly edited version of "Christian Universalism," in *Either/Or: The Gospel or Neopaganism*, ed. Carl E. Braaten and Robert W. Jenson (Grand Rapids: Wm. B. Eerdmans Publishing Co., 1995), 37–48. It is reprinted here by kind permission of Wm. B. Eerdmans Publishing Co.
2. Paul Knitter has advanced his position on this issue in the widely read book *No Other Name? A Critical Survey of Christian Attitudes toward Other Religions* (Maryknoll, N.Y.: Orbis Books, 1985). John Hick has recently restated his position in *An Interpretation of Religion: Human Respondents to the Transcendent* (New Haven, Conn.: Yale University Press, 1989). With Knitter, Hick edited an influential volume of essays, *The Myth of Christian Uniqueness: Toward a Pluralistic Theology of Religions* (Maryknoll, N.Y.: Orbis Books, 1987), in which the pluralist case is pressed from a variety of standpoints. For responses to these essays and to pluralism generally, see Gavin D'Costa, *Christian Uniqueness Reconsidered: The Myth of a Pluralistic Theology of Religions* (Maryknoll, N.Y.: Orbis Books, 1990).
3. For a historical perspective on this debate, see Francis A. Sullivan, *Salvation outside the Church? Tracing the History of the Catholic Response* (New York: Paulist Press, 1992). For a reliable survey of the current discussion, though from a largely inclusivist vantage point, see Gavin D'Costa, *Theology and Religious Pluralism* (Oxford: Basil Blackwell, 1986).
4. See J. A. DiNoia, *The Diversity of Religions: A Christian Perspective* (Washington, D.C.: Catholic University of America Press, 1992).
5. See, for instance, the discussion of the uniqueness of the Buddha's discovery and teaching of the dharma in Sangharakshita, *A Survey of Buddhism*, 5th ed. (Boulder, Colo.: Shambhala Publications, 1980), 37–38.
6. In his *Doctrines of Religious Communities* (New Haven, Conn.: Yale University Press, 1987), 186, William A. Christian, Sr., has observed, "There seems to be a deep-seated tendency in the major religious communities to develop a comprehensive pattern of life . . . which bears on all human interests . . . and on all situations in which human beings find themselves."
7. Sundays in Ordinary Time, Preface 7, *The Sacramentary* (New York: Catholic Book Publishing, 1974), 443.
8. The statement of my argument here is deliberately hypothetical. My purpose is not to present an account of Buddhism, though I have striven to be accurate about Buddhist doctrines. Rather, it is to render plausible the claim, funda-

mental to my argument, that *nirvana* and *salvation* seem to designate significantly different aims of life, and thus call forth distinctive patterns of life in the members of Buddhist and Christian communities respectively, and to render implausible the pluralist claim that salvation encompasses what Christians mean by ultimate communion with the triune God and what Buddhists (seem to) mean by nirvana.

9. For a philosophical analysis of religious diagreements, see William A. Christian, Sr., *Oppositions of Religious Doctrines* (New York: Seabury Press, 1972). For a discussion of the kinds of arguments that such disagreements might give rise to in interreligious dialogue, see Paul J. Griffiths, *An Apology for Apologetics: A Study in the Logic of Interreligious Dialogue* (Maryknoll, N.Y.: Orbis Books, 1991).

Chapter 9: Where Are We Going?

1. For classic statements of the positions, see, for futuristic eschatology, Johannes Weiss, *Jesus' Proclamation of the Kingdom of God*, trans. Richard Hydes Hiers and David Larrimore Holland (Philadelphia: Fortress Press, 1971); and, for realized eschatology, C. H. Dodd, *The Parables of the Kingdom*, rev. ed. (New York: Charles Scribner's Sons, 1961).
2. Joachim Jeremias, *The Parables of Jesus*, trans. S. H. Hooke (New York: Charles Scribner's Sons, 1963), 148.
3. See Plato, *Phaedo* 64a, trans. David Gallop (Oxford: Oxford University Press, 1993), 9; and Seneca, *Ad Lucilium Epistulae Morales* 24.18, trans. Richard M. Gummere (New York: G. P. Putnam's Sons, 1917), 177.
4. Tertullian, *On the Resurrection of the Flesh* 9, in *Ante-Nicene Fathers* (Peabody, Mass.: Hendrickson Publishers, 1994), 3:551–52; Athenagoras, *The Resurrection of the Dead* 15, in *Ante-Nicene Fathers,* 2:157.
5. Thomas Aquinas, *Summa Theologica* 1a.76.1 ad 6, trans. Fathers of the English Dominican Province (Westminster, Md.: Christian Classics, 1981), 372.
6. See Norman Cohn, *In Pursuit of the Millennium* (Fairlawn, N.J.: Essential Books, 1957).
7. The relevant texts are 1 Thess. 4:16–17 and Matt. 25:40.
8. See Weiss, *Jesus' Preaching*; and Albert Schweitzer, *The Quest of the Historical Jesus*, 1st complete ed., trans. W. Montgomery et al. (Minneapolis: Fortress Press, 2001).
9. Pierre Teilhard de Chardin, *The Divine Milieu*, rev. ed. (New York: Harper, 1968).
10. John D. Barrow and Frank J. Tipler, *The Anthropic Cosmological Principle* (New York: Oxford University Press, 1986).
11. "The Creed of S. Athanasius," in *The Faith of Christendom,* ed. B. A. Gerrish (Cleveland: Meridian Books, 1963), 64.
12. Origen, *On First Principles* 3.6, trans. G. W. Butterworth (New York: Harper Torchbooks, 1966), 251.
13. Ibid. 2.10, 146.
14. In favor of universal salvation, see Acts 3:21; Rom. 5:18; 11:32; 1 Cor. 15:25–28; Eph 1:10; Phil. 2:10–11; Col. 1:20. Opposed to universal salvation, see Matt. 7:13–27; 12:32; 25:31–46; Mark 9:45–48; 16:1–6; Luke 16:23; John 3:16, 36; 1 Cor. 1:18; 2 Cor. 2:15; Phil. 3:19.
15. See Karl Barth, *Church Dogmatics* IV/3, trans. G. W. Bromiley (Edinburgh: T. & T. Clark, 1962), 918, 931–32; Hans Urs von Balthasar, *Mysterium Paschale*, trans. Aidan Nichols (Edinburgh: T. & T. Clark, 1990), 177; Karl Rahner, *Foundations of Christian Faith*, trans. William V. Dych (New York: Seabury Press, 1978), 444.

Richard J. Mouw's Essay

1. This sort of decoding is provided in rich detail by the notes in the Scofield Bible. See, for example, the notes for Gen. 10:2 and Ezek. 38:2, as well as those that provide a running commentary of the whole book of Revelation. The *Scofield Reference Bible* was first published by Oxford University Press in 1909.
2. There is much literature available on the Fatima prophecies. For a concise account of their role and impact in twentieth-century Catholicism, see Sandra L. Zimdars-Swartz, *Encountering Mary: From La Salette to Medjugorje* (Princeton, N.J.: Princeton University Press, 1991), 190–219.
3. For a fascinating account of various strands of recent Catholic apocalypticism, see Michael W. Cuneo, *The Smoke of Satan: Conservative and Traditionalist Dissent in Contemporary American Catholicism* (New York: Oxford University Press, 1997), 121–77.
4. Paul G. Hiebert, "The Flaw of the Excluded Middle," *Missiology: An International Review* 10, no. 1 (January 1982): 44–46.
5. The schools of thought I am briefly describing here are spelled out in many theological works. For a good sampling of how representatives of each perspective state their case, see Robert G. Clouse, ed., *The Meaning of the Millennium: Four Views* (Downers Grove, Ill.: InterVarsity Press, 1977). The "four views" include both the dispensationalist and nondispensationalist versions of premillennialism.
6. Stanley J. Grenz, *The Millennnial Maze: Sorting Out Evangelical Options* (Downers Grove, Ill.: InterVarsity Press, 1992), 184, 187.
7. George Eldon Ladd, *A Theology of the New Testament* (Grand Rapids: Wm. B. Eerdmans Publishing Co., 1974), 630.
8. Heidelberg Catechism, question 1, in *The Creeds of Christendom*, ed. Philip Schaff, vol. 3 (Grand Rapids: Baker Book House, 1996), 307.
9. Ibid., questions 50 and 51, pp. 323.
10. Ibid., question 52, pp. 323–24.

Ted Peter's Essay

1. Oscar Cullmann, "Immortality of the Soul or Resurrection of the Dead?" in *Immortality and Resurrection*, ed. Krister Stendahl (New York: Macmillan, 1965), 14.
2. "The post-resurrectional confession is not simply 'We have seen Jesus' but 'We have seen *the Lord*' (John 20:18, 25; 21:7; Luke 24:34). Since 'Lord' is a christological evaluation of Jesus, the evangelists are telling us that the witnesses enjoyed not only the *sight* of Jesus but also and even primarily *insight*." Raymond E. Brown, *The Virginal Conception and Bodily Resurrection of Jesus* (New York: Paulist Press, 1973), 112, emphasis in original.
3. I am assuming here *subjective immortality*—that is, that the person being raised experiences the event subjectively. This stands in contrast to *objective immortality*, according to which we are objectively remembered by God everlastingly but do not ourselves continue to have experiences. See the debate between Schubert M. Ogden, "The Meaning of Christian Hope," *Union Seminary Review* 30, no. 2 (Winter-Summer 1975): 153–64, and Marjorie Suchocki, "The Question of Immortality," *Journal of Religion* 57, no. 3 (July 1977): 288–306.
4. See John Polkinghorne and Michael Welker, *The End of the World and the Ends of God: Science and Theology on Eschatology* (Harrisburg, Pa.: Trinity Press International, 2000); and Robert John Russell, "Time in Eternity: Special Relativity and Eschatology," *Dialog* 39, no. 1 (Spring 2000): 46–55.

5. See Paul Ricoeur, *The Symbolism of Evil*, trans. Emerson Buchanan (Boston: Beacon Press, 1967), 348.
6. Westminster Shorter Catechism, question 38, in *The Creeds of Christendom*, ed. Philip Schaff, (Grand Rapids: Baker Book House, 1996), 3:684.
7. On proleptic presence of the future ahead of time, see Wolfhart Pannenberg, *Systematic Theology*, vol. 3, trans. Geoffrey W. Bromiley (Grand Rapids: Wm. B. Eerdmans Publishing Co., 1998), 627.
8. Thomas Aquinas, *Summa Theologica* supp.70.3, trans. Fathers of the English Dominican Province (Westminster, Md.: Christian Classics, 1981), 2829.
9. Karl Rahner, "Hell," *Encyclopedia of Theology* (New York: Seabury Press, 1975), 603.
10. See John Hick, *Death and Eternal Life* (San Francisco: Harper & Row, 1976), 201; Hans Küng, *Eternal Life?* (New York: Doubleday, 1984), 136; and John S. Mbiti, *New Testament Eschatology in an African Background* (Oxford: Oxford University Press, 1971), 70.
11. Timothy Ware, *The Orthodox Church* (New York: Penguin Books, 1963), 266.
12. Karl Barth, *Church Dogmatics,* II/2, trans. G. W. Bromiley et al. (Edinburgh: T. & T. Clark, 1957), 417.
13. Karl Rahner, *Foundations of Christian Faith*, trans. William V. Dych (New York: Seabury Press, 1978), 444.

Index